W9-CCD-807

No Stress Tech Guide To
Crystal Reports Basic
For Visual Studio 2008 For Beginners

By Dr. Indera E. Murphy

Tolana Publishing
Teaneck, New Jersey

No Stress Tech Guide To Crystal Reports Basic For Visual Studio 2008 For Beginners

Published By:
Tolana Publishing
PO Box 719
Teaneck, NJ 07666 USA

Find us online at www.tolanapublishing.com
Inquiries may be sent to the publisher: tolanapub@yahoo.com

Our books are available online at amazon.com, www.barnesandnoble.com www.alibris.com and
www.lulu.com/tolanapub

ISBN-10: 0-9773912-8-0
ISBN-13: 978-0-9773912-8-8

Library of Congress Control Number: 2008901627

Printed and bound in the United States Of America

Notice of Liability
Every effort has been made to ensure that this book contains accurate and current information.
However, the publisher and author shall not be liable to any person or entity with respect to any loss or damage
caused or alleged to be caused directly or indirectly, as a result of any information contained herein or by the
computer software and hardware products described in it.

Trademarks
All companies and product names are trademarks or registered trademarks of their respective companies. They are
used in this book in an editorial fashion only. No use of any trademark is intended to convey endorsement or other
affiliation with this book.

Cover designed by Mary Kramer, owner of Milkweed Graphics, www.milkweedgraphics.com

Quantity Discounts

Discounts are available for corporations, non-profit organizations, libraries, wholesalers,
bookstores, distributors and educational institutions for fundraising or resale. Please check our
website for more information.

Discount On Future Books

To be notified when new titles are released, send an email with the subject "New Book Release".
This will entitle you to a pre-publish discount, for new titles when they are released.

Who The Book Is For

This book is primarily for end-users and developers that have never used the version of Crystal Reports that comes with Visual Studio 2008 before and people that have used a previous version and want to learn about the features of Crystal Reports Basic for Visual Studio 2008. You do not have to know Visual Basic or Visual C++ to use this workbook. You will learn how to create a basic form that will be used to display reports.

About The No Stress Tech Guide Series

The No Stress Tech Guide To Crystal Reports Basic For Visual Studio 2008 For Beginners, is part of a growing series of computer software training workbooks that are designed to be used in a classroom setting, an online class or as a self-paced learning tool. This workbook can also be used as a textbook supplement or reference guide. The workbooks contain an abundance of screen shots to help reduce the "stress" often associated with learning new software.

Tolana Publishing believes that the following principals are important when it comes to computer software training workbooks:

⇒ The text should be large enough that the reader does not have to squint.
⇒ The step-by-step instructions should really work and not leave something out.
⇒ Features or options that do not work as intended should be pointed out, not to bash the software company, but so that you don't think that you are crazy <smile>.
⇒ That there should be a realistic mix of theory, real world examples and hands-on exercises. It is important to know the past, because it helps you transition into the future with ease and dignity.

Why A Book On Crystal Reports Basic For Visual Studio 2008

After reading the Users Guide that comes with Visual Studio 2008, I felt that users, especially new users would prefer to have more assistance in learning how to get the most out of the version of Crystal Reports that comes with Visual Studio 2008. I also did not see a book specifically for this version of Crystal Reports. The Users Guide provides a starting point of reference, but often the Users Guide refers you to the Help System to get more information. As a professor and author, I do not feel that flipping between a book and the Help System is the most ideal way to learn how to use a software package.

I know that many books claim to have "step-by-step instructions". If you have tried to follow books that make this claim and you got lost or could not complete a task as instructed, it may not have been your fault. When I decided to write computer books, I vowed to really have step-by-step instructions that actually included every step.
This includes steps like which file to open, which menu option to select, when to save a document and more.
In my opinion, it is this level of detail that makes a computer book easy to follow. I hope that you feel the same way.

Other Titles In The Series

Microsoft Works 7	ISBN-10: 0977391221	ISBN-13: 978-0-9773912-2-6
Microsoft Works 8 & 8.5	ISBN-10: 0977391213	ISBN-13: 978-0-9773912-1-9
Windows XP	ISBN-10: 0977391205	ISBN-13: 978-0-9773912-0-2
Crystal Reports XI:		
For Beginners	ISBN-10: 097739123X	ISBN-13: 978-0-9773912-3-3
OpenOffice.org Writer 2	ISBN-10: 0977391248	ISBN-13: 978-0-9773912-4-0
ACT! 2007	ISBN-10: 0977391256	ISBN-13: 978-0-9773912-5-7
Microsoft Works 9	ISBN-10: 0977391272	ISBN-13: 978-0-9773912-7-1
Crystal Reports For		
Visual Studio 2005	ISBN-10: 0977391264	ISBN-13: 978-0-9773912-6-4

Forthcoming Titles

Crystal Reports 2008
ACT! 2008

About The Author

Dr. Indera Murphy is an author, educator and IT professional that has over 18 years of experience in the Information Technology field. She has held a variety of positions including, programmer, consultant, technical writer, web designer, course developer and project leader. Indera has designed and developed software applications and web sites, as well as, manage IT Projects. In addition to being an Executive Director and consultant, Indera is also an online adjunct professor. She teaches courses in a variety of areas including technical writing, information processing, Access, HTML, Windows, project management, spreadsheets, Dreamweaver and critical thinking.

TABLE OF CONTENTS

GETTING STARTED WITH CRYSTAL REPORTS BASIC FOR VISUAL STUDIO 2008

The easiest and fastest way to overcome an obstacle is to have someone that has been there, to be by your side every step of the way. That is the goal of this workbook - to be by your side every step of the way through learning Crystal Reports Basic for Visual Studio 2008.

A hands-on approach is usually the best way to learn most things in life. This workbook is a visual guide that shows you how to create or modify over 175 reports. There are over 600 illustrations that practically eliminate the guess work and let you know that you are creating the steps correctly.

The table of contents takes the **HOW TO** approach, which makes it easier to find exactly what you are looking for. There is more to Crystal Reports than knowing how to open and print a report. Crystal Reports is robust and has a lot of features.

One goal of this workbook is to discuss report design issues and potential solutions on how to resolve them. The good thing is that you have taken a great first step towards learning Crystal Reports Basic for Visual Studio 2008 by purchasing this workbook. Now all you have to do is use this workbook to learn how to overcome the hurdles. From time to time, I will point out functionality that may not work as expected. When I do this, I am not complaining, merely pointing out things that you should be aware of.

It is my sincere hope that whatever your current skill level is with Crystal Reports, that you will learn more about features that you are already familiar with as you go through this workbook and that you learn about features that you did not know existed. While you can jump to exercises that cover something you need to know now, I hope that you complete the exercises in the order that they are presented because you will get more from the exercises. Learning new tips and shortcuts will let you work faster and smarter. The more you know about Crystal Reports, the easier your day to day report design experiences will be. So sit back and lets get started.

Thank you for purchasing this workbook!

LESSON 1

About Crystal Reports Basic For Visual Studio 2008

Crystal Reports is a software package that allows you to create reports. It is the report writing software that many companies use. Almost all businesses today that maintain data have a need for reports to help them get their job done and to make business decisions. Reports allow one to be able to read and make sense of large amounts of data that is most often stored in a database. Most databases have limited reporting capabilities and only allow reports to be created in that "type" of database. Database types include Sybase, Microsoft SQL Server and Oracle, to name a few. These are often called SQL databases and are usually stored on a database server. Some of them do provide a desktop version that is often used for learning purposes. If you need to create a report that has data (information) in both Oracle and Sybase databases for example, you would have to use Crystal Reports because neither database allows you to create reports that have data in other types of databases.

Crystal Reports allows you to use data from a variety of database types and combine the data in one report. Crystal Reports can use databases of any size. In addition to the SQL databases mentioned above, you can also use mainframe databases and what I call desktop or PC databases like Microsoft Access and Visual FoxPro. This type of database usually contains a lot less data than the SQL databases and do not have the capacity to support hundreds or thousands of end-users like SQL databases do. Crystal Reports comes bundled with a lot of software development tools including Visual Studio. It also comes bundled with several leading software packages like PeopleSoft, SAP, JD Edwards and many others. In addition to creating paper reports, you can export reports to Word, Excel and PDF formats. You can create almost any type of report that you can dream up.

Normally, Crystal Reports is a read-only program, meaning that when you create or modify reports, the data in the database is not changed. You can however, include SQL commands in the report, which will allow the report to edit, delete and add records to a database.

The primary goal of Crystal Reports is to allow a wide range of users to work with the raw data in databases to be able to create reports that allow data to be interpreted and analyzed. Crystal Reports makes creating basic reports easy enough for less technical people to use through the use of report wizards, which are similar to wizards that you may have used in other software packages. You can also create complex reports that include formulas, charts and much more.

Workbook Objectives

This workbook is written to accommodate classroom and online training, as well as, to be used as a self-paced training course. While there are no required prerequisites to successfully complete the exercises in this workbook, having a general knowledge of any of the following would be helpful.

- ☑ Other versions of Crystal Reports
- ☑ Database structures
- ☑ Basic programming
- ☑ Report design

Step-by-step instructions are included throughout this workbook. This workbook takes a hands-on, performance based approach to teaching you how to use Crystal Reports in the Visual Studio environment and provides the skills required to create reports efficiently. After completing this workbook you will be able to perform the following tasks and more:

- ☑ Utilize report design and planning techniques
- ☑ Understand database concepts
- ☑ Use the report wizards and create reports from scratch
- ☑ Modify existing reports
- ☑ Use multiple tables to create a report
- ☑ Format and edit reports
- ☑ Create report selection criteria
- ☑ Sort and group data

☑ Create charts
☑ Create reports that have subtotals, counts, running totals and summary information
☑ Export reports to other file formats
☑ Add Special Fields to reports
☑ Incorporate drill-down techniques in reports
☑ Create mailing labels using a wizard
☑ Create Cross-Tab reports
☑ Use the Formula Workshop to create formulas and use functions
☑ Use the Highlighting and Section Experts to format data conditionally
☑ Change the default report options
☑ Create If...Then...Else Statements
☑ Create parameter fields

Lesson 1 Objectives

After completing the exercises in this lesson you will be able to:

☑ Create an icon on your desktop for Visual Studio
☑ Understand the options on the menu and toolbars
☑ Check for updates for Crystal Reports
☑ Remove toolbars
☑ Create a project

Conventions Used In This Workbook

I designed the following conventions to make it easier for you to follow the instructions in this workbook.

☑ The `Courier font` is used to indicate what you should type.
☑ **Drag** means to hold down the left mouse button while moving the mouse.
☑ **Click** means to press the left mouse button once, then release it immediately.
☑ **Double-click** means to quickly press the left mouse button twice, then release it.
☑ **Right-click** means to press the right mouse button once to open a shortcut menu.
☑ Click **OK** means to click the OK button on the dialog box.
☑ Press **Enter** means to press the Enter key on your keyboard.
☑ Press **Tab** means to press the Tab key on your keyboard.
☑ SMALL CAPS are used to indicate an option to click on or to bring something to your attention.
☑ The blinking cursor is the marker that is in the document and appears to the right of where you are typing. This is also known as the INSERTION POINT or KEYBOARD CURSOR. This is different then the pointer that is controlled by the mouse. The MOUSE POINTER looks like an I-beam when not in use.
☑ This icon indicates a tip or additional information about the topic that is being discussed.
☑ This icon indicates a shortcut or another way to complete the task being discussed.
☑ This icon indicates a warning that you need to pay attention to.
☑ NEW This icon represents a new or modified feature if you are upgrading from Crystal Reports For Visual Studio 2005.
☑ Press CTRL + V means to press and hold down the Ctrl key, then press the V key.
☑ When you see "YOUR SCREEN SHOULD LOOK LIKE THE ONE SHOWN IN FIGURE X.X", or something similar in the exercises, check to make sure that your screen does look like the figure. If it does, continue with the next set of instructions. If your screen does not look like the figure, redo the steps that you just completed so that your screen does match the figure. Not doing so may cause you problems when trying to complete exercises later in the workbook.

☑ The instruction "Right-click on a field" means to right-click on the field in the details section of the report, unless noted otherwise.

☑ The instruction "Select the database" means to select the Xtreme database that comes with Crystal Reports. You will learn about this database in Lesson 2.

☑ The section heading **EXERCISE X.Y:** (where x equals the lesson number and y equals the exercise number) represents exercises that have step-by-step instructions that you should complete. You will also see sections that have step-by-step instructions that are not an exercise. Completing them as you go through the workbook is optional, but recommended.

☑ [See Lesson 2, Figure 2-8] refers to a screen shot that you can use as a reference for the current topic that is being discussed.

☑ [See Lesson 2, Database Concepts] refers to a section that you can use as a reference for the topic that is being discussed.

☑ "Clear the (name of option) option" means to remove the check mark from the option specified in the instruction.

☑ "L2.1 Report Name" is the naming convention for reports that you will create. L2.1 stands for Lesson 2, Exercise 1. You may consider some of the report file names to be long. I did this on purpose, so that it is easier to know what topic the report covers. If you do not like to type or do not want to type the full report name, you can just type the first part as the file name (Example, L5.8, L7.2 etc). That way when you have to find a report to complete another exercise, you will be able to find the correct report. For example, if the report name is L5.5 Orders Shipped Between 4-1-2001 and 6-30-2001, you can save the report as L5.5.

☑ "Save the L4.5 report as" means to open the L4.5 report and save it with the new report name that is specified in the instructions. Doing this lets you keep the original report.

☑ At the end of each lesson is a section called **TEST YOUR SKILLS**. These exercises help reinforce what is covered in the lesson. If you are not familiar with working from what is known as "Business Requirements" or "Report Specs", these exercises will help you become familiar with this process because these types of documents do not include step-by-step instructions like the exercises have. Many of the reports created in this section are used in other lessons as a starting point, which means that you need to complete them before going to the next lesson.

☑ **FILE** ⇒ **NEW** ⇒ **PROJECT** means to open the **FILE** menu, select the option **NEW**, then select the option **PROJECT**, as illustrated in Figure 1-1.

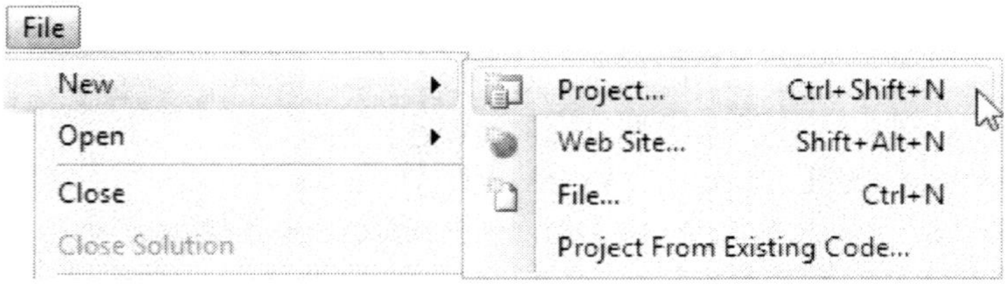

Figure 1-1 Menu navigation technique illustrated

All of the web sites referenced in this workbook are listed on this page on our website: www.tolana.com/books/2008/cr_vs2008/links.html. You can go to this page and click on the link that you want, instead of having to type the link in. See how nice I am. If you plan to use this page on our website, it is probably a good idea to bookmark the page, so that you can get to it quickly.

Assumptions

(Yes, I know one should never assume anything but . . . .)

☑ You have Visual Studio 2008 Professional (or higher) installed, which includes Crystal Reports. The standard version of Visual Studio 2008 does not include Crystal Reports.

☑ You are familiar with the Windows environment.

☑ You are comfortable using a mouse.

☑ You have access to a printer, if you want to print any of the reports that you will create. This is not a requirement for completing the exercises.

☑ You have access to the Internet to download any files that you may need to complete the exercises and to download any updates to Crystal Reports that are available.

☑ You know that the operating system used to write this workbook is Windows Vista. If you have Windows XP or a different operating system, it is possible that some of the screen shots may have a slightly different look.

☑ You have Visual Studio open at the beginning of each lesson.

☑ Optional: That you have Microsoft Word and Excel installed if you want to view the reports that will be exported to these formats. If you don't have either of these software packages, other options are covered in Lesson 8.

Interactive Messages

Like many other software packages, Crystal Reports will display interactive messages that require a response from you to confirm an action. Table 1-1 shows the three types of interactive message symbols and what they mean.

Symbol	Type	This interactive message type . . . . .
(i)	Information	Provides information about an action that you just performed.
⚠	Warning	Usually requires you to make a decision.
✖	Critical	Requires you to make a decision before moving on to the next step.

Table 1-1 Interactive message types explained

Installing Crystal Reports

Crystal Reports is installed by default when Visual Studio is installed. You should see it as one of the installed components.

Product Support Options

Below are some of the more popular support options for Crystal Reports.

Service Packs

These are updates to a software package. Service packs fix many of the bugs in the software. They can also include new functionality for the software. You can check for service pack updates by going to the Business Objects web site or you can check for updates using a menu option in Crystal Reports, which you will learn how to do later in this lesson.

Hot Fix Announcement

Hot fixes are updates to a software package. They do not contain as many bug fixes as service packs because they are released once a month. If you want to receive the free monthly hot fix e-mail announcement for Crystal Reports, click on the link **SUBSCRIBE TO MONTHLY HOT FIX NOTIFICATIONS**. You can also sign up on the link at the end of this paragraph. Signing up here will also allow you to post questions in the forums, which are explained in the next section.

https://secure.businessobjects.com/login/login.asp

Crystal Reports Forums

If you have a question about Crystal Reports, you can post a message in one of the forums on the BusinessObjects.com web site by opening the Support menu and selecting Forums. If you do not already have an account you will be prompted to create one. It's free.

The questions are primarily answered by other Crystal Reports users. There seems to be staff answering some questions in the moderated forum.

Microsoft has a forum specifically for the version of Crystal Reports that comes with Visual Studio. It is part of the MSDN (Microsoft Development Network). The link below is for the forum home page. You will need to create a user account if you do not already have a Microsoft Passport account.

http://forums.microsoft.com/MSDN/

Newsgroups

There are newsgroups on the Internet that are specifically for the version of Crystal Reports that comes with Visual Studio. You can post questions and receive answers. You will also learn how other people are living with and using Crystal Reports. Like the forum listed above, the questions on this newsgroup are also answered by other users. The reason Microsoft has a newsgroup for Crystal Reports is because it comes bundled with Visual Studio.

The newsgroup host is **MSNEWS.MICROSOFT.COM**.
The name of the newsgroup is **MICROSOFT.PUBLIC.VB.CRYSTAL**.

You can use a newsgroup reader like the one in Microsoft Outlook Express to use the newsgroups.
You can also access the newsgroups online at Microsoft's web site. The link below is for the home page of newsgroups on Microsoft's web site.

http://www.microsoft.com/communities/newsgroups/default.mspx

I was personally disappointed when I first started using Crystal Reports to find out that there really is not a newsgroup or forum that has staff dedicated to answering our questions. This is one reason why I decided to write a book on Crystal Reports Basic for Visual Studio 2008, so that I would be able to provide as many tips and helpful information as possible. Hopefully by reading and completing the exercises in this workbook you will not have to go through all of the trials and tribulations that I went through when I first learned Crystal Reports years ago.

Access The Newsgroups With Email Software

Many people prefer to use email software like Outlook Express (which you already have on your computer in you have Windows XP), that has a newsgroup reader to access the newsgroups instead of logging on to a website to access the newsgroups. If you want to do this, the link below provides instructions for setting up Outlook Express to use newsgroups. Don't worry, it is not difficult to set up.

http://www.microsoft.com/communities/guide/newsgroups.mspx

> If you plan to participate in newsgroups either from the web site or using software like Outlook Express, you should not use your real email address. Most people that use their real email address suddenly wind up with more spam then they can handle. My advise is to set up a free email account and use that email account to post messages in newsgroups. If your ISP offers multiple email accounts, you can create another account under your primary account and use that one.

Create A Shortcut Icon For Visual Studio/Crystal Reports

If you want to create an icon on your desktop for Visual Studio/Crystal Reports, follow the steps below after you minimize all open windows.

1.   Start ⇒ All Programs ⇒ Microsoft Visual Studio 2008, as shown in Figure 1-2.

Microsoft Visual Studio 2008
Microsoft Visual Studio 2008 Docum
Microsoft Visual Studio 2008
Visual Studio Remote Tools
Visual Studio Tools
Microsoft Windows SDK v6.0A
Microsoft Works

◀   Back

Figure 1-2 Path to Visual Studio 2008

2. Using the right mouse button, drag the Microsoft Visual Studio 2008 menu option to the desktop, then release the mouse button. You will see the shortcut menu shown in Figure 1-3. Select **CREATE SHORTCUTS HERE**. You should see an icon for Visual Studio 2008 on your desktop.

Copy Here
Move Here
Create Shortcuts Here

Cancel

Figure 1-3 Shortcut menu

If you want this icon on your Quick Launch bar on the Taskbar in Windows XP instead of on your desktop, drag it there with the **RIGHT** mouse button. You will see a shortcut menu similar to the one shown above in Figure 1-3. Select **MOVE HERE**. If you want the shortcut on your desktop and on the Quick Launch bar, select **COPY HERE**.

Opening Visual Studio

If this is the first time that you have opened Visual Studio, you will see the dialog box shown in Figure 1-4. Select the **GENERAL DEVELOPMENT SETTINGS** option, then click the Start Visual Studio button.

The reason that I had you select this option is because you do not need any features of a specific development tool to use Crystal Reports. This option is also best because it allows you to develop applications in more than one programming language.

If you have already opened Visual Studio, Tools ⇒ Import and Export Settings, will let you reset the environment settings back to the ones when the software was first installed.

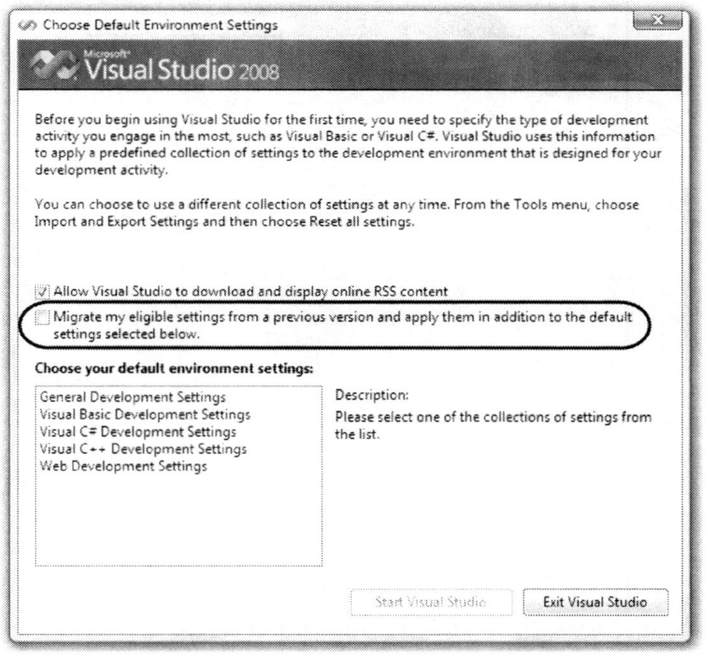

Choose Default Environment Settings

Visual Studio 2008

Before you begin using Visual Studio for the first time, you need to specify the type of development activity you engage in the most, such as Visual Basic or Visual C#. Visual Studio uses this information to apply a predefined collection of settings to the development environment that is designed for your development activity.

You can choose to use a different collection of settings at any time. From the Tools menu, choose Import and Export Settings and then choose Reset all settings.

☑ Allow Visual Studio to download and display online RSS content

☐ Migrate my eligible settings from a previous version and apply them in addition to the default settings selected below.

Choose your default environment settings:

General Development Settings
Visual Basic Development Settings
Visual C# Development Settings
Visual C++ Development Settings
Web Development Settings

Description:
Please select one of the collections of settings from the list.

Start Visual Studio   Exit Visual Studio

Figure 1-4 Choose Default Environment Settings dialog box

If you have a previous version of Visual Studio installed, you can check the option illustrated above in Figure 1-4 to have your settings copied to this version of Visual Studio.

Start Page Overview

Once Visual Studio is open you should see the **START PAGE** window shown in Figure 1-5. The Start Page window provides a lot of options that you may find helpful when using a development tool in the Visual Studio environment.

The **RECENT PROJECTS** section lists the last X number of projects that you have opened. X is determined by an environment option that you select on the Options dialog box. [See Lesson 5, Visual Studio Options]

The **GETTING STARTED** section has links to topics that would be of interest to people using Visual Studio for the first time.

The **VISUAL STUDIO HEADLINES** and **MSDN: VISUAL STUDIO** sections contain links to articles about Visual Studio and Crystal Reports. This is a good way to stay current.

> Depending on the security that you have set in your firewall software, you may be prompted to grant Visual Studio access to the Internet. It is probably a good idea to grant the access so that you can check for updates.

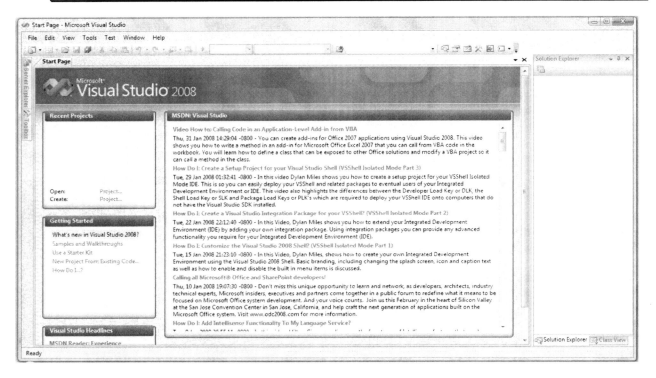

Figure 1-5 Visual Studio Start Page tab

Start Page Tab Menu And Toolbar Options

These options are for Visual Studio and are not for Crystal Reports specifically.

The one option that you may find helpful for Crystal Reports is Help ⇒ About Microsoft Visual Studio. This option will open the dialog box shown in Figure 1-6. This lets you know what version of each component of Visual Studio you have installed including Crystal Reports.

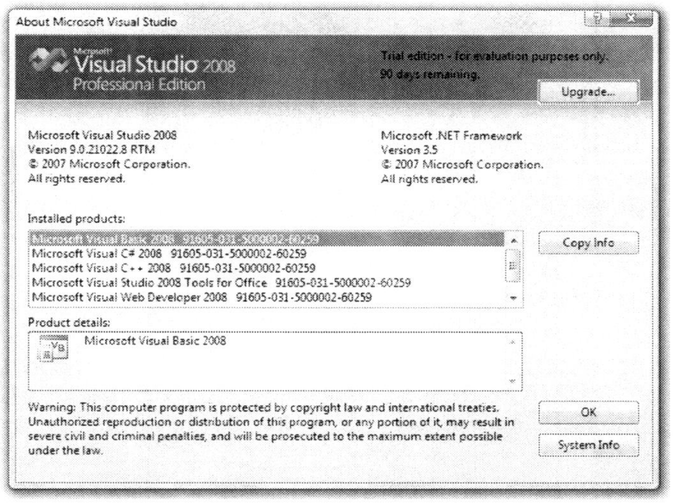

Figure 1-6 About Microsoft Visual Studio dialog box

> If you close the Start Page tab either on purpose or by accident, you can still get to all of the options on the Start Page tab through the menu, toolbar or shortcuts.

Creating A Project

If you have already created an application in Visual Studio, you already know how to create a project. The reports that you create must be stored in a project. The primary types of projects that you can create are based on the programming language used for the application.

As shown in Figure 1-7, there are three programming languages available in Visual Studio: Visual Basic, Visual C# and Visual C++.

The functionality of Crystal Reports is the same for each type of project. How you connect to a database, the types of databases that you can use or how you deploy a report may be slightly different, but it doesn't effect how you create a report.

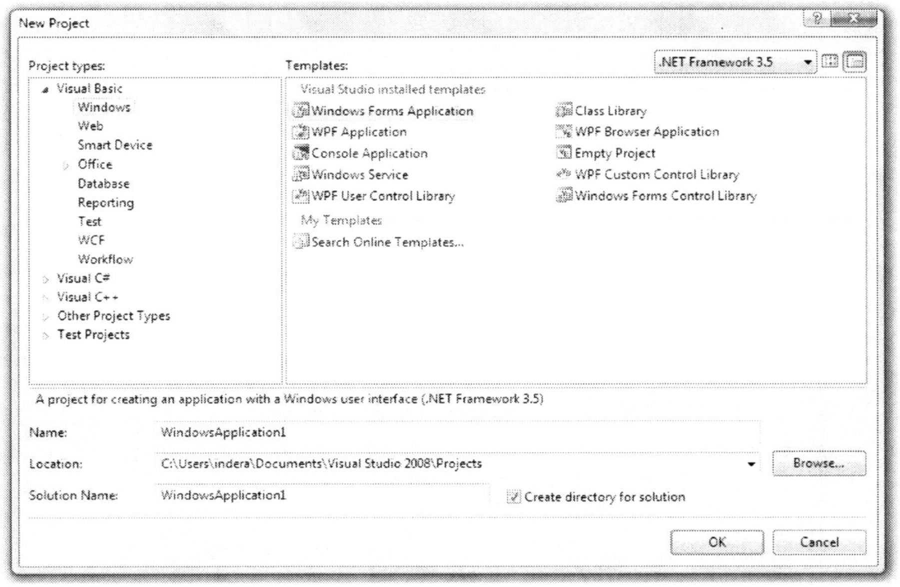

Figure 1-7 New Project dialog box

There is often a debate over why computer book authors select Visual Basic as the project type for creating reports. I doubt that it is done to offend the C++ and C# programmers or report writers. I use Visual Basic for the project type for two reasons: 1) I know Visual Basic better then any of the other programming languages and 2) more people use Visual Basic then any of the others. On that note, lets get started learning how to create reports in the Visual Studio/Crystal Reports environment.

The project that you will create in this exercise will be used to save all of the reports that you create and modify in this workbook. I am aware of the fact that some readers think that authors should have you create a new project for each chapter in the book. I personally think that is unnecessary. You have better things to do then create 13 projects for this workbook. The report naming convention that I use for reports will let you easily know which chapter each report was created or modified in.

1. File ⇒ New ⇒ Project. You will see the dialog box shown above in Figure 1-7.

2. Select the **REPORTING** option under Visual Basic on the left, then click on the Crystal Reports Application template option on the right.

3. In the Name field type `My_CrystalReports_VS2008_Project`.

4. If you do not want to save your project in the folder that is displayed in the **LOCATION** field, click the Browse button. Navigate to and click on the folder that you want to save this project in, then click the Select Folder button.

5. Type `CrystalReports_Workbook` in the **SOLUTION NAME** field.

6. Make sure that the **CREATE DIRECTORY FOR SOLUTION** option is checked. You should have the options shown at the bottom of Figure 1-8. The only difference may be the path in the Location field. Click OK. It will take a few seconds for the project to be created.

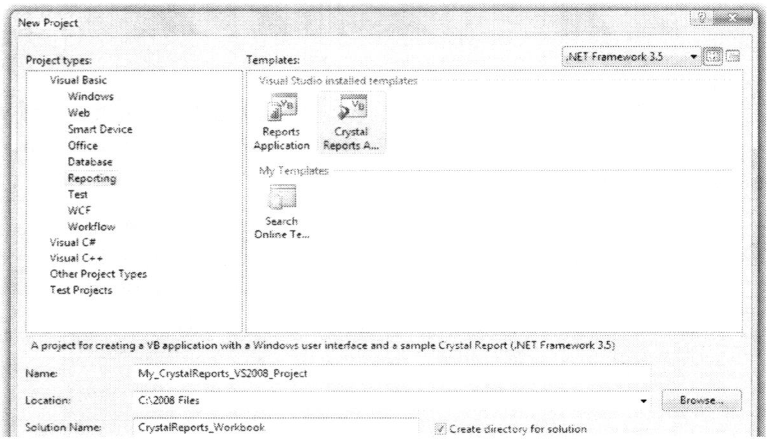

Figure 1-8 Options to create a project and add a report to the project

7. If you have not used Crystal Reports for Visual Studio 2008 before, you will see the Crystal Reports End User License dialog box. Select the option to accept the License Agreement, then click OK.

8. You will see the dialog box shown in Figure 1-9. Click the X in the upper right corner of the dialog box. If you have not used Crystal Reports before, the **TOOLBOX** will be initialized.

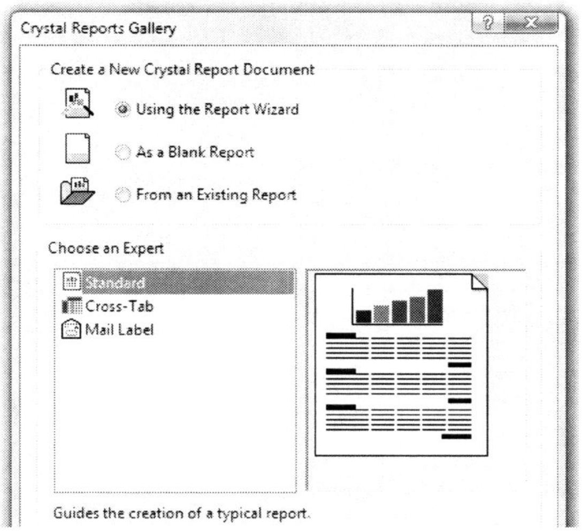

Figure 1-9 Crystal Reports Gallery dialog box

All of the reports created in this workbook are in a zip file named cr_vs2008.zip. (http://www.tolana.com/d/cr_vs2008/crfiles.html) They are provided as a reference in case you really get stuck. If you follow each step in the exercises, you probably will not need to look at these files. The zip file also contains reports that I created that are referenced in the workbook to illustrate a concept.

Crystal Reports Toolbars

There are three toolbars that are enabled by default in Crystal Reports: Standard, Crystal Reports - Main and Crystal Reports - Insert, as discussed below. They are right below the menu bar. The other toolbars that you may want to enable are the **REPORT BORDERS** and **REPORT FORMATTING** toolbars. They are not needed to complete any exercise in this workbook. Like toolbars in other applications, you can rearrange the toolbars by clicking on the dots at the beginning of the toolbar with the left mouse button and dragging the toolbar to a new location in the window. You can add or delete buttons on the toolbars. You can create your own toolbar. If you have used other Windows based applications, you are already familiar with many of the toolbar options.

Standard Toolbar

The buttons on the Standard toolbar contain general options. Table 1-2 explains the purpose of each button on the Standard toolbar.

Button	Purpose
	Create a new project.
	Add a new or existing object to the project. If you click on the arrow at the end of the button, you will see all of the objects that you can add.
	Opens a file.
	Saves the report.
	Saves all open reports and projects that have been changed.
	Deletes the selected object(s).
	Copies the selected object(s).
	Pastes object(s) from the clipboard into the report.
	Undoes an action.
	Redoes the last action that was undone.
	Navigate backward. (1)
	Navigate forward. (1)
	Starts the debugger. (1)
Debug	Selects the solution configuration. (1)
Any CPU	Selects the solution platform. (1)
	Opens the Find and Replace dialog box, which will let you search for files in the project or search for words in files and replace them.
	The Quick search option lets you search in the open report.
	Displays or hides the Solution Explorer window.
	Displays or hides the Properties window.
	Opens the Object Browser. (1)
	Displays or hides the Toolbox.
	Switches to the Start Page tab.
	Opens the Command window. (1)

Table 1-2 Standard toolbar buttons explained

(1)   This option is used for debugging an application.

Crystal Reports - Main Toolbar

The buttons on the Crystal Reports - Main toolbar provide access to the experts, including the select, group and sort experts. The buttons on this toolbar open dialog boxes that provide options to complete a task. Table 1-3 explains the purpose of each button on the toolbar.

Button	Purpose
	The Toggle Field View button opens and closes the Field Explorer.
	Opens the Select Expert which lets you create criteria to filter the records that will appear on the report.
	Opens the Group Sort Expert, which will let you find the Top or Bottom N records or lets you sort the data on summary fields.
	Opens the Record Sort Expert which lets you set the order that the detail records will be sorted in.
	Opens the appropriate Format Editor, which will let you modify the formatting properties of the selected object.
100%	Sets the zoom level for viewing a report. If you need a zoom percent that is not in the list, you can type in the percent you need over the 100 and press Enter.
Arial	Lets you select a font.
10	Lets you change the size for the font that is currently selected.
B	Makes the selected object bold.
I	Makes the selected object italic.
U	Underlines the selected object.
	Aligns the selected object flush left.
	Centers the data in the selected object.
	Aligns the data in the selected object flush right.
$	Adds or removes the currency symbol in the selected numeric field.
,	Adds or removes the comma in the selected numeric field.
%	Adds or removes the percent sign in the selected numeric field.
	Moves the decimal point in the selected numeric field one place to the right each time this button is clicked. (2)
	Moves the decimal point in the selected numeric field one place to the left each time this button is clicked. (2)

Table 1-3 Crystal Reports - Main toolbar buttons explained

(2) Rounding is set to the number of decimal places in the field.

Crystal Reports - Insert Toolbar

The buttons on the Crystal Reports - Insert toolbar contain options that let add objects to the report. Table 1-4 explains the purpose of each button on the Crystal Reports - Insert toolbar. These options are also on the shortcut menu.

Button	Purpose
Σ	Opens the Insert Summary dialog box which is used to create a calculated (summary) field.
〈目	Opens the Insert Group dialog box which is used to create a group.
団	Opens the Insert Subreport dialog box which is used to create a new report that will be used as a subreport or select an existing report to use as a subreport.
⬛	Opens the Chart Expert which is used to create a new chart.
⬛	Lets you add an image or picture file to the report.

Table 1-4 Crystal Reports - Insert toolbar buttons explained

Keep in mind that the buttons on the toolbars are available based on what you are doing and the object that is selected.

How To Remove Toolbars

Like many features in Crystal Reports, there is more than one way to remove toolbars. There are two ways to remove a toolbar, as discussed below.

① Tools ⇒ Customize. You will see the dialog box shown in Figure 1-10. Clear the check mark for the toolbar option that you do not want and click Close.

② View ⇒ Toolbars or right-click near the toolbars at the top of the Crystal Reports window. You will see the **TOOLBAR SHORTCUT MENU** shown in Figure 1-11. Click on the toolbar that you want to remove. Notice the **CUSTOMIZE** option at the bottom of the shortcut menu. Selecting this option will open the Toolbars dialog box shown in Figure 1-10.

Figure 1-10 Toolbars tab on the Customize dialog box

The arrow at the bottom of the menu means that there are more options that are not visible.

Click on the arrow and you will see the additional options.

	Build
	Class Designer
✔	Crystal Reports - Insert
✔	Crystal Reports - Main
	Data Design
	Database Diagram
	Debug
	Debug Location
	Device
	Dialog Editor
	Formatting
	Help
	HTML Source Editing
	Image Editor
	Layout
	Microsoft Office Excel 2003
	Microsoft Office Excel 2007
	Microsoft Office Word 2003
	Microsoft Office Word 2007
	Query Designer
	Report Borders
	Report Formatting
	Source Control
✔	Standard
	Style Application
	Style Sheet
	Table Designer
	Test Tools
	Text Editor
	View Designer
	▼

Figure 1-11 Toolbar shortcut menu

The Online Help File

The Help file in Crystal Reports is quite extensive. When you open the Help file, it opens in a new window instead of opening on the right side of the application window, like it does in other applications. To open the Help file, follow the instructions below.

1. Help ⇒ Contents. You will see the Document Explorer window. Click the Search button.

2. Type Crystal Reports in the Search field, then click the SEARCH button at the end of the field. You should see results similar to those shown in Figure 1-12. Click on the link that best meets your needs.

3. Close the Document Explorer window. If you are going to Lesson 2 now, leave Visual Studio and Crystal Reports open.

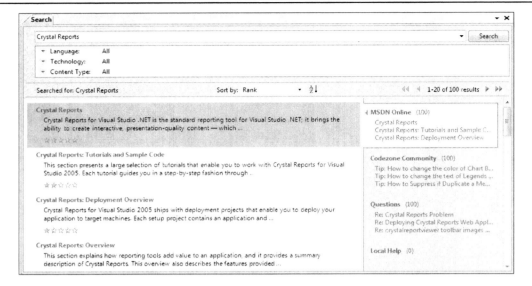

Figure 1-12 Search results

Getting Help On Dialog Boxes

Many of the dialog boxes have a question mark in the upper right corner as illustrated in Figure 1-13.

If you click on this button, the Document Explorer window will open and display the help page for the dialog box as shown in Figure 1-14.

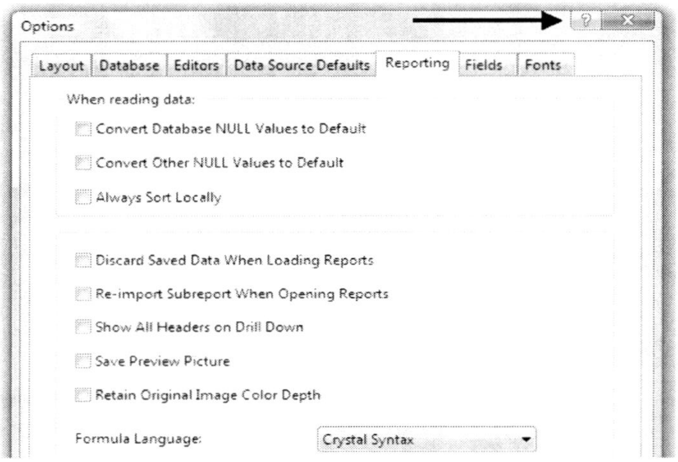

Figure 1-13 Dialog box with help button

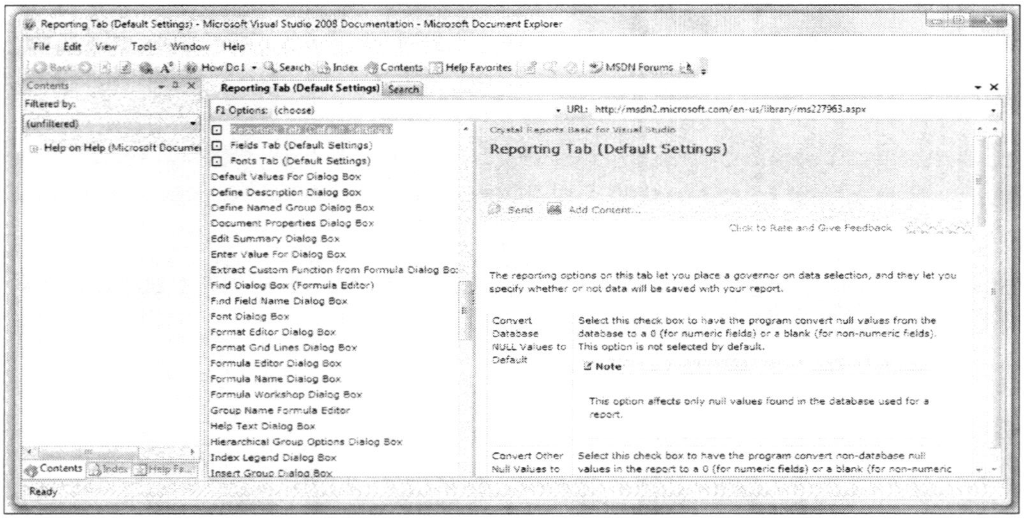

Figure 1-14 Help page for the options on the dialog box

Checking For Crystal Reports Software Updates

There are two ways to get the updates for Crystal Reports. You can download and install the Business Objects Update Service software (crupdate.msi). This service is suppose to notify you when updates are available. This exercise will show you how to check for and install updates. You need to be connected to the Internet before checking for updates. You have to have Crystal Reports and the design window open to check for updates. You will also learn how to check for updates manually.

 At press time, there were no updates for Crystal Reports Basic for Visual Studio 2008. The figures and instructions below are based on the version of Crystal Reports in Visual Studio 2005.

Use The Business Objects Crystal Reports Update Service

In this exercise you will download and install the update service software. You only have to install the software once (step 2 below), then you can check for updates using the menu option in Crystal Reports.

1. Crystal Reports ⇒ Check for Updates as shown in Figure 1-15.

2. Click on the **CRUPDATE.MSI** link, then click Run. I did not see any message saying the installation was complete.

3. Close the browser window after you install this software and select the Check for Updates option shown in Figure 1-15, you will see a dialog box similar to the one shown in Figure 1-16 that lets you know whether or not there are updates.

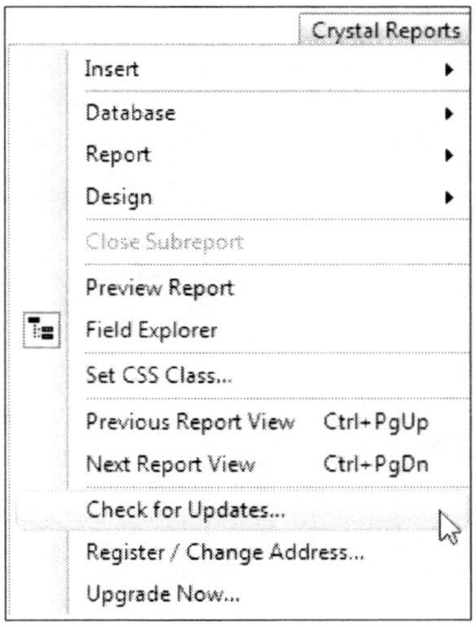

Figure 1-15 Update option

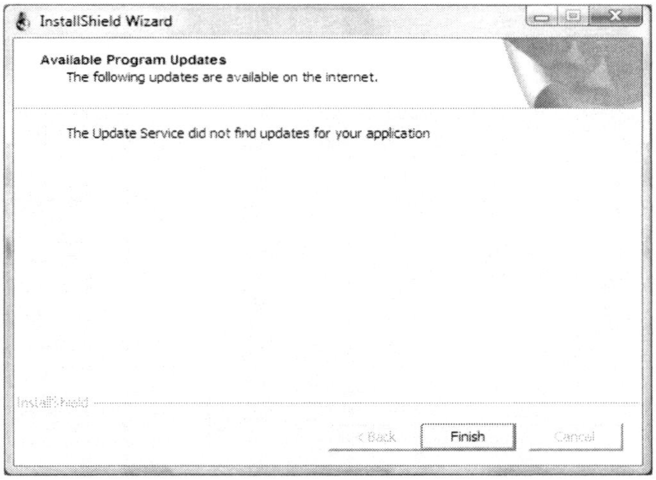

Figure 1-16 Available Program Updates dialog box

How To Check For Updates Manually

You can get the updates for Crystal Reports manually by going to the link below and downloading the update.
The link is for all of the updates for all versions of Crystal Reports. Scroll down the page and look for the Crystal Reports Basic for Visual Studio 2008 option. It should look similar to the one illustrated in Figure 1-17 for Visual Studio 2005.

http://support.businessobjects.com/downloads/
service_packs/crystal_reports_en.asp

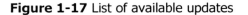

Crystal Reports 9

⬦ Service Pack 7 - EXE 69 MB - released July 2006
   Readme - PDF 0.3 MB

⬦ Service Pack 6 - EXE 68 MB - released January 2006
   Readme - PDF 0.3 MB

Crystal Reports 8.5

⬦ Service pack 3 - EXE 30 MB - released January 2004
   Readme - PDF 0.2MB

⬦ Service Pack 2 - EXE 30 MB - released October 2003
   Readme - PDF 0.2MB

Crystal Reports for Visual Studio .NET 2005

⬦ Service Pack 1 - EXE 107 MB - released November 2007
   Readme - PDF - 0.3 MB

Figure 1-17 List of available updates

Backing Up Your Work

I cannot stress how important it is to back up your work frequently. Doing so will save you frustration, aggravation and stress in the event a power failure occurs or if you have a hardware failure. The majority of times that you lose work it can't be recovered or if it can, it may cost you a few hundred dollars or more to recover it.

If you aren't already, you should also be saving your work to an external source like a CD, DVD, external hard drive or USB drive. Windows has a backup utility that you can use. I tell my students this in every class and it never fails that a student loses some, if not all of their work. Don't say that I didn't warn you <smile>.

Test Your Skills

1. Which toolbar has the option to let you open the Select Expert?

2. How many ways can you get updates for Crystal Reports?

3. Which toolbar has the option to open the Properties window?

4. What does the Crystal Reports Gallery allow you to do?

5. Which toolbar has the option to let you add a Summary field?

CREATE YOUR FIRST REPORT

In addition to creating your first report, after completing the exercises in this lesson you will be able to:

☑ Have a foundation of database terminology
☑ Understand data types
☑ Have a foundation of Crystal Reports terminology
☑ Understand the report design process
☑ Understand the sections of a report
☑ Understand the report creation options
☑ Understand the save data report options
☑ Use the Group Tree
☑ Use the design and preview windows

LESSON 2

Database Terminology

Below are key terms that you need to understand about databases in order to work with them effectively. It is important to note that there are different types of physical database structures.

① **Field** A field contains one piece of information and is stored in a record. Examples of fields include customer name and customer address.

② **Record** A record has one or more fields. Each of the fields in a record are related. A record looks like a row of data in a spreadsheet.

③ **Table** A table is stored in a database and is a collection of records. Most databases have more than one table. Related tables are linked on similar fields. Tables may remind you of a spreadsheet when viewed, because SQL databases have rows and columns, which Crystal Reports refers to as records and fields. Each table contains information about a specific topic. For example, a customer table would only contain information about customers. The customer table would not contain information about products.

④ **Relational Database** A relational database is a collection of **RELATED** information that is stored in one or more tables.

⑤ **Database** A database is a collection of information that is stored in one or more tables.

Database Concepts

There are several database concepts that you need to be aware of. Having an understanding of these concepts is necessary to create reports effectively.

Data Source A data source is where the data is stored. Examples of data sources are databases/tables, views and spreadsheets. You will learn more about data sources in Lesson 3.

Data Dictionary A data dictionary contains detailed information about a data source and includes the following types of information: database and table names, field names, field types, sizes, indexes and related files. A data dictionary can be a handwritten or typed document. It can also be generated by some database software packages.

Relationship A relationship is how two or more tables are joined (linked). Tables can be joined when they have at least one field that is the same in each table. For example, an invoice table can be joined to a products table because each invoice record will have at least one item from the products table. Crystal Reports has a feature that will automatically join tables that have related information. Crystal Reports also has a built-in visual utility that will help you link tables.

Length Is used to set what the contents of the field cannot be longer than. If the length of a field is set to 20, the contents in the field cannot have more than 20 characters.

Null Any of the field data types discussed later in this lesson can be null (empty). Null means that the field does not have a value. Depending on the data source, an empty string may or may not be set to null. An empty numeric field is not equal to zero by default.

Index The purpose of indexes is to make the retrieval of records from tables faster. Knowing which fields in the table are indexed is important when you need to optimize a report. Crystal Reports can indicate which fields are indexed in some types of databases and in other types of databases it can't. If Crystal Reports does not recognize the indexes in the table(s) that you are using, you can get the information from the data dictionary for the database.

 PRIMARY KEY FIELDS should always be indexed. **FOREIGN KEY FIELDS** are usually indexed. Fields in a table that are used frequently to retrieve (select) records should be indexed. Fields that fall into this category are fields that are used to sort, group or link data.

Databases that have too many indexes will retrieve records slower. Indexes are usually created by the DBA (Data Base Administrator). If you need to have an index created contact the DBA, unless you have the rights to do so.

Data Types

Each field must have a data type. The data type determines what type of information can be stored in the field and how the data can be formatted. Table 2-1 explains the data types that are available in most databases.

Data Type	Description
Text	Text fields primarily contain alpha numeric characters. Text fields can also have numbers, spaces and other special characters. Text fields are also known as **STRING FIELDS**. Numeric data that is stored in a string field is treated like text because there is no need to use the data in any type of calculation. An example of numeric data that is treated like text is zip codes. Numeric data stored in a string field cannot be formatted with any number data type formatting options. (1)
Number	This data type can only contain numbers and decimal points. This data type can be used in a calculation like addition, multiplication and formulas. (1)
Currency	This data type can only contain monetary data. You can use currency fields in calculations, just like number fields. Currency is a special number data type. By default, Crystal Reports will automatically display and print a dollar sign with this data type. (1)
Date	Date fields are used to store dates, which can be stored in several formats. Date fields contain the month, day and year. (1)
Time	This data type is used to store time, which can be stored in several formats. Time fields contain hours, minutes and seconds. Crystal Reports does not recognize fractional seconds even if the underlying data source has them. (1)
Date and Time	Displays the date and time in one field, in this format - MM/DD/YYYY HH:MM:SS. You can suppress the time portion of this data type on reports if you need to. (1)
Boolean	Boolean fields are used to set a logical value of true/false, yes/no or 1/0. (1)
Memo	The memo data type is a free form text field, meaning that it can store almost any type of information. This data type may not be available in all databases. Memo fields can contain large amounts of data and embedded formatting. Crystal Reports can recognize **RICH TEXT (RTF)** and **HTML FORMATTING** in memo fields. A common use for memo fields is to store comments about the data in the other fields in the record.
OLE Object	This data type can store an image file. Crystal Reports recognizes the following image file types: BMP, JPEG, TIFF, PNG and WMF. Some databases refer to this data type as a **BLOB** (Binary Large Object).

Table 2-1 Data types explained

(1) Can also be used as an unbound field. Unbound fields do not have a data source.

Crystal Reports recognizes all of the data types listed above. If you use a database that has data types other then the ones listed above in Table 2-1, they will be mapped to a data type that Crystal Reports recognizes.

Crystal Reports Terminology

Below are some key terms that you need to understand about Crystal Reports in order to work with databases effectively. The four field types discussed below are not stored in a table like the data types discussed above are.

① **Formula Fields** Formula fields can include any of the 200+ built-in functions that Crystal Reports has, or you can create a formula from scratch. The result of a calculated field is created on the fly, meaning that each time the report is run, the formula field will be recalculated. Formula fields are covered in detail in Lesson 9.

② **Special Fields** Special fields contain information that is system generated. Examples of system generated fields include the date the report was printed and page numbers. There are 18 special fields that you can use.

③ **Summary Fields** Summary fields are calculated fields and like formula fields, they are also calculated on the fly, each time the report is run. You create summary fields.

④ **Text Object Fields** This is a free form field that is used to place information on the report that can't be added to the report by any of the fields discussed above. Text objects are often used to create a report title or a heading for fields that you create.

Report Design Process

I know that you are anxious to create your first report, but there are several items that need to be addressed and worked out before you create a report, whether this is your first report or your 100th report. This section is an overview of the report design process and planning. Report design could be an entire chapter or two all by itself, but I am giving you the abridged version. The report design process is part of what is known as the "Business Requirements" phase of a project. As you gain experience, you will see that if you do not get the business requirements right, the project will be delayed, potentially be over budget and not produce the results that the business owner (requestor) or client is looking for. Many call this a "bad career move".

When you learn the concepts presented in this lesson, it will be easier for you to create reports. You should write down the answers to the questions that will be presented in the report design process. The more planning that you do before you create the report, the less you will have to modify a report after it is created. There are four primary steps to the report design process. Each step can have multiple tasks. You will see how these steps come together through the exercises in this workbook.

When creating reports, especially reports that other people use, it is imperative that you fully understand the requirements of the report, which often requires asking a lot of questions. This is not a task that you can be bashful about. Not asking questions or worse, asking the wrong questions will more then likely cause you grief down the road.

Step 1: Define The Purpose Of The Report

Yes, I know what you are saying - "How hard can it be to figure out the purpose of a report?". The answer is it depends on how well the person or group of people are able to explain what they want the report to provide and how well you understand what they tell you.

The majority of reports that you create will be used by someone other than yourself, which means that you should meet with the person or group of people that will use the report. These meetings are part of the requirement gathering process. Keep in mind that you may have to have more than one meeting to get a good idea of what the report needs to include, because the users may not tell you or be able to clearly articulate their needs in the one meeting. Reports are often used as a decision making tool, which means that poor decisions will be made or the decision making process will be ineffective due to missing or incorrect data that is presented on the report. The data must be presented in a logical manner in order to be an effective decision making tool.

Keep in mind that one report can be used by people at different levels in the company. This means that at each level, people can have slightly different needs. If this is the case, you will have to plan and design the report accordingly, so that it meets the needs for all of the users.

Your role as the report designer is to gather the information needed, which will help the user(s) of the report to be able to read it easily, as well as, understand the data on the report. If the information is not presented in a way that works for the users, trust me, they will let you know and you will be spending a lot of time modifying the report(s).

In my opinion and experiences that I have had, the more that users have you modify a report, the quicker your credibility goes down hill. That is not something that you want to happen. What I have discovered, as well as, many other Information Technology professionals, is that if you create a prototype (which is discussed later in this lesson) of the report for the users, they can discuss what they like and do not like about the prototype report. Usually, you will gain valuable information that is often hard to get users to discuss in a regular meeting. The worst thing that you can do in many cases, is give the users the impression that you know more about their needs then they do. I am not saying that in some cases that you won't know more about their data, just don't give them that impression, if you know what I mean.

To define the expected outcome of the report, write a descriptive sentence or two about the purpose of the report or what the report needs to accomplish. Below are some sample purpose statements.

① The purpose of the report is to compare last years sales data to this years sales data by region.
② The purpose of the report is to show products that are low on inventory and need to be reordered.
③ The purpose of the report is to show the top 10 best selling products by sales team.

In addition to defining the expected outcome of the report you have to take into consideration who will be using the report. It is very possible that managers and their staff will request similar reports. In many cases it is better to create separate reports, even if there is only one field that is different, then to try and get multiple parties to try and come up with one report that works for both groups of users. As you gain report design experience, understand business requirements and know the requestors, you will be able to quickly determine which is the best option.

Step 2: Determine The Layout Of The Report

Now that you have determined the purpose of the report, you need to determine where each piece of data should be placed on the report. If you are creative you will like this step. In addition to determining where the data should be placed you need to determine some or all of the following:

① Create a list of fields that need to appear on the report. If you know what database or table each field is in, include that on the list. If the data does not currently exist, include it on the list also. You will use this list to complete tasks in future steps in the report design process.
② What should the report title be and where should it be placed on the report. Should it only be printed on the first page or on all pages of the report?
③ Does the report need page numbers or dates? If so, what format should they be in and where should they be placed on the report - in the page header or footer section or someplace else?
④ Are any Special Fields other than the page number or date needed on the report?
⑤ Which fields or sections of the report need totals, summary, statistical information or some other type of calculated field? (**Hint**: Summary fields do not currently exist in a table).
⑥ An important question to answer during this step is what format(s) the report needs to be in. This is known as the **DELIVERY METHOD** (for example, paper, PDF or web based). The way that a report needs to be distributed can influence the layout of a report. You should also determine if the report needs to be distributed in more than one format.

Step 3: Find The Data For The Report

This step is very important because without the data there is no report. As the person creating the report, life will be much easier for you if you are familiar with the data needed for the report and how it is organized. If you are not familiar with the data or are not technical, you may have to rely on Information Technology specialists like database administrators to help you with the tasks in this step. There are three tasks that you have to work on to complete this step successfully.

Task 1 The first task that you have to complete is to find out which databases and tables contain the data that you need for the report. Use the list of fields that you created in step 2 to find the databases and tables. You may also have to find out what servers the databases are on. There are several types of databases that the data can be stored in. The data may also be stored in a Crystal dictionary or something other then a database like an Excel spreadsheet. This task is known as finding the DATA SOURCE.

Task 2 This task involves selecting the actual fields in the tables that are needed for the report. Use the list that you created in step 2. Once the fields are selected, determine the formatting for each field and how the fields should be displayed on the report. You also have to determine if the field names in the table are the best choice for the field headings on the report. One example of when a field heading needs to be changed on a report is for fields that are commonly known as ID fields, which you will learn about in Lesson 3.

Task 3 Now that you have found some of the data in the tables, there are probably fields left on the list that you created in step 2 that you have not found. Some may be special fields that you read about earlier in this lesson. More than likely, many of the fields that are left on the list are calculated fields. This task involves writing out the formulas for the calculated fields. Some calculated fields may use a built-in function and others require a field that is in a data source, but will not be placed on the report.

In order to be able to create calculated fields, you have to become familiar with the database field types and the Crystal Reports fields discussed earlier in this lesson. Several of the Crystal Reports functions are designed to only work with specific types of data. Examples of calculated fields include:

① Sales price times quantity
② Number of days between the order date and the ship date
③ How long the person has been employed at the company

Step 4: Organize The Data

This step involves organizing all of the data. Many of the options that you decide on in task 1 below, will automatically dictate which section of the report certain fields will be placed in.

Task 1 To complete this task you have to organize all of the data, both from the tables and calculated fields, as well as, any other data source. Organizing the data means at a minimum, answering the following questions.

① Does the data need to be sorted? If so, which field(s) should the data be sorted on?
② Does the data need to be grouped? If so, which field(s) should the data be grouped on?
③ Does the report need summary data? Summary data is a calculated field, like grand totals, averages and counts.
④ Does the report need to have any data flagged? If so, how should the data be flagged?
The primary reason data would be flagged is so that it can be easily identified on a report. Make a list of any data that needs to be flagged. Crystal Reports has several options including borders, symbols, changing the font size and other formatting techniques that you can use to indicate that the data is flagged.
⑤ Decide if the report needs any of the following: charts, cross-tabs or a logo.

Task 2 To complete this task you have to determine which section of the report each field should be placed in. Task 1 had you make decisions on how to organize the data at a high level. There are several sections of a report that the data and objects can be placed in. The sections of a report are discussed later in this lesson.

Task 3 One way that you organize the data is selecting which records will actually appear on the report. This is important because most reports do not require that all records in a table appear on the report. For example, if the report needs to display sales (orders) for a specific sales rep, you would create selection criteria that would only allow orders for the particular sales rep to appear on the report. Another example would be to display all customers that purchased a specific product or group of products.

In addition to record selection, it may be necessary to create parameter fields which will make the report more flexible in terms of record selection. Parameter fields allow the person running the report to select the criteria that will be used to retrieve the records that will appear on the report. Parameter fields allow one report to be run with a variety of selection criteria. An example of this would be an order report. If the report had parameter fields for the order date, order amount and sales rep fields, all of the following reports and more, could be run from the same report.

① A report to print all orders on a specific date.
② A report to print orders for a specific sales rep.
③ A report to print orders over or under a specific total order amount.
④ A report to print all orders in a date range.
⑤ A report to print all orders in a date range for a specific sales rep.

Task 4 Depending on the company, it may be necessary to have the person or group of people sign a document that states that all of the tasks discussed above will produce the report that they need.

Report Prototype

Even though you will go through the entire report design process, it is very possible that the users are still somewhat unclear or cannot visualize what the finished report will look like. If that is the case, creating a report prototype will be a life saver. A prototype can be hand drawn on paper or you can create a sample report that displays the data based on the information that you gather during the report design process.

Some report designers create this prototype as each of the steps and tasks that were discussed above are completed. Other report designers will create the prototype right after the report design process is over. The reason prototypes are helpful is because the users will get a pretty good idea of what the finished report will look like, based on the information that they supplied.

The feedback that you receive from the users about the prototype is invaluable because users get to "see" what they asked for. I have found this process to be a very effective way for users to tell me what they like, don't like, need and don't need.

Sections Of A Report

There are seven sections of a report that you can place data and other objects in. If you place the same calculated field in different sections of the report it will produce different results. It is important that you understand how each section of the report functions because they function independently of each other. Keep the following items in mind when deciding where to place fields and objects on the report.

① Not all sections are needed for every report.
② If you create a report using a wizard, the majority of fields are automatically placed in an appropriate section of the report.
③ All of the report sections discussed below except the group header and footer, will automatically appear in all reports, whether you use them or not. Grouping is optional.
④ The order of the default sections of a report cannot be changed.

⑤ If a report does not need a section, it can be suppressed so that it does not display blank space on the report.

⑥ Sections can be resized as needed.

Formulas, charts and cross-tabs will display different results, depending on which section of the report they are placed in. These differences are explained below in each report section.

Section 1: Report Header

Data fields and other objects placed in this section will only print on the first page of the report. It is quite possible that many of the reports that you create will not have anything in this section. Something that you may want to include in this section of the report is the criteria and parameters of the report. If the report needs a cover page, the report header section can be used for the cover page. If this is what you need to do, add a page break after this section so that the actual report starts on a new page.

FORMULAS are calculated for the entire report.
CHARTS and **CROSS-TABS** will contain data for the entire report.

 If the report header section requires more than one page, the information in the page header and footer sections will not print until all of the information in the report header section has printed.

Section 2: Page Header

On the first page of the report, this section is right below the report header section. From the second page on in the report, the page header section appears at the top of each page. Data fields and other objects placed in this section will appear at the top of every page in the report, except the report header page if it prints on a page by itself. This is where most people put the report title. Other objects that are commonly placed in this section include the date, page number and headings for the fields in the details section of the report. Report wizards will automatically place field headings and the system generated "print date" field in this section.

FORMULAS are calculated at the beginning of every page of the report.
CHARTS and **CROSS-TABS** cannot be placed in this section.

Section 3: Group Header

This section is only used if data is grouped in the report. Data fields and other objects placed in this section will print at the beginning of each group section of the report. Each time the data in the field the group is based on changes, another group header and footer section is dynamically created. This section is always right above the details section. If a report is grouped on two or more fields, a new group header and footer section will be created for each field that the report is grouped on.

FORMULAS are calculated one time at the beginning of the group, based on the data in the group, not all of the data in the report.
CHARTS and **CROSS-TABS** will only display information based on the data in the group.

Section 4: Details

Data fields and other objects placed in this section will print for each record that meets the selection criteria. The data fields and other objects in this section usually have field headings in the page header section. This section is automatically repeated once for each record that will be printed on the report.

FORMULAS are calculated for each record in this section, unless the record does not meet the condition of the formula.
CHARTS and **CROSS-TABS** cannot be placed in this section.

Section 5: Group Footer

This section is only used if data is grouped in the report. Data fields and other objects placed in this section will print at the end of each group. The group footer section often includes subtotals and other summary data for the group. This section is always right below the details section.

FORMULAS are calculated one time at the end of the group, based on the data in the group, not on all of the data in the report.
CHARTS and **CROSS-TABS** will only display information based on the data in the group.

Section 6: Report Footer

Data fields and other objects placed in this section will print once at the end of the report. This is usually where grand totals and other types of report summary information is placed.

FORMULAS are calculated once at the end of the report.
CHARTS and **CROSS-TABS** will contain data for the entire report.

If the report footer section requires more than one page to print information, the page header and footer sections will print on the additional pages that the report footer needs. This is the opposite of what happens if the report header requires more than one page. If you think about it though, that makes sense because by the time the report footer section is printed, the "switch" if you will, for the page header and footer sections is turned on.

Section 7: Page Footer

Data fields and other objects placed in this section will print at the bottom of each page of the report. The page footer section is similar to the page header section. Page numbers are often placed in this section. Report wizards will automatically place the page number in this section.

FORMULAS are calculated at the end of every page of the report. This would be useful if the report needs to have totals by page.
CHARTS and **CROSS-TABS** cannot be placed in this section.

The five default sections of a report in order are: Report Header, Page Header, Details, Report Footer and Page Footer.

Report Creation Options

There are three ways (wizards, from an existing report and from scratch) that you can create a report. Each option has pros and cons. Once you understand all of the options, you can select the one that best meets the needs for each report that you have to create.

Wizards

This is the easiest way to create a new report. The wizards will walk you through all of the steps required to create a report. The wizards are helpful when learning the basics of Crystal Reports. Experienced report designers often only use the wizards to save time to create a basic report and then add advanced features manually. Keep in mind that the wizards do not provide all of the functionality that is needed to create many features that reports need. The wizards are limited because they use default options which often do not meet the needs of the report that you are creating. One of the things that comes to mind are the titles that summary fields and other total fields are given.

Based on your selections on the wizard screens, the fields are placed in the most appropriate section of the report. This does not mean that if you make a mistake when using the wizard, that the wizard will correct the mistake. It is possible to create a report that displays results that are different then you intended when using a wizard. There are three report wizards that you can select from, that are discussed later in this lesson. What you will find, depending on the options that you select, is that additional fields are automatically added to the report, which you may not need. If you create a report with a wizard that groups data, the fields will not appear in the same order that you selected them in. If either of these issues happen you can delete the field(s) once you have the report open in the design window.

Create A Report Based Off Of An Existing Report

If a report exists that is similar to the report that you now need to create, select this report creation option. Save the existing report with a new name and make the necessary changes to the new report. An example of when to create a report based off of an existing report would be when two groups of people need to see the majority of the same fields and one group of people needs additional information that the other group does not need, or when one group needs the same fields in a different layout.

Create A Report From Scratch

This option gives you the most flexibility to create a report. You start with a blank canvas so to speak and add the fields, formulas and other objects without any assistance. For many, this can be intimidating especially in the beginning, but being the fearless person that you are, I'm sure that when you get to the exercises that have you create a report from scratch, you will do just fine.

Wizard Types

As mentioned earlier, there are three report wizards that you can select from to create reports. They are discussed below.

① **Standard** This is probably the most used wizard because it provides the majority of options needed to create a wide variety of reports. The report wizards discussed below create specific types of reports.

② **Cross-Tab** This wizard will create a report that presents data in a grid. Cross-Tab reports resemble spreadsheets because they have rows and columns. The grid often contains totals at the end of each row and column. An example of when a cross-tab should be used would be if you needed to know how many of specific products were sold by each sales rep. You should only use this wizard if the cross-tab will be the only object on the report.

③ **Mail Label** This wizard will walk you through the process of creating mailing labels. While you can format a report created with the Standard wizard to print labels, the advantage of using the mailing label wizard is that it has an option to select the label size that you need. This means that you will not have to manually format the report to match the dimensions of the label size that you need.

Xtreme Database

The Xtreme database comes with Crystal Reports. This is the database that you will use as the basis for all of the reports that you will create in this workbook. It also contains sample reports, which you can use to get ideas for reports that you may need to create.

When Crystal Reports was installed, the Xtreme database also was installed. It is a Microsoft Access database. This database contains the data for a fictitious company called Xtreme Mountain Bikes. As the company name suggests, they sell mountain bikes and accessories. The database has tables that store the following types of information: Customers, Employees, Orders, Suppliers and Products.

Figure 2-1 shows the data model for the Xtreme database. The fields in bold are the Primary Key fields. Table 2-2 contains information for each table in the database that will be helpful when creating reports. You will learn more about primary keys in the next lesson.

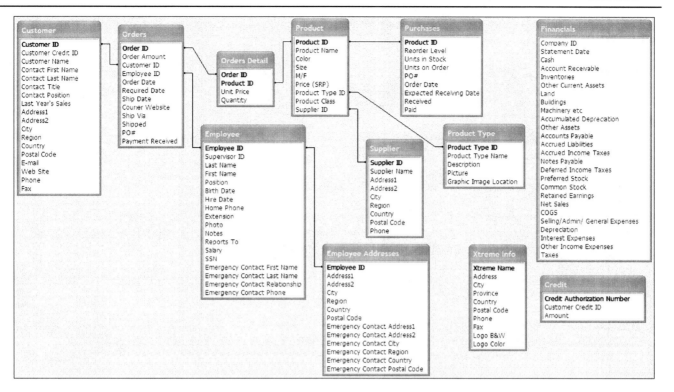

Figure 2-1 Xtreme database data model

Table	Primary Key	Indexed Fields	Records
Credit	Credit Authorization Number	Credit Authorization Number, Customer Credit ID	322
Customer	Customer ID	Customer ID, Postal Code	269
Employee	Employee ID	Employee ID, Supervisor ID, Reports To	15
Employee Address	Employee ID	Employee ID, Postal Code, Emergency Contact Postal Code	15
Financials	Company ID	Company ID	4
Orders	Order ID	Order ID, Customer ID, Employee ID	2,192
Orders Detail	Order ID, Product ID	Order ID, Product ID	3,684
Product	Product ID	Product ID, Product Type ID, Supplier ID	115
Product Type	Product Type ID	Product Type ID	8
Purchases	Product ID	Product ID	44
Supplier	Supplier ID	Supplier ID, Postal Code	7
Xtreme Info	Xtreme Name	Xtreme Name, Postal Code	1

Table 2-2 Xtreme database table information

Xtreme Database Tables Explained

In order to help you become more familiar with the data contained in each table, this section provides a description of the data in each table. The table name is in bold.

Credit Contains credit limit information for customers.

Customer Contains contact and address information for all of the companies customers.

Employee Contains information for each employee. Some of the employees are sales reps for the company.

 The Supervisor ID field in the Employee table contains the Employee ID of a different person in the Employee table. The Supervisor ID field contains who the employee reports to. This is known as a **RECURSIVE JOIN**, which you will learn about in the next lesson.

Employee Addresses Contains the home address and emergency contact information for each person in the Employee table.

Financials Contains accounting information for the company.

Orders Contains information about each customer order. Fields that apply to the entire order, like the order date and order amount are in this table. This table is often referred to as the **ORDER HEADER** table. This table does not contain information about the items on the order.

Orders Detail Contains information about each item in each order. This is one of the smaller tables in the database in terms of the number of fields.

Product Contains information for each item that Xtreme sells. Each product only has one product type and supplier. This does not mean that there cannot be two suppliers that have the same product. For example, Supplier A has blue hats. Supplier B has blue hats and brown hats. There would be a record in the Product table for each of these three hats.

Product Type Contains the general categories for the products like gloves, locks and helmets.

Purchases Contains information about purchases that Xtreme makes from their suppliers.

Supplier Contains information about the companies that Xtreme purchases the products from that they sell. Contact and address information for each supplier is stored in this table.

Xtreme Info Contains the Xtreme company contact information and the logo.

Viewing The Sample Reports

If you haven't already viewed any of the sample reports that come with the Xtreme database, this exercise will show you how to view them.

1. Click the **OPEN FILE** button on the Standard toolbar. Navigate to the sample reports in this location. C:\Program Files\Microsoft Visual Studio 9.0\Crystal Reports\Samples\en\Reports.

2. You should see two folders, **FEATURE EXAMPLES** and **GENERAL BUSINESS**. Double-click on the General Business folder. You will see the list of reports shown in Figure 2-2.

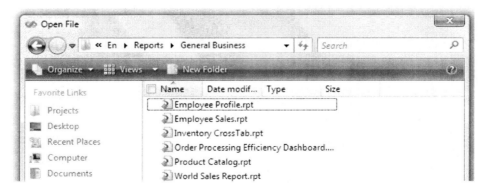

Figure 2-2 Reports in the General Business folder

3. Double-click on the Product Catalog report. Click on the **MAIN REPORT PREVIEW** tab below the report. The report should look similar to the one shown in Figure 2-3. The only difference should be the date and time under the report title.

Notice that the report opened on it's own tab. The tab name is the report file name.

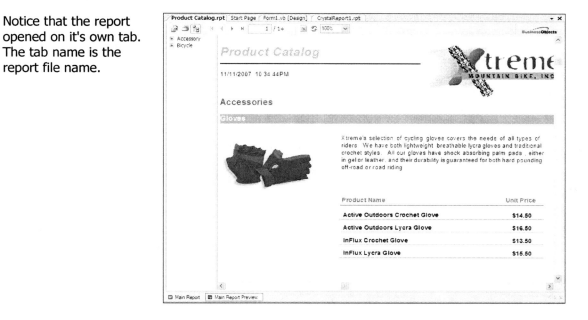

Figure 2-3 Product Catalog report

Design And Preview Windows

These two windows are available for each report, as illustrated at the bottom of Figure 2-3 shown above. The **MAIN REPORT** window is where you create an modify reports. I will refer to this window as the design window. The **MAIN REPORT PREVIEW** window is where you view reports. I will refer to this window as the preview window. The preview window lets you view the report as it will look when it is printed. Reports can look different in this window depending on the printer that is selected. Also notice the following:

① Some of the toolbar options that you learned about in Lesson 1 are now available in the design window.

② The report has it's own navigation toolbar right above the report as shown above in Figure 2-3. You can use the options on this toolbar to move from one page to another and to refresh the data in the report. The navigation toolbar also lets you know what page of the report you are currently viewing and how many pages in total the report has.

Design And Preview Window Differences

As much as these windows have in common, there are some differences that you should be aware of as discussed below.

① Only the preview window has the group tree, page controls and refresh data options.

② If you select a field in the preview window, every occurrence of the field in the report is selected.

③ The design window has a vertical and horizontal ruler.

Report Navigation Toolbar

Earlier I mentioned that the preview tab has it's own toolbar. It is located on the preview window above the report. The buttons on this toolbar contain options to navigate in a report. This toolbar is activated once you preview a report. This toolbar is shown in Figure 2-4. Table 2-3 explains the purpose of each button on the toolbar.

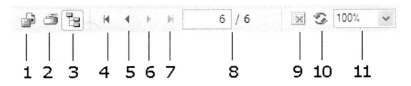

Figure 2-4 Report navigation toolbar

Button	Description
1	Exports the report to another file format.
2	Prints the report.
3	Hides and displays the Group Tree.
4	Displays the first page of the report.
5	Displays the previous page of the report.
6	Displays the next page of the report.
7	Displays the last page of the report.
8	Displays the current page of the report and the total number of pages the report has. If you want to go to a specific page number, you can type it in this field and press Enter. The plus sign in **1 OF 1+** shown in Figure 2-5 lets you know that Crystal Reports has not formatted all of the pages in the report. This means that the total number of pages is currently unknown.
9	Stops the processing of data and only displays the report with the data that has been processed, prior to clicking this button. This is helpful if the report has a lot of pages and you only need to see the first few pages of the report.
10	Refreshes the data in the report.
11	Sets the zoom level for viewing a report. If you need a zoom percent that is not in the list, you can type over the 100 that is displayed and press Enter. You have to use the percent sign.

Table 2-3 Report navigation toolbar buttons explained

Figure 2-5 Report page number field

> 🔆 If you see **1 OF 1+** and want to know how many pages the report has, click the **GO TO LAST PAGE** button on the report navigation toolbar. As shown earlier in Figure 2-4, the page indicator lets you know that there are six pages in the report.

1. Click the Go to last page button on the Report navigation toolbar. You should see the last page of the report.

2. Close the Product Catalog report by right-clicking on the tab for it. You will see the shortcut menu shown in Figure 2-6. Each type of tab has different options on the shortcut menu. Figure 2-7 shows the shortcut menu for the Start Page tab. Select the **CLOSE** option. You may see the dialog box shown in Figure 2-9.

Report Tab Shortcut Menu

The report tab has a shortcut menu as shown in Figure 2-6. These options are available from the design and preview windows. The options are explained in Table 2-4.

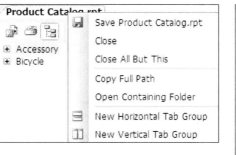

Figure 2-6 Report tab shortcut menu

Figure 2-7 Start Page tab shortcut menu

Option	Description
Save	Saves the report on the tab.
Close	Closes the report on the tab.
Close All But This	Closes all report files that are open, except the one on the tab.
Copy Full Path	Lets you copy the path of the report and paste it in a document.
Open Containing Folder	Opens the folder that the report on the tab is in.
New Horizontal Tab Group	Opens a tab group below the one the report is in and moves the report to the new tab group as shown in Figure 2-8.
New Vertical Tab Group	Opens a tab group to the right of the current tab group and moves the report to the new tab group.

Table 2-4 Report tab shortcut menu options explained

The **RECENT PROJECTS** section of the Start Page tab will display the last six projects that you opened by default.

You should see the project that you created, as shown in Figure 2-8. You will see additional projects listed if you opened them prior to starting this exercise. The first project listed is the last one that you opened.

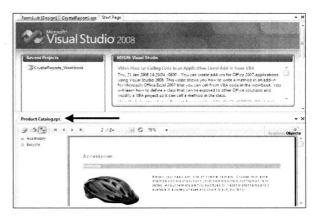

Figure 2-8 Horizontal tab group

Closing Visual Studio

When you close Visual Studio you will see the dialog box shown in Figure 2-9 if you did not click the Save All button after you made the last change.

Figure 2-9 Save project and report changes dialog box

When you create or modify reports in a project, the project files (which are different then the report files) are updated. If you click the **SAVE ALL** button on the Standard toolbar right before you close Visual Studio, the reports that you create or modify are saved, as well as, the project files.

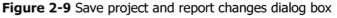

Depending on what you have touched in the report, Crystal Reports will think that you have made changes. In this case, you did not make any changes and if you did, you would not want to save them in the sample report.

3. Click **NO** on the dialog box shown above in Figure 2-9. The report window will close.

The Group Tree

The options shown down the left side of the preview window are the groups that the report has. This section is called the **GROUP TREE**. It displays all of the groups and subgroups in the report. You can customize the group name, which you will learn how to do later in the workbook. The group tree is helpful when you need to navigate through a report that has a lot of groups. Clicking on an option in the group tree will jump to the corresponding section in the report.

If a group has a subgroup, you will see a plus sign (+) in front of the group name, as shown in Figure 2-10. Clicking on the plus sign will expand the group and show the subgroup(s) as shown in Figure 2-10. The plus sign is also known as the **EXPAND BUTTON**. The minus sign is also known as the **COLLAPSE BUTTON**.

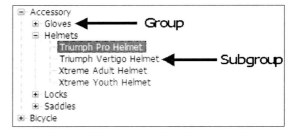

Figure 2-10 Group tree expanded

To show or hide the group tree, click the **TOGGLE GROUP TREE** button on the Report navigation toolbar or right-click in the Group tree section of the report and select **GROUP TREE** as shown at the bottom of Figure 2-11.

By default, the group tree is enabled even if the report does not have any groups.

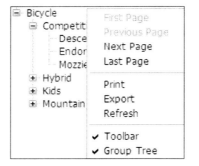

Figure 2-11 Group tree shortcut menu

Resizing The Group Tree Section

If you can't see the groups on the left side of the window, place the mouse pointer on the bar as illustrated in Figure 2-12 and drag the bar over to the right as much as needed.

Figure 2-12 Mouse pointer in position to resize the Group Tree section

Drilling-Down In A Report

If you double-click on an item in the report, another window will open that displays the detail information for the item that you double-clicked on, in this example a product shown in Figure 2-13. This technique is known as **DRILLING-DOWN** in a report.

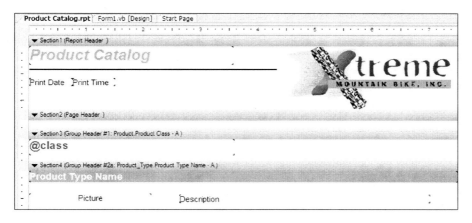

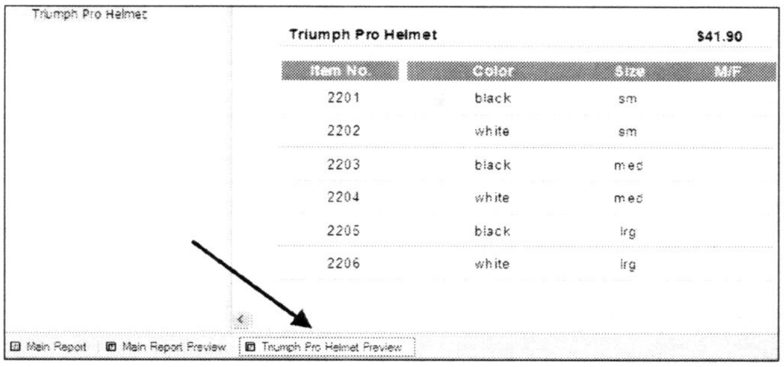

Figure 2-13 Detail information for a specific product in the report

If you want more space for the report on the screen, close the Document Outline section on the left of the window by clicking on the X in that window.

Overview Of The Design Window

1. File ⇒ Recent Files. Select the Product Catalog report. You will see the window shown in Figure 2-14.

Figure 2-14 Design (Main Report) window

The design window is where you will create and modify reports, as well as, see the structure of the report. Figure 2-15 illustrates the parts of the design window. Table 2-5 explains the parts of the design window.

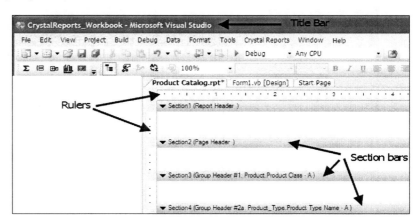

Figure 2-15 Parts of the design window illustrated

Report tabs that have a * after the file name as shown in Figure 2-15, indicates that changes have been made to the report, but the changes have not been saved.

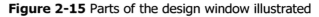

Option	Description
Title bar	Displays the solution name of the project.
Section bar	Like other parts of the design window, each section has a shortcut menu, which you access by right-clicking on the section bar that you want to work on. These are the report sections that you learned about earlier in this lesson.
Rulers	The rulers help you place fields in a specific location on the report.
Design area	This is white space under each section bar where you can add, change and format fields and other objects. The design area has a shortcut menu, that has different options then the section bars. You can place objects as close to the edge of this area as necessary because this area is inside of the page margins.

Table 2-5 Parts of the design window explained

Everything on a report is an object. Each object has its own set of properties. Almost all of these properties can be modified. The properties can also be modified based on a condition that you set. You will learn about conditional formatting in Lesson 9.

Report Sections

As shown above in Figure 2-15, the design window is divided into sections. The sections are divided by **SECTION BARS**. The sections can be resized by moving the section bar up or down. Figure 2-16 shows a smaller page header section and a larger report section, then shown above in Figure 2-15.

If you do not need to display data in a section of the report, you can **SUPPRESS** (hide) the section and it will not appear on the preview window or on the printed report. To resize a section of the report, place the mouse pointer over the section bar for the section that you need to resize, as illustrated in Figure 2-17. The mouse pointer will change to a double arrow as illustrated. Drag the section bar up or down.

▼ Section1 (Report Header)

▼ Section2 (Page Header)

▼ Section3 (Group Header #1: Product.Product Class - A)

Figure 2-16 Sections of a report resized

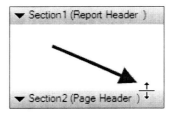

▼ Section1 (Report Header)

▼ Section2 (Page Header)

Figure 2-17 Mouse pointer in position to move the section bar

You cannot make a section of the report smaller than the objects that are in the section.

View Another Sample Report

1. Click on the Start Page tab, then click the Open File button. If necessary, navigate to the sample reports folder.

2. Double-click on the Feature Examples folder, then double-click on the Group report. You will see the report shown in Figure 2-18 in preview mode.

3. Close the Group report by right-clicking on the tab and selecting Close. If you see the dialog box shown earlier in Figure 2-9 click No.

File ⇒ Close, will also close the active report window.

4. Close the Form1.vb and CrystalReport1 tabs.

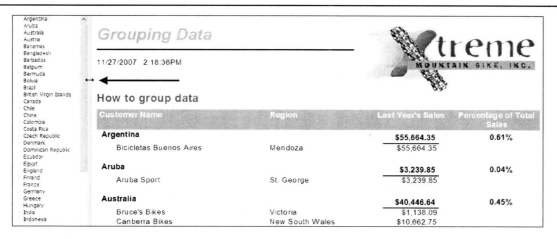

Figure 2-18 Grouping report

Learning To Create Reports

For some, learning to create reports can be intimidating. **LEARNING TO CREATE REPORTS REQUIRES TIME, PATIENCE, DEDICATION AND ATTENTION TO DETAIL.** Crystal Reports is a very robust package and has a lot of features and options. As you go through the hands-on exercises in this workbook, take your time and try to understand how the concepts that you are learning can be applied to reports that you will create on your own, once you have completed this workbook. It is possible to go through this entire workbook in a few days if you already have above average report design experience with another report writing software package or if you have used a previous version of Crystal Reports and have a solid foundation of relational databases. What you will appreciate about Crystal Reports is that you can create very robust reports without having to write a lot of code. You will write very little code to complete the exercises in this workbook.

The reality is that you will make some mistakes along the way. If you have a fear of making mistakes, this is the time to let go of the fear because the fear will prevent you from learning. It is also normal to initially get confused on what to do next. Even though you may not understand why you are being instructed to do something, the steps in each exercise will allow you to achieve the expected result. This is how you will begin to build a foundation for creating reports and learning Crystal Reports.

The first time that a concept or technique is presented, a lot of information is provided. Each subsequent time that you have to perform the same task, less and less information (aka hand holding) will occur. As you will see, there are a lot of repetitive tasks involved in creating reports. These are the tasks that less and less information will be provided for as you go through the workbook. The purpose behind this learning technique is to allow you to rely more on your knowledge instead of flipping through this workbook to find the answer, which in turn allows you to complete an exercise in less time.

Exercise 2.1: Create Your First Report

I suspect that this is the moment that you have been waiting for; to create your first report. The first report that you will create is a report that only uses data from one table. The report layout is basic, but you will use almost every screen on the Standard Report wizard dialog box so that you can become familiar with all of the options.

Step 1: Add A New Report To The Project

1. Click on the arrow on the **ADD NEW ITEM** button on the Standard toolbar and select **ADD NEW ITEM** as illustrated in Figure 2-19.

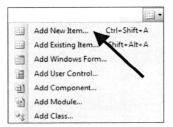

Figure 2-19 Add Component button options

2. Click on the Reporting option on the left, then click on the Crystal Report option. Notice that the default name for the report is **CRYSTAL REPORT**. You can use this name, but you should save the report with a file name that is more meaningful. Type `L2.1 My First Report.rpt` in the Name field as shown at the bottom of Figure 2-20. Click Add.

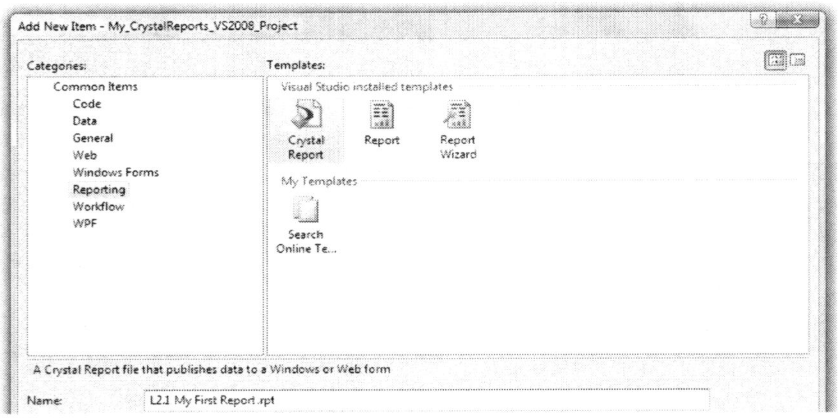

Figure 2-20 Add New Item dialog box

> The default file extension for reports is **.RPT** in Crystal Reports. Report file names can have up to 255 characters and can include spaces and special characters. Reports can be stored in almost any folder on your hard drive or server. However, you should not store reports or any files for that matter in operating system folders.

3. Accept the Report Wizard and Standard Expert options on the Crystal Reports Gallery dialog box, then click OK.

Why Do I Have To Connect To A Data Source?

A data source contains the underlying data for the report that you will create or modify. The most common data source is a database. In addition to there being several types of data sources that you can connect to, sometimes there are multiple ways to connect to the same data source including the Xtreme database. You can connect to this database via the Access/Excel (DAO) connection type or the ODBC connection type. There are two reasons that you would need to connect to a data source as discussed below.

① Earlier in this lesson you viewed two of the reports that come with the Xtreme sample database. The reason that you were able to view data for these reports is because the reports were saved with the data. You will learn more about saving data with reports later in this lesson. If the data is not saved with the report, you would have to create a connection to the database(s) that the report gets its data from, to view data with the report.

② If you want to create a new report or modify an existing report that does not have the data saved with it.

Step 2: Create A Connection To The Data Source

There are several types of data sources that you can use in Crystal Reports. Figure 2-21 shows the categories of connection options that are available. Table 2-6 explains some of the more popular connection options.

Figure 2-21 Available connection options illustrated

> You may see different data source options depending on the data components that were selected when you installed Visual Studio/Crystal Reports. You will also see data source options that you have added.

Connection Option	Connects To . . .
Access/Excel (DAO)	Access databases and Excel files.
Database Files	Standard PC databases including FoxPro, Paradox, Clipper and dBASE.
ODBC (RDO)	Any ODBC complaint database including Oracle, Sybase, Access and Visual FoxPro.
OLE DB (ADO)	Data link files that contain connection information that is saved in a file.
More Data Sources	Databases through ODBC drivers including ACT!, Btrieve, Informix, Oracle, Sybase and Web/IIS log files.

Table 2-6 Connection options explained

If you haven't created a connection, either for the Access/Excel (DAO) or the ODBC (RDO) connection type for the Microsoft Access Xtreme sample database that comes with Crystal Reports, you will have to do that first. Follow the steps below to create an Access/Excel (DAO) connection. When Crystal Reports is installed, an ODBC connection for the Xtreme database should have been created. You can go to section, Step 3: Select The Tables, if you already have a connection to the Xtreme database.

How To Create An Access/Excel (DAO) Connection

1. Click on the plus sign in front of the **CREATE NEW CONNECTION** Data Source option, then click on the plus sign in front of the Access/Excel (DAO) folder. If this is the first Access/Excel (DAO) connection that you are creating, you will see the Access/Excel (DAO) connection dialog box shown in Figure 2-22.

Figure 2-22 Access/Excel (DAO) Connection dialog box

2. Click the button at the end of the **DATABASE NAME** field on the Access/Excel (DAO) dialog box, then navigate to the following path:
C:\Program Files\Microsoft Visual Studio 9.0\Crystal Reports\Samples\en\databases, as illustrated in Figure 2-23. If you changed the default folders when you installed Visual Studio, navigate to the destination folder that you selected during the installation.

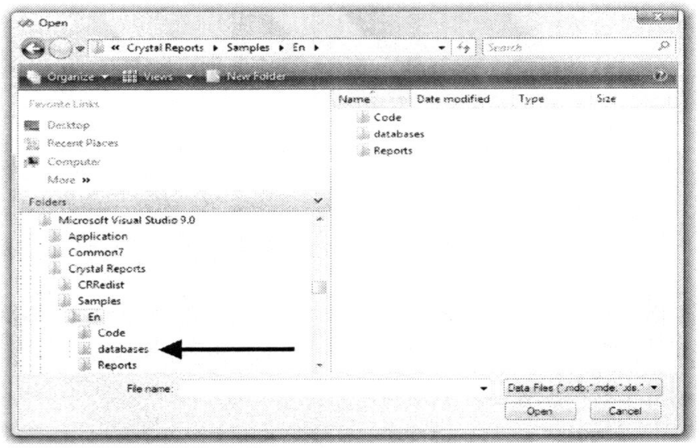

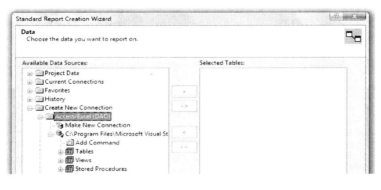

Figure 2-23 Path to the Xtreme sample database

3. Double-click on the **XTREME.MDB** database file. The database should have been added to the Database Name field on the dialog box as shown in Figure 2-24.

If you want to make sure that you added the correct database, click in the Database Name field and press the **END** key. You will be able to see the database name at the end of the field, as shown in Figure 2-24.

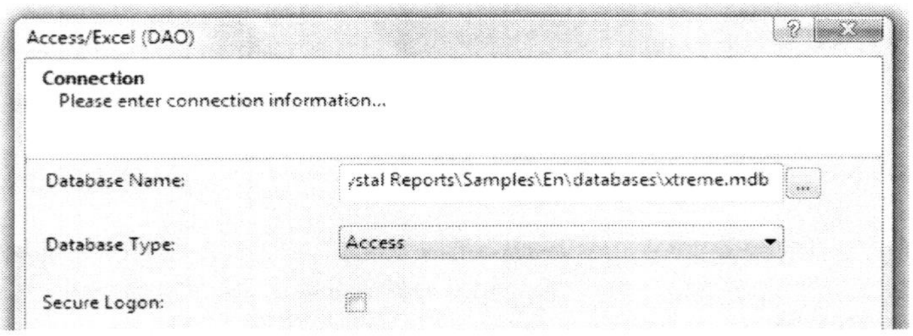

Figure 2-24 Xtreme database added to the Connection dialog box

If the database required logon information, you would check the **SECURE LOGON** option shown above in Figure 2-24. The remaining fields on the dialog box would become available for you to enter the password information.

4. Click **FINISH**. You have completed creating your first connection to a database in Crystal Reports. That wasn't so bad, was it? You should see the connection to the database as shown in Figure 2-25.

Figure 2-25 Connection to Xtreme database

Step 3: Select The Tables

1. Click on the plus sign in front of the Tables folder, shown above in Figure 2-25. You should see the tables shown in Figure 2-26. These are all of the tables that are in the Xtreme database. They are the tables that are used in the sample reports that you viewed earlier in this lesson.

Figure 2-26 Tables in the Xtreme database

> The only reason that I can think of to click the **CANCEL** button on a screen in the wizard is if you decide that you no longer want to create the report. You will lose all of the options that you have selected if you click the Cancel button. It is better to use the **BACK** button to go back and make changes because you cannot reopen the wizard to make changes or pick up where you left off.

2. Click on the **PRODUCT** table, then click the **>** button. The Product table should now be in the **SELECTED TABLES** section, as shown in Figure 2-27. Click Next.

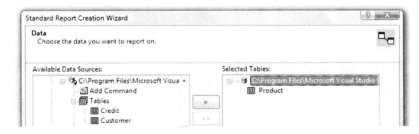

Figure 2-27 Product table selected

View The Data In A Field

The **BROWSE DATA** button on the Fields screen will let you view data that is in the field that you select. Being able to view the data in a field is helpful if you are not familiar with the data. This button is on several dialog boxes in Crystal Reports.

1. Click on the plus sign in front of the Product table. Click on the **PRODUCT NAME** field, then click the Browse Data button. You will see the dialog box shown in Figure 2-28. This is the data in the Product Name field.

Figure 2-28 Data in the Product Name field

> Notice that the field **TYPE** and **LENGTH** are displayed at the top of the dialog box shown above in Figure 2-28. This information is helpful because you can learn more about the field and the data stored in it.

2. Click the Close button when you are finished viewing the data.

> You can also view the data on the design window. By default, the first 500 distinct values in the field are displayed. This default number of values cannot be changed from the dialog box, but the actual values that you see can be changed, by clearing the **SELECT DISTINCT DATA FOR BROWSING** option on the Database tab on the Options dialog box or on the Report Options dialog box if you only want the change to be for the report that you are currently working on.
>
> Ok, that's the way that it is suppose to work, but it doesn't. If this actually worked, it probably is not a good idea to turn this option off because you can see duplicate data in the Browse Data dialog box shown above in Figure 2-28. But since it doesn't work, turning it off has no effect. If you want to view more or less records you have to modify this registry entry: HKEY_CURRENT_USER\Software\Business Objects\10.5\Crystal Reports Designer Component\DatabaseServer. Change the **MAXNBROWSEVALUES** key to the maximum number of records that you want to see.

How To Find A Field

The **FIND FIELD** button will open the dialog box shown in Figure 2-29. You can search for a field in the table. You will see this button on a few dialog boxes in Crystal Reports. I'm not sure that I understand the purpose of this button because all of the fields in a table are displayed on the wizard screens. It could be helpful if you didn't know which table a field is in and there were a lot of tables being used to create the report.

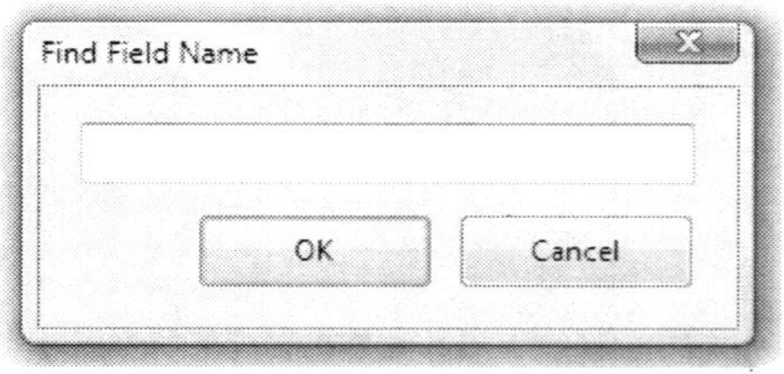

Figure 2-29 Find Field Name dialog box

The Find Field button will only find the first field that matches the text that you enter in the dialog box. You can also enter a partial field name. If the same field name is in more than one table, it does not continue searching. If you were creating a report on your own, in the report design process you would have already written down a list of fields and where they are located because you learned to do this earlier in this lesson <smile>.

Step 4: Select The Fields

1. Click on the Product Name field if it is not already selected, then click the > button. You should see the field in the **FIELDS TO DISPLAY** list.

2. Add the following fields to the Fields To Display list: Size, Price (SRP) and Product Class. Figure 2-30 shows the fields that should have been added. Click Next.

To add all of the fields in the table at the same time click the **>>** button. You do not have to select any fields before clicking this button.

To remove a field that you do not need on the report click on the field in the Fields to Display list, then click the **<** button.

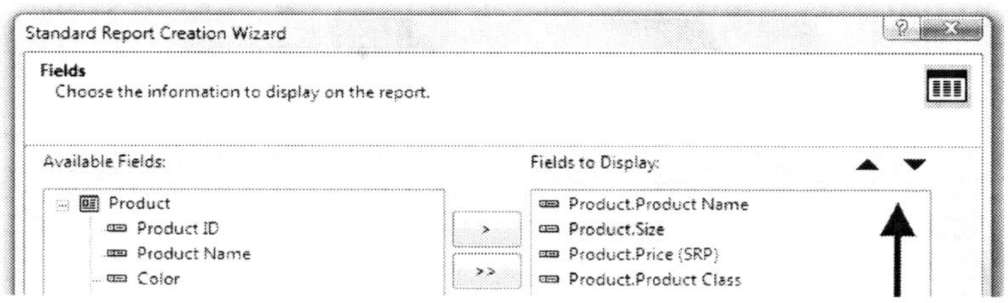

Figure 2-30 Fields selected

To remove all of the fields from the Fields to Display list click the **<<** button.

> You can add several fields at the same time by clicking on the first field that you want to add, then hold down the **CTRL** key and click on the other fields, one by one that you want to add. When you have all of the fields selected that you want to add, click the **>** button.

The order that you add the fields to the Fields to Display list is the order that they will appear on the report in the details section from left to right. If you discover that the fields are not in the order that you want them to appear in on the report, click on the field in the Fields to Display list and click the **UP** or **DOWN** arrow buttons illustrated above in Figure 2-30 to move the field to where it should be.

> The order that the fields are in will change automatically if at least one field is selected to group on. Fields that are grouped on are moved to the beginning of the details section. You can rearrange the fields after the wizard has created the report. This does not happen when you create a report from scratch that has groups.

Notice in Figure 2-30 above that fields in the Fields to Display list have the table name in front of the field name. This is done to let you know which table the field is in. This is helpful when you are using more than one table to create the report. Primary key fields in tables often have the same field name when the tables have related information. Without adding the table name you would not know which table a field is in.

> Primary key fields are fields that are used to link one table to another table.

Step 5: Select The Grouping Options

As you learned earlier, grouping allows you to organize and sort the data. Grouping data forces all records that are related by the field that is being grouped on to print together. Grouping data makes reports that have a lot of data easier to read. Grouping the data in a report is optional. You can group on more than one field. You can group on fields that have already been selected to print on the report or you can select fields to group on that will not print on the report.

The Product Catalog report that you viewed earlier in this lesson uses the grouping option. That report is grouped on the Product Class field.

1. Add the Product Class field to the Group By list. The grouping option **IN ASCENDING ORDER** is correct. Figure 2-31 shows the grouping options that you should have selected. Click Next.

There are two options that you can select from to group the records by, as discussed below. This is how you sort the values that are in the field that is being grouped on.

IN ASCENDING ORDER This is the default grouping option. The values in the field being grouped on will be sorted in A-Z order if the field is a string field. If the field being used to group on is numeric, the values will be sorted in 0-9 order.

IN DESCENDING ORDER The values in the field being grouped on will be sorted in Z-A order if the field is a string field. If the field being used to group on is numeric, the values will be sorted in 9-0 order.

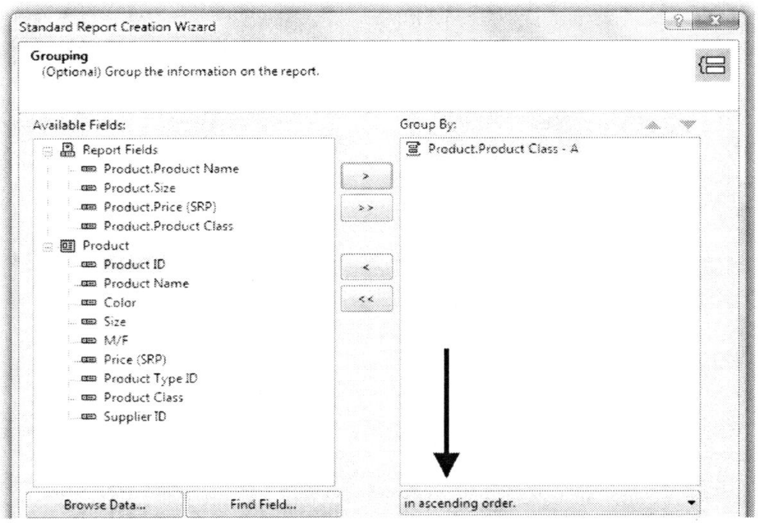

Figure 2-31 Field added to the Group By list

Step 6: Select The Summary Options

Creating summary fields is optional. Summary options usually involve calculated fields. By default, the wizard will create a summary field for all numeric fields that were selected to print on the report.

There are 25 built-in summary functions that you can use. Many of them are shown at the bottom of Figure 2-32. The number of summary options that you see in the list depends on the data type of the field that you are summarizing on. Not all data types can use all of the summary function options. Many of the summary functions are only for numeric fields.

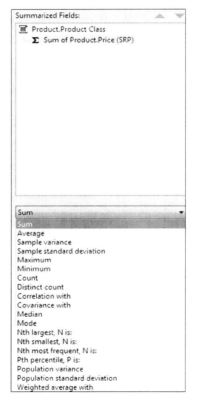

Figure 2-32 Summary options illustrated

1. Add the Product Class field to the **SUMMARIZED FIELDS** list.

2. Open the drop-down list shown above in Figure 2-32 and select **COUNT**. Notice that the Product Class field has different options in the drop-down list, then those shown above for the Product Price (SRP) field. Figure 2-33 shows the summary options that should be selected. Click Next.

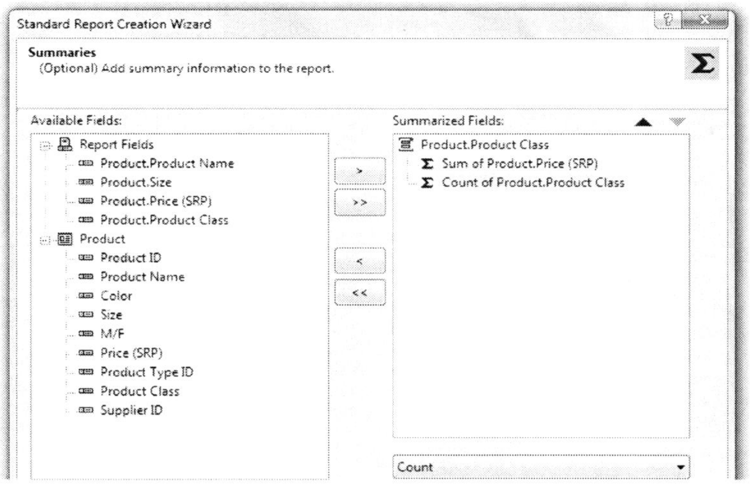

Figure 2-33 Summary options for the Product Class field

3. Select the **TOP 5 GROUPS** option, then select the Price field in the Summary values drop-down list. Figure 2-34 shows the Group Sorting options that should be selected. Click Next.

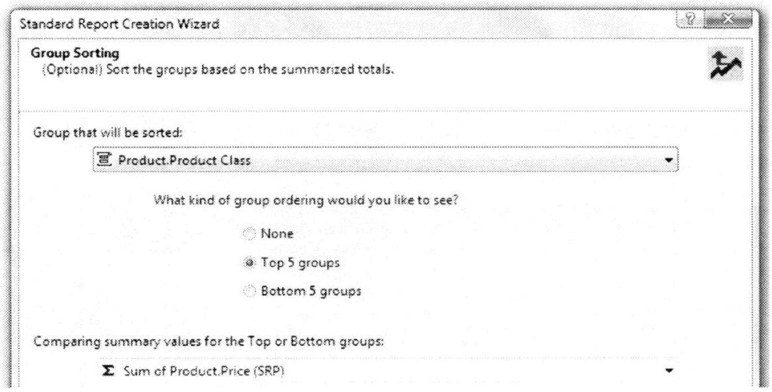

Figure 2-34 Group Sorting options

The Top 5 Groups option will only display data for the five groups that have the highest value in the field selected in the **SUMMARY VALUES** field at the bottom of the Group Sorting screen. This is accomplished by sorting the groups based on the summary field in descending order for the Top N groups or sorting the groups in ascending order for the Bottom N groups. Selecting **NONE**, which is the default, will display all groups. It is possible that you will not get the five groups that you think should appear on the report. This is because of the way that Crystal Reports processes data. In Lesson 7 you will create a Top 5 group report that illustrates unexpected results because a wizard was used to create the report.

Step 7: Select The Chart Type

Adding a chart to a report is optional. Once you select a chart type the wizard will fill in information for the other fields on the screen. If you are not sure what options to select, accept the defaults, preview the report and then decide which chart options need to be modified.

1. Select the **PIE CHART** option, then select the Price field in the Show summary drop-down list. Figure 2-35 shows the chart options that should be selected. Click Next.

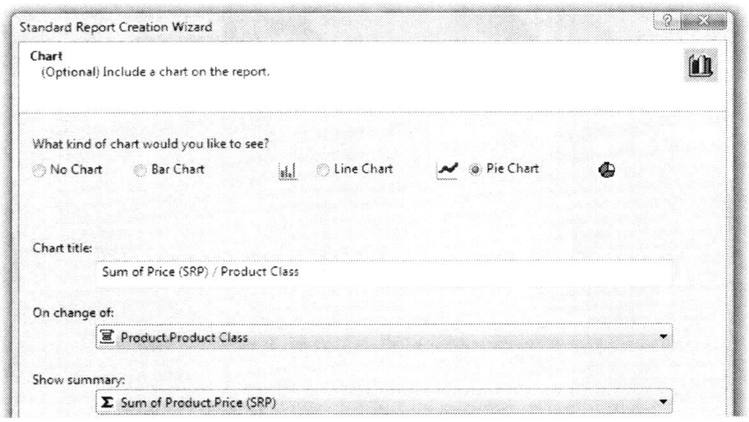

Figure 2-35 Chart options

Step 8: Select The Fields To Filter On

Creating filters is optional. Filters are another way that you can narrow down the number of records that will appear on the report. You can create as many filters as you need. In this step you will create a filter for the Product Size field to only display records that have a size that is in a specific range.

1.   Add the Product Size field to the **FILTER FIELDS** list, then open the drop-down list and select **IS BETWEEN**.

2.   Open the next drop-down list and select 16. Open the last drop-down list and select **XLRG**. Figure 2-36 shows the filter options that should be selected. Click Next.

The data in the last two drop-down lists is actual data in the field that you are creating this filter for.

The filter that you just created will only display products that have a size that is between 16 and XLRG.

The filter options shown in Figure 2-36 are the same as what you would select on the **SELECT EXPERT** tool that you will learn how to use in Lesson 5.

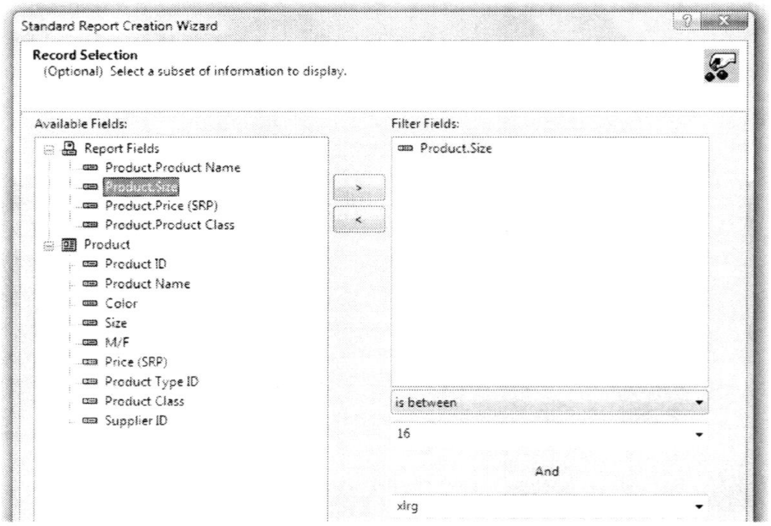

Figure 2-36 Record Selection options

Step 9: Select A Report Style

Report styles apply formatting to the report. The styles are like templates, which allow you to quickly change the appearance of a report. You can preview what the other style options look like by clicking on them.

1. Select the **EXECUTIVE, TRAILING BREAK** style as shown in Figure 2-37, then click Finish. The first page of the report should look like the one shown in Figure 2-38. The top of the second page of the report should look like the one shown in Figure 2-39. As you scroll through the report you may see things that you would like to rearrange on the report.

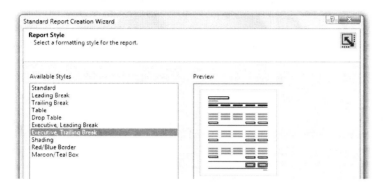

Figure 2-37 Report style options

Because grouping options were selected in Step 5, the **GROUP TREE** is displayed with the report. Clicking on the options in the group tree will take you to that section of the report.

If for some reason the group tree is not visible or you do not want to see it, you can click the **TOGGLE GROUP TREE** button on the report navigation toolbar to turn it on or off.

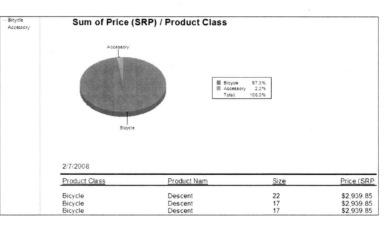

Figure 2-38 Page 1 of the L2.1 report

2/7/2008			
Product Class	Product Nam	Size	Price (SRP
Bicycle	Wheeler	16	$539.85
Bicycle	Wheeler	18	$539.85
Bicycle	Wheeler	20	$539.85
Bicycle	Wheeler	22	$539.85
Bicycle	SlickRock	16	$764.85
Bicycle	SlickRock	18	$764.85
Bicycle	Endorphin	22	$899.85
Bicycle	**$50,215.80**	**48**	
Accessory	InFlux Lycra Glove	lrg	$15.50
Accessory	Triumph Vertigo Helmet	lrg	$53.90

Figure 2-39 Page 2 of the L2.1 report

NEW In the previous version, the entire Print Date field would not display the entire year by default. You would have to resize it. Now the entire field is displayed automatically, as shown above in Figures 2-38 and 2-39.

Step 10: Save The Report

In addition to giving the report a meaningful name, you have to decide whether or not you want to save the data with the report, which is discussed below.

Save The Report With Data

Unless you changed the default options after Visual Studio was installed, the data is saved with the report by default. There are pros and cons to saving data with a report as discussed below. As stated earlier, saving the data with the report is the default option. You can preview and print reports faster with this option selected because the data does not have to be retrieved. This option is also useful if you need to send the report to someone that does not have access to the data. One downside to saving the data with the report is that the report requires more hard drive or server space. A second downside is that anyone that runs the report with saved data will not be using the most current data. A third downside occurs if the database has security. Unless the report has been published to Crystal Reports Server, the security is bypassed and anyone that opens the report will have access to the data, whether they should or not.

Save The Report Without Data

Selecting this option requires less disk space. With this option you will be using live data each time the report is run. The downside is when you need to preview or print the report, it will take a little longer to process, because the data has to be retrieved. Most of the time, you will not notice the delay. To save the report without data, check the **DISCARD SAVED DATA WHEN LOADING REPORTS** option on the Reporting tab of the Options dialog box.

> From a report developers perspective if you have the space, it will save time, a considerable amount of time if there are thousands of records, if you save the data with the report while you are creating and modifying it. The danger that some developers have <not us of course> is that they forget to change the save data option before putting the report into production. Another danger is not testing the report with live data. Remember that most data is volatile, meaning that it changes frequently. Not testing with live data before putting the report into production could be a bad career move, if you know what I mean. Testing with live data before putting the report into production, also means that it won't go into production with the saved data.

Refreshing Report Data

As you just learned, you have to decide whether to save the data with the report or not. If you decide to normally save data with a report to save processing time while designing the report that's fine. Anytime that you want to work with the current data, click the **REFRESH** button on the report navigation toolbar.

If the changes that you make to a report fall in the formatting category, like changing fonts, moving fields around on the report or adding titles to summary fields that were already saved with the report, you do not have to refresh the data.

Automatic Data Refreshing

If any of the items below occur after a report have been saved, the data will automatically be refreshed, regardless of the save data option that is associated with the report.

    ① A new field is added to the report.
    ② If a formula is added to the report that uses a field that was not already being used on the report.
    ③ If an existing formula is modified that uses a field that was not already being used on the report.
    ④ If any report criteria or parameter fields are added or changed that include a field that was not already being used on the report.
    ⑤ If the grouping is not done on a server, the detail record data will be refreshed.

If you drill-down on hidden data, the data is not a full refresh. If the grouping is taking place on a server, drilling down in the details section will only retrieve the new data required by the drill-down for the details section.

Yes, I can sense that you are shaking your head about the save data with report options. Keep in mind that only the fields on the report and fields needed for formulas or functions that the report uses are saved with the report. Other fields in the table are not saved with the report. As you become more familiar with modifying reports, you will know which save data option is best suited for each report that you are modifying or creating.

Real World Data

Many companies have what is known as a "development server" that has a copy of "live data" and applications (live data is also known as production data). This is done so that anyone that is creating new applications, modifying existing applications or testing software, can do so without putting the companies data in danger. If this is the type of environment that you working in, keep in mind while going through this workbook, the differences between "live" and "refreshed" data, when these terms are referenced.

When creating reports on a development server and you click the **REFRESH** button in Crystal Reports, you are not getting a copy of the data from a production server. You are getting another copy of the data from the development server. The same is true if you have placed a copy of the production data on your hard drive. Usually, data on a development server is refreshed from a production server at pre-defined intervals (ex. daily, weekly monthly). If you want to know when the data on a development server is refreshed, ask the DBA or the person that manages the databases that you are using.

Save The Report

1. Right-click on the L2.1 tab and select Save L2.1 My First report.

 You can also click the **SAVE** button on the Standard toolbar.

Additional Ways To Select A Data Source

In the previous exercise you selected the data source (in this case a database) under the **CREATE NEW CONNECTION** folder. There are other ways to select a data source that you have already created a connection for as discussed below.

① If you opened the data source after you opened the current session of Crystal Reports, you can select the data source under the **CURRENT CONNECTIONS** folder shown in Figure 2-40. Once you close Crystal Reports, all data source connections in the Current Connections folder are closed.

```
Current Connections
    C:\Program Files\Microsoft Visual Stu
        Add Command
    Tables
    Views
    Stored Procedures
```

Figure 2-40 Current Connections folder option

② If you know that you will be using a data source on a regular basis, you should add it to the **FAVORITES** folder by right-clicking on the data source under another folder and selecting **ADD TO FAVORITES**, as illustrated in Figure 2-41. If you open the Favorites folder you will see the data source that you added.

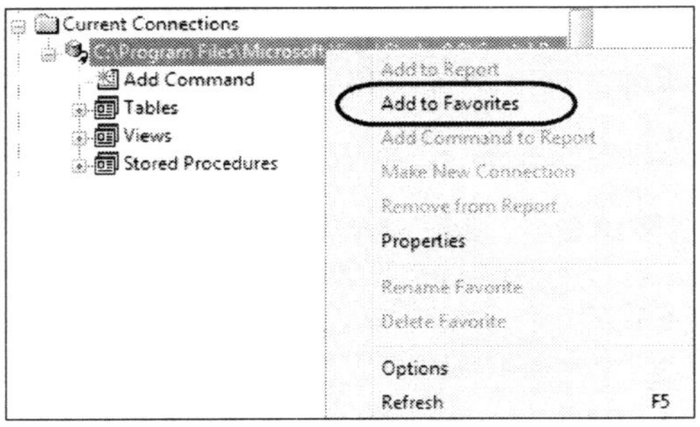

Figure 2-41 Add to Favorites option illustrated

③ The **History** folder contains the last five data sources that were opened.

> ☼ All of the reports that you will create in this workbook will use the Xtreme database, so make sure that you have a connection to it.

> ☼ When creating a new report for exercises in this workbook, select the Report Wizard and Standard option on the Crystal Reports Gallery dialog box, unless instructed otherwise.

Create A Report From An Existing Report

There are three ways to create a report from an existing report as discussed below.

① Open the report that you will base the new report from. File ⇒ Save As. Type in the new report name.
② Open a new report, then open the Crystal Reports Gallery and select the **FROM AN EXISTING REPORT** option. Click OK, then double-click on the existing report that you want to use. This produces the same results as the option above.
③ Project ⇒ Add Existing Item. This option is similar to the option in 2 above. The difference is that this option does not use the Crystal Reports Gallery dialog box.

Exercise 2.2: Create A Product List Report

In this exercise you will create a product list report that will print the Product ID, Product Name and Price fields.

1. Create a new report and save it as L2.2 Product list.

2. Add the Product table to the Selected Tables list on the Data screen, then click Next.

3. Add the Product ID, Product Name and Price (SRP) fields to the Fields to Display list, then click Finish because the report does not require any of the options on the other wizard screens. Save the report. It should look like the one shown in Figure 2-42.

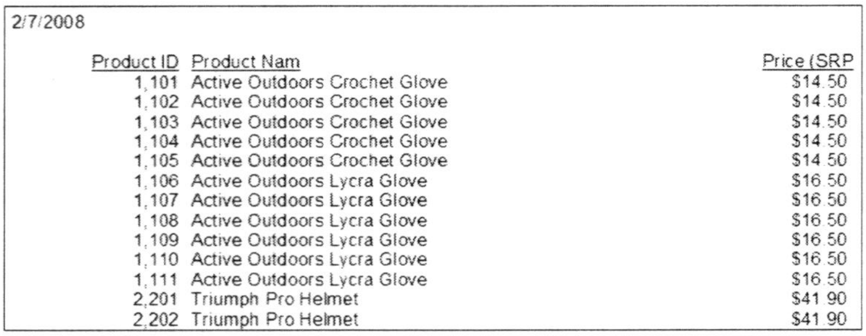

2/7/2008		
Product ID	Product Nam	Price (SRP
1,101	Active Outdoors Crochet Glove	$14.50
1,102	Active Outdoors Crochet Glove	$14.50
1,103	Active Outdoors Crochet Glove	$14.50
1,104	Active Outdoors Crochet Glove	$14.50
1,105	Active Outdoors Crochet Glove	$14.50
1,106	Active Outdoors Lycra Glove	$16.50
1,107	Active Outdoors Lycra Glove	$16.50
1,108	Active Outdoors Lycra Glove	$16.50
1,109	Active Outdoors Lycra Glove	$16.50
1,110	Active Outdoors Lycra Glove	$16.50
1,111	Active Outdoors Lycra Glove	$16.50
2,201	Triumph Pro Helmet	$41.90
2,202	Triumph Pro Helmet	$41.90

Figure 2-42 L2.2 Product list report

Exercise 2.3: Create An Employee Contact List Report

The fields that are needed to create this report are stored in two tables. This report will be grouped by the Supervisor ID field so that each supervisor can have a list of their employees.

1. Create a new report and save it as L2.3 Employee contact list.

2. Add the Employee and Employee Addresses tables, then click Next.

Linking Tables

You will see the screen shown in Figure 2-43. You will only see this screen if two or more tables have been added to the report. The options on this screen allow you to select the appropriate links for the tables that you have selected.

Most of the time, the link that is automatically created is the one that you need. Fields are automatically linked if they have the same name and compatible data type. In this exercise the tables should be linked by the Employee ID field.

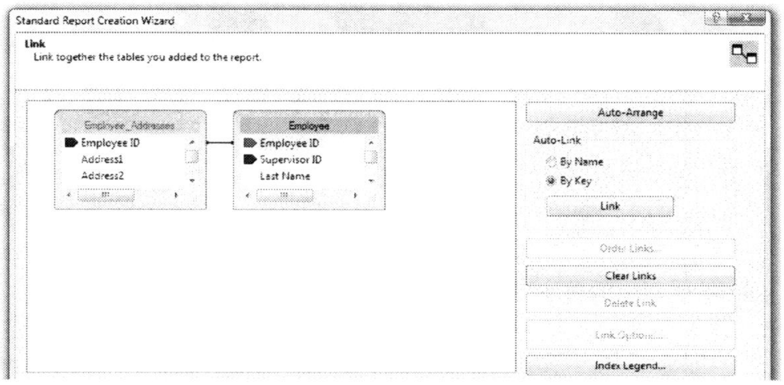

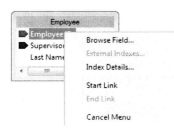

Figure 2-43 Link screen

 Link Screen Tips

① You may need to make the dialog box wider to see both tables. To make the dialog box wider, place the mouse pointer on the right side of the dialog box and drag the border of the dialog box to the right. You can also make the tables longer if you want to see all of the fields.

② If you right-click on a field and select **BROWSE FIELD**, as shown in Figure 2-44, you will be able to see the first 500 unique values for the field that you selected. If you see more than one occurrence of the same value, it means that you have turned off the Select Distinct Data For Browsing option on the Database tab on the Options dialog box or on the Report Options dialog box.

Figure 2-44 Link screen field shortcut menu

Index Legend

As you can see in Figure 2-44 above, there are arrows next to some fields. If you click on the **INDEX LEGEND** button you will see the index that each color represents as shown in Figure 2-45.

Fields in tables are indexed to reduce the time it takes to retrieve the records needed to create the report. Fields that are used in the record selection criteria are often used as an index.

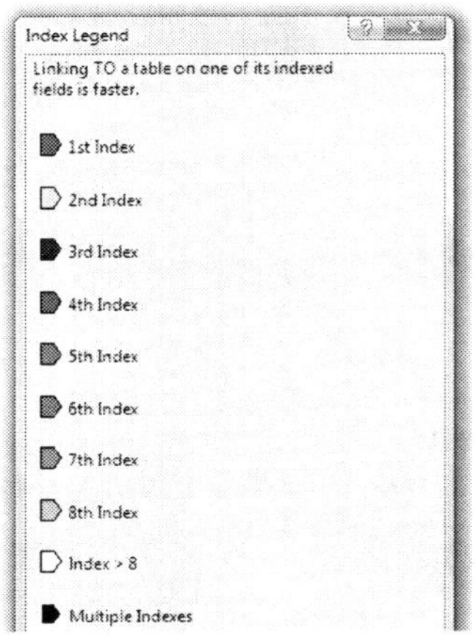

Figure 2-45 Index Legend dialog box

Add The Fields To The Report

1. Click Next on the Link screen, then add the fields in Table 2-7 to the Fields to Display list. Figure 2-46 shows the order that the fields should be in. Click Next.

Employee	Employee Addresses
Supervisor ID	Region
First Name	
Last Name	
Home Phone	

Table 2-7 Fields to add to the report

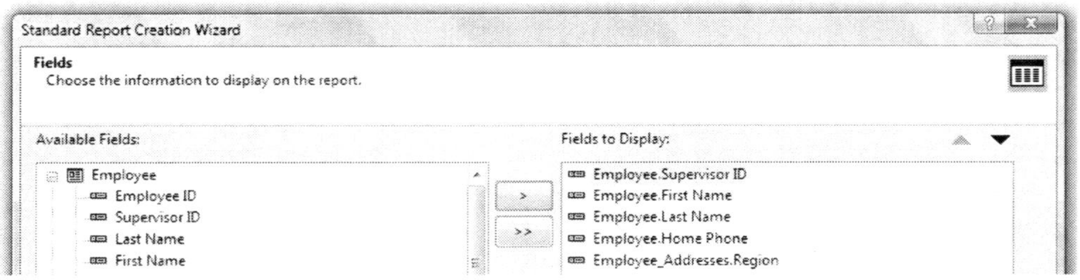

Figure 2-46 Fields selected for the report

Select The Grouping Options

This report would look better if it was grouped on the Supervisor ID field and within each Supervisor ID group, the employee names were sorted by last and first name. It would also be helpful if there was a count of employees per supervisor.

1. Add the Supervisor ID field to the **GROUP BY** list, then click Next.

2. Add the Employee ID field to the **SUMMARIZED FIELDS** list. This field is in the Employee table.

3. Open the drop-down list and select **COUNT**. Figure 2-47 shows the summary options that should be selected.

This option will count the number of employee ID's under each Supervisor ID. When you want a count of records, you should select a field that has unique values. Each employee is assigned a unique ID.

Think of ID's as being the equivalent of social security numbers, where each persons social security number is unique.

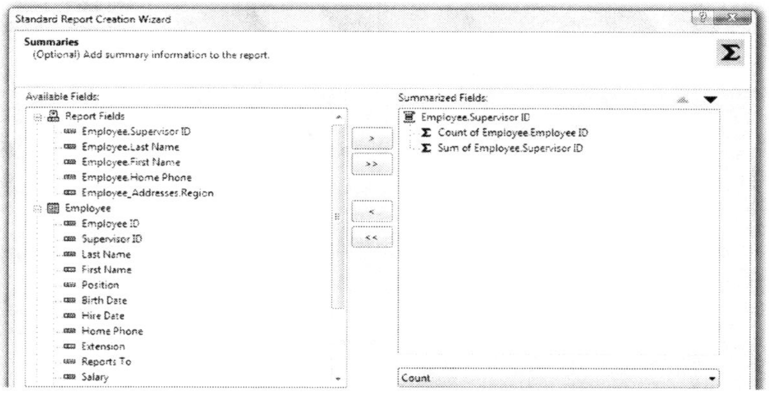

Figure 2-47 Summary options

4. Click Next. Click Next again on the Group Sorting dialog box because you do not need to change any of the options.

Select The Chart Options

1. Select the **BAR CHART** option.

2. Type `Count of employees per supervisor` in the **CHART TITLE** field. Figure 2-48 shows the chart options that should be selected. Click Next.

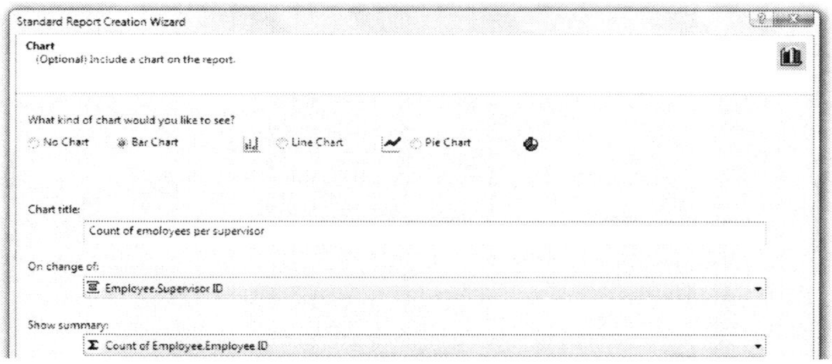

Figure 2-48 Chart options

Finish The Report

1. Click Next on the Record Selection screen because the report does not require any filters.

2. Select the Standard Style if it is not already selected, then click Finish. Your report should look like the one shown in Figure 2-49 (on the next page). It looks okay, but it needs to be modified. You will learn how to modify reports later in the workbook. Save and close the report.

Report Processing Model

Reports in Crystal Reports are processed in three passes. The first pass reads all of the records, calculates the formulas and summary fields, suppresses fields and creates a temporary data file. This temporary file only contains the records needed for the report, not all of the records in the database. The second pass sorts records, calculates totals for groups, calculates running totals, generates charts, maps, cross-tabs, OLAP grids and subreports as needed. The second pass also formats the pages. The third pass calculates the total page count and Page N of M special fields if necessary.

Formulas can be placed in all sections of a report. Formulas are not processed in report section order. The processing model uses the following criteria to help determine the order to process formulas.

① Formulas that use database fields are processed while the records are being read in the first pass.

② There is no order to how formulas are processed in the same section of the report.

③ Formulas that only use variables are processed before records are read.

④ Formulas that use summary and group fields are processed after the records are read.

⑤ Cross-Tab summary fields are calculated in the first pass.

The link below provides more information on the processing model that Crystal Reports uses.
http://msdn2.microsoft.com/en-us/library/ms225477.aspx

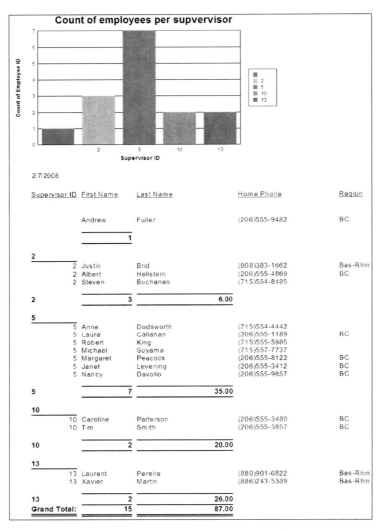

Figure 2-49 L2.3 Employee contact list report

Saving An Existing Report With A New File Name

This is a task that you will do a lot in this workbook. The steps below will show you how.

1. Open the report that you want to save with a new file name.

2. File ⇒ Save (report name) As, as illustrated in Figure 2-50.

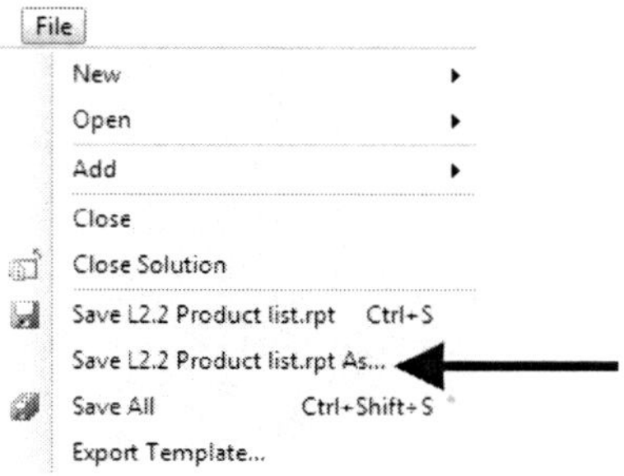

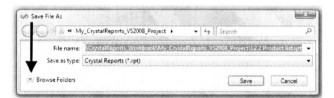

Figure 2-50 Save As option illustrated

3. If you want to save the report in a different folder, click the arrow next to the Browse Folders option shown in Figure 2-51. The Save As dialog box will look like the one shown in Figure 2-52.

Figure 2-51 Browse Folders option illustrated

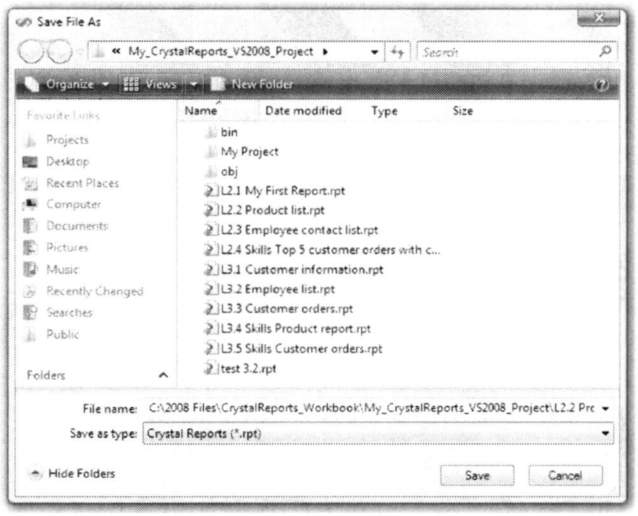

Figure 2-52 Save File As dialog box

4. Navigate to the folder using the options on the left of Figure 2-52 above to find the folder where you want to save the new copy of the report.

5. When you select the folder, you should highlight the text in the **FILE NAME** field, then type in the name for the new report as shown in Figure 2-53, then press Enter or click the Save button.

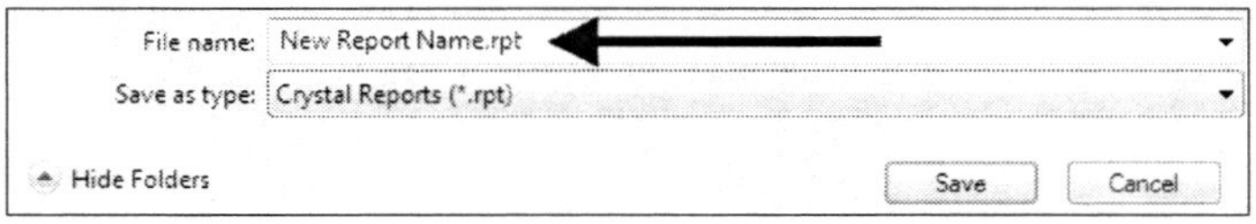

Figure 2-53 New file name

Test Your Skills

1. Create a report using the Standard Wizard. The report should look like the one shown in Figure 2-54.

    - Save the report as L2.4 Skills Top 5 customer orders with chart.
    - Add the Customer table.
    - Add the Customer ID, Customer Name and Last Year's Sales fields to the report.
    - Group on the Last Years Sales field.
    - Select the Top 5 groups sorting option.
    - Create a bar chart and type Top 5 Customer Orders as the chart title name.

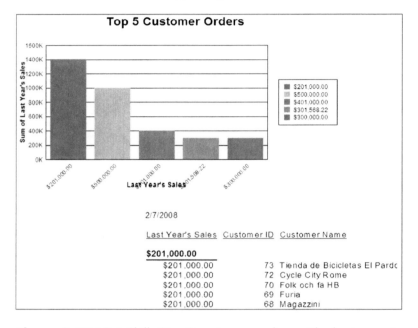

Figure 2-54 L2.4 Skills Top 5 customer orders with chart report

CREATING REPORTS FROM SCRATCH

After completing the exercises in this lesson you will be able to:

- ☑ Create basic reports from scratch
- ☑ Use the Database Expert
- ☑ Use the Field Explorer
- ☑ Add and remove tables in the Field Explorer window
- ☑ Dock and undock the explorer windows
- ☑ Understand relational databases
- ☑ Understand the different types of relationships
- ☑ Understand Linking and Join Types techniques

LESSON 3

The Database Expert

The Database Expert shown in Figure 3-1 will display the options to select the data source that you need for the report.

Crystal Reports ⇒ Database ⇒ Database Expert will open this dialog box.

As you can see, this dialog box is very similar to the Data screen in the Standard wizard that you used in the previous lesson. Like the Data screen, the Database Expert has a Links screen.

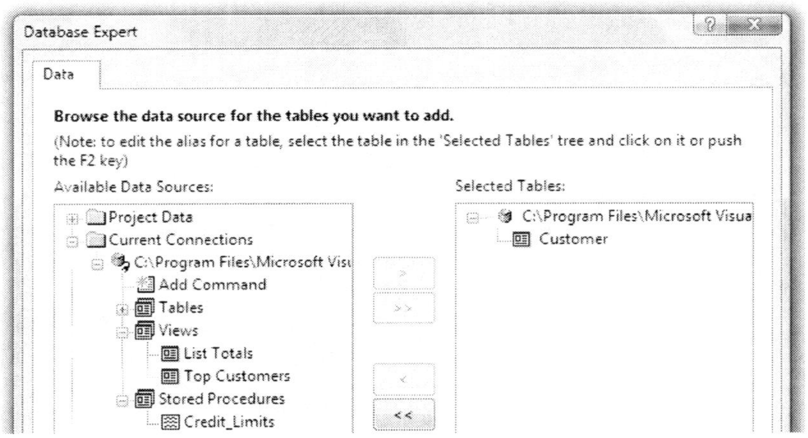

Figure 3-1 Database Expert dialog box

Data Source Options

Each of the four data source options (Commands, Tables, Views and Stored Procedures) provide a different way to access data for the reports that you create. As the report designer, for the most part, you will not be required to create or maintain the data sources. You do however, need a good understanding of them so that you can select the best option, based on the requirements for the report.

Commands are queries (code that retrieves data from tables) that are created with a **STRUCTURED QUERY LANGUAGE (SQL)** and have been brought into Crystal Reports. These queries are often complex. They are usually created (by a DBA or programmer) in another software package.

Using a command as a data source allows the report to process faster, because the selection of records for the report is already done before the report that you create is run. Commands are very useful when you (the report designer) need data from several databases to create one report.

SQL (stands for Structured Query Language) This is the language that is most used to interact with databases. It is used to create and populate tables with data, modify data and retrieve data from a database. The **SQL SELECT** command is what is used to retrieve data. This is also known as a **QUERY**. Before you start to frown, the answer is no, you do not have to learn how to write SQL code to retrieve the data that you need for the reports that you will create in this workbook. Crystal Reports provides tools, like the Select Expert and Group Expert, that allow you to retrieve the data from the tables. At some point you may have requests for functionality that these tools can't provide, which means that you will have to write code.

Tables are probably the most used of the four data sources because accessing the tables does not require any code or programming skills, like the other three data source options require.

Views Business Views is the real name of this option. Business Views are a set of components, (Data Connections, Dynamic Data Connections, Data Foundations and Business Elements) that report designers and end-users can use to access the data that is needed to create the report. Business Views are created in the Business View Manager by a System Administrator, report designer or someone that has administrator rights to the databases. Business Views allow one to gather data from a variety of databases and combine the data into a "view". This makes it easier to access the data.

Many databases have the ability to present different views of the data. A view is a **RECORDSET** (the result) of a query. Views usually display a subset of the data in a data source. Views are stored in the database and are like tables, but they do not have the physical characteristics of a table. For example, records cannot be added or deleted from a view, fields cannot be added to a view or the length of a field cannot be changed in a view.

Views are less complex queries then the ones in the Command section. These queries are similar to what you can create in Crystal Reports when you use the sorting, grouping and data selection options to create a report. Views are created when the same recordset, calculation or query needs to be used in several reports. If you know that you will create several reports that use the same sorting, grouping or data selection options, you could create and save a view, if you have the appropriate administrator rights to do so. Doing this means that you would not have to select the same options over and over again for each report. Instead of selecting all of the tables, fields and options, select the view that already has all of this information.

Views are one way to optimize reports that use tables that have a lot of data. For example, a customer table will hold all customers world wide. If there is a need to create several reports that are specific to a certain country for marketing or sales analysis purposes, create a view (a query) that retrieves all of the customer records for the country. When the reports are created for that country, select the "country view" if you will, as the data source, instead of the customer table. The report will run faster because it does not have to read the entire customer table to find the records for the specific country. Instead, the "view" is read. The Xtreme database comes with two business views that you can use. Figure 3-1 above shows the views. They are explained below.

① **List Totals** This view calculates the total order amount by multiplying the Quantity times the Unit Price. Both of these fields are in the Orders Detail table.

② **Top Customers** This view contains customers that have purchased $50,000 or more worth of products. The fields in this view are from the Customer table.

Stored Procedures These are mini programs that are stored (saved). They are created when it is difficult to retrieve the data from a table or when a view cannot handle the processing that is needed. Stored procedures are saved on a database server. From a report designers perspective, they function and have the same characteristics as a view. Don't worry, most report designers do not create stored procedures. If you have to create a complex report and have trouble getting the data the way that you need it, talk to the DBA to get their recommendation for the best way to get the data that you need or to create the stored procedure for you.

Stored procedures, like Commands and Views, do not contain data. They contain queries that are more complex then views, but less complex than commands. The majority of the time, stored procedures are created by a DBA or programmer. The Xtreme database comes with one stored procedure that you can use. Figure 3-1 above shows the stored procedure. It is explained below.

Credit_Limits This view contains customer credit limits. It also has a parameter field that will let you specify the range limit that you need for the report that you are creating. The reason this view is in the stored procedure section is because views cannot have parameter fields in most databases. When Crystal Reports recognizes that a view has a parameter field, the view will be placed in the stored procedure section, because stored procedures can store a parameter field.

 Think of these tools (Commands, Views and Stored Procedures) as query generators. They let you "visually" select criteria that will be used to retrieve the records based on the criteria that you create.

Explorers

Crystal Reports comes with two explorers that you can use to help create and manage reports. The one that you will probably use the most is the Field Explorer, shown in Figure 3-2. The Solution Explorer is shown in Figure 3-3. The explorers are discussed below.

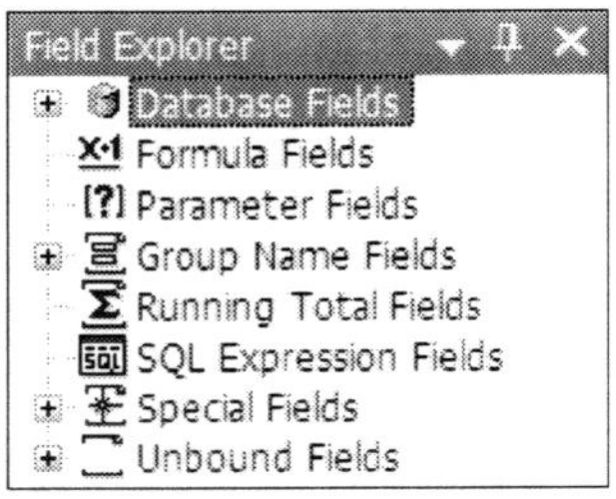

Figure 3-2 Field Explorer

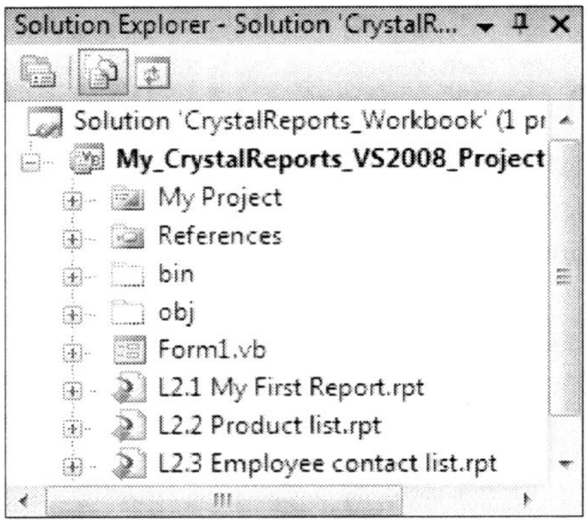

Figure 3-3 Solution Explorer

1. If the Field and Solution Explorers are not visible, display them now.

> By default, the Field Explorer docks on the left side of the design window. Pay attention to the symbols (icons) that are next to each of the options in the Field Explorer. You will see them again when you learn how to create formulas.

Solution Explorer

The Solution Explorer lets you view and open the objects in the project, as well as set properties for the project. Table 3-1 explains the buttons on the Solution Explorer window.

Button	Description
Properties	Displays the Properties window for the object that is selected.
Show All Files	Displays all of the files in the project. By default, only the report files are displayed.
Refresh	Redisplays the objects in the window.

Table 3-1 Solution Explorer buttons explained

> Reports that are created from an existing report do not appear in the Solution Explorer window without clicking the Show All Files button.

Field Explorer

The Field Explorer lets you add the eight types of fields shown above in Figure 3-2, to a report. Table 3-2 explains each of the field types.

Field Type	Description
Database	The fields in this folder come from tables and are usually placed in the details section of the report. This is the only field type in the Field Explorer that is stored in a database.
Formula	These are calculated fields that you create using the Formula Workshop. [See Lesson 9, Formula Workshop Overview] They are recalculated every time the report is run or previewed. (1)

Table 3-2 Field types explained

Field Type	Description
Parameter	This field type is one that you create. Parameter fields prompt the person running the report to provide information. The information gathered from the parameter fields is used to query the tables to select records that meet the information in the parameter fields. Parameter fields allow the person running the report to produce several versions of the report from one report file. An example of parameter fields are the questions that you answer when you use an ATM machine to withdraw or deposit money. (1)
Group Name	This field type is automatically created for each group that the report has. When a group is created, by default the group name field is added to the group header section of the report and will display the value in the field. You can customize the group name to display something other than the value in the field. [See Lesson 6, How To Create A Custom Group Name] (1)
Running Total	This is a formula field that sums (adds) the values in a numeric field (or column of data). Running Total fields can be placed in the details section of the report and will provide a total up to the current record. Running Total fields can be reset to zero. They can be used to create totals by group or for the entire report. Summary fields can only be placed in the group header and footer, report header and footer sections of the report. (1)
SQL Expression	This type of field is written in a language called SQL. This field type queries (searches) tables to select records that meet the criteria in the query. They are stored on and run from a server. (1)
Special	These are system generated fields. Some of the more popular special fields include page number, print date and Page N of M. Special Fields can be formatted like the other field types discussed in this table. [See Lesson 4, Special Fields] (1)
Unbound	These fields were explained in Lesson 2, Table 2-1. (1)

Table 3-2 Field types explained (Continued)

(1) This field type is not stored in a database.

Field Type Symbols And Naming Conventions

In Table 3-2, you learned about several field types that you can add to a report. Five of these field types: Formula, SQL Expression, Parameter, Running Total and Unbound, are fields that you create. Crystal Reports will add a symbol to the beginning of the field name as discussed below. This is done to help you know what type of field it is when you are viewing the field in the design window. Figure 3-4 shows what each field type looks like when displayed in the design window.

   ① **@ symbol** Is a formula or Unbound field.
   ② **% sign** Is an SQL Expression field.
   ③ **? question mark** Is a parameter field.
   ④ **# sign** Is a Running Total (or summary) field.

Employee Name	Position	Birth Date	Hire Date
@Employee Name	%Position	?Birth Date	#Hire Date

Figure 3-4 Field types and symbols

Do not use the field type symbols discussed above as part of a field name that you create.

Formula, SQL Expression, Parameter, Running Total and Unbound fields must have a unique name within each field type. Therefore, it is possible to use the same field name for a parameter, formula and running total field in the same report. This is why understanding what the field type symbols represent is important.

Docking Explorer Windows

There are three ways that you can dock explorer windows as explained in Table 3-3.

Docking explorers is not a requirement to complete the exercises in this workbook, but doing so will make the explorer windows easier to find and use. I find it easier to dock the explorers in the same section on the right side of the window as shown in Figure 3-5.

To rearrange your explorer windows to look like the ones in the figure, follow the steps below. Doing this is optional.

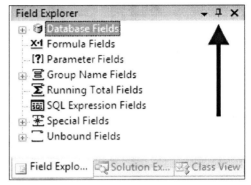

Figure 3-5 Docked explorer windows

Docking Type	Description
Floating	Free form placement. You can move the window to any location on the screen.
Dockable	Two or more explorer windows share the same space as shown above in Figure 3-5.
Tabbed Document	Will put the selected explorer window on a tab where the Start Page tab is.

Table 3-3 Explorer window docking types explained

1. Open the Field Explorer window if it is not already open. (Crystal Reports ⇒ Field Explorer)

2. Click on the down arrow illustrated in Figure 3-6 and select **FLOATING**.

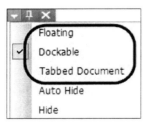

Figure 3-6 Explorer window position options

3. With the left mouse button, drag the Field Explorer window over to the Solution Explorer window and release the mouse button. Drag it so that it is on top of the Solution Explorer window.

4. Right-click on the Title bar and select **DOCKABLE**. You should see tabs for both explorers, as shown at the bottom of Figure 3-5 shown earlier.

Docking Tips

Below are several tips that you should find useful when using the explorers. It could be me, but when I mistakenly move an explorer window, I have difficulty getting it back to where it was. This truly drives me nuts. I hope a solution is available soon. The reason that I am telling you this is so that if you have trouble getting the explorers exactly where you want them, you know that you aren't the only one that this bothers.

① To select the explorer that you want to use, click on the tab for it at the bottom of Figure 3-5 shown earlier.
② If you double-click on an explorer's title bar, it will toggle between being in docked and free floating modes.
③ If you double-click on the title bar of a free floating explorer window, it will go back to where it was the last time that you used Crystal Reports.
④ In free-floating mode, the explorer window can be moved to a new location in the Crystal Reports window.
⑤ The Data Sources window can also be docked with the explorers as shown earlier in Figure 3-5. I like to keep all three explorer windows in the same location because it frees up space on the screen that I use to make the report window larger.

The Push Pin

If you click on the push pin illustrated in the upper right corner of Figure 3-5 shown earlier, you will open the toolbar shown in Figure 3-7. This toolbar will give you more space to work on reports.

To access one of the explorers from this toolbar, hold the mouse over the icon and the corresponding explorer window will open.

To close the toolbar and return to the docked explorer windows, open an explorer window from the toolbar and click on the push pin.

Click the push pin again to restore the windows.

Figure 3-7 Explorer toolbar

Exercise 3.1: Create Your First Report From Scratch

Don't panic, but you are going to learn how to create a report without using the wizard.

1. Create a new report and save it as `L3.1 Customer information`.

2. Select the **BLANK REPORT** option, then click OK. Crystal Reports ⇒ Database ⇒ Database Expert.

3. Add the Customer table to the **SELECTED TABLES** list, then click OK. You will see an empty design window.

How To Add Fields To A Report

There are several ways to add fields in the Field Explorer to a report as discussed below. If you are not familiar with the techniques discussed, take some time to try them and see which one you like the best.

① Drag the field to the report.
② Select the field. Press Enter, then click in the report where you want to place the field.
③ Right-click on the field that you want to add to the report and select **INSERT TO REPORT** on the shortcut menu, then click in the report where you want to place the field.

Add The Fields To The Report

1. Click on the plus sign in front of the **DATABASE FIELDS** option on the Field Explorer window. You will see all of the tables that you have added to the report. Clicking on the plus sign in front of a table name will display all of the fields in that table. Click on the plus sign in front of the Customer table.

2. Click on the Customer Name field with the left mouse button and drag the field to the **DETAILS** section. Notice that a field heading is automatically added to the page header section.

 If you add a field to a section other then the details section, a field heading will not automatically be added to the page header section. Field headings are only added automatically when the field is added to the details section.

As a general rule, the brackets for one field should not be inside of the brackets for another field unless you are combining objects and fields. Overlapping fields, as illustrated in Figure 3-8 will cause the fields to print on top of each other, as shown in Figure 3-9.

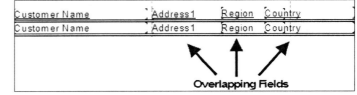

Figure 3-8 Fields overlapped in the report layout

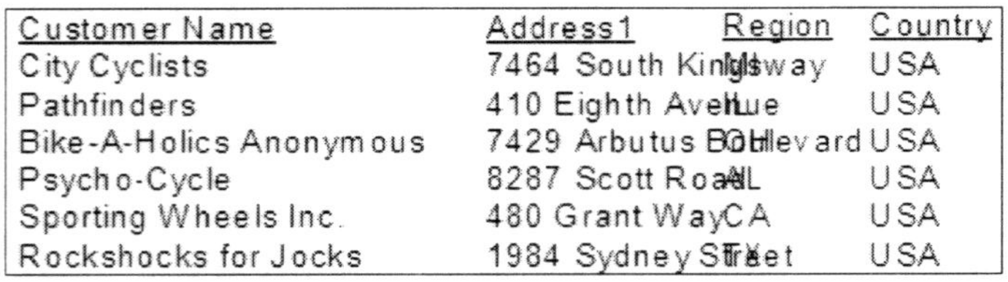

Customer Name	Address1	Region	Country
City Cyclists	7464 South Kingsway		USA
Pathfinders	410 Eighth Avenue		USA
Bike-A-Holics Anonymous	7429 Arbutus Boulevard		USA
Psycho-Cycle	8287 Scott Road		USA
Sporting Wheels Inc.	480 Grant Way	CA	USA
Rockshocks for Jocks	1984 Sydney Street		USA

Figure 3-9 Overlapped fields illustrated in print preview

3. Add the following fields to the **DETAILS** section: Address1, Region, Country and Postal Code. When you are finished, the report layout should look like the one shown in Figure 3-10.

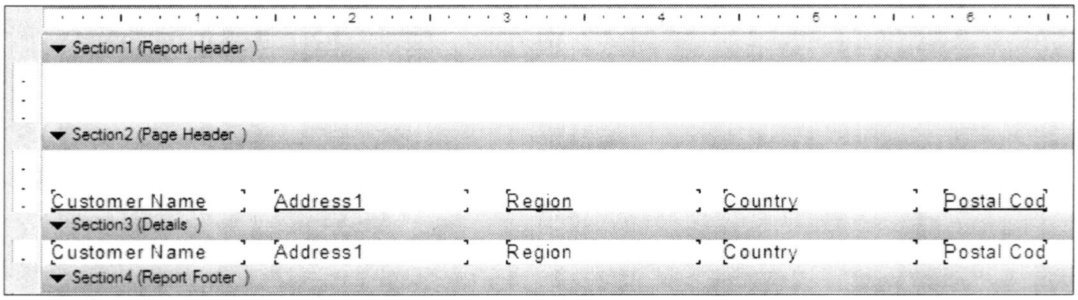

Section1 (Report Header)				
Section2 (Page Header)				
Customer Name	Address1	Region	Country	Postal Cod
Section3 (Details)				
Customer Name	Address1	Region	Country	Postal Cod
Section4 (Report Footer)				

Figure 3-10 Report layout

The green check marks illustrated in the Field Explorer in Figure 3-11 indicate that the field has been added to the report or is being used in a formula field that is being used on the report.

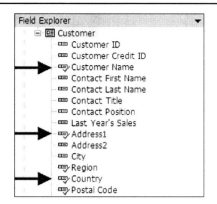

Figure 3-11 Checked fields illustrated

Preview The Report

1. Save the report. It should look like the one shown in Figure 3-12. Not bad for your first time creating a report from scratch.

Customer Name	Address1	Region	Country	Postal Cod
City Cyclists	7464 South Kingswa	MI	USA	48358
Pathfinders	410 Eighth Avenue	IL	USA	60148
Bike-A-Holics Anony	7429 Arbutus Boulev	OH	USA	43005
Psycho-Cycle	8287 Scott Road	AL	USA	35818
Sporting Wheels Inc	480 Grant Way	CA	USA	92150
Rockshocks for Jock	1984 Sydney Street	TX	USA	78770
Poser Cycles	8194 Peter Avenue	MN	USA	55360
Spokes 'N Wheels L	3802 Georgia Court	IA	USA	50305
Trail Blazer's Place	6938 Beach Street	WI	USA	53795
Rowdy Rims Compa	4861 Second Road	CA	USA	91341

Figure 3-12 L3.1 Customer information report

2. Close the report. If prompted to save the changes, click Yes.

Exercise 3.2: Create A Report Using Multiple Tables

In the previous exercise the report that you created was based on one table. Many of the reports that you will need to create will use two or more tables. The report that you will create in this exercise will use more than one table.

Select The Tables

1. Create a new report using the report wizard option and save it as L3.2 Employee list.

2. Add the Employee, Employee Addresses and Orders tables as shown in Figure 3-13 to the report.

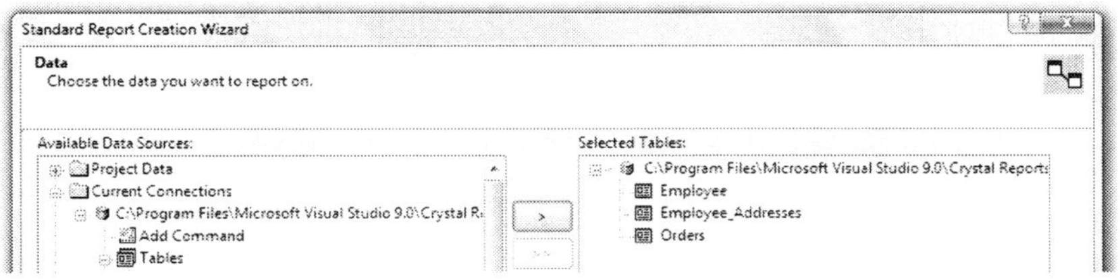

Figure 3-13 Tables selected for the report

> You can add more than one table at the same time by clicking on the first table that you want to add, then press and hold down the Shift key and select the other tables. You can also double-click on the table in the **AVAILABLE DATA SOURCES** section to add it to the Selected Tables list.

3. Click Next. Make the Link window larger. This will make it easier to see how the tables are linked. Notice that all of the tables have an Employee ID field.

 The Database Expert calls the screen that you link tables on, the **LINKS** screen. The wizards call the same screen the **LINK** screen. They both do the exact same thing, so I don't know why they have slightly different names.

The **ORDER LINKS** button opens the dialog box shown in Figure 3-14. It allows you to verify the order of how the tables are connected. Most of the time, the order that is selected is what you need.

When you are using several tables it is a good idea to check the link order to make sure that the links are correct, because an incorrect linking order will produce an outcome different then what you expect.

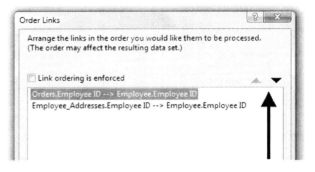

Figure 3-14 Order Links dialog box

If you need to rearrange the order of the links, click on the link that you need to move, then click the **UP** or **DOWN** arrow to move the link, as illustrated above in Figure 3-14.

If you are using a command or query as the basis of the report you do not have to create or have links, because the links are created and stored in the command or query. Linking data in tables is an important concept to understand and will be covered in detail after you finish creating this report.

4. Close the Order Links dialog box, then click Finish to close the Standard Report Creation wizard dialog box.

Add The Fields To The Report

1. Delete the Print Date field in the page header section.

2. Add the following fields in the Employee table to the details section: Photo, First Name and Last Name.

3. Add the following fields in the Employee Addresses table to the details section: Address1 and Region. Figure 3-15 shows the report layout.

Figure 3-15 Fields from the Employee and Employee Addresses tables added to the report

4. Save the report and leave it open to complete the next exercise.

How To Add And Remove Databases And Tables

It is possible that during the report design process you may need to add a database or table or delete one. You just realized that you do not need any fields from the Orders table and want to remove the table from the report. You can make changes like this in the Field Explorer window by following the steps below.

1. Right-click on the **DATABASE FIELDS** option in the Field Explorer. You will see the shortcut menu shown in Figure 3-16.

Figure 3-16 Field Explorer shortcut menu for databases, tables and fields

2. Select the **DATABASE EXPERT** option on the shortcut menu.

> **Other Ways To Open The Database Expert**
>
> ① Right-click on a table in the Field Explorer and select Database Expert.
> ② Right-click on a field in the Field Explorer and select Database Expert.
> ③ Crystal Reports ⇒ Database ⇒ Database Expert.

3. Click on the Orders table in the **SELECTED TABLES** list, then click the **<** button.

> If you need to add a table select it from the **AVAILABLE DATA SOURCES** section and add it to the Selected Tables section of the Database Expert dialog box.

4. Click OK twice to close the Database Expert dialog box. Your report should look like the one shown in Figure 3-17. Save the changes and close the report.

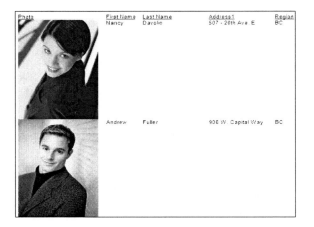

Figure 3-17 L3.2 Employee list report

Relational Databases

Earlier in this lesson you learned a little about linking tables. The reason tables can be linked is because there is a relationship (at least one field in common) between them, thus the term "Relational Databases". Yes, this is a complicated topic and there are a lot of books on the concepts associated with relational databases and how to create them, so I won't bore you with the details, but please hear me out and don't skip this section.

If the databases that you will use out in the real world are created properly, you will not have to learn a lot about linking or relational databases, because Crystal Reports will create the links that you need. This doesn't mean that you do not have to learn anything about these topics. A good introduction to databases would be to read the chapter "Understanding Databases" in the Crystal Reports User Guide. Search Businessobjects.com for the file name "usergde" or look in the product documentation for the latest version of Crystal Reports. The more of that chapter that you understand, the easier it will be for you to create meaningful reports.

While databases are not the primary focus of this workbook, it is important that you understand a little more than the fundamentals that were covered in Lesson 2. The reason that you need to understand databases is because they are the foundation for the reports that you will create and modify. If you have never created a database, or have very little experience creating them, the next few sections in this lesson will be your crash course in databases, relationships and linking. In Lesson 2 you learned the basic database terminology. Now you will learn how all of the components fit together. Figures 3-18 and 3-19 illustrate the layout of two tables.

Orders			
Order ID	Order Date	Order Amount	Cust ID
1000	1/2/2005	$263.99	48
1001	1/2/2005	$322.45	57
1002	1/3/2005	$196.00	3
1003	1/4/2005	$124.99	48

Figure 3-18 Orders table layout

Orders Detail		
Order ID	Product ID	Quantity
1000	43	4
1000	76	2
1001	76	3
1001	10	2
1003	10	1
1004	25	3

Figure 3-19 Orders Detail table layout

Primary Key Fields

In Lesson 2 you saw a table that listed the primary keys for the tables in the Xtreme database. [See Lesson 2, Xtreme Database] The fields in the Primary Key column are the ID fields. You will see these two terms used interchangeably. I prefer to use the term ID field because primary key fields usually have "ID" as part of the field name.

> ID is short for identification. It is jargon that the programming community uses to reference a field that can be used to link the data in one table to the data in another table.

All of the tables that you will use in the Xtreme database have at least one ID field. Hopefully, you will find that this is also true out in the real world. The reason ID fields are used is because by design they provide a way for each record in the table to have a unique way to be identified.

I have taught several database classes and almost without fail, this topic causes a lot of confusion. For some reason, people want to create links on string (text fields). Please don't do that. It can cause you problems.

If you needed to create a report that showed all of the orders and what items were on each order, you would need a way to link the Orders and Orders Detail tables. Think of "linking" as having the ability to combine two or more tables "virtually" and being able to display the result of this "virtual linking" on a computer screen or on a printed report.

In Figures 3-18 and 3-19 above, the common ID field is the Order ID field. If you look at the data in the Orders Detail table, you will see that some records have the same Order ID number. That's okay.

This means that some customers placed orders with more than one item. Each record in the Orders Detail table represents one item that a customer ordered. If you were to "virtually" join the data in the tables shown in Figures 3-18 and 3-19 above, it would look like the table shown in Figure 3-20.

Orders				Orders Detail		
Order ID	Order Date	Order Amount	Cust ID	Order ID	Product ID	Quantity
1000	1/2/2005	$263.99	48	1000	43	4
1000	1/2/2005	$263.99	48	1000	76	2
1001	1/2/2005	$322.45	57	1001	76	3
1001	1/2/2005	$322.45	57	1001	10	2
1002	1/3/2005	$196.00	3			
1003	1/4/2005	$124.99	48	1003	10	1
				1004	25	3

Figure 3-20 Virtually joined tables

This "virtual" join is what happens when tables are LINKED. If all of this data was stored in one table instead of two, at the very minimum, the Order Date and Order Amount fields would be repeated for every record that is in the Orders Detail table. Repetition of data is why this information is stored in two tables instead of one. It is considered poor table design to have the same information (other than fields that are used to join tables) stored in more than one table.

> More then likely if you see a record in the Orders Detail table, like Order ID 1004 shown above in Figure 3-20, or any child table that is in a parent-child relationship, there is a problem with the data in at least one of the tables because all of the records in the child table should have at least one matching record in the parent table. Parent tables are used to get data from a child table.

Types Of Relationships

The Employee report that you just created required two tables. These tables are linked by a common field, the Employee ID field. This field is what connects (joins) data from both tables and allows you to use data from both tables.

The Employee ID field in the Employee table is how you find the matching record (known as a ONE-TO-ONE RELATIONSHIP) or records (known as a ONE-TO-MANY RELATIONSHIP, which is the most popular type of relationship) in the Employee Addresses table. These are two of the most common types of relationships. The MANY-TO-MANY RELATIONSHIP is a third type of relationship. It is not used as much as the other two.

How Linking Works

More than likely, most reports that you create will require data from more than one table. Reports like the Product List report that you created in Lesson 2 only used one table, so there is no linking involved. For reports that require two or more tables, the tables need to be linked. The tables are usually linked in the database. The links that you see on the Link screen are the same as the links in the database. When you create a report and need to view or modify the links, you can do so by opening the Database Expert and clicking on the Link tab. Even though most of the time the links that you need are created for you, it is important to understand what is going on behind the scenes, as they say.

The best way to understand the basic concept of linking tables is to look at the records or a portion of the records in the tables that need to be linked. When you create a report that you are not familiar with the data that is needed, you should take the time to look at the data in the tables. Figures 3-21 and 3-22 show the records in the Employee and Employee Addresses tables. As mentioned earlier, the field that these tables have in common is the Employee ID field, as shown below.

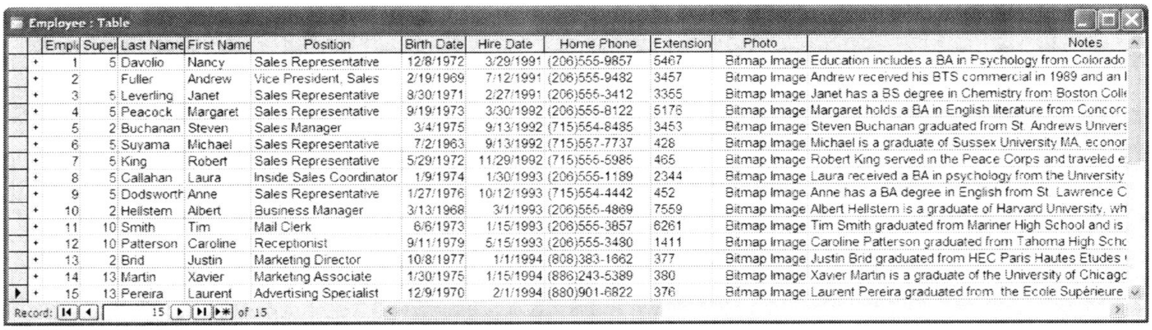

Employee : Table

Empl	Super	Last Name	First Name	Position	Birth Date	Hire Date	Home Phone	Extension	Photo	Notes
1	5	Davolio	Nancy	Sales Representative	12/8/1972	3/29/1991	(206)555-9857	5467	Bitmap Image	Education includes a BA in Psychology from Colorado
2		Fuller	Andrew	Vice President, Sales	2/19/1969	7/12/1991	(206)555-9482	3457	Bitmap Image	Andrew received his BTS commercial in 1989 and an I
3	5	Leverling	Janet	Sales Representative	8/30/1971	2/27/1991	(206)555-3412	3355	Bitmap Image	Janet has a BS degree in Chemistry from Boston Coll
4	5	Peacock	Margaret	Sales Representative	9/19/1973	3/30/1992	(206)555-8122	5176	Bitmap Image	Margaret holds a BA in English literature from Concorc
5	2	Buchanan	Steven	Sales Manager	3/4/1975	9/13/1992	(715)554-8485	3453	Bitmap Image	Steven Buchanan graduated from St. Andrews Univers
6	5	Suyama	Michael	Sales Representative	7/2/1963	9/13/1992	(715)557-7737	428	Bitmap Image	Michael is a graduate of Sussex University MA, econor
7	5	King	Robert	Sales Representative	5/29/1972	11/29/1992	(715)555-5985	465	Bitmap Image	Robert King served in the Peace Corps and traveled e
8	5	Callahan	Laura	Inside Sales Coordinator	1/9/1974	1/30/1993	(206)555-1189	2344	Bitmap Image	Laura received a BA in psychology from the University
9	5	Dodsworth	Anne	Sales Representative	1/27/1976	10/12/1993	(715)554-4442	452	Bitmap Image	Anne has a BA degree in English from St. Lawrence C
10	2	Hellstern	Albert	Business Manager	3/13/1968	3/1/1993	(206)555-4869	7559	Bitmap Image	Albert Hellstern is a graduate of Harvard University, wh
11	10	Smith	Tim	Mail Clerk	6/6/1973	1/15/1993	(206)555-3857	6261	Bitmap Image	Tim Smith graduated from Mariner High School and is
12	10	Patterson	Caroline	Receptionist	9/11/1979	5/15/1993	(206)555-3480	1411	Bitmap Image	Caroline Patterson graduated from Tahoma High Schc
13	2	Brid	Justin	Marketing Director	10/8/1977	1/1/1994	(808)383-1662	377	Bitmap Image	Justin Brid graduated from HEC Paris Hautes Etudes
14	13	Martin	Xavier	Marketing Associate	1/30/1975	1/15/1994	(886)243-5389	380	Bitmap Image	Xavier Martin is a graduate of the University of Chicagc
15	13	Pereira	Laurent	Advertising Specialist	12/9/1970	2/1/1994	(880)901-6822	376	Bitmap Image	Laurent Pereira graduated from the Ecole Supérieure

Record: 15 of 15

Figure 3-21 Data in the Employee table

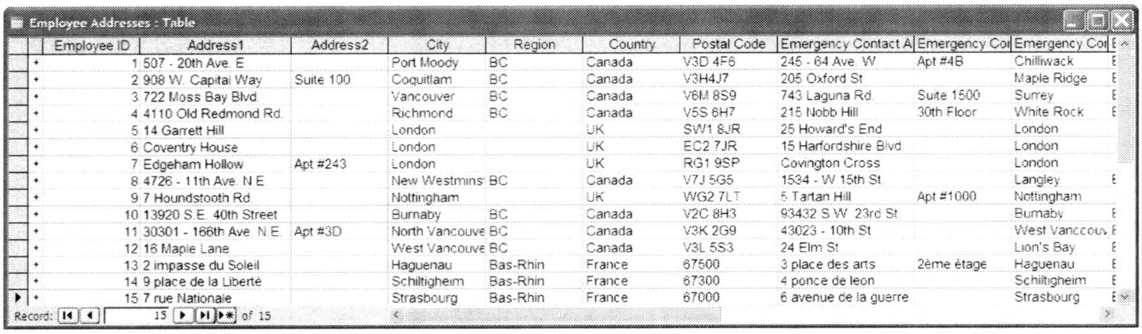

Employee Addresses : Table

Employee ID	Address1	Address2	City	Region	Country	Postal Code	Emergency Contact A	Emergency Co	Emergency Co	E
1	507 - 20th Ave. E		Port Moody	BC	Canada	V3D 4F6	245 - 64 Ave. W	Apt #4B	Chilliwack	E
2	908 W. Capital Way	Suite 100	Coquitlam	BC	Canada	V3H4J7	205 Oxford St		Maple Ridge	E
3	722 Moss Bay Blvd.		Vancouver	BC	Canada	V6M 8S9	743 Laguna Rd.	Suite 1500	Surrey	E
4	4110 Old Redmond Rd.		Richmond	BC	Canada	V5S 6H7	215 Nobb Hill	30th Floor	White Rock	E
5	14 Garrett Hill		London		UK	SW1 8JR	25 Howard's End		London	
6	Coventry House		London		UK	EC2 7JR	15 Harfordshire Blvd		London	
7	Edgeham Hollow	Apt #243	London		UK	RG1 9SP	Covington Cross		London	
8	4726 - 11th Ave. N.E.		New Westmins	BC	Canada	V7J 5G5	1534 - W 15th St.		Langley	E
9	7 Houndstooth Rd.		Nottingham		UK	WG2 7LT	5 Tartan Hill	Apt #1000	Nottingham	
10	13920 S.E. 40th Street		Burnaby	BC	Canada	V2C 8H3	93432 S.W. 23rd St.		Burnaby	E
11	30301 - 166th Ave. N.E.	Apt #3D	North Vancouve	BC	Canada	V3K 2G9	43023 - 10th St		West Vanccouv	E
12	16 Maple Lane		West Vancouve	BC	Canada	V3L 5S3	24 Elm St		Lion's Bay	E
13	2 impasse du Soleil		Haguenau	Bas-Rhin	France	67500	3 place des arts	2ème étage	Haguenau	E
14	9 place de la Liberté		Schiltigheim	Bas-Rhin	France	67300	4 ponce de leon		Schiltigheim	E
15	7 rue Nationale		Strasbourg	Bas-Rhin	France	67000	6 avenue de la guerre		Strasbourg	E

Record: 15 of 15

Figure 3-22 Data in the Employee Addresses table

Fields that are used to link tables must be the same data type. [See Lesson 2, Table 2-1] You could not create a link between a date field and a string field.

Depending on the table structure, tables can have more than one field that they can be linked by. An example of this would be the Orders Detail table. This table has an ID field that would let you link it to the Orders table. There is a Product ID field in the Orders Detail table that would let you retrieve the Product Name from another table (the Product table) to print on the report, instead of printing the Product ID number. Displaying the product name on the report is more meaningful to the people that read the report then the Product ID field, which contains a number. If you are asking why the Product Name is not stored in the Orders Detail table, there are three reasons.

① The ID field takes up less space, thereby keeping the size of the Orders Detail table smaller.

② The Product Name data takes up more space than the ID data does, thereby making the size of the Orders Detail table and any other table that stored the Product Name larger than it needs to be.

③ If a Product Name has to be changed for any reason, it only has to be changed in the Product table. Every place that the Product Name field is used on any report would automatically be updated with the revised product name. If the product name was stored in the Orders Detail table, every record in the Orders Detail table that had that product name would have to be changed, as well as, any other table that stored the product name. That would be a lot extra of work.

Join Types

Hopefully you are still with me. Don't worry, the relational database "lecturette" is almost over. There are several types of links that can be created. Figure 3-23 shows the link options. These different types of links are called **JOIN TYPES**. Crystal Reports has several join types that you can select from. Each join type will return different recordsets from the same tables, which you will see in Figures 3-25 to 3-28. **INNER** joins are the most common. If you use any of the three **OUTER** join types discussed below, the order that the tables are added to the report is important. The four join types that are explained in Table 3-4 are the ones that are automatically created and are the most common. The other join types have to be created manually. They are covered later in this lesson.

To open this dialog box, right-click on the line between the tables as shown in Figure 3-24, then select **LINK OPTIONS** on the shortcut menu. You can also open the Link Options dialog box by clicking on the link between the tables and click the Link Options button shown in Figure 3-24.

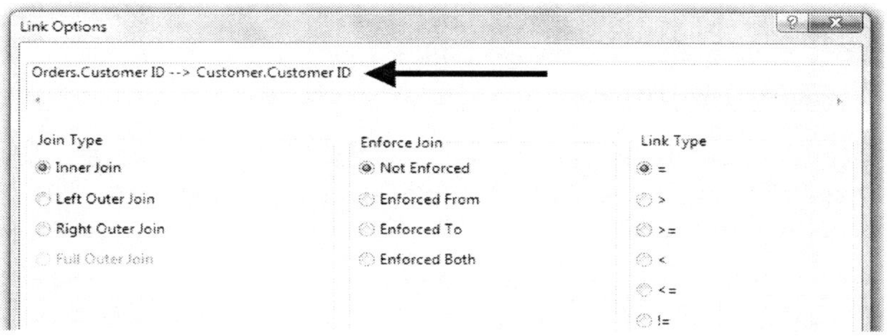

Figure 3-23 Link Options dialog box

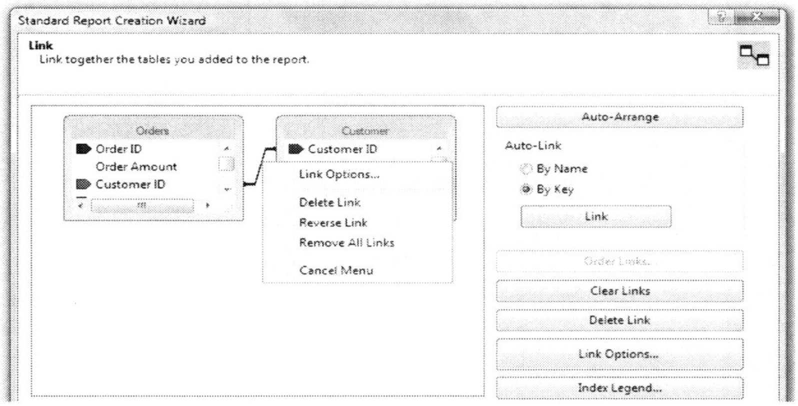

Figure 3-24 Link screen

Join Type	Description
Inner	Records that have matching records in both tables, as illustrated in Figure 3-25.
Left-Outer	Selects all records from one table (usually the left most table on the Links tab) and only matching records in the table on the right, as illustrated in Figure 3-26.
Right-Outer	Selects all records from the right table and only matching records from the table on the left, as illustrated in Figure 3-27. This join type works the opposite of the Left-Outer join type.
Full-Outer	Selects all records from both tables whether or not there are matching records in the other table, as illustrated in Figure 3-28. Full-Outer joins are also known as a **UNION** join type.

Table 3-4 Join types explained

 The "matching" discussed above in Table 3-4 is usually done on **ID** fields.

In the Orders and Orders Detail tables, the Orders table is known as the LEFT table and should be added to the list of tables for the report first. The Orders Detail table is known as the RIGHT table and should be added to the list of tables after the Orders table. The reason the tables need to be added in this order is because for each record in the Orders table, there can be multiple records in the Orders Detail table that have the same ID. Earlier in this lesson you learned about the Order Links dialog box. If the tables were added incorrectly you can use the options on the Order Links dialog box to change the order.

Join Type Examples

When walking through these examples compare the data in Figures 3-25 to 3-28 to the data shown earlier in Figure 3-20. The data shown in these examples only represent the data that would be retrieved from the tables in Figure 3-20. The examples in this section illustrate how the same data would be retrieved differently depending on the join type that is selected. This is why it is important to understand linking and join types.

In Figure 3-25, the record for Order ID 1002 in the Orders table would not be retrieved in an Inner join because there is no related record in the Orders Detail table. The arrows between the tables represent the flow of the data.

Orders					Orders Detail		
Order ID	Order Date	Order Amount	Cust ID		Order ID	Product ID	Quantity
1000	1/2/2005	$263.99	48		1000	43	4
1001	1/2/2005	$322.45	57		1000	76	2
1003	1/4/2005	$124.99	48		1001	76	3
					1001	10	2
					1003	10	1

Figure 3-25 Inner join recordset

In Figure 3-26, the record for Order ID 1004 would not be retrieved from the Orders Detail table in a Left-Outer join because there is no related record in the Orders table.

Orders					Orders Detail		
Order ID	Order Date	Order Amount	Cust ID		Order ID	Product ID	Quantity
1000	1/2/2005	$263.99	48		1000	43	4
1001	1/2/2005	$322.45	57		1000	76	2
1002	1/3/2005	$196.00	3		1001	76	3
1003	1/4/2005	$124.99	48		1001	10	2
					1003	10	1

Figure 3-26 Left-Outer join recordset

In Figure 3-27, the record for Order ID 1002 in the Orders table would not be retrieved in a Right-Outer join because there is no related record in the Orders Detail table.

Orders					Orders Detail		
Order ID	Order Date	Order Amount	Cust ID		Order ID	Product ID	Quantity
1000	1/2/2005	$263.99	48		1000	43	4
1001	1/2/2005	$322.45	57		1000	76	2
1003	1/4/2005	$124.99	48		1001	76	3
					1001	10	2
					1003	10	1
					1004	25	3

Figure 3-27 Right-Outer join recordset

In Figure 3-28, all records would be retrieved in a Full-Outer join whether there is a related record in the other table or not.

Orders					Orders Detail		
Order ID	Order Date	Order Amount	Cust ID		Order ID	Product ID	Quantity
1000	1/2/2005	$263.99	48		1000	43	4
1001	1/2/2005	$322.45	57		1000	76	2
1002	1/3/2005	$196.00	3		1001	76	3
1003	1/4/2005	$124.99	48		1001	10	2
					1003	10	1
					1004	25	3

Figure 3-28 Full-Outer join recordset

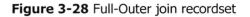

Tables Without A Link

If you added the Orders and Orders Detail tables to a report but did not link them, Crystal Reports would not know which record in the Orders table went with which record in the Orders Detail table. The result would be that each order record would be displayed (matched) with each of the records in the Orders Detail table as shown in Figure 3-29. In total, 24 records would print on the report. When a report uses more than one table, this is usually not what you want.

Orders					Orders Detail		
Order ID	Order Date	Order Amount	Cust ID		Order ID	Product ID	Quantity
1000	1/2/2005	$263.99	48		1000	43	4
1000	1/2/2005	$263.99	48		1000	76	2
1000	1/2/2005	$263.99	48		1001	76	3
1000	1/2/2005	$263.99	48		1001	10	2
1000	1/2/2005	$263.99	48		1003	10	1
1000	1/2/2005	$263.99	48		1004	25	3
1001	1/2/2005	$322.45	57		1000	43	4
1001	1/2/2005	$322.45	57		1000	76	2
1001	1/2/2005	$322.45	57		1001	76	3
1001	1/2/2005	$322.45	57		1001	10	2
1001	1/2/2005	$322.45	57		1003	10	1
1001	1/2/2005	$322.45	57		1004	25	3
1003	1/4/2005	$124.99	48		1004	25	3

Figure 3-29 Tables not joined recordset

The reports shown in Figures 3-30 and 3-31 have the same three fields: Customer Name, Product ID and Order ID. The report shown in Figure 3-30 has the **LEFT-OUTER** join between the Customer and Orders tables. The report shown in Figure 3-31 has the **RIGHT-OUTER** join between the Orders and Orders Detail tables. As you can see, the output is completely different for these reports. Hopefully, these reports demonstrate why understanding table structures, types of relationships, linking and join types is important. [See the L3 Left outer join and L3 Right outer join reports in the zip file]

Customer Name	Product ID	Order ID
City Cyclists	2,201	1
Deals on Wheels	5,205	1,002
Deals on Wheels	102,181	1,002
Warsaw Sports, Inc.	2,213	1,003
Warsaw Sports, Inc.	5,402	1,003
Bikes and Trikes	402,002	1,004
SAB Mountain	1,101	1,005
Poser Cycles	1,107	1,006
Poser Cycles	5,208	1,006
Poser Cycles	5,402	1,006
Spokes	1,109	1,007

Figure 3-30 Left-Outer join report

Customer Name	Product ID	Order ID
City Cyclists	2,209	1,387
City Cyclists	3,305	1,387
City Cyclists	302,201	1,387
City Cyclists	1,108	2,277
City Cyclists	2,207	2,277
City Cyclists	1,101	1,033
City Cyclists	1,105	1,033
City Cyclists	102,181	1,033
City Cyclists	2,214	2,402
City Cyclists	7,402	2,402
City Cyclists	301,161	2,772
City Cyclists	301,201	1,366

Figure 3-31 Right-Outer join report

Recursive Join

In addition to the join types discussed above, there is another join type called **RECURSIVE JOIN**. This type of join is not always obvious when looking at the table structures. A recursive join occurs when the same data is stored in two different ID fields in the same table. This is not the same as a parent/child (also known as a master/detail) relationship because this type of relationship does not require two tables like the Orders and Orders Detail tables that you read about earlier in this lesson.

An example of a recursive join is in the Employee table. The Supervisor ID field in the Employee table contains the Employee ID of another record in the Employee table. This is because supervisors are also employees. Refer back to Figure 3-21. Seven employees have the number 5 in the Supervisor ID field (the second field from the left). This is because they all have the same supervisor, Steven Buchanan, whose Employee ID is number 5. Recursive joins are used to create hierarchical reports, which you will learn how to create in Lesson 13.

View The Current Links

1. Open a blank report and name it what you want, then add the Customer, Orders and Orders Detail tables.

2. On the Links tab click the **CLEAR LINKS** button. Click Yes, when prompted if you are sure.

How To Manually Create Links

When you have the need to manually create links, follow the steps below.

1. Select a field in one table and drag it to the field in the other table. In this example, select the Quantity field in the Orders_Detail table and drag it to the Customer Name field in the Customer table, then release the mouse button.

 Both fields must have the same data type. If there is something wrong with the link that you are trying to create, you will see a warning message similar to the one shown in Figure 3-32. This message lets you know that the link that you are trying to create is not valid.

Figure 3-32 Link error warning message

2. Click OK to close the Visual Linking Editor message window shown above in Figure 3-32. Leave the Database Expert open to complete the next exercise.

Manual Join Types

As discussed earlier, there are other join and link types that can be used to link tables. Table 3-5 explains the enforce join type options. Table 3-6 explains the link types.

Enforce Join Type	Description
Not Enforced	Selecting this option doesn't mean that the link will be included in the SQL statement. At least one field must be used to join tables in order for the linking criteria to be included in the SQL statement.
Enforced From	Selecting this option forces the link to the right table. When a field from the right table is used, but not one from the left table, the SQL statement requires that both tables be referenced.
Enforced To	This option forces the link from the left table, whether or not a field is used from the right table. This means that the SQL statement will include both tables.
Enforced Both	This option forces the link between the tables, regardless of where the fields that are used in the report are stored.

Table 3-5 Enforce Join types explained

Link Type	Description
Equal Link =	Creates a recordset where the link field has related records in the left and right tables.
Greater Than Link >	Creates a recordset where the link field from the left table is greater than the linked field in the right table.
Greater Than or Equal To Link >=	Creates a recordset where the link field from the left table is greater than or equal to the linked field in the right table.
Less Than Link <	Creates a recordset where the link field from the left table is less than the linked field in the right table.
Less Than or Equal To Link <=	Creates a recordset where the link field from the left table is less than or equal to the linked field in the right table.
Not Equal Link !=	Creates a recordset where the link field from the left table does not match the linked field in the right table.

Table 3-6 Link Types explained

Exercise 3.3: Create A Customer Orders Report

In this exercise you will create a report that displays customers and their orders.

1. You should still have the report open from the previous example. Go back to the Data tab and remove the Orders Detail table, then click OK.

2. Delete the Print Date field from the report. Add the Customer Name field in the Customer table to the details section.

3. Add the Order Date and Ship Date fields in the Orders table to the details section.

Add Another Table

You have decided that the report would look better if it also had fields from the Orders Detail table. To add a table to the report, follow the steps below.

1. Right-click on the **DATABASE FIELDS** option in the Field Explorer, then select Database Expert.

2. Add the Orders Detail table and click OK. When you see the **LINKS** tab, Click OK. You will see the Orders Detail table in the Field Explorer window.

Add More Fields

1. Add the Order ID, Unit Price and Quantity fields in the Orders Detail table to the details section. Your report layout should look like the one shown in Figure 3-33.

Figure 3-33 Customer orders report layout

2. Save the changes. The report should look like the one shown in Figure 3-34. Close the report.

Customer Name	Order Date	Ship Date	Order ID	Unit Price	Quantity
City Cyclists	12/2/2000 12:00:0(	12/10/2000 5:32:2	1	$41.90	1
Deals on Wheels	12/2/2000 12:00:0(	12/2/2000 6:45:32	1,002	$33.90	3
Deals on Wheels	12/2/2000 12:00:0(	12/2/2000 6:45:32	1,002	$1,652.86	3
Warsaw Sports, Inc.	12/2/2000 12:00:0(	12/5/2000 12:10:12	1,003	$48.51	3
Warsaw Sports, Inc.	12/2/2000 12:00:0(	12/5/2000 12:10:12	1,003	$13.78	3
Bikes and Trikes	12/2/2000 12:00:0(	12/2/2000 3:24:54	1,004	$274.35	3
SAB Mountain	12/3/2000 12:00:0(	12/3/2000 1:54:34	1,005	$14.50	2
Poser Cycles	12/3/2000 12:00:0(	12/5/2000 7:58:01	1,006	$16.50	1
Poser Cycles	12/3/2000 12:00:0(	12/5/2000 7:58:01	1,006	$33.90	1

Figure 3-34 L3.3 Customer orders report

The reason that the information in the Customer Name, Order Date, Ship Date and Order ID fields is repeated, is because on some orders the customer ordered more than one item. (See Order ID 1002 and 1003). As you can see, all of the reports that you have created in Lessons 2 and 3 need to be edited and formatted, so that they are more presentable. You will learn how to edit reports in the next lesson.

How To Rename A Report

When you created this report, I did not give you a name for it. In this part of the exercise you will learn how to rename the report.

1. Right-click on the report name in the Solution Explorer window that you named and select Rename.

2. Type L3.3 Customer orders.rpt as the file name, then press Enter. You should see the new report name in the Solution Explorer window.

Test Your Skills

1. Create a Product report from scratch that uses the Product, Supplier and Product Type tables. Save it as `L3.4 Skills Product report`. Add the fields in Table 3-7 in the order they are shown in the report. The report should look like the one shown in Figure 3-35.

Product	Supplier	Product Type
Product ID	Supplier Name	Product Type Name
Product Name		

Table 3-7 Fields to add to the report

Product ID	Product Name	Product Type Name	Supplier Name
1,101	Active Outdoors Cro	Gloves	Active Outdoors
1,102	Active Outdoors Cro	Gloves	Active Outdoors
1,103	Active Outdoors Cro	Gloves	Active Outdoors
1,104	Active Outdoors Cro	Gloves	Active Outdoors
1,105	Active Outdoors Cro	Gloves	Active Outdoors
1,106	Active Outdoors Lycr	Gloves	Active Outdoors
1,107	Active Outdoors Lycr	Gloves	Active Outdoors
1,108	Active Outdoors Lycr	Gloves	Active Outdoors
1,109	Active Outdoors Lycr	Gloves	Active Outdoors
1,110	Active Outdoors Lycr	Gloves	Active Outdoors
1,111	Active Outdoors Lycr	Gloves	Active Outdoors
2,201	Triumph Pro Helmet	Helmets	Triumph
2,202	Triumph Pro Helmet	Helmets	Triumph
2,203	Triumph Pro Helmet	Helmets	Triumph

Figure 3-35 L3.4 Skills Product report

2. Create a Customer Orders report from scratch that uses the Customer, Employee and Orders tables. Save it as `L3.5 Skills Customer orders`. Add the fields in Table 3-8 in the order they are shown in the report. The Last Name field may not fit on the report. It's okay to let it hang off of the right edge of the report for now. Later you will learn how to resize fields so that they fit on the report. The report should look like the one shown in Figure 3-36.

Customer	Employee	Orders
Customer Name	First Name	Order ID
	Last Name	Order Date
		Order Amount
		Ship Via

Table 3-8 Fields to add to the Customer orders report

Customer Name	Order ID	Order Date	Order Amount	Ship Via	First Name	Last Name
City Cyclists	1	12/2/2000 12:00:00	$41.90	UPS	Nancy	Davolio
Deals on Wheels	1,002	12/2/2000 12:00:00	$5,060.28	Pickup	Janet	Leverling
Warsaw Sports, Inc.	1,003	12/2/2000 12:00:00	$186.87	UPS	Margaret	Peacock
Bikes and Trikes	1,004	12/2/2000 12:00:00	$823.05	Pickup	Margaret	Peacock
SAB Mountain	1,005	12/3/2000 12:00:00	$29.00	Loomis	Janet	Leverling
Poser Cycles	1,006	12/3/2000 12:00:00	$64.90	Purolator	Margaret	Peacock
Spokes	1,007	12/3/2000 12:00:00	$49.50	Parcel Post	Anne	Dodsworth
Clean Air Transporta	1,008	12/3/2000 12:00:00	$2,214.94	Purolator	Margaret	Peacock
Extreme Cycling	1,009	12/3/2000 12:00:00	$29.00	Loomis	Margaret	Peacock
Cyclopath	1,010	12/3/2000 12:00:00	$14,872.30	UPS	Nancy	Davolio
BBS Pty	1,011	12/3/2000 12:00:00	$29.00	Purolator	Margaret	Peacock
Piccolo	1,012	12/3/2000 12:00:00	$10,259.10	Loomis	Nancy	Davolio
Pedals Inc.	1,013	12/3/2000 12:00:00	$1,142.13	Parcel Post	Margaret	Peacock
Spokes 'N Wheels L	1,014	12/4/2000 12:00:00	$29.00	Purolator	Nancy	Davolio
Cycle City Rome	1,015	12/4/2000 12:00:00	$43.50	UPS	Anne	Dodsworth
SAB Mountain	1,016	12/4/2000 12:00:00	$563.70	FedEx	Janet	Leverling
Tyred Out	1,017	12/5/2000 12:00:00	$72.00	Purolator	Margaret	Peacock
Has Been Bikes (cor	1,018	12/5/2000 12:00:00	$115.50	Loomis	Janet	Leverling

Figure 3-36 L3.5 Skills Customer orders report

FORMATTING AND EDITING 101

As the title of this lesson indicates, you will learn basic formatting and editing techniques that you can use to make the reports that you create look better. Lessons 9 and 10 will teach you other ways to format reports. After completing the exercises in this lesson you will be able to:

- ☑ Understand the formatting options on various shortcut menus
- ☑ Select objects
- ☑ Align objects
- ☑ Understand the purpose of the Grid
- ☑ Resize objects
- ☑ Add graphics to a report
- ☑ Use the Format Editor
- ☑ Use the Section Expert
- ☑ Add Special Fields to a report

LESSON 4

Shortcut Menus

Crystal Reports has several shortcut menus that you can use instead of selecting menu options or clicking on toolbar buttons. As you will see, you will spend a lot of time formatting and editing reports. A great time saver in completing these tasks is using the options on the shortcut menus.

The options on the shortcut menu will change depending on the object that is right-clicked on.

In addition to the object shortcut menu, there is a general shortcut menu available when you right-click on an empty space in the design window as shown in Figure 4-1. These are the same options that are on the Crystal Reports menu.

[See Lesson 5, Crystal Reports Menu] Several of the options on this shortcut menu are explained in detail later in this lesson.

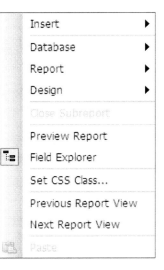

Figure 4-1 General shortcut menu

Selecting Fields And Objects

A lot of the report editing that you will do requires fields and other objects to be selected. Often, you will have the need to apply the same changes to several fields or objects. To select a single field or object, click on it with the left mouse button. When an object is selected you will see a frame around it, as illustrated in Figure 4-2. You will also see squares. These squares are called **SIZE HANDLERS**.

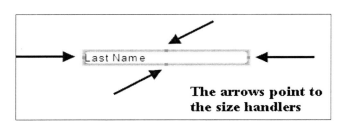

Figure 4-2 Field selected and size handlers illustrated

They allow you to change the size of the object to make it wider, longer, shorter or smaller. You will learn how to resize objects later in this lesson.

> In the Visual Studio environment everything on a report is considered an object, including fields, text boxes, lines and images. When I use the word "field", I am referring to a field in the details section of the report, or a field from a table or a calculated field that you create. "Objects" refer to items like the field heading, a text field or an image.

Selecting Multiple Fields And Objects

There are two ways to select the fields in the report that you need, as discussed below.

① Click on one field or object. Press and hold down the **CTRL** or **SHIFT** key, then click on the other fields or objects that you need to select.

② Draw what is called a **MARQUEE** or **LASSO** around the fields or objects with the mouse. To do this successfully, the objects need to be near each other, either side by side or up and down from each other. Click outside of the first field or object. Hold the left mouse button down, then draw around the objects that you need to select. You will see a frame being drawn. When you are finished selecting the objects and release the mouse button, you will see that several objects have been selected. To use this technique no objects on the report can already be selected.

Exercise 4.1: Moving Objects

One of the tasks that you will do from time to time is rearrange fields and other objects on a report. This exercise will show you how to move fields and objects on a report.

1. Save the L3.4 report as `L4.1 Moving fields`. Make sure that you save the report in the Crystal Reports_Workbook project.

2. Click on the **PRODUCT ID** field in the details section and move it to the left, as close to the edge as possible. Notice that the field heading moved with the field.

3. Move the Product Name and Product Type Name fields to the left, then delete the Print Date field.

Aligning Objects

In addition to moving objects, you will have the need to have multiple objects line up. The **ALIGNMENT** option will help you line up several objects at the same time. Follow the steps below to learn how to align objects. Because everything on the report is currently aligned, you need to move an object to get it out of alignment to complete this exercise.

1. Click on the Product Type Name field heading and drag it to the right as shown in Figure 4-3.

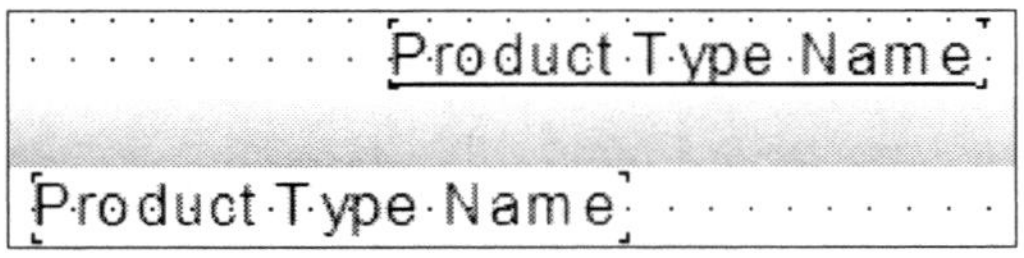

Figure 4-3 Field heading moved to the right

2. Select the Project Type Name field and heading, then right-click on the Project Type Name field.

> In the step 2, you have to right-click on the object that has the alignment that you want duplicate. In this exercise you want to align the field heading with the field in the details section. If you right-clicked on the field heading in the step above and selected Align ⇒ Rights, the field in the details section would have been aligned on the right with the field heading.

3. Align ⇒ Lefts, as shown in Figure 4-4. The field and heading should be where it was before you started this exercise. Table 4-1 explains the alignment options.

> At the top of the shortcut menu if you see the words **FORMAT MULTIPLE OBJECTS**, it means that you have more than one object selected. When selecting multiple fields or objects, whatever change you make will be applied to all of the selected fields or objects as long as the change can be applied to the data type. Not all data types can have the same changes.

You can right-click on any object and select the **ALIGN** option. Just remember which object that you right-click on before selecting an align option, because you may get results different then what you expected. The alignment of the object that you right-click on will be applied to the other objects that are selected.

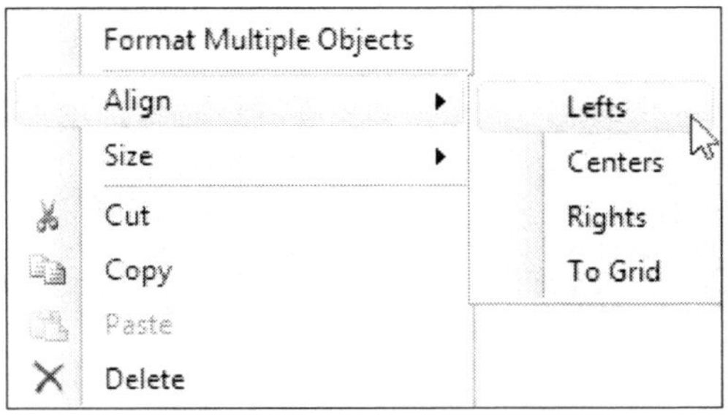

Figure 4-4 Alignment options illustrated

Align Option	How It Aligns
Lefts	Aligns on the left side of the object.
Centers	Aligns on the center of the object.
Rights	Aligns on the right side of the object.
To Grid	Aligns to the closest grid point of the object that you right-click on. You need to have the **GRID** option turned on to see how this feature works.

Table 4-1 Alignment options explained

    4.   Save the changes and leave the report open to complete the next exercise.

Aligning Objects Horizontally

This type of alignment is very similar to the alignment options that you just learned about. The horizontal alignment option is useful when you manually add fields or objects to a report. If you rush and add fields to a report like I do, meaning that you just drop them on the report without paying attention to whether or not they are lined up properly, you will really appreciate this exercise. In order to demonstrate how this feature works, you need to rearrange objects on the report first.

    1.   Drag the Product ID and Product Type Name field headings up in the page header section, as shown in Figure 4-5.

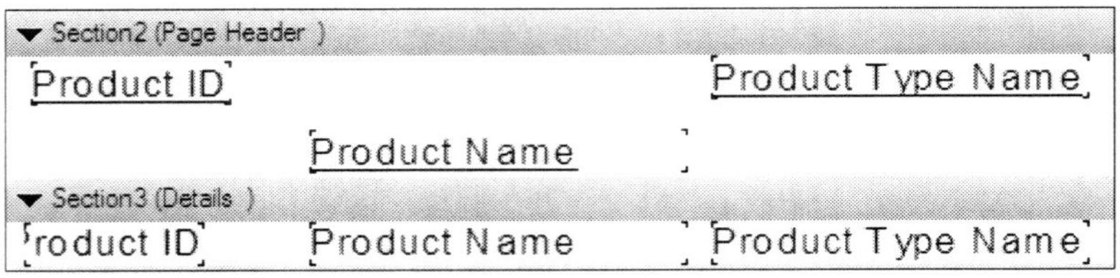

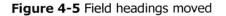

Figure 4-5 Field headings moved

    2.   Select the Product ID, Product Name and Product Type Name field headings, then right-click on the Product Name heading.

    3.   Align ⇒ Bottoms, as shown in Figure 4-6. The field headings should be back where they were before you started this exercise. Table 4-2 explains the options on the shortcut menu.

The alignment options shown in Figure 4-6 are only available when all of the selected objects are in the same section of the report.

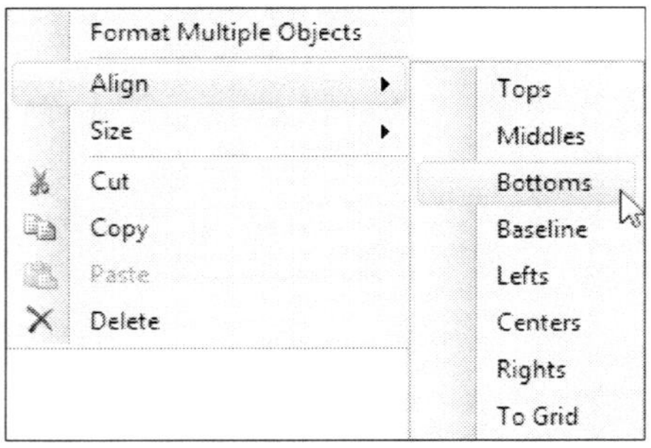

Figure 4-6 Horizontal alignment options

    4.   Move the Product Type Name field to the right, then save the changes and leave the report open to complete the next exercise.

Align Option	How It Aligns
Tops	Aligns on the top of the object.
Middles	Aligns on the middle of the object.
Bottoms	Aligns on the bottom of the object.
Baseline	Aligns on the bottom of the text, not the bottom of the frame like all of the other alignment options discussed in this table. The baseline alignment option is useful when you are aligning objects that have a different font, font size or frame size.
Lefts	Aligns on the left side of the object.
Centers	Aligns on the center of the object.
Rights	Aligns on the right side of the object.
To Grid	Aligns to the closest grid point of the object that you right-click on. You need to have the GRID option turned on to see how this works.

Table 4-2 Horizontal alignment options explained

Using The Grid

When you need to have greater precision over lining up objects on a report, you can turn on the GRID option. This option is not on by default. In addition to the grid option, turning on the SNAP TO GRID option provides additional precision.

The grid is the dot pattern in the background. When new fields or objects are added to the report manually, they are automatically placed on the closest grid position to where you release the mouse button. If you need to change any of the grid settings, they are located on the Layout tab on the Options dialog box.

Crystal Reports ⇒ Design ⇒ Grid will turn on the grid on the design window, as shown in Figure 4-7.

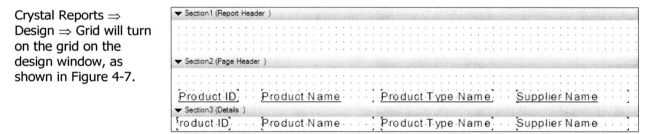

Figure 4-7 Report layout with the grid option turned on

It could be me, but I have noticed that if the snap to grid option is on and I create a report with a wizard, the objects are not always placed on a gridline. If you need to line these objects up with a gridline to make the spacing better or because you have manually added more fields, often it cannot be done. Instead, I use the Align options if I used a wizard to create a report.

Sizing Objects

When fields are added to a report, the size is the larger of the field or the field heading. It appears that Crystal Reports estimates the horizontal space needed for string fields. Sometimes this works and sometimes the data in a string field in the details section of the report gets cut off using this method.

Product ID	Product Name		Product Type Name
1,101	Active Outdoors Crochet Glo		Gloves
1,102	Active Outdoors Crochet Glo		Gloves
1,103	Active Outdoors Crochet Glo	Truncated Data	Gloves
1,104	Active Outdoors Crochet Glo		Gloves
1,105	Active Outdoors Crochet Glo		Gloves
1,106	Active Outdoors Lycra Glove		Gloves
1,107	Active Outdoors Lycra Glove		Gloves

Figure 4-8 Truncated data illustrated

I suspect this happens because there is not enough space in the row to display all of the fields, so text fields are often truncated. This is what happened with the Product Name field on the report illustrated in Figure 4-8. To fix this you need to resize the field. Depending on how close you placed the fields on the report, you may have to move the Product Type Name and Supplier Name fields to the right, before starting this exercise. To resize a field, follow the steps below.

1. Click on the field that you need to resize. In this exercise, click on the Product Name field.

2. Place the mouse pointer on the right side of the field as illustrated in Figure 4-9. The mouse pointer will change to a double headed arrow as shown. Drag the **RESIZE HANDLE** that you saw earlier in Figure 4-2 to the right. Notice that the field heading was also resized.

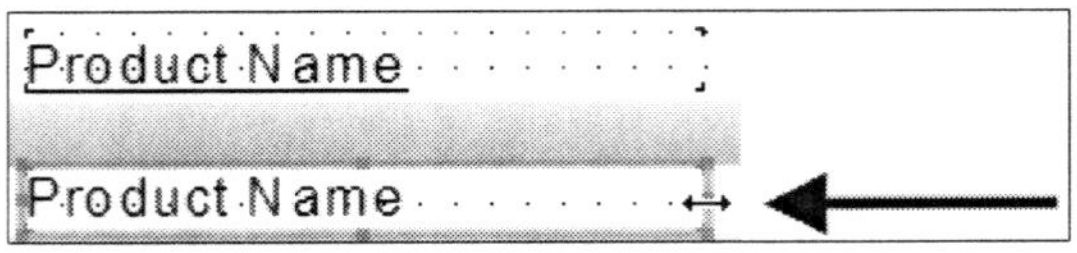

Figure 4-9 Mouse pointer in position to resize the field

3. Preview the report to see if you can now see all of the data in the Product Name field as shown in Figure 4-10. Save the changes and leave the report open to complete the next exercise.

If the Product Name field is selected on the preview window, click on a blank space in the report to deselect it. To keep this from happening, click on a blank space in the design window before previewing the report.

Product ID	Product Name	Product Type Name
1,101	Active Outdoors Crochet Glove	Gloves
1,102	Active Outdoors Crochet Glove	Gloves
1,103	Active Outdoors Crochet Glove	Gloves
1,104	Active Outdoors Crochet Glove	Gloves
1,105	Active Outdoors Crochet Glove	Gloves
1,106	Active Outdoors Lycra Glove	Gloves
1,107	Active Outdoors Lycra Glove	Gloves

Figure 4-10 Product Name field resized

It is a good idea to scan through several pages of the report while previewing it, to make sure that you do not see any data cut off (truncated) in the field that you are resizing. It is possible that the resized field may still not be wide enough.

Nudging Objects

So far in this lesson you have learned how to move and resize objects using the mouse. You can also move and resize objects using the keyboard. This is helpful if you use a laptop and do not use a mouse. Using the keyboard to move or resize objects is known as **NUDGING** an object.

If the **SNAP TO GRID** option is turned on, the arrow key will move the object one grid point each time you press an arrow key.

How To Move An Object By Nudging It

1. Select the object that you want to move.

2. Use one of the four arrow keys on the keyboard to move the object in the direction that you need to reposition it.

How To Resize An Object Using The Nudge Feature

1. Click on the object that you need to resize, then press and hold down the SHIFT key.

2. Use the arrow key that points in the direction that you want to resize the object. If you used the nudging feature on the L4.1 report, close the report but do not save the changes.

Formatting And Editing Overview

It can take an hour or more to create a report. You may struggle to write the formulas, make sure that the sorting and grouping options meet the report requirements and come up with an appropriate title for the report. You are pleased that you were able to accomplish all of these tasks and give a copy of the report to the person that requested it. You see them frown, but can't figure out why, especially because you checked the formulas by hand and know that the data is correct. You ask why they are frowning and they say, "Some of the fields are not lined up and there are too many fonts." As they say, "Perception is everything." Take from this what you will.

Crystal Reports provides a variety of options that you can use to make the reports that you design look better. You can draw boxes, apply templates, add color (probably best suited for reports that will be viewed as a web page or printed on a color printer) and more. You can also apply formatting conditionally to fields or sections of the report depending on whether the value in a field meets specific criteria. This type of formatting can be applied to any field that is on the report including summary, formula, group name, running total and SQL Expression fields.

Earlier in this workbook you learned that everything on a report is an object, including charts, data fields, headings and formulas. I realize that this may take some getting use to. The good news is that each type of object has it's own set of properties that you can modify. The options on the Standard, Crystal Reports - Main and Crystal Reports - Insert menus shown in Figures 4-11, 4-12 and 4-13 respectively, contain many of the options that are covered in the next few exercises in this lesson.

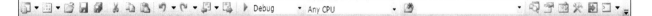

Figure 4-11 Standard toolbar

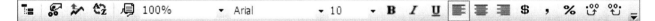

Figure 4-12 Crystal Reports - Main toolbar

Figure 4-13 Crystal Reports - Insert toolbar

Adding And Editing Text Objects

Text objects are used to add additional information to a report. Text objects include field headings, report titles or any text that you want to add to a report that is not created based on a field in a table.

Crystal Reports does not have a spell checker.

Exercise 4.2: How To Edit Text Objects

In this exercise you will learn how to edit text objects.

1. Save the L3.5 report as L4.2 Text objects. Delete the Print Date field.

The majority of the field headings on the report are clear and easy to understand. The one field heading that would be easier to understand is the Order ID field. Most end-users (people that will read the report) would not understand the term "ID", so it would be better to change this field heading.

2. Right-click on the Order ID field heading in the page header section and select **EDIT TEXT OBJECT**.

 You can also double-click on the Order ID field heading to change the text.

3. Select (highlight) the text shown in Figure 4-14, then type Order # and click on a blank space on the report.

Figure 4-14 Text selected to change

 You can also select a portion of the text in a field and change that. For example, you could select "ID" in Figure 4-14 above and just change that.

Pressing the **ENTER** key does not end the editing session like it does in other software packages. Pressing Enter in Crystal Reports starts a new line in the text object. When you finish adding or editing text, click outside of the text object to end the edit session.

Make The Page Header Section Longer

The report that you have open does not have a report title. As you can see, there is not a lot of space in the page header section above the field headings to add the report title. The page header section needs to be longer. Follow the steps below to learn how to make a section of the report longer.

1. Click on the details section bar. The mouse pointer is in the right position when you see the double headed arrow illustrated in Figure 4-15. Drag the section bar down to the top of the report footer section.

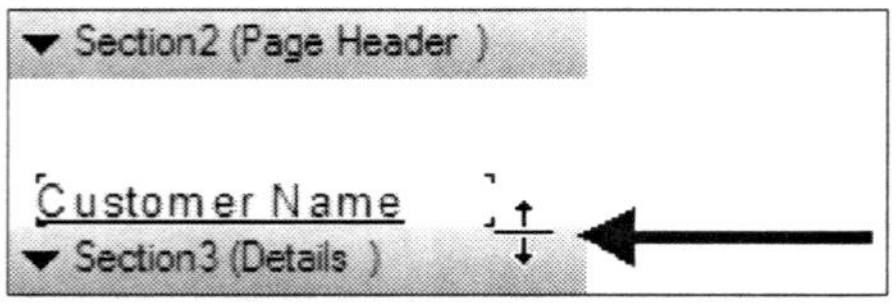

Figure 4-15 Mouse pointer in position to make the page header section longer

2. Move all of the field headings in the page header section down, then click on a blank space on the report.

 The easiest way to move all of the field headings at one time is to select all of them first and then move them at the same time.

If you need to make a section in the report shorter, drag the section bar up.

How To Add A Text Object

1. Right-click in the report. Insert ⇒ Text Object. The mouse pointer will have a field attached to it as shown in Figure 4-16.

Figure 4-16 Text object ready to be placed on a field

2. Click in the page header section above the field titles and type `Customer Orders Report` in the text object, then click on a blank space on the report.

When selecting fonts to use on a report, it is best to use the default fonts that come with Windows, otherwise the report will look different on computers that do not have the font that you selected. If you have to use a font that does not come with Windows, you should export the report to Adobe PDF format. Doing that will allow the report to be seen with the font that you selected.

How To Format A Text Object

As you can see, the text object is too small for the text that you entered. Follow the steps below to learn how to format a text object.

1. Click on the object that you want to apply formatting to. In this exercise, click on the report title that you just created.

2. Click the **BOLD** button and change the font size to 14, then make the object longer and wider so that you can see all of the text.

3. Move the report title so that it is centered (left to right) across the page header section. The top of the report should look like the one shown in Figure 4-17. Save the changes and close the report.

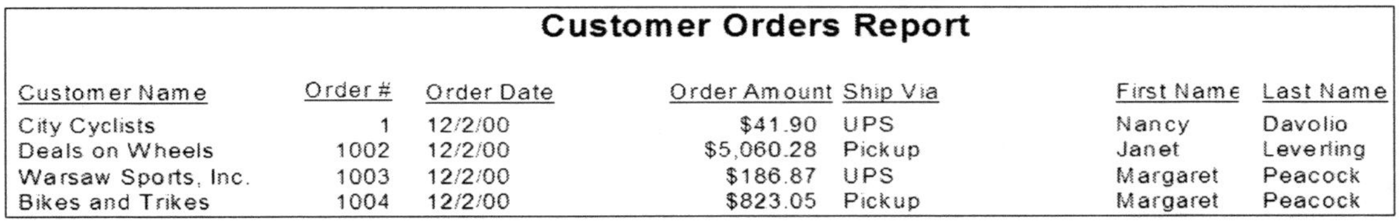

Customer Orders Report						
Customer Name	Order #	Order Date	Order Amount	Ship Via	First Name	Last Name
City Cyclists	1	12/2/00	$41.90	UPS	Nancy	Davolio
Deals on Wheels	1002	12/2/00	$5,060.28	Pickup	Janet	Leverling
Warsaw Sports, Inc.	1003	12/2/00	$186.87	UPS	Margaret	Peacock
Bikes and Trikes	1004	12/2/00	$823.05	Pickup	Margaret	Peacock

Figure 4-17 Modified page header section

I use to find it difficult to center a report title across the page. I finally came up with the steps below to center a report title across the page.

① Make the report title object the width of the report as shown in Figure 4-18.

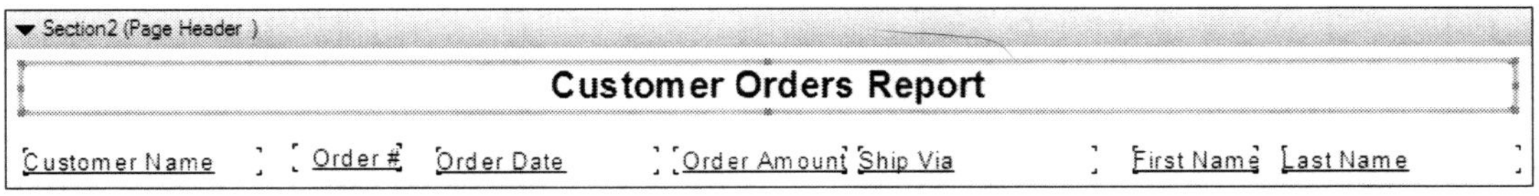

▼ Section2 (Page Header)						
Customer Orders Report						
Customer Name	Order #	Order Date	Order Amount	Ship Via	First Name	Last Name

Figure 4-18 Text object resized to the width of the report

② Click the **CENTER** button.

If you do not see the font size that you need in the **FONT SIZE** drop-down list, you can type it in. In the font drop-down list, there is no option for font size 15. You can type it into the field on the toolbar and press Enter as shown in Figure 4-19.

Figure 4-19 Font size changed to one not in the drop-down list

How To Import A Text File Into A Text Object

If there is text in a file that you want to add to a text object in the report, you can, by following the steps below.

1. Add a text object to the report, then double-click in the text object to go into edit mode.

2. Right-click in the text object and select **INSERT FROM FILE** as shown in Figure 4-20.

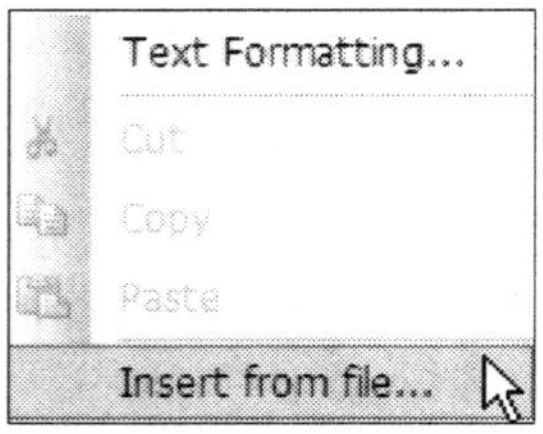

	Text Formatting...
✄	Cut
🗐	Copy
📋	Paste
	Insert from file...

Figure 4-20 Text object shortcut menu

3. Find the file on your hard drive or in another location and double-click on it. The content of the text file will be added to the text object. Save the changes.

Combining Text Objects And Database Fields

Text objects are more powerful then they may appear. If you have spent any time trying to get a text object and a field to line up side by side with spacing that looks right, but have had trouble doing so, you are in luck. Text objects can have data fields embedded in them. Text objects will automatically resize to accommodate the embedded field so that there is no extra space. The steps below explain how to embed a database field in a text object.

1. Add a text object to the report, then add the text to the object.

2. Drag a database field either from the report or from the Field Explorer into the text object as shown in Figure 4-21, then release the mouse button.

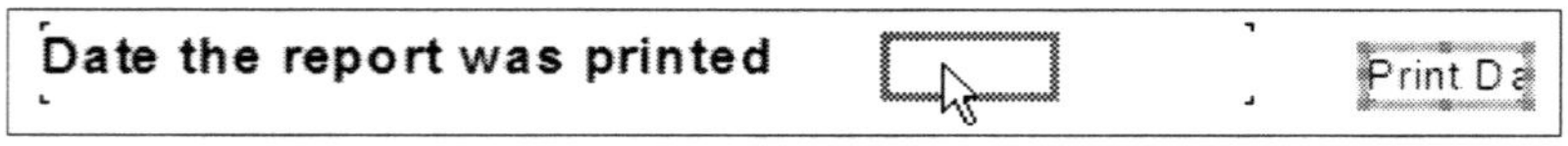

Date the report was printed   Print Da

Figure 4-21 Database field being added to a text object

💡 **Combining Text Objects Tips**

① You can edit the combined field or add more text or another database field to the text object.
② You can format part of a text object. If this is what you need to do, only select (highlight) the part that you want to format.
③ If you discover that you have added the wrong field to the text object, click on the text object and move it away from the database field. Click on the database field, then press the **DEL** key.

Exercise 4.3: Adding Graphics To A Report

The sample reports that you viewed in Lesson 2 had a logo. Believe it or not, the logo that you saw in the sample reports does not come with the sample files for Crystal Reports. This exercise will show you how to add a logo or any graphic file to a report. There are two ways to add a graphic to a report as discussed below.

① Click the **PICTURE** button on the Crystal Reports - Insert toolbar.
② Crystal Reports ⇒ Insert ⇒ Picture.

💡 Because the logo file was not included with the sample files you can open a sample report that has the logo, like the Product Catalog report in the General Business sample reports folder and copy it to the report that you create.

1. Save the L3.4 report as `L4.3 Insert picture`. Delete the Print Date field.

2. Make the page header section longer by dragging the details section bar down almost to the end of the page footer section. You will need that amount of space for the logo. Move the field headings down.

3. Open one of the sample reports. Right-click on the logo and select Copy. Close the sample report.

4. Right-click in the page header section and select Paste. The mouse pointer should change to a shadow box (which is the actual size of the graphic), as shown in Figure 4-22.

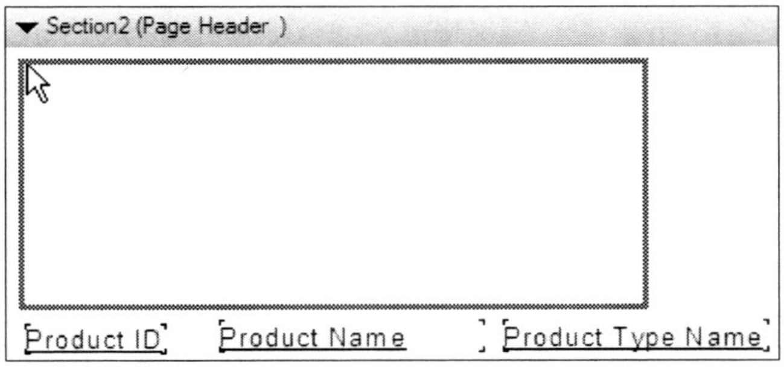

Figure 4-22 Mouse pointer in the Insert Picture mode

5. Click in the upper left corner of the page header section. You should see the logo.
   Save the changes and leave the report open to complete the next part of the exercise.

How To Resize A Graphic

The logo would look better if it were smaller. The default size of the logo is too large. Follow the steps below to resize the logo.

1. Select the logo if it is not already selected. If the Product ID and Product Name field headings are covered by the logo, click on the lower right corner of the logo and drag the mouse up and over to the left until you can see the field headings.

2. The report should look like the one shown in Figure 4-23. If you look at other pages in the report, you will see the logo at the top of the page because it was placed in the page header section, which prints on every page. Save the changes and close the report.

Figure 4-23 L4.3 Insert picture report with the logo added

Exercise 4.4: Adding Graphics From Fonts

In addition to being able to add graphic images to a report, you can also add graphics that are stored in fonts like the Wingdings font. Fonts that have graphics can be accessed from the Character Map application in Windows. These graphics have to be placed in a text object. In this exercise you will add a graphic from a font to a report.

1. Save the L4.2 report as L4.4 Graphics from fonts.

2. Delete the first and last name fields from the report.

3. Click the Start button ⇒ All Programs (or Programs) ⇒ Accessories ⇒ System Tools ⇒ Character Map.

4. Open the Font drop-down list on the Character Map dialog box and select **WINGDINGS**, if it is not already selected. You should see the dialog box shown in Figure 4-24.

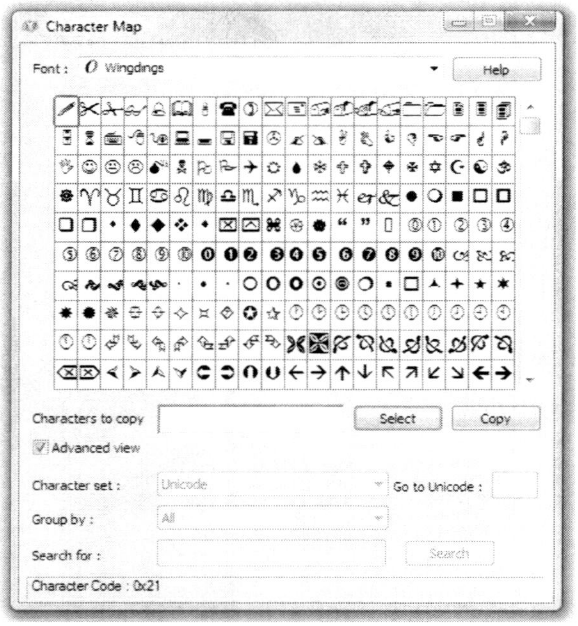

Figure 4-24 Character Map dialog box

5. Double-click on the document picture (the third picture from the right in the first row), then click the Copy button and close the dialog box.

6. Add a text object to the details section after the Ship Via field, then press the CTRL+ V keys to paste the picture in the text object. Click on a blank space on the report. Save the changes. The report should look like the one shown in Figure 4-25.

One reason to add an image next to each detail record is to create a hyperlink to another section of the report or to open a document or another report that has information that relates to the detail record.

Customer Orders Report

Customer Name	Order #	Order Date	Order Amount	Ship Via	
City Cyclists	1	12/2/2000 12:00:00	$41.90	UPS	
Deals on Wheels	1,002	12/2/2000 12:00:00	$5,060.28	Pickup	
Warsaw Sports, Inc.	1,003	12/2/2000 12:00:00	$186.87	UPS	
Bikes and Trikes	1,004	12/2/2000 12:00:00	$823.05	Pickup	

Figure 4-25 L4.4 Graphics from fonts report

The Format Editor

So far in this lesson all of the formatting that you have learned about is considered basic formatting. For many reports that is all of the formatting that is required. When you need to create additional formatting, you can use the Format Editor dialog box shown in Figure 4-26. If the standard options on the Format Editor do not handle your needs you can write conditional formulas. As you will see, many options on the Format Editor have a Formula button. Clicking on this button will let you apply conditional formatting to a field or object. You will learn how to do this in Lesson 10. The Format Editor provides a lot of options for changing how objects look on a report.

The options that are on the Format Editor dialog box will vary, depending on the type of object that is selected. When you open the Format Editor you will only see tabs that can be used for the field type that is selected. Table 4-3 explains all of the tabs on the Format Editor. In the next few exercises you will learn how to use the Format Editor.

Figure 4-26 Common tab options

Tab	Data Type	Purpose
Common	All	The options shown above in Figure 4-26 can be used by most objects on a report. Table 4-4 explains the options on the Common tab.
Border	All	Add lines and drop shadows to fields.
Font	All except OLE & graphic objects	Select font, font size, font color, underlining, strike out and character spacing. Most of the options on this tab are also on the Crystal Reports - Insert toolbar.
Paragraph	String & Memo fields	Formats paragraphs that are stored in string or memo fields.
Hyperlink	All	Lets you use the selected object as a link to a web site, file, email address or a field on a web page.
Number	Number & currency	Lets you apply formatting options that are only for number fields. (1)
Date & Time	Date & Time fields	Lets you apply formatting options that are only for date and date/time fields. (1)
Picture	Graphic	Lets you crop, scale, reset and resize graphic images.
Boolean	Boolean	Lets you select how Boolean values will be displayed.

Table 4-3 Format Editor tab options explained
(1) Options on this tab support custom formatting.

Option	Description
Object Name	This field is filled in by default. You can accept the default name unless you have a need to use it in a formula and want to use a shorter or more descriptive name. It is not necessary to change the object name.
CSS Class Name	If the field will be formatted with a style sheet, enter the CSS Class Name that should be applied to the object.
Repeat on Horizontal Pages	This option is mostly used with a cross-tab or OLAP grid that will print horizontally across more than one page.
Suppress	Hides the object. When an object is suppressed it is grayed out. When a section is suppressed, it has diagonal lines through the section.
Horizontal Alignment	Lets you select the alignment options that you learned about in Table 4-1.
Keep Object Together	Keeps the object from printing on more than one page. The object will be printed on the next page if it does not fit on the current page.
Close Border on Page Break	This option is used for fields that will print on more than one page and have a border. This option will print the bottom of the border of the object on the first page and print another border around the remaining data in the field that prints on the next page.
Can Grow	Lets the field expand vertically to accommodate more data.
Tool Tip Text	Enter text in this field that you want displayed when the mouse pointer hovers over the field in Preview mode.
Text Rotation	Lets you change the angle of the field.
Suppress If Duplicated	Hides the object if it has the same value as the one in the prior record. In Figure 4-27, this option is turned on for the Product Name field.
	The Formula button opens the Formula Workshop, which lets you create a formula to use with the option. You can also attach an existing formula to the option. You would use a formula when you need to control when the option is turned on or off, based on a condition. For example, if you wanted to highlight the order amount field on records that were in a certain dollar amount range.

Table 4-4 Common tab options explained

Product ID	Product Name	Product Type Name	Supplier Name
1,101	Active Outdoors Crochet	Gloves	Active Outdoors
1,102		Gloves	Active Outdoors
1,103		Gloves	Active Outdoors
1,104		Gloves	Active Outdoors
1,105		Gloves	Active Outdoors
1,106	Active Outdoors Lycra G	Gloves	Active Outdoors
1,107		Gloves	Active Outdoors

Figure 4-27 Suppress If Duplicated option illustrated

If you need to make the same change to several objects, select all of the objects that need the same change, prior to opening the Format Editor.

If you create a report with the wizard and do not add anything to a section of the report, the empty section will be suppressed. Sections that are suppressed have diagonal lines as shown in Figure 4-28. If you later add data to a suppressed section, as shown, it will not be displayed on the report. To remove the suppression, right-click on the section bar and select DON'T SUPPRESS, as illustrated.

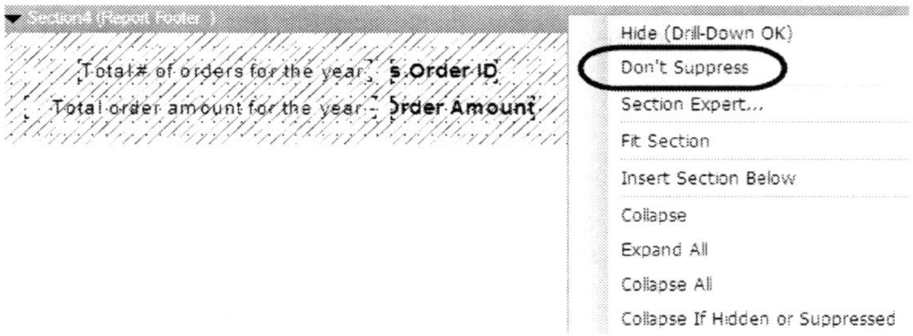

Figure 4-28 Suppressed section

The Toolbox

The Toolbox shown in Figure 4-29 contains options that you can use to enhance reports.

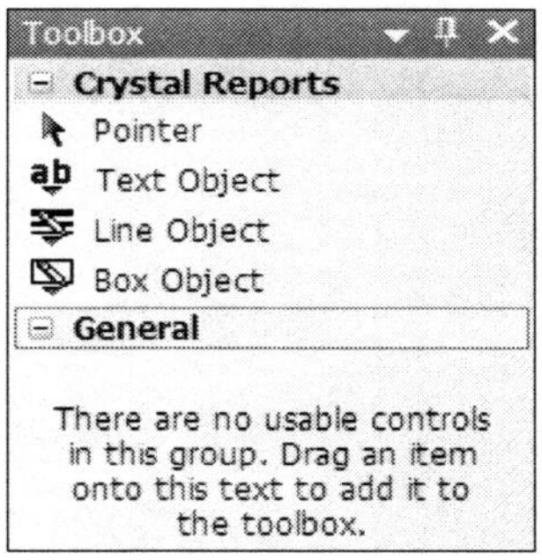

The **TEXT OBJECT** option is the same one that you have already learned about.

The **LINE OBJECT** will let you draw a line on the report.

The **BOX OBJECT** will let you draw a box around an object on the report. This option is also available on the shortcut menu when you right-click in the report.

Figure 4-29 Toolbox

All of these options are also on the Crystal Reports ⇒ Insert menu. You can also access these options by right-clicking on a blank space in the report and selecting the Insert submenu. There are two ways to open the Toolbox as listed below.

    ① View ⇒ Toolbox.
    ② Click the Toolbox button on the Standard toolbar.

Format A Text Object

1. Open the L4.2 report and right-click on the report title, then select **FORMAT OBJECT**.

2. On the **BORDER** tab you will see the options shown in Figure 4-30. Table 4-5 explains the options on this tab. Change the **LINE STYLE** to single for the Left, Right and Top options. Notice at the bottom of the dialog box in the **SAMPLE** section that you can see the options that you have applied to the object.

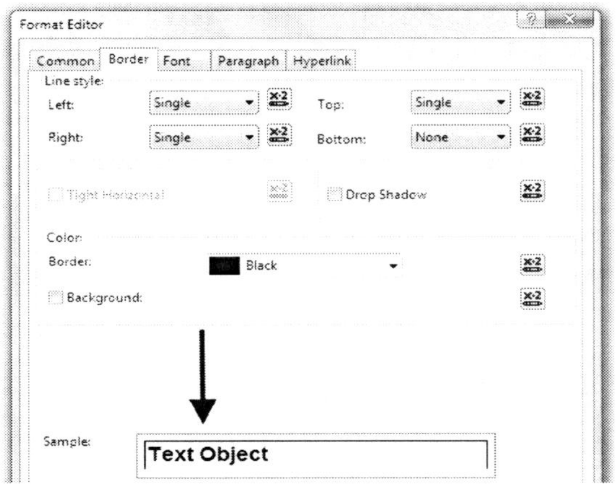

Figure 4-30 Border tab options on the Format Editor dialog box

Option	Description
Line Style	These four options let you select the line style for each side of the object.
Tight Horizontal	Moves the border of the object closer to the object.
Drop Shadow	Adds the shadow effect to the lower right corner of the object.
Border Color	Lets you select a color for the border and drop shadow.
Background Color	Lets you select the color for the background of the object.

Table 4-5 Border tab options explained

3. Check the **DROP SHADOW** and **BACKGROUND** options, then open the drop-down list across from the Background option and select **YELLOW** as shown in Figure 4-31.

Figure 4-31 Background color options

 If selected, the **MORE** option shown above in Figure 4-31 will open the Color dialog box, which will let you select additional colors or create a custom color.

4. Click OK to close the Format Editor. The report should look like the one shown in Figure 4-32. Save the changes and leave the report open.

Customer Orders Report						
Customer Name	Order #	Order Date	Order Amount	Ship Via	First Name	Last Name
City Cyclists	1	12/2/2000 12:00:0(	$41.90	UPS	Nancy	Davolio
Deals on Wheels	1,002	12/2/2000 12:00:0(	$5,060.28	Pickup	Janet	Leverling
Warsaw Sports, Inc.	1,003	12/2/2000 12:00:0(	$186.87	UPS	Margaret	Peacock
Bikes and Trikes	1,004	12/2/2000 12:00:0(	$823.05	Pickup	Margaret	Peacock

Figure 4-32 L4.2 report with formatting applied to a text object

The Can Grow Option

Earlier in this exercise I mentioned that one reason data gets truncated is because there may not be enough room in the section of the report to accommodate all of the data. In the part of the exercise that you just completed, there was enough room to make the field longer. If you have tried everything possible to get all of the data to fit, the **CAN GROW** option should fix the problem. This option will cause the data in the field to wrap to a new line, only when needed. Fields that have this option enabled, will only grow longer, not wider. Follow the steps below to learn how to turn this option on.

 The Can Grow option can only be used with string fields, text objects and memo fields.

1. Open the L4.3 report. Right-click on the object(s) that you want to apply the Can Grow option to and select **FORMAT OBJECT**. You will see the Format Editor dialog box. For this exercise, right-click on the Product Name field.

 You can also click on the field and then click the **OBJECT PROPERTIES** button on the Crystal Reports - Main toolbar to open the Format Editor.

2. On the Common tab check the **CAN GROW** option, then click OK.

If you want to limit the maximum number of lines that a field can print on the report, enter it in the **MAXIMUM NUMBER OF LINES** field to the right of the Can Grow field. For example, if you are applying the Can Grow option to a memo field that could have 500 characters or more of text, you may not want to have all of the text in the field print on the report. If this is the case, you would enter a number in the Maximum number of lines field so that only the first two or three lines of information in the field will actually print on the report. The Can Grow option, even when enabled will only be activated when needed. It does not force every record to expand to the number entered in the field.

If you use the Can Grow option on a field and there is another field below it, it is possible that the field below will be overwritten. To prevent this, the following options are available.

    ① Put the field with the Can Grow option at the bottom of the section.

    ② Not as effective as the first option, but you can check the spacing to make sure that the field with the Can Grow option is not close to other fields.

3. Resize the Product Name field so that it ends at the 2.5 inch mark. The report should look similar to the one shown in Figure 4-33. Save the changes.

Product ID	Product Name	Product Type Name	Supplier Name
1,101	Active Outdoors Crochet Glove	Gloves	Active Outdoors
1,102	Active Outdoors Crochet Glove	Gloves	Active Outdoors
1,103	Active Outdoors Crochet Glove	Gloves	Active Outdoors

Figure 4-33 Report with the Can Grow option applied to the Product Name field

Text Rotation

There may be times when some of the text on a report will look better if it is rotated. Figure 4-34 shows the degrees that you can rotate text. Select the text that you want to rotate, then select the degree rotation and click OK. Figure 4-35 shows the Product ID heading rotated 90 degrees.

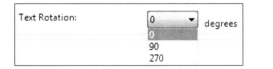

Figure 4-34 Text rotation options illustrated

Figure 4-35 Product ID heading rotated 90 degrees

Format Editor Paragraph Tab

When you are applying formatting to a text object, string or memo field, you will see the Paragraph tab shown in Figure 4-36. The options on this tab let you select how text fields that have multiple lines of data or text will be formatted.

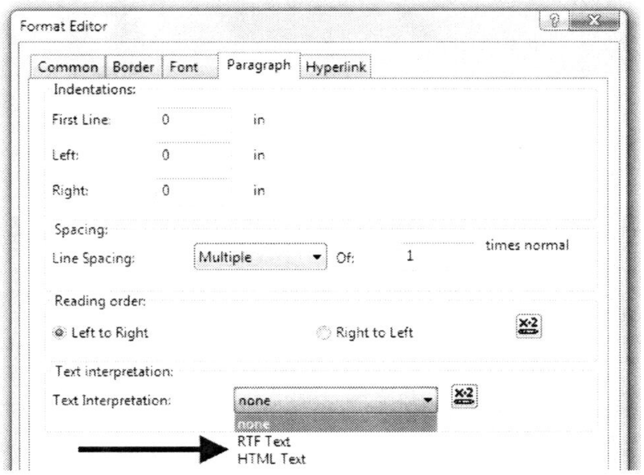

Figure 4-36 Paragraph tab on the Format Editor

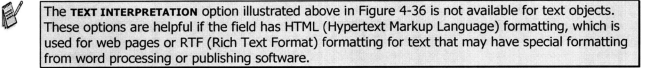

The **TEXT INTERPRETATION** option illustrated above in Figure 4-36 is not available for text objects. These options are helpful if the field has HTML (Hypertext Markup Language) formatting, which is used for web pages or RTF (Rich Text Format) formatting for text that may have special formatting from word processing or publishing software.

Format A Numeric Object

Usually, order numbers do not have any formatting. As you saw earlier in Figure 4-32, the Order Number field has a comma. This field would look better if it did not have any formatting. Follow the steps below to change the formatting of the Order Number field.

1.   Open the L4.2 report. Right-click on the Order ID field in the details section and select **FORMAT OBJECT**. You will see the dialog box shown in Figure 4-37.

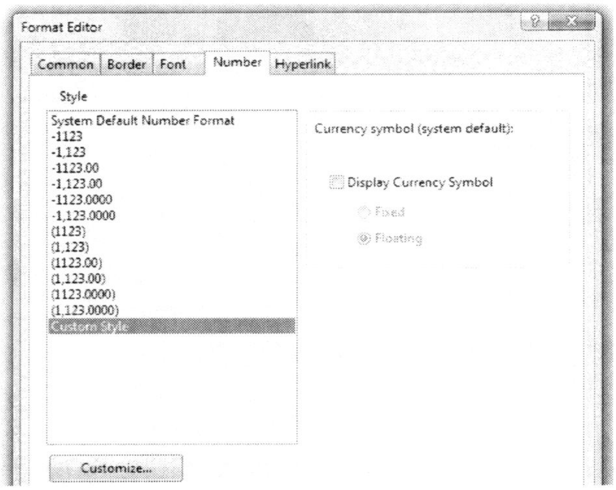

Figure 4-37 Number tab options

2.   Click on the second option **-1123** from the top. The minus sign will only print if the number is negative. Click OK and preview the report. The Order ID field should not have a comma in it. Save the changes and leave the report open to complete the next part of the exercise.

If none of the options shown above in Figure 4-37 meet your needs to format currency or number fields, click the **CUSTOMIZE** button.

You will see the options shown in Figure 4-38 if the field that you are formatting is a currency field. You will see the options shown in Figure 4-39 if the field that you are formatting is a number field.

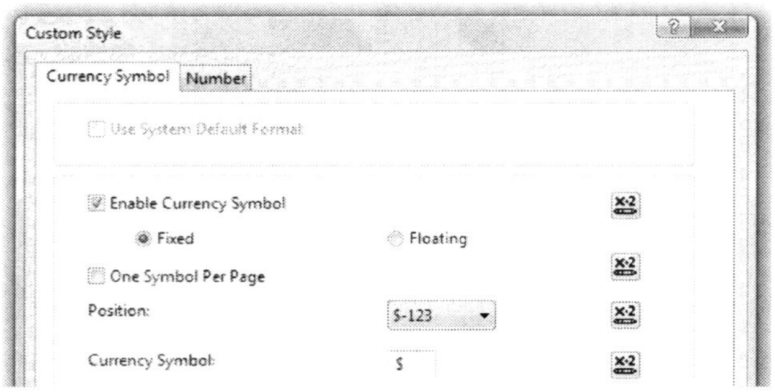

Figure 4-38 Currency symbol custom style options

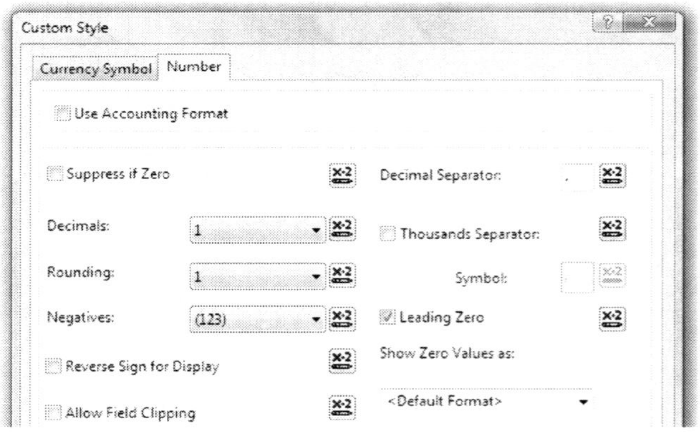

Figure 4-39 Number custom style options

Usually, the **DECIMALS** and **ROUNDING** options shown above in Figure 4-39 are set to the same number of decimal places.

If you think determining if a field is a string field or a numeric field based on the name is difficult or confusing, you can select the **SHOW FORMAT SYMBOLS** option on the Layout tab of the Options dialog box. [See Lesson 5, Figure 5-45] This option will display X's in text fields and 5's in numeric fields as shown in Figure 4-40.

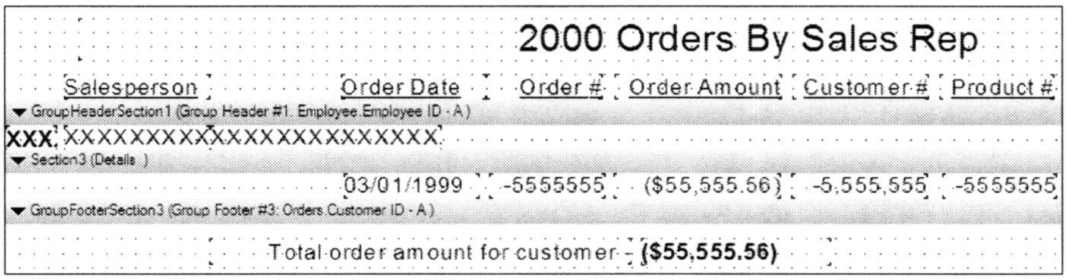

Figure 4-40 Fields without field names

Format A Date Field

Displaying the time as part of the Order Date field is not needed on the report that you are working on. To keep the time portion of the field from printing on the report, the data needs to be formatted. Follow the steps below to change the formatting of the Order Date field.

1. Right-click on the Order Date field and select Format Object. You will see the dialog box shown in Figure 4-41.

If you click the **CUSTOMIZE** button you will see the dialog box shown in Figure 4-42, which will let you change the formatting for a date field or the date portion of a date/time field. The options shown on Figure 4-43 let you change the formatting for the time portion of a date/time field.

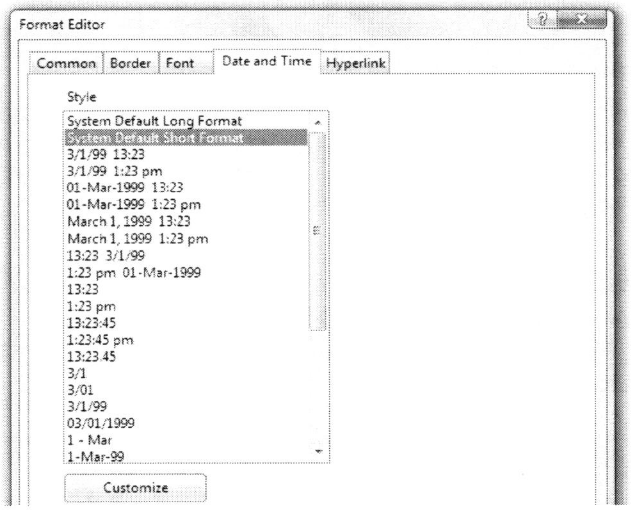

Figure 4-41 Date and Time tab options

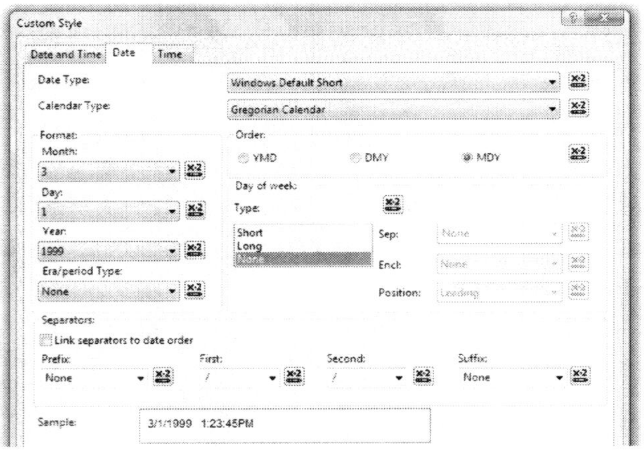

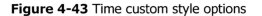

Figure 4-42 Date custom style options 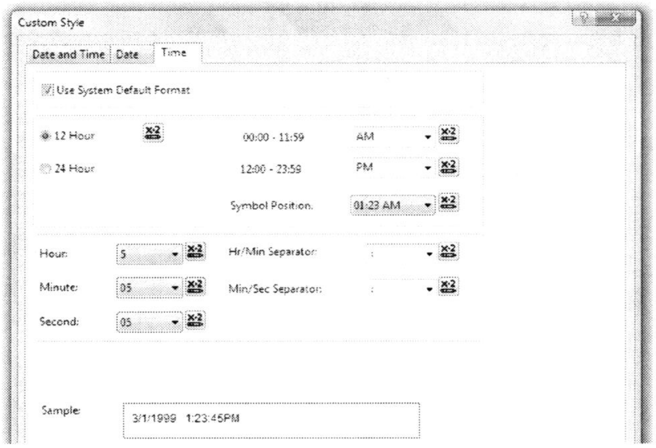   **Figure 4-43** Time custom style options

2. Click on the option **3/1/99** on the Date and Time tab, then click OK. The report should look like the one shown in Figure 4-44. You should not see the time on the Order Date field like you did earlier in Figure 4-32. Save the changes and close the report.

Customer Orders Report

Customer Name	Order #	Order Date	Order Amount	Ship Via	First Name	Last Name
City Cyclists	1	12/2/00	$41.90	UPS	Nancy	Davolio
Deals on Wheels	1002	12/2/00	$5,060.28	Pickup	Janet	Leverling
Warsaw Sports, Inc.	1003	12/2/00	$186.87	UPS	Margaret	Peacock
Bikes and Trikes	1004	12/2/00	$823.05	Pickup	Margaret	Peacock

Figure 4-44 L4.2 Text objects report with the Order Number and Order Date fields modified

The Picture Tab

Earlier in this lesson you added a logo (graphic) to the L4.3 Insert Picture report. The logo would look better if it had a border and was scaled down. The options on the Picture tab will let you scale an image, as well as, crop and resize the image. The Picture object supports the following image formats: JPG, usually used for photos, TIFF, PNG and BMP, which is not used much these days.

Resize The Logo

1. Open the L4.3 report, then right-click on the logo and select Format Object. Click on the **PICTURE** tab. You will see the dialog box shown in Figure 4-45. Table 4-6 explains the options on the Picture tab.

Figure 4-45 Picture tab options

Option	Description
Crop From	Allows you to remove part of the image. The part of the image that is removed, is the part on the outside of the crop lines that are created when you enter the dimensions in any or all of the four crop options (left, right, top or bottom).
Scaling	Allows you to enlarge or reduce the image by a percent.
Size	Allows you to change the width and height of the image.
Reset	Removes all of the formatting that was applied to the image on the Picture tab. When you crop, scale or size an image, the original image file is not changed. It is only displayed differently on the report, based on the options that are selected.

Table 4-6 Picture tab options explained

2. Change the scaling **WIDTH** option to 40, then change the scaling **HEIGHT** option to 40 and click OK. Figure 4-46 shows the logo before it was scaled. Figure 4-47 shows the logo after scaling. Save the changes and leave the report open to complete the next part of the exercise.

Figure 4-46 L4.3 Insert picture report with the image before scaling

Figure 4-47 L4.3 Insert picture report with the image after scaling

Add A Border To The Logo

1. Click on the logo, then open the Format Editor and click on the Border tab.

2. Change all four **LINE STYLE** options to Dotted, then click OK. The logo should look like the one shown in Figure 4-48. Save the changes and leave the report open to complete an exercise later in this lesson.

Figure 4-48 Image border modified

Exercise 4.5: Format A Boolean Field

In this exercise you will change how the data in a Boolean field is displayed on a report.

1. Create a new report and save it as L4.5 Boolean formatting.

2. Add the following fields from the Orders table: Order ID, Order Date, Shipped and Payment Received. The report should look like the one shown in Figure 4-49.

The Shipped and Payment Received fields are Boolean fields. As you can see, they both are displaying true or false. You will format these fields so that they display Yes and No instead. Doing this does not change the data in the table.

Order ID	Order Date		Shipped	Payment Received
1	12/2/2000	12:00:00A	True	True
1,002	12/2/2000	12:00:00A	True	True
1,003	12/2/2000	12:00:00A	True	True
1,004	12/2/2000	12:00:00A	True	True
1,005	12/3/2000	12:00:00A	True	True
1,006	12/3/2000	12:00:00A	True	True

Figure 4-49 L4.5 Boolean formatting report

3. Select both Boolean fields, then right-click and select Format Multiple Objects.

4. On the Boolean tab open the **BOOLEAN TEXT** drop-down list and select Yes or No as shown in Figure 4-50, then click OK. The value in the Shipped and Payment Received fields is now displayed as Yes or No instead of True and False. If you go to page 30 of the report, you will see that not all of the data in these fields is Yes, as shown in Figure 4-51. Save the changes and close the report.

> Instead of clicking on the right arrow 29 times, you can type `30` in the navigation toolbar as illustrated in Figure 4-51 and press Enter.

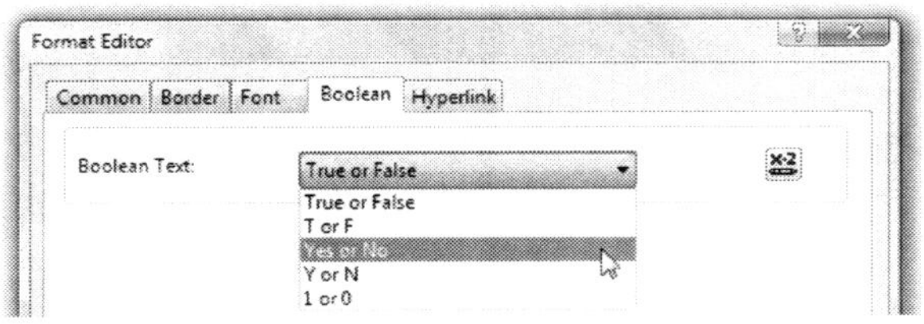

Figure 4-50 Boolean tab options

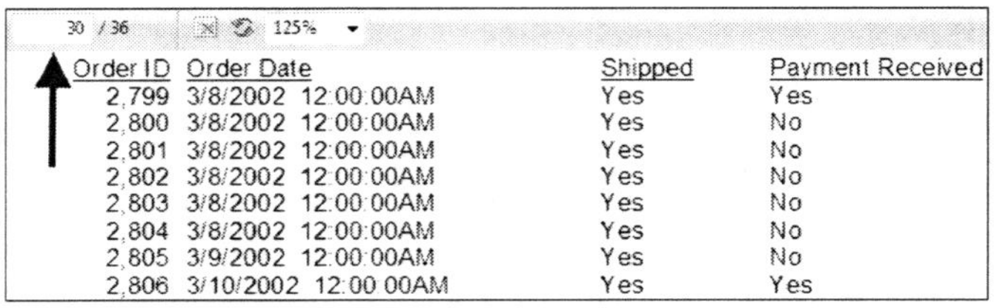

Order ID	Order Date	Shipped	Payment Received
2,799	3/8/2002 12:00:00AM	Yes	Yes
2,800	3/8/2002 12:00:00AM	Yes	No
2,801	3/8/2002 12:00:00AM	Yes	No
2,802	3/8/2002 12:00:00AM	Yes	No
2,803	3/8/2002 12:00:00AM	Yes	No
2,804	3/8/2002 12:00:00AM	Yes	No
2,805	3/9/2002 12:00:00AM	Yes	No
2,806	3/10/2002 12:00:00AM	Yes	Yes

Figure 4-51 Boolean fields displayed differently on the L4.4 report

Exercise 4.6: Center Data Under A Heading

The report would look better if the following changes were made.

① Center the region field under the heading.
② Put a line under each detail record to make the report easier to read.

1. Save the L3.1 report as `L4.6 Modified customer information.`

2. Select the Region field and heading, then click the **CENTER** button on the Crystal Reports - Main toolbar.

3. Make the Region field and heading smaller. The data should now be centered under the heading.

How To Add Horizontal Lines To A Report

One way to make the data in the details section of a report easier to read is to place a line under the fields in this section. Like other objects, you can format lines that you add to a report. There are three ways to open the **LINE** tool as discussed below.

① Right-click in the report ⇒ Insert ⇒ Line.
② Crystal Reports ⇒ Insert ⇒ Line.
③ Select if from the Toolbox.

Follow the steps below to add a line to the details section.

1. Move the details section bar down a little.

2. Open the **LINE** tool. The mouse pointer will change to a pencil. Draw a line under the fields in the details section.

> It is easier to draw a long line like this if you can see the entire width of the report. To do this, I often change the **ZOOM** option on the Crystal Reports - Main toolbar to 75%.

Format The Line

Follow the steps below to learn how to format a line.

1. Right-click on the line and select **FORMAT OBJECT**. You will see the dialog box shown in Figure 4-52.

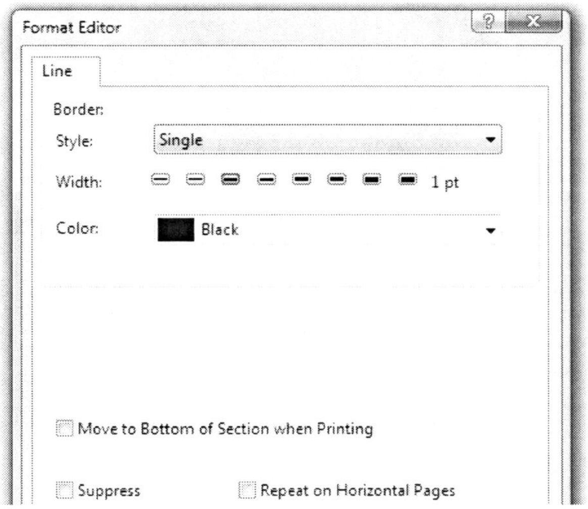

Figure 4-52 Format Editor line options

> The **MOVE TO BOTTOM OF SECTION WHEN PRINTING** option is often used for lines in a section of the report that has a field with the Can Grow option turned on, like a Notes field. Checking this option will force the line to print at the bottom of the section, which is what you usually want. You can test how this option works by checking this option and making the section of the report longer that has the line and preview the report.

2. Open the **STYLE** drop-down list and select Single, if it is not already selected.

3. Click on the first button in the **WIDTH** section. You should see the word **HAIRLINE** at the end of the Width options. Click OK. The report should look like the one shown in Figure 4-53. Notice that the Region field data is centered under the heading. Save the changes and close the report.

Customer Name	Address1	Region	Country	Postal Cod
City Cyclists	7464 South Kingswa	MI	USA	48358
Pathfinders	410 Eighth Avenue	IL	USA	60148
Bike-A-Holics Anonymous	7429 Arbutus Boulev	OH	USA	43005
Psycho-Cycle	8287 Scott Road	AL	USA	35818
Sporting Wheels Inc.	480 Grant Way	CA	USA	92150
Rockshocks for Jocks	1984 Sydney Street	TX	USA	78770

Figure 4-53 L4.6 Modified customer information report with the details section modified

Exercise 4.7: Add Vertical Lines To A Report

In the previous exercise you learned how to add horizontal lines to a report. In this exercise you will learn how to add vertical lines to a report.

1. Save the L3.1 report as L4.7 Vertical lines.

2. Make the Region and Country fields smaller, then move the Country and Postal Code fields over to the left.

3. Open the Line tool. Draw a vertical line in the details section, after the Customer Name field.

4. Right-click on the vertical line that you just created and select Copy, then right-click anyplace in the report and select Paste. The mouse pointer will have a picture of the line next to it.

5. Repeat step 4 to place a vertical line after every field in the details section except the Postal Code field, then save the changes. The report should look like the one shown in Figure 4-54. Close the report.

Customer Name	Address1	Region	Country	Postal Code
City Cyclists	7464 South Kingsway	MI	USA	48358
Pathfinders	410 Eighth Avenue	IL	USA	60148
Bike-A-Holics Anonymo	7429 Arbutus Boulevard	OH	USA	43005
Psycho-Cycle	8287 Scott Road	AL	USA	35818
Sporting Wheels Inc.	480 Grant Way	CA	USA	92150
Rockshocks for Jocks	1984 Sydney Street	TX	USA	78770

Figure 4-54 L4.7 Vertical lines report

You can also draw vertical lines through sections of the report. In the report that you just added vertical lines to, make the vertical lines longer by clicking on the line and dragging the top blue square on the line up, so that it is above the field heading in the page header section. The report should look like the one shown in Figure 4-55.

Customer Name	Address1	Region	Country	Postal Code
City Cyclists	7464 South Kingsway	MI	USA	48358
Pathfinders	410 Eighth Avenue	IL	USA	60148
Bike-A-Holics Anonymo	7429 Arbutus Boulevard	OH	USA	43005
Psycho-Cycle	8287 Scott Road	AL	USA	35818
Sporting Wheels Inc.	480 Grant Way	CA	USA	92150
Rockshocks for Jocks	1984 Sydney Street	TX	USA	78770

Figure 4-55 L4.7 Vertical lines report with lines extended into the page header section

In previous versions of Crystal Reports, if an object has the Can Grow option turned on, the object will grow, but the vertical line will not grow by default, as shown in Figure 4-56. You will see breaks in the vertical line. To fix this, check the **EXTEND TO BOTTOM OF SECTION WHEN PRINTING** option for the line object as shown in Figure 4-57. This appears to have been fixed.

Customer Name	Address1	Region	Country	Postal Code
City Cyclists	7464 South Kingsway	MI	USA	48358
Pathfinders	410 Eighth Avenue	IL	USA	60148
Bike-A-Holics Anonymous	7429 Arbutus Boulevard	OH	USA	43005
Psycho-Cycle	8287 Scott Road	AL	USA	35818
Sporting Wheels Inc.	480 Grant Way	CA	USA	92150

Figure 4-56 Can Grow option and vertical lines

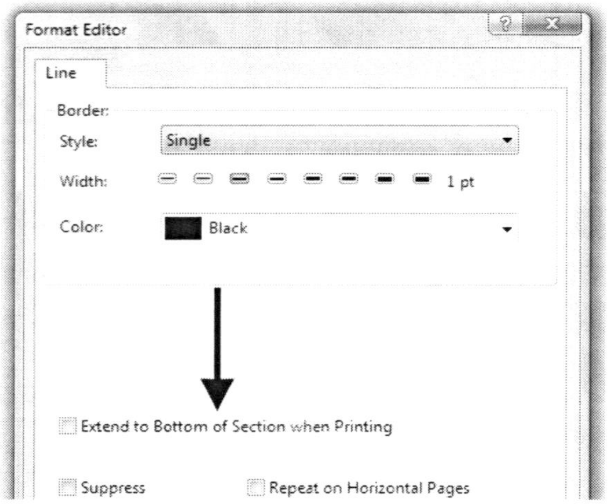

Figure 4-57 Format Editor options for a vertical line

Subsections

As you saw in the L3.5 Skills Customer orders report, all of the fields in the details section did not fit. Crystal Reports allows you to split any section of the report into **SUBSECTIONS**.

One reason that you would create subsections is to be able to spread the fields out so that they are easier to read. This allows fields to be in multiple rows. Yes, you can make the section longer, but depending on the requirements of the report, creating subsections may be a better solution. One reason that comes to mind that this is a better solution is because you may need to apply conditional formatting to some fields in a section. When a section of the report is split, the subsections are labeled, a, b, c, etc, as shown in Figure 4-58.

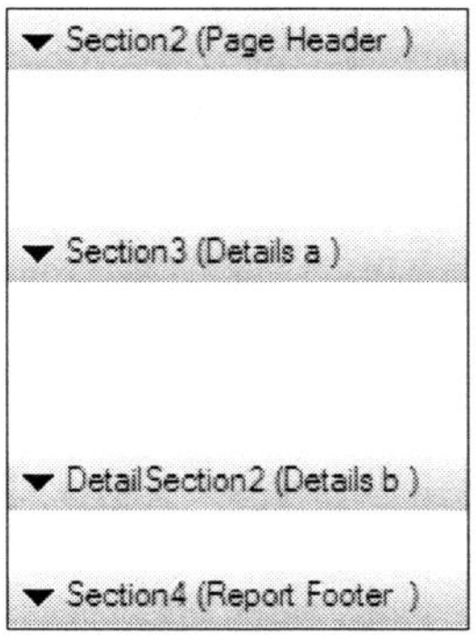

▼ Section2 (Page Header)

▼ Section3 (Details a)

▼ Detail Section2 (Details b)

▼ Section4 (Report Footer)

Figure 4-58 Details subsections

How To Add A Subsection

There are three ways to add subsections to a report as described below.

    ① Use the Section bar shortcut menu. Right-click on the section that you want to split and select **INSERT SECTION BELOW**, as shown in Figure 4-59.

    ② Right-click in the report and select Insert ⇒ Section.

    ③ Crystal Reports ⇒ Report ⇒ Section Expert.

Depending on the section and attributes already applied to the section, the options on the shortcut menu will be slightly different.

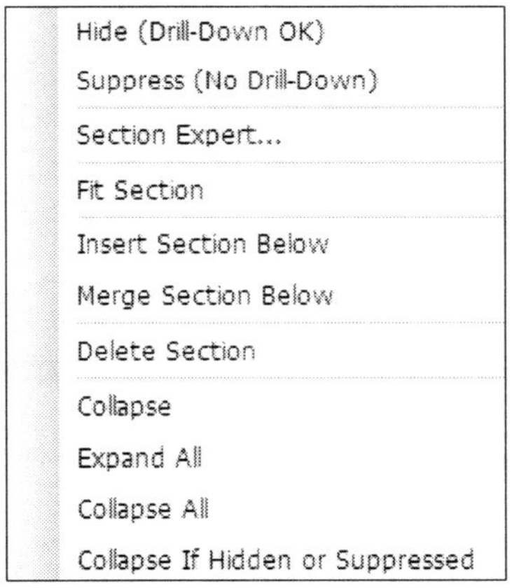

Hide (Drill-Down OK)

Suppress (No Drill-Down)

Section Expert...

Fit Section

Insert Section Below

Merge Section Below

Delete Section

Collapse

Expand All

Collapse All

Collapse If Hidden or Suppressed

Figure 4-59 Section bar shortcut menu

Exercise 4.8: How To Create Subsections

1. Save the L3.5 report as `L4.8 Subsections`.

2. Open the Section Expert and click on the report section that you want to add a section to as shown in Figure 4-60, then click the **INSERT** button. For this exercise, select the details section. You will see the section that you added, as illustrated in Figure 4-61.

The benefit of using the Section Expert to add a new section to the report is that you can apply other options to the section. These options are on the right side of Figure 4-60. You will learn about the options on the Section Expert in Lesson 10.

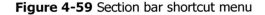

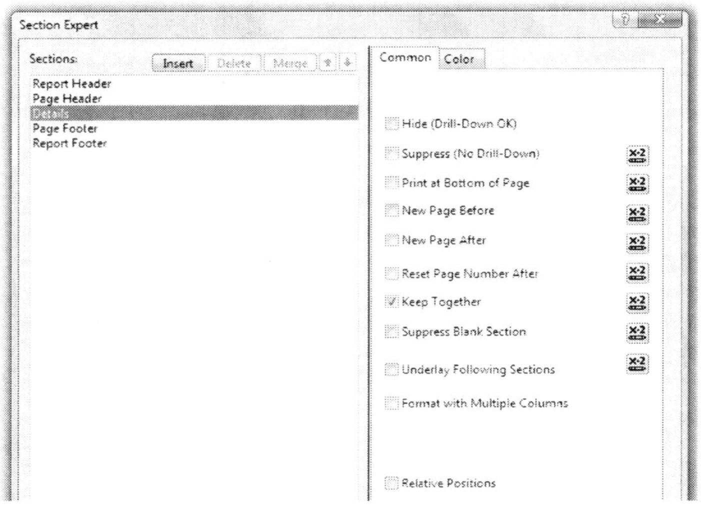

Figure 4-60 Section Expert

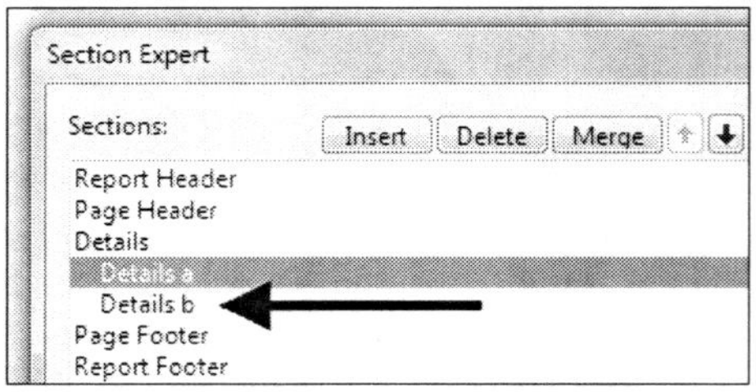

Figure 4-61 Section added to the details section

3. Add a new section to the page header section, then click OK to close the Section Expert. Delete the Print Date field. The report layout should look like the one shown in Figure 4-62.

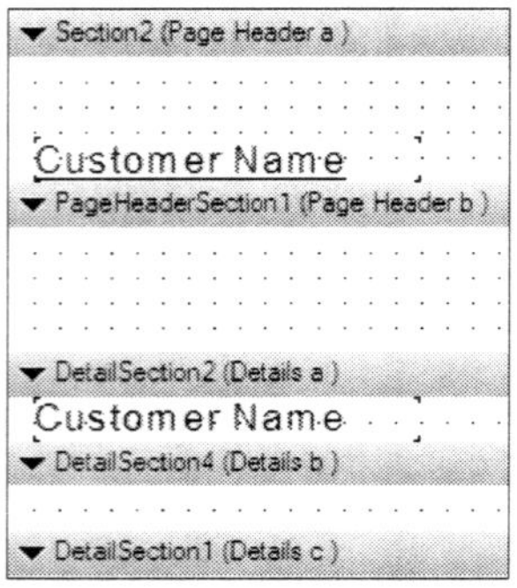

Figure 4-62 L4.8 Subsections report with new sections

4. Rearrange the fields in the details section as shown in Figure 4-63, then save the changes.

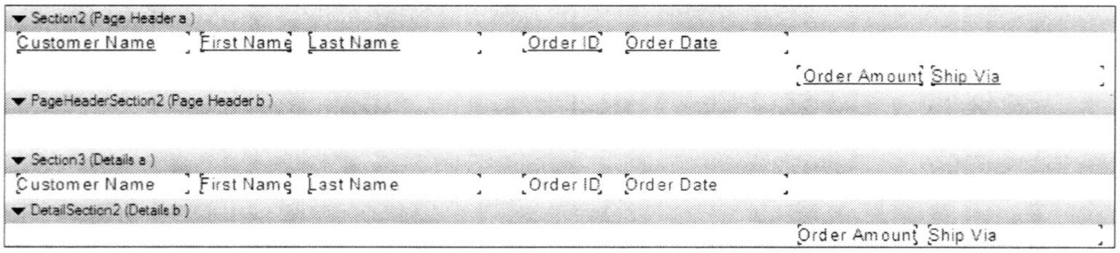

Figure 4-63 Fields rearranged in the details section

Exercise 4.9: Add A Background Color To A Report Section

In some of the sample reports that come with Crystal Reports, the field headings have a background color applied. Many reports have other objects in the page header section in addition to the field headings. If you applied a background color to the page header section, all of the objects in the section would have the background. Usually, this is not what you want. Fortunately, there is a solution for this. If you only want the background color applied to the field headings and not the other objects in the page header section, you have to create another page header section and move some of the fields to it.

1. Save the L4.3 report as L4.9 Section background color.

2. Insert a new page header section using the Section Expert, then click on the Color tab for the new section (Page header b).

3. Check the Background Color option, then open the drop-down list and select the color Gray. Click OK.

4. Select all of the field headings and change the color to white. (**Hint**: Use the Font tab on the Format Editor.) Remove the underline and move the fields to the new page header section. Save the changes. The report should look like the one shown in Figure 4-64.

Product ID	Product Name	Product Type Name	Supplier Name
1,101	Active Outdoors Crochet Glove	Gloves	Active Outdoors
1,102	Active Outdoors Crochet Glove	Gloves	Active Outdoors

Figure 4-64 L4.9 Section background color report

Exercise 4.10: Add A Border To A Field

So far in this lesson you have learned several formatting techniques that you can use to make reports look better. Another technique that you can use is to put borders around a field. Borders are often used to make a field stand out on the report. In this exercise you will add a border to the Notes field. Earlier in this lesson you learned about the Can Grow option. A good field to use this option on is a Notes field.

1. Save the L4.8 report as `L4.10 Border around field`.

2. Add the Notes field in the Employee table to the details b section of the report under the Customer Name field. Make the Notes field longer and wider. Delete the Notes field title.

3. Right-click on the Notes field and select Format Object. Check the **CAN GROW** option on the Common tab if it is not already checked.

4. On the Border tab check the **DROP SHADOW** option.

5. Change the Line Style to **DOTTED** for the Left and Right options, then change the Top and Bottom Line Style options to **SINGLE**. You should have the options selected that are shown in Figure 4-65. Click OK and save the changes. The report should look like the one shown in Figure 4-66. Close the report.

> It may be a good idea to check the **CLOSE BORDER ON PAGE BREAK** option on the Common tab on the Format Editor for fields that have a border because it is possible that the field could print on more than one page, especially a field that has the Can Grow option turned on and the section does not have the Keep together option turned on.

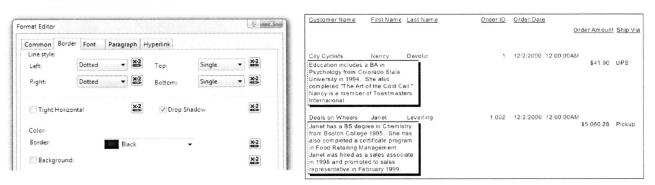

Figure 4-65 Border options

Figure 4-66 L4.10 Border around field report

Exercise 4.11: Adding Boxes To A Report

Earlier in this lesson you learned how to add lines to a report. If you need to make something on a report stand out or you want to put a more decorative border around a field or heading then the border options that you learned about in Exercise 4.10, you can use the options on the Box tab on the Format Editor. The options on this tab let you change the style, width and color of the box. In this exercise you will add a box to a field and a box to a report title. There are three ways to open the Box tool as discussed below.

    ① Right-click in the report ⇒ Insert ⇒ Box.
    ② Crystal Reports ⇒ Insert ⇒ Box.
    ③ Select it from the Toolbox.

Add The Box

1. Save the L4.8 report as L4.11 Box around objects.

2. Add the Notes field in the Employee table to the details b section of the report under the Customer Name field. Make the Notes field longer and wider. Leave space in the section above and below the Notes field.

3. Open the Box tool and draw a box around the Notes field.

4. Right-click on the box (not the field) and select Format Object. As you can see, the Box tab has many of the same options that the Line tab has that you saw earlier in Figure 4-57. Table 4-7 explains the options that are different on the Box tab.

Box Option	Description
Fill Color	If checked, this option will let you apply a background color to the box.
Close Border on Page Breaks	This option will close a box by adding additional lines if a box prints on more than one page. The box at the bottom of the page will have a bottom line added to the border. The box at the top of the next page will have a line at the top of the box added automatically.
Extend to Bottom of Section when Printing	Checking this option will allow the box to extend to the bottom of the section as the field that it is being used for, extends (grows).

Table 4-7 Box tab options explained

5. Select the **DOTTED** Border Style, then check the **FILL COLOR** option and select Silver as the color.

6. Check the **EXTEND TO BOTTOM OF SECTION WHEN PRINTING** option. You should have the options selected that are shown in Figure 4-67. Leave the Format Editor open to complete the next part of the exercise.

Use The Rounding Options

The options on the Rounding tab will let you change the corners of the box to make them round.

1. On the Rounding tab change the **ROUNDING PERCENT** to 50. It's easier to type in the percent. You should have the options selected that are shown in Figure 4-68.

2. Click OK and save the changes. Leave the report open to complete the next part of the exercise.

If you move the slider all the way to the right, the box will change to a circle.

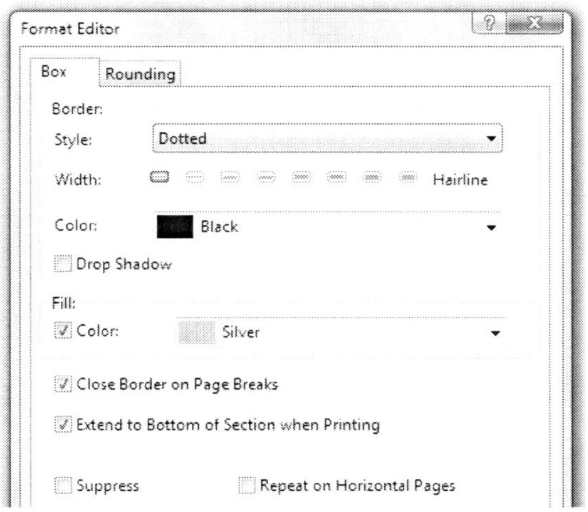

Figure 4-67 Box tab options

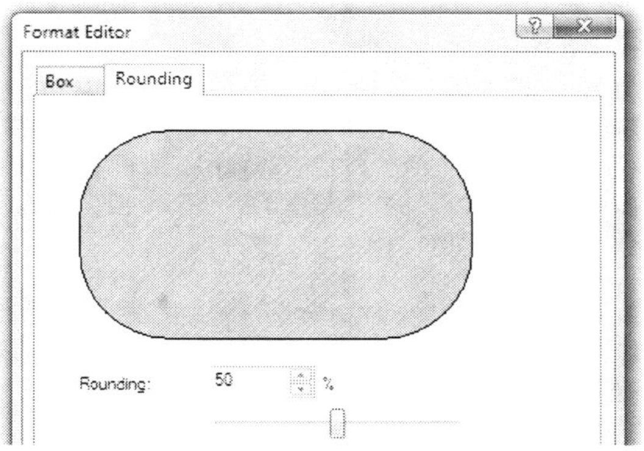

Figure 4-68 Rounding tab options

Add A Box Around A Text Object

Just like you can place a box around a field, you can place a box around a text object.

1. Turn off the suppression in the report header section if necessary, then add a text object to the report header section. Type `Customer Orders` in the text object.

2. Make the border of the text object smaller, so that it is close to the words in it.

3. Draw a box around the text object, then open the Format Editor for the box.

4. Accept the default options on the Box tab. Change the rounding percent to 100 on the Rounding tab. Click OK and save the changes. The report should look like the one shown in Figure 4-69. Close the report.

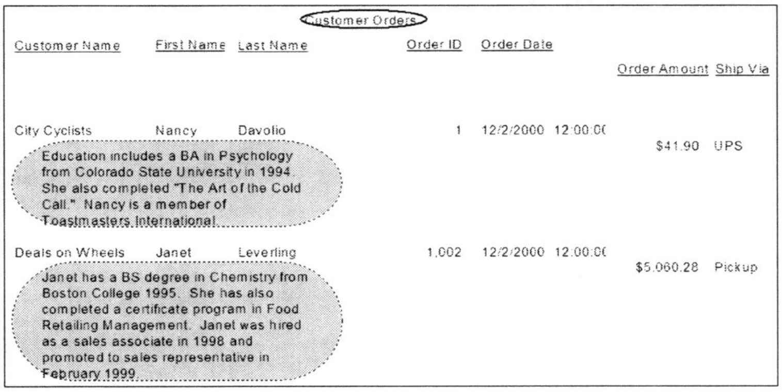

Figure 4-69 L4.11 Box around objects report

Deleting Objects From The Report Layout

There are three ways to delete one object or several objects from a report as discussed below.
When deleting fields in the details section, the field heading in the page header section is also deleted.

① Right-click on the object(s), then select Delete.
② Select the object(s), then press the Delete key.
③ Select the object(s), then Edit ⇒ Delete.

Special Fields

Crystal Reports has 18 built-in fields that you can add to reports. You can drop and drag these fields from the Field Explorer to the report, just like you drop and drag fields from tables in the Field Explorer to the report.

Figure 4-70 shows the Special Fields that you can add. Because these are system fields, the data can change each time the report is run. Table 4-8 explains the data that each of the Special Fields contains.

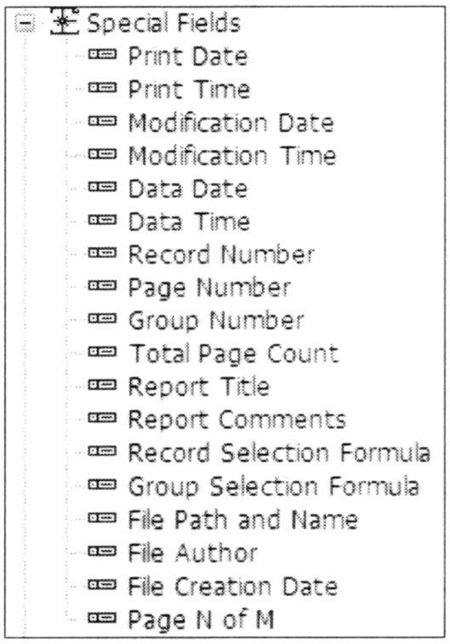

Figure 4-70 Special Fields

> Special fields, like the fields from a table that are added to the details section, have headings automatically created in the page header section.

Special Field	The Field Will Print The . . .
Data Date	Date the data was last refreshed in the report.
Data Time	Time the data was last refreshed in the report.
File Author	Information in the **AUTHOR** field. (3)
File Creation Date	Date the report was first created.
File Path And Name	File path and name of the report. (The location on the hard drive or server). For example: C:\Crystal Reports Workbook\L3.2 Employee list.rpt.
Group Number	Number of each group in the group header or footer. If the report does not have any groups, this field will print a "1".
Group Selection Formula	Group selection formula if applicable.
Modification Date	Date the report was last modified. This would be helpful during the report creation and modification process.
Modification Time	Time the report was last saved.
Page N of M	Page number and total number of pages in this format - Page 3 of 24. (4)
Page Number	Current page number.
Print Date	Date the report was printed. (2)
Print Time	Time the report was printed. (2)
Record Number	System generated number that is a counter for each detail record. It is based on the sort order in the report.
Record Selection Formula	Record Selection formula that was created in the Record Selection Formula Editor.
Report Comments	Information in the **COMMENTS** field. (3)
Report Title	Information in the **TITLE** field. (3)
Total Page Count	Total number of pages in the report. (4)

Table 4-8 Special Fields explained

(2) This data comes from the computer that the report is run from.
(3) This data comes from the Summary tab on the Document Properties dialog box shown in Figure 4-71.

(4) This field adds to the processing time when the report is generated. If the report has hundreds of pages, you may notice a delay while the data is being processed, but it is bearable.

Crystal Reports ⇒ Report ⇒ Summary Information, will let you view the dialog box shown in Figure 4-71.

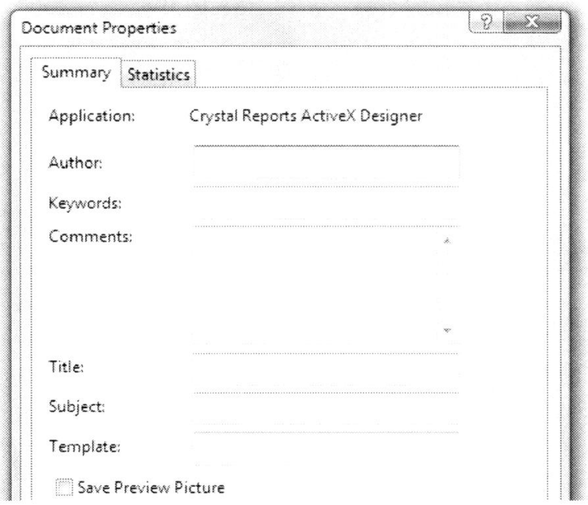

Figure 4-71 Summary tab options

Exercise 4.12: Add Special Fields To A Report

As you learned in Table 4-8 above, there are several "Date" and "Time" fields. To better understand what each of these fields will print, you will add all of them to one report in this exercise.

1. Save the L3.4 report as `L4.12 Date special fields`.

2. Make the report header section longer by dragging the section bar down to the top of the details section. Turn off the suppression in this section if necessary.

3. Open the Special Fields section in the Field Explorer and drag the **DATA DATE** field to the upper right corner of the report header section.

4. Drag the **DATA TIME** field to the upper right corner of the report header section and place it below the Data Date field.

Adding Text Objects

As you noticed, the headings were not created for the special fields that you added to the report header section. You have two options for using a text object with Special Fields, as discussed below. I tend to use the second option because I find it easier to move the objects when they are combined, but you can use either option.

① Create a text object. Enter a title for the field and place the text object next to the special field.
② Complete ① above, then press the **SPACE BAR** and drag the special field into the text object.

1. Create two text objects in the report header section.
   Type `Date the data was last refreshed:` in one of the text objects.
   Type `Time the data was last refreshed:` in the other text object.
   Make both text objects bold.

2. Rearrange the fields and text objects so that they look like the ones shown in Figure 4-72. Save the changes and leave the report open to complete the next part of the exercise.

You may need to use the **ALIGN** options that you learned about earlier in this lesson to line up the objects that you just added to the report. This would be a good use of the Align ⇒ Baseline option so that you can line up the text object and the corresponding field because the text object is bold and the field is not.

| | Date the data was last refreshed: | 11/15/2007 |
| | Time the data was last refreshed: | 11:57:27AM |

Product ID	Product Name	Product Type Name	Supplier Name
1,101	Active Outdoors Cro	Gloves	Active Outdoors
1,102	Active Outdoors Cro	Gloves	Active Outdoors

Figure 4-72 Fields and text objects arranged on the report

Add More Date And Time Special Fields

1. In the report header section, add the Special Fields and Text Objects in Table 4-9. Arrange the objects so that they look like the ones shown in Figure 4-73.

Special Field	Text For The Text Object
File Creation Date	Date the report was designed:
Modification Date	Date the report was last saved:
Modification Time	Time the report was last saved:
Print Date	Date the report was printed:

Table 4-9 Fields and text objects to add to the report

▼ Section1 (Report Header)

	Date the report was last saved:	Modificatio	Date the data was last refreshed:	Data Date
	Time the report was last saved:	Modification	Time the data was last refreshed:	Data Time
	Date the report was printed:	Print Date	Date the report was designed:	File Creation

▼ Section2 (Page Header)

| Product ID | Product Name | Product Type Name | Supplier Name |

Figure 4-73 Special Fields and text objects arranged on the report

2. Save the changes. Make any changes that are needed. The report should look similar to the one shown in Figure 4-74. Write down the dates and times that are displayed in the report.

Date the report was last saved:	11/15/2007	Date the data was last refreshed:	11/15/2007
Time the report was last saved:	12:15:42PM	Time the data was last refreshed:	12:16:06PM
Date the report was printed:	11/15/2007	Date the report was designed:	11/13/2007

Product ID	Product Name	Product Type Name	Supplier Name
1,101	Active Outdoors Cro	Gloves	Active Outdoors
1,102	Active Outdoors Cro	Gloves	Active Outdoors

Figure 4-74 L4.12 Date special fields report run on day one

3. Tomorrow, run this report twice as follows:

① Run the report without refreshing the data. Compare the dates and times to those that you wrote down in step 2 above. My report looks like the one shown in Figure 4-75. The only fields that should have changed are the **DATE THE REPORT WAS PRINTED, DATE THE DATA WAS LAST REFRESHED** and **TIME THE REPORT WAS LAST REFRESHED.**

② Move the Print Date field and title to the upper left corner of the report and save the changes. Refresh the data and run the report. Compare the data to what you wrote down in step 2 above. My report looks like the one shown in Figure 4-76. The only field that should still have the same data is the **DATE THE REPORT WAS DESIGNED,** as shown in Figure 4-74 above.

Date the report was last saved: 11/15/2007	**Date the data was last refreshed:** 11/17/2007	
Time the report was last saved: 12:15:42PM	**Time the data was last refreshed:** 10:01:20PM	
Date the report was printed: 11/17/2007	**Date the report was designed:** 11/13/2007	

Product ID	Product Name	Product Type Name	Supplier Name
1,101	Active Outdoors Cro	Gloves	Active Outdoors
1,102	Active Outdoors Cro	Gloves	Active Outdoors

Figure 4-75 L4.12 Date special fields report run on day two without modifications

Date the report was printed: 11/17/2007	**Date the report was last saved:** 11/17/2007	**Date the data was last refreshed:** 11/17/2007
	Time the report was last saved: 7:08:47PM	**Time the data was last refreshed:** 10:05:00PM
		Date the report was designed: 11/13/2007

Product ID	Product Name	Product Type Name	Supplier Name
1,101	Active Outdoors Cro	Gloves	Active Outdoors
1,102	Active Outdoors Cro	Gloves	Active Outdoors

Figure 4-76 L4.12 Date special fields report run on day two with modifications

4. Save the changes and close the report.

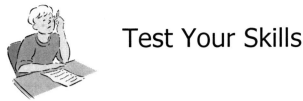

Test Your Skills

1. Save the L4.6 report as `L4.13 Skills Customer information`. Make the changes below. Your report should look like the one shown in Figure 4-77.

   - Add space below the field headings.
   - Change the Line Style to Dotted in the details section.
   - Move the Country field over to the left and make it smaller.
   - Move the Postal Code field over to the left.
   - Apply the Can Grow option to the Customer Name and Address1 fields. Do not limit the number of lines.

Customer Name	Address1	Region	Country	Postal Code
City Cyclists	7464 South Kingsway	MI	USA	48358
Pathfinders	410 Eighth Avenue	IL	USA	60148
Bike-A-Holics Anonymous	7429 Arbutus Boulevard	OH	USA	43005
Psycho-Cycle	8287 Scott Road	AL	USA	35818
Sporting Wheels Inc.	480 Grant Way	CA	USA	92150
Rockshocks for Jocks	1984 Sydney Street	TX	USA	78770
Poser Cycles	8194 Peter Avenue	MN	USA	55360

Figure 4-77 L4.13 Skills Customer information report

2. Save the L4.2 report as `L4.14 Skills Editing`. Make the changes below. Your report should look like the one shown in Figure 4-78.

   - Center the Order ID field under the heading.
   - Make the Order Date and Ship Via fields smaller.
   - Add the logo to the upper right corner of the page header section above the report title. (You can copy the logo from the L4.3 report.)
   - Add the Page N of M special field below the logo.
   - Apply the Can Grow option to the Customer Name field.
   - Change the Top border line style of the report title to Dotted.
   - Change the report title border color to red.
   - Move the Order Amount, Ship Via, First Name and Last Name fields over to the left so that they fit on the page.

Xtreme

Page 1 of 61

Customer Orders Report

Customer Name	Order #	Order Date	Order Amount	Ship Via	First Name	Last Name
City Cyclists	1	12/2/00	$41.90	UPS	Nancy	Davolio
Deals on Wheels	1002	12/2/00	$5,060.28	Pickup	Janet	Leverling
Warsaw Sports, Inc.	1003	12/2/00	$186.87	UPS	Margaret	Peacock
Bikes and Trikes	1004	12/2/00	$823.05	Pickup	Margaret	Peacock
SAB Mountain	1005	12/3/00	$29.00	Loomis	Janet	Leverling
Poser Cycles	1006	12/3/00	$64.90	Purolator	Margaret	Peacock
Spokes	1007	12/3/00	$49.50	Parcel Post	Anne	Dodsworth
Clean Air Transportation Co.	1008	12/3/00	$2,214.94	Purolator	Margaret	Peacock
Extreme Cycling	1009	12/3/00	$29.00	Loomis	Margaret	Peacock
Cyclopath	1010	12/3/00	$14,872.30	UPS	Nancy	Davolio

Figure 4-78 L4.14 Skills Editing report

3. Save the L4.3 report as `L4.15 Skills Product report`. Make the changes below. Your report should look like the one shown in Figure 4-79.

  - Change the Product ID heading to `Product #`.
  - Format the Product ID field to not have a comma.
  - Make the field headings italic and bold.
  - Remove the underline from the headings.
  - Add the Print Date field above the logo in the page header section.
  - Add the Record Number special field in front of the Product ID field. Change the font on the Record Number field and heading to the one that the other fields and headings use.
  - Add a double border line above and below the field headings.
  - Add a Page Number to the page footer section in the lower left corner.

Record Number	Product #	Product Name	Product Type Name	Supplier Name
1	1101	Active Outdoors Crochet Glove	Gloves	Active Outdoors
2	1102	Active Outdoors Crochet Glove	Gloves	Active Outdoors
3	1103	Active Outdoors Crochet Glove	Gloves	Active Outdoors
4	1104	Active Outdoors Crochet Glove	Gloves	Active Outdoors
5	1105	Active Outdoors Crochet Glove	Gloves	Active Outdoors
6	1106	Active Outdoors Lycra Glove	Gloves	Active Outdoors
7	1107	Active Outdoors Lycra Glove	Gloves	Active Outdoors
8	1108	Active Outdoors Lycra Glove	Gloves	Active Outdoors
9	1109	Active Outdoors Lycra Glove	Gloves	Active Outdoors
10	1110	Active Outdoors Lycra Glove	Gloves	Active Outdoors
11	1111	Active Outdoors Lycra Glove	Gloves	Active Outdoors
12	2201	Triumph Pro Helmet	Helmets	Triumph
13	2202	Triumph Pro Helmet	Helmets	Triumph

11/15/2007

Figure 4-79 L4.15 Skills Product report

4. Create a new report. This report will print orders by sales rep. Save the report as `L4.16 Skills Orders by sales rep`. Your report should look like the one shown in Figure 4-80.

  - Add the tables and fields in Table 4-10 to the report.

Employee	Orders	Order Details
Employee ID	Order ID	Product ID
First Name	Order Date	Unit Price
Last Name		Quantity

Table 4-10 Tables and fields for the Orders by sales rep report

  - Add the logo to the center of the page header section.
  - Print the date in the left corner, across from the logo.
  - Add the Page number to the upper right corner of the page header section.
  - Format the Order Date, Order ID and Product ID fields as shown in the report.

12/6/2007   Page 1 of 64

First Name	Last Name	Order Date	Order ID	Product ID	Unit Price	Quantity
Nancy	Davolio	12/02/2000		2201	$41.90	1
Janet	Leverling	12/02/2000	1002	5205	$33.90	3
Janet	Leverling	12/02/2000	1002	102181	$1,652.86	3
Margaret	Peacock	12/02/2000	1003	2213	$48.51	3
Margaret	Peacock	12/02/2000	1003	5402	$13.78	3
Margaret	Peacock	12/02/2000	1004	402002	$274.35	3
Janet	Leverling	12/03/2000	1005	1101	$14.50	2

Figure 4-80 L4.16 Skills Orders by sales rep report

SELECTING RECORDS

After completing the exercises in this lesson you will be able to use the following techniques to control which records will appear on a report:

- ☑ Select, filter and query records
- ☑ Create report summary information
- ☑ Add summary information to a report

LESSON 5

Selecting Records Overview

So far you have learned to create a variety of basic reports. All of the reports that you created without a wizard retrieved all of the records in the tables. As you saw, many of the reports contained 500 or more detail records. Most of the time reports provide specific information, which means that all of the records in the tables selected should not be on every report that is created. For reports that use tables similar to the size of the ones in the Xtreme database this may not be a problem, but if the report is using tables or other data sources with thousands or millions of records (think credit card statements), the report will take a long time to run. Not only will you notice this on your computer, which may run out of memory, the network will also take a performance hit.

One way that Crystal Reports lets you narrow down the records that will appear on the report is through a selection process. This selection process uses the **SELECT EXPERT**. This tool allows you to specify which records will appear on the report by entering **CRITERIA** that a record must meet. Records that do not meet the criteria will not appear on the report. This process is also known as **FILTERING RECORDS** or **QUERYING THE DATABASE**. Other ways to select records include writing formulas and using functions.

In Lesson 2 when you used a wizard to create the L2.1 report, you created a filter on the Record Selection screen. [See Lesson 2, Figure 2-36] The Record Selection screen has similar functionality to the Select Expert that you will learn how to use in this lesson.

Examples of the types of information that can be retrieved when selecting, filtering records or querying the database, include the following:

① Orders that were placed during a specific date range, like the month of June.
② Customers that purchased a specific product.
③ Orders that are over a certain dollar amount.
④ Products that need to be reordered.

Selecting, filtering or querying the database lets you ask a question about the data and then retrieve the records that meet the criteria that you specify. The records that are retrieved are known as a **RECORDSET**. The examples above are only asking one question. You can ask more than one question in the same query. You can ask the following types of multi-part questions.

① Orders that were placed during a specific date range and are more than $500.
② Customers that purchased a specific product and live in a specific state.
③ Orders that are over a certain dollar amount that are for a specific salesperson.
④ Customers that have a credit limit of $1,000 or more and have placed at least one order over $2,500, that shipped during a specific date range.
⑤ Orders that were placed or shipped during a specific date range.

In Lesson 3 you learned a little about SQL. Like SQL, the selection process produces the same results. Think of the Select Expert as an SQL code generator, without actually having to write code. The Select Expert creates the SQL code for you (as shown later in Figure 5-40), which makes the Select Expert easy to use. The SQL code is what Crystal Reports uses to select records for the report.

In addition to selecting individual records, the Select Expert can also select groups. A group selection example would be to only display records in states that have an order total amount between $100,000 and $400,000.

The Select Expert provides two ways to select records as discussed below:

① Use the built-in **OPERATORS**. Table 5-1 explains the operators that are available. Not all of the operators listed in the table are available for all field types.
② **FORMULAS** let you write the SQL code. This is not a contradiction to what I said earlier about not having to write code to use the Select Expert, because writing code in the Select Expert is not mandatory.

Operator	This Operator Selects Records That . . .
Is Equal To	Are equal to (the same as) the value that you specify.
Is Not Equal To	Are not equal to the value that you specify. This operator works the opposite of the "Is Equal To" operator.
Is One Of	Match at least one of the values that you specify. If the criteria is NY, NJ or PA for the state field, any record that has one of these values in the state field would appear on the report.
Is Not One Of	Are not one of the values that you specify. This operator works the opposite of the "Is One Of" operator.
Is Less Than	Are less than the value that you specify. If you want to see products that have a reorder level of less then 10 items in stock, enter 10 in the criteria field and the report will display products with a reorder level of nine or less. (1)
Is Less Than Or Equal To	(Works similar to "Is Less Than"). The difference is that this operator will also select records that have the value that you specify. In the less than example above, the report would not display records with a reorder level of 10 items. The less than or equal to operator will. (1)
Is Greater Than	Are greater than the value that you specify. If you want to see all orders with an order amount over $500, enter $500 in the criteria field and the report will display records with an order amount of $500.01 or more.
Is Greater Than Or Equal To	(Works similar to "Is Greater Than"). The difference is that this operator will also select records that have the value that you specify. In the greater than example above, the report would not display records with an order amount of exactly $500. The greater than or equal to operator will.
Is Between	Fall between two values. If you want to see order amounts between $1,000 and $5,000 or orders between 6/1/05 and 6/15/05, this is the operator that you would use. This operator also selects records equal to the two values that you enter for the range.
Is Not Between	Are not in the range of values that you enter. This operator works the opposite of the "Is Between" operator. It will retrieve records outside of the range that you selected.
Starts With	Begins with a specific character or set of characters. If you want to retrieve records of employees whose last name starts with the letter "M", use this operator. (2)
Does Not Start With	Do not start with the character or set of characters that you specify. This operator works the opposite of the "Starts With" operator. (2)
Is Like	Meet the wildcard criteria that you specify. The wildcard characters that you can use are a ? (question mark) and an * (asterisk). (2)
Is Not Like	Do not meet the criteria that you specify with the wildcards. This operator works the opposite of the "Is Like" operator. (2)
Is In The Period	Meet the criteria of one of the functions explained in Table 5-2. These functions will save you a lot of time because you do not have to figure out what the formula should be. (3)
Is Not In The Period	Are not in the period that you select. This operator works the opposite of the "Is In The Period" operator. (3)
Is True	Have a value of true in the Boolean field. (4)
Is False	Have a value of false in the Boolean field. (4)
Formula	Lets you write the code for the records that need to be selected for the report.

Table 5-1 Select Expert operator options explained

(1) This operator can also be used with a string field.
(2) This operator can only be used with a string field.
(3) This operator can only be used with date and date/time fields.
(4) This operator can only be used with a Boolean field.

> In addition to the operators listed above in Table 5-1, there is another operator, IS ANY VALUE, which is the default operator that you see when the Select Expert is first opened. This operator does not apply any condition to the field that it is associated to. In reports that you create and do not select any criteria for the report, this is the operator that is used by default when the report is run.

The functions in Table 5-2 provide a date range. You can create the same criteria using the "Is Between" operator, but using the built-in functions is easier and does not require dates to be hard coded.

Function	When It Starts And Ends
Week To Date From Sun	From last Sunday to today.
Month To Date	From the beginning of the current month to today.
Year To Date	From the first day of the current year to today.
Last 7 Days	From 7 days ago to today.
Last 4 Weeks To Sun	From 4 weeks prior to last Sunday to last Sunday.
Last Full Week	From Sunday of last week to Saturday of last week.
Last Full Month	From the first day of last month to the last day of last month.
All Dates To Today	From the earliest date in the table up to and including today.
All Dates To Yesterday	From the earliest date in the table up to and including yesterday.
All Dates From Today	From today forward.
All Dates From Tomorrow	From yesterday forward.
Aged 0 To 30 Days	From 30 days ago to today.
Aged 31 To 60 Days	From 31 days ago from today to 60 days ago.
Aged 61 To 90 Days	From 61 days ago from today to 90 days ago.
Over 90 Days	More than 90 days ago.
Next 30 days	From today to 30 days in the future.
Next 31 To 60 Days	From 31 days from today to 60 days in the future.
Next 61 To 90 Days	From 61 days from today to 90 days in the future.
Next 91 To 365 Days	From 91 days from today to 365 days in the future.
Calendar 1st Qtr	From January 1 of the current year to March 31 of the current year.
Calendar 2nd Qtr	From April 1 of the current year to June 30 of the current year.
Calendar 3rd Qtr	From July 1 of the current year to September 30 of the current year.
Calendar 4th Qtr	From October 1 of the current year to December 31 of the current year.
Calendar 1st Half	From January 1 of the current year to June 30 of the current year.
Calendar 2nd Half	From July 1 of the current year to December 31 of the current year.
Last Year MTD	From the first day of the current month last year to the same month and day last year.
Last Year YTD	From January 1 of last year to today's month and day last year.

Table 5-2 Is in the period criteria functions explained

Using The Select Expert

For the most part, using the Select Expert is point and click. The only time that you have to type, is if the value that you want to use is not in the drop-down list. When this happens, it is usually because the drop-down list only displays the first 500 unique values in a field. Any field that has multiple values that are identical will only display the value once in the drop-down list. An example of this would be a date field, because it is possible that multiple records have the same date in the same field.

If you want to create a customer order report and only want to display records for the Wheels Company, this company name may not appear in the drop-down list because there could be more than 500 companies in the table and this company name is near the end of the alphabet. This is an example of when you would have to type something in the Select Expert.

The other time that you would need to type something in the Select Expert is if you are using a value that you know is not one of the values for the field. For example, if you want to select records that have an order amount greater than $600. You may have to type 600 in the field if the order amount field does not have that value in any of the first 500 values that are in the drop down list.

There are three ways to open the Select Expert as discussed below:

① Right-click on the field that you want to create criteria for and select, **SELECT EXPERT**.
② Click the **SELECT EXPERT** button on the Crystal Reports - Main toolbar.
③ Crystal Reports ⇒ Report ⇒ Select Expert.

If you click on the field that you want to create the criteria for before you select option two or three above, the Select Expert will open with the field selected and you can start to create the selection criteria.

The first nine exercises in this lesson will teach you how to create a variety of queries using the operators that you learned about earlier in Table 5-1. Hopefully, this will make you feel comfortable using the Select Expert.

Exercise 5.1: Using The Is Equal To Operator

In this exercise you will use the Select Expert to find customers that are in the CA region. The region field contains the same data as a state field.

1. Save the L4.6 report as `L5.1 Region = CA`.

2. Add the Record Number special field to the report footer section. Preview the report. Go to the last page of the report. Notice that there are 269 records in the report.

3. Use one the last two options discussed earlier to open the Select Expert. You will see the dialog box shown in Figure 5-1. You will learn how to use the first option in the next exercise.

The reason that you see the Choose Field dialog box is because a field was not selected in the report prior to opening the Select Expert.

The **REPORT FIELDS** section at the top of the dialog box lists the fields that are currently on the report. Below that section you will see all of the data sources that are connected to the report.

You can use any field in the Choose Field dialog box as a field for the selection criteria, whether or not it is being displayed on the report.

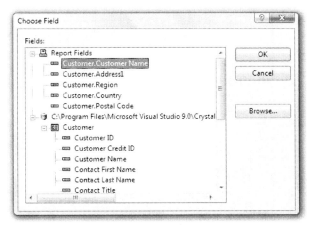

Figure 5-1 Choose Field dialog box

Selecting Records Limitation

You cannot use summary fields or formula fields that use summary fields as selection criteria. This is because of the three pass data collection model that Crystal Reports uses. As you read in Lesson 2, summary fields are not calculated until the second pass. Selecting records for the report is done in the first pass, which means that the summary field calculations have not been processed when the records are being selected. The work around is to create group selection summary fields which you will learn about in Lesson 6, Exercise 6.8.

4. Click on the **CUSTOMER.REGION** field in the Report Fields section, then click OK. You will see the dialog box shown in Figure 5-2.

Notice that the field that you selected is the name on the first tab. Multiple tabs means that there is more than one set of selection criteria for the report.

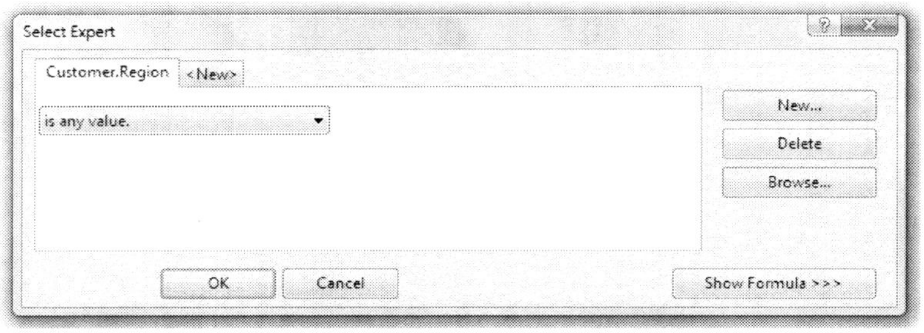

Figure 5-2 Select Expert dialog box

The **NEW** button opens the Choose Field dialog box.
The **DELETE** button deletes the tab that is selected.
The **BROWSE** button will let you view data in the field that is selected.
The **SHOW FORMULA** button will display the formula that was created by the selection criteria.

5. Open the drop-down list and select **IS EQUAL TO**.

You will now see another drop-down list. This drop-down list is connected to the field that is selected. The values in the second drop-down list are from the Region field in the table, as shown in Figure 5-3.

Figure 5-3 Data from the Region field illustrated

6. Select **CA** from the drop-down list shown above in Figure 5-3. Figure 5-4 shows the criteria that should be selected. When the report is run, it will use this criteria to find records that have CA (the state) in the Region field.

Figure 5-4 Criteria for the report

If you were creating this report and using live data, you would probably click the Refresh button the first time that you run the report after creating the selection criteria. Keep in mind that refreshing data can take a little longer than using saved data if there are thousands of records in the table. Under certain conditions you may have to refresh the data, regardless of how long it takes. Don't worry, even with thousands of records, it only takes a few seconds. If the record selection criteria changes, Crystal Reports does not know if the database has to be re-queried.

If you changed the selection criteria to include more records then the original selection criteria, you should refresh the data unless you know for sure that the Discard saved data when loading reports option is checked. It is possible that no records will be displayed on the report depending on the revised selection criteria, if the data is not refreshed.

7. Click OK. The report should look like the one shown in Figure 5-5. Notice that there are six records displayed on the report. This means that there are only six records in the Customers table in the CA region. Save the changes and close the report.

Customer Name	Address1	Region	Country	Postal Code
Sporting Wheels Inc.	480 Grant Way	CA	USA	92150
Rowdy Rims Company	4861 Second Road	CA	USA	91341
Changing Gears	1600 Hyde Crescent	CA	USA	92750
Off the Mountain Biking	192 St. Luke Bouleva	CA	USA	92725
Tyred Out	3687 Kerrisdale Stre	CA	USA	92721
Bike Shop from Mars	7071 Dundas Cresce	CA	USA	91338

Figure 5-5 L5.1 Region = CA report

Exercise 5.2: Using The Is One Of Operator

In the previous exercise you used the "Is Equal To" operator to find customers in one region. In this exercise you will use the Is One Of operator to find customers that are in the OH or FL region.

1. Save the L4.6 report as L5.2 Region = OH or FL.

2. Right-click on the **REGION** field and select, **SELECT EXPERT**.

3. Open the drop-down list and select **IS ONE OF**, then open the next drop-down list and select **OH**.

> If you type in the first letter of the value that you are looking for in the drop-down list after you open the list, it will jump to the first value that starts with that letter that you type in. You can also type in the exact value that you want.

4. Open the same drop-down list that you just used and select **FL**. Figure 5-6 shows the criteria that should be selected. Click OK.

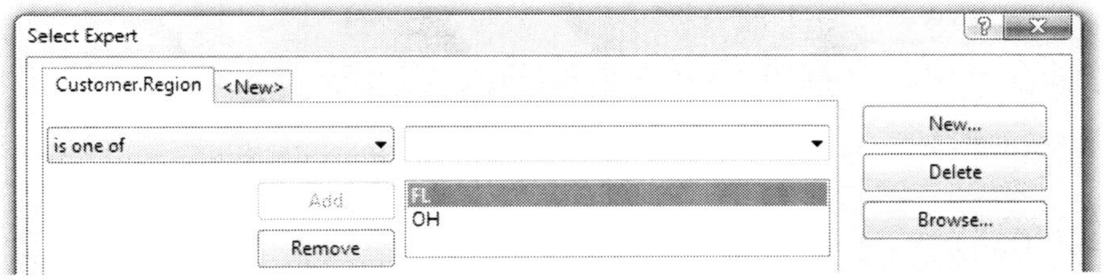

Figure 5-6 Criteria for the report

5. If necessary, move the Postal Code field over to the left so that it fits on the page. You may need to make the Country field smaller, so that the Postal Code field will fit on the page. Your report should look like the one shown in Figure 5-7. Save the changes and close the report.

Customer Name	Address1	Region	Country	Postal Code
Bike-A-Holics Anonymous	7429 Arbutus Boulev	OH	USA	43005
Wheels and Stuff	2530 Bute Avenue	FL	USA	34666
Uni-Cycle	1008 Kerr Street	OH	USA	43042
Extreme Cycling	1925 Glenaire Avenu	FL	USA	34638
Karma Bikes	1516 Ohio Avenue	OH	USA	43092

Figure 5-7 L5.2 Region = OH or FL report

Exercise 5.3: Using The Is Greater Than Or Equal To Operator

In this exercise you will use the "Is Greater Than Or Equal To" operator to find all orders that were placed on or after 6/24/2001.

1. Save the L3.3 report as `L5.3 Order Date GTE 6-24-2001`.
   (GTE is an abbreviation for greater than or equal to that I made up).

2. Add the Record Number special field to the report footer section. Save the changes. The report should have 3,683 records.

3. Open the Select Expert to use with the Order Date field.

4. Select the "Is greater than or equal to" operator, then open the next drop-down list and select 6/24/2001. You can type the value in if you want to. Figure 5-8 shows the criteria that should be selected. You can type in a date that is not in the list.

If you select the date from the drop-down list, you will also see the time next to the date.

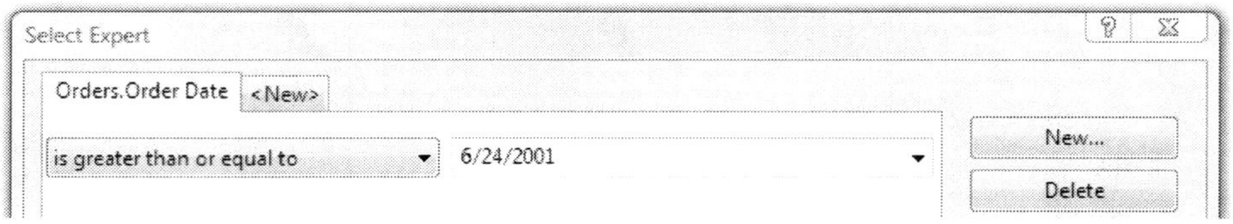

Figure 5-8 Criteria for the report

5. Click OK. Your report should look like the one shown in Figure 5-9. The report should have 2,199 records. Notice that there are fewer records then before the selection criteria was applied. Save the changes and leave the report open to complete the next exercise.

Customer Name	Order Date	Ship Date	Order ID	Unit Price	Quantity
Alley Cat Cycles	6/24/2001 12:00:0(	7/2/2001 12:00:00/	1,761	$21.90	1
Alley Cat Cycles	6/24/2001 12:00:0(	7/2/2001 12:00:00/	1,761	$539.85	1
Alley Cat Cycles	6/24/2001 12:00:0(	7/2/2001 12:00:00/	1,761	$329.85	3
Piccolo	6/24/2001 12:00:0(	6/29/2001 12:00:0(	1,762	$2,939.85	2
City Cyclists	6/24/2001 12:00:0(	6/30/2001 12:00:0(	1,763	$41.90	2
City Cyclists	6/24/2001 12:00:0(	6/30/2001 12:00:0(	1,763	$764.85	3
Hercules Mountain E	6/24/2001 12:00:0(	6/27/2001 12:00:0(	1,764	$37.90	2

Figure 5-9 L5.3 Order Date GTE 6-24-2001 report

Exercise 5.4: Modify Selection Criteria

In the previous exercise you created criteria to find orders that have an order date greater than or equal to a specific date. In this exercise you will add to this criteria to filter out orders that have an order amount greater than $2,500.00.

Adding additional criteria via the Select Expert will reduce or increase the number of records that will appear on the report. As you have probably noticed, the report that you just added selection criteria to does not have the order amount field. If you need to have additional fields on the report you can add them at anytime. If you need to create a filter on a field, but do not need to see the field on the report, you can create a filter without adding the field to the report.

> Creating the criteria IS GREATER THAN 2499.99 will produce the same results as creating the criteria, IS GREATER THAN OR EQUAL TO 2500.00.

1. Save the L5.3 report as
   `L5.4 Order Date GTE 6-24-01 and Order Amt GT 2499.99`.

2. Delete the Quantity field. Add the Order Amount field from the Orders table and place it after the Ship Date field as shown in Figure 5-10. Save the changes.

▼ Section2 (Page Header)					
Customer Name	Order Date	Ship Date	[Order Amount]	[Order ID]	[Unit Price]
▼ Section3 (Details)					
Customer Name	Order Date	Ship Date	[der Amount]	[Order ID]	[Unit Price]

Figure 5-10 Order Amount field added to the report

3. Open the Select Expert to use with the Order Amount field. Notice that you see existing criteria on the Select Expert dialog box. This is the criteria that you created in the previous exercise. Open the drop-down list and select **IS GREATER THAN**, then type 2499.99 in the next drop-down list. Figure 5-11 shows the criteria that should be selected.

Select Expert				
Orders.Order Amount	Orders.Order Date	<New>		
is greater than ▼	$2,499.99		▼	New...
				Delete

Figure 5-11 Criteria for the report

4. Click OK. Your report should look like the one shown in Figure 5-12. The report should have 724 records. Save the changes and close the report.

Customer Name	Order Date		Ship Date		Order Amount	Order ID	Unit Price
Piccolo	6/24/2001	12:00:00	6/29/2001	12:00:00	$5,879.70	1,762	$2,939.85
The Great Bike Shop	6/24/2001	12:00:00	6/28/2001	12:00:00	$7,829.29	1,765	$2,939.85
The Great Bike Shop	6/24/2001	12:00:00	6/28/2001	12:00:00	$7,829.29	1,765	$809.87
The Great Bike Shop	6/24/2001	12:00:00	6/28/2001	12:00:00	$7,829.29	1,765	$329.85
Trail Blazer's Place	6/24/2001	12:00:00	6/26/2001	12:00:00	$2,989.35	1,767	$16.50
Trail Blazer's Place	6/24/2001	12:00:00	6/26/2001	12:00:00	$2,989.35	1,767	$2,939.85
Trail Blazer's Place	6/24/2001	12:00:00	6/24/2001	12:00:00	$5,994.94	1,768	$14.50
Trail Blazer's Place	6/24/2001	12:00:00	6/24/2001	12:00:00	$5,994.94	1,768	$2,645.87

Figure 5-12 L5.4 Order Date GTE 6-24-2001 and Order Amt GT 2499.99 report

Exercise 5.5: Using The Is Between Operator

In this exercise you will use the "Is Between" operator to find all of the orders that were shipped between 4/1/2001 and 6/30/2001.

1. Save the L3.3 report as
   L5.5 Orders shipped between 4-1-2001 and 6-30-2001.

2. Add the Record Number special field to the report footer section, then open the Select Expert to use with the Ship Date field.

3. Select the "Is between" operator, then open the top drop-down list on the right and select 4/1/2001.

4. Open the bottom drop-down list and select 6/30/2001. Click OK. The report should have 780 records. Save the changes and close the report.

Exercise 5.6: Using Multiple Selection Criteria

In this exercise you will create a new report that selects records that meet the following criteria:
Country = USA, the Order Date is between 4/1/2002 and 4/30/2002 and the order was not shipped.

☑ Save the report as L5.6 US orders not shipped in April 2002.

☑ Table 5-3 contains the tables and fields for the report. The table names are in bold.

☑ Figure 5-13 shows the report layout.

☑ Figure 5-14 shows the selection criteria formula. Click the **SHOW FORMULA** button on the Select Expert dialog box to view the formula. Depending on the tab that is selected prior to clicking the Show Formula button, the formula will be in a different order then what is shown. The Country tab was selected for this exercise.

☑ Figure 5-15 shows the report, which should have 44 records.

Customer	Orders
Customer Name	Order Date (5)
Country	Order Amount
	Shipped

Table 5-3 Tables and fields to add to the report

(5) Change the format of this field to xx/xx/xxxx on the report.

Steps

① Create a new report, then add the tables and fields.

② Add the selection criteria.

③ Save the report.

Customer Name	Country	Order Date	Order Amount	Shipped
Customer Name	Country	Order Date	Order Amount	Shipped

Figure 5-13 L5.6 report layout

 Once you open the Select Expert and create the first set of criteria, you do not have to close it to add additional criteria. Click on the **NEW** tab to add more criteria.

If the syntax in your formula looks different then what is shown in Figure 5-14 and your report looks exactly like the one shown in Figure 5-15, you are probably using the **BASIC SYNTAX** formula language instead of **CRYSTAL SYNTAX**. [See Lesson 9, Syntax]

The zeros at the end of the date/time fields in the formula shown in Figure 5-14 represent the time in HH MM SS format (hours, minutes, seconds).

```
{Customer.Country} = "USA" and
not {Orders.Shipped} and
{Orders.Order Date} in DateTime (2002, 04, 01, 00, 00, 00) to DateTime (2002, 04, 30, 00, 00, 00)
```

Figure 5-14 L5.6 Selection criteria formula

Customer Name	Country	Order Date	Order Amount	Shipped
City Cyclists	USA	04/29/2002	$63.90	False
Pathfinders	USA	04/26/2002	$3,185.42	False
Rockshocks for Jocks	USA	04/25/2002	$8,933.25	False
Rockshocks for Jocks	USA	04/30/2002	$31.00	False
Poser Cycles	USA	04/14/2002	$83.80	False
Trail Blazer's Place	USA	04/18/2002	$107.80	False
Trail Blazer's Place	USA	04/25/2002	$39.80	False
Hooked on Helmets	USA	04/20/2002	$2,797.25	False
Hooked on Helmets	USA	04/25/2002	$1,971.53	False

Figure 5-15 L5.6 US orders not shipped in April 2002 report

Using Wildcard Characters As Selection Criteria

Earlier in the lesson you learned that you could use the ? and the * as selection criteria using the "Is Like" and "Is Not Like" operators. Wildcard characters provide another way to retrieve records. Wildcards are characters that you can use to substitute all or part of the data in a field. You can also use wildcards to search for data that has a pattern. You can use these wildcard characters as shown in Figure 5-16 at the beginning or end of the search criteria that you enter.

① The question mark is used to replace one character in the data. If you entered t?n in the criteria field, the selection criteria would return records that have ten, tan, tune and ton, but not toon.

② The asterisk is used to replace more than one character in the data. If you entered s*r in the criteria field, the selection criteria would return records that have star, start and sour, or any records that had the letter "s" come before the letter "r" in the field that the selection criteria is for. This wildcard character selection criteria is more flexible, but often returns a lot of results that are not needed.

Figure 5-16 Wildcard characters illustrated

Viewing Formulas

Earlier in this lesson you created criteria that selected an order date greater than or equal to 6/24/2001. In another exercise you modified that criteria to only retrieve records that had an order amount greater than $2,499.99. To view the formula click the **SHOW FORMULA** button on the Select Expert. The formulas for the selection criteria are similar.

Figure 5-17 shows the formula that was created for the selection criteria shown earlier in Figure 5-8. Figure 5-18 shows the formula that was created for the report shown earlier in Figure 5-12. It shows all of the criteria that must be met. At the end of the first line of the formula, you see the word **AND**. If you changed the "and" to **OR**, the report would look like the one shown in Figure 5-19. If you made this change and ran the report, you would see that there are 2,637 records in this report, compared to the 724 records in the report shown earlier in Figure 5-12.

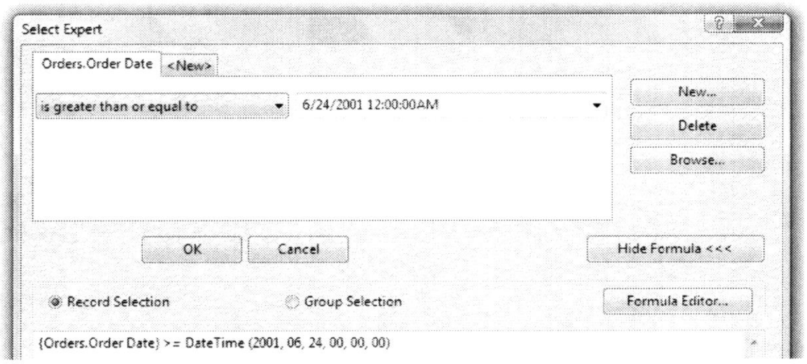

Figure 5-17 Formula for the selection criteria shown earlier in Figure 5-8

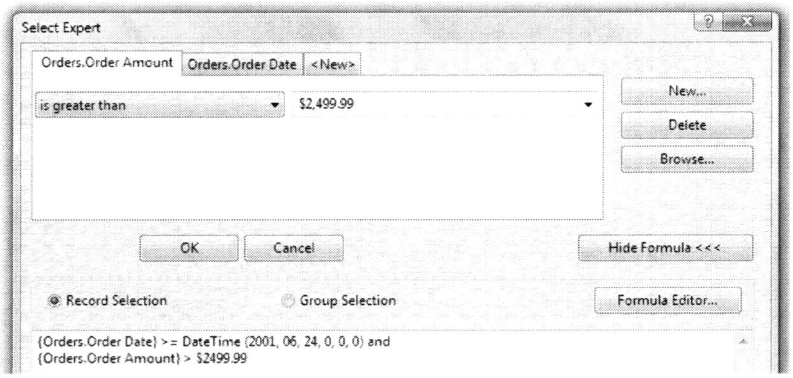

Figure 5-18 Formula for the selection criteria for the report shown earlier in Figure 5-12

Customer Name	Order Date		Ship Date		Order Amount	Order ID	Unit Price
Piccolo	6/24/2001	12:00:0(	6/29/2001	12:00:0(	$5,879.70	1,762	$2,939.85
The Great Bike Shop	6/24/2001	12:00:0(	6/28/2001	12:00:0(	$7,829.29	1,765	$2,939.85
The Great Bike Shop	6/24/2001	12:00:0(	6/28/2001	12:00:0(	$7,829.29	1,765	$809.87
The Great Bike Shop	6/24/2001	12:00:0(	6/28/2001	12:00:0(	$7,829.29	1,765	$329.85
Trail Blazer's Place	6/24/2001	12:00:0(	6/26/2001	12:00:0(	$2,989.35	1,767	$16.50
Trail Blazer's Place	6/24/2001	12:00:0(	6/26/2001	12:00:0(	$2,989.35	1,767	$2,939.85
Trail Blazer's Place	6/24/2001	12:00:0(	6/24/2001	12:00:0(	$5,994.94	1,768	$14.50
Trail Blazer's Place	6/24/2001	12:00:0(	6/24/2001	12:00:0(	$5,994.94	1,768	$2,645.87
Trail Blazer's Place	6/24/2001	12:00:0(	6/24/2001	12:00:0(	$5,994.94	1,768	$329.85
Bikes and Trikes	6/25/2001	12:00:0(	6/28/2001	12:00:0(	$2,939.29	1,770	$39.81
Bikes and Trikes	6/25/2001	12:00:0(	6/28/2001	12:00:0(	$2,939.29	1,770	$9.00

Figure 5-19 L5.4 Order Date GTE 6-24-2001 **OR** Order Amt GT 2499.99 report

> As you have learned, a report can have more than one selection criteria. When this is the case, in order for records to appear on the report, they have to meet all of the selection criteria. That is because by default, Crystal Reports uses the logical **AND** operator on the Select Expert. If you need to create selection criteria where only one of the selection criteria options must be true in order for a record to appear on the report, you have to use the logical **OR** operator. To change the operator, you have to manually edit the selection formula that is created by the Select Expert.

How To Delete Selection Criteria

After you have created selection criteria you may decide that one or more of the criteria that you set up is not needed. You do not have to delete everything and start over. The steps below will show you how to delete specific criteria on the Select Expert dialog box.

1. Open the report that has the selection criteria that you want to delete.

2. Open the Select Expert. Click on the tab that has the selection criteria that you want to delete, then click the **DELETE** button shown earlier in Figure 5-18.

3.   Click OK to close the Select Expert and save the changes.

Understanding How Date/Time Fields Work In Selection Criteria

In Exercise 5.4, a date/time field was used as part of the selection criteria. You entered a date and the records that have an order date greater than or equal to 6/24/2001 were retrieved, even though you did not enter a time for the date that you selected. That is because Crystal Reports will use midnight as the time when a date is entered without a time. This is fine for selection criteria that only uses a date/time field once. If the selection criteria uses the **IS BETWEEN** operator for example (or any operator that requires that two dates be entered for the selection criteria), the records that are retrieved may not be exactly what you are expecting.

The first date in the selection criteria will be compared to midnight as the time, meaning that all records that have a time of midnight or later will be included. So far, so good. The problem is with the second date in the selection criteria. If a time is not entered for the second date, only records that have midnight as the time will be retrieved. This means that a record that has the same date as the second date field in the criteria but the time is something other then midnight will not appear on the report. To include all records on the date in the second date field, you should enter 23:59:59 or 11:59:59 PM as the time after the date. If you enter 17:00:00 or 05:00:00 PM as the time for the second date, records that have a time that is greater than 5 PM will not be included on the report.

If you were going to modify the L5.6 report to show all of the orders that were shipped between 1/1/2001 and 1/15/2001, Figure 5-20 shows what many people would enter as the selection criteria. When the report is run with this selection criteria, 49 records will be retrieved. This is incorrect because it does not account for records that have a time other than midnight on the Ship Date field.

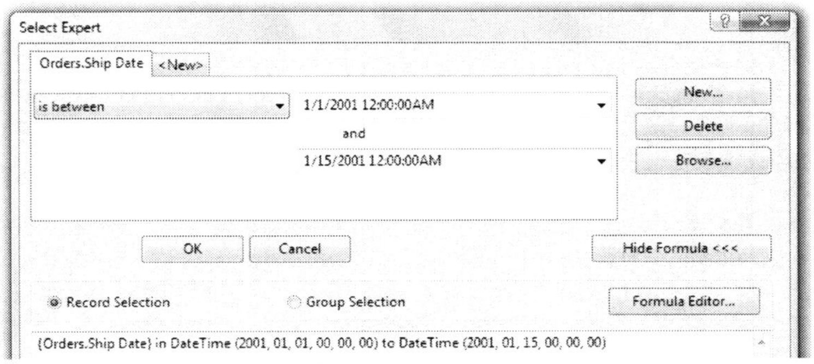

Figure 5-20 Incorrect selection criteria

If the selection criteria shown in Figure 5-21 was entered, the report would retrieve 58 records. As you can see in Figure 5-22, the times on the Ship Date field are different. Notice that there are nine records that have a ship date of 1/15/2001.

Figure 5-21 Correct selection criteria

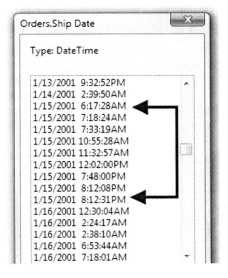

Figure 5-22 Ship Date field data

If the second Ship Date field has the time entered as 03:00:00 PM as shown in Figure 5-23, the last three records on the 15th shown above in Figure 5-22 would not be displayed on the report because the time for these three records is after 3 PM.

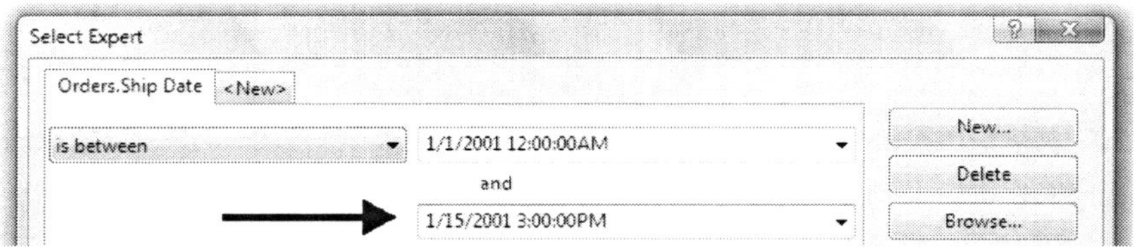

Figure 5-23 Criteria to show orders that were shipped between 1/1/2001 and 1/15/2001 by 3 PM

If you want to try this yourself, save the L5.6 report as L5.6A Time Problem (Incorrect Criteria). Delete all of the current selection criteria, then create the criteria shown above in Figure 5-20. Type in the dates. Add the Ship Date field to the report and sort this field in ascending order. Refresh the data and run the report. If you scroll to the end of the report you will see that the last record on the report has a ship date of 1/14/2001. There are no records with a ship date of 1/15/2001 on the report.

Save the L5.6A report as L5.6B Time Problem (Correct Criteria). Use the criteria shown above in Figure 5-21. If you scroll to the end of the report you will see that there are nine records on 1/15/2001. These are the records that you were expecting to appear on the report when you entered the criteria shown above in Figure 5-20.

Save the L5.6A report as L5.6C Time criteria with a specific time. Use the criteria shown above in Figure 5-23. If you scroll to the end of the report you will see that there are 55 records on the report. This is what you were expecting because the time on the criteria was 3 PM. There are three records with a time after 3 PM on the 15th. [See bottom of Figure 5-22]

I don't know about you, but when I first figured this out it was somewhat scary. You have two options. You can always type in the time that you need on the second date field or you can type in the day after the last day that you want to include records for on the report. Instead of typing 1/15/2001 for the second date, you could type 1/16/2001 and let the time default to 12:00:00 AM and you will get the same result. Keep this in mind when you are creating reports on your own. In an effort to save time, when you create reports in this workbook that have similar selection criteria, you do not have to enter a time on the Select Expert dialog box.

Being able to enter a time is helpful for reports that are time sensitive. If you needed to create a report that displayed a list of medications that were dispensed to patients between 8 AM and 2 PM, you could enter the times as part of the selection criteria.

More Practice Creating Report Criteria

By now you have probably figured out how important it is to understand how to create selection criteria to meet the requirements of the report. If the wrong criteria is created for the report, the output will not be what the user is expecting. This means that they could make decisions based on incorrect data and not know that the data is incorrect. If you aren't familiar with the data, it is a good idea to open the tables and look at the raw data. The next three exercises will allow you to gain more practice creating report selection criteria.

Each of the three practice exercises below is worded slightly different on purpose to help you learn how to take report specs and create selection criteria from them. Remember that each person that requests a report or asks for changes to an existing report will convey their needs differently.

Exercise 5.7: Practice Exercise 1

In this exercise you will create a new report that will find all products that the suppliers Craze and Triumph offer.

☑ Save the report as L5.7 Products that suppliers Craze and Triumph offer.
☑ Table 5-4 contains the tables and fields for the report.
☑ Figure 5-24 shows the report layout.
☑ Figure 5-25 shows the selection criteria formula.
☑ Figure 5-26 shows the report, which should have 86 records.

Product	Supplier
Product Name	Supplier Name
M/F	
Price (SRP)	

Table 5-4 Tables and fields to add to the report

```
▼ Section2 (Page Header )
  Product Name          M/F        Supplier Name            Price (SRP)
▼ Section3 (Details )
  Product Name          M/F        Supplier Name            Price (SRP)
```

Figure 5-24 L5.7 Report layout

{Supplier.Supplier Name} in ["Craze", "Triumph"]

Figure 5-25 Selection criteria formula

Product Name	M/F	Supplier Name	Price (SRP)
Triumph Pro Helmet		Triumph	$41.90
Triumph Pro Helmet		Triumph	$41.90
Triumph Pro Helmet		Triumph	$41.90
Triumph Pro Helmet		Triumph	$41.90
Triumph Pro Helmet		Triumph	$41.90
Triumph Pro Helmet		Triumph	$41.90
Triumph Vertigo Helmet		Triumph	$53.90
Triumph Vertigo Helmet		Triumph	$53.90
Triumph Vertigo Helmet		Triumph	$53.90
Triumph Vertigo Helmet		Triumph	$53.90
Triumph Vertigo Helmet		Triumph	$53.90
Triumph Vertigo Helmet		Triumph	$53.90
Triumph Vertigo Helmet		Triumph	$53.90
Triumph Vertigo Helmet		Triumph	$53.90
Xtreme Adult Helmet		Craze	$33.90
Xtreme Adult Helmet		Craze	$33.90

Figure 5-26 L5.7 Products that suppliers Craze and Triumph offer report

Exercise 5.8: Practice Exercise 2

In this exercise you will add selection criteria to the L3.5 report. You will modify the report so that it will only retrieve customers whose order amount is between $2,000 and $5,000 and was not shipped via the carrier Purolator.

☑ Save the L3.5 report as L5.8 Orders between 2-5000 and not shipped by Purolator.
☑ Figure 5-27 shows the report, which should have 281 records.

The report needs the following criteria and changes.

    ① Change the format of the Order Date field to look like the one shown in the report.
    ② The Order Amount is between $2,000 and $5,000.
    ③ The order was not shipped by Purolator.

Customer Name	Order ID	Order Date	Order Amount	Ship Via	First Name	Last Name
Belgium Bike Co.	1,022	12/07/2000	$2,792.86	Parcel Post	Janet	Leverling
The Great Bike Shop	1,027	12/07/2000	$2,972.85	UPS	Michael	Suyama
City Cyclists	1,033	12/08/2000	$3,520.30	Loomis	Janet	Leverling
The Bike Cellar	1,036	12/10/2000	$2,014.20	Loomis	Michael	Suyama
Cyclopath	1,043	12/11/2000	$2,179.83	UPS	Margaret	Peacock
The Bike Cellar	1,045	12/11/2000	$3,764.04	FedEx	Michael	Suyama
Cycle City Rome	1,055	12/12/2000	$2,459.40	Parcel Post	Nancy	Davolio
Cycle City Rome	1,057	12/12/2000	$3,638.01	Loomis	Janet	Leverling
To The Limit Biking (	1,063	12/12/2000	$2,497.05	Loomis	Anne	Dodsworth

Figure 5-27 L5.8 Orders between 2-5000 and not shipped by Purolator report

Exercise 5.9: Practice Exercise 3

In this exercise you will add selection criteria to the L3.5 report. This report will only retrieve orders from 2001 that were shipped by the carrier Purolator or were picked up.

    ☑ Save L3.5 the report as `L5.9 2001 Orders shipped by Purolator or Pickup`.
    ☑ Figure 5-28 shows the report, which should have 483 records.

The report needs the following criteria and changes.

    ① Change the format of the Order Date field to look like the one shown in the report.
    ② The Ship Via field must have Pickup or Purolator.
    ③ The Order Date is in 2001.

Customer Name	Order ID	Order Date	Order Amount	Ship Via	First Name	Last Name
Clean Air Transportation Co.	1,123	01/02/2001	$5,219.55	Pickup	Janet	Leverling
Off the Mountain Biking	1,124	01/02/2001	$59.70	Purolator	Margaret	Peacock
BBS Pty	1,127	01/02/2001	$520.35	Pickup	Robert	King
Paris Mountain Sports	1,134	01/05/2001	$43.80	Pickup	Anne	Dodsworth
C-Gate Cycle Shoppe	1,136	01/05/2001	$3,209.53	Pickup	Michael	Suyama
Furia	1,137	01/05/2001	$6,040.95	Purolator	Margaret	Peacock
Cyclopath	1,147	01/06/2001	$1,830.35	Purolator	Michael	Suyama
Magazzini	1,148	01/07/2001	$157.11	Pickup	Janet	Leverling
Biking's It Industries	1,150	01/08/2001	$83.80	Pickup	Robert	King

Figure 5-28 L5.9 2001 Orders shipped by Purolator or Pickup report

Edit An Existing Formula

In Exercise 5.9, the criteria for the Ship Via field is that it has to contain one of two values. If you needed to add another value, you could use the Select Expert to add the value from the drop-down list or you could edit the formula that is at the bottom of the Select Expert dialog box.

If you type in the **FORMULA** field, Crystal Reports will disable the top portion of the Select Expert dialog box as shown in Figure 5-29. Compare this to the Select Expert dialog box shown earlier in Figure 5-18.

In Figure 5-29 you do not see anything in the top portion of the dialog box. That is because I typed "UPS" in the formula field at the bottom of the dialog box.

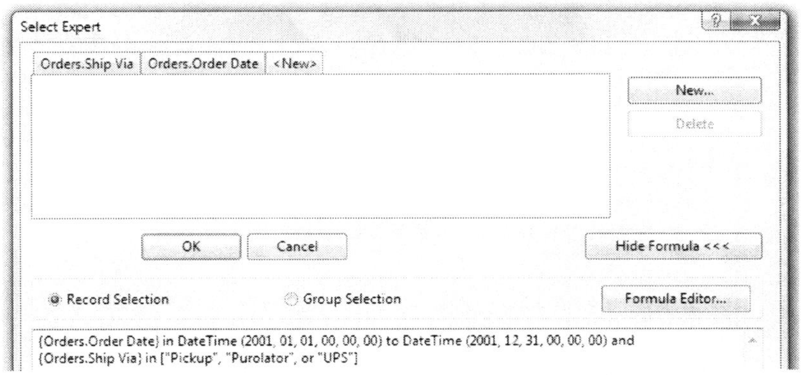

Figure 5-29 Top half of the Select Expert dialog box disabled

The reason Crystal Reports disables the top half of the Select Expert when you create or edit a formula at the bottom of the dialog box is because the formula can't be duplicated by the options that the Select Expert has at the top of the dialog box.

Opening The Formula Editor From The Select Expert

If you can create or edit the formula at the bottom of the Select Expert shown above in Figure 5-29, you do not have to use the Formula Editor. If you cannot remember the function or need help creating the formula, there are two ways that you can open the Formula Editor from the Select Expert as discussed below. You will learn more about the Formula Editor in Lesson 9.

① Click the **FORMULA EDITOR** button shown above in Figure 5-29.
② Open the operator drop-down list, scroll to the bottom of the list and select the **FORMULA** option illustrated in Figure 5-30. The Select Expert will change as illustrated in Figure 5-31 to let you create a formula.

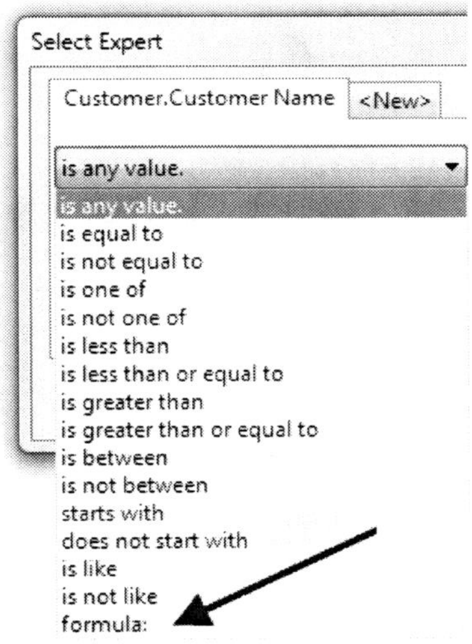

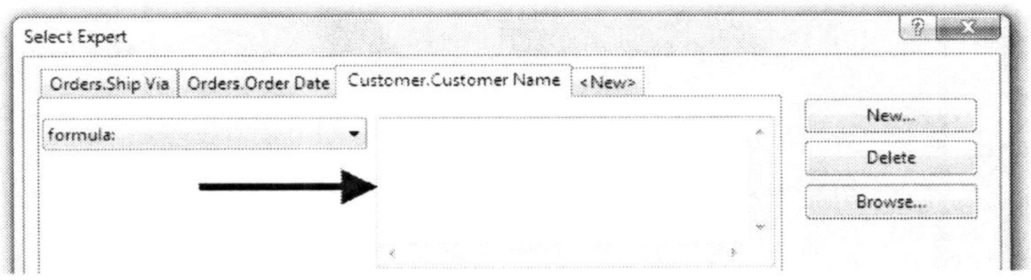

Figure 5-31 Select Expert with formula field

Figure 5-30 Formula option illustrated

Record Selection Performance Considerations

The type of database that the report is using determines the record selection process that Crystal Reports uses. Databases that are stored on a database server or desktop databases that use an ODBC connection have more performance issues than desktop databases that are local or are on a network drive, as discussed below.

① If the database is on a server, Crystal Reports creates a WHERE clause and adds the clause to the query and sends the query to the database server. The query is run on the server and returns the records to Crystal Reports to use, to generate the report. If the database is on a server, performance improves if this record selection process is used.

② If the database is local or is a desktop database that is stored on a network drive (which is different then a database server), Crystal Reports runs the query that is created from the record selection criteria itself. Depending on the number of records, the report selection process can take some time.

Making changes to a formula created with the Select Expert via the **SHOW FORMULA** button can really slow down the record selection process if the database is on a database server, especially if the underlying tables have a lot of records.

The **USE INDEXES OR SERVER FOR SPEED** option if selected, will improve performance. If you want to use this option for the current report, it is on the Report Options dialog box. [See Lesson 8, Report Options] If you want this option to be the default for all reports that you will create going forward, select the option on the Database tab of the Options dialog box, which you will learn about later in this lesson.

In Lesson 2 you read about indexes. Using indexed fields will improve performance during the record selection process, especially when using tables that have a lot of records. When possible, you should use indexed fields for the record selection process because the fields index stores all of the values that are in the field, in sorted order, which makes it faster to retrieve records.

Case Sensitive Considerations

When Crystal Reports is installed, case insensitivity is set as the default. This means that entering "new orleans" or "New Orleans" will retrieve the same records. When creating selection criteria on text fields, keep the following in mind.

① PC and SQL databases that are connected to via an ODBC connection usually ignores case sensitivity in Crystal Reports.

② Some databases and ODBC drivers may not support case insensitivity when used with Crystal Reports, even though the **DATABASE SERVER IS CASE-INSENSITIVE** option is checked.

③ If the server that the database is stored on is set to be case sensitive, you cannot override it by checking the Database server is case-insensitive option. If you select the same option on the Report Options dialog box, you can turn the option on, only for the report that you are currently working with. If this is the case, you would have to convert the text field that you need to create the selection criteria for to all upper case and enter the criteria to support all upper case.

④ If the database is not stored on a server that is set to case sensitive and the database is set for case insensitivity, you can use the Database server is case-insensitive option to control what the selection criteria returns.

If you want the **DATABASE SERVER IS CASE-INSENSITIVE** option applied to reports that have already been created, you have to open each of the reports and select the option on the Report Options dialog box.

Document Properties

In Lesson 4 you learned about **SPECIAL FIELDS** and that they can be added to a report. You also learned that some of the special fields come from the Summary tab on the Document Properties dialog box. The next two exercises will show you how to create summary information and save it, as well as, add the summary information to a report.

Exercise 5.10: How To Create Report Summary Information

1. Save the L5.1 report as L5.10 Region = CA with summary info.

2. Crystal Reports ⇒ Report ⇒ Summary Info. Type your name in the **AUTHOR** field.

3. Type This report has summary information in the **COMMENTS** field, then type L5.10 Region = CA in the **TITLE** field. Figure 5-32 shows the options that should be filled in.

The information that is entered on this tab is used for identification purposes. These are properties of Windows files and are not specific to Crystal Reports. Other software packages have similar dialog boxes. For example, Microsoft Word has the "Properties" dialog box.

The **TITLE** field does not appear on the tab in place of the report file name like it does in the full version of Crystal Reports.

The **TEMPLATE** field shown in Figure 5-32 currently does not provide any use. It does not let you apply a template to the report or save the active report as a template. If the report is based off of a template, you could enter the template name in this field so that you will know which template the report is using.

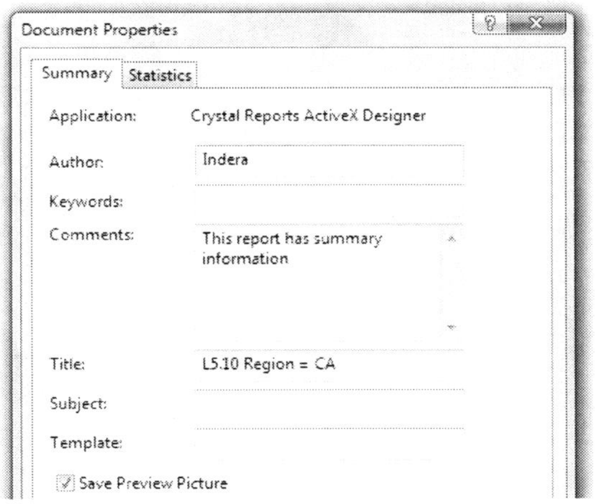

Figure 5-32 Summary tab options

In Windows XP, the **SAVE PREVIEW PICTURE** option if checked, will let you view a thumbnail size picture of the first page of the report in the Open dialog box of Crystal Reports.

4. Click OK and save the changes. Leave the report open to complete the next part of the exercise.

Statistics Tab

1. Open the Document Properties dialog box and click on the Statistics tab.

The options shown in Figure 5-33 are **READ-ONLY**, which means that you cannot modify them manually.

The **REVISION NUMBER** is incremented each time the report is saved. If you are modifying a report that you did not create, the information on this tab may be helpful. The **TOTAL EDITING TIME** field lets you know how long the report has been open and whether it has been edited.

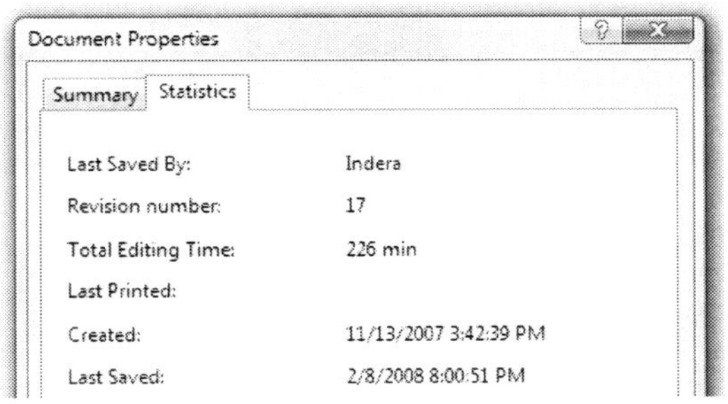

Figure 5-33 Statistics tab options

2. Close the Document Properties dialog box.

Add Summary Information To A Report

1. Add the **FILE AUTHOR** and **REPORT TITLE** Special Fields to the report header section of the L5.10 report. The report should look similar to the one shown in Figure 5-34. Save the changes and close the report.

Indera		L5.10 Region = CA		
Customer Name	Address1	Region	Country	Postal Code
Sporting Wheels Inc.	480 Grant Way	CA	USA	92150
Rowdy Rims Company	4861 Second Road	CA	USA	91341

Figure 5-34 L5.10 Region = CA report with summary information added

Crystal Reports Menu

When Crystal Reports is installed in the Visual Studio environment, one menu for Crystal Reports is installed. You have already read about and used many of the options on this menu. Table 5-5 explains all of the options on the menu shown in Figure 5-35.

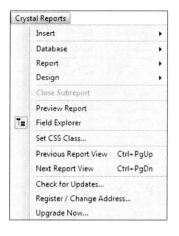

Figure 5-35 Crystal Reports menu

Menu Option	Description
Insert	Opens the submenu shown in Figure 5-36. Table 5-6 explains the Insert submenu options.
Database	Opens the submenu shown in Figure 5-37. Table 5-7 explains the Database submenu options.
Report	Opens the submenu shown in Figure 5-38. Table 5-8 explains the Report submenu options.
Design	Opens the submenu shown in Figure 5-39. Table 5-9 explains the Design submenu options.
Close Subreport	If you double-click on a subreport object in the main report, the subreport will open on it's own tab. This menu option is only available when viewing the subreport on it's own tab. Select this option to close the subreport tab.
Preview Report	Lets you view what the report will look like when printed.
Field Explorer	Opens and closes the Field Explorer window.
Set CSS Class	Lets you create HTML style sheets which are used for reports that will be displayed on the web.
Previous Report View	Toggles between the design and preview tabs.
Next Report View	Toggles between the design and preview tabs.
Check for Updates	Lets you check for updates for Crystal Reports.
Register/Change Address	Lets you register your copy of Crystal Reports with Business Objects. Doing this gives you additional resources, if you need help.
Upgrade Now	Goes to the Business Objects web site to see if there are any newer versions of Crystal Reports available for purchase.

Table 5-5 Crystal Reports menu options explained

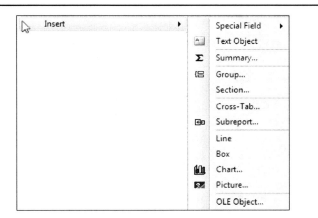

Figure 5-36 Insert submenu

Figure 5-37 Database submenu

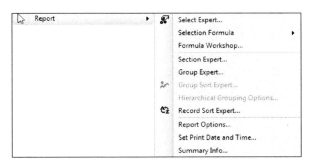

Figure 5-38 Report submenu

Figure 5-39 Design submenu

Menu Option	Description
Special Field	Add system fields to the report.
Text Object	Add a text object to the report.
Summary	Add a summary field to the report.
Group	Add a group to the report.
Section	Add a section to the report.
Subreport	Opens the Insert Subreport dialog box, which lets you create a subreport or select an existing report to use as a subreport.
Line	Lets you draw lines on the report. You can draw horizontal or vertical lines. Lines can also be drawn across sections of the report.
Box	Lets you draw a box on the report. Boxes can also be drawn across sections of the report.
Chart	Lets you create a chart using the Chart Expert.
Picture	Lets you add graphic files to a report. The supported file types are BMP, JPG, PNG, TIFF and WMF.
OLE Object	Lets you add an OLE object like a chart or sound file to the report.

Table 5-6 Insert submenu options explained

Menu Option	Description
Database Expert	Opens the Database Expert, which is used to add or delete data sources to or from the report.
Set Datasource Location	Lets you select a different database for the report or a different location for the database that the report is currently using. This option is useful when you are using a copy of the database to create and test the report(s) and are now ready to move the report(s) into production (go live). For example, this feature will let you change the database to point to the one on a production server.
Log On or Off Server	Lets you log on or off of an SQL or ODBC server, set database options and maintain the Favorites folder. Most of the tasks that you can complete on the Data Explorer window can be done another way.
Verify Database	Lets you compare the structure of the data source that is used in the report to the structure of the actual database.
Verify on Every Print	This option works almost the same as the Verify Database option. Either of these options can cause a processing delay and usually is not needed during development.
Show SQL Query	This option will let you view SQL queries if the report is using any. Parameter fields are included if they are used in the selection formula. Figure 5-40 shows the dialog box.

Table 5-7 Database submenu options explained

Each of the exercises that you have completed so far in this lesson created an SQL query, similar to the one shown in Figure 5-40.

Figure 5-40 Show SQL Query dialog box

Menu Option	Description
Select Expert	Opens the Select Expert which lets you create selection criteria to filter records.
Selection Formula	The **RECORD** option opens the Record Selection Formula Editor, which lets you edit the record selection formula. The **GROUP** option opens the Group Selection Formula Editor, which lets you edit the group selection formula.
Formula Workshop	Opens the Formula Workshop, which allows you to create, edit and view formulas and functions.
Section Expert	Opens the Section Expert which lets you format any section of the report. [See Lesson 10, The Section Expert]
Group Expert	Opens the Group Expert which is used to create, modify and delete groups.
Group Sort Expert	Lets you sort the groups in the report by group summary fields.
Hierarchical Grouping Options	Lets you create a hierarchical report. [See Lesson 13, Hierarchical Group Reports]
Record Sort Expert	Opens the Record Sort Expert which lets you select the order that the detail records will be sorted in. [See Lesson 6, Sorting Records]
Report Options	Opens the Report Options dialog box, which lets you override or set how data is retrieved for the report. [See Lesson 8, Report Options]
Set Print Date and Time	Lets you override the values that would print if the Print Date or Print Time special fields are on the report. [See Lesson 8, Using The Set Print Date And Time Options]
Summary Info	Opens the Document Properties dialog box shown earlier in Figure 5-33.

Table 5-8 Report submenu options explained

Menu Option	Description
Printer Setup	Opens the Print Setup dialog box which lets you change the orientation and paper size options.
Page Setup	Opens the Page Setup dialog box so that you can change the report margins.
Default Settings	Opens the Options dialog box that you will learn about in the next section.
Ruler	Displays or hides the rulers in the design window.
Grid	Displays or hides the grid in the design window. The grid is used to make it easier to line up objects.

Table 5-9 Design submenu options explained

Customizing Crystal Reports Design Environment

If you need to customize the design environment you can, by following the steps below. These options let you set the default settings for the majority of features that you will use to create and modify reports. Once you have used the software for a while and find yourself always having to change an option, you should come back to this section and review all of the options on the Options dialog box and change the ones that you use, to better meet your needs.

Modifying these options will save you time because they will automatically be applied as you are creating and editing reports. Some of the options that you may want to change would be the field formats and default fonts.

While looking at the options, pay particular attention to the options on the layout, database and reporting tabs. They contain the options that you are likely to need to change first, because they are the options that most effect the functionality in the design window.

The changes that you make on the Options dialog box effect all of the reports that you create or modify once the changes on this dialog box are saved. Any changes that are made will not be picked up by reports that were saved prior to the changes made on the Options dialog box. If you want to apply changes that you make on the Options dialog box to existing reports, delete the object from the report that the change will effect and then add the object back to the report.

1. Crystal Reports ⇒ Design ⇒ Default Settings. You will see the dialog box shown in Figure 5-41.

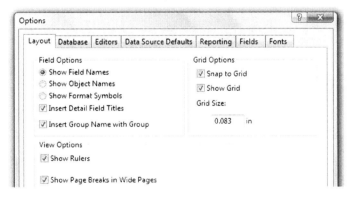

Figure 5-41 Layout tab options

The Layout options determine how reports are displayed on the design window.

The options in the Field Options section determine how fields are displayed in the design window.

The options in the Grid Options section determine how the grid will or will not be displayed in the design window.

If the **SHOW FORMAT SYMBOLS** option is checked, characters will be displayed in fields in the design window instead of the field name as shown in Figure 5-42.

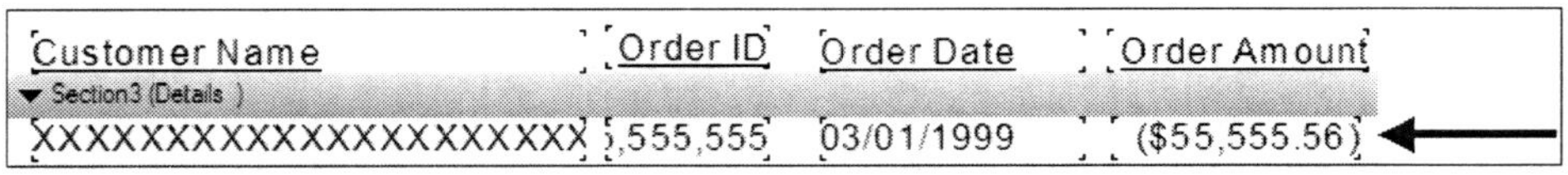

Customer Name	Order ID	Order Date	Order Amount
▼ Section3 (Details)			
XXXXXXXXXXXXXXXXXXXXX	),555,555	03/01/1999	($55,555.56) ←

Figure 5-42 Format symbols in the design window

2. Figures 5-43 to 5-48 show all of the other options that you can change. When you are finished viewing the options, close the dialog box.

The Database options determine how data appears and how queries are processed.

The options in the Tables and Fields section let you configure how tables and fields are displayed.

The options in the Data Explorer section determine how database objects are displayed in the Field Explorer.

The options in the Advanced Options section help resolve performance issues, like determine how queries will be run and when changes in the database structure will be checked. The first two options are only available for SQL tables, not queries.

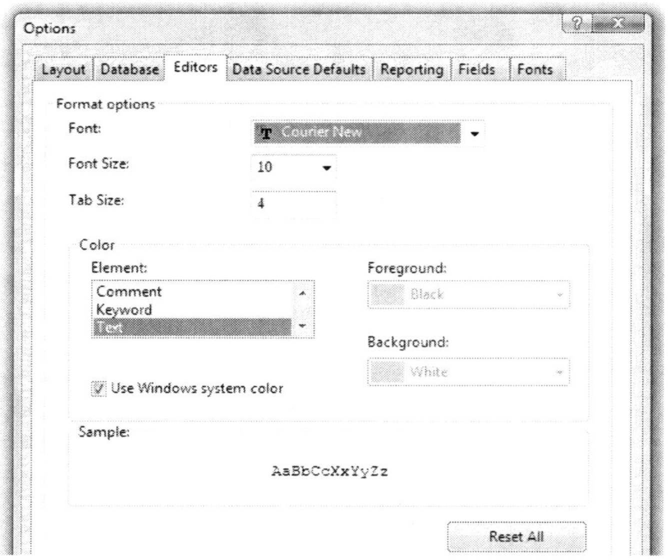

Figure 5-43 Database tab options

The Editors options let you customize the fonts and colors used in the Formula Editor. [See Lesson 9, Formula Editor]

Figure 5-44 Editors tab options

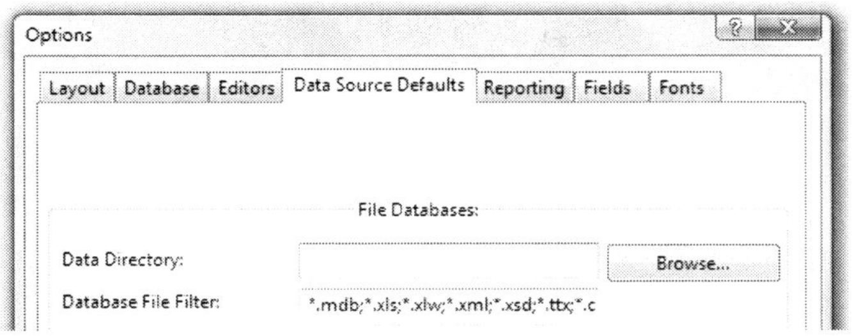

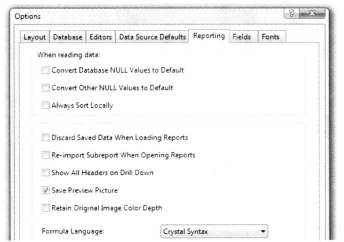

Figure 5-45 Data Source Defaults tab options

Lets you select the default folder for the database files. The folder that you select will be the folder that is displayed by default when the Open dialog box is opened.

Figure 5-46 Reporting tab options

The Reporting options determine how the data is stored and retrieved in the report. These settings can be changed on a report by report basis on the Report Options dialog box. [See Lesson 8, Report Options]

The options in the When reading data section determine how null values and sorting features will be handled.

The **FORMULA LANGUAGE** drop-down list will let you select the default syntax language for the formulas that you create. [See Lesson 9, Syntax]

The remaining options apply to a variety of report features.

Figure 5-47 Fields tab options

The Field format options let you select the default options for the field types that Crystal Reports supports. (6)

You may want to click on these buttons now to become familiar with the default options. One option that you may want to change after completing the exercises in this workbook is the default date format if you think that you will use the same date format for the majority of reports that you will create. You do not have to change anything to complete the exercises in this workbook.

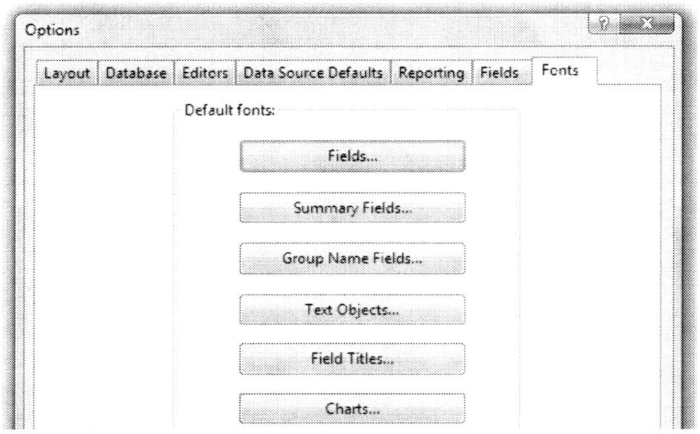

Figure 5-48 Fonts tab options

The Font options let you select the default font options for a variety of fields and objects that Crystal Reports supports. (6)

(6)   The options that you select will only be applied to objects that are added to a report after you make changes to this dialog box. The changes will not be applied to existing reports.

Customizing The Toolbars

In addition to being able to change the default values and options in Crystal Reports that you just read about you can also customize the toolbars. They are on the lower half of the Toolbars dialog box, that you read about in Lesson 1.

1. Tools ⇒ Customize.

The options shown in Figure 5-49 are the toolbars that you can add. You can also create your own toolbar by clicking the New button, then adding the buttons (commands) that you want to it. Most of the toolbars are for building applications. The options shown in Figure 5-50 are all of the options that you can add to a menu or toolbar. The options shown are for Crystal Reports.

Some of the buttons (commands) that I added to the Crystal Reports - Main toolbar are the Page N of M, Print Date, Preview Report and Text Object because I use them all the time. I found having the Preview Report tab at the bottom of the screen very awkward.

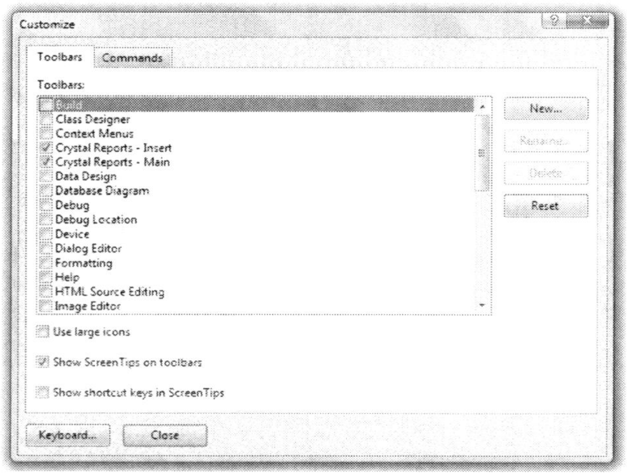

Figure 5-49 Toolbars tab

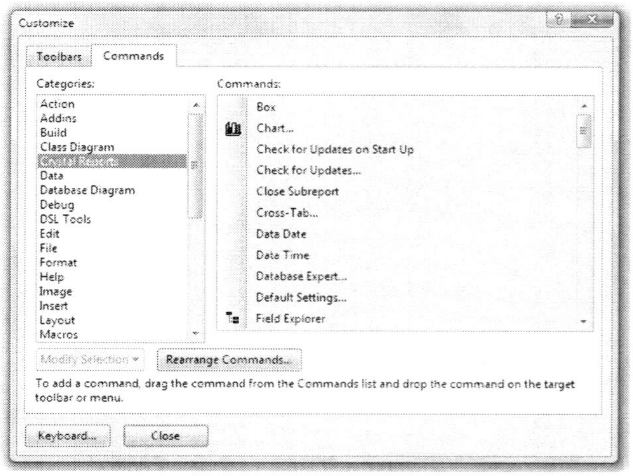

Figure 5-50 Commands tab

2. Make any changes that you want, then close the Customize dialog box.

Visual Studio Options

In Lesson 2 you viewed the File ⇒ Recent Files submenu. The default number of files displayed on the submenu is six. You can change the number of files that are displayed by following the steps below.

1. Tools ⇒ Options. Select the General option that is illustrated if necessary. You will see the dialog box shown in Figure 5-51.

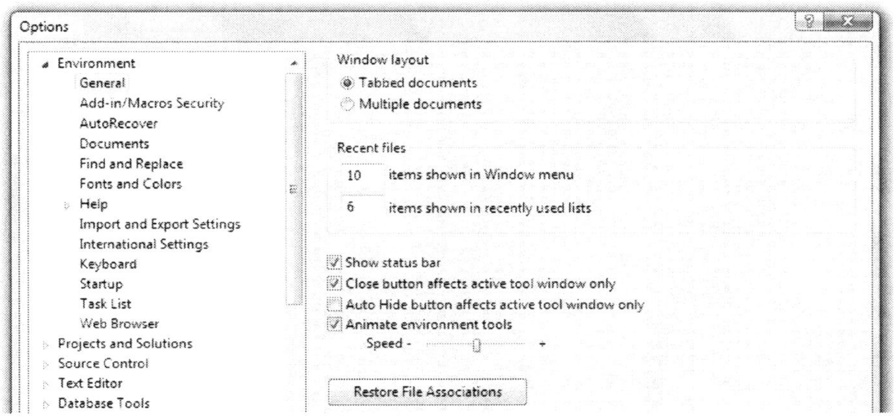

Figure 5-51 Options dialog box

2. Change the number in the **ITEMS SHOWN IN RECENTLY USED LISTS** option to the maximum number of files that you want to be able to select from. This option also applies to the File ⇒ Recent Projects submenu. Click OK.

Test Your Skills

You should refresh the data before previewing the reports that have selection criteria.

1. Save the L4.1 report as L5.11 Skills Product type filter.

    - Create a filter that only displays the gloves, saddles and kids product types.

    Your report should look like the one shown in Figure 5-52 and have 33 records.

Product ID	Product Name	Product Type Name	Supplier Name
401,001	Mini Nicros	Kids	Craze
401,002	Mini Nicros	Kids	Craze
402,001	Micro Nicros	Kids	Craze
402,002	Micro Nicros	Kids	Craze
1,101	Active Outdoors Crochet Glove	Gloves	Active Outdoors
1,102	Active Outdoors Crochet Glove	Gloves	Active Outdoors
1,103	Active Outdoors Crochet Glove	Gloves	Active Outdoors
1,104	Active Outdoors Crochet Glove	Gloves	Active Outdoors

Figure 5-52 L5.11 Skills Product type filter report

2. Save the L3.5 report as L5.12 Skills Ship Via filter.

    - Create a filter that displays all orders where the Ship Via field does not have **PICKUP** or **LOOMIS**.

    Your report should look like the one shown in Figure 5-53 and have 1,445 records.

Customer Name	Order ID	Order Date	Order Amount	Ship Via	First Name	Last Name
City Cyclists	1	12/2/2000 12:00:0(	$41.90	UPS	Nancy	Davolio
Warsaw Sports, Inc.	1,003	12/2/2000 12:00:0(	$186.87	UPS	Margaret	Peacock
Poser Cycles	1,006	12/3/2000 12:00:0(	$64.90	Purolator	Margaret	Peacock
Spokes	1,007	12/3/2000 12:00:0(	$49.50	Parcel Post	Anne	Dodsworth
Clean Air Transporta	1,008	12/3/2000 12:00:0(	$2,214.94	Purolator	Margaret	Peacock
Cyclopath	1,010	12/3/2000 12:00:0(	$14,872.30	UPS	Nancy	Davolio
BBS Pty	1,011	12/3/2000 12:00:0(	$29.00	Purolator	Margaret	Peacock
Pedals Inc.	1,013	12/3/2000 12:00:0(	$1,142.13	Parcel Post	Margaret	Peacock
Spokes 'N Wheels L`	1,014	12/4/2000 12:00:0(	$29.00	Purolator	Nancy	Davolio
Cycle City Rome	1,015	12/4/2000 12:00:0(	$43.50	UPS	Anne	Dodsworth
SAB Mountain	1,016	12/4/2000 12:00:0(	$563.70	FedEx	Janet	Leverling
Tyred Out	1,017	12/5/2000 12:00:0(	$72.00	Purolator	Margaret	Peacock
Spokes for Folks	1,019	12/5/2000 12:00:0(	$43.50	Parcel Post	Anne	Dodsworth
Extreme Cycling	1,020	12/5/2000 12:00:0(	$67.80	FedEx	Robert	King
Canal City Cycle	1,021	12/6/2000 12:00:0(	$5,237.55	Purolator	Robert	King
Belgium Bike Co.	1,022	12/7/2000 12:00:0(	$2,792.86	Parcel Post	Janet	Leverling
SAB Mountain	1,025	12/7/2000 12:00:0(	$8,819.55	Parcel Post	Nancy	Davolio

Figure 5-53 L5.12 Skills Ship Via filter report

3. Save the L4.2 report as L5.13 Skills Order filter.

    - Create a filter that displays order amounts that are >= $1,000 and were **SHIPPED** between 1/01/01 and 1/31/01 in the USA.
    - Delete the First and Last Name fields. Add the Region field after the Ship Via field.

    Your report should look like the one shown in Figure 5-54 and have 40 records.

Customer Orders Report

Customer Name	Order #	Order Date	Order Amount	Ship Via	Region
City Cyclists	1246	1/30/01	$3,884.25	Pickup	MI
Bike-A-Holics Anonymous	1097	12/27/00	$1,439.55	Loomis	OH
Sporting Wheels Inc.	1181	1/15/01	$5,912.96	UPS	CA
Sporting Wheels Inc.	1220	1/22/01	$5,879.70	UPS	CA
Rockshocks for Jocks	1161	1/11/01	$1,799.70	Parcel Post	TX
Rowdy Rims Company	1090	12/22/00	$1,529.70	Loomis	CA
Rowdy Rims Company	1186	1/15/01	$1,110.70	Purolator	CA
Clean Air Transportation Co.	1123	1/2/01	$5,219.55	Pickup	PA
Clean Air Transportation Co.	1228	1/25/01	$2,181.86	Loomis	PA
Hooked on Helmets	1122	1/1/01	$1,025.40	Loomis	MN
C-Gate Cycle Shoppe	1136	1/5/01	$3,209.53	Pickup	VA

Figure 5-54 L5.13 Skills Order filter report

4. Save the L3.5 report as `L5.14 Skills Employee report`.

   - Create a filter that displays orders that do not have an Order Date in 2001.
   - Do not display the time on the Order Date field.

   The last page of your report should look like the one shown in Figure 5-55 and have 629 records.

Customer Name	Order ID	Order Date	Order Amount	Ship Via	First Name	Last Name
Hikers and Bikers	3,192	12/12/2000	$959.70	UPS	Nancy	Davolio
Mountain View Sport	3,193	12/12/2000	$23.80	Parcel Post	Nancy	Davolio
			629			

Figure 5-55 L5.14 Skills Employee report

GROUPING, SORTING AND SUMMARIZING RECORDS

After completing the exercises in this lesson you will be able to use the following techniques to control which records appear on a report and how they are organized.

- ☑ Grouping records
- ☑ Sorting records
- ☑ Create summary subtotals and group totals
- ☑ Organize the records that will appear on the report
- ☑ Create percent calculations
- ☑ Create a custom group name
- ☑ User defined sort order
- ☑ User defined groups
- ☑ Use the Group Expert

LESSON 6

Grouping And Sorting Overview

Sorting rearranges the order that records will appear on the report without changing the layout or structure of the report. Grouping takes sorting one step further by displaying records that have the same value in a field or a value that is in a range of values together. Grouping changes the structure of the report by automatically creating another group header and group footer section for each group. If either of these group sections are not needed, you can suppress them. You can also create formulas that determine if or when the section is displayed or hidden. After all of the records in a group print, there are often totals or some type of summary information about the records in the group. You can sort records whether or not there are groups on the report.

Grouping Records

Grouping displays records together that meet specific criteria. Consider the following two examples:

① In the L5.2 Region = OH or FL report, at a glance, it is hard to tell how many records are in the OH region versus how many are in the FL region. If the report was modified to print all of the records in the same region together, it would be easier to see how many records are in each region. This is known as grouping records.

② In the L5.6 US orders not shipped in April 2002 report, you cannot tell how many orders were not shipped on any particular day. If the records were grouped by ship date, you would be able to create a count summary field to show how many orders were not shipped by day. You could also have a total by day of the total dollar amount, based on the order amount field, of orders that were not shipped.

There are three main tasks that need to be completed when records in a report need to be grouped. The three tasks are listed below and are discussed in detail in this lesson.

① Select the fields to group on. [See Lesson 2, Report Design Process Step 4]
② Decide if the detail records in each group need to be sorted.
[See Lesson 2, Report Design Process Step 4]
③ Decide if any fields in the details section of the report need summary information.
[See Lesson 2, Report Design Process Step 2]

You learned about the group header and footer sections in Lesson 2. The name of the group is usually placed in the group header section. The summary information, which is not a requirement, is usually placed in the group footer section.

Being able to add this type of functionality to reports will make them much more useful in many cases, then the reports that were created in Lesson 5. Reports that have groups can also use the drill-down feature. In addition to creating the groups, Crystal Reports also provides summary functions including statistical, averaging and totals that you can add to a report.

Records are placed together because they have the same value in a field (or fields). This is how the group header and footer sections are automatically re-created each time the value in a field the report is grouped on changes. You will not see this in the design window. The process of creating another group each time the value changes is dynamic processing that happens behind the scenes, as they say. This is how you can create totals for a group. If you are shaking your head, after you complete the first exercise in this lesson, this should make more sense.

Grouping Tips

Below are some tips that I follow to help determine if a report needs a group and if so, which field(s) to group on.

① Reports that retrieve hundreds or thousands of records probably would be easier to read, if nothing else, if there were one or two groups.
② If you need to provide a count or subtotal for a field.

③ If the report needs statistical information.

Insert Group Dialog Box

The options on the **COMMON** tab are used to create the groups. At a minimum, the field to group on (the first drop-down list shown in Figure 6-1) and the sorting order of the group (the second drop-down list shown in Figure 6-1) have to be selected. Date and Boolean fields have an additional option that can be set. The **OPTIONS** tab will be discussed later. There are three ways to open the **INSERT GROUP** dialog box, as discussed below.

① Click the **INSERT GROUP** button on the Crystal Reports - Insert toolbar.
② Right-click on a blank space on the report and select Insert ⇒ Group.
③ Crystal Reports ⇒ Insert ⇒ Group.

The **GROUP BY** field is the first drop-down list on the Common tab. It contains all of the fields that the report can be grouped by. This list contains the fields that are on the report and the fields in tables that are connected to the report. You can also use formula fields as the field to group on.

The **GROUP SORT ORDER** field is the second drop-down list on the Common tab. The sort order determines the order that the groups will appear on the report. Table 6-1 explains the group sorting options.

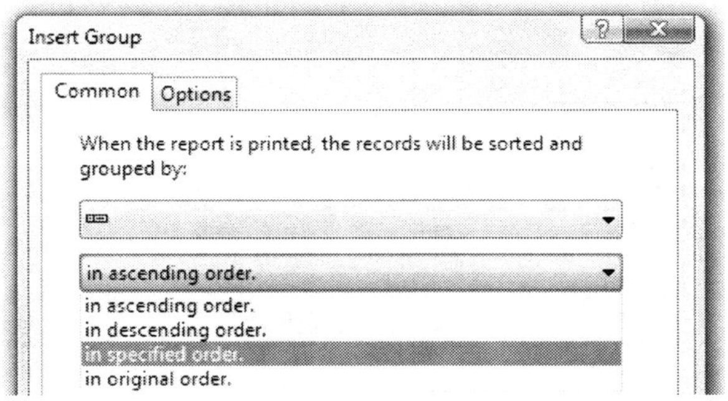

Figure 6-1 Insert Group dialog box

> Memo fields will not appear in the group by drop-down list because they cannot be used as a field to group on.

Sorting Option	Description
In Ascending Order	Text fields will be sorted in A-Z order. Numeric fields will be sorted in low to high order. Date group fields will be sorted in oldest to most recent date order.
In Descending Order	Text fields will be sorted in Z-A order. Numeric fields will be sorted in high to low order. Date group fields will be sorted in most recent to oldest date order.
In Specified Order	This option allows you to select the order of the groups. This is known as **CUSTOM GROUPING** and is discussed below. An example of a custom group would be to rank customers by the amount of sales they placed last year. The option causes two tabs (Specific Order and Other) to appear on the dialog box.
In Original Order	This option will leave the data in the order that it is retrieved from in the database. It may be me, but I don't find this option very useful.

Table 6-1 Group sorting options explained

> Once a field is selected to be grouped on, it will appear under the text, **THE SECTION WILL BE PRINTED ON ANY CHANGE OF** at the bottom of the Insert Group dialog box.

The **DATE/TIME** option is only available when a date, time or date/time field is selected in the Group By drop-down list. Figure 6-2 shows the options for date/time fields.

The **BOOLEAN** group sort order option is only available when a Boolean field (ex. true/false or yes/no field) is selected in the group by drop-down list. The Boolean sort process does not work like the other sort options. Boolean fields sort false before true, when the ascending sort order option is selected. The groups are created when there are changes from yes to no, or from true to false in the report data. The exception to this is the **ON ANY CHANGE** option. Figure 6-3 shows the group sorting options for Boolean fields. Table 6-2 explains the Boolean field group sorting options.

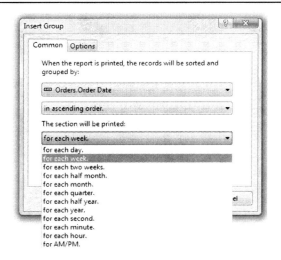

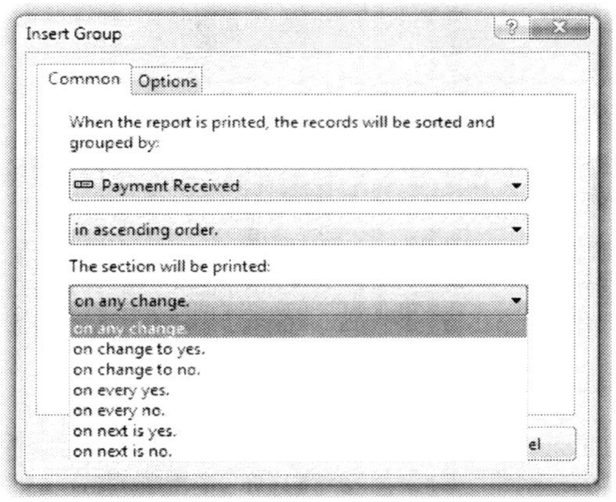

Figure 6-3 Boolean field group sorting options

Figure 6-2 Date/Time field group sorting options

> In addition to using the Insert Group dialog box to create and edit groups, you can also use the Group Expert to create and edit groups.

Option	Description
On any change	This is the default option and will sort the values and place them next to each other.
On change to yes	Creates a new group each time a **True** value comes after a False value. (1)
On change to no	Creates a new group each time a **False** value comes after a True value. (1)
On every yes	This option creates a group that always ends with a True value and includes any records in the middle that have a False value, back to the previous True value. (1)
On every no	This option creates a group that always ends with a False value and includes any records in the middle that have a True value, back to the previous False value. (1)
On next is yes	This option creates groups that always start with a True value and includes all records in the middle that have a False value until the next record with a True value is found. (1)
On next is no	This option creates groups that always start with a False value and includes all records in the middle that have a True value until the next record with a False value is found. (1)

Table 6-2 Boolean field group sorting options explained

(1) The records are not sorted if this option is selected.

Custom Grouping

If the ascending and descending sort options are not sufficient, you can create custom groups by selecting the **IN SPECIFIED ORDER** option in the second drop-down list shown earlier in Figure 6-1. There are two custom group options available on the Insert Group dialog box: User defined sort order and User defined groups.

User Defined Sort Order

When you select this option, a tab called **SPECIFIED ORDER** will appear on the Insert Group dialog box as shown in Figure 6-4. The options on this tab let you create the list of how the values in the groups will be sorted.

The **NAMED GROUP** drop-down list contains all of the values for the group field. Select the values that you want the groups to appear in on the report, as shown at the bottom of Figure 6-5.

You can change the order of the values by clicking on the value that you want to move, then click the Up or Down arrow to the right of the list.

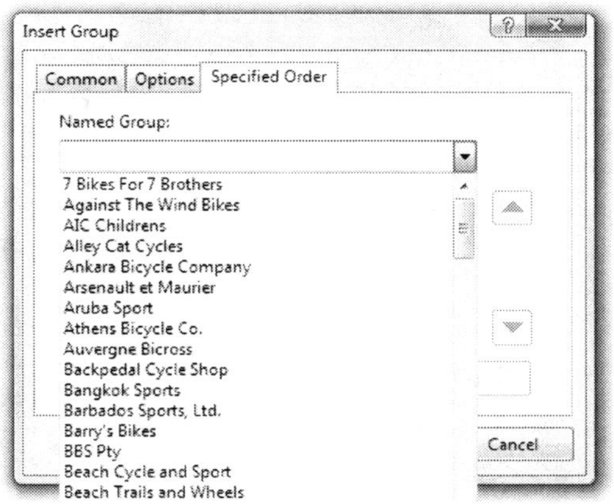

Figure 6-4 Specified Order tab

In addition to being able to select individual values in a field that will be used as a group, you can also create your own groups. To do this, click the New button on the Specified Order tab to create a named group. Named groups let you specify a range that a value has to be in to be added to the group. For example, if you want to group order records by the week that they were shipped, you would create named groups in seven day intervals. The operators that are available to create the selection criteria for the group range are a subset of the select operators that you saw in Lesson 5, Table 5-1.

Once you add one value to the Named Group list, the **OTHERS** tab shown in Figure 6-6 will open. The options on this tab allow you to determine what you want to happen to the group values that are not added to the Named Group list on the Specified Order tab. Table 6-3 explains the options on the Others tab.

 You do not have to order all of the group values. You can select just the ones that you need.

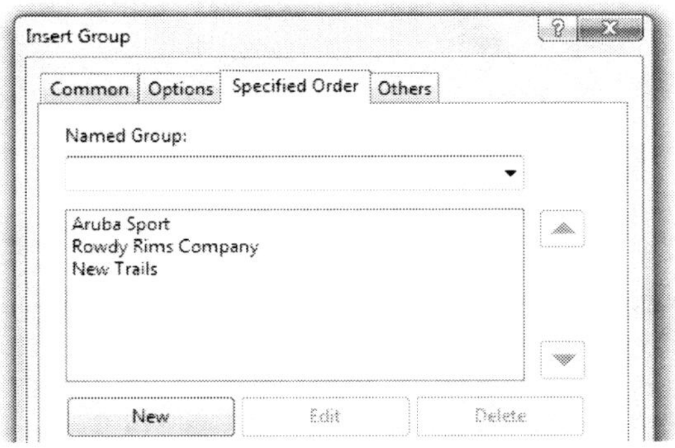

Figure 6-5 Values placed in order

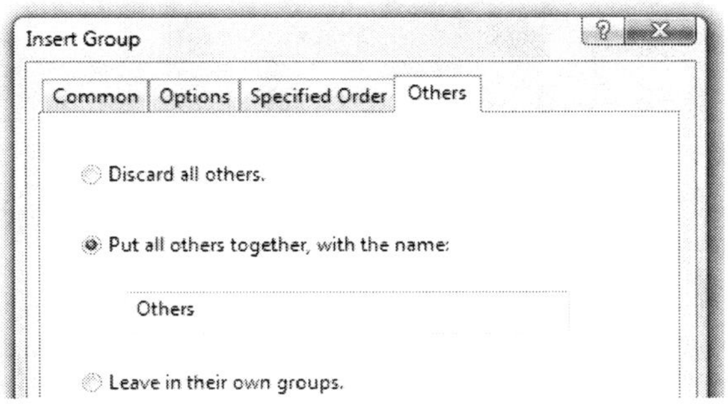

Figure 6-6 Others tab options

Option	Description
Discard all others	Selecting this option causes the group values (and their detail records) that are not selected on the Specified Order tab to not be displayed on the report.
Put all others together, with the name	Selecting this option allows you to put all of the group values that are not selected on the Specified Order tab together under one group name that you type in the text box.
Leave in their own groups	Selecting this option will print all of the group values that you selected on the Specified Order tab first on the report. The remaining group values will be printed after, in ascending order.

Table 6-3 Others tab options explained

Sorting Records

Sorting records is the second task that has to be completed. Like grouping, sorting allows you to rearrange the order that records appear on the report. Data can be sorted by any database field, formula or SQL Expression. Data cannot be sorted by a memo field. The data can be sorted on more than one field including fields that are not on the report. There are two types of sorting, as discussed below.

① You can sort the report as it is. The L5.1 report could be sorted by customer name. Another way to sort this report would be by postal code.

② You can sort the records within a group. After the groups for a report have been determined, you may decide that the report would be more meaningful if the detail records in the group were sorted. If you do not specify a sort order, the records in each group will print in the order that they are retrieved from the table.

The **RECORD SORT EXPERT** dialog box shown in Figure 6-7 lets you select the options to sort the records in the details section of the report.

The Record Sort Expert will show group fields in the Sort Field list. This is done to show that the detail records will be sorted within the group. Group field sorting is done before detail record sorting.

Figure 6-7 Record Sort Expert dialog box

This expert does not sort groups. You can sort in ascending or descending order on each field. There are three ways to open the dialog box as discussed below.

① Click the **RECORD SORT EXPERT** button on the Crystal Reports - Main toolbar.
② Crystal Reports ⇒ Report ⇒ Record Sort Expert.
③ Right-click on a blank space on the report, then select Report ⇒ Record Sort Expert.

> In addition to clicking on a field in the Available Fields list and clicking the arrow button to add it to the Sort Fields list, you can also drag fields to the Sort Fields list.

What I found interesting is that if you click on a group field in the Sort Fields list, all of the buttons become disabled on the dialog box. I suspect that this is because Crystal Reports is trying to protect you from changing the group order. Don't worry. If you need to change the order of the groups, you can change them on the design window by dragging them or you can use the Group Expert.

> The order that fields are added to the **SORT FIELDS** list of the Record Sort Expert is the order that the records will be sorted in. If you discover that the fields are in the wrong order in the Sort Fields list, click on the field that is not in the correct place, then click the Up or Down arrow buttons that are across from the words "Sort Fields", to move the field to the correct location.

Summary Information

This is the third task that has to be completed when groups are created. One reason that groups are created is to make the report easier to read. Another reason groups are created is to provide summary information for fields in the details section of the report.

These summary calculated fields are usually placed in the group footer section of the report. As you learned in Lesson 2, formulas, in this case summary fields can also be placed in the group header section. Students have asked me how it is possible that summary fields that are in the group header section contain accurate totals. The answer is somewhat beyond the scope of this workbook, but I will answer the question because it may help you understand and allow you to use summary fields in the group header section with confidence, when needed.

Crystal Reports actually builds (processes) the entire report before it is printed. This means that values for summary fields, regardless of where they are placed on the report, are calculated before the report prints.

The two types of calculations that you can perform on text (string) data is counting records in a group and determining the frequency of records in the group. These summary calculations are often also placed in the report footer section to create what is known as a grand total or report total. Summary fields have some similarities of **RUNNING TOTAL** fields, which you will learn about in Lesson 13. Summary fields that are in the report header or footer section are not dependant on groups. You can create summary calculation fields in the report header and footer if the report does not have any groups. Summary fields in the report header and footer contain totals for all records on the report.

Instead of having to manually count the number of orders that are printed on a report for each customer, a calculated field can be added to the report that would count the number of orders and display the number on the report. Each summary field has to be created separately.

 To create a group summary field, the report must have at least one group. If you select the option to create a summary field and the report does not have a group, you will be prompted to create a group. If you place the same summary field in different sections of the report it will produce different total amounts, which is what should happen.

There are three ways to open the Insert Summary dialog box shown in Figure 6-8 **AFTER** you have selected the field that you need to create a summary field for, as discussed below. If the field that you need to create a summary calculation for is not on the report, you have to select option two or three below.

① Right-click on a field or blank space on the report and select Insert ⇒ Insert Summary.
② Click the **SUMMARY** button on the Crystal Reports - Insert toolbar.
③ Crystal Reports ⇒ Insert ⇒ Summary.

Figure 6-8 Insert Summary dialog box

There are two categories of summary calculations that you can create, as discussed below.

① The **Text** field summary calculation options are explained in Table 6-4. Text fields can only create the calculations in Table 6-4.
② The **Numeric** field summary calculation options are explained in Table 6-5. They can also be used with currency fields. Numeric fields can also create the calculations in Table 6-4.

Text Summary Calculation Options	
Calculation	**Description**
Count	Counts the detail records. By default, if the field that is being used to count on is **NULL**, it will not be included in the count. Select the **CONVERT DATABASE TO NULL VALUES TO DEFAULT** option on the Report Options dialog box.
Distinct Count	Counts all of the unique values in the field.
Maximum	Finds the highest value in the field.
Minimum	Finds the lowest value in the field.
Mode	Finds the most frequently used value in the field.
N^{th} Largest, N is:	Lets you select a number (the N is a value) and calculate the Nth largest value in the selected field. An example would be if you wanted to find out what the third largest (N^{th} largest) order amount (N) is in the group.
N^{th} Most Frequent, N is:	Lets you select a number (the N is a value) and calculate the Nth most frequently occurring value in the selected field. An example would be if you wanted to find out which product was ordered the most in the group, you would enter a 1 in this field. This is similar to the Mode function, but it is not limited to the frequent occurrences.
N^{th} Smallest, N is:	Lets you select a number (the N is a value) and calculate the Nth smallest occurring value in the selected field. An example would be if you wanted to find out what the fifth (N^{th} smallest) smallest order amount (N) is in the group. You would enter a 5 in this field.

Table 6-4 Text summary calculation options explained

Numeric Summary Calculation Options	
Calculation	**Description**
Average	Finds the average value of all of the values in the field.
Correlation With	Finds the relationship between the selected field and another field in the database or on the report.
Covariance With	Finds the difference (often called the variance) between the selected field and another field in the database or on the report.
Median	Finds the middle value of all the values in the field.
Mode	Finds the most frequently used value in the field.
P^{th} percentile, P is:	Lets you select a percent (the P is value) between 0 and 100 and calculates that percentile of the values in the field.
Population Standard Deviation	Calculates how far from the mean (the average) each value in the selected field deviates.
Population Variance	Divides the sum of the number of items in the population. The result is the population variance.
Sample Standard Deviation	Calculates the mean (the average) value for the items in the sample.
Sample Variance	Calculates the square of the standard deviation of the sample.
Sum	Adds the values in the selected field to get a total.
Weighted Average With	Calculates the average, by the number of times the value is in the selected field.

Table 6-5 Numeric summary calculation options explained

Date and Boolean fields can only be used in the following types of calculations: count, distinct count, maximum, minimum, mode, N^{th} largest, N^{th} most frequent and N^{th} smallest.

In addition to the summary options that you learned about in Tables 6-4 and 6-5 above, the summary options in Table 6-6 are also available. They are located at the bottom of the Insert Summary dialog box.

Option	Description
Summary Location	This option allows you to select the section of the report where you want to place the summary field. If you open the drop-down list you will see the options that are available. The good thing is that you are not limited to the options in the drop-down list. You can manually copy or move the summary field to another section of the report in the design window.
Show as a percentage of	This option will calculate a comparison of the percent of one group that is part of a larger group. If selected, this option lets you select the group or total that you want the comparison to be based on. For example, this option can calculate the percent of sales for June compared to the sales for the entire year. The result that would display will tell you (out of 100%) what percent the sales in June accounted for, compared to the sales for the entire year. This option is not available for all types of calculations. (2)
Summarize across hierarchy	On reports that have hierarchical groups (groups that have parent/child relationships), an identical summary field will be added to all subgroups under the primary hierarchical group. An example of a report that could have hierarchical groups would be one that displays a list of department managers (the parent group) and the employees (the child group) that are in each department.

Table 6-6 Summary options explained

(2) Percentage summaries cannot be placed in the report footer section.

Headings are not automatically created for group summary fields like they are for fields in the details section. By default, summary fields are usually placed in a section below the field that it is summarizing. The exception would be if the summary field is placed in the group header section.

Many of the exercises in this lesson will have you create a title for the report or a title for a field. When you see the phrase "Create a title", that means to add a text object to the report and type in the specified text. Report titles should be placed in the page header section unless stated otherwise. They should also be centered across the report.

If all of the summary calculation options seem a little confusing right now don't worry, you will only see options in the drop-down list that are available for the field type that you select to create the calculation for.

Summary Field Limitations

While summary fields allow you to create a variety of totals, counts and averages, there are some things that you should be aware of as discussed below.

① Summary fields cannot be placed in the details section.
② Summary field calculations include suppressed records.

Creating Groups

The first five reports that you modify in this lesson will show you how to apply a variety of group and sorting options effectively. The name of each exercise describes how the data will be grouped. You will also learn more formatting techniques. As you will see, the more data that you add to a report, the more the report needs to be formatted.

Exercise 6.1: Group Customer Information By Region

In this exercise you will modify a report to include the following group and sorting options. These options also allow you to create totals for the group.

① Group the data by the region field and sort the group in ascending order.
② Sort the detail records in each group in ascending order by the Postal Code field.

③ Create a count of detail records in each group.

1. Save the L4.13 report as `L6.1 Customer info by region`.

2. Open the Insert Group dialog box. Open the first drop-down list and select the **REGION** field from the Customer table, then click OK.

Notice that a **GROUP HEADER** and **GROUP FOOTER** section have been added to the report, as illustrated in Figure 6-9. If you also wanted to group this report on a second field, you would see a second set of group header and footer sections, as shown in Figure 6-10.

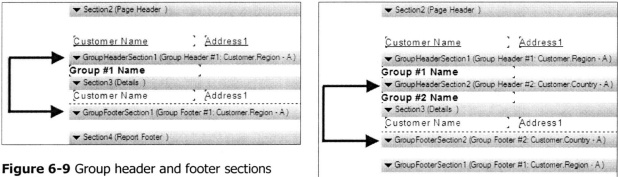

Figure 6-9 Group header and footer sections added to the report

Figure 6-10 Two sets of group header and footer sections

3. Save the changes. The report should look like the one shown in Figure 6-11.

	Customer Name	Address1	Region	Country	Postal Code
Abu Dhabi					
AL	**Abu Dhabi**				
Alsace	UAE Cycle	Post Box: 278	Abu Dhabi	United Arab Em	3453
Ankara					
Aquitaine	**AL**				
AR	The Great Bike Shop	1922 Beach Crescent	AL	USA	35857
Auckland					
Auvergne	Benny - The Spokes	1020 Oak Way	AL	USA	35861
Avon	Person				
AZ	Psycho-Cycle	8287 Scott Road	AL	USA	35818
Bangkok					
Basse Normandie					
Bayern	**Alsace**				
BC	Sports Alsace	11, rue Clemenceau	Alsace	France	67100
Belo Horizonte					
Berkshire	Mulhouse Vélos	4 avenue de la Liberation	Alsace	France	68100
Berlin					
Bourgogne					
Bridgetown	**Ankara**				
Brussels	Ankara Bicycle Company	PO Box 2121	Ankara	Turkey	443665
Bucharesti					
Budapest					
CA					
Cairo					
Cambridgeshire					

Figure 6-11 Customer information grouped by region

Notice that the group name is bold on the report. This makes it easier to know where each group starts. If you look in the group tree section on the left of Figure 6-11 above, you will see all of the groups that the report has. If you scroll down the list of groups and click on the **PA** group, that section of the report will be displayed, as shown in Figure 6-12.

> By default, group name fields are added to the group header section of the report. If at some point you decide that you do not want the group name to automatically be added to the group header section, you can turn the **INSERT GROUP NAME WITH GROUP** option off on the Layout tab on the Options dialog box. If you turn this option off and then need to add a group name to a specific report, you can, without turning this option back on.

9 / 9+				
OR				
Rad Bikes	8217 Prince Edward Place	OR	USA	97068
Whistler Rentals	4501 Third Street	OR	USA	97051
PA				
Insane Cycle	5198 Argus Place	PA	USA	19442
Backpedal Cycle Shop	743 Three Rivers Way	PA	USA	19178
Clean Air Transportation Co.	1867 Thurlow Lane	PA	USA	19453
Tek Bikes	8018 Meacon Crescent	PA	USA	19144
Rocky Roadsters	1430 Hastings Boulevard	PA	USA	19440

Figure 6-12 Customers in the PA region

Sort The Detail Records

As you can see in Figure 6-11 shown earlier, the detail records in each group are not sorted on any field. Unless you specify a sort order, the detail records will appear in the report based on the order they are retrieved from the database. In this part of the exercise you will sort the detail records by the Postal Code field.

1. Open the Record Sort Expert dialog box and click on the Postal Code field in the **AVAILABLE FIELDS** list, then click the **>** button. Select the **ASCENDING** sort order, if it is not already selected. Figure 6-13 shows the sort options that you should have selected. Click OK.

Notice that the group information for the report is the first entry in the **SORT FIELDS** section of the Record Sort Expert dialog box shown in Figure 6-13. This is done to outline the sort order for the entire report. The first way that the report will be sorted is by group. Remember that the group is sorted in ascending order, which is denoted by the **A** at the end of the group field. If the field was sorted in descending order, you would see a **D** at the end of the field.

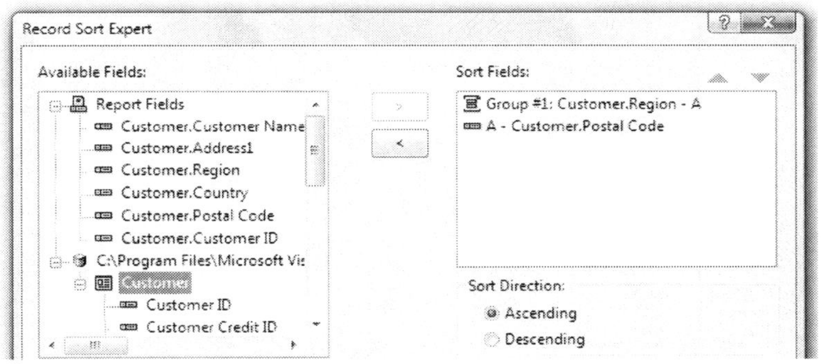

Figure 6-13 Report sort options

> If you need to sort a report by a persons name and the name is in two fields, you should sort on the last name field first, then sort on the first name field.

The detail records in each group will be sorted in ascending order by the Postal Code field. If you wanted to sort on other fields in the group you can do that also, as shown in Figure 6-14. In this example, adding the Country field means that within each group, the detail records would be sorted by Postal Code first and then within each Postal Code in the group, the records would be sorted by Country. In reality, these sort options would produce strange results. It is shown here for illustration purposes only.

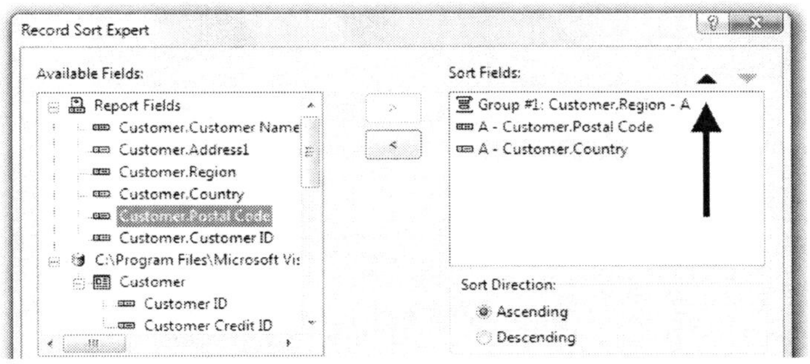

Figure 6-14 Second field in group to be sorted on

A better way to sort on these two fields would be to sort on the Country field first in each group, because there are several Postal Codes within each Country. If you wanted to sort on the Country field first instead of the Postal Code field, you would click on the Country field, then click the **UP** arrow. This would move the Country field up, as shown in Figure 6-15.

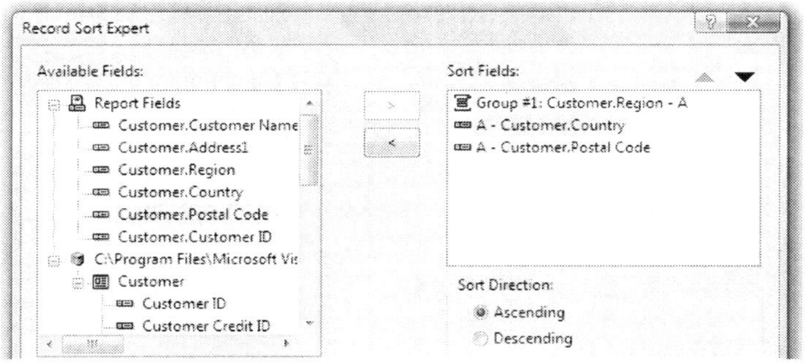

Figure 6-15 Sort order of the detail records changed

When you make changes to groups or sorting options, you should refresh the data by clicking the **REFRESH** button on the report navigation toolbar because you may not have all of the data based on the modified sorting and grouping options that have been selected.

2. Save the changes and preview the report. Go to the PA group. You should see the records shown in Figure 6-16. Notice the different order of the detail records in this version of the report, compared to the order of the detail records in the report shown earlier in Figure 6-12. Leave the report open to complete the next part of the exercise.

PA					
Tek Bikes	8018 Meacon Crescent	PA	USA		19144
Backpedal Cycle Shop	743 Three Rivers Way	PA	USA		19178
Rocky Roadsters	1430 Hastings Boulevard	PA	USA		19440
Insane Cycle	5198 Argus Place	PA	USA		19442
Clean Air Transportation Co.	1867 Thurlow Lane	PA	USA		19453

Figure 6-16 Report with detail record sort order added

Count Summary Field Overview

As you learned earlier in this lesson, creating summary fields is the third step in the grouping and sorting process. In this part of the exercise you will create a summary field that will count the number of detail records in each group.

Create The Count Summary Field

1. On the Insert Summary dialog box open the first drop-down list and select the Customer ID field.

2. Open the second drop-down list and select **COUNT**. You should see all of the options that were discussed earlier in Tables 6-4 and 6-5 for Customer ID field because it is a numeric field.

Notice that you can create a group from this dialog box. If you click the **INSERT GROUP** button, you will see the Insert Group dialog box that you saw earlier in Figure 6-1.

3. Open the **SUMMARY LOCATION** drop-down list and select the Group 1 option. Figure 6-17 shows the summary options that you should have selected.

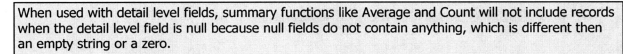

Figure 6-17 Summary options

4. Click OK. The summary field should be in the group footer section. Save the changes. The report should look like the one shown in Figure 6-18. The number in bold below the dotted lines is the count field that you just created.

Customer Name	Address1	Region	Country	Postal Code
Abu Dhabi				
UAE Cycle	Post Box: 278	Abu Dhabi	United Arab Em	3453
1				
AL				
Psycho-Cycle	8287 Scott Road	AL	USA	35818
The Great Bike Shop	1922 Beach Crescent	AL	USA	35857
Benny - The Spokes Person	1020 Oak Way	AL	USA	35861
3				
Alsace				
Sports Alsace	11, rue Clemenceau	Alsace	France	67100
Mulhouse Vélos	4 avenue de la Liberation	Alsace	France	68100
2				

Figure 6-18 Report with the summary field added

When used with detail level fields, summary functions like Average and Count will not include records when the detail level field is null because null fields do not contain anything, which is different then an empty string or a zero.

For example, if you were creating a summary field that counts on the city field and some records did not have any data in the city field and the database was set to use **NULL VALUES**, records that fall into this category would print on the report, but would not be included in the count summary calculation.

Often, this may not be what you want to happen. If this is the case, checking the **CONVERT DATABASE NULL VALUES TO DEFAULT** option on the Report Options dialog box will automatically convert the null values in the database to an empty string for string fields or zero for numeric fields. Selecting this option will include records in the count or average summary calculation. If you want this to be the default option for all reports, check the same option on the Reporting tab on the Options dialog box.

If you need to change the options for a summary field on the report, right-click on the summary field and select Change Summary Operation. This will open the Edit Summary dialog box shown in Figure 6-19, which looks like the Insert Summary dialog box shown earlier in Figure 6-17.

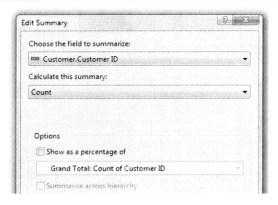

Figure 6-19 Edit Summary dialog box

Modify The Report

The report would look better if the following changes were made.

    ① Add a report title, print date and page number.
    ② Change the Postal Code heading to Zip Code.
    ③ Change the Address1 heading to Address.
    ④ Delete the Region field from the details section of the report. The field is not needed in this section because it is the field that the report is grouped on.
    ⑤ Create a title for the summary field that you created.
    ⑥ Create a grand total for the number of customers that are displayed on the report. Place this field in the report footer section.
    ⑦ Rearrange the fields in the details section so that the report is easier to read.

Add A Report Title, Print Date And Page Number

1. Make the page header section of the report longer, so that you will have room to add the report titles. Move all of the headings in the page header section down.

2. Create a report title and type `Customer Information Grouped By Region` in the object. Make the font size 16 and make the title bold.

3. Create a second report title and type `Sorted By Zip Code` in the object. Change the font size to 14 and make the title bold.

4. Center both of these titles across the page.

5. Add the Print Date special field to the page header section below the second report title on the left, then add the Page N of M special field across from the Print Date field on the right. Right align the Page Number field.

Change The Field Headings And Delete Fields

1. Change the Address1 field heading to `Address`, then change the Postal Code field heading to `Zip Code`.

2. Delete the Region field.

3. Move the Address field and heading over to the right and make the Customer Name field wider.

Create A Title For The Summary Field

1. Create a title for the summary field in the group footer section and type
   `Total # of customers in region` – in the object. Right align the title.

2. Move the summary field over and place the field title that you just created before it, then remove the bold from the summary field and left align the field.

3. Make the group footer section a little longer so that there will be more blank space on the report before the next group prints.

Create A Grand Total Summary Field

Grand totals are also known as **RUNNING TOTALS** because they keep a total for all of the detail records that are included on the report. Earlier in this lesson you learned how to create group summary totals, which are also known as "subtotals". The difference between a group summary total and a running total is that a running total field cannot be summarized.

Another difference between group summary total fields and running total fields is that group summary total fields are automatically reset to zero each time a new group is started, as shown earlier in Figure 6-18. Running Total fields have the option of being reset to zero.

Grand or running total fields that are placed in the report footer section include all of the records in the report, regardless of which group the detail records are in. Earlier in this lesson, I stated that depending on the section of the report that the summary field is placed in, you will get different results. The summary field that you will copy to the report footer section in this exercise will demonstrate this.

1. Right-click on the summary field in the group footer section and select **COPY**.

2. Right-click in the report and select **PASTE**, then click in the report footer section where you want to place the field.

3. Create a title for the summary field in the report footer section and type
   `Grand Total # of customers on this report` – in the object. Start this title at the two inch mark. Move the grand total field to the right of the title.

> You could create another summary field by using the Insert Summary dialog box, just like the one you created for the group footer section and place it in the report footer section. I find it easier to copy the field and place the second field in the section that I need it in.

Rearrange The Fields

1. Move the fields in the details section to the right so that the Customer Name field starts at the half inch mark.

2. Delete the dotted line in the details section. The report layout should look like the one shown in Figure 6-20. Save the changes.

   Page 1 of the report should look like the one shown in Figure 6-21. The last page of the report should look like the one shown in Figure 6-22. The total number of pages in the report depends on the spacing that you have in each section of the report. Adjust the spacing if necessary, so that it is readable.

▼ Section2 (Page Header)

Customer Information Grouped By Region
Sorted By Zip Code

Print Date   Page N of M

Customer Name   Address   Country   Zip Code
▼ GroupHeaderSection1 (Group Header #1: Customer.Region - A)
Group #1 Name
▼ Section3 (Details)
Customer Name   Address1   Country   Postal Cod
▼ GroupFooterSection1 (Group Footer #1: Customer.Region - A)
Total # of customers in region - Count of C

▼ Section4 (Report Footer)

Grand Total # of customers on this report - Count of C

Figure 6-20 L6.1 Report layout

Customer Information Grouped By Region
Sorted By Zip Code

11/16/2007   Page 1 of 18

Customer Name   Address   Country   Zip Code
Abu Dhabi
    UAE Cycle   Post Box: 278   United Arab Em 3453
Total # of customers in region - 1

AL
    Psycho-Cycle   8287 Scott Road   USA   35818
    The Great Bike Shop   1922 Beach Crescent   USA   35857
    Benny - The Spokes Person 1020 Oak Way   USA   35861
Total # of customers in region - 3

Figure 6-21 First page of the L6.1 Customer info by region report

---

Customer Information Grouped By Region
Sorted By Zip Code

11/16/2007   Page 18 of 18

Customer Name   Address   Country   Zip Code
Grand Total # of customers on this report - 269

Figure 6-22 Last page of the L6.1 Customer info by region report

3. If you open the Field Explorer and click on the plus sign in front of the **GROUP NAME FIELDS** option, you will see the Region group that you created, as illustrated in Figure 6-23. Close the report.

You can drag a group name field from the **GROUP NAME FIELDS** section of the Field Explorer on to the report. If you prefer to keep the data in the group header or footer section visible, but not display it on the report, you can suppress the section.

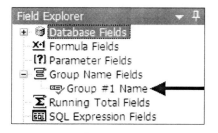

Figure 6-23 Group Name Fields section of the Field Explorer illustrated

Exercise 6.2: Group Orders By Customer

In this exercise you will modify a report to include the following group and sorting options.

① Group on the Customer Name field and sort the group in ascending order.
② Sort the detail records in each group in ascending order by Order Date.
③ Provide a count of detail records for each customer in each group.
④ Create a total amount per customer based on the order amount field. This will let the person reading the report know the total amount of the orders placed by each customer.

These options will create counts and totals for the group. The changes that you will make to the report will place all of the orders for each customer together. This will make the report more effective, because you will be able to see all of a customers orders in one place.

In Exercise 6.1 you created a group based on a field that was not being printed on the report. Groups are often created on fields that are printed on the report, but it is not a requirement.

1. Save the L5.4 report as `L6.2 Orders by customer.`

2. On the Insert Group dialog box open the first drop-down list and select the **CUSTOMER NAME** field, if it is not already selected, then click OK. The report should look like the one shown in Figure 6-24.

Customer Name	Order Date	Ship Date	Order Amount	Order ID	Unit Price
Alley Cat Cycles					
Alley Cat Cycles	2/19/2002 12:00:0(	2/22/2002 12:00:0(	$8,819.55	2,735	$2,939.85
Alley Cat Cycles	9/28/2001 12:00:0(	9/30/2001 12:00:0(	$2,559.63	2,157	$313.36
Alley Cat Cycles	1/31/2002 12:00:0(	2/3/2002 12:00:00/	$9,290.30	2,664	$2,792.86
Alley Cat Cycles	1/31/2002 12:00:0(	2/3/2002 12:00:00/	$9,290.30	2,664	$455.86
Alley Cat Cycles	9/28/2001 12:00:0(	9/30/2001 12:00:0(	$2,559.63	2,157	$539.85
Alley Cat Cycles	10/27/2001 12:00:(	11/6/2001 12:00:0(	$2,699.55	2,272	$899.85
Alley Cat Cycles	2/19/2002 12:00:0(	2/22/2002 12:00:0(	$8,819.55	2,735	$2,939.85
Backpedal Cycle Shop					
Backpedal Cycle Shc	12/18/2001 12:00:(	12/19/2001 12:00:(	$6,226.05	2,507	$329.85
Backpedal Cycle Shc	1/4/2002 12:00:00/	1/5/2002 12:00:00/	$9,612.47	2,560	$832.35
Backpedal Cycle Shc	1/4/2002 12:00:00/	1/5/2002 12:00:00/	$9,612.47	2,560	$2,792.86

Figure 6-24 Orders grouped by customer

Sort The Detail Records

As you can see in Figure 6-24 above, the report is now grouped by customer. The detail records in each group are not sorted. Because orders are entered into the database in the order that they are received, they are often already in date order. There are exceptions to this, including orders that may get changed some how during the ordering process.

Other exceptions that have to be accounted for include how the tables are linked and how the database sends the records to Crystal Reports. To be on the safe side, it is best to control the sort order. In this exercise that means that you should sort the records by the Order Date field to ensure that they are in date order, if that is what the requirement of the report calls for.

1. On the Record Sort Expert dialog box click on the Order Date field, then click the **>** button.

2. Select the ascending sort order, if it is not already selected. Figure 6-25 shows the sort options that should be selected. Click OK, then save the changes.

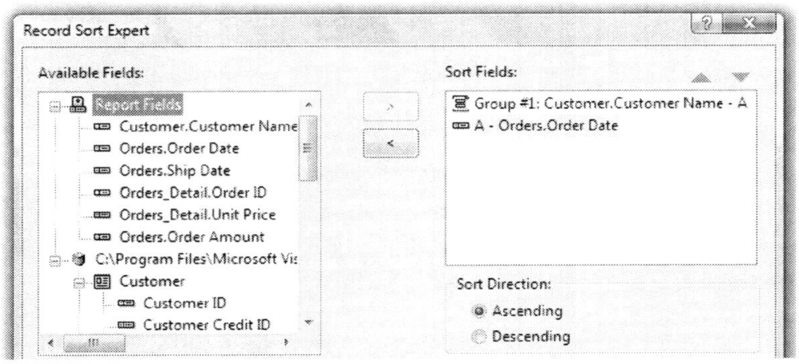

Figure 6-25 Sort options

Total Summary Fields Overview

In this part of the exercise you will create a summary field that will create a total dollar amount of orders for each customer. You will also create a count to show the number of orders for each customer.

 The default summary type is **SUM** for numeric fields.
The default summary type is **MAXIMUM** for Boolean, date and string fields.

Create The Total Summary Field

This summary field will create a total dollar amount of orders for each customer.

1. On the Insert Summary dialog box open the first drop-down list and select the Order Amount field, then open the second drop-down list and select **SUM**.

2. Open the Summary Location drop-down list and select the Group 1 option. Figure 6-26 shows the summary options that should be selected. Click OK. The order amount summary field should be in the group footer section.

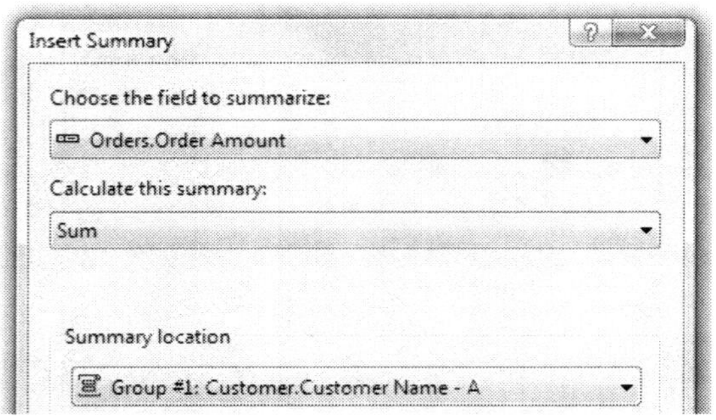

Figure 6-26 Summary options

Create The Count Summary Field

This summary field will create a count of the number of orders for each customer.

1. On the Insert Summary dialog box open the first drop-down list and select the Order ID field, then open the second drop-down list and select **COUNT**.

2. Open the Summary Location drop-down list and select the Group 1 option, then click OK. The count summary field should be in the group footer section.

Create The Distinct Count Summary Field

The distinct count summary will only count the information in a field once. If there are 20 orders for one customer, the distinct count calculation will only count that customer once. This will let you create a count for the total number of customers that are on the report.

1. On the Insert Summary dialog box open the first drop-down list and select the Customer Name field, if it is not already selected, then open the second drop-down list and select **DISTINCT COUNT**. Notice that the only options that are available for this text field are the ones discussed earlier in Table 6-4.

2. Open the Summary Location drop-down list and select the **GRAND TOTAL (REPORT FOOTER)** option, if it is not already selected. The distinct count only needs to appear once, at the end of the report. Figure 6-27 shows the summary options that should be selected. Click OK. The distinct count summary field should be in the report footer section.

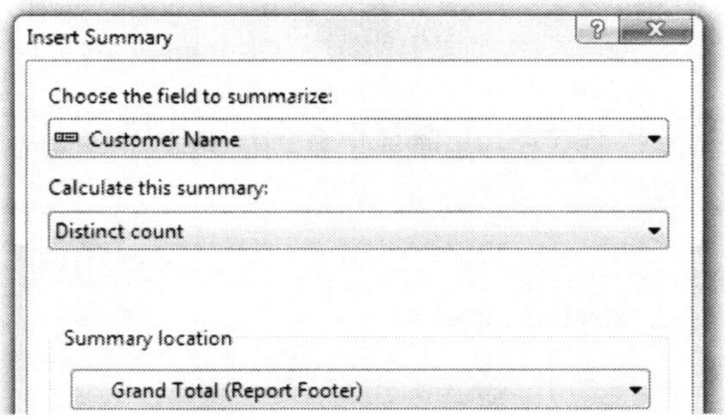

Figure 6-27 Distinct count summary options

3. Save the changes. The report should look like the one shown in Figure 6-28. As you can see, the report needs a little work.

Customer Name	Order Date	Ship Date	Order Amount	Order ID	Unit Price
Alley Cat Cycles					
Alley Cat Cycles	9/28/2001 12:00:0(	9/30/2001 12:00:0(	$2,559.63	2,157	$539.85
Alley Cat Cycles	9/28/2001 12:00:0(	9/30/2001 12:00:0(	$2,559.63	2,157	$313.36
Alley Cat Cycles	10/27/2001 12:00:(	11/6/2001 12:00:0(	$2,699.55	2,272	$899.85
Alley Cat Cycles	1/31/2002 12:00:0(	2/3/2002 12:00:00/	$9,290.30	2,664	$455.86
Alley Cat Cycles	1/31/2002 12:00:0(	2/3/2002 12:00:00/	$9,290.30	2,664	$2,792.86
Alley Cat Cycles	2/19/2002 12:00:0(	2/22/2002 12:00:0(	$8,819.55	2,735	$2,939.85
Alley Cat Cycles	2/19/2002 12:00:0(	2/22/2002 12:00:0(	$8,819.55	2,735	$2,939.85
			$44,038.51	**7**	

Figure 6-28 Orders by customer report

If you view the last page of the report you will see the number 78. This is the distinct count summary field that you just created, which shows how many customers are on the report. In the next part of this exercise you will create a title for this field.

Modify The Report

The report would look better if the following changes were made.

① Add a report title, print date and page number.
② Create titles for the summary fields.
③ Create a grand total field and title for the order amount field and for the grand total count of order summary field. Place these fields in the report footer section.
④ Remove the time from the order date and ship date fields.
⑤ Add a line above all of the summary fields.
⑥ Rearrange the fields in the details section so that the report is easier to read.

1. Create a report title and type `Customer Orders` in the object. Make the font size 16 and the title bold. Center the title across the page.

> If a report has selection criteria, it is a good idea to incorporate the selection criteria in the report. Doing this lets the reader know what criteria the report is using. This report will print records for orders that were placed after a specific date and have a specific minimum order amount. How, or if you incorporate this information is up to you and the requestors of the report. Keep in mind that business decisions are based off of the data in reports, so providing as much helpful and useful information as possible is a good thing.

2. Add the Print Date special field to the page header section below the report title on the right. Add the Page N of M special field to the page footer section in the right corner and right align this field.

3. Copy both of the summary fields in the group footer section and place them in the report footer section.

> If you select both fields before you select the **COPY** command, you can copy both fields at the same time.

4. Create the field titles in Table 6-7 for the summary fields. The section column in the table refers to the section in the report where the title should be placed. Make all of the titles bold.

Summary Field	Section	Title
Order Amount	Group Footer	Total $ amount of orders -
Order ID	Group Footer	Total # orders -
Customer Name	Report Footer	Total # of customers on this report -
Order Amount	Report Footer	Grand Total $ amount of all orders -
Order ID	Report Footer	Grand Total # of orders -

Table 6-7 Field titles for Exercise 6.2

> If I know that the report needs several field titles with the same formatting, I create one and then copy it and just change the text. Over time, you will find a process that works best for you.

> I usually right align titles for calculated fields, when the title is placed to the left of the calculated field. Doing this reduces the amount of white space between the title and the calculated field. When I do this, I also left align the calculated field to further reduce the space between the field and the title. The other option is to drag the calculated field into the text object.

5. Remove the time from the Order Date and Ship Date fields.

6. Delete the Customer Name field in the details section. Delete the Record Number field from the report footer section. Remove the bold from the Group Name field.

> Group Name objects can be formatted like any other object in the report.

7. Change the Order ID heading to `Order #`, then format the Order ID and Order ID count summary fields to display as a whole number without a comma.

8. Add a line at the bottom of the group footer section. Change the size of the line to 0.5 pt. Save the changes and leave the report open to complete the next part of the exercise.

Add A Line Above The Summary Fields

1. Move the summary fields in the group footer section down, so that you have room to add the line.

2. Right-click on the Order Amount summary field in the group footer section and select **FORMAT OBJECT**. On the Border tab open the **TOP** drop-down list, select **SINGLE**, then click OK.

The advantage of using the line option on the Border tab for a field is that if you move or resize the field, the line is automatically re-adjusted. You can also use the **LINE** tool to draw a line. If you use the Line tool and you move or resize the field, you will also have to move or resize the line.

3. Rearrange the fields so that they look like the layout shown in Figure 6-29.

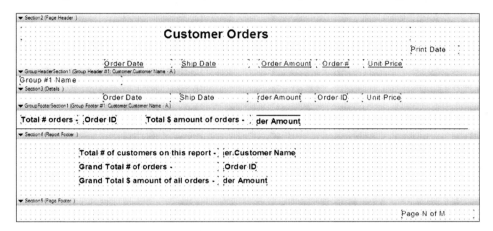

Figure 6-29 L6.2 Report layout

4. Save the changes. Page 1 should look like the one shown in Figure 6-30. The report footer section on the last page should have the totals shown in Figure 6-31.

If you see **###'s** in a field, make the field wider.

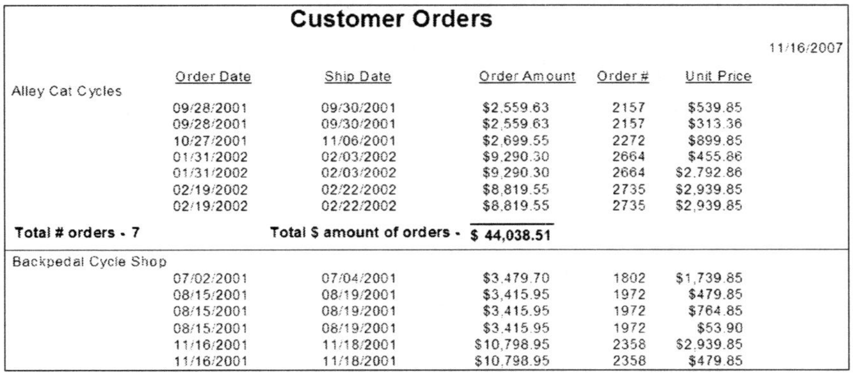

	Order Date	Ship Date	Order Amount	Order #	Unit Price
					11/16/2007
Alley Cat Cycles					
	09/28/2001	09/30/2001	$2,559.63	2157	$539.85
	09/28/2001	09/30/2001	$2,559.63	2157	$313.36
	10/27/2001	11/06/2001	$2,699.55	2272	$899.85
	01/31/2002	02/03/2002	$9,290.30	2664	$455.86
	01/31/2002	02/03/2002	$9,290.30	2664	$2,792.86
	02/19/2002	02/22/2002	$8,819.55	2735	$2,939.85
	02/19/2002	02/22/2002	$8,819.55	2735	$2,939.85
Total # orders - 7		Total $ amount of orders -	$ 44,038.51		
Backpedal Cycle Shop					
	07/02/2001	07/04/2001	$3,479.70	1802	$1,739.85
	08/15/2001	08/19/2001	$3,415.95	1972	$479.85
	08/15/2001	08/19/2001	$3,415.95	1972	$764.85
	08/15/2001	08/19/2001	$3,415.95	1972	$53.90
	11/16/2001	11/18/2001	$10,798.95	2358	$2,939.85
	11/16/2001	11/18/2001	$10,798.95	2358	$479.85

Customer Orders

Figure 6-30 Page 1 of the L6.2 Orders by customer report

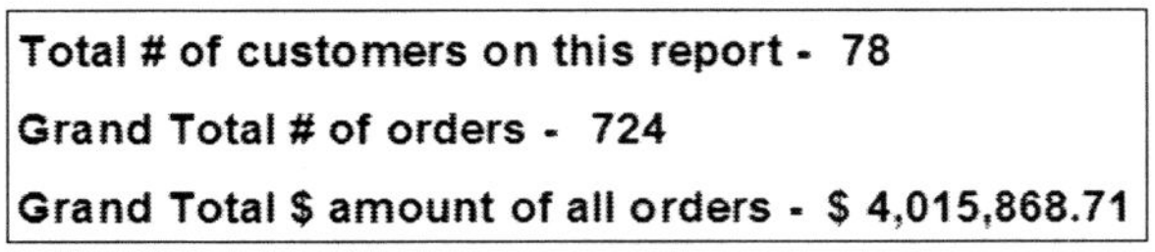

Total # of customers on this report - 78

Grand Total # of orders - 724

Grand Total $ amount of all orders - $ 4,015,868.71

Figure 6-31 Last page of the L6.2 Orders by customer report

5. Make any changes that are needed. Leave the report open to complete the next exercise.

Exercise 6.3: Group Orders By Customer With Averages

It may be useful to the reader of the report to know the average order amount for each customer. The steps below will show you how to create an average summary field.

1. Save the L6.2 report as `L6.3 Orders by customer with averages`.

2. On the Insert Summary dialog box open the first drop-down list and select the Order Amount field. Open the second drop-down list and select **AVERAGE**. Open the Summary Location drop-down list and select the Group 1 option, then click OK. The order amount average summary field should be in the group footer section.

3. Move the average summary field over to the right, then copy the average summary field in the group footer section and place the copy in the report footer section below the last summary field.

4. Create a title for the Order Amount average summary field in the group footer section and type `Average order amount for customer -` in the object. Make the title bold.

5. Create a title for the Order Amount average summary field in the report footer section and type `Average order amount for all customers -` in the object. Make the title bold. Save the changes. The last page of the report should look like the one shown in Figure 6-32. If you need to make any changes make them now, then close the report.

Customer Orders

11/16/2007

Order Date	Ship Date	Order Amount	Order #	Unit Price
01/30/2002	01/31/2002	$8,819.55	2662	$2,939.85
02/28/2002	03/06/2002	$5,321.25	2770	$33.90
02/28/2002	03/06/2002	$5,321.25	2770	$1,739.85
02/28/2002	03/06/2002	$5,321.25	2770	$33.90

Total # orders - 9   Total $ amount of orders - $ 59,951.48

Average order amount for the customer - $6,661.28

Total # of customers on this report - 78
Grand Total # of orders - 724
Grand Total $ amount of all orders - $ 4,015,868.71
Average order amount for all customers - $ 5,546.78

Figure 6-32 L6.3 Orders by customer with averages report

Exercise 6.4: Group 2001 Orders By Shipping Method

In this exercise you will modify a report to include the following group and sorting options. These options also allow you to create totals for the group.

① Group on the Ship Via field and sort the groups in ascending order.
② Sort the detail records in ascending order on the Order Date field.
③ Create a count of orders in each ship via group.
④ Create a total per customer in each ship via group.

This report currently only displays orders between $2,000 and $5,000. All of the shipping methods are selected, except for Purolator. In order to get a count of detail records for each group and a total per customer, two groups need to be created. To get an accurate count of orders for each shipping method in 2001, the existing selection criteria needs to be deleted and new criteria has to be created.

Create The Ship Via And Customer Name Groups

1. Save the L5.8 report as `L6.4 2001 Orders by shipping method`.

2. On the Insert Group dialog box open the first drop-down list, select the **SHIP VIA** field, then click OK.

3. On the Insert Group dialog box open the first drop-down list and select the CUSTOMER NAME field, if it is not already selected, then click OK. You should have two groups in the report layout as shown in Figure 6-33.

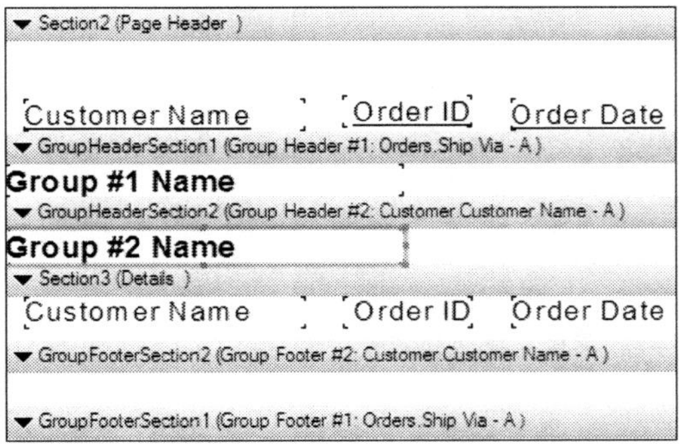

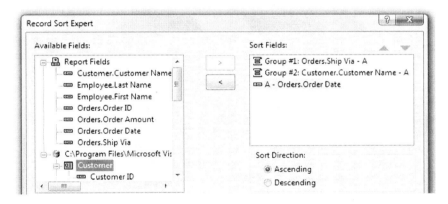

Figure 6-33 Two groups added to the report

Sort The Detail Records

1. On the Record Sort Expert dialog box click on the Order Date field, then click the > button.

2. Select the Ascending sort order, if it is not already selected. Figure 6-34 shows the sort options that should be selected. Click OK and save the changes.

Figure 6-34 Sort options

Change The Selection Criteria

The report that this one is based off of, has selection criteria that is not needed in the report that you are modifying now. This report needs criteria to only display records from 2001.

1. Open the Select Expert and delete all of the current criteria.

2. Create criteria to only include orders placed in 2001.

Create The Summary Fields

This report requires two summary fields: a count of orders and a total dollar amount of orders per customer.

Create The Order ID Count Summary Field

This count summary field will create a total number of orders per customer. It will also be copied to the report footer section to create a grand total number of orders on the report.

1. On the Insert Summary dialog box open the first drop-down list and select the Order ID field. Open the second drop-down list and select COUNT. Open the Summary Location drop-down list and select the Group 2 option. This will place the summary field in the customer name group footer section. Click OK.

Create The Order Amount Summary Field

This summary field will create a total dollar amount per customer. It will also be copied to the report footer section to create a grand total order amount on the report.

1. On the Insert Summary dialog box open the first drop-down list and select the Order Amount field, then open the second drop-down list and select SUM. Open the Summary Location drop-down list and select the Group 2 option, then click OK.

Summary fields are available in the FORMULA WORKSHOP. They are not available in the Field Explorer.

2. Save the changes. The report should look like the one shown in Figure 6-35.

Customer Name	Order ID	Order Date	Order Amount	Ship Via		First Name	Last Name
FedEx							
Alley Cat Cycles							
Alley Cat Cycles	2,207	10/11/2001	$72.00	FedEx		Janet	Levering
Alley Cat Cycles	2,301	10/31/2001	$1,664.70	FedEx		Michael	Suyama
Alley Cat Cycles	2,361	11/17/2001	$389.65	FedEx		Robert	King
	3		$2,126.35				
Backpedal Cycle Shop							
Backpedal Cycle Sh(	1,311	02/19/2001	$6,233.05	FedEx		Robert	King
Backpedal Cycle Sh(	1,802	07/02/2001	$3,479.70	FedEx		Anne	Dodsworth
Backpedal Cycle Sh(	2,198	10/08/2001	$93.50	FedEx		Janet	Levering
	3		$9,806.25				
BBS Pty							
BBS Pty	1,776	06/25/2001	$5,913.60	FedEx		Margaret	Peacock
BBS Pty	2,067	09/03/2001	$51.60	FedEx		Michael	Suyama

Figure 6-35 L6.4 Orders by shipping method report

Modify The Report

The report would look better if the following changes were made.

① Add a report title, print date and page number.
② Create titles for the summary fields.
③ Create a grand total field and title for the order amount and count of orders summary fields. Place the fields in the report footer section.
④ Rearrange the fields in the details section so that the report is easier to read.

1. Create a report title in the page header section and type
    2001 Orders By Shipping Method in the object. Change the font size to 16.

2. Add the Print Date field to the page header section below the report titles on the right, then add the Page N of M field to the page footer section in the right corner. Right align the field.

3. Add the logo to the upper left corner of the page header section. Change the Order ID field heading to Order #. Format the Order ID field to display as a whole number without a comma.

4. Delete the Customer Name and Ship Via fields from the details section. Remove the bold from the Group 2 Header field. Remove the bold from the summary fields in the Group 2 Footer section. Delete the Record Number field from the report footer section.

5. Move the First Name and Last Name fields over to the left. Delete the Last Name field header. Change the First Name field header to `Salesperson`. Center this header over the two name fields in the details section.

6. Copy both of the summary fields in the Group 2 Footer section and place them in the Group 1 Footer and report footer sections.

7. Add a line under the totals in the Group 1 and 2 Footer sections. Change the line in the Group 1 Footer section to dotted. Change the size of the line in the Group 2 Footer section to 0.5.

8. Create the field titles in Table 6-8 for the summary fields.

Summary Field	Section	Title
Order Amount	Group 1 Footer	Total order amount for customers -
Order ID Count	Group 1 Footer	Total # orders for customers
Order Amount	Group 2 Footer	Total order amount for customer -
Order ID Count	Group 2 Footer	Total # orders for customer -
Order Amount	Report Footer	Total order amount for all customers -
Order ID	Report Footer	Total # orders for all customers -

Table 6-8 Field titles for Exercise 6.4

9. Copy the Group 1 Header field and place the copy in the Group 1 Footer section, then remove the bold from the field in the Group 1 Footer section.

10. Create a title for the Group 1 Footer section and type `Totals For:` in the object. Create a title for the report footer section and type `Report Grand Totals:` in the object. Make both objects bold.

11. Arrange the fields so that they look like the layout shown in Figure 6-36. Save the changes. Page 1 should look like the one shown in Figure 6-37.

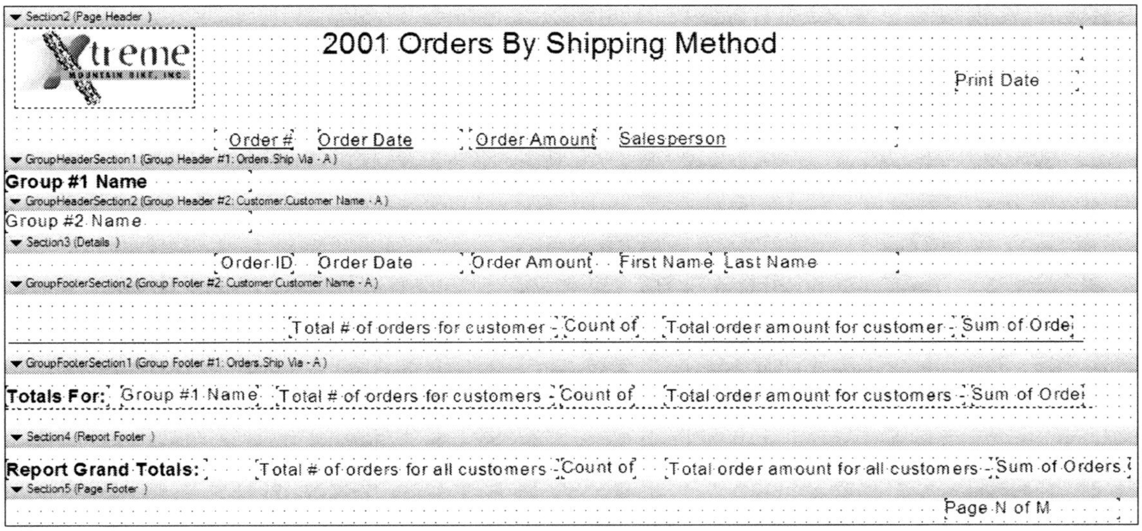

Figure 6-36 L6.4 report layout

Figure 6-37 Page 1 of the L6.4 2001 Orders by shipping method report

12. Open the FedEx option in the group tree. Click on the company Yue Xiu Bicycles. You should see the page shown in Figure 6-38. Notice the totals for the shipping method for FedEx. The last page should look like the one shown in Figure 6-39. Leave the report open to complete the next exercise.

Figure 6-38 FedEx information on the L6.4 2001 Orders by shipping method report

Figure 6-39 Last page of the L6.4 2001 Orders by shipping method report

Exercise 6.5: Change The Group Order

The L6.4 report that you just completed is grouped on two fields: Ship Via and Customer Name. If after viewing the report you decide that the groups should be in the opposite order, meaning that the first group should be the Customer Name, follow the steps below.

1. Save the L6.4 report as L6.5 Change group order.

2. Open the Group Expert. Click on the Ship Via group on the right, then click the down arrow button. Click OK.

Notice that Group Header 1 is now grouped on the Customer Name field. This is now the first field that the report will be grouped on, as shown in Figure 6-40. Refer back to Figure 6-37. If you look at the last page of the report, you will see that the report grand totals are the same, but in the L6.5 report, the totals for the shipping method are per customer.

			2001 Orders By Shipping Method		
					11/16/2007
	Order #	Order Date	Order Amount	Salesperson	
7 Bikes For 7 Brothers					
Parcel Post					
	3054	05/26/2001	$53.90	Janet	Leverling
Totals For: Parcel Post		Total # of orders for customers - 1		Total order amount for customers - $ 53.90	
		Total # of orders for customer - 1		Total order amount for customer - $ 53.90	
Against The Wind Bikes					
Purolator					
	3055	05/26/2001	$479.85	Michael	Suyama
Totals For: Purolator		Total # of orders for customers - 1		Total order amount for customers - $ 479.85	
		Total # of orders for customer - 1		Total order amount for customer - $ 479.85	

Figure 6-40 Page 1 of the L6.5 Change group order report

If you open the Alley Cat Cycles group in the group tree you will see options for different types of shipping methods, as shown in Figure 6-41. This means that this company has deliveries from each of these shipping methods. You will see totals for each shipping company if you click in it in the group tree. If you go to the next page of the report, you will see the totals illustrated in Figure 6-42. These are the grand totals for the company.

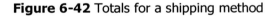

Alley Cat Cycles
FedEx
Loomis
Parcel Post
Pickup
Purolator
UPS

Figure 6-41 Shipping method options for a group

UPS					
	1204	01/19/2001	$1,583.05	Margaret	Peacock
	1260	02/04/2001	$33.90	Robert	King
	1701	06/09/2001	$113.70	Nancy	Davolio
	2153	09/27/2001	$43.50	Margaret	Peacock
	2455	12/06/2001	$43.50	Margaret	Peacock
Totals For: UPS		Total # of orders for customers - 5		Total order amount for customers - $ 1,817.65	
		Total # of orders for customer - 21		Total order amount for customer - $ 25,781.75	

Figure 6-42 Totals for a shipping method

3. Save the changes and close the report.

Exercise 6.6: Another Change The Group Order Report

You have already learned that if the same summary field is placed in different sections of the report, it will display a different total. This exercise will demonstrate the differences when the same summary field is placed in different group footer sections of the report.

1. Create a new report. Save the report as L6.6 Change group order. Add the Customer Name, Region and Country fields from the Customer table to the report.

2. Delete the date field in the page header section if you created the report using the Standard wizard, then create a group for the region. Insert another group for the country.

3. Create a summary count field for the region field and place it in the Group Footer 1 section. Create a summary count field for the country field and place it in the Group Footer 1 section.

4. Format the country summary field so that it only displays whole numbers (meaning no decimal points), then duplicate the country summary count field and place it in the Group Footer 2 section.

5. Left align the three summary count fields. The report should look like the one shown in Figure 6-43.

Customer Name	Region	Country
Abu Dhabi		
United Arab Emirates		
UAE Cycle	Abu Dhabi	United Arab Emirates
		1
	1	1
AL		
USA		
The Great Bike Shop	AL	USA
Benny - The Spokes Person	AL	USA
Psycho-Cycle	AL	USA
		3
	3	3
Alsace		
France		
Sports Alsace	Alsace	France
Mulhouse Vélos	Alsace	France
		2
	2	2

Figure 6-43 L6.6 Change group order report with summary count fields

6. Open the Group Expert. Click on the Region group on the right, then click the down button. The report should look like the one shown in Figure 6-44.

Customer Name	Region	Country
Argentina		
Mendoza		
Bicicletas Buenos Aires	Mendoza	Argentina
	1	1
		1
Aruba		
St. George		
Aruba Sport	St. George	Aruba
	1	1
		1
Australia		
New South Wales		
Canberra Bikes	New South Wales	Australia
Down Under Bikes	New South Wales	Australia
	2	2
Queensland		
Koala Road Bikes	Queensland	Australia
	1	1

Figure 6-44 L6.6 Change group order report with the group sections rearranged

If you moved the region count summary field to the Group Footer 1 section, the report would look like the one shown in Figure 6-45. Notice the difference in totals at the bottom of the reports shown in Figures 6-44 and 6-45. This is why it is important to understand what the report specifications require. Just by looking at the two reports, you can't tell which is the one that is being requested.

Customer Name	Region	Country
Argentina		
Mendoza		
Bicicletas Buenos Aires	Mendoza	Argentina
		1
	1	1
Aruba		
St. George		
Aruba Sport	St. George	Aruba
		1
	1	1
Australia		
New South Wales		
Canberra Bikes	New South Wales	Australia
Down Under Bikes	New South Wales	Australia
		2
Queensland		
Koala Road Bikes	Queensland	Australia
		1

Figure 6-45 L6.6 Change group order report with the region count field moved to the Group Footer 1 section

7. Save the changes and close the report.

Custom Group Names

So far in this lesson the group names used come from the field that the report is grouped on. In Crystal Reports there are options that let you customize the group name as discussed below.

① Use a different field as the group name.
② Create a custom group name.
③ Create a user defined group name.
④ Create a formula to display the group name.

Use A Different Field As The Group Name

The custom group name option lets you use one field to create the group and a different field to display as the group name. In Exercise 6.2, the report is grouped on the Customer Name field. If that report was grouped on the Customer ID field, the group name would be displayed as shown in Figure 6-46. If you selected the options shown in Figure 6-47 on the Options tab for the Customer ID group field, the report would look like the one shown in Figure 6-48.

	Order Date	Ship Date	Order Amount	Order #	Unit Price
1					
	09/01/2001	09/02/2001	$4,078.95	2054	$899.85
	09/01/2001	09/02/2001	$4,078.95	2054	$329.85
	09/01/2001	09/02/2001	$4,078.95	2054	$539.85
	01/26/2002	01/26/2002	$2,939.85	2640	$2,939.85
	04/09/2002	04/16/2002	$5,549.40	2900	$1,739.85
	04/09/2002	04/16/2002	$5,549.40	2900	$329.85
2					
	07/21/2001	07/27/2001	$3,526.70	1883	$1,739.85
	07/21/2001	07/27/2001	$3,526.70	1883	$23.50

Figure 6-46 Report grouped by the Customer ID field

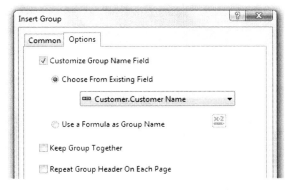

Figure 6-47 Options to use a different field as the group name

	Order Date	Ship Date	Order Amount	Order #	Unit Price
City Cyclists					
	09/01/2001	09/02/2001	$4,078.95	2054	$899.85
	09/01/2001	09/02/2001	$4,078.95	2054	$329.85
	09/01/2001	09/02/2001	$4,078.95	2054	$539.85
	01/26/2002	01/26/2002	$2,939.85	2640	$2,939.85
	04/09/2002	04/16/2002	$5,549.40	2900	$1,739.85
	04/09/2002	04/16/2002	$5,549.40	2900	$329.85
Pathfinders					
	07/21/2001	07/27/2001	$3,526.70	1883	$1,739.85
	07/21/2001	07/27/2001	$3,526.70	1883	$23.50

Figure 6-48 Report using a different field as the group name

Exercise 6.7: Group 2001 Orders By Month

In this exercise you will modify a report to include the following group and sorting options. These options also allow you to create totals and counts so that the records will be grouped by the month the orders were placed.

① Group on the Order Date field.
② Sort the detail records in ascending order on the Order Date field.
③ Provide a count of orders per month.

The goal of this exercise is to create a report that displays all of the orders from 2001 and to have a subtotal for each month. In order to create a subtotal of orders for each month, the report needs to be grouped on the Order Date field.

As you will see, when you group on a date or date/time field, the Insert Group dialog box will display the option, **THE SECTION WILL BE PRINTED**. This option will allow you to create the group by month, day, quarter, year and more.

Create The Order Date Group

1. Save the L4.16 report as `L6.7 2001 Orders by month`.

2. On the Insert Group dialog box open the first drop-down list and select the **ORDER DATE** field. Open the last drop-down list and select **FOR EACH MONTH**. Figure 6-49 shows the group options that should be selected. Click OK.

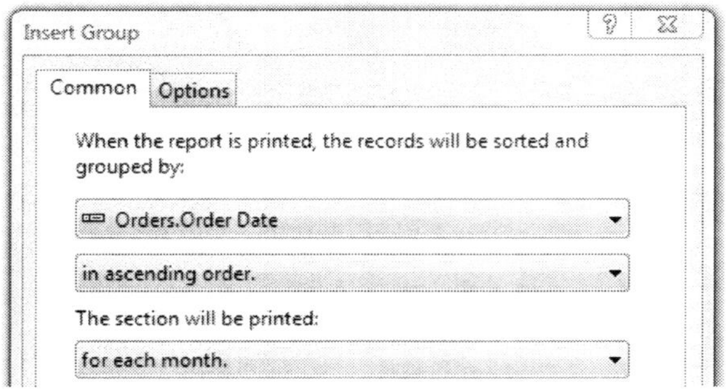

Figure 6-49 Group options

Sort The Detail Records

1. On the Record Sort Expert click on the Order Date field, then click the > button.

2. Select the Ascending sort order, if it is not already selected. Click OK and save the changes.

Select The Records

In this part of the exercise you will create criteria to select all of the orders in 2001.

1. Click on the Order Date field in the details section.

2. Open the Select Expert and select the **IS BETWEEN** operator, then type `01/01/2001` in the first field. Type `12/31/2001` in the last field, then click OK.

Create The Order ID Count Summary Field

This count summary field will create a total for the number of orders per month. It will also be copied to the report footer section to create a grand total of orders for the entire report.

1. Add the Order Amount field in the Orders table to the report. Place it after the Order ID field in the details section.

2. On the Insert Summary dialog box open the first drop-down list and select the Order ID field, then open the second drop-down list and select **DISTINCT COUNT**. Open the Summary Location drop-down list and select the Group 1 option, then click OK.

Create The Order Amount Summary Field

This summary field will create a total dollar amount per month. It will also be copied to the report footer section to create a grand total order amount.

1. Delete the Product ID, Unit Price and Quantity fields from the report.

2. On the Insert Summary dialog box open the first drop-down list and select the Order Amount field, then open the second drop-down list and select **SUM**. Open the Summary Location drop-down list and select the Group 1 option, then click OK.

How To Create Percent Calculations

Percent calculations are very useful when you have the need to show what percent each group on the report represents in comparison to the grand total value on the report. For example, on a report that shows the sales for an entire year, there could be a percent calculation by month on the Order Amount field. This would tell the person that reads the report the percent of sales each month represents for the year. Another example on a yearly sales report would be the percent of sales each salesperson had per month, per year or both.

> You can only create percent calculations on summary fields that have a numeric value. This means that if you are creating a count summary of customers based on the Customer Name field which is a text field, you can create a percent calculation, because the count calculation field is a numeric value.

Each percent calculation on a report requires its own percent summary calculation field. The process of creating a percent summary calculation starts off the same as the calculations that you have already created in this lesson. The options to create percent calculations are at the bottom of the Insert Summary dialog box. To create a percent calculation check the **SHOW AS A PERCENTAGE OF** option, then select the group or total that you want the percent comparison based on.

> If you need a total field and a percent calculation field that are based off of the same field, you have to create two summary calculation fields: one for the total amount and one for the percent.

In the previous part of the exercise you created the Order Amount summary field. Now you will create the Order Amount percent calculation field.

1. On the Insert Summary dialog box open the first drop-down list and select the Order Amount field, then open the second drop-down list and select **SUM**. Open the Summary Location drop-down list and select the Group 1 option, then check the **SHOW AS A PERCENTAGE OF** option. Figure 6-50 shows the summary options that should be selected. Click OK.

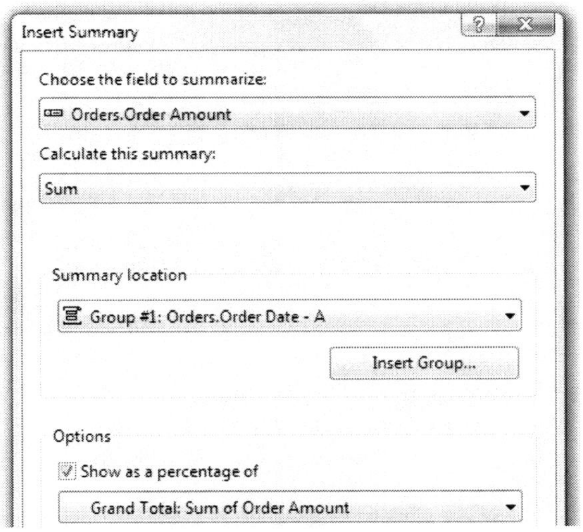

Figure 6-50 Insert Summary dialog box options

2. Move the percent summary field over to the right. On my report, it is currently on top of the Order Amount summary field that you just created. Save the changes. The third page of the report should look like the one shown in Figure 6-51. Notice that the percent summary field is already formatted with a percent sign.

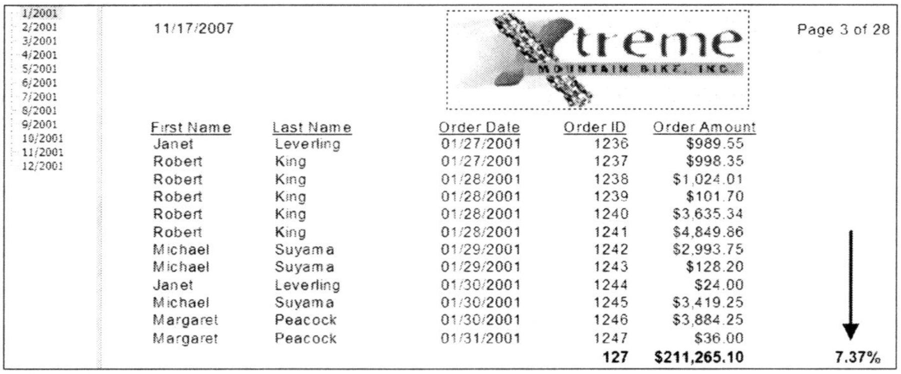

First Name	Last Name	Order Date	Order ID	Order Amount	
Janet	Leverling	01/27/2001	1236	$989.55	
Robert	King	01/27/2001	1237	$998.35	
Robert	King	01/28/2001	1238	$1,024.01	
Robert	King	01/28/2001	1239	$101.70	
Robert	King	01/28/2001	1240	$3,635.34	
Robert	King	01/28/2001	1241	$4,849.86	
Michael	Suyama	01/29/2001	1242	$2,993.75	
Michael	Suyama	01/29/2001	1243	$128.20	
Janet	Leverling	01/30/2001	1244	$24.00	
Michael	Suyama	01/30/2001	1245	$3,419.25	
Margaret	Peacock	01/30/2001	1246	$3,884.25	
Margaret	Peacock	01/31/2001	1247	$36.00	
			127	$211,265.10	7.37%

Figure 6-51 L6.7 2001 Orders by month report with percent calculation

How To Check Or Edit Summary Fields

Sometimes reports will have more than two or three summary fields and you may not remember what each summary field is calculating. If a summary field is not producing the output that you think it should, it is possible that you selected an option that you should not have. If either of these is the case, all is not lost. You do not have to delete the field and start over. You can follow the steps below.

1. Right-click on the percentage summary field and select **CHANGE SUMMARY OPERATION** as shown in Figure 6-52. You will then see the dialog box shown in Figure 6-53. You can make any changes that are necessary.

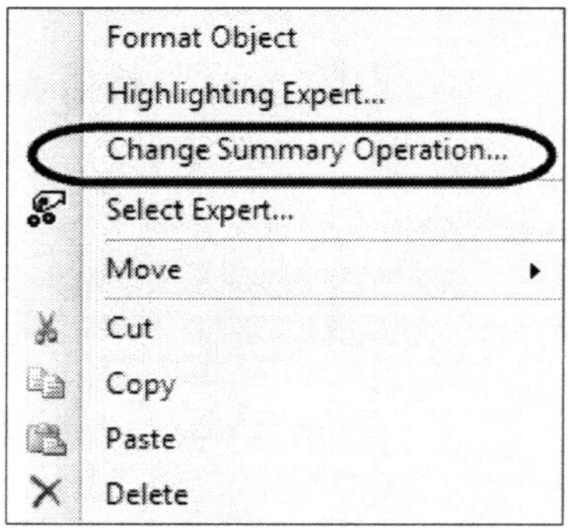

Figure 6-52 Change Summary Operation option illustrated on the shortcut menu

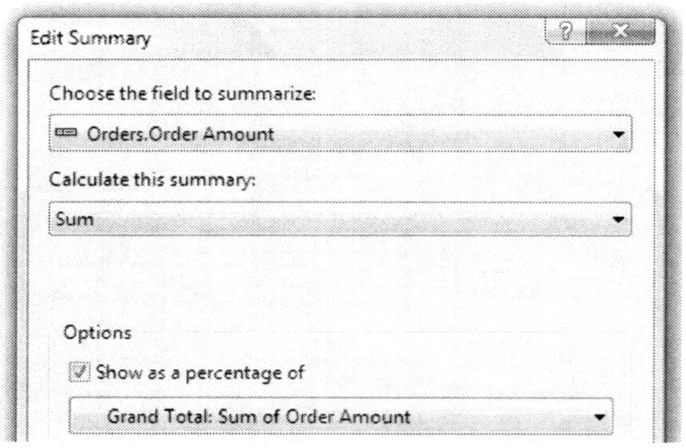

Figure 6-53 Edit Summary dialog box

The Edit Summary dialog box is almost identical to the Insert Summary dialog box. The difference is that you cannot change the location of the summary field. If you need to move a summary field from one section of the report to another, you will have to do it manually.

Modify The Report

The report would look better if the following changes were made.

① Add a report title.
② Create titles for the summary fields.
③ Create a grand total field and title for the order amount and count of orders summary fields. Place the fields in the report footer section.
④ Rearrange the fields in the details section so that the report is easier to read.

1. Create a report title and type `2001 Orders By Month` in the object. Make the font size 16 and place the title above the field headings.

2. Change the Order ID field heading to `Order #` and center the Order ID field.

3. Delete the Last Name field heading. Change the First Name field heading to `Salesperson`. Center this heading over the two name fields in the details section.

4. Format the Order ID field in the Group 1 Footer section to display as a whole number without a comma.

5. Copy the Order ID and Order Amount summary fields in the Group 1 Footer section and place the copies in the report footer section.

6. Add a line under the totals in the Group 1 Footer section. Change the size of the line to 0.5.

7. Create the field titles in Table 6-9 for the summary fields.

Summary Field	Section	Title
Order Amount	Group 1 Footer	Total order amount for the month -
Order ID Count	Group 1 Footer	Total # orders for the month
Order Amount Percent	Group 1 Footer	Percent of yearly sales -
Order Amount	Report Footer	Total order amount for the year -
Order ID	Report Footer	Total # orders for the year -

Table 6-9 Field titles for Exercise 6.7

8. Copy the Group 1 Header field and place the copy in the Group 1 Footer section. Remove the bold from the field in the Group 1 Footer section.

9. Create a title for the Group 1 Footer section and type `Totals For:` in the object. Create a title for the report footer section and type `Report Grand Totals:` in the object.

10. Arrange the fields so that they look like the layout shown in Figure 6-54. Save the changes. Leave the report open to complete the next part of the exercise.

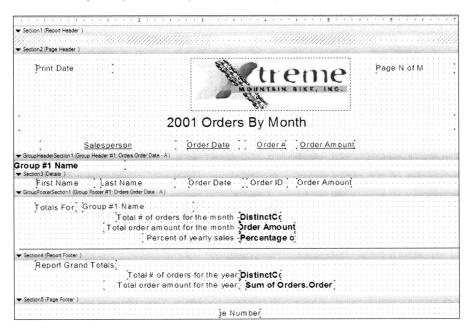

Figure 6-54 L6.7 report layout

When you preview the report you will see the months in the group tree section of the report. If you click on the 1/2001 group as illustrated in Figure 6-55, you will see the orders that were placed in January. Later in this lesson you will change the group name to display the name of the month instead of the month number. The Percent of yearly sales field lets you know that the orders in January represent 7.37% of the total sales in 2001.

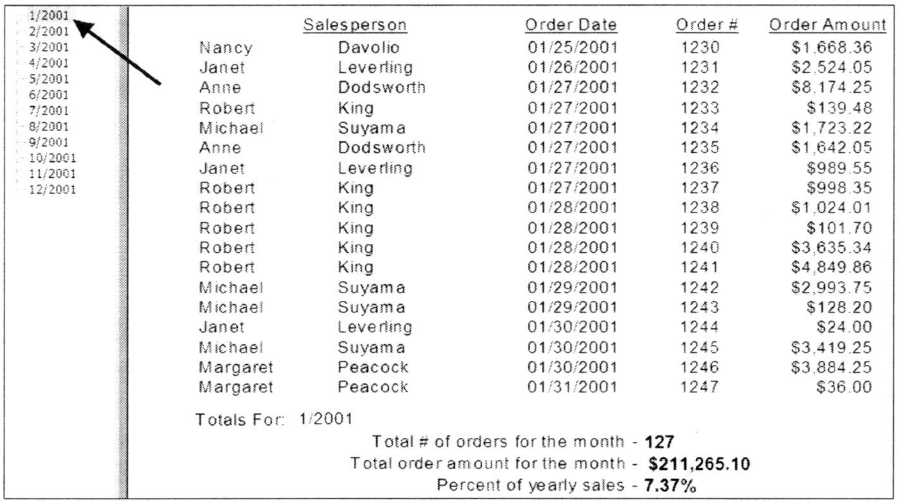

		Salesperson	Order Date	Order #	Order Amount
1/2001					
2/2001					
3/2001	Nancy	Davolio	01/25/2001	1230	$1,668.36
4/2001	Janet	Leverling	01/26/2001	1231	$2,524.05
5/2001	Anne	Dodsworth	01/27/2001	1232	$8,174.25
6/2001	Robert	King	01/27/2001	1233	$139.48
7/2001	Michael	Suyama	01/27/2001	1234	$1,723.22
8/2001	Anne	Dodsworth	01/27/2001	1235	$1,642.05
9/2001	Janet	Leverling	01/27/2001	1236	$989.55
10/2001	Robert	King	01/27/2001	1237	$998.35
11/2001	Robert	King	01/28/2001	1238	$1,024.01
12/2001	Robert	King	01/28/2001	1239	$101.70
	Robert	King	01/28/2001	1240	$3,635.34
	Robert	King	01/28/2001	1241	$4,849.86
	Michael	Suyama	01/29/2001	1242	$2,993.75
	Michael	Suyama	01/29/2001	1243	$128.20
	Janet	Leverling	01/30/2001	1244	$24.00
	Michael	Suyama	01/30/2001	1245	$3,419.25
	Margaret	Peacock	01/30/2001	1246	$3,884.25
	Margaret	Peacock	01/31/2001	1247	$36.00

Totals For: 1/2001

Total # of orders for the month - **127**
Total order amount for the month - **$211,265.10**
Percent of yearly sales - **7.37%**

Figure 6-55 Page 3 of the L6.7 2001 Orders by month report

How To Create A Custom Group Name

The report would look better if the group name displayed the actual month name instead (January, February, March, etc.). The Format Editor has an option that you can use to display the month name. You could create a formula to accomplish this task, but using the Format Editor is easier. The steps below will show you how to create a custom group name.

1. Right-click on the **GROUP 1 NAME** field in the group header section, then open the Format Editor. Click the **CUSTOMIZE** button on the Date and Time tab.

2. Open the **ORDER** drop-down list and select Date. Figure 6-56 shows the option that you should have selected.

Figure 6-56 Date and Time tab options

3. On the Date tab open the Month drop-down list and select **MARCH**, then select **NONE** for the Day and Year options. Figure 6-57 illustrates the options that you should have selected. Click OK twice, to close both dialog boxes.

4. Format the Group Name field in the group footer section to have the same formatting as the one in the group header section and save the changes. Go to the last page of the report. The totals for December and the report grand totals should look like the ones shown in Figure 6-58. Leave the report open to complete the next exercise.

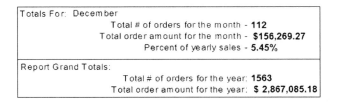

Figure 6-57 Date tab options illustrated

```
Totals For:  December
                 Total # of orders for the month - 112
                 Total order amount for the month -  $156,269.27
                        Percent of yearly sales - 5.45%

Report Grand Totals:
                 Total # of orders for the year: 1563
                 Total order amount for the year:  $ 2,867,085.18
```

Figure 6-58 Last page of the L6.7 2001 Orders by month report

Exercise 6.8: Create Selection Criteria On Summary Fields

In Lesson 5 you learned about record selection. **GROUP SELECTION** is similar. The difference is that group selection is done on summary fields, instead of fields in the details section. If a report is grouping the orders by state, each state would include an order total amount.

In Exercise 6.7 you created a report that grouped the orders by month. At the end of each month are summary calculations for the total number of orders and total order amount for the month. In this exercise you will learn how to create selection criteria on group summary fields. The report that you created in Exercise 6.7 displays data for every month in 2001. In this exercise you will use the Select Expert to modify that report to only display months where the total monthly sales is greater than $250,000.

1. Save the L6.7 report as `L6.8 2001 Monthly total orders over 250K`.

2. Right-click on the Sum of Orders field in the group footer section and select, Select Expert.

3. Open the drop-down list and select **IS GREATER THAN OR EQUAL TO**, then type `250000` in the second field and click OK. Notice that the field name on the tab does not display a table name. Instead it displays information that lets you know that this is a summary field.

4. Change the report title to `2001 Monthly Total Orders Over $250,000`, then save the changes.

As shown in Figure 6-59, the first page of the report is for June. Notice that all of the groups are still visible in the group tree. If you click on the 02/2001 option in the group tree, you will not see the data for February. That is because the monthly total for February is less than $250,000. I don't know about you, but I would prefer that the only options that appear in the group tree are the ones that meet the criteria. This happens because of the way Crystal Reports processes data. Remember that the group header information is processed before the totals for the summary calculations in the group footer are processed. This is why all of the months appear in the group tree.

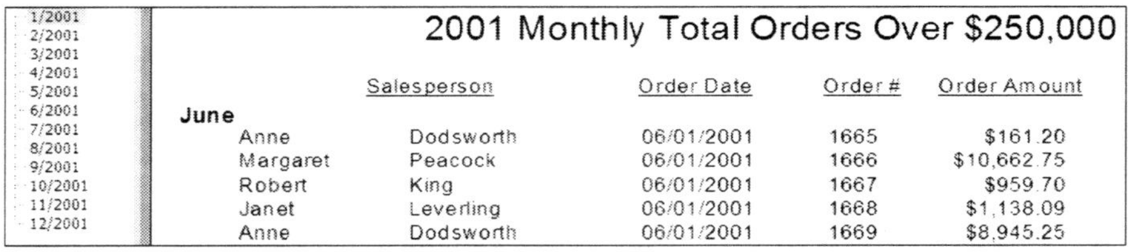

Figure 6-59 L6.8 2001 Monthly total orders over 250K

Using The Group Expert

All of the groups that you have created in this lesson were created using the Insert Group dialog box. You can also create and edit groups using the Group Expert shown in Figure 6-60.

There are two ways to open the Group Expert as discussed below.

① Right-click on the group header or footer section bar and select Group Expert.
② Crystal Reports ⇒ Report ⇒ Group Expert.

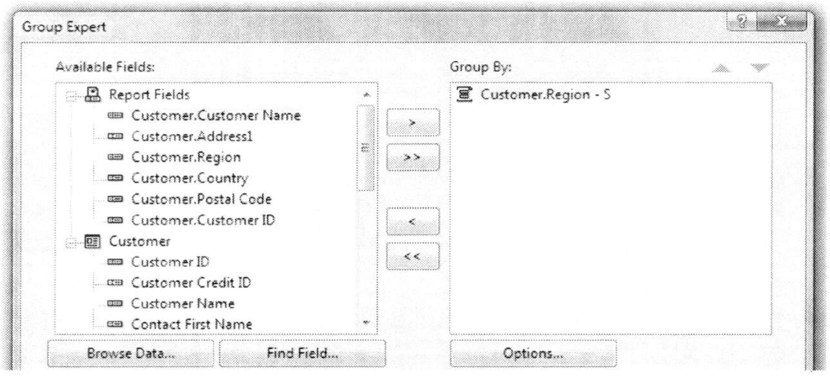

Figure 6-60 Group Expert

The **OPTIONS** button on the Group Expert will open the Change Group Options dialog box shown in Figure 6-61. It is similar to the Insert Group dialog box shown earlier in Figure 6-49.

One benefit of using the Group Expert is that you can create all of the groups for the report without having to re-open a dialog box to create each group. Another benefit is if you need to see the data in a field, you can click the Browse Data button.

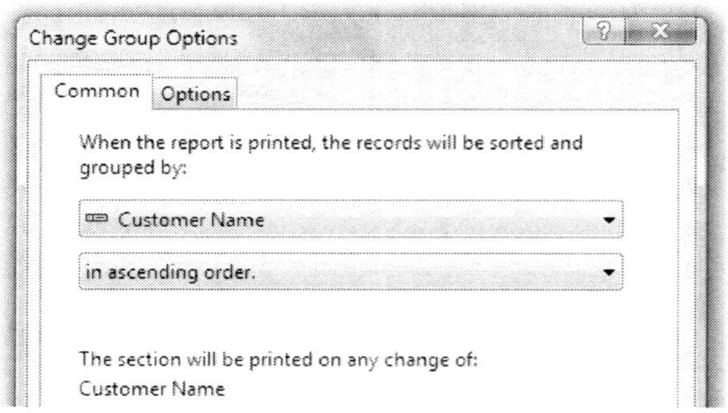

Figure 6-61 Change Group Options dialog box

User Defined Groups

Earlier in this lesson you learned about the User defined sort order. In Exercise 6.7 you learned how to create a custom group name. Custom group names allow you to rename existing group names. Custom groups must be based on a single field in the report. User defined groups are similar to custom group names. The major difference is that the user defined group name is free form. In addition to being able to create a free form group name, you can create custom groups. Below are examples of user defined groups.

① Orders placed between the first and the 15th of the month.
② Group customers based on their year to date sales (Example Gold, Bronze and Silver levels).
③ Create sales territories and associate states to a territory (Example Northeast, Southeast and Midwest).

There are four steps to creating a user defined group as discussed below:

① Select the field that you want to create the user defined group for, then select the option, **IN SPECIFIED ORDER** in the second drop-down list on the Common tab of the Insert Group dialog box. Once this option is selected, other tabs (the Specified Order and Others tabs) will appear on the dialog box.

② Type in the name for the first group name that you need in the **NAMED GROUP** drop-down list shown in Figure 6-62, then click the **NEW** button.

③ The **DEFINE NAMED GROUP** dialog box is similar to the Select Expert. One difference is that each tab on the Define Named Group dialog box is for the same field. User defined groups cannot use parameter fields and the formula cannot be modified. You would type in the criteria for the user defined group, as shown in Figure 6-63. The other difference is that these filters or selection criteria use the **OR** operand, meaning that the detail record can meet the criteria for filter 1 or filter 2 or filter 3.

④ Click OK and repeat steps 2 and 3 until you have created all of the user defined groups that the report needs.

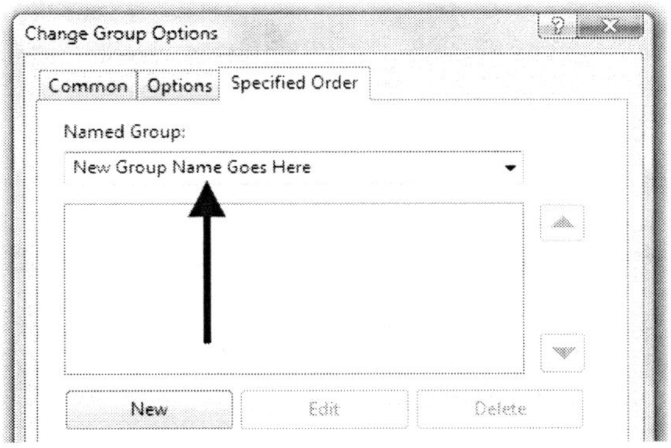

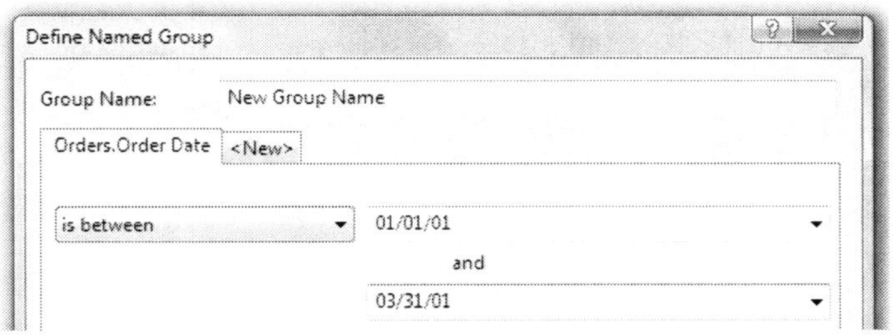

Figure 6-62 Specified Order tab options

Figure 6-63 Criteria for a user defined group

If you wanted to group orders by specific order date ranges like 1/1/01 to 1/15/01, 2/1/01 to 2/15/01 and 3/1/01 to 3/15/01, you would create three named groups, for example, Jan 01, Feb 01 and Mar 01.
For each named group you would select the Order Date field, the operator "Is between" and the date range for the named group. The report would show the three groups and the detail records that have an order date that falls into one of the three date ranges.

If one group or all groups need additional criteria, click on the New tab and add the next piece of criteria for the group. You can only add criteria for the same field. For example, if you also wanted to see orders for 1/15/01 to 1/25/01, you would add this criteria on the New tab shown in Figure 6-64. The criteria for each group name is joined using the **OR** operand. This means that as long as the record meets one of the sets of criteria for the group name, it will appear on the report.

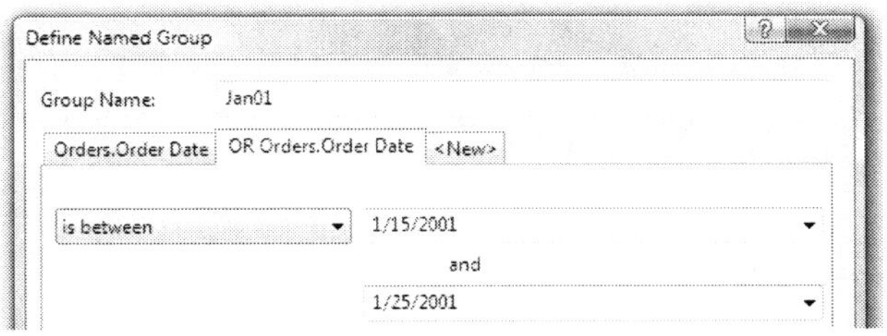

Figure 6-64 Additional criteria added to the named group

The options on the Others tab, which you will learn about in the next exercise will let you select what you want to do with the records that do not meet the criteria for any of the named groups.

Exercise 6.9: Create A User Defined Group Report

In this exercise you will modify the L6.1 report to include the following region user defined groups: CA, IL and PA.

1. Save the L6.1 report as `L6.9 User defined groups`.

2. Right-click on the group header section bar and select **GROUP EXPERT**, then click the Options button.

3. Select the option **IN SPECIFIED ORDER** in the second drop-down list on the Change Group Options dialog box. You should now see the **SPECIFIED ORDER** tab.

4. Select CA, IL and PA in the **NAMED GROUP** drop-down list. Make sure that the states are in the order shown in Figure 6-65. If they are not in the order shown, use the up and down arrow buttons to put the states in the order shown.

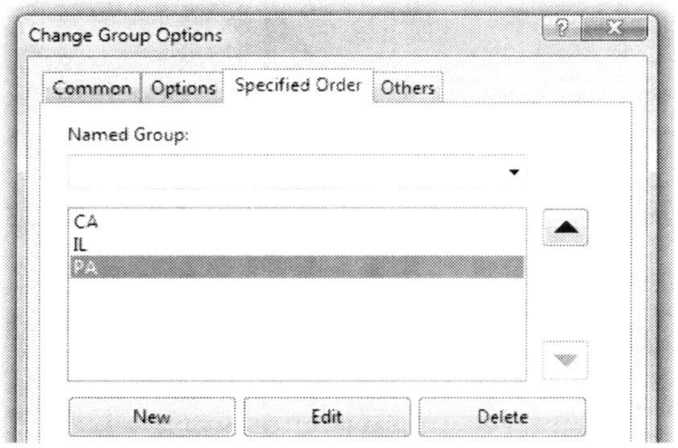

Figure 6-65 Change Group Options dialog box

5. On the **OTHERS** tab select the option **DISCARD ALL OTHERS**, as shown in Figure 6-66. Click OK twice to close both dialog boxes.

Selecting the Discard all others option means that records that are not in any of the groups listed on the Specified Order tab will not appear on the report.

The **PUT ALL OTHERS TOGETHER, WITH THE NAME** option, will put all of the other records that do not meet the criteria on the Specified Order tab in the report under a new group name that you enter on the field below the option. This group will appear at the end of the report.

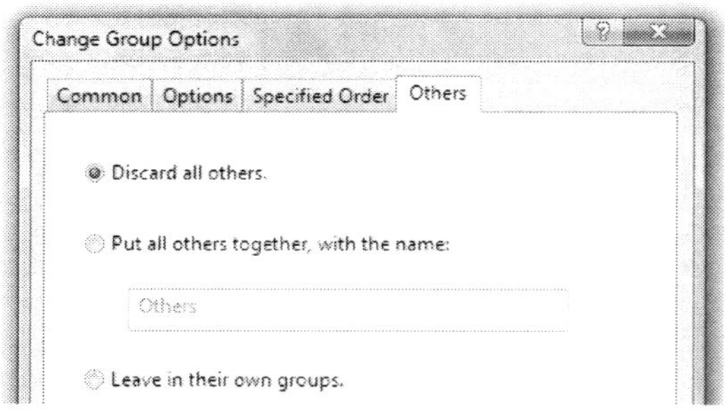

Figure 6-66 Others tab options

6. Preview the report. You should only see the CA, IL and PA groups in the group tree as shown in Figure 6-67. Save the changes and leave the report open to complete the next exercise.

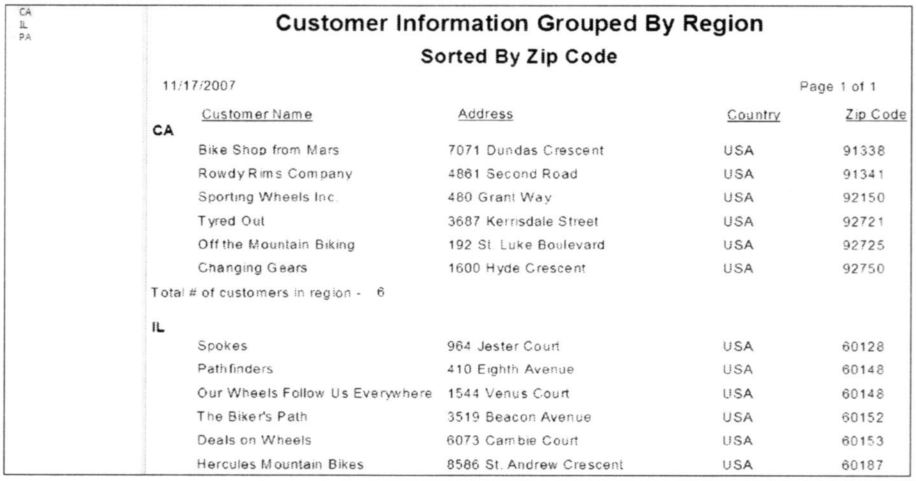

Customer Information Grouped By Region

Sorted By Zip Code

11/17/2007 Page 1 of 1

Customer Name	Address	Country	Zip Code
CA			
Bike Shop from Mars	7071 Dundas Crescent	USA	91338
Rowdy Rims Company	4861 Second Road	USA	91341
Sporting Wheels Inc.	480 Grant Way	USA	92150
Tyred Out	3687 Kerrisdale Street	USA	92721
Off the Mountain Biking	192 St. Luke Boulevard	USA	92725
Changing Gears	1600 Hyde Crescent	USA	92750
Total # of customers in region - 6			
IL			
Spokes	964 Jester Court	USA	60128
Pathfinders	410 Eighth Avenue	USA	60148
Our Wheels Follow Us Everywhere	1544 Venus Court	USA	60148
The Biker's Path	3519 Beacon Avenue	USA	60152
Deals on Wheels	6073 Cambie Court	USA	60153
Hercules Mountain Bikes	8586 St. Andrew Crescent	USA	60187

Figure 6-67 L6.9 User defined groups report

Exercise 6.10: Create A Custom Group Name Report

In the previous exercise, the User Defined Group report displayed the two character state name. In this exercise you will modify that report so that the state names are spelled out.

1. Save the L6.9 report as L6.10 Custom group name.

2. Right-click on the group header report section and select **GROUP EXPERT,** then click the Options button.

3. Delete all of the Named Groups on the Specified Order tab.

4. Click the **NEW** button and type California in the Group Name field. Open the first drop-down list and select **IS EQUAL TO**, then select CA from the second drop-down list. You should have the options selected that are shown in Figure 6-68. Click OK.

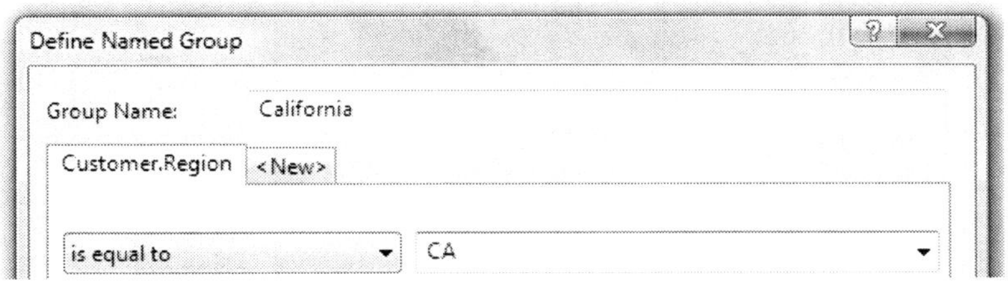

Figure 6-68 Defined Name Group options for CA

5. Repeat the steps above for IL and PA. Leave the Change Group Options dialog box open when you are finished.

6. On the **OTHERS** tab select the option **PUT ALL OTHERS TOGETHER, WITH THE NAME,** then type Other States, as shown in Figure 6-69.

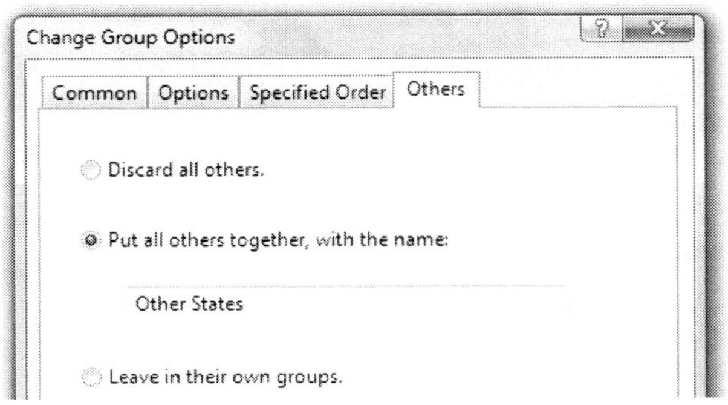

Figure 6-69 Others tab options

7. Click OK twice to close both dialog boxes, then save the changes. The report should look like the one shown in Figure 6-70. Notice that the state names are spelled out in the group tree and on the report. Also notice that there is a new group called **OTHER STATES** in the group tree. This group contains all of the records that meet the selection options for the report, but are not in CA, IL or PA.

California
Illinois
Pennsylvania
Other States

Customer Information Grouped By Region

Sorted By Zip Code

11/17/2007   Page 1 of 8

Customer Name	Address	Country	Zip Code
California			
Bike Shop from Mars	7071 Dundas Crescent	USA	91338
Rowdy Rims Company	4861 Second Road	USA	91341
Sporting Wheels Inc.	480 Grant Way	USA	92150
Tyred Out	3687 Kerrisdale Street	USA	92721
Off the Mountain Biking	192 St. Luke Boulevard	USA	92725
Changing Gears	1600 Hyde Crescent	USA	92750

Total # of customers in region - 6

Customer Name	Address	Country	Zip Code
Illinois			
Spokes	964 Jester Court	USA	60128
Pathfinders	410 Eighth Avenue	USA	60148
Our Wheels Follow Us Everywhere	1544 Venus Court	USA	60148
The Biker's Path	3519 Beacon Avenue	USA	60152
Deals on Wheels	6073 Cambie Court	USA	60153
Hercules Mountain Bikes	8586 St. Andrew Crescent	USA	60187

Figure 6-70 L6.10 Custom group name report

Test Your Skills

1. Modify the monthly report so that it is grouped by quarter, instead of by month.
   Save the L6.7 report as `L6.11 Skills 2001 orders by quarter`.

   - Change the report title to `2001 Orders By Quarter`.
   - Modify the report to group by quarter instead of by month.
   - Change the titles in the group footer section to `Quarter` instead of month.
   - Delete the Group 1 field in the group footer section.
   - Add `Quarter` to the end of the "Totals For The" text object in the group footer section.

   Figure 6-71 shows the last page of the report. Notice the Quarter totals and that the report grand totals are the same as the ones shown earlier in Figure 6-58. Also notice that there are only four groups instead of 12.

1/2001	Robert	King	12/30/2001	2551	$5,879.70
4/2001	Margaret	Peacock	12/31/2001	2552	$2,644.20
7/2001					
10/2001					

   Totals For The Quarter:
   Total # of orders for the quarter - **381**
   Total order amount for the quarter - **$653,638.42**
   Percent of yearly sales - **22.80%**

   Report Grand Totals:
   Total # of orders for the year: **1563**
   Total order amount for the year: **$ 2,867,085.18**

   Figure 6-71 Last page of the L6.11 Skills 2001 orders by quarter report

2. Modify the report to include the salary field and a group by region. Save the L3.2 report as `L6.12 Skills Employee list`.

   - Delete the Photo field and make the details section shorter.
   - Move all of the fields over to the left in the details section.
   - Add the Salary field after the Region field. Center the Salary heading over the field.
   - Group the report by region.
   - Sort the report on the salary field in descending order in each region.

   Your report should look like the one shown in Figure 6-72, which should have 15 records.

First Name	Last Name	Address1	Region	Salary
Steven	Buchanan	14 Garrett Hill		$50,000.00
Robert	King	Edgeham Hollow		$37,000.00
Anne	Dodsworth	7 Houndstooth Rd.		$35,000.00
Michael	Suyama	Coventry House		$30,000.00
Bas-Rhin				
Justin	Brid	2 impasse du Soleil	Bas-Rhin	$75,000.00
Xavier	Martin	9 place de la Liberté	Bas-Rhin	$50,000.00
Laurent	Pereira	7 rue Nationale	Bas-Rhin	$45,000.00

   Figure 6-72 L6.12 Skills Employee list report

3. Modify the Orders By Employee report so that it only displays orders in 2001, grouped by sales rep. Save the L4.16 report as `L6.13 Skills 2001 monthly orders by sales rep`.

   - Create selection criteria that displays orders that have an order date in 2001.
   - Group the report by the Employee ID field.
   - Sort the records by Order Date in descending order.

Create the following three summaries in the group footer section.

① A count of Customer Orders (use the Order ID field).
② A total amount per customer.
③ A sum order amount field to calculate a total of the number of pieces shipped per customer.

   - Format the fields appropriately.
   - Move the Employee Name fields to the group header section.
   - Change the First Name field heading to `Salesperson`. Delete the Last Name field heading.

The last page of the report should look like the one shown in Figure 6-73, which should have 2,617 records.

Totals for:	Anne Dodsworth	
	Total # of orders -	**434**
	Total # of pieces shipped -	**888**
	Total amount of orders -	**$ 1,076,651.52**
Report Totals:	Total # of orders -	**2,617**
	Total # of pieces shipped -	**5,395**
	Total amount of orders -	**$ 5,835,909.95**

Figure 6-73 L6.13 Skills 2001 Monthly orders by sales rep report

4. Modify the sort order of a report. Save the L6.1 report as
   `L6.14 Skills Customers sorted by country and zip code`.

   - Change the existing sort criteria to sort by Country first and then by Postal Code.

Preview the **DISTRITO FEDERAL** region section of the report. It should look like the one shown in Figure 6-74.

Distrito Federal			
Brasilia Bikes Inc.	Rua Fernando, 991	Brazil	23293-300
Bicycles Alex	Rufino Tamayo 395	Mexico	03853
Deportes Mexico City	Via Morelos 3343	Mexico	24421
Tienda de Repuestos Caracas	Av San Jorge 2011	Venezuela	32111
Harare Cycle	4290 Shell Aveneue	Zimbabwe	403943
Total # of customers in region - 5			

Figure 6-74 L6.14 Skills Customers sorted by country and zip code report

5. Modify the report to only display months that have less than 125 orders. Save the L6.7 report as `L6.15 Skills Monthly number of orders under 125`.

   - Change the report title to `2001 Months With Less Than 125 Orders`.
   - Create selection criteria to only display months where the total number of orders is less than 125.
   - The report should look like the one shown in Figure 6-75. The only months that should appear on the report are February, March, April, July, September and December, even though all 12 months are in the group tree.

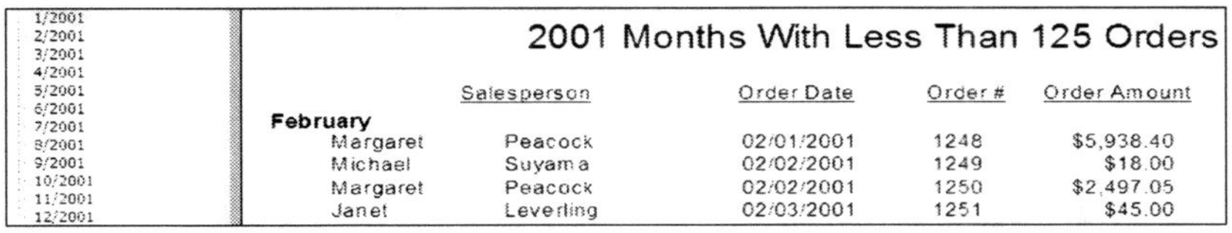

Figure 6-75 L6.15 Skills Monthly number of orders under 125 report

6. Modify the report to create groups and summary fields. Save the L4.16 report as
`L6.16 Skills 2000 orders by sales rep.`

   - Add the Order Amount field after the Order ID field.
   - Add the Customer ID field after the Order Amount field.
   - Group on the Employee ID field, then group on the Order Date field, then group on the Customer ID field. Sort the groups in ascending order. (Use the Group Expert)
   - Sort the detail records on the Customer ID, Order Amount and Order Date fields in ascending order.
   - Create a count of orders per day, per sales rep. Place the count in the Order Date and Employee ID group footer sections and in the report footer section. (Use the Order ID field)
   - Create a total amount of orders per day, per sales rep (Employee). Place the total in all three group footer sections and in the report footer section. (Use the Order Amount field).
   - Create selection criteria to only include orders in 2000.
   - Create a report title and type `2000 Orders By Sales Rep` in the object. Make the font size 16. Make the title bold and center the title across the page.
   - Add a line under the totals in all of the group footer sections. Change the size of the line to 0.5.
   - Center the Quantity field.
   - Move the First Name and Last Name fields to the Group Header 1 section. Change the field heading to `Salesperson`.
   - Change the Order ID field heading to `Order #` and center the field.
   - Change the Customer ID field heading to `Customer #` and center the field.
   - Change the Product ID field heading to `Product #`.
   - Create titles for all of the summary fields.

The layout should look similar to the one shown in Figure 6-76.
Page 1 should look like the one shown in Figure 6-77.
The last page of the report should look like the one shown in Figure 6-78. Notice the totals for the sales rep. As you can see, the total order amount for each customer is not correct. You will modify this report in Lesson 9.

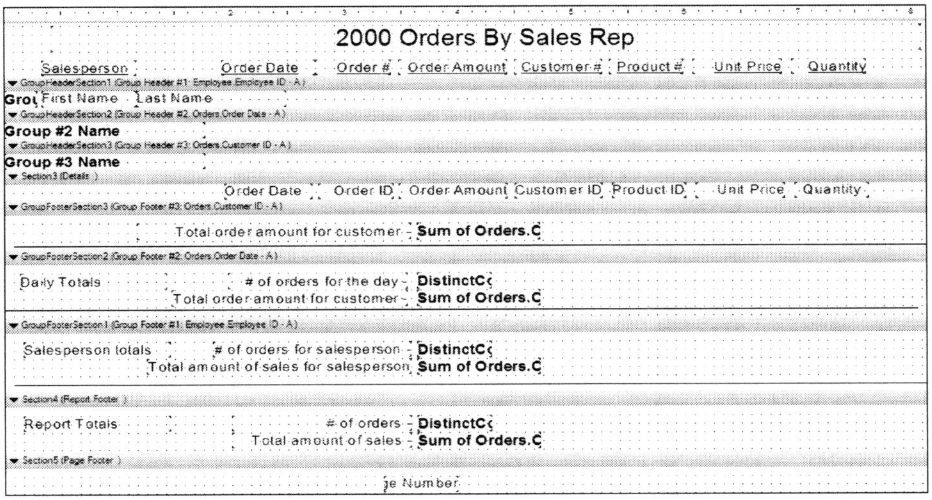

Figure 6-76 Report layout

		2000 Orders By Sales Rep						
⊞ 2/13/2000								
⊞ 2/20/2000								
⊞ 2/27/2000	Salesperson	Order Date	Order #	Order Amount	Customer #	Product #	Unit Price	Quantity
⊞ 11/26/2000	1 Nancy Davolio							
⊞ 12/3/2000	**2/13/2000**							
⊞ 12/10/2000	**30**							
⊞ 12/17/2000		02/19/2000	1310	$58.00	30	1101	$14.50	3
⊞ 12/24/2000		02/19/2000	1310	$58.00	30	1104	$14.50	1
⊟ 3	Total order amount for customer - **$ 116.00**							
⊞ 2/20/2000								
⊞ 2/27/2000	**75**							
⊞ 11/26/2000		02/19/2000	1312	$789.51	75	302162	$479.85	1
⊞ 12/3/2000		02/19/2000	1312	$789.51	75	401001	$267.76	1
⊞ 12/10/2000		02/19/2000	1312	$789.51	75	2202	$41.90	1
⊞ 12/17/2000	Total order amount for customer - **$ 2,368.53**							
⊞ 12/24/2000								
⊞ 12/31/2000	Daily Totals	# of orders for the day - **2**						
⊞ 4	Total order amount for customer - **$ 2,484.53**							
⊞ 6								
⊞ 7								
⊞ 9								

Figure 6-77 Page 1 of the L6.16 Skills 2000 orders by sales rep report

	2000 Orders By Sales Rep						
Salesperson	Order Date	Order #	Order Amount	Customer #	Product #	Unit Price	Quantity
	Total order amount for customer - **$ 170.70**						
33							
	12/27/2000	1101	$982.65	33	2204	$41.90	3
	12/27/2000	1101	$982.65	33	402002	$274.35	3
	12/27/2000	1101	$982.65	33	5204	$33.90	1
	Total order amount for customer - **$ 2,947.95**						
Daily Totals	# of orders for the day - **4**						
	Total order amount for customer - **$ 3,202.65**						
Salesperson totals	# of orders for salesperson - **37**						
	Total amount of sales for salesperson **$ 54,138.44**						
Report Totals	# of orders - **181**						
	Total amount of sales - **$ 515,252.18**						

Figure 6-78 Last page of the L6.16 Skills 2000 orders by sales rep report

7. Modify the report to include a custom group.
    Save the L5.11 report as L6.17 Skills Supplier custom group.

    -   Group the report on the Supplier Name field.
    -   Create a custom group called Top Suppliers.
    -   Add the following suppliers to the Defined Named Group dialog box using the **IS ONE OF** operator: Craze, Roadster, Triumph and Vesper. Group all of the other suppliers under the group Other Suppliers.
    -   The report should look like the one shown in Figure 6-79.
        The **TOP SUPPLIERS** and **OTHER SUPPLIERS** groups should look like the ones shown in Figure 6-79.

Top Suppliers	Product ID	Product Name	Product Type Name	Supplier Name
Other Suppliers	**Top Suppliers**			
	401,001	Mini Nicros	Kids	Craze
	401,002	Mini Nicros	Kids	Craze
	402,001	Micro Nicros	Kids	Craze
	402,002	Micro Nicros	Kids	Craze
	5,401	Xtreme Anatomic Mens Saddle	Saddles	Craze
	5,402	Xtreme Anatomic Ladies Saddle	Saddles	Craze
	5,403	Xtreme Wide MTB Saddle	Saddles	Craze
	5,404	Xtreme Gellite Mens Saddle	Saddles	Craze
	5,405	Xtreme Gellite Ladies Saddle	Saddles	Craze
	6,401	Roadster Jr BMX Saddle	Saddles	Roadster
	6,402	Roadster Micro Mtn Saddle	Saddles	Roadster
	6,403	Roadster Mini Mtn Saddle	Saddles	Roadster
	7,401	Vesper Comfort ATB Saddle	Saddles	Vesper
	7,402	Vesper Comfort Ladies Saddle	Saddles	Vesper
	7,403	Vesper Gelflex ATB Saddle	Saddles	Vesper
	7,404	Vesper Gelflex Ladies Saddle	Saddles	Vesper
	Other Suppliers			
	1,101	Active Outdoors Crochet Glove	Gloves	Active Outdoors
	1,102	Active Outdoors Crochet Glove	Gloves	Active Outdoors
	1,103	Active Outdoors Crochet Glove	Gloves	Active Outdoors

Figure 6-79 L6.17 Skills Supplier custom group report

REPORT WIZARDS AND TEMPLATES

Lesson 2 provided an overview of how to create reports and charts using a wizard. In this lesson you will learn more about the wizards. In the last few lessons all of the reports that you created were created from scratch. I figured that I would give you a break in this lesson from creating reports from scratch. After completing the exercises in this lesson you will be able to:

☑ Understand the options on the common wizard screens
☑ Know the types of reports that each wizard can create
☑ Use the Mail Label wizard
☑ Use the Cross-Tab wizard

LESSON 7

Report Wizard Overview

Now that you have used several report creation and modification features and were able to see the completed reports, many of the options on the wizard screens will hopefully make more sense. Selecting the wrong option in the wizard or not selecting an option that you need will cause you to have to fix the report manually. That's okay though, as wizards can be used as a starting point for a report that you can modify as needed. I think that it is important to understand sorting, grouping and summary options before using a wizard to create a report. One reason that I think this is important is because many of the wizard screens are scaled down versions of an expert screen. This is why this lesson comes after lessons that had you create reports that demonstrate how to sort, group and summarize records.

Table 7-1 explains the type of report that each wizard creates. As you learn to use each of the report wizards you will see that they have a core set of common screens. Table 7-2 illustrates the common screens and the screens that are unique to a specific report wizard.

Wizard	Type Of Report It Creates
Standard	Allows you to create a variety of reports because it is a generic report wizard. It is similar to creating a report from scratch.
Cross-Tab	Allows you to create reports that look like spreadsheets.
Mail Label	Allows you to create reports in a column layout, which can be used to create any size mailing label that you need.

Table 7-1 Report Wizards explained

Screen	Standard	Cross-Tab	Mail Label
Data	X	X	X
Link	X	X	X
Fields	X		X
Grouping	X		
Summaries	X		
Group Sorting	X		
Record Selection	X	X	X
Chart	X	X	
Report Style	X		
Cross-Tab		X	
Grid Style		X	
Label			X

Table 7-2 Report wizard screens

You should be familiar with many of the wizard screens because in Exercise 2.1 you created a report using a wizard that selected options on every screen on the Standard wizard. This was done to demonstrate all of the options in the wizard. The reports that you create with wizards in this lesson will be more focused. Many of the reports that you will create in this lesson are reports that you have already created from scratch. The reason for this is two-fold:

① So that you will be able to determine which method (by wizard or by scratch) is better suited for a specific type of report.
② So that you can decide which way you like best.

The wizards are designed to make what may seem like a complicated task, a little easier to complete. What you may not realize is that there is often more going on behind the scenes of a wizard then you realize. By that I mean, wizards can have default options that you may not be aware of. In Exercise 7.7 you will see an example of this.

Unless you are very familiar with the data that is being used to create the report, you or the person using the report may not know that the data on the report is not 100% accurate. I personally try not to use wizards because of this. I may reconsider using wizards if there was documentation that thoroughly explains the inner workings and defaults that are set.

Common Wizard Screens

As you saw above in Table 7-2, several of the report wizards use the same screens. The majority of reports that you will create with a wizard will be created using the standard wizard. This section will explain the purpose and features of the screens that provide the foundation for many of the wizards.

Some of the wizard screens including the Record Selection, Chart and Cross-Tab have less functionality then the "Expert" that it was taken from. If you find that there is a task that you can't complete using the wizard, check the options on the Expert to see if there is an option that will help you complete the task.

I would like to have the ability to preview the report before the wizard creates it. This would let you know how "close" you are to getting the output that you want.

If you make a mistake or leave something out, you would not have to start all over again because you could click the Back button and fix the mistake or add what you need, because you could see what the report would look like before clicking the Finish button.

Data Screen

Figure 7-1 shows the Data screen. This is the first screen that wizards use. This screen is used to select the data sources that are needed to create the report. The Data screen provides the same functionality as the Database Expert that you learned about. [See Lesson 3, The Database Expert]

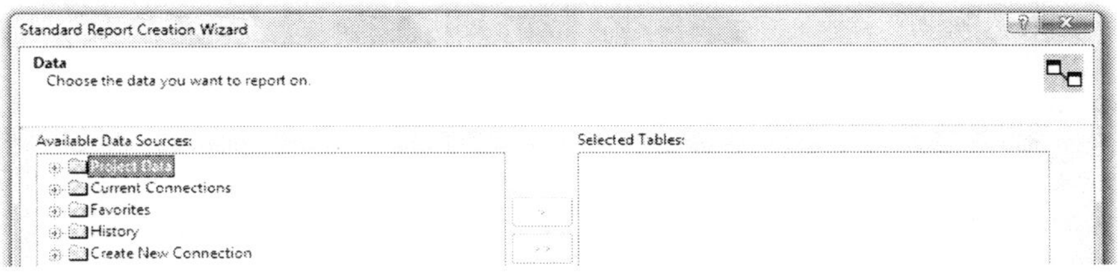

Figure 7-1 Data screen

Fields Screen

Figure 7-2 shows the Fields screen. This is where you select the fields that are needed for the report.

The fields that you select on this screen will be placed in the details section of the report.

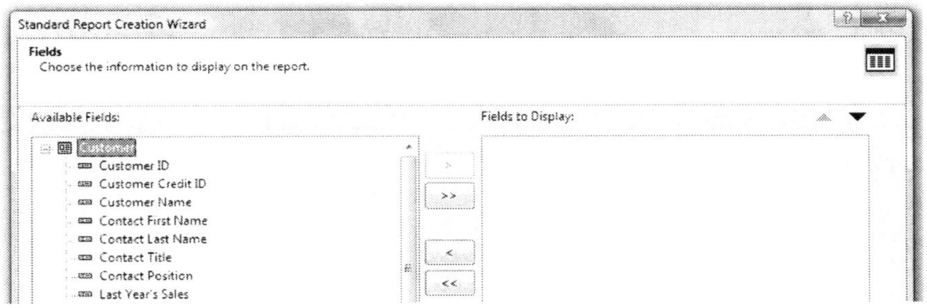

Figure 7-2 Fields screen

Grouping Screen

Figure 7-3 shows the Grouping screen. The options on this screen let you select the fields to group the data by. Creating groups is optional. Grouping options if selected, will create the group header and footer sections of the report. This screen is the equivalent of the Insert Group dialog box that you learned about in Lesson 6.

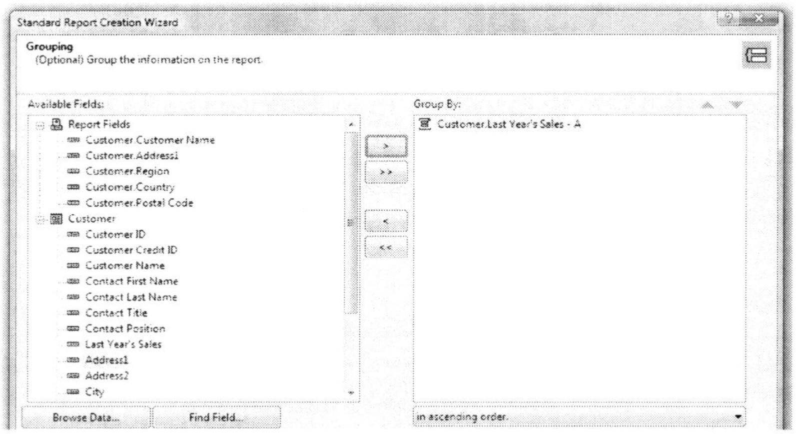

Figure 7-3 Grouping screen

You cannot sort the detail records on this wizard screen. If you need to sort records in a report that does not have a group, you will have to do that through the Record Sort Expert, after the report has been created with the wizard.

 Keep in mind that when you create a group using the wizard, the field(s) that are being grouped on, are automatically moved to the beginning of the report. The fields do not stay in the order that you add them to the report on the Fields screen.

Summaries Screen

The Summaries screen is only available if at least one field is being grouped on. By default, the numeric fields that you select on the Grouping screen are automatically added to the **SUMMARIZED FIELDS** section, as shown in Figure 7-4. The fields in the Summarized Fields section will automatically have grand total fields created and placed in the report footer section of the report.

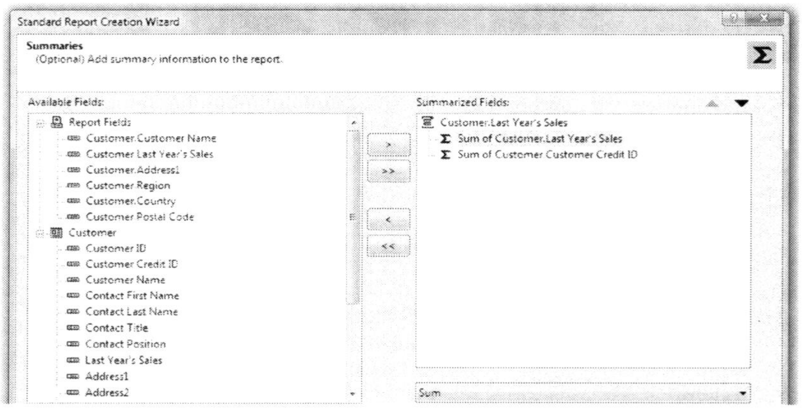

Figure 7-4 Summaries screen

The Summaries screen is the equivalent of the Insert Summary dialog box. If you do not need a summary field for a field that is in the Summarized Fields section, click on the summary field that is not needed, then click the < button. If you need to add a field to summarize on, select it here.

Group Sorting Screen

The Group Sorting screen is only available if at least one field was selected on the Grouping and Summaries screens. Figure 7-5 shows the options that you can select as needed to change the order of the groups based on the value from the selection on the Summaries screen. The Group Sorting screen is a scaled down version of the Group Sort Expert.

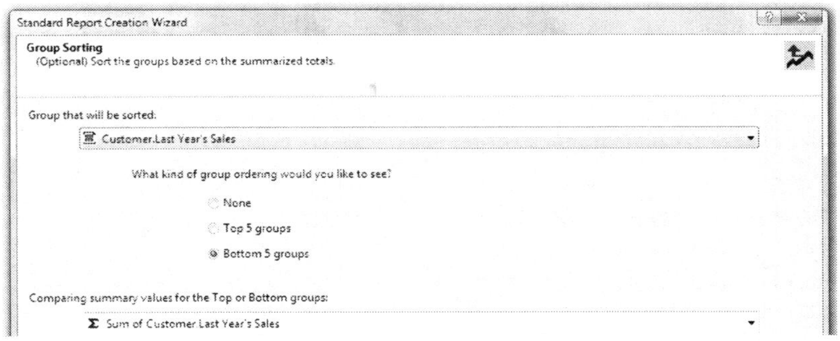

Figure 7-5 Group Sorting screen

There are three group ordering options that you can select from, as discussed below.

① **None** This is the default group ordering option. This option will leave the group order the way it is. Most of the time, this is the option that you want.
② **Top 5 Groups** This option will only print the five groups that have the highest value in the field that is being grouped on. The other groups will not print on the report.
③ **Bottom 5 Groups** This option will only print the five groups that have the lowest value in the field that is being grouped on. The other groups will not print on the report.

If the Top 5 groups or Bottom 5 groups option is selected, the **COMPARING SUMMARY VALUES FOR THE TOP OR BOTTOM GROUPS** option is turned on. This option lets you select the summarized field to base the sort on. The options available in the drop-down list come from the summary fields that you created on the Summaries screen.

Top and Bottom N reports, commonly known as Top N reports, allow you to show the first N or bottom N records in a group. Instead of displaying all orders in a certain date range, you could only show the largest 10 orders in the date range. The wizard does not allow you to select the value of N. It always uses five. If you use the Group Sort Expert to create a Top or Bottom N report, you can select the value of N, by typing it in or using a parameter field to get the value of N each time the report is run. [See Lesson 12, Parameter Fields Overview] You can use the Group Sort Expert to edit a Top N report that was created with a wizard. [See Lesson 13, Group Sort Expert]

Chart Screen

The options shown in Figure 7-6 will let you add a chart to the report. Adding a chart is optional. In order to add a chart, the report has to have at least one group.

Compared to the Chart Expert, the options and chart types on the Chart screen are limited, which means that most of the time you will have to modify the chart after the wizard creates it.

Figure 7-6 Chart screen

The other major drawback to creating a chart using a report wizard is that you have to create the chart from fields that will print on the report. The Chart Expert allows you to create a chart with fields that do not print on the report. Once you select a chart type in the wizard, the three options discussed below are available to help you customize the chart.

① **Chart Title** The information that you enter here will be printed above of the chart.

② **On Change Of** This option defaults to a field that the report is being grouped on.

③ **Show Summary** This option defaults to the summary field for the field that is in the On Change Of field.

Record Selection Screen

The options shown in Figure 7-7 allow you to create selection criteria like you did in Lesson 5 when you learned how to use the Select Expert. Selecting options on this screen is optional. As you saw in Lesson 5, a formula is created when you use the Select Expert. A formula is created on the Record Selection screen if criteria is added.

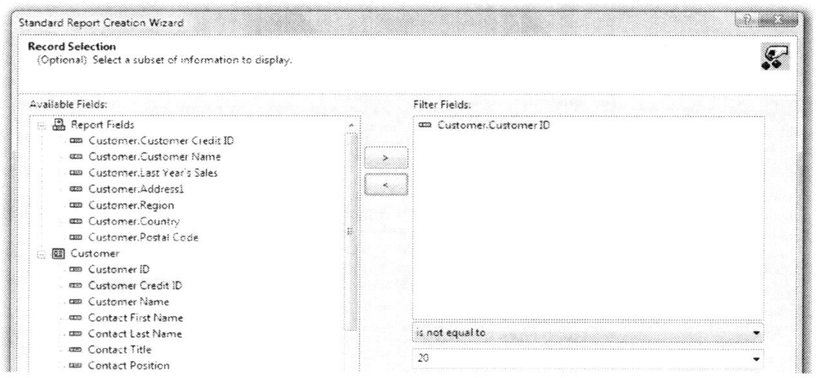

Figure 7-7 Record Selection screen

The difference is that you cannot see the formula that is created from the wizard screen. You can view it after the report is created with the wizard by opening the Select Expert. This will let you edit the formula if necessary. Like the Select Expert, you can create as many filters as you need.

Report Style Screen

The options shown in Figure 7-8 allow you to apply a style which is similar to a template to the report. Applying a style to a report is optional.

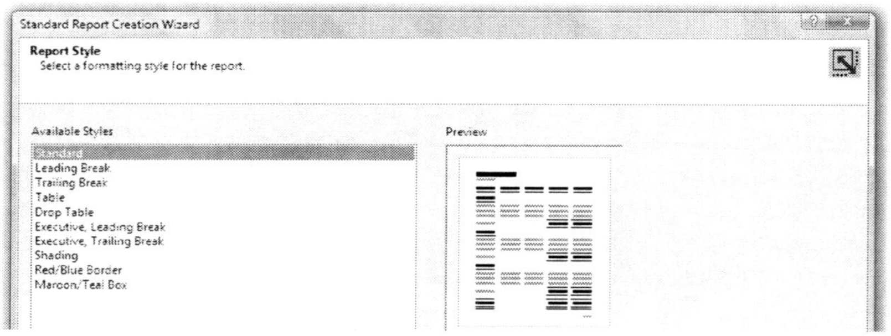

Figure 7-8 Report Style screen

Exercise 7.1: Create The Region = OH Or FL List Report

As you learned in Lesson 2, list reports are one of the easiest types of reports to create. In Lesson 6 you learned how to select records. The report that you will create in this exercise is a list report that selects certain records. The L2.2 list report that you created displayed all of the product records. In this exercise you will select options on the wizard that will filter the data in the customers table to retrieve customers that are in OH or FL.

1. Create a new report and save it as `L7.1 Region = OH or FL list`. Open the Standard Report Wizard and add the Customer table, then click Next.

2. Add the following fields: Customer Name, Address1, Region, Country and Postal Code, then click Next.

3. Click Next on the Grouping screen because this report does not have any grouping requirements. Add the Region field to the **FILTER FIELDS** list on the Record Selection screen.

4. Open the drop-down list and select **IS ONE OF**, then open the next drop-down list and select **OH** or you can type it in. Open the same drop-down list that you just used and select **FL** or you can type it in. Figure 7-9 shows the filter options that should be selected.

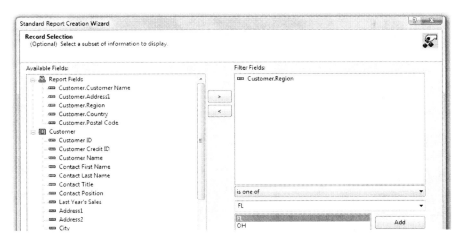

Figure 7-9 Record Selection screen options

5. The report does not require a report style. Click **FINISH**. Your report should look like the one shown in Figure 7-10. Notice that a date field was automatically added to the report. Save the changes and close the report.

2/12/2008				
Customer Na	Address	Region	Country	Postal Code
Bike-A-Holics Anonymo	7429 Arbutus Boulevarc	OH	USA	43005
Wheels and Stuff	2530 Bute Avenue	FL	USA	34666
Uni-Cycle	1008 Kerr Street	OH	USA	43042
Extreme Cycling	1925 Glenaire Avenue	FL	USA	34638
Karma Bikes	1516 Ohio Avenue	OH	USA	43092

Figure 7-10 L7.1 Region = OH or FL list report

Exercise 7.2: Create The Order Date And Order Amount Report

In this exercise you will create a report that selects criteria on fields in different tables. You will create a filter that will select records that have an order date greater than or equal to 6-24-01 and has an order amount greater than 2499.99. [See Exercise 5.4]

1. Create a new report and save it as `L7.2 Order Date GTE 6-24-2001 and Order Amt GT 2499.99`. Open the Standard Report Wizard and add the Customer, Orders and Orders Detail tables, then click Next. The reason that you see the **LINK** screen is because more than one table is being used to create the report. The default links between the tables are correct. Click Next.

2. Add the following fields: Customer Name, Order Date, Ship Date, Order Amount, Order ID and Unit Price, then click Next.

3. Click Next on the Grouping screen because this report does not have any grouping requirements. Add the Order Date field to the **FILTER FIELDS** list.

4. Open the drop-down list and select **IS GREATER THAN OR EQUAL TO**. Open the next drop-down list and select **6/24/2001** or you can type in the date.

5. Add the Order Amount field to the **FILTER FIELDS** list, then open the drop-down list and select **IS GREATER THAN**.

6. Type 2499.99 in the next drop-down list, then click **FINISH**. Your report should look like the one shown in Figure 7-11. Save the changes and close the report.

2/12/2008				
Customer Name	Order Date	Ship Date	Order Amou	Order ID	Unit Price
Piccolo	6/24/2001 12:00:00A	6/29/2001 12:00:00A	$5,879.70	1,762	$2,939.85
The Great Bike Shop	6/24/2001 12:00:00A	6/28/2001 12:00:00A	$7,829.29	1,765	$2,939.85
The Great Bike Shop	6/24/2001 12:00:00A	6/28/2001 12:00:00A	$7,829.29	1,765	$809.87
The Great Bike Shop	6/24/2001 12:00:00A	6/28/2001 12:00:00A	$7,829.29	1,765	$329.85
Trail Blazer's Place	6/24/2001 12:00:00A	6/26/2001 12:00:00A	$2,989.35	1,767	$16.50
Trail Blazer's Place	6/24/2001 12:00:00A	6/26/2001 12:00:00A	$2,989.35	1,767	$2,939.85
Trail Blazer's Place	6/24/2001 12:00:00A	6/24/2001 12:00:00A	$5,994.94	1,768	$14.50
Trail Blazer's Place	6/24/2001 12:00:00A	6/24/2001 12:00:00A	$5,994.94	1,768	$2,645.87
Trail Blazer's Place	6/24/2001 12:00:00A	6/24/2001 12:00:00A	$5,994.94	1,768	$329.85

Figure 7-11 L7.2 Order Date GTE 6-24-2001 and Order Amt GT 2499.99 report

Exercise 7.3: Create A Group Report

In Lesson 6 you learned how to create reports that had groups. In this exercise you will create a report that has a group. The records will be grouped by the product that was ordered.

1. Create a new report and save it as L7.3 Orders grouped by product name. Open the Standard Report Wizard and add the Orders Detail and Product tables, then click Next. The reason that you are adding the Product table is so that you can print the name of the product instead of the Product ID number that is in the Orders Detail table. Click Next on the Link screen because the link options do not need to be changed.

2. Add the following fields: Product Name, Quantity and Order ID, then click Next.

3. Add the Product Name field to the Group By list. The default sort order for the group will cause the Product Names to be sorted in ascending order. No other options need to be selected. Click Finish. Your report should look like the one shown in Figure 7-12. Save the changes and close the report.

Active Outdoors Croch ^	2/12/2008		
Active Outdoors Lycra			
Descent			
Endorphin	Product Name	Quantity	Order ID
Guardian "U" Lock			
Guardian ATB Lock	**Active Outdoors Crochet Glove**		
Guardian Chain Lock	Active Outdoors Crochet Glove	2	1,326
Guardian Mini Lock	Active Outdoors Crochet Glove	1	1,891
Guardian XL "U" Lock	Active Outdoors Crochet Glove	1	1,850
InFlux Crochet Glove	Active Outdoors Crochet Glove	1	1,655
InFlux Lycra Glove	Active Outdoors Crochet Glove	3	1,610

Figure 7-12 L7.3 Orders grouped by product name report

Exercise 7.4: Create A Summary Report

The report that you just created lets you see how many orders for each product there are. If you wanted to know how many customers ordered a specific product you would have to manually count the detail records in each group. You can add a count summary field to the report that will display the total number of orders for each product. In this exercise you will create a report that has a count summary field.

1. Repeat the first three steps in Exercise 7.3. Save the report as L7.4 Product summary. Click Next on the Grouping screen in step 3, instead of clicking the Finish button.

As you can see in Figure 7-13, two summary fields were automatically added to the Summarized Fields section.

Figure 7-13 Group and summary options

You need to remove the fields in the Summarized Fields section that you do not need. To count the number of orders for each product, you can use the Order ID field or the Product Name field because each will print in the details section of the report. The Quantity summary field is not needed.

2. Remove the Quantity summary field, then click on the Sum Order ID field.

3. Open the drop-down list below the Summarized Fields list and select Count. You should have the options selected that are shown in Figure 7-14. Click Finish. Your report should look like the one shown in Figure 7-15. Save the changes and close the report.

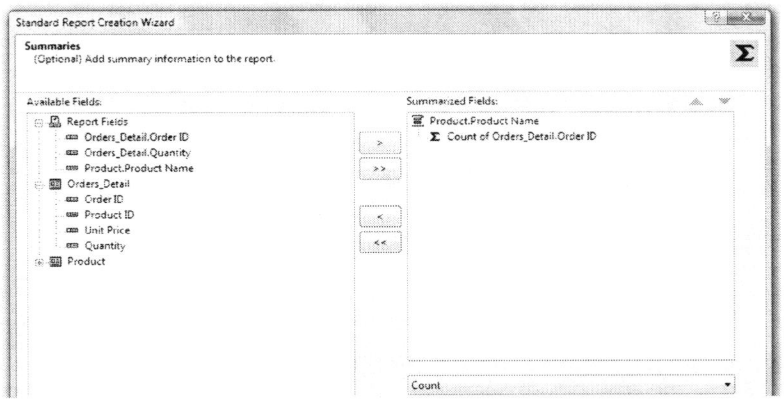

Figure 7-14 Modified summary options

If you look in the group tree you will see a list of all of the products that were purchased by product name, instead of by Product ID number. This makes it easy to find out how many orders were placed for a certain product.

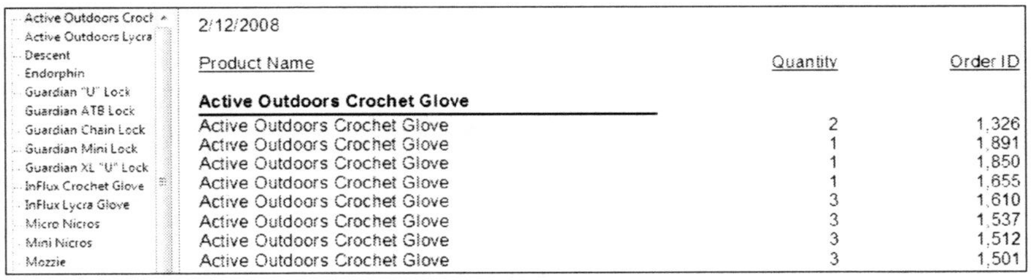

Figure 7-15 L7.4 Product summary report

Figure 7-16 shows the total number of orders for the first product on the report.

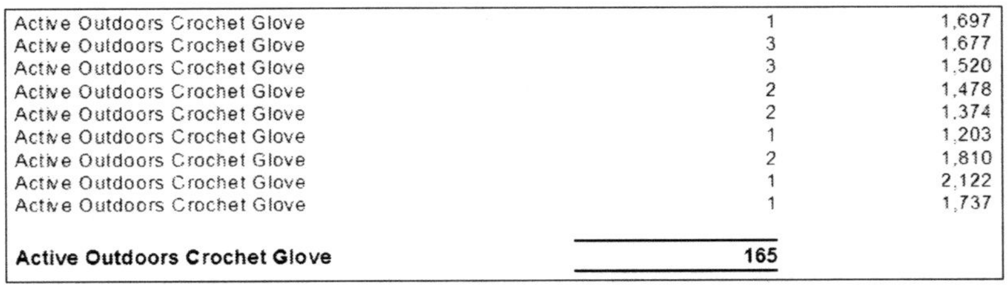

Figure 7-16 Total number of orders for the first product on the report

Exercise 7.5: Create The Customer Information By Region Report

In this exercise you will create a report that groups the data by region. The report will also have summary information and a bar chart.

1. Create a new report and save it as `L7.5 Customer information by region with chart`. Open the Standard Report Wizard, then add the Customer table and click Next.

2. Add the following fields: Customer Name, Address1, Region, Country and Postal Code, then click Next.

3. Add the Region field to the GROUP BY list. Within each region, the report needs to be sorted by Postal Code. Add the Postal Code field to the Grouping screen. Figure 7-17 shows the options that should be selected.

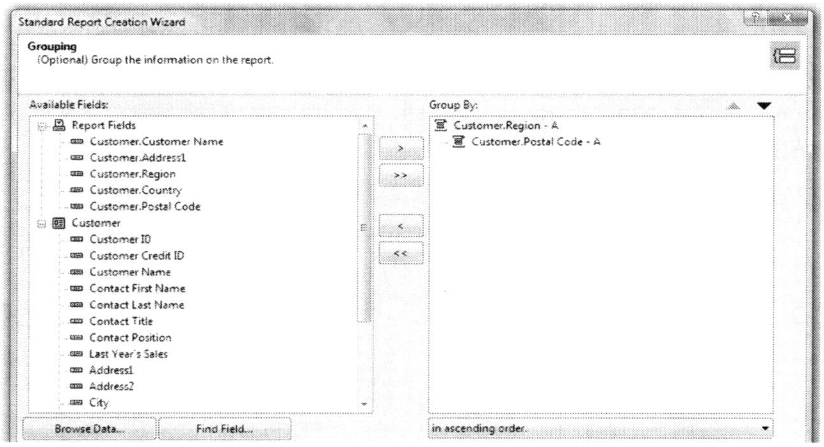

Figure 7-17 Grouping and sorting options selected

4. Click Next and add the Customer ID field, then open the drop-down list and select COUNT.
    Click Next. You will see the Group Sorting screen. No options need to be selected on this screen.

5. Click Next, then select the BAR CHART option on the Chart screen and type
    `Customers Per Region` in the Chart Title field. Figure 7-18 shows the options that should be selected.

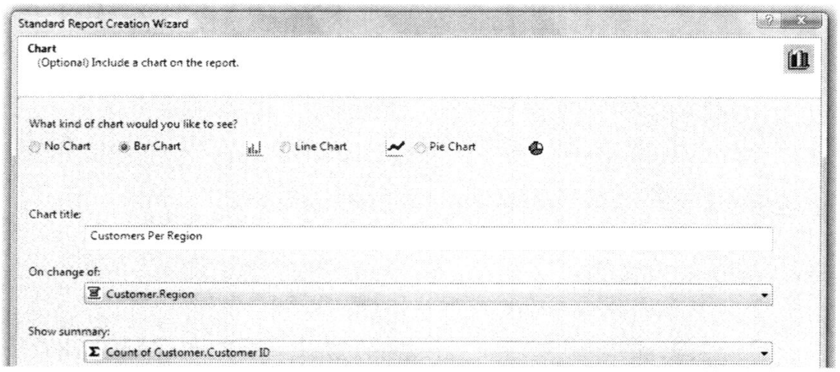

Figure 7-18 Chart screen options

6. This report does not require any filters or selection criteria. Click Finish. Your report should look like the one shown in Figure 7-19. Save the changes and close the report.

Notice that the fields are not in the same order on the report as the order that you added them to the Fields to Display section on the Fields screen. The wizard rearranges the fields and puts the fields that are being grouped on, at the beginning of the details section. As you can see, the chart would need to be modified to be meaningful.

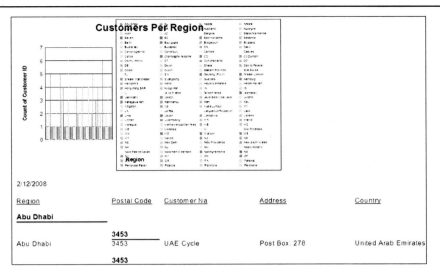

Figure 7-19 L7.5 Customer information by region with chart report

Exercise 7.6: Create The Orders By Customer Report

The report that you will create in this exercise is similar to the report that you created in Exercise 6.2.

1. Create a new report and save it as L7.6 Orders by customer. Open the Standard Report Wizard and add the Customer, Orders and Orders Detail tables. Click Next, then click Next on the Link screen.

2. Add the following fields: Customer Name, Order Date, Ship Date, Order Amount, Order ID and Unit Price, then click Next.

3. Add the Customer Name field to the **GROUP BY** list, then click Next.

4. Click on the Order ID field in the Summarized Fields list and select **COUNT** from the drop-down list, then remove the Unit Price field from the Summarized Fields section.

5. Click on the Order ID field in the **AVAILABLE FIELDS** list, then click the **>** button. This will let you create another summary for the Order ID field.

6. With the second Order ID field still selected, open the drop-down list and select **DISTINCT COUNT**. Figure 7-20 shows the Summarized Field options that should be selected.

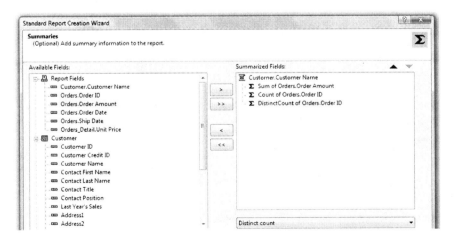

Figure 7-20 Summaries screen options

7. Click Next. Click Next again because none of the options on the Group Sorting screen are needed for this report. Click Next again because none of the options on the Chart screen are needed for this report.

8. Add the Order Date field to the Filter Fields list. Open the drop-down list and select **IS GREATER THAN OR EQUAL TO**, then open the next drop-down list and select **6/24/2001** or you can type it in.

9. Add the Order Amount field to the Filter Fields list. Open the drop-down list and select **IS GREATER THAN**, then type 2499.99 in the next drop-down list and click Finish. Your report should look like the one shown in Figure 7-21. Have you noticed that you can't create a title for the report in the wizard? Close the report.

2/12/2008					
Customer Name	Order Date	Ship Date	Order Amou	Order ID	Unit Price
Alley Cat Cycles					
Alley Cat Cycles	2/19/2002 12:00:00A	2/22/2002 12:00:00A	$8,819.55	2,735	$2,939.85
Alley Cat Cycles	9/28/2001 12:00:00A	9/30/2001 12:00:00A	$2,559.63	2,157	$313.36
Alley Cat Cycles	1/31/2002 12:00:00A	2/3/2002 12:00:00AN	$9,290.30	2,664	$2,792.86
Alley Cat Cycles	1/31/2002 12:00:00A	2/3/2002 12:00:00AN	$9,290.30	2,664	$455.86
Alley Cat Cycles	9/28/2001 12:00:00A	9/30/2001 12:00:00A	$2,559.63	2,157	$539.85
Alley Cat Cycles	10/27/2001 12:00:00,	11/6/2001 12:00:00A	$2,699.55	2,272	$899.85
Alley Cat Cycles	2/19/2002 12:00:00A	2/22/2002 12:00:00A	$8,819.55	2,735	$2,939.85
Alley Cat Cycles	$44,038.51		7	4	

Figure 7-21 L7.6 Orders by customer report

Exercise 7.7: Create A Top N Report

In previous exercises in this lesson you created reports that grouped data. By default, the groups are sorted on the value in the group field. For example, in Exercise 7.6 the orders were grouped by the values (the actual customer names) in the summary customer name field.

There is another way to sort groups on a report. In Lesson 5 you learned how to filter (select) which records would appear on the report. Just like you filtered the detail records in Lesson 5, you can filter the groups. One way to explain Top N reports is that this sort method is sorting the groups on the value of a group summary field instead of the values in the group by field. Top N reports do not display all of the groups. They only display the number of groups that N has. Top N reports rank the groups based on the summary field values. For example, if N=7, only the seven highest groups based on the value of the summary field would be displayed on the report.

> The grand totals that appear on a report when the top or bottom five group sorting option is used, are not the real totals for the detail records on the report. They are the totals for all records that meet the other report criteria before the top or bottom five group sort option is applied.

In this exercise you will create a report that will display the top five days in June 2001 with the largest daily order totals. You will also create a pie chart that displays the top five order days.

1. Create a new report and save it as L7.7 Top 5 order days in June 2001. Open the Standard Report Wizard, then add the Customer and Orders tables and click Next. Click Next on the Link screen.

2. Add the following fields: Customer Name, Order ID, Order Amount and Order Date, then click Next.

3. Add the Order Date field to the **GROUP BY** list, then click Next.

4. Remove the Order ID field from the Summarized Fields list, then click Next.

5. Select the **TOP 5 GROUPS** option on the Group Sorting screen, then click Next.

6. Select the Pie chart option on the Chart screen and type
`Top 5 Order Days In June 2001` in the Chart Title field, then click Next.

7. Add the Order Date field to the Filter Fields list on the Record Selection screen. Open the drop-down list and select **IS BETWEEN**, then type `6/01/2001` in the next drop-down list. In the last drop-down list type `6/30/2001`. Figure 7-22 shows the options that should be selected.

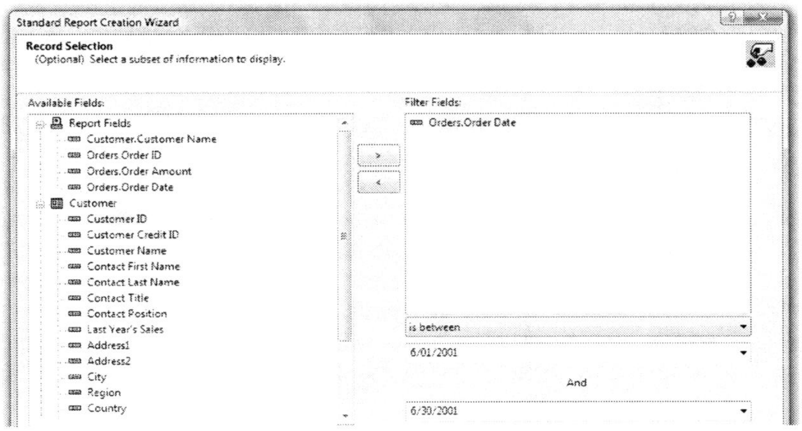

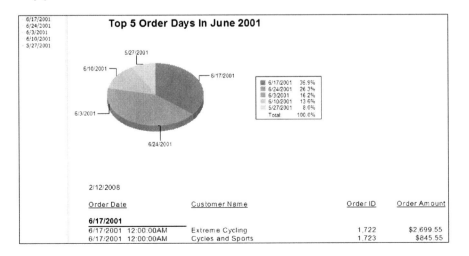

Figure 7-22 Record Selection options

8. Click Finish. Your report should look like the one shown in Figure 7-23. You will only see detail information for the top five order days. Save the changes and leave it open to complete the next exercise.

As you can see, one of the dates in the group tree is in May. If you click on that link, you will see orders for June. No, I did not lead you astray. This is one of the features of the wizard that does not work as intended and is why many report designers tend to stay away from the report wizards. There are options that are preset that you don't know about, that can produce unexpected results. If you plan to use this wizard on a regular basis for something other then a basic report, hopefully you see how important it is to understand the data that the report should produce. That should lead you in the direction of how to fix any problem that the wizard creates.

Figure 7-23 L7.7 Top 5 order days in June 2001 report

Exercise 7.8: How To Fix The L7.7 Top 5 Order Days Report

When I looked at the data in the report, I noticed that each of the five groups actually had more than one days worth of data. Each group actually had a weeks worth of data, even though I was expecting to only see data for one day in each group. Because the data is grouped on the Order Date field, I realized that the wizard must have a group default set to weekly. I opened the Group Expert and sure enough, the option was set to weekly.

This is an example of how a wizard will produce unexpected results. What scares me is that I get the feeling that because the majority of people that use wizards use them without questioning the results, this is something that could easily be missed. What would be helpful on the Standard Wizard would be if the Group Sorting wizard screen had an option to let you select how you want the data to be grouped, by day, week, month, year etc. After looking at the options on the Group Sort Expert, I noticed that it did not have this option either, so because the Group Sorting wizard screen is a subset of the Group Sort Expert, it made a little sense.

Even though the wizard produces results that you may not want, I do not know about you, but I can do without this type of "help" from a wizard. The best advise that I can give you if you insist on using a wizard is after the wizard creates the report, open each corresponding expert for a screen that you selected options on in the wizard and look at the options. While this is good advise, if you think for a minute, you will realize that even that advise would not have helped you detect this error because options from the Group Expert are not used in this wizard. The good news is that this report can be fixed by following the steps below.

1. Save the L7.7 report as `L7.8 Fixed Top 5 order days in June 2001`.

2. Open the Group Expert, then click the **OPTIONS** button. You will see the Change Group Options dialog box. In the last drop-down list you will see that the option **FOR EACH WEEK IS** selected.

3. Open **THE SECTION WILL BE PRINTED** drop-down list and select **FOR EACH DAY** as shown in Figure 7-24. As you can see, knowing about this option would allow you to create a variety of reports just by changing this option. Click OK twice to close both dialog boxes. The report should look like the one shown in Figure 7-25. You should now see five days in June (opposed to four as shown earlier in Figure 7-23) in the group tree section of the report. All of the detail records in each group should have the same order date. Save the changes and close the report.

Figure 7-24 Change Group Options dialog box

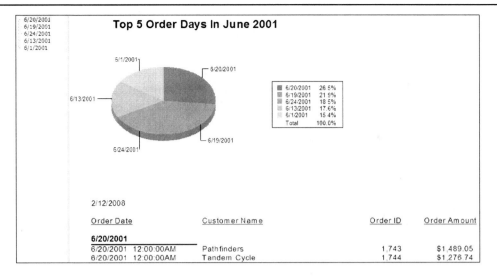

Figure 7-25 L7.8 Fixed Top 5 order days in June 2001 report

Exercise 7.9: Use The Mail Label Report Wizard

This wizard allows you to create a column layout report which many people use to print labels. You can use this wizard to create other types of columnar reports besides mailing labels. In this exercise you will learn how to create a report that can be used to print labels. The report will print shipping labels for customers that placed an order in June 2001, that are in the US. Many of the screens in this wizard are the same as the ones that you have used in the Standard Report wizard.

1. Create a new report and save it as L7.9 Customer labels for June 2001.
    Open the Mail Label Report wizard and add the Customer and Orders tables, then click Next. Click Next again, because the links are correct.

2. Add the following fields: Customer Name, Address1, Address2, City, Region and Postal Code, then click Next.

3. Open the **MAILING LABEL TYPE** drop-down list and select Avery 5163. Figure 7-26 shows the options that should be selected.

The **MAILING LABEL TYPE** drop-down list has an option, **USER-DEFINED LABEL**, that will let you create a custom size label.

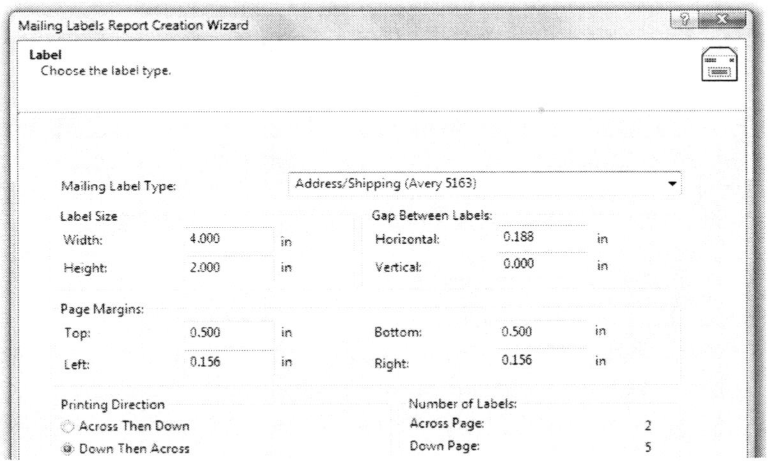

Figure 7-26 Label screen options

4. Click Next and add the Country field to the Filter Fields list. Open the drop-down list and select **IS EQUAL TO**, then open the next drop-down list and select **USA** or type it in.

5. Add the Order Date field to the Filter Fields list. Open the drop-down list and select **IS BETWEEN**, then type `6/01/2001` in the first drop-down list.

6. Type `6/30/2001` in the last drop-down list. Click Finish. Your report should look like the one shown in Figure 7-27, which should have 108 records. Close the report.

Because the date criteria is for a month, you see duplicate customer names. More than likely, the labels would be printed daily, which means that you would not see duplicate customer names in the labels unless a customer placed more than one order on the same day.

City Cyclists 7464 South Kingsway Suite 2006 Sterling Heights MI 48358	Psycho-Cycle 8287 Scott Road Huntsville AL 35818
City Cyclists 7464 South Kingsway Suite 2006 Sterling Heights MI 48358	Psycho-Cycle 8287 Scott Road Huntsville AL 35818
Pathfinders 410 Eighth Avenue DeKalb IL 60148	Psycho-Cycle 8287 Scott Road Huntsville AL 35818

Figure 7-27 L7.8 Customer labels for June 2001 report

 This label report uses two address lines. What many people do is modify the label layout and put both address fields on the same line. That is not a requirement for this exercise.

Cross-Tab Reports

As you saw earlier in Table 7-2, the Cross-Tab wizard has many of the same screens as the Standard Report wizard. The major differences between the Standard and Cross-Tab wizards/reports are discussed below.

① There are no detail records in a cross-tab report.
② The functionality of the Standard wizards grouping and summary screens are combined on one Cross-Tab wizard screen.
③ Cross-Tabs are most often placed in the report header or footer section, but they can be placed in other sections.

Cross-Tabs, like the Select Expert allow you to retrieve records that meet specific criteria. The cross-tab report takes the Select Expert that you learned about in Lesson 5 one step further because it allows you to summarize the data that is in the detail section of standard reports. Cross-Tab reports are often used for comparison analysis. Examples of cross-tab reports are:

① Sales by sales rep by year.
② Sales by region.
③ Summarizing how many orders by year and by zip code, each sales rep has.
④ Sales of a specific product by sales rep, by month.
⑤ Summarizing how many customers by region purchased certain products by month or by year.

Cross-Tab reports often give new report designers difficulty. I suspect that this is because this type of report requires one to think in dimensions. Like spreadsheets, cross-tab reports have rows and columns. Each cell in a spreadsheet contains one piece of data. In a cross-tab object, the cell contains one piece of summary data (count, sum, average etc) that is the equivalent of the sub totals for each group that are usually in the group footer section.

Behind the scenes, cross-tab reports take the detail records that you are use to seeing, as well as, the groups and summarizes the detail data and places the result in a cell. Hopefully, the following scenario will make the concept of cross-tab reports easier to understand.

Going From Standard Reports To Cross-Tab Reports

This scenario will use the first cross-tab example mentioned above; Sales by sales rep by year. The goal of this cross-tab report from a standard report perspective is to show sales for a year by sales rep.

The report shown in Figure 7-28 is a basic list report that sorts the sales, by sales rep and by year. [See the L7 Cross-tab basic sort report combined in the zip file]

		Sales By Rep By Year		
Last Name	First Name	Order Date	Order Amount	Customer Name
Davolio	Nancy	02/19/2000	$58.00	Spokes for Folks
Davolio	Nancy	02/19/2000	$789.51	Belgium Bike Co.
Davolio	Nancy	02/26/2000	$68.90	Mountain Madmen Bicycles
Davolio	Nancy	02/27/2000	$2,698.53	Pedals Inc.
Davolio	Nancy	02/27/2000	$1,079.70	Mountain Madmen Bicycles
Davolio	Nancy	02/27/2000	$1,529.70	Cycle City Rome
.				
.				
.				
Last Name	First Name	Order Date	Order Amount	Customer Name
Suyama	Michael	03/30/2002	$43.50	Whistler Rentals
Suyama	Michael	03/30/2002	$7,483.06	Rockshocks for Jocks
Suyama	Michael	04/03/2002	$43.50	Crazy Wheels
Suyama	Michael	04/03/2002	$55.80	Uni-Cycle
Suyama	Michael	04/06/2002	$32.73	Cycles and Sports
Suyama	Michael	04/06/2002	$1,028.55	Uni-Cycle

Figure 7-28 Basic sorted report of sales by sales rep by year

The report shown above in Figure 7-28 contains all of the data one would need to determine sales by sales rep, by year, but because there aren't any totals for the groups, it would take a while to manually do the math, especially if there were hundreds of sales reps. Yes, I know what you are thinking, create a report that groups the data by sales rep, then by year. Figure 7-29 shows that report.

Can you tell me how many saddles Robert King sold in total? Or can you tell me who had the lowest number of sales in 2001? Okay, I'll wait while you open the report shown in Figure 7-29 and get a calculator to add up the totals for the two sales reps.
[See the L7 Cross-tab grouped report in the zip file] I can wait. I have patience <smile>.

Like the report shown above in Figure 7-28, the report in Figure 7-29 has all of the information that you need to answer these questions.

		Sales By Rep By Year		
Last Name	First Name	Order Date	Order Amount	Customer Name
Nancy Davolio				
2000				
Davolio	Nancy	02/19/2000	$58.00	Spokes for Folks
Davolio	Nancy	02/19/2000	$789.51	Belgium Bike Co.
Davolio	Nancy	02/26/2000	$68.90	Mountain Madmen Bicycles
Davolio	Nancy	02/27/2000	$1,529.70	Cycle City Rome
Davolio	Nancy	02/27/2000	$2,698.53	Pedals Inc.
Davolio	Nancy	02/27/2000	$1,079.70	Mountain Madmen Bicycles
Davolio	Nancy	12/02/2000	$41.90	City Cyclists
Davolio	Nancy	12/03/2000	$10,259.10	Piccolo
.				
.				
.				
Davolio	Nancy	05/01/2002	$238.63	Hercules Mountain Bikes
Davolio	Nancy	05/02/2002	$1,082.50	Warsaw Sports, Inc.
		$138,028.42	# of orders for the current year	73
		$660,756.95	# of orders for the sales rep	360
Janet Leverling				
2000				
Leverling	Janet	02/21/2000	$8,819.55	Bikes, Bikes, and More Bikes
Leverling	Janet	02/21/2000	$5,219.55	Tienda de Bicicletas El Pardc
Leverling	Janet	02/25/2000	$2,246.25	Folk och fä HB
Leverling	Janet	02/26/2000	$61.35	Bike Shop from Mars
Leverling	Janet	02/26/2000	$267.76	Hooked on Helmets
Leverling	Janet	02/27/2000	$1,529.70	Pedals Inc.

Figure 7-29 Data grouped by sales rep by year

The problem is that it is spread out over several pages in the report which makes it difficult for comparison analysis. As you will see after completing Exercise 7.10, this same data in a cross-tab report will be in an easy to read format. With a cross-tab report you can quickly answer questions like how many sales Robert King had for three products and who had the lowest number of sales in 2001.

How To Create This Cross-Tab

Yes, I hear you grumbling and saying, "Great, I now see the advantages of creating a cross-tab report, but how do I get the data shown earlier in Figures 7-28 and 7-29 into cross-tab format?" Okay, here goes:

① Usually, the field down the left side of a cross-tab (that creates the rows) is the data element that there are more occurrences of. In this example, there are more sales reps then years. You can put the sales reps across the top and still get the same results.

② The field that goes across the top (that creates the columns) represents the data element that there are less occurrences of.

③ The cells in the middle of the cross-tab are the sum (in this example, a count) of orders that the sales rep had for the year. This is the equivalent to grouping and sorting data.

④ The totals at the bottom of the cross-tab report will tell you how many sales are for each year and a grand total number of sales for the entire report in the lower right corner of the cross-tab. These totals are automatically calculated in a cross-tab report.

⑤ I have saved the best for last - the placement of the fields on the Cross-Tab screen. The fields for the row and column were answered above. That leaves the field for the cells in the middle of the cross-tab report. Recall the original statement - Sales by sales rep, by year. You have already determined that the sales rep field (the Employee Name field), is what will be used for the rows. You have also determined that the Order Date will be used for the columns. The only field left is the sales (the orders). This is what goes in the Summary field section of the Cross-Tab screen. In this example, the cells represent a count of orders. The default calculation is Sum. You would change that to **DISTINCT COUNT** for the Order ID field.

Cross-Tab Screen

Now that you have a foundation of cross-tab reports, the options on the Cross-Tab and Grid Style screens will hopefully make sense. Figure 7-30 shows the Cross-Tab screen. Figure 7-31 shows the Grid Style screen.

The **AVAILABLE FIELDS** section lets you select the fields that are needed to create the report.

The **ROWS** section contains the field(s) that will be displayed down the left side of the report.

The **COLUMNS** section contains the field(s) that will be displayed across the top of the report.

The **SUMMARY FIELDS** section contains the field(s) that will have the calculation (sum, count, average etc).

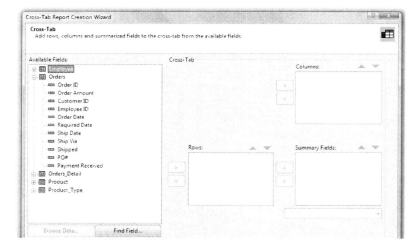

Figure 7-30 Cross-Tab screen

At least one field is required in the rows, columns and summary fields sections to create a cross-tab report.

> Text fields cannot be printed in the cells of a cross-tab without selecting a summary type that works with a text field like count, distinct count, minimum or maximum.

The Grid Style screen contains options that let you add formatting to the report, similar to templates.

Like other reports, you can format a cross-tab report manually.

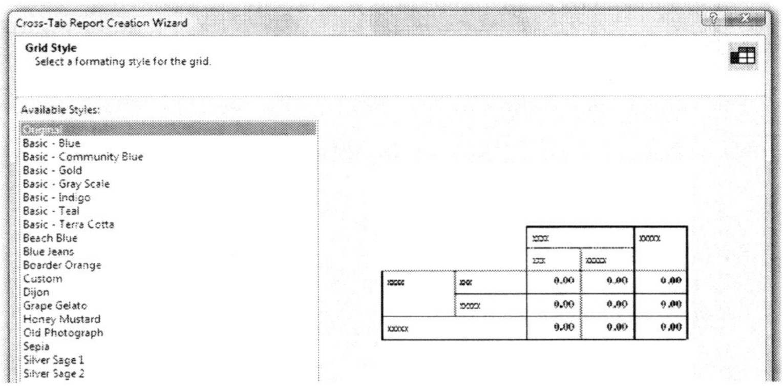

Figure 7-31 Grid Style screen

Exercise 7.10: Create A Cross-Tab Product Report

In this exercise you will create a cross-tab report that shows the number of sales for three classes of products: gloves, kids and saddles by sales rep.

1. Create a Cross-Tab report and save it as `L7.10 Cross-Tab`. Select the Cross-Tab Expert option, then click OK.

2. Add the Employee, Orders, Orders Detail, Product and Product Type tables, then click Next. Click Next on the Link screen.

3. Click on the Last Name field in the Employee table, then click the right arrow button next to the **ROWS** list.

4. Add the Product Type Name field in the Product Type table to the **COLUMNS** list, then add the Quantity field in the Orders Detail table to the **SUMMARY FIELDS** list.

> You can click on the field in the Available Fields list and drag it to the section of the Cross-Tab screen that you need.

5. Select **COUNT** from the drop-down list under the Summary Fields section. The Cross-Tab screen should have the options selected that are shown in Figure 7-32.

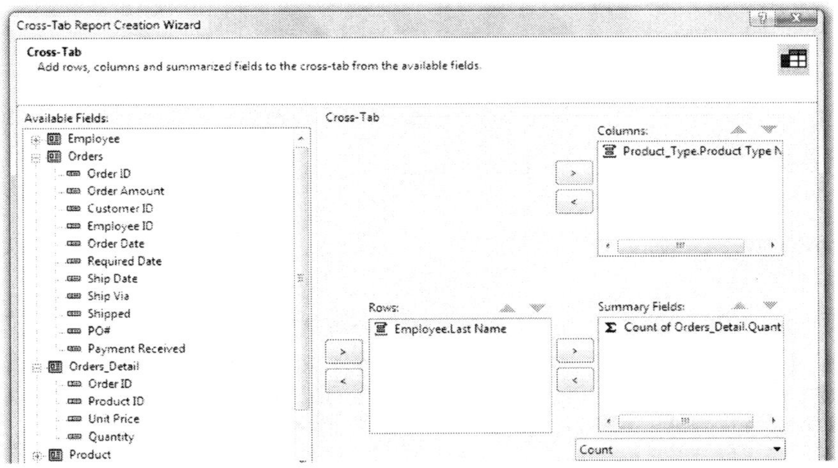

Figure 7-32 Cross-Tab screen options

6. Click Next. Select the **NO CHART** option, if it is not already selected, then click Next.

> The reason that you added the Orders table and did not use any fields from the table is because it is the "link" between the Orders Detail table and the Employee table to get the Employee Name for each order.

7. This report needs to be filtered because you only want totals for three classes of products: gloves, kids and saddles. Add the Product Type Name field from the Product Type table to the Filter Fields list, then open the drop-down list and select **IS ONE OF**.

8. Open the next drop-down list and select gloves, kids and saddles. You should have the options selected that are shown in Figure 7-33.

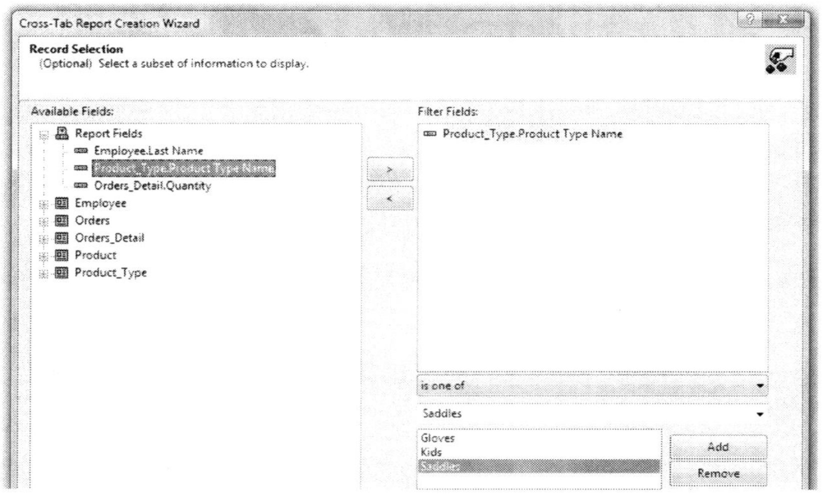

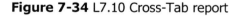

Figure 7-33 Record Selection options

9. Click Next, then click on the **ORIGINAL** grid style if it is not already selected, as shown earlier in Figure 7-31. Click Finish. Your report should look like the one shown in Figure 7-34. Now can you tell me how many saddles Robert King sold in total? Close the report.

	Gloves	Kids	Saddles	Total
Davolio	85	18	49	152
Dodsworth	101	19	58	178
King	97	23	58	178
Leverling	84	25	56	165
Peacock	105	20	59	184
Suyama	84	25	56	165
Total	556	130	336	1,022

Figure 7-34 L7.10 Cross-Tab report

Exercise 7.11: Create A Sales Per Year Per Sales Rep Cross-Tab Report

Earlier I asked if you could tell how many sales in total Robert King had and who had the lowest total sales in terms of the order amount. I was wondering if you came up with the answer yet? If not, this exercise will show you how to find out how many sales per year each sales rep had.

1. Create a Cross-Tab report and save it as
   `L7.11 Sales Per Year Per Sales Rep Cross-Tab`.

2. Add the Employee and Orders tables, then click Next. Click Next on the Link screen.

3. Add the Last Name field in the Employee table to the **ROWS** list. Add the Order Date field to the **COLUMNS** list.

4. Open the drop-down list under the Columns section and select **FOR EACH YEAR**. This will create a column for each year that there are orders in the Orders table.

5. Add the Order Amount field to the Summary Fields list. You should have the options selected that are shown in Figure 7-35. This cross-tab report does not need to select (filter) any records because you want to create totals for all of the orders in the database. Click Finish. Your report should look like the one shown in Figure 7-36. Leave the report open to complete the next part of the exercise.

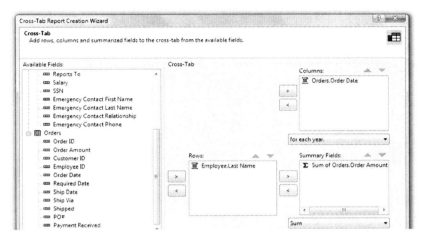

Figure 7-35 Cross-Tab screen options

If the Orders table had 10 years worth of data and you only wanted to show some of the years on the report, you would select the Order Date field on the Record Selection screen and enter the date range for the years that you wanted to display on the report.

	2000	2001	2002	Total
Davolio	,862.70	,865.83	,028.42	ı,756.95
Dodsworth	,049.94	,545.52	,253.75	ı,849.21
King	,093.75	,406.60	,255.59	ı,755.94
Leverling	.121.64	,235.19	,745.16	ı,101.99
Peacock	,458.39	,150.56	,190.82	,799.77
Suyama	,804.22	,881.48	,715.78	ı,401.48
Total	,390.64	,085.18	,189.52	,665.34

Figure 7-36 Sales by year cross-tab report

Modify The Cross-Tab Report

As you can see, the grid is too small to handle the sales total amounts. This part of the exercise will show you how to modify the cross-tab report.

1. In the design window, select all four of the Order Amount fields as shown in Figure 7-37, then make the fields wider by dragging them to the right. The border around the Cross-Tab will expand as you make the fields wider.

	Column #1 N	Total
Row #1 Name	der Amount	der Amount
Total	der Amount	der Amount

Figure 7-37 Order Amount fields selected

2. Center the Column #1 Name and Total column headings. Save the changes. The report should look like the one shown in Figure 7-38. Now you should be able to figure out who had the lowest sales amount each year. Close the report.

	2000	2001	2002	Total
Davolio	$71,862.70	$450,865.83	$138,028.42	$660,756.95
Dodsworth	$29,049.94	$513,545.52	$140,253.75	$682,849.21
King	$21,093.75	$512,406.60	$215,255.59	$748,755.94
Leverling	$44,121.64	$447,235.19	$157,745.16	$649,101.99
Peacock	$38,458.39	$446,150.56	$147,190.82	$631,799.77
Suyama	$54,804.22	$496,881.48	$158,715.78	$710,401.48
Total	$259,390.64	$2,867,085.18	$957,189.52	$4,083,665.34

Figure 7-38 L7.11 Sales Per Year Per Sales Rep Cross-Tab report

Test Your Skills

1. Create the L5.11 Skills Product type filter report using the Standard Wizard. Your report should look similar to the one shown in Figure 7-39. The report should have 33 records.

   - Save the report as `L7.12 Skills Product type filter`.
   - The Product, Product Type and Supplier tables are needed to create this report.
   - Create a filter that only displays the gloves, saddles and kids product types.
   - Apply the Drop Table style to the report.

	2/12/2008	
Product ID	Product Name	Supplier Name
1,101	Active Outdoors Crochet Glove	Active Outdoors
1,102	Active Outdoors Crochet Glove	Active Outdoors
1,103	Active Outdoors Crochet Glove	Active Outdoors
1,104	Active Outdoors Crochet Glove	Active Outdoors
1,105	Active Outdoors Crochet Glove	Active Outdoors
1,106	Active Outdoors Lycra Glove	Active Outdoors
1,107	Active Outdoors Lycra Glove	Active Outdoors
1,108	Active Outdoors Lycra Glove	Active Outdoors
1,109	Active Outdoors Lycra Glove	Active Outdoors
1,110	Active Outdoors Lycra Glove	Active Outdoors
1,111	Active Outdoors Lycra Glove	Active Outdoors
2,201	Triumph Pro Helmet	Triumph
2,202	Triumph Pro Helmet	Triumph

Figure 7-39 L7.12 Skills Product type filter report

2. Create the L5.12 Skills Ship Via filter report using the Standard Wizard. Your report should look similar to the one shown in Figure 7-40. The report should have 40 records.

   - Save the report as `L7.13 Skills Orders filter`.
   - The Customer and Orders tables are needed to create this report.
   - Create a filter that displays order amounts that are >= $1,000 and were shipped between 1/1/2001 and 1/31/2001 in the USA.

Customer Name	Order ID	Order Date	Order Amou	Ship Via	Region
City Cyclists	1,246	1/30/2001 12:00:00.	$3,884.25	Pickup	MI
Bike-A-Holics Anonymous	1,097	12/27/2000 12:00:0	$1,439.55	Loomis	OH
Sporting Wheels Inc.	1,181	1/15/2001 12:00:00.	$5,912.96	UPS	CA
Sporting Wheels Inc.	1,220	1/22/2001 12:00:00.	$5,879.70	UPS	CA
Rockshocks for Jocks	1,161	1/11/2001 12:00:00.	$1,799.70	Parcel Post	TX
Rowdy Rims Company	1,090	12/22/2000 12:00:0	$1,529.70	Loomis	CA
Rowdy Rims Company	1,186	1/15/2001 12:00:00.	$1,110.70	Purolator	CA
Clean Air Transportation C	1,123	1/2/2001 12:00:00A	$5,219.55	Pickup	PA
Clean Air Transportation C	1,228	1/25/2001 12:00:00.	$2,181.86	Loomis	PA
Hooked on Helmets	1,122	1/1/2001 12:00:00A	$1,025.40	Loomis	MN
C-Gate Cycle Shoppe	1,136	1/5/2001 12:00:00A	$3,209.53	Pickup	VA

Figure 7-40 L7.13 Skills Orders filter report

3. Create a report using the Standard Wizard that groups and counts employees by position. Your report should look like the one shown in Figure 7-41. The report should have 15 records.

   - Save the report as `L7.14 Skills Employees by position`.
   - Add the following fields from the Employee table: Position, First Name, Last Name, Hire Date and Reports To.

Advertising Specialist Business Manager Inside Sales Coordinator Mail Clerk Marketing Associate Marketing Director Receptionist Sales Manager Sales Representative Vice President, Sales	Position	First Name	Last Name	Hire Date	Reports To
	Advertising Specialist				
	Advertising Specialist	Laurent	Pereira	2/1/1994 12:00:00AM	
	Advertising Specialist	1			
	Business Manager				
	Business Manager	Albert	Hellstern	3/1/1993 12:00:00AM	2
	Business Manager	1			
	Inside Sales Coordinator				
	Inside Sales Coordinator	Laura	Callahan	1/30/1993 12:00:00Al	2
	Inside Sales Coordinator	1			

Figure 7-41 L7.14 Skills Employees by position report

4. Create a report using the Standard Wizard to create a Bottom N report that only selects records in the Customer table in the USA. Your report should look like the one shown in Figure 7-42.

- Save the report as L7.15 Skills Bottom 5 orders.
- Add the following fields from the Customer table: Customer ID and Customer Name.
- Add the following fields from the Orders table: Order Amount, Order Date and Ship Via.
- Group on the Order Amount field.
- Remove the Customer ID summary field.
- The orders must have Pickup in the Ship Via field.
- Use the Bottom 5 groups option and sort the groups on the order amount field.

Order Amount	Customer ID	Customer Name	Order Date	Ship Via
$10.71				
$10.71	40	Cyclist's Trail Co.	1/24/2001 12:00:00AI	Pickup
$10.71	**$10.71**			
$13.50				
$13.50	36	Road Runners Paradise	10/20/2001 12:00:00/	Pickup
$13.50	**$13.50**			
$13.95				
$13.95	31	To The Limit Biking Co.	11/27/2001 12:00:00/	Pickup
$13.95	**$13.95**			
$14.50				
$14.50	55	Tandem Cycle	8/8/2001 12:00:00AM	Pickup
$14.50	**$14.50**			
$14.73				
$14.73	9	Trail Blazer's Place	4/4/2001 12:00:00AM	Pickup
$14.73	**$14.73**			
Grand Total:	**$505,586.64**			

Figure 7-42 L7.15 Skills Bottom 5 orders report

PRINTING AND EXPORTING

You have created and modified a lot of reports in the previous lessons. So far, the reports that you have created have not been printed or shared with anyone. As the report designer, after you create the reports, they are put into production so that other people can use them.

There are several ways that other people can use the reports, including: printing them if they have Crystal Reports installed, use a Crystal Reports viewer, attach them to a Visual Basic or Visual C++ form or export the reports to a file type that other people can use. Most users will not have Crystal Reports installed on their computer, so they will not be able to open the report file and print it like you can.

After completing the exercises in this lesson you will be able to use the following printing and exporting options and techniques:

- ☑ Page Setup dialog box options
- ☑ Print options
- ☑ Use the Set print date and time options
- ☑ Diagnose printing problems
- ☑ Report Options dialog box
- ☑ Export reports to a variety of file formats

LESSON 8

Printing Options

Crystal Reports has the majority of printing options for reports that you have already used in word processing and other types of software packages. As you learned, most people that will run the reports that you create will not have Crystal Reports installed. Even if they do have Crystal Reports installed, do you think that every user will be able to set the printing and page setup options correctly without calling you? And if they can, you should still select the appropriate printing options so that the report will print as you intended it to.

Page Setup Options

As shown in Figure 8-1, the options on this dialog box let you change the page margins. The options shown are the defaults that are set when Crystal Reports is installed.

Crystal Reports ⇒ Design ⇒ Page Setup will open this dialog box.

If checked, the **ADJUST AUTOMATICALLY** option will cause the margins to change automatically, when the paper size or orientation is changed.

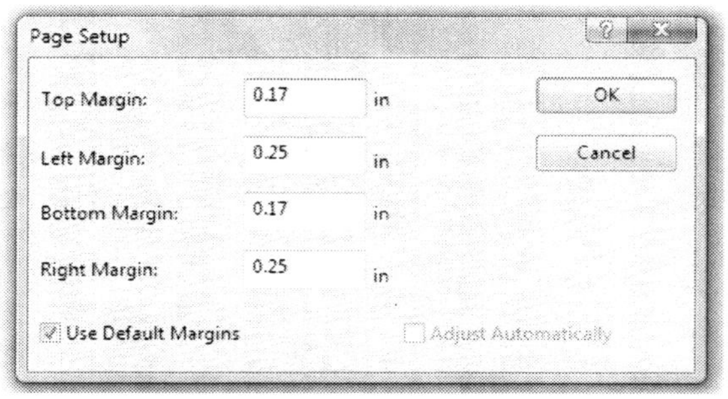

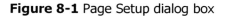

Figure 8-1 Page Setup dialog box

Print Options

The options shown in Figure 8-2 let you select a printer and its options, which are the same options that you have probably used in other software packages. Crystal Reports ⇒ Design ⇒ Printer Setup will open this dialog box. Select the **NO PRINTER** option if the report will not be printed. This option will optimize the report to be viewed on a screen. It can also be used to resolve printing problems, as you will learn later in this lesson.

The default paper size is **LETTER**. Some reports, in particular, financial reports may need to be printed on legal paper. To switch to legal paper open the Print Setup dialog box and change the Paper Size to **LEGAL**, then change the Orientation to **LANDSCAPE**. You can fit more fields across the page if the orientation is **LANDSCAPE**. Some of the reports that you have created had a field that was hanging off of the right side of the report. When you previewed the report all of the data in the last field could not be displayed.

If you have more than one printer installed, the default printer that you have selected in Windows will appear in the **NAME** drop-down list shown above in Figure 8-2. If the printer shown is not the one that you want to use, open the drop-down list and select the printer that you want. Clicking the **PROPERTIES** button will open the Properties dialog box for the selected printer, as shown in Figure 8-3. You can select the options for the printer.

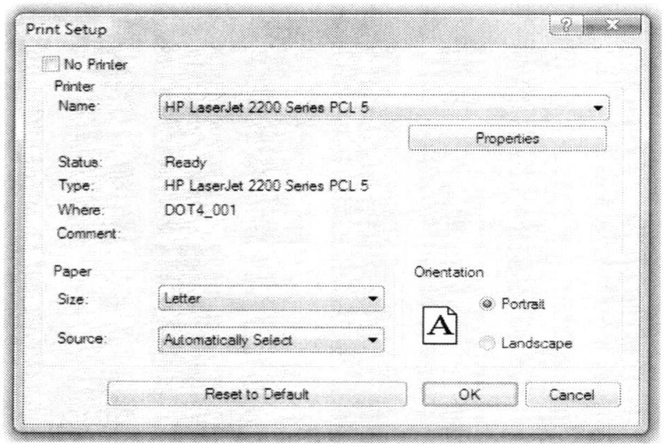

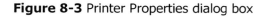

Figure 8-2 Printer options dialog box

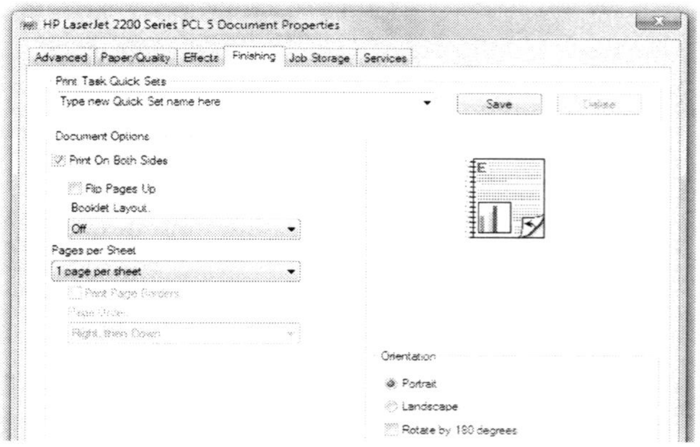

Figure 8-3 Printer Properties dialog box

Figure 8-4 shows the print dialog box that you will see if you click the print button on the report preview toolbar. It allows you to select options for the active report.

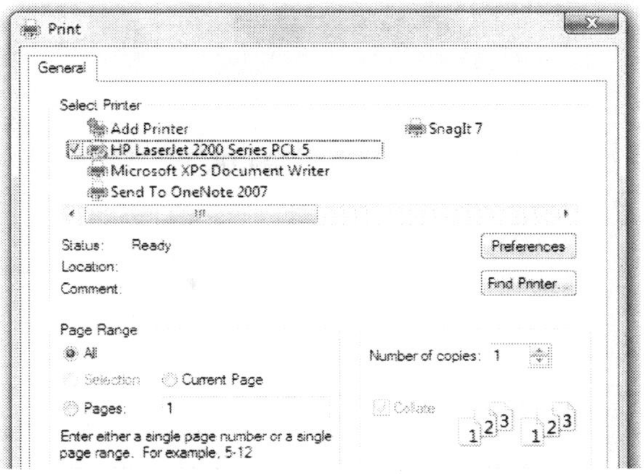

Figure 8-4 Print dialog box

Printing Problems

If you have an ink jet printer and have opened a document that was created by someone that has a laser jet printer, you may have noticed that sometimes the spacing is off. If so, the topics discussed in this section will be helpful. If you have experienced formatting issues (when it comes to printing a document) using other software, many of those problems are also found in Crystal Reports, as discussed below.

While the reports that you create may look good on your computer monitor and look good when you print them, that may not be the case when the reports go into production. This is because information like printer drivers and monitor resolution come from the options that are on your computer. Technical people tend to install printer and video driver updates, while end-users do not. This can cause reports to print differently even if you have the same model printer as the person printing the report.

This information is saved with the report. This is why someone that does not have the same exact settings on their computer as you do, will sometimes get different printed or visual screen results when they run the report. The list below discusses several printing concepts that you should be aware of that can effect how the reports that you create, look on a computer monitor and how they look when printed.

① Crystal Reports uses information from the printer driver that was the default, when the report was created (meaning the one on your computer). The printer driver determines the character width and height of the information printed on a report.

② The video driver resolution and operating system used when the report was created can also effect the report when it is viewed on a different monitor.

③ It is important to note that some of the layout options of reports that you create come from the options on the Page Setup and Print Setup dialog boxes. The default margins from the Page Setup dialog box are used for the reports that you create.

④ The length of the report page comes from the type of printer that is selected, which is usually your default printer. This is important to know because each printer model has limits on how close to the edge of the paper it can print.

Okay, I can imagine that the information that you just read is cause for concern. The suggestions below will help resolve many of the printing problems discussed above.

① Set the margins for the report instead of using the default printer driver margins.

② Use the **CAN GROW** option for fields that contain a lot of data, like memo fields.
Putting memo fields in their own subsection of the report would also be helpful.

③ Use common True Type fonts, like Arial, Garamond and Times New Roman, that come standard on Windows based computers. If you need to use a non standard font, you should export the report to Adobe Acrobat PDF format, which you will learn about later in this lesson. Creating a PDF file is the best option to use, because this file type can be read on any computer that has the free Adobe Acrobat Reader.

④ Select the **NO PRINTER** option shown earlier in Figure 8-2. Selecting this option is best if the report will be printed on several different printer models. Doing this helps keep the formatting generic enough so that the report can be printed on a variety of printers. If you know that a report will be printed on a printer that is different from the printer that you have, select the No Printer option.

⑤ Select the computer monitor video resolution that most of the people that will view the report have. If this is not possible, consider exporting the report to PDF format, so that more people can view the report as intended.

Report Viewers

If you do not have Microsoft Word or Excel, you can download the free viewers and use them to view some of the exported reports that you will create later in this lesson. If the web pages listed below have changed and you can't find the files, search for the file name in parenthesis on Microsoft's web site.

Word 2003 Viewer - (wdviewer.exe)
office.microsoft.com/search/redir.aspx?AssetID=DC011320141033&Origin=HH100152641033&CTT=5

Excel 2003 Viewer - (xlviewer.exe) office.microsoft.com/downloads/2000/xlviewer.aspx

Exercise 8.1: Use The Set Print Date And Time Options

The Set Print Date and Time options are useful when you use the Print Date or Print Time special fields on a report and have the need to override these dates when the report is printed. The options on the dialog box will let you set these fields to a date or time, other than the current date or time.

1. Save the L4.12 report as `L8.1 Set print date`.

2. Preview the report. Notice the date in the **DATE THE REPORT WAS PRINTED** field. It should be today's date.

3. Crystal Reports ⇒ Report ⇒ Set Print Date and Time. Select the **OTHER** option and type `1/1/2001` in the Date field as shown in Figure 8-5.

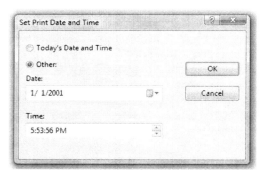

Figure 8-5 Set Print Date and Time dialog box

4. Click OK and save the changes, then preview the report. You should see 1/1/2001 in the Date the report was printed field, as shown in Figure 8-6.

Date the report was printed:	Date the report was last saved:	11/18/2007	Date the data was last refreshed:	11/18/2007
1/1/2001	Time the report was last saved:	5:55:15PM	Time the data was last refreshed:	5:55:28PM
			Date the report was designed:	11/13/2007

Figure 8-6 L8.1 Set print date report with the print date changed

5. Close the report. The 2001 date will print every time the report is run until you remove it from the Set Print Date and Time dialog box.

Report Options Dialog Box

The options that you see checked like the **DATABASE SERVER IS CASE-INSENSITIVE**, when you open the dialog box shown in Figure 8-7 are selected by the settings on the Options dialog box. [See Lesson 5, Customizing Crystal Reports Design Environment] The pre-selected options are automatically applied to every report that you create. The purpose of this dialog box is to let you select options for the current report. Changes to this dialog box are set on a report by report basis.

Crystal Reports ⇒ Report ⇒ Report Options will open this dialog box.

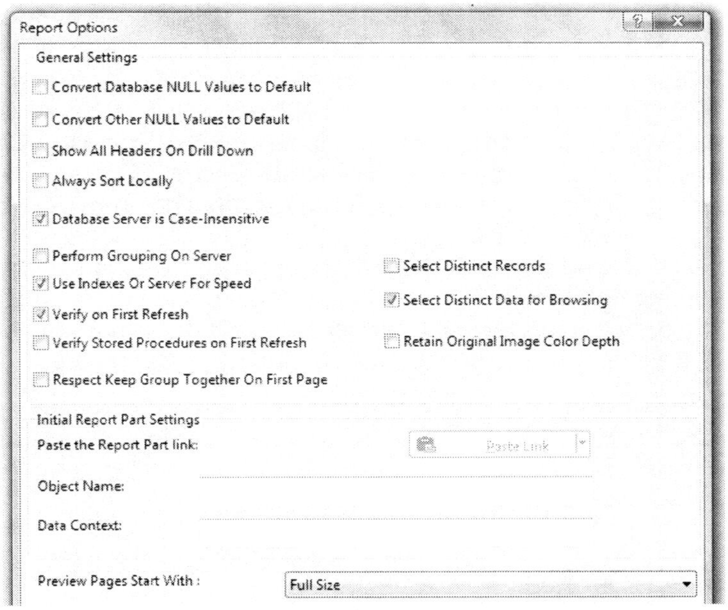

Figure 8-7 Report Options dialog box

> Changes that you make on the Reporting tab on the Options dialog box will change the default options on the Report Options dialog box. The options selected on the Report Options dialog box override the corresponding option on the Options dialog box (when applicable), for the active report. This means that the options on the Report Options dialog box will always be applied to the report, while the options on the Options dialog box will only be applied if there is no corresponding option on the Report Options dialog box.

Export Report Overview

A report designer is not only responsible for creating and modifying reports, they can also be responsible for distributing the reports. There are five main ways that an end-user can access and run reports that you create, as discussed below.

① Purchase and install Crystal Reports for every end-user that needs to run a report. This is probably not the best solution, especially if there are hundreds or thousands of people in the company that need to run or print reports. This option could cost tens of thousands of dollars in hardware upgrades, software purchases, training and tech support.

② Hire someone to run reports all day, print them and send them via inter-office mail or email to end-users. This may sound good until you realize that end-users may not get the reports in a timely manner if they are sent via inter-office mail.

③ If the reports are part of an application that is being developed in a software package like Visual Basic or C++, the reports can be attached to forms in the application. If this is the case, that's great, because your job is done, unless you are the person that is creating the application.

④ Save the reports to a Crystal Reports Server or the Business Objects Enterprise.

⑤ If none of the options discussed above are appropriate, all is not lost. There is another option. Exporting reports is cost effective and is something that a report designer can set up. The DBA would have to create a script that runs the exported report and places it on a server. The only downside to this solution is that the reports will not necessarily have the most current data. If this is a problem, you will have to select one of the options above.

Export Format Options

Crystal Reports supports six export formats. Exporting reports is a two step process, as discussed below.

① Select the **EXPORT** format. This determines the format that the exported report will be saved in.
② Select the **DESTINATION**. This determines where the report will be saved.

Reports can be exported to more than one format if needed. Some export formats are better suited for certain types of reports then others. For example, some Word and Excel export format options are better suited for reports that may need to be edited by the end-user. Table 8-1 explains the export format options. The software in brackets in the description column in the table is the most commonly used software to open the corresponding exported file format.

Some of the formats in the table do a better job of duplicating the report then others. I've noticed that sometimes reports that are exported to Excel get shifted a little. If the data does not need to be edited by the person using the exported report, the best format to use is PDF because it retains all of the formatting that you see when the report is viewed in Crystal Reports.

Format	Description
Adobe Acrobat (PDF)	This format will create a PDF file (Portable Document File), which is one of the most popular export formats because it can be read by both PC and MAC computers. If you want the report to retain its look after it is exported, select this format. [Adobe Acrobat or the free Adobe reader] (1)
Crystal Reports (RPT)	This format can only be read by Crystal Reports or a report viewer from Crystal Reports Server, the Report Application Server (RAS) or a program that was created in Visual Basic, C++ or another application development tool that supports a runtime viewer. [Crystal Reports]
MS Excel 97-2000 (XLS)	Select this format if you want to export the report to a spreadsheet and keep as much of the formatting as possible. This format will not include any formulas from the report, just the result of the formula. [Microsoft Excel]
MS Excel 97-2000 (XLS) Data Only	Select this format if you want to export the report to a spreadsheet. Don't select this format if the report has charts or maps that you also need to export. Any data that is suppressed will not be exported. [Microsoft Excel]
MS Word	This format will create an RTF document, which requires Microsoft Word or the viewer. RTF stands for Rich Text Format. [Microsoft Word]
Rich Text Format (RTF)	This RTF export option retains the formatting of the report including graphics. Select this option if the report will be opened in a word processor other than Word. [Microsoft Word]

Table 8-1 Export format options explained

(1) The drill-down feature and hyperlinks will not work with this report format.

There are two ways to open the Export dialog box shown in Figure 8-8, as discussed below. Figure 8-9 shows the export format options.

① Click the **EXPORT** button on the report preview toolbar.
② Right-click on the report in preview mode and select Export.

Export Destination Option

In addition to selecting an export format, a destination for the report also has to be selected. **DISK FILE** is the only export destination option in this version of Crystal Reports. This option lets you select a folder, either on a hard drive or a server (which is also known as a Network drive), where the exported report will be placed. This destination option does not automatically open the application associated with the export file type.

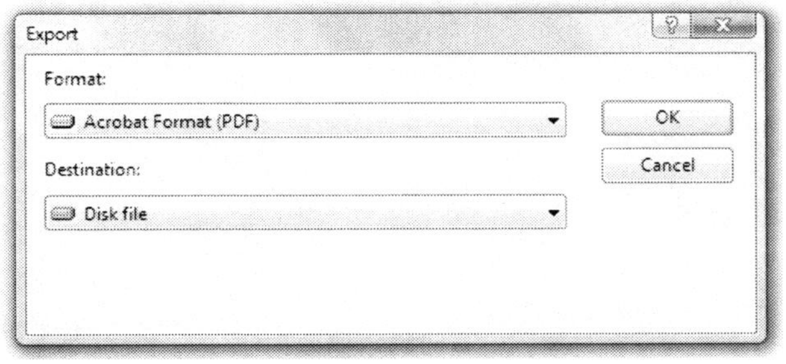

Figure 8-8 Export dialog box

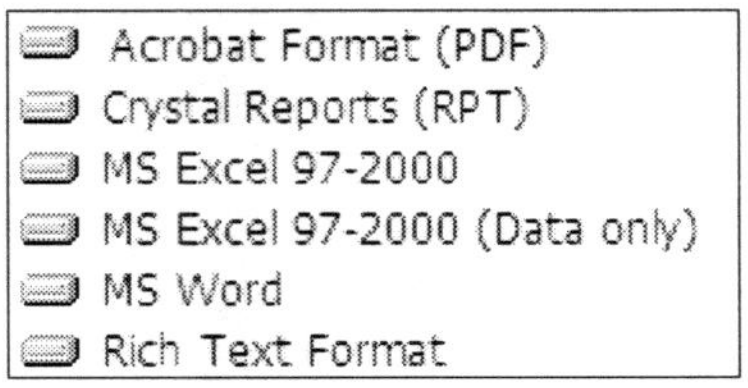

Figure 8-9 Export options

Export Formatting Tips

I have found that by making sure that the export format tips listed below are followed, the exported file, regardless of the format, will look more like the report does in Crystal Reports.

① Make sure that all of the data fields in the same column have the same alignment (left or right). This is especially important for number and currency fields. If the fields in the same column have a different alignment option, some fields may appear in a different column in the exported report.

② Remove any space that is not needed in each section of the report by moving all of the objects in each section up, as much as possible.

Report Export Formats

The exercises in this lesson will show you how to export reports. The L6.7 2001 Orders by month report is the report that you will use to create all of the export reports. You should open this report and then open the Export dialog box shown earlier in Figure 8-8, prior to starting each exercise, unless instructed otherwise. Unless stated otherwise, save each exported report in the project folder that you created.

Exercise 8.2: Create An Adobe Acrobat PDF Export File

This export file type will create a PDF file of the report. End-users that need to open reports in this file type will need to have the Adobe Acrobat Reader installed. This software is free and can be downloaded from http://www.adobe.com/products/acrobat/readstep2.html. You do not have to download and install any other software that is shown on this web page for the Acrobat Reader software to work. This export file type can also be opened and viewed with Adobe Acrobat, which is the full version of the software that lets you create PDF files.

1. Select the Adobe Acrobat (PDF) format, if it is not already selected. Figure 8-8 shown earlier, has the export options that should be selected. Click OK.

The dialog box shown in Figure 8-10 will let you select whether you want to include all or some of the pages from the report in the PDF export file that you are about to create. If you were going to send each sales rep their stats for the month from the report, you would enter the corresponding page numbers in the From and To fields in the dialog box. If the report has **PARAMETER FIELDS**, you would not have to do this to get a specific sales reps stats. Parameter fields are covered in Lesson 12.

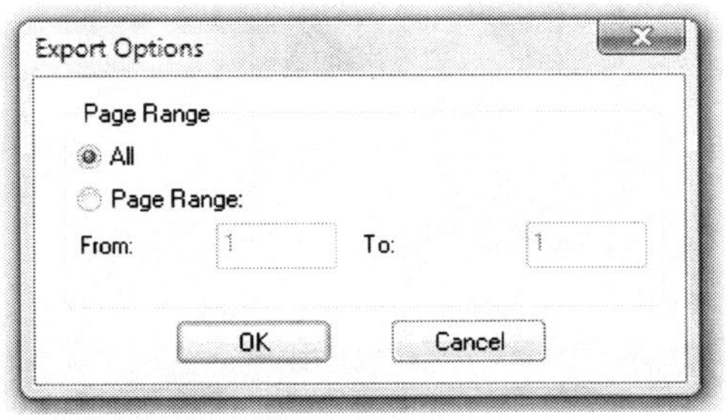

Figure 8-10 Export page range options

2. Click OK to include all of the pages. You will see the dialog box shown in Figure 8-11. This dialog box lets you select where you want to store the export file.

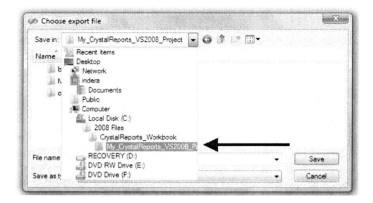

Figure 8-11 Choose Export File dialog box

3. Navigate to your project folder, as shown above in Figure 8-11.
    Type `L8.2 2001 Orders By Month exported PDF file` as the file name at the bottom of the dialog box and press Enter or click the Save button.

You will see the dialog box shown in Figure 8-12. This dialog box lets you know that the export file is being created and how many records will be exported. When the export is complete, you can open the PDF file in either the Adobe Acrobat Reader or Adobe Acrobat. The exported PDF file should look similar to the one shown in Figure 8-13.

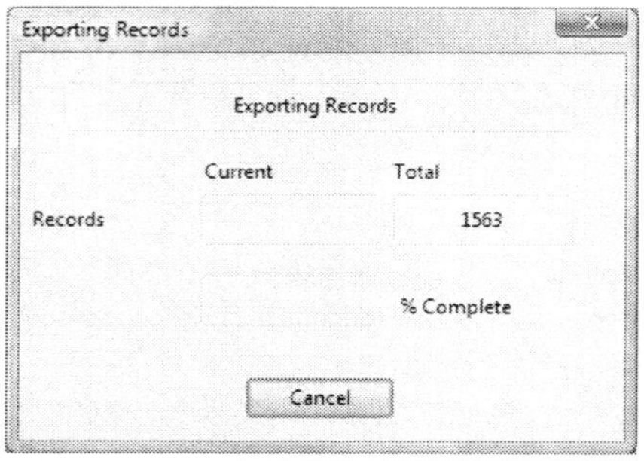

Figure 8-12 Exporting Records dialog box

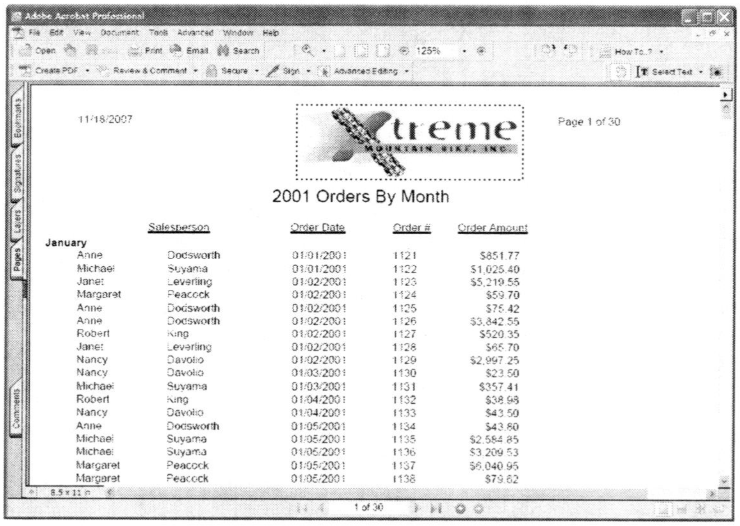

Figure 8-13 L8.2 2001 Orders By Month exported PDF file

4. Close the PDF report.

Exercise 8.3: Create An Excel 97-2000 Export File

This export file type will create an Excel file of the report. To open this exported file type, Microsoft Excel or the free Excel viewer needs to be installed. As you read in Table 8-1, there are two Excel export formats. The Excel export format options provide a different output of the data. You will use both export options so that you can see the differences.

1. Select the first Excel 97-2000 format, then click OK.

You will see the dialog box shown in Figure 8-14. As you can see there are several options that you can select, which will determine how the data will be formatted in Excel. Table 8-2 explains the options.

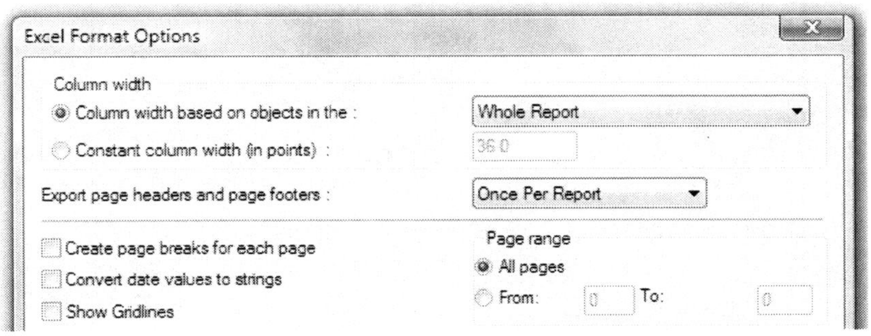

Figure 8-14 Excel 97-2000 Format Options dialog box

Option	Description
Column Width	These options let you select the column widths in Excel. ① The **COLUMN WIDTH BASED ON OBJECTS IN THE** option lets you select the column width in Excel based on a section in the report. ② The **CONSTANT COLUMN WIDTH (IN POINTS)** option lets you select a free form column width.
Export page headers and page footers	This option lets you select whether or not the information in the page header and footer sections on the report will be exported to Excel. If the page header and footer information is exported, the options in the drop-down list determine where the information will be placed in the Excel file. ① **ONCE PER REPORT** causes the header information to only print at the top of the first page and the footer information to only print at the bottom of the last page. ② **ONCE PER PAGE** causes the header and footer information to print on each page of the report like it does in Crystal Reports.
Create page breaks for each page	If selected, page breaks will be added to the exported Excel file in the same place they would appear in Crystal Reports. This may cause the report to break someplace other then at the end of the printed page. If you want the page breaks to happen automatically in Excel, do not check this option.
Convert date values to strings	If selected, this option will keep the date formatting in Crystal Reports when the report is exported to Excel. If this option is not checked, the formatting for the date fields when the report is exported will come from the date formatting options in the copy of Excel that the exported file is opened with. This means that if different people have different date settings in their copy of Excel, the dates in the exported file will appear differently. This is something that you may want to control.
Show Gridlines	If selected, this option forces gridlines in the exported copy of the report.
Page range	These options let you select how many pages of the report will be exported.

Table 8-2 Excel 97-2000 export format options explained

2. Select the **SHOW GRIDLINES** option shown above in Figure 8-14, then click OK.

3. You will see the Select Export File dialog box. Navigate to your project folder, if necessary. Type L8.3 2001 Orders by month exported file as the file name, then press Enter. You will see the records being processed/exported. When the export is complete, open Excel to view the report shown in Figure 8-15.

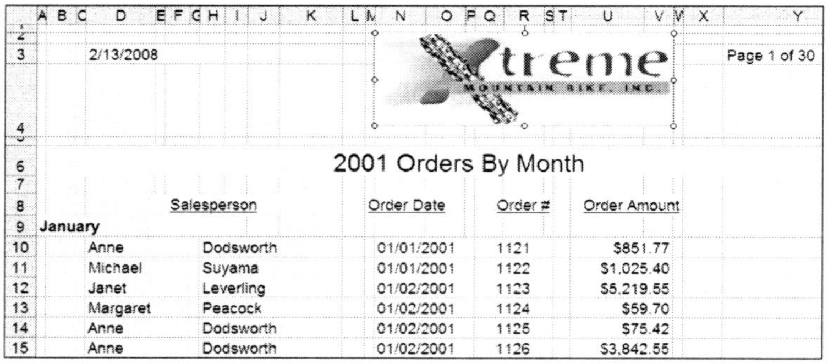

Figure 8-15 L8.3 2001 orders by month exported Excel file

4.   Scroll down to row 139, then click in the cell illustrated in Figure 8-16, the Total # of orders for the month cell. It may be a different cell then the one shown.

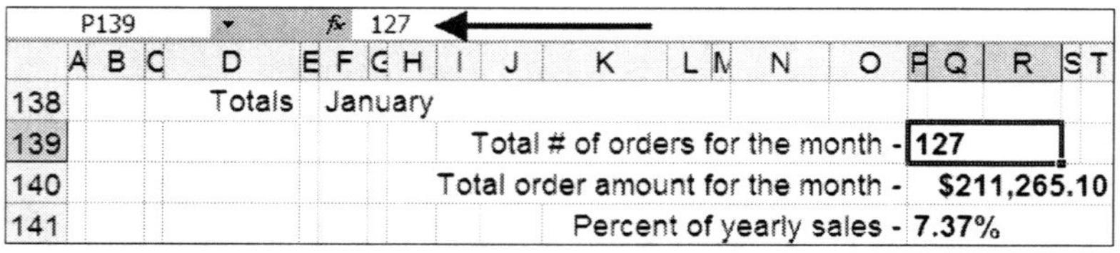

Figure 8-16 Formula Bar illustrated

If you look in the Formula Bar at the top of the spreadsheet shown above in Figure 8-16, you will not see the summary calculation (formula). One reason to use this export format is if you do not want the end-user to be able to change or see the formulas. For other end-users, it would be helpful if the formulas that are used in the report were also exported. You will learn how to export formulas in the next exercise.

5.   Close the spreadsheet.

Exercise 8.4: Create An Excel 97-2000 Data Only Export File

As you noticed in the previous exercise, the calculations were not included in the spreadsheet.
In order to have the calculations in the export file, you have to select the Excel Data Only export format.

If the **DETAILS** option was selected in the Column Width drop-down list on the Excel Format Options dialog box instead of the **WHOLE REPORT** option shown earlier in Figure 8-14, the spreadsheet would look the way that many Excel users are use to seeing it. They would just have to turn the **GRIDLINES** option on.

1.   Select the **EXCEL 97-2000 (DATA ONLY)** format, then click OK. You will see the dialog box shown in Figure 8-17. The typical and minimal options pre-select some options on the bottom portion of the Excel Format Options dialog box for you. Table 8-3 explains the Excel format options.

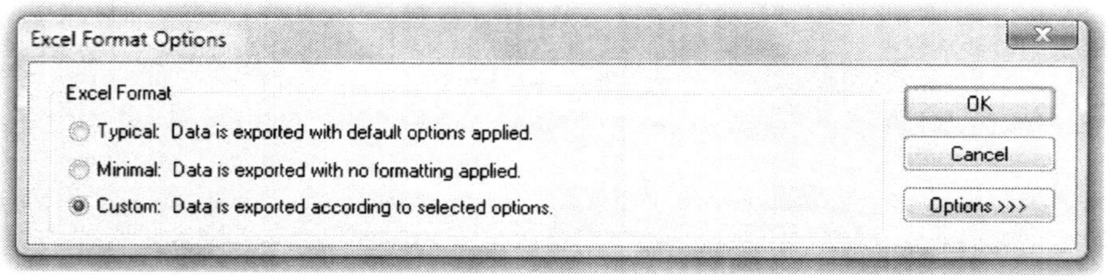

Figure 8-17 Top section of the Excel Only Format Options dialog box

Format	Description
Typical	This option pre-selects the most common options in the bottom section of the dialog box, which are shown in Figure 8-18.
Minimal	This option pre-selects the basic options shown in Figure 8-19, to export the report without any formatting options.
Custom	This option lets you select the export options.

Table 8-3 Excel Data Only export format options explained

Changing an option after selecting the typical or minimal option changes the format to custom.

The pre-selected options shown in Figures 8-18 and 8-19 can be used as a starting point. You can select one of these options and then add or remove options as needed. This may be helpful if one of these export formats has a few of the options already selected that you need. Selecting one of these options and then making changes to it may save you some time.

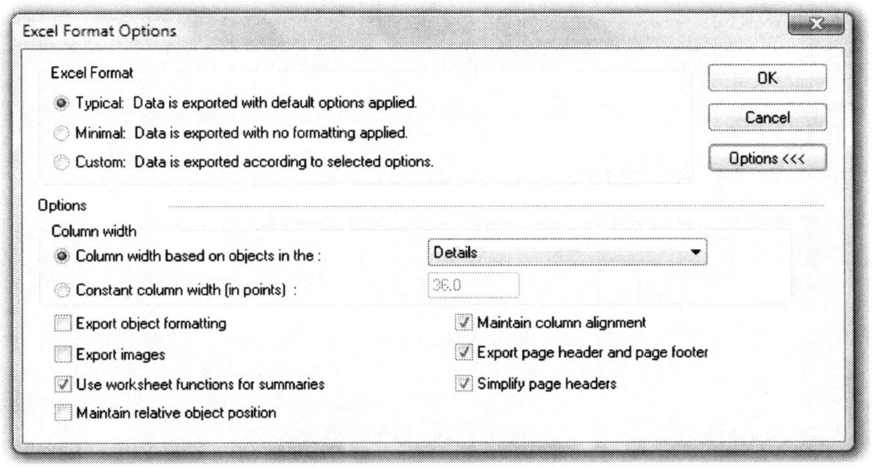

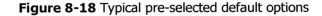

Figure 8-18 Typical pre-selected default options

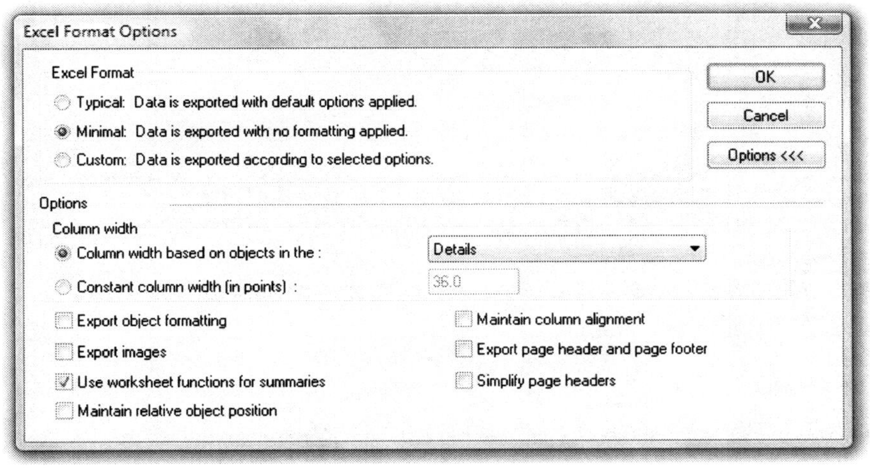

Figure 8-19 Minimal pre-selected default options

2. Click the **OPTIONS** button. You will see the options shown in Figure 8-20. Table 8-4 explains the options.

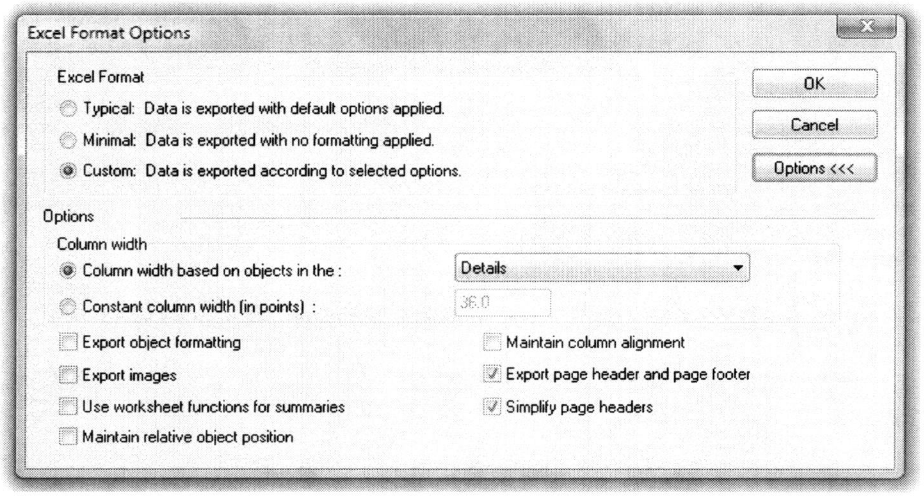

Figure 8-20 Custom pre-selected default options

Option	Description
Column Width	These options let you select the column widths in Excel. ① The **COLUMN WIDTH BASED ON OBJECTS IN THE** option lets you select the column width in Excel based on a section in the report. ② The **CONSTANT COLUMN WIDTH (IN POINTS)** option lets you select a free form column width.
Export object formatting	Check this option to export as much of the formatting that is in the report as possible.
Export images	Check this option to export any images that are in the report.
Use worksheet functions for summaries	Check this option if you want Crystal Reports to try and convert summary fields to Excel functions. If a matching function is not found, the summary field will be exported as a number without the formula.
Maintain relative object position	Check this option if you want Crystal Reports to add rows and columns as needed to keep objects in the exported Excel file in the same location/position that they are in the report.
Maintain column alignment	Check this option to force summary fields to appear in the correct column in Excel. By default, the export process ignores blank spaces to the left of fields, which causes fields to be shifted.
Export page header and page footer	Check this option if you want the information in the page header and footer sections to be exported.
Simplify page headers	Check this option if you only want the last row of the page header section to be exported. Usually the last row of the page header section contains the field headings.

Table 8-4 Excel Data Only export options explained

3. Check the option **USE WORKSHEET FUNCTIONS FOR SUMMARIES**, then click OK. Save the exported file as `L8.4 2001 orders by month data only exported file`.

4. Open the L8.4 2001 orders by month data only spreadsheet in Excel and make columns A through H wider.

5. Scroll down to row 130 and click in cell F130, then look in the Formula Bar. You will see the equivalent of the summary calculation that was created in the report, as illustrated in Figure 8-21. Save the changes and close the spreadsheet.

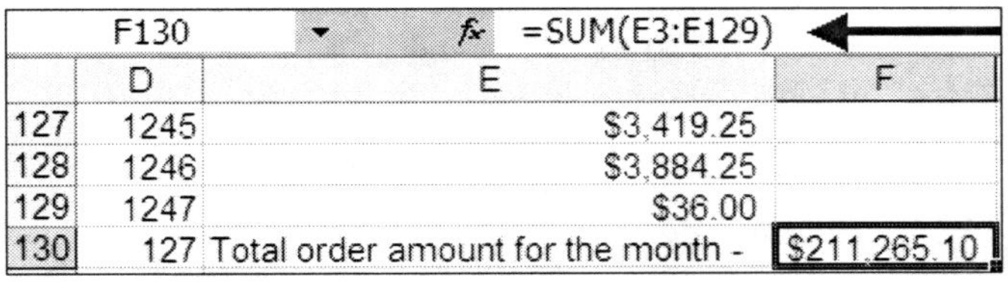

Figure 8-21 Summary calculation in the Formula Bar illustrated

Exercise 8.5: Create A Word Export File

This file type will export the report to a Word document. To open this exported file type, Microsoft Word or the free Word viewer needs to be installed. In this exercise you will only select the first 10 pages of the report to be exported to Word.

1. Select the MS Word format, then click OK.

2. Select the page options shown in Figure 8-22.

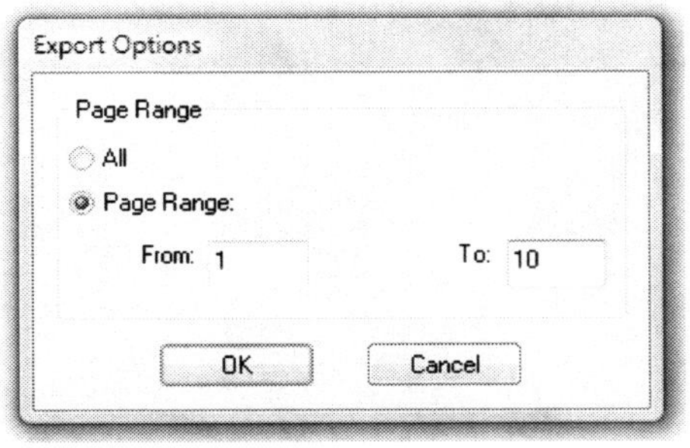

Figure 8-22 Page range export options

3. Click OK to export the pages in the report. Save the exported file as L8.5 2001 orders by month report in Word exported file. The report will now be exported to a Word document in .doc format. When you open the exported file in Word (or the viewer), you will see the report shown in Figure 8-23. If you scroll down to page 3, you will be able to see the totals for January.

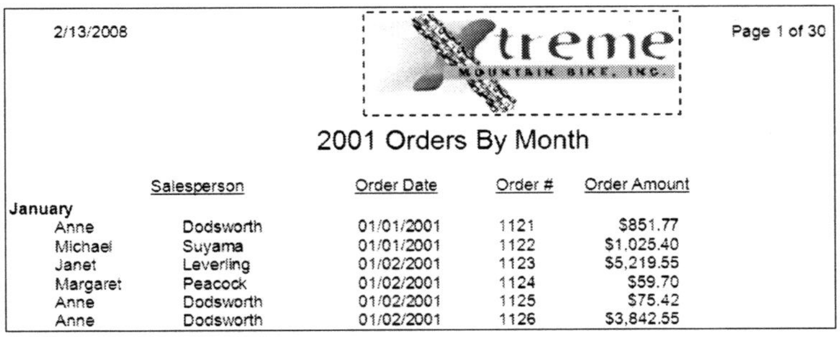

Figure 8-23 L8.5 2001 orders by month exported file in Word format

4. Close the Word document.

> If you wanted to save the report in a different file format, File ⇒ Save As, then open the **SAVE AS TYPE** drop-down list at the bottom of the Save As dialog box and select the format that you need, as illustrated in Figure 8-24.

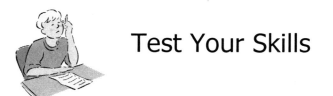

Figure 8-24 Save as type options illustrated

Test Your Skills

1. Create a PDF file for the L7.8 report. Save the PDF file as `L8.6 Skills Top 5 orders PDF export file`. The PDF should look like the one shown in Figure 8-25.

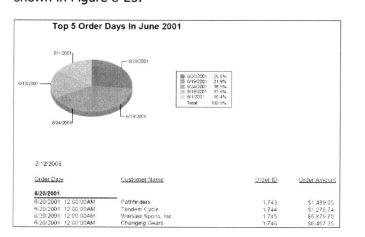

Figure 8-25 L8.6 Skills Top 5 orders PDF export file

2. Create an Excel export file for the L7.7 report.
Save the Excel file as `L8.7 Skills Top 5 orders export file`. The report should look like the one shown above in Figure 8-25.

FORMULAS AND FUNCTIONS

After completing the exercises in this lesson you will be able to:

- ☑ Understand the difference between formulas and functions
- ☑ Know what the formula rules are
- ☑ Select a Syntax Editor
- ☑ Use the Formula Workshop and know the purpose of its toolbar buttons
- ☑ Customize the Formula Workshop window
- ☑ Use the Workshop Tree
- ☑ Understand the formula evaluation order
- ☑ Create numeric formulas
- ☑ Create string formulas
- ☑ Use functions in string formulas
- ☑ Create date formulas
- ☑ Use the Truncate function

LESSON 9

Formulas And Functions Overview

Formulas and functions are some of the most powerful features in Crystal Reports. Ironically, many people that are first learning Crystal Reports think that they are one of the most dreaded features because there is math and logic involved. If you fall into this category, hopefully this lesson will help you overcome some of the fear.

In Lesson 2 as part of the report design process, you learned that not all fields that are needed for a report exist in tables. In Lesson 6 you learned how to create summary fields which are not stored in tables. While summary fields provide a quick way to create totals, that's about as far as they go.

For example, summary fields will not let you add the values in two fields together, nor can you multiply a field in a table by a constant value, like calculating the sales tax for an order. When you have exhausted all other math related options, it's time to turn to formulas and functions. Formulas are created in the Formula Workshop, which you will learn about in this lesson.

Actually, you have two options for creating formulas: The Formula Workshop and writing SQL Expressions. This type of field is what would be placed in the SQL Expression Fields section of the Field Explorer. If you are already freaking out about creating formulas, for now you should focus on using the Formula Workshop, because you would need to learn the version of SQL that works with the database that you are using for the reports that you are creating or modifying. If you recall, in Lesson 1, I listed several types of databases. They use different versions of SQL. Also keep in mind that some companies use a variety of database types from the list. [See Lesson 1, About Crystal Reports Basic For Visual Studio 2008]

While creating SQL Expressions is more efficient than creating formulas in the Formula Workshop, SQL Expressions are evaluated (processed) on the server and sent back to Crystal Reports. The SQL for some types of databases is limited and can have fewer options than Crystal Reports has. For example, if you have to create a formula that needs to process or refer to (as in lookup) a record, other than the current record, you would have a problem if the database does not have any analytical functionality. I'm not saying this to scare you away from learning SQL, merely pointing out something that you may not be aware of.

What Is The Difference Between Formulas And Functions?

One of the questions that I am asked a lot is, "What is the difference between formulas and functions?" Formulas are calculations or some type of data manipulation that you create. Functions are built-in formulas or procedures that have already been created. If there is a built-in function that meets your needs, use it because there is no point reinventing the wheel, as they say. If you have created or used formulas or functions in spreadsheet software, you are already familiar with the basics of creating them in Crystal Reports.

Formula Overview

Formulas let you create new fields. If you need to include data on a report that is not stored in the tables, many times you will need to create a formula to get the data. An example of this would be the line item total on an order report. Line item information is not stored in an Order Detail table, but the price and quantity ordered are stored in the table. These are the fields that you would use to create the formula to calculate the line item total. A line item total is sometimes referred to as the "Extended Price". Formulas allow you to create the following types of calculations, comparisons, manipulations and much more.

① Solve math problems
② Convert data from one format to another
③ Compare or evaluate data
④ Join two or more text fields into one field
⑤ Join text and data fields

You may be thinking or asking why all of this information is not stored in tables. There are many reasons including the following, why data that falls into these categories is not stored in tables.

① It would take a lot of hard drive or server space to store all of the data for these fields.

② Applications that share data have slightly different data needs, which means that some tables would have empty fields.

③ Some data is only needed once or the data changes constantly, so it is more efficient to calculate it when it is needed.

④ The more data that has to be written (added or changed) to a table or tables, the slower the application will run. This slowness is often referred to as a "performance hit".

Syntax Rules

Formulas have rules (also known as syntax rules) that have to be followed. Basically, the rules require that items be placed in a certain order, so that the formula will work. Table 9-1 provides the rules for Crystal Syntax, that if followed, will make learning how to write formulas easier. The items listed below are the parts of the formula.

Item	Syntax
//	The double slash lets you add comments to a formula. This is helpful when you need to document the formula. (1)
Case Sensitive	Formulas are not case sensitive.
Hard Returns	Pressing the Enter key to continue the formula on another line to make the formula more readable is acceptable. This is usually done on long formulas to make them easier to read. The one time that this will cause an error is if there is a hard return between quotation marks in a formula.
Operators	Placing a space before or after an operator is acceptable, but is not required. Many people include spaces to make the formulas easier to read. The spaces are ignored when the formula is executed. The operators are similar to the ones that you learned about in Lesson 5. The difference is that symbols are used in formulas instead of words. = < > + - are some of the operators that you can use when creating formulas.
Fields	They must be surrounded by braces. For example, {Table.Field Name}.
Functions	Each function requires at least one argument. Each argument must be followed by a comma, except the last one. Arguments must be entered in this format: FunctionName (Argument 1, Argument 2).
Numbers	Numbers must be entered without any formatting. 5600 or 56000 is correct. 5,600 or 56,000.00 is incorrect.
Text	Text must be entered inside of quotation marks. Examples: "Help" would be printed as Help. ' "Help" ' would be printed as "Help". Notice the difference in the output when different types of quotes are used.

Table 9-1 Syntax rules explained

(1) Comments should be added to formulas to explain the purpose of the formulas and to provide documentation. If the comment needs more than one line, each line must start with two slashes, otherwise Crystal Reports will treat the line as part of the formula, which will generate a syntax error. You may think that you will remember what the formula does six months from now, but it may take you a minute or so to remember, if you're lucky <smile>. I have learned that it is easier to add comments and give formulas a descriptive name when they are first created.

Functions Overview

Functions are prewritten, built-in formulas or procedures. Software that supports functions have built-in functions, plus allow you to create your own. Functions have been thoroughly tested and from what I can tell, they are error free in Crystal Reports. However, this does not mean that if there is bad data in a table that you won't have a problem with the function. If you do not follow the syntax rules or fill in the arguments correctly when using the function, you will get an error.

Crystal Reports has over 200 functions that you can use. Sum, Average, Count and Distinct Count are functions that you have already learned to use. Many of the Special Fields that you have learned about are also functions, as are the Document Properties that you learned about. You also read about the Date Range functions. [See Lesson 5, Table 5-2] This lesson covers some of the more popular functions that you may have a need to use.

Syntax

You can select the syntax language that you want to use. If you are already familiar with one, by all means continue to use it. If you have used a previous version of Crystal Reports, you may already be familiar with Crystal Syntax. You can create formulas and incorporate functions in both languages and both can be used in the same report. The good thing is that you do not have to be a programmer to create formulas or use functions in the Formula Workshop. Each language has its own rules for the Control Structures, functions and other syntax. In order to create a formula, you need to select one of the following languages:

① **Crystal Syntax** This language has been included in every version of Crystal Reports and is the default language that is selected when Crystal Reports is installed. The formulas that you viewed at the bottom of the Select Expert dialog box were written in Crystal Syntax, unless you changed the default language to Basic Syntax prior to working on the exercises in this workbook. Some say that Crystal syntax is more user-friendly than Basic syntax. The exercises in this workbook use Crystal Syntax.

② **Basic Syntax** If you have developed applications in Visual Basic, you will find this syntax language familiar. The main difference that you will notice between Visual Basic and Basic Syntax is that the Basic Syntax language has extensions for creating reports. Figures 9-1 and 9-2 show the same formula using different syntax editors.

```
// This formula combines the Supplier ID and Supplier Name field
ToText ({Supplier.Supplier ID}, 0) + " - " + {Supplier.Supplier Name}
```

Figure 9-1 Formula created using Crystal Syntax

```
'This formula combines the Supplier ID and Supplier Name field
formula = ToText ({Supplier.Supplier ID},0)+ " - " + {Supplier.Supplier Name}
```

Figure 9-2 Formula created using Basic Syntax

Statements Depending on the environment that you work in, you may hear the term "Statement" and have a different interpretation of what a statement is then the context that I will present it in. That's fine, I just don't want you to think that either interpretation is incorrect. You may have also heard the term EXPRESSION. I believe that the terms statement and expression mean the same thing, but some will argue that there is a difference. Formulas in Crystal Reports and other software tools as well, consider a statement a combination of fields, operators, functions and other variables that provide an answer or value. I think of statements in Crystal Reports as sentences. Formulas have at least one statement.

Control Structures are how Crystal Reports processes a formula. The process starts at the beginning of the formula and moves from one statement to the next. Control structures evaluate expressions or conditions. The result of this evaluation is known as the RETURN VALUE. Formulas must return a value. The result of the last statement executed in the formula contains the result value. It is important to note that the last statement executed may not be the last physical line of code in the formula.

Types of control structures include WHILE DO/DO WHILE, SELECT CASE STATEMENTS and IF STATEMENTS, which are also known as If Then Else or Nested If statements. You will learn to create If Then Else statements in Lesson 10.

Formula Workshop Overview

The Formula Workshop shown in Figure 9-3 is the tool that you will use to create and manage formulas. You can also work with record and group selection formulas in the Formula Workshop. Notice that it does not have any menus. Depending on how you open the Formula Workshop, you will either see the Formula Editor as shown in Figure 9-3 or the Formula Expert. If you do not like the toolbars at the top of the window, you can move them. Each section of the Formula Workshop is explained below.

Table 9-2 explains the General Formula Workshop toolbar buttons. Table 9-3 explains the Expressions Editor toolbar buttons. Table 9-4 explains the Workshop Tree toolbar buttons.

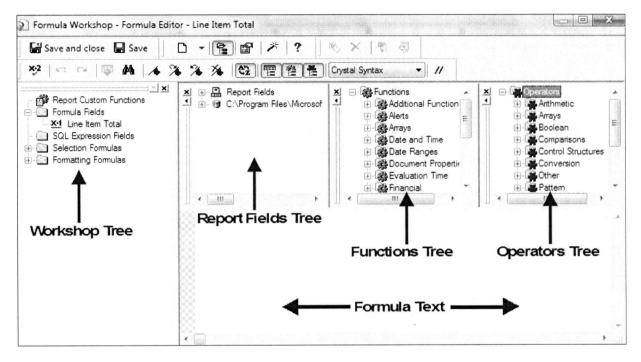

Figure 9-3 Formula Workshop

Button	Purpose
Save and close	Closes the Formula Editor and returns to the report design window after prompting you to save changes if necessary. (2)
Save	Saves the formula and leaves the Formula Workshop open. (2)
☐ ▾	The New button lets you create a new formula based on the option selected on the drop down list shown in Figure 9-4. If a formula is open prior to clicking this button, the syntax is checked and the current formula is saved.
🗐	The Show/Hide Workshop Tree button shows or hides the Formula Workshop Tree.
🖺	The Toggle Properties Display button toggles between the Custom Function Editor and Custom Function Properties dialog box.
⚒	The Use Expert/Editor button toggles between the Formula Editor and the Formula Expert. Use the Formula Expert to create a formula based on a custom function.
?	Opens the online help for the Formula Workshop, Formula Editor or Formula Expert, depending on which is currently displayed or where the cursor is.

Table 9-2 General Formula Workshop toolbar buttons explained

(2)   When you save the changes, the formula or SQL Expression is checked for errors.

Formula...

Custom Function...

Formatting Formula...

SQL Expression...

Record Selection Formula

Group Selection Formula

Figure 9-4 New Formula options drop-down list

Button	Purpose
x·2	The Check button tests the syntax of the formula or custom function and identifies syntax errors.
↶	The Undo button undoes the last action made to the formula.
↷	The Redo button redoes the last action that was made to the formula.
	The Browse Data button lets you view the data in a field in the Report Fields window.
🔍	The Find or Replace dialog box shown in Figure 9-5 searches the formula, fields, functions or operators for words or expressions. You can also replace text in formulas using this dialog box. The **EDIT TEXT** option is where you type in the formula.
	The Bookmark button inserts a bookmark in the current line of the selected formula. Click the button again to remove the bookmark. Bookmarks let you mark a line of code as important. The bookmark feature is helpful in long formulas when you have to go from one part of the formula to another.
	The Next Bookmark button will place the cursor at the next bookmark in the formula.
	The Previous Bookmark button will place the cursor at the previous bookmark in the formula.
	The Clear All Bookmarks button deletes all bookmarks in the current formula.
	This toggle button sorts the options in the Report Fields, Functions and Operators trees in alphabetical order or returns them to their original order.
	Displays or hides the Report Fields tree.
	Displays or hides the Functions tree.
	Displays or hides the Operators tree.
Crystal Syntax	Lets you to select **CRYSTAL SYNTAX** or **BASIC SYNTAX** as the formula syntax editor.
//	Lets you add comments to a formula. Commented lines are not evaluated as part of the formula. I type the // into the Formula Text section when writing the formula because I find it faster then clicking this button.

Table 9-3 Expressions Editor toolbar buttons explained

💡 If you close or undock a toolbar by mistake, close the Formula Workshop, then reopen it to get the toolbar back.

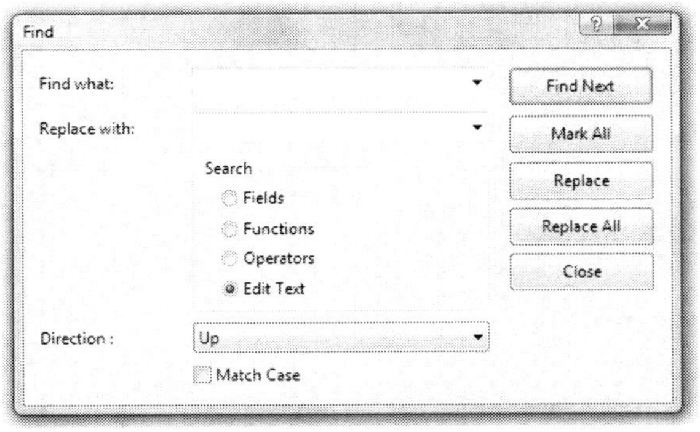

Figure 9-5 Find dialog box

Button	Purpose
	Lets you rename the selected formula, custom function, or SQL Expression.
 ✕	Deletes the selected formula, custom function, or SQL Expression.
	Expands the selected node(s) in the Workshop Tree.
	The Show Formatting Formulas button shows or hides all of the report objects in the Formatting Formulas folder or only the objects that have a formatting formula.

Table 9-4 Workshop Tree toolbar buttons explained

Formula Editor

The Formula Editor itself is not new. What's new is that it has been incorporated into the Formula Workshop interface. The contents of each of the trees in the Formula Editor change to show the options that are available for the type of database that the report is based on. The Formula Editor allows you to create formulas by double-clicking on the functions, operators and fields that you need to include in the formula. The Formula Editor will allow you to create at least 90% of the formulas that you need. The Formula Editor contains the three trees discussed below. You may want to open some of the categories (nodes) in each tree to become familiar with the options.

① **Report Fields Tree** This tree displays all of the fields that are on the report, including groups, summary fields, running totals, parameters, formulas and the tables that the report uses. This tree is similar to the Field Explorer. You can use any of these fields in a formula.

② **Functions Tree** This tree contains the built-in functions. The functions are divided into categories, which makes it easier to find the function that you need. What you will notice is that the same function categories will not be available depending on the property that you selected before opening the Format Editor. This is determined based on the property that you are working on. For example, Figure 9-6 shows the functions for a string field if you clicked on a Format button in the Line style section on the Border tab. If you click on the Format button in the Color section on the Border tab you will see the functions shown in Figure 9-7.
Refer back to Figure 9-3. Notice that the options illustrated in Figures 9-6 and 9-7 are not in Figure 9-3. That is because a formula field is selected. Line style and Color constants functions will not work with a formula field.

③ **Operators Tree** This tree contains all of the operators (logical and mathematical) that you can use to create formulas. The operators are grouped by type to make them easier to find. Operators use symbols instead of words.

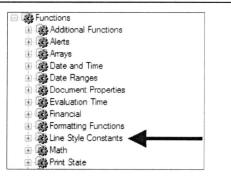

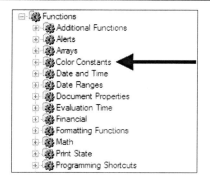

Figure 9-6 Available functions when a line style property is selected

Figure 9-7 Available functions when a color property is selected

 When you open the Formula Workshop without creating a new field or editing an existing field first, you will not see the Formula Editor. You can do either of the following to open the Formula Editor.

① Select a field in the Formula Fields, SQL Expression Fields or Selection Formulas section of the Workshop Tree.
② Select one of the formula or function options on the New button menu shown earlier in Figure 9-4.

Formula Text Window

In addition to the three trees, the blank section below the trees is where you type in the formula. This section is called the Formula Text window. By default, the font is automatically color coded as follows:

① Green is used for comments that you type in.
② Blue is used for reserved words like functions.
③ Black is used for constants and variables.

You can use the **AUTO COMPLETE** feature in the formula text window by typing in the first few letters of the function that you need and then press the **CTRL + SPACE BAR** keys. You will see a list that has functions that start with the letters that you typed in, as shown in Figure 9-8. If you type in enough letters to only display the function that you want, the drop-down list will not be displayed. Instead, the function will be filled in for you. If you press the CTRL + Space bar keys before typing any letters, you will see all of the functions in the list.

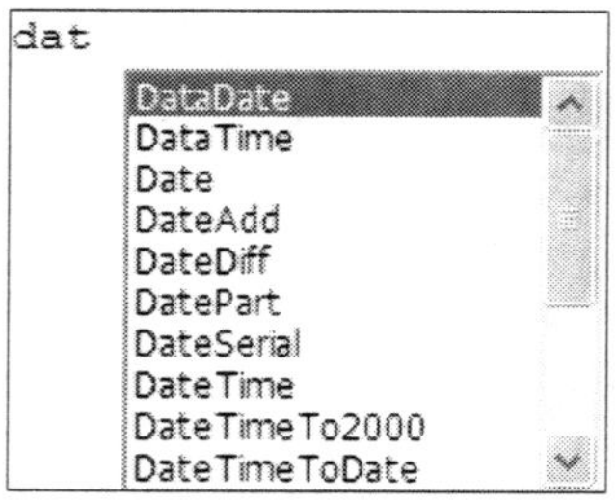

```
dat
   DataDate
   DataTime
   Date
   DateAdd
   DateDiff
   DatePart
   DateSerial
   DateTime
   DateTimeTo2000
   DateTimeToDate
```

Figure 9-8 Auto complete list

Formula Expert

The Formula Expert shown in Figure 9-9 allows you to create custom functions. By design, the Formula Expert will help you create a formula without having to use the Crystal Reports syntax programming language. While this may sound appealing to those that are new to Crystal Reports or do not want to write code, the Formula Expert only creates formulas that use one custom function. You cannot use the math operators or the Crystal Reports syntax programming language in the Formula Expert.

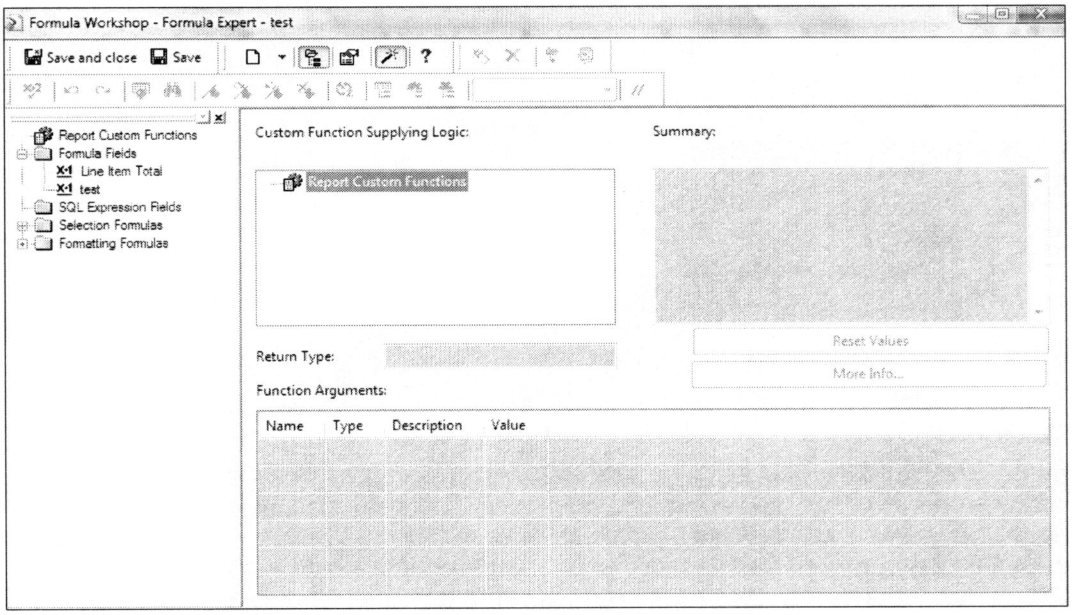

Figure 9-9 Formula Expert

Formula Editor Versus Formula Expert

The main difference between the two is that formulas created in the Formula Editor are saved with the report that they are created in and can only be used in that report. Formulas created in the Formula Expert can be saved as a **CUSTOM FUNCTION** and can be used in any report.

If you find yourself creating the same formula in several reports, copy it to the Formula Expert and save it as a custom function. I often also save the custom functions that I create in a Microsoft Word document because I find it easier to get to them that way. If you work from home, you will understand what I mean. Many will say that this is not a good technique <smile>. There are valid reasons not to save custom functions in a document. I will leave it up to you to decide what works best for you in the environment that you will create reports in.

How To Open The Formula Workshop

Like many other tools in Crystal Reports, there is more than one way to open the this tool. The Formula Workshop is no exception. This tool has more ways that it can be opened then most tools.

① Crystal Reports ⇒ Report ⇒ Formula Workshop.
② Right-click on a formula or SQL Expression field in the design window and select Edit Formula.
③ Right-click on a formula or SQL Expression field in the Field Explorer and select New or Edit.
④ Click the **FORMULA** button on any tab of the Format Editor dialog box.
⑤ Open the Select Expert, click the Show Formula button, then click the **FORMULA EDITOR** button.

Customizing The Formula Editor

You can customize the Formula Editor by doing any or all of the following:

① You can resize any of the tree sections by dragging the bar illustrated in Figure 9-10 left or right.

② Close a tree by clicking on the ⊠ button to the left of the section that you want to close.

③ Expand a tree by clicking on the ◂ button to the left of the section that you want to expand.

④ Make the Formula text window longer or shorter by dragging the section bar above it, up or down.

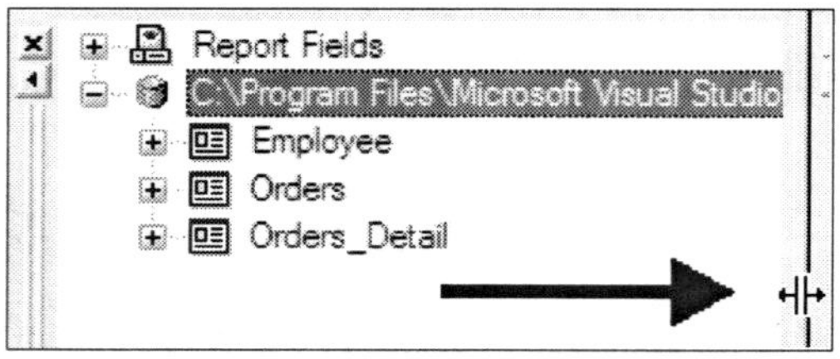

Figure 9-10 Mouse pointer in position to resize a tree

The Workshop Tree

As you saw earlier in Figure 9-3, the Workshop Tree contains several sections called **NODES** or **CATEGORY** folders that formulas can be saved in. This section of the Formula Workshop contains all of the formulas that are in the report. Items under the Selection Formulas folder are the ones that you have created with the Select Expert. In addition to being able to create formulas, you can also rename and delete formulas, just like you can in the Field Explorer. Each of the categories in the Workshop Tree is explained below.

① **Report Custom Functions** The functions that you create are stored in this folder. The functions in this category can be used by any formula in your report. Custom functions are used in reports just like the built-in functions that come with Crystal Reports.

② **Formula Fields** The formulas in this category and are the same ones that are in the Field Explorer in the Formula Fields, Parameter Fields, Running Total Fields and Group Name Fields sections.

③ **SQL Expression Fields** The formulas in this category are the same expression fields that are in the SQL Expression Fields section of the Field Explorer. If you create a new expression or modify an existing expression, the SQL Expression Editor will open in the Formula Workshop instead of the Formula Editor. The options in the Report Fields Tree, Functions Tree and Operators Tree will change and display the options that are available for the type of database that the report is using. It has been reported that the SQL Expression Editor may not reflect all of the operators and functions that are really available for certain database types.

④ **Selection Formulas** The formulas in this category are created when you use the Select Expert or the selection formula options on the Report menu. You can also create selection formulas in the Formula Workshop. If you click on the Group Selection option, the **GROUP SELECTION FORMULA EDITOR** will open. If you click on the Record Selection option, the **RECORD SELECTION FORMULA EDITOR** will open. The only difference that you will notice is that the title bar of the Formula Workshop will change as shown in Figure 9-11. Compare this title bar to the one shown earlier in Figure 9-3.

Figure 9-11 Record Selection Formula Editor title bar

⑤ **Formatting Formulas** This category has a folder for each section of the report. All of the objects from each section of the report are listed here. Formatting formulas like changing the color, font or font size for objects in the report are stored in this category.

Formula Evaluation Order

Many of the formulas that you will create will use more than one operator. The order that the formula is written in from left to right may not be the order that the formula is calculated or evaluated in. Some operations are processed first, regardless of where they are in the formula. This is known as the ORDER OF PRECEDENCE. The formula evaluation order is:

   ① The portion of the formula that is in parenthesis.
   ② Exponential.
   ③ Multiplication and division. (3) (4)
   ④ Integer division.
   ⑤ MOD.
   ⑥ Addition and subtraction. (3)

   (3) If the operators (3 and 6 above) are on the same level, they are evaluated from left to right. See the examples below.

Example #1: 3 + 4 / (2 + 19) = 3.19
Example #2: 3 + (4 / 2) + 19 = 24

The first example calculates the (2+19) first, then divides that by 4 and then adds 3.

The second example calculates the (4/2) first, then adds 3 and then adds 19.

(4) In Crystal syntax, percents are evaluated at the same level as multiplication and division.

> You may find it helpful to write the formula on paper and use data in the tables to test the formulas to see if you get the results that you are expecting from the formula. As you saw in the examples above, the same data and operators can produce different results.
>
> I have noticed in the workplace and in classes that I teach that this is one area where many people have a lot of trouble. I think this is because they are not willing to write out the formula and test it prior to opening the Formula Workshop. Yes, I am fully aware that doing this takes more time up front, but experience shows that the more time you spend "preparing", the less time you will spend debugging reports in the future. Keep the following in mind when creating formulas:
>
> ① Formulas must have an equal number of left and right parenthesis.
> ② Arguments must be the same data type.

Formula Naming Conventions

The naming conventions for formulas is free form. You should use as descriptive a name as possible, one that will make sense to you a year from now. The name you select is what you will see when the formula field is added to the report. Formula names can be up to 256 characters. You can use upper and lower case letters, spaces and the underscore. You should not use characters like the slash, dollar or percent sign in the formula name.

The company that you work for may have naming conventions. You should check to find out.
One convention that many companies have is that they do not want spaces in object names. When this is the case, most companies use the underscore in place of spaces in object names.

Create Numeric Formulas

The exercises in this section will teach you how to create numeric formulas.

Exercise 9.1: Create A Formula Field

In Exercise L6.16, you created a report that displayed an order total per customer. As you saw, the order total was not correct. In this exercise you will modify the report and create a formula that will calculate the amount for each item. This is known as the line item amount. The formula is Unit Price * Quantity. This will allow the report to have the correct total amount.

1. Save the L6.16 report as `L9.1 Formula field for line item totals`.

2. Right-click on the **FORMULA FIELDS** option in the Field Explorer, then select **NEW**.

3. Type `Line Item Total` in the dialog box as shown in Figure 9-12, then click the Use Editor button.

Figure 9-12 Formula Name dialog box

4. In the Report Fields tree, double-click on the Unit Price field in the Orders Detail table. You should see the field in the Formula text window in the Formula Editor, as shown at the bottom of Figure 9-13.

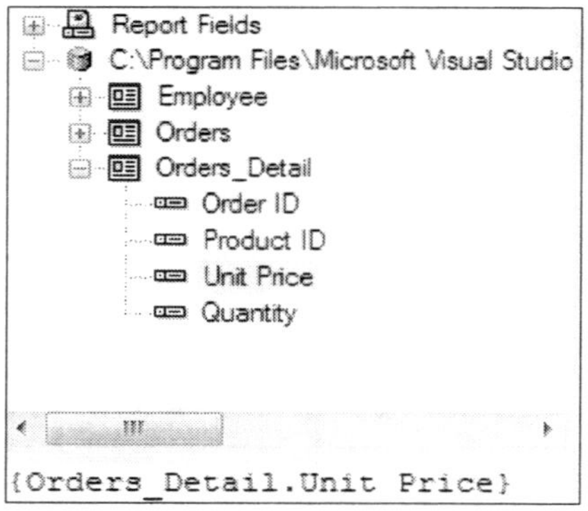

Figure 9-13 Field added to the Formula text window

> You can also drag the field to the Formula text window in the Format Editor.

5. Type a * after the Unit Price field, then double-click on the Quantity field.

> You can use the **MULTIPLY** Arithmetic operator illustrated in Figure 9-14 instead of typing the operator.

6. Add a blank line above the formula and type the following comment.
   `// This formula calculates the Line Item Total.`

   Your formula should look like the one shown in Figure 9-15.

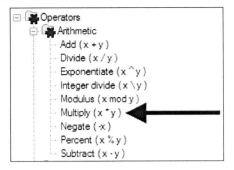

Figure 9-14 Multiply arithmetic operator illustrated

```
// This formula calculates the Line Item Total
{Orders_Detail.Unit Price} *{Orders_Detail.Quantity}
```

Figure 9-15 Line Item Total formula

Notice that the comment line is a different color then the formula line. This is one way to know that you have entered the comment correctly. Comments do not have to go at the beginning of a formula.

7. Click the **CHECK (X-2)** button on the Expressions Editor toolbar. You should see the message shown in Figure 9-16.

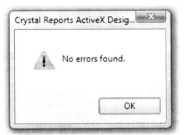

Figure 9-16 No errors found message

The message shown above in Figure 9-16 means that Crystal Reports did not find a syntax error. This does not mean that the formula will produce the results that you are expecting.

If you do not see the message in Figure 9-16, there is an error in your formula. Check to make sure that your formula looks like the one shown earlier in Figure 9-15. Figure 9-17 shows one error message that you could see. If there is an error, the flashing insertion bar will be at the location in the formula where Crystal Reports thinks the error is.

Figure 9-17 Formula error message

The part of the formula where the syntax checker stopped understanding the formula will also be highlighted, as illustrated in Figure 9-17. You are not required to fix the error immediately. You can save it as is and work on something else. Just don't forget to come back and fix it.

8. Click OK, then click the **SAVE AND CLOSE** button.

 If you need to work on another formula, click the **SAVE** button instead of the Save and close button. Doing this will leave the Formula Workshop open. When you save a formula it becomes a field, which you can then add to the report or use in another formula.

Using Formula Fields In Reports

You can use formula fields in reports, just like you use fields from a table. Formula fields can be placed in any section of the report. You can create counts and summary fields that are based on formula fields. You can also use formula fields as selection criteria.

Add The Line Item Formula Field To The Report

In this part of the exercise you will add the formula field that you just created to the report.

1. Delete the Order Amount field and heading, then move the four fields after the Order Amount field over to the left.

2. Add the Line Item Total field to the report. (**Hint:** The field is in the Field Explorer in the Formula Fields section.) The report should look like the one shown in Figure 9-18. Save the changes and leave the report open to complete the next exercise.

Salesperson		Order Date	Order #	Customer #	Product #	Unit Price	Quantity	Line Item Total
1 Nancy	Davolio							
2/13/2000								
30								
		02/19/2000	1310	30	1101	$14.50	3	$43.50
		02/19/2000	1310	30	1104	$14.50	1	$14.50
		Total order amount for customer - **$ 116.00**						
75								
		02/19/2000	1312	75	302162	$479.85	1	$479.85
		02/19/2000	1312	75	401001	$267.76	1	$267.76
		02/19/2000	1312	75	2202	$41.90	1	$41.90
		Total order amount for customer - **$ 2,368.53**						
Daily Totals		# of orders for the day - **2**						
		Total order amount for customer - **$ 2,484.53**						

Figure 9-18 L9.1 Formula field for line item totals added to the report

As you can see, the Total Order Amount for each customer is still not correct. That is because the Total Order Amount field is adding the values in the Order Amount field. The Total Order Amount field should be adding the values in the Line Item Total formula field. One of the skills exercises in this lesson will have you modify this.

Exercise 9.2: Create A Sales Tax Formula

Many orders (or purchases) require sales tax to be collected. This exercise will show you how to create a sales tax formula. You will create a formula that calculates 6% of the line item total. As you know, not all items are taxable. If all items were taxable, you could create a sales tax formula that used the order total times the sales tax rate. In this exercise, you will modify a customer order report and create a sales tax formula that will use the Line Item Total field instead of the Order Total field.

 In the real world, the product table would have a field that is used to signify if each product is taxable or not. In that case, you would have to create a conditional formula that checked the field to see if the product is taxable. If it is taxable, then calculate the sales tax.

1. Save the L9.1 report as L9.2 Sales tax formula.

2. Create a formula field and name it Line Item Sales Tax, then open the Formula Workshop.

3. Double-click on the Line Item Total field in the Report Fields tree, then type `*.06` at the end of the field. Check the formula to make sure that the syntax is correct by clicking the Check (X-2) button. Your formula should look like the one shown in Figure 9-19. Save the formula and close the Formula Workshop.

```
{@Line Item Total} * .06
```

Figure 9-19 Line Item Sales Tax formula

4. Move all of the fields except for the Salesperson field to the left, then add the Line Item Sales Tax field at the end of the details section.

5. Change the field heading for the Line Item Sales Tax field to `Sales Tax`. Your report should look similar to the one shown in Figure 9-20. Save the changes and leave the report open to complete the next exercise.

Salesperson	Order Date	Order #	Customer #	Product #	Unit Price	Quantity	Line Item Total	Sales Tax
1 Nancy Davolio								
2/13/2000								
30								
	02/19/2000	1310	30	1101	$14.50	3	$43.50	$2.61
	02/19/2000	1310	30	1104	$14.50	1	$14.50	$0.87
	Total order amount for customer - **$ 116.00**							
75								
	02/19/2000	1312	75	302162	$479.85	1	$479.85	$28.79
	02/19/2000	1312	75	401001	$267.76	1	$267.76	$16.07
	02/19/2000	1312	75	2202	$41.90	1	$41.90	$2.51
	Total order amount for customer - **$ 2,368.53**							
Daily Totals	# of orders for the day - **2**							
	Total order amount for customer - **$ 2,484.53**							

Figure 9-20 L9.2 Sales tax formula report

Exercise 9.3: Create A Summary Formula

In Lesson 6 you learned how to create summary fields. All of the summary fields that you created were based off of fields in a table. In this exercise you will create a summary field that is based off of a formula field.

1. Save the L9.2 report as `L9.3 Summary formula`.

2. Right-click on the Line Item Sales Tax formula field in the details section, then select Insert ⇒ Summary.

3. Select the Average summary type, then select the Group 2 Orders Date Summary location as the section to place the field in and click OK. You will see the average sales tax amount for the daily totals as illustrated in Figure 9-21. If you want, you can add a title for the field so that the person reading the report knows what the number is. Save the changes and close the report.

75								
	02/19/2000	1312	75	302162	$479.85	1	$479.85	$28.79
	02/19/2000	1312	75	401001	$267.76	1	$267.76	$16.07
	02/19/2000	1312	75	2202	$41.90	1	$41.90	$2.51
	Total order amount for customer - **$ 2,368.53**							
Daily Totals	# of orders for the day - **2**			Average Sales Tax			**$10.17**	
	Total order amount for customer - **$ 2,484.53**							
2/20/2000								
48								
	02/26/2000	1354	48	2202	$41.90	1	$41.90	$2.51
	02/26/2000	1354	48	6402	$9.00	3	$27.00	$1.62
	Total order amount for customer - **$ 137.80**							
Daily Totals	# of orders for the day - **1**			Average Sales Tax			**$2.07**	
	Total order amount for customer - **$ 137.80**							

Figure 9-21 L9.3 Summary formula report

Exercise 9.4: Create A Weekly Salary Formula

In this exercise you will create a formula that will calculate each employees weekly salary. The annual salary field is stored in the Employee table. You will use this field to calculate the weekly salary.

1. Save the L6.12 report as `L9.4 Employee list with weekly salary formula`.

2. Create a formula field and name it `Weekly Salary`, then open the Formula Workshop.

3. Double-click on the Salary field in the Employee table, then drag the **DIVIDE (X/Y)** Arithmetic Operator to the Formula text section.

4. Type `52` after the slash. Check the formula to make sure that the syntax is correct. Your formula should look like the one shown in Figure 9-22. Save the formula and close the Formula Workshop.

```
{Employee.Salary} / 52
```

Figure 9-22 Weekly Salary formula

5. Delete the Region field, then add the Weekly Salary formula field before the Salary field. The report should look like the one shown in Figure 9-23. Save the changes and leave the report open to complete the next exercise.

First Name	Last Name	Address1	Weekly Salary	Salary
Steven	Buchanan	14 Garrett Hill	$961.54	$50,000.00
Robert	King	Edgeham Hollow	$711.54	$37,000.00
Anne	Dodsworth	7 Houndstooth Rd.	$673.08	$35,000.00
Michael	Suyama	Coventry House	$576.92	$30,000.00

Figure 9-23 L9.4 Employee list with weekly salary formula report

Exercise 9.5: Use A Formula Field As Selection Criteria

Earlier you learned that you can use a formula field as selection criteria. In this exercise you will use the Weekly Salary formula field to only display employees that have a weekly salary between $500 and $750.

1. Save the L9.4 report as `L9.5 Formula field used as selection criteria`.

2. Create the selection criteria for the Weekly Salary formula field. The report should look like the one shown in Figure 9-24. There should be five records on the report. Save the changes and close the report.

First Name	Last Name	Address1	Weekly Salary	Salary
Robert	King	Edgeham Hollow	$711.54	$37,000.00
Anne	Dodsworth	7 Houndstooth Rd.	$673.08	$35,000.00
Michael	Suyama	Coventry House	$576.92	$30,000.00
BC				
Margaret	Peacock	4110 Old Redmond Rd.	$673.08	$35,000.00
Janet	Leverling	722 Moss Bay Blvd.	$634.62	$33,000.00

Figure 9-24 L9.5 Formula field used as selection criteria report

Create String Formulas

The exercises in this section will teach you how to create formulas that use String (text) fields or literals. Some of the most used string formulas allow you to convert date and numeric fields to text, select specific portions of a field and trim fields. A common string formula that is used is one that will concatenate (combine) the first and last name fields. Names are usually stored in two or more fields in a table. There are several string formula operators and functions that you can use, as explained in Tables 9-5 and 9-6.

Operator	What It Does
+ or &	These are known as concatenation operators. They are used to combine text fields. The plus sign requires that all arguments be string fields. Crystal Reports will automatically convert every argument to a string when the ampersand (&) operator is used.
[ ]	Subscript operators let you select specific characters from a text field.
" " or ' '	Quotes will treat the text inside of them as a literal. If a string or text field contains numeric data and you need to use it in a formula, you have to put the numeric data in quotes.
If Then Else	This operator allows different actions to be taken based on a condition. (5)

Table 9-5 String operators explained

Date/Time literals must be in one of these formats: #6/24/2005# or #June 24, 2005#.

Keep in mind that while the + (plus sign) operator allows you to join text and data fields, it does not add a space between the fields that are being joined. You have to type + " " + to add a space between the fields that you are joining. There is a space between the quotes in the syntax above.

Function	What It Does
Is Null	This function checks to see if a field has a value. It is often used with the If...Then...Else operator. If the function is used alone, it returns a value of True or False (Boolean). (5)
Length (str)	This function counts the number of characters in a string. It can be used to determine the length of the value in a field.
Lower Case (str)	This function converts the text to all lower case letters. Use **LOWERCASE** for Crystal Syntax. Use **LCASE** for Basic Syntax.
Picture (str, picture)	This function lets you format a string field. This is similar to the "mask" feature that some database software packages support.
To Text	This function is used to convert non text fields like Date, Number and Currency to a text string. This function can have multiple arguments, as shown in Figure 9-25. The only argument that requires a value is X.
Trim (str)	This function removes spaces before and after the data in a string argument. Use **TRIMLEFT** if you only want to remove spaces on the left of the string argument. Use **TRIMRIGHT** if you only want to remove spaces on the right of the string argument.
Upper Case (str)	This function converts the text to all upper case letters. Use **UPPERCASE** for Crystal Syntax. Use **UCASE** for Basic Syntax.

Table 9-6 String functions explained

(5) You will learn how to use this operator in Lesson 10.

```
⊟ ToText
    ToText (x)
    ToText (x, y)
    ToText (x, y, z)
    ToText (x, y, z, w)
    ToText (x, y, z, w, q)
```

Figure 9-25 To Text functions

Exercise 9.6: Combine Two String Fields

Earlier in this lesson you modified an employee report. That report would look better if the employee first and last names were closer together. This produces the same result as dragging one field into another as you learned in Lesson 4. One reason that you would write code to combine the name fields is if you only needed to combine fields if a certain condition was met. Another reason to write code to combine fields is if there is a possibility that at least one of the fields is null.

1. Save the L9.1 report as `L9.6 Combine string fields`.

2. Create a formula field and name it `Employee Full Name`, then add the First Name field from the Employee table to the Formula text window.

3. Click after the First Name field and type + " " +
   This will add a space after the First Name. Make sure that there is a space between the quotes, then add the Last Name field to the formula.

4. Add a blank line above the formula and type `// This formula combines 2 fields`, then check the formula for errors. The formula should look like the one shown in Figure 9-26. Save the formula and close the Formula Workshop.

```
// This formula combines 2 fields
{Employee.First Name}+ " " +{Employee.Last Name}
```

Figure 9-26 String formula

Add The Employee Full Name Formula Field To The Report

1. Delete the First and Last name fields in the Group Header 1 section. Add the Employee Full Name field in place of the two fields that you just deleted.

2. Create a field title and call it `Employee`. Place it above the Employee Full Name field.
   The report should look like the one shown in Figure 9-27. Save the changes and leave the report open to complete the next exercise.

Employee	Order Date	Order #	Customer #	Product #	Unit Price	Quantity	Line Item Total
1 Nancy Davolio 2/13/2000 30							
	02/19/2000	1310	30	1101	$14.50	3	$43.50
	02/19/2000	1310	30	1104	$14.50	1	$14.50
	Total order amount for customer - **$ 116.00**						

Figure 9-27 L9.6 Combine string fields report

Exercise 9.7: Use The Subscript Operator

The subscript operator allows you to extract specific characters in a field based on their position in the field. In Exercise 9.6 you learned how to combine the first and last name fields. If you needed to modify that formula to only display the first letter of the first name, you would use the subscript operator. The subscript [1] means to select the first character in the field from the left. Subscript [3] means to select the third character in the field from the left. In this exercise you will add the subscript operator to an existing formula.

1. Save the L9.6 report as `L9.7 Subscript`.

2. Right-click on the Employee Full name field in the report and select **EDIT FORMULA**.
   Modify the Employee Full Name formula so that it looks like the one shown in Figure 9-28.

```
// This formula combines 2 fields and only uses the first letter
// of the First Name field
{Employee.First Name} [1] + " " +{Employee.Last Name}
```

Figure 9-28 Subscript formula

3. Save the changes. The report should look like the one shown in Figure 9-29. Notice that only the first letter of the first name is displayed. Close the report.

Employee	Order Date	Order #	Customer #	Product #	Unit Price	Quantity	Line Item Total
1 N Davolio							
2/13/2000							
30							
	02/19/2000	1310	30	1101	$14.50	3	$43.50
	02/19/2000	1310	30	1104	$14.50	1	$14.50
Total order amount for customer - **$ 116.00**							

Figure 9-29 L9.7 Subscript report

Exercise 9.8: Combine A Text And Numeric Field

In the reports that you have created with totals, you created a text object for the title of the summary field. If you had trouble either getting the text object and total field to line up or getting the two fields to be close together, this exercise will show you how to combine these fields using a formula, which means that you will not have to align the field and text object.

> If the numeric field that you will use needs to be formatted, you should not combine it with a text field because text fields cannot be formatted with numeric formatting options.

1. Save the L6.1 report as `L9.8 Combine text and numeric fields`.

2. Create a formula field and name it `Total Field`.

3. Add the comment `This formula combines text with a numeric field`.

4. Type `"Total # of customers in region - "` in the Formula text section.

5. Open the **STRINGS** operator node and drag the **CONCATENATE (X&Y)** operator illustrated on the right in Figure 9-30, to the formula.

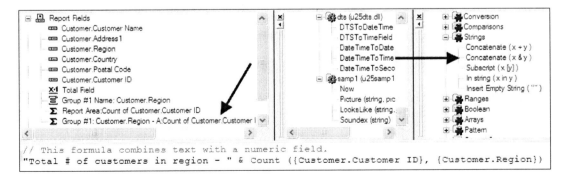

Figure 9-30 Group 1 Customer ID field added to the formula

6. Add the Group 1 Customer ID field illustrated above in Figure 9-28 to the formula, then check the formula for errors. Save the formula and close the Formula Workshop.

Add The Total Formula Field To The Report

1. Delete everything in the group footer section.

2. Add the Total Field formula field to the group footer section. The report should look like the one shown in Figure 9-31. Notice that there is a decimal point in the number. You cannot format the number. Save the changes and close the report.

Customer Information Grouped By Region
Sorted By Zip Code

2/12/2008			Page 1 of 15
Customer Name	Address	Country	Zip Code
Abu Dhabi			
UAE Cycle	Post Box: 278	United Arab Em	3453
Total # of customers in region - 1.00			
AL			
Psycho-Cycle	8287 Scott Road	USA	35818
The Great Bike Shop	1922 Beach Crescent	USA	35857
Benny - The Spokes Person	1020 Oak Way	USA	35861
Total # of customers in region - 3.00			

Figure 9-31 L9.8 Combine text and numeric fields report

Use Functions In String Formulas

You may have the need to combine data that is stored in different data types or format data differently then it is stored in the table. The next two exercises will show you how to incorporate functions in string formulas.

Exercise 9.9: Use The Picture Function

The phone numbers in the Supplier table are stored in the format shown in Figure 9-32. Notice that there are also international phone numbers in the table. When you want to print US phone numbers, they will look better if they are printed like this **(555) 555-5555**. In this exercise you will use the Picture function to format phone numbers in the Supplier table.

Supplier.Phone

Type: String
Length: 20

313 555-5735
44 171 555-2222
503 555-9931
514 555-9022
604 681 3435
81 3 3555-5011
81 6 431 -7877

Close

Figure 9-32 Phone numbers stored in the table

1. Create a new report and save it as `L9.9 Picture function`. Add the Supplier table, but do not add any fields to the report.

2. Create a formula field and name it `Supplier Phone`, then add the comment `This formula formats the Phone Number field` to the formula.

3. Open the Report Fields tree, then open the Supplier table.

4. Open the **ADDITIONAL FUNCTIONS** category in the Functions tree, then open the **SAMP1** category and double-click on the **PICTURE** function, as illustrated in Figure 9-33.

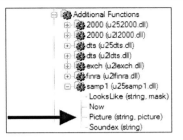

Figure 9-33 Picture function illustrated

5. Double-click on the Phone field in the Report Fields tree, then click after the comma in the formula and type " (XXX)XXXXXXX". Your formula should look like the one shown in Figure 9-34. Save the formula and leave the Formula Workshop open to complete the next part of the exercise.

```
// This formula formats the Phone Number field
Picture ({Supplier.Phone},"(XXX)XXXXXXX")
```

Figure 9-34 Phone number formula

> The brackets { } in a formula are used for data fields. The parenthesis ( ) are used to control the order that the formula is evaluated in.

In Figure 9-32 shown earlier, you saw the phone numbers that are stored in the Supplier table. All of the phone numbers will not work with the mask that you just created in the formula. In order to be able to accommodate international phone numbers, the formula would have to be modified to also use the **LENGTH** function and have another mask to accommodate phone numbers of a different length. This is known as conditional formatting, which you will learn how to do in the next lesson.

Use The ToText Function

The ToText function is one of the more popular functions. It lets you convert dates, numbers and more to a string/text field. In this part of the exercise you will combine the Supplier ID and Supplier Name fields. In order to combine a numeric and string field, you have to convert the numeric field to text. The **TOTEXT** function will let you do this.

1. Click the New button on the toolbar and type Supplier ID & Name as the formula name.

2. Add the comment
   This formula combines the Supplier ID and Supplier Name fields
   to the formula.

3. Open the Strings category in the Functions tree and double-click on the ToText (x,y) function.

4. Click inside of the parenthesis, then add the Supplier ID field.

5. Click after the right of the comma in the formula and type a zero. The zero means that the number should not display any decimal places if there are any in the field.

6. Click outside of the formula on the right and type + " - " +, then add the Supplier Name field. Your formula should look like the one shown in Figure 9-35. Save the formula and close the Formula Workshop.

```
//This formula combines the Supplier ID and Supplier Name fields
ToText ({Supplier.Supplier ID}, 0) + " - " + {Supplier.Supplier Name}
```

Figure 9-35 Supplier ID and Name formula

7. Add both of the formula fields to the details section of the report. The report should look like the one shown in Figure 9-36. Save the changes and close the report.

Supplier ID & Name	Supplier Phone
1 - Active Outdoors	(503) 555-9931
2 - Triumph	(313) 555-5735
3 - Guardian	(81)3 3555-5011
4 - InFlux	(81)6 431-7877
5 - Craze	(604) 681 3435
6 - Roadster	(44)171 555-2222
7 - Vesper	(514) 555-9022

Figure 9-36 L9.9 Picture function report

Using The Ampersand To Concatenate Strings

In the exercise that you just completed, you used the ToText function and the plus sign operator to concatenate string fields. The benefit of using the ToText function with the plus sign is that you can control the formatting. If you do not need to control the formatting, use the ampersand operator instead of the plus sign.

Formatting Strings With A Mask

In Exercise 9.8 you formatted a phone number field with the Picture function, which used a mask to format the field. Masks use characters including d, m and y as placeholders for the data, which determines how the data will be formatted when it is converted to a string. Table 9-7 lists some of the mask placeholders that are used the most for date fields. Table 9-8 provides placeholder examples for the date 6/1/05.

Placeholder	Description
d	Day of the month in numeric format without a leading zero.
dd	Day of the month in numeric format with a leading zero if necessary.
dddd	Name of the day spelled out.
M	Month in numeric format without a leading zero.
MM	Month in numeric format with a leading zero if necessary.
MMMM	Name of the month spelled out.
y	Last two digits of the year.
yyyy	Four digit year.

Table 9-7 Placeholder options

Mask	Displays
dd, MM, yy	01, 06, 05
MMMM dd yyyy	June 01 2005
dddd MMMM d, yyyy	Wednesday June 1, 2005
M, d, yy	6, 1, 05

Table 9-8 Mask options

Create Date Formulas

Table 9-9 provides an overview of some of the date functions. The exercises in this section will show you how to create some of the more popular date formulas using functions.

Function	Description
ChrW(x)	This function returns the character that represents the Unicode value of (x).
CurrentDate	This function uses the system date on your computer.
DateAdd	This function allows you to increment a date field by intervals, including days, weeks, months and years.
DateDiff	Calculates the difference between the start and end dates in the function. (6)
Day	Extracts the day from a Date or Date/Time field and returns a whole number.
Month	Extracts the month from a Date or Date/Time field and returns a whole number.
ToText	This function allows you to format any or all parts of a date field. This function also allows you to convert a date field to a text value.
Year	Extracts the year from a Date or Date/Time field and returns a whole number.

Table 9-9 Date functions explained

(6) The **DATEDIFF** function has arguments that you can use to determine how to calculate the difference between two date fields. The most common arguments are:

D will calculate the difference in days
M will calculate the difference in months
YYYY calculate the difference in years

Exercise 9.10: Create A Date Formula To Calculate The Order Processing Time

In this exercise you will create a formula to find out how long it is between the day an order is placed and when the order was shipped. This is known as the order processing time.

1. Save the L5.3 report as `L9.10 Calculate order processing time`.

2. Create a formula field and name it `Delay In Days To Ship`.

3. Expand the Date and Time function category, then expand the **DATEDIFF** category and double-click on the first DateDiff function.

4. Type "d" before the first comma in the formula.

5. Add the Order Date field to the formula after the first comma, then add the Ship Date field to the formula after the second comma. Your formula should look like the one shown in Figure 9-37. Check the formula for errors, then save the formula and close the Formula Workshop.

```
DateDiff ("d",{Orders.Order Date},{Orders.Ship Date})
```

Figure 9-37 Delay in days to ship formula

Add The Delay In Days To Ship Formula Field To The Report

1. Remove the time from the Order Date and Ship Date fields. Make these fields smaller, then move them to the left.

2. Add the Delay In Days To Ship formula field to the report and format it so that it does not have any decimal places. The report should look like the one shown in Figure 9-38. Save the changes and close the report.

Customer Name	Order Date	Ship Date	Order ID	Unit Price	Quantity	Delay In Days To Ship
Alley Cat Cycles	06/24/2001	07/02/2001	1,761	$21.90	1	8
Alley Cat Cycles	06/24/2001	07/02/2001	1,761	$539.85	1	8
Alley Cat Cycles	06/24/2001	07/02/2001	1,761	$329.85	3	8
Piccolo	06/24/2001	06/29/2001	1,762	$2,939.85	2	5
City Cyclists	06/24/2001	06/30/2001	1,763	$41.90	2	6
City Cyclists	06/24/2001	06/30/2001	1,763	$764.85	3	6

Figure 9-38 L9.10 Calculate order processing time report

A zero in the Delay In Days To Ship Field means that the order was shipped within 24 hours of when it was placed. Depending on the time an order was placed and shipped, the Ship Date could be the next day and still have a zero in the Delay In Days To Ship field because the order was shipped in less than 24 hours. Remember that the fields used in this formula are Date/Time fields.

Exercise 9.11: Calculate The Employee Age

One of the more popular date functions will allow you to calculate a persons age if you have their date of birth. In this exercise you will create an employee birthday list report. You will create a formula to calculate the age of the employees. In the Formula Overview section earlier in this lesson, I listed four reasons why certain types of data are not saved in a table. A persons age is a good example of the type of data that should not be saved in a table. The reason is because the age changes every year. This would mean that the field would have to be updated once a year on each persons birthday. This is why it is best to calculate the age, each time the report is run.

1. Create a new report and save it as `L9.11 Calculate age formula`. Add the following fields from the Employee table: Position, Birth Date and Hire Date.

2. Remove the time from the Birth Date and Hire Date fields, then save the changes.

3. Create a formula field to combine the first and last name fields. Name the formula `Employee Name`.

4. Create another formula field and save it as `Age`.

5. Add the Current Date function in the Date and Time category to the Age formula, then type a – (minus sign).

6. Add the Birth Date field to the formula, then check the formula for errors. Save the formula and close the Formula Workshop.

Modify The Report

1. Add the Employee Name formula field to the beginning of the details section, then add the Age formula field to the report after the Birth Date field.

2. Sort the report by the Last Name field. The report should look like the one shown in Figure 9-39. Save the changes.

Employee Name	Position	Birth Date	Age	Hire Date
Justin Brid	Marketing Director	10/08/1977	10,998.00	01/01/1994
Steven Buchanan	Sales Manager	03/04/1975	11,947.00	09/13/1992
Laura Callahan	Inside Sales Coordinator	01/09/1974	12,366.00	01/30/1993
Nancy Davolio	Sales Representative	12/08/1972	12,763.00	03/29/1991
Anne Dodsworth	Sales Representative	01/27/1976	11,618.00	10/12/1993

Figure 9-39 Age field added to the report

Modify The Age Formula

As you can see, the formula did not return the age in the format that you expected. The age shown on the report is in days, not years. This is because the Current Date function calculates in days. The formula will have to be modified so that the age is displayed in years.

1. Right-click on the Age formula field and select Edit Formula.

You may be thinking that the only thing that you have to do is click after the Birth Date field and type /365 and the age would be converted to years. Just adding this to the formula will not calculate the age in years. Instead, you will see the message shown in Figure 9-40.

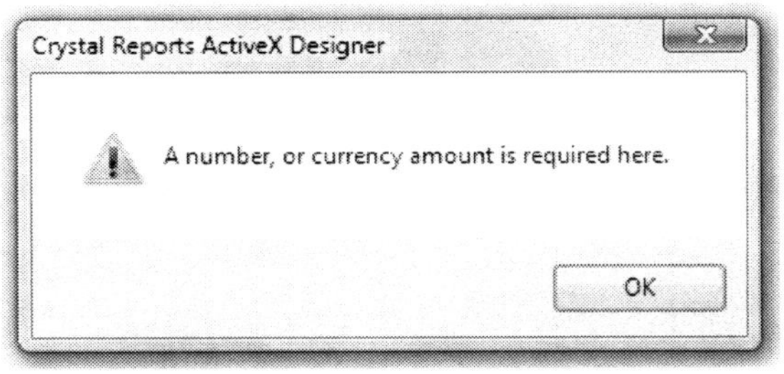

Figure 9-40 Calculation warning message

The reason that you will see this message is because you are trying to divide the Birth Date field which is a Date/Time field by 365, which is a numeric field. As you learned earlier, arguments must be the same data type to use them in a formula. This is not the case in this formula.

Another reason that this formula will not work is because of the formula evaluation order. The evaluation order must be forced in this formula. The way to force it is by adding parenthesis around the portion of the formula that has to be evaluated first. The order needed is to force the Birth Date to be subtracted from the Current Date **BEFORE** the division takes place.

2. Type parenthesis around the formula, then type /365 after the last parenthesis and check the formula.

Use The Truncate Function

When you previewed the report you saw that the age field has a decimal place, as shown earlier in Figure 9-37. The decimal place represents part of the year. This is not what you want. The Truncate function will remove that portion of the data.

1. Add the comment `This formula calculates the employees age.`

2. Expand the Math category, then expand the Truncate category.

3. Click at the beginning of the formula, then double-click on the Truncate (x) function.

TRUNCATE(X) truncates a field. **TRUNCATE (X, #PLACES)** determines how many decimal places to keep before truncation occurs.

4. After the truncate function, you will see parenthesis. Delete the right parenthesis and add it to the end of the formula. Your formula should look like the one shown in Figure 9-41. Check the formula for errors, then save and close the formula.

```
// This formula calculates the age of each employee
Truncate ((CurrentDate-{Employee.Birth Date})/365)
```

Figure 9-41 Age formula

5. Format the Age field so that it does not have any decimal places, then save the changes. The report should look like the one shown in Figure 9-42.

Employee Name	Position	Birth Date	Age	Hire Date
Justin Brid	Marketing Director	10/08/1977	30	01/01/1994
Steven Buchanan	Sales Manager	03/04/1975	32	09/13/1992
Laura Callahan	Inside Sales Coordinator	01/09/1974	33	01/30/1993
Nancy Davolio	Sales Representative	12/08/1972	34	03/29/1991
Anne Dodsworth	Sales Representative	01/27/1976	31	10/12/1993
Andrew Fuller	Vice President, Sales	02/19/1969	38	07/12/1991

Figure 9-42 L9.11 Calculate age formula report

You may see a different age for some or all of the employees. This will happen if you run the report after an employees birthday has past. For example, I ran the report shown above in Figure 9-42 in mid November 2007. I ran the report shown in Figure 9-43 in mid January 2008. Notice that the age for some of the employees has changed. That is because some people had a birthday since I ran the report shown above in Figure 9-42.

Employee Name	Position	Birth Date	Age	Hire Date
Justin Brid	Marketing Director	10/08/1977	30	01/01/1994
Steven Buchanan	Sales Manager	03/04/1975	32	09/13/1992
Laura Callahan	Inside Sales Coordinator	01/09/1974 ➝	34	01/30/1993
Nancy Davolio	Sales Representative	12/08/1972 ➝	35	03/29/1991
Anne Dodsworth	Sales Representative	01/27/1976	31	10/12/1993

Figure 9-43 L9.11 Calculate age formula report run two months later

If you need to use the same formula in more than one report, you can copy it from one report and paste it in another report.

Test Your Skills

1. Save the L9.4 report as `L9.12 Skills Calculate monthly salary.`

   - Create a formula to calculate the employees monthly salary and name it `Monthly Salary`. Place the formula on the report after the Weekly Salary formula field.
   - Create a formula called `Combined Name` that combines the Employee ID, first and last name fields. (**Hint:** Use the ToText (x,y) function)
   - Add a dash after the Employee ID field in the formula.
   - Create a title on the report for the field called `Employee`.
   - Delete the Address1 field.
   - Change the sort order to sort on the Employee ID field.
   - The report should look like the one shown in Figure 9-44.

Employee	Weekly Salary	Monthly Salary	Salary
5 - Steven Buchanar	$961.54	$4,166.67	$50,000.00
6 - Michael Suyama	$576.92	$2,500.00	$30,000.00
7 - Robert King	$711.54	$3,083.33	$37,000.00
9 - Anne Dodsworth	$673.08	$2,916.67	$35,000.00
Bas-Rhin			
13 - Justin Brid	$1,442.31	$6,250.00	$75,000.00
14 - Xavier Martin	$961.54	$4,166.67	$50,000.00
15 - Laurent Pereira	$865.38	$3,750.00	$45,000.00

   Figure 9-44 L9.12 Skills Calculate monthly salary report

2. Save the L9.6 report as `L9.13 Skills Calculate sales tax.`

   - Modify the Total order amount for customer, Total amount of sales for the day, Total amount of sales for salesperson and Total amount of sales fields to use the Line Item Total field for the summary, instead of the Order Amount field. (**Hint:** Use the Change Summary option)
   - Create a `Sales Tax` formula field that calculates 8.25% sales tax. Use the Group 3 Sum of Line Item Total field.
   - Create a formula field called `Order Total`. Add the Group 3 Sum of Line Item Total field and the Sales Tax field.
   - Add the Sales Tax and Order Total fields to the report. Place them in the Group 3 Footer section after the summary field.
   - Move the Total order amount for customer title in front of the Order Total field.
   - Create a field title called `Sub Total` and place it in front of the first summary field in the Group 3 Footer section. Take the bold off of the summary field in this section.
   - Create a field title called `Sales Tax` and place it in front of the Sales Tax field.

   Page 1 of the report should look like the one shown in Figure 9-45.
   The last page of the report should look like the one shown in Figure 9-46.

Employee	Order Date	Order #	Customer #	Product #	Unit Price	Quantity	Line Item Total
1 Nancy Davolio							
2/13/2000							
30							
	02/19/2000	1310	30	1101	$14.50	3	$43.50
	02/19/2000	1310	30	1104	$14.50	1	$14.50
	Sub Total $ 58.00		Sales Tax $ 4.79		Total order amount for customer -		$62.79
75							
	02/19/2000	1312	75	302162	$479.85	1	$479.85
	02/19/2000	1312	75	401001	$267.76	1	$267.76
	02/19/2000	1312	75	2202	$41.90	1	$41.90
	Sub Total $ 789.51		Sales Tax $ 65.13		Total order amount for customer -		$854.64

Figure 9-45 Page 1 of the L9.13 Skills Calculate sales tax report

Employee	Order Date	Order #	Customer #	Product #	Unit Price	Quantity	Line Item Total
	Sub Total $ 42.00		Sales Tax $ 3.47		Total order amount for customer -		$45.47
5							
	12/30/2000	1115	5	3301	$4.50	2	$9.00
	12/29/2000	1112	5	2215	$53.90	3	$161.70
	Sub Total $ 170.70		Sales Tax $ 14.08		Total order amount for customer -		$184.78
33							
	12/27/2000	1101	33	2204	$41.90	3	$125.70
	12/27/2000	1101	33	402002	$274.35	3	$823.05
	12/27/2000	1101	33	5204	$33.90	1	$33.90
	Sub Total $ 982.65		Sales Tax $ 81.07		Total order amount for customer -		$1,063.72
Daily Totals	# of orders for the day - **4**						
	Total order amount for customer - **$ 1,195.35**						
Salesperson totals	# of orders for salesperson - **37**						
	Total amount of sales for salesperson **$ 29,049.94**						
Report Totals	# of orders - **181**						
	Total amount of sales - **$ 259,390.64**						

Figure 9-46 Last page of the L9.13 Skills Calculate sales tax report

If you refer back to Exercise 6.16, Figures 6-77 and 6-78, you will see the difference in the total amounts. Hopefully after completing this exercise you realize how easy it is to produce a report that looks good, but does not display the correct data. Many of the calculations in the L6.16 report are incorrect, which in this case inflated the totals.

People reading the L6.16 report would think that the orders were a lot higher then they really are. Whatever decisions that would be made from the data on that report may not be correct. Remember that the people reading the report normally do not see the formulas that are used in the report. This is why I know that it is important for the report designer (you) to understand the data for the report and to take the time to test the calculations to ensure that the calculations are correct. Okay, I will get off of my soap box now, as hopefully I have proven my point.

3. Save the L9.10 report as L9.14 Skills Ship delay GT 2 days.

   - Create selection criteria to only show orders that have a shipping delay of two or more days.

   Your report should look like the one shown in Figure 9-47, which should have 1,217 records.

Customer Name	Order Date	Ship Date	Order ID	Unit Price	Quantity	Delay In Days To Ship
Alley Cat Cycles	06/24/2001	07/02/2001	1,761	$21.90	1	8
Alley Cat Cycles	06/24/2001	07/02/2001	1,761	$539.85	1	8
Alley Cat Cycles	06/24/2001	07/02/2001	1,761	$329.85	3	8
Piccolo	06/24/2001	06/29/2001	1,762	$2,939.85	2	5
City Cyclists	06/24/2001	06/30/2001	1,763	$41.90	2	6
City Cyclists	06/24/2001	06/30/2001	1,763	$764.85	3	6
Hercules Mountain Bikes	06/24/2001	06/27/2001	1,764	$37.90	2	3
Hercules Mountain Bikes	06/24/2001	06/27/2001	1,764	$23.50	2	3
Hercules Mountain Bikes	06/24/2001	06/27/2001	1,764	$832.35	2	3
The Great Bike Shop	06/24/2001	06/28/2001	1,765	$2,939.85	2	4
The Great Bike Shop	06/24/2001	06/28/2001	1,765	$809.87	2	4
The Great Bike Shop	06/24/2001	06/28/2001	1,765	$329.85	1	4
Changing Gears	06/24/2001	06/26/2001	1,766	$53.90	2	2

Figure 9-47 L9.14 Skills Ship delay GT 2 days report

4. In this exercise you will combine two address fields and add the combined field to the report. You will also create totals for the report.

    -   Save the L9.4 report as `L9.15 Skills Combined address fields`.
    -   Create a formula field called `Full Address` that combines the two address fields.
    -   Create a count of employees per region.
    -   Create a total dollar amount of weekly and monthly salaries per region.
    -   Create a field title called `Totals for region –` and place it in the Group 1 Footer section.
    -   Create a field title called `# of employees` and place it in the Group 1 Footer section.
    -   Add a line at the top and bottom of the Group 1 Footer section.

    Your report should look like the one shown in Figure 9-48. Notice that most of the addresses did not print on the report. That is because at least one of the address fields is null (empty). In order to properly combine and print both address fields, conditional formatting needs to be applied that will force the address fields to print. You will learn how to create conditional formatting in the next lesson.

First Name	Last Name	Address	Weekly Salary	Salary
Steven	Buchanan		$961.54	$50,000.00
Robert	King	Edgeham Hollow	$711.54	$37,000.00
Anne	Dodsworth		$673.08	$35,000.00
Michael	Suyama		$576.92	$30,000.00
Totals for region -		# of employees 4	$576.92	$30,000.00
Bas-Rhin				
Justin	Brid		$1,442.31	$75,000.00
Xavier	Martin		$961.54	$50,000.00
Laurent	Pereira		$865.38	$45,000.00
Totals for region -		# of employees 3	$865.38	$45,000.00

Figure 9-48 L9.15 Skills Combined address fields report

 When you create a formula that is combining fields and one or more fields in the formula is null, or could be null, the formula will fail, which is what happened in this exercise. Any field that is not a required data entry field can be null.

5. Save the L4.15 report as `L9.16 Skills Convert case`.

   - Create a formula called `ProductTypeLowerCase` that changes the case of the Product Type Name field to all lower case letters.
   - Create a formula called `SupplierNameUpperCase` that changes the case of the Supplier Name field to all upper case letters.
   - Replace the existing Product Type Name and Supplier Name fields on the report with the formula fields.

   Your report should look like the one shown in Figure 9-49.

Record Number	Product #	Product Name	Product Type	Supplier Name
1	1101	Active Outdoors Crochet Glove	gloves	ACTIVE OUTDOORS
2	1102	Active Outdoors Crochet Glove	gloves	ACTIVE OUTDOORS
3	1103	Active Outdoors Crochet Glove	gloves	ACTIVE OUTDOORS
4	1104	Active Outdoors Crochet Glove	gloves	ACTIVE OUTDOORS
5	1105	Active Outdoors Crochet Glove	gloves	ACTIVE OUTDOORS
6	1106	Active Outdoors Lycra Glove	gloves	ACTIVE OUTDOORS
7	1107	Active Outdoors Lycra Glove	gloves	ACTIVE OUTDOORS
8	1108	Active Outdoors Lycra Glove	gloves	ACTIVE OUTDOORS
9	1109	Active Outdoors Lycra Glove	gloves	ACTIVE OUTDOORS
10	1110	Active Outdoors Lycra Glove	gloves	ACTIVE OUTDOORS
11	1111	Active Outdoors Lycra Glove	gloves	ACTIVE OUTDOORS
12	2201	Triumph Pro Helmet	helmets	TRIUMPH

Figure 9-49 L9.16 Skills Convert case report

CONDITIONAL FORMATTING

After completing the exercises in this lesson you will be able to use the following tools and techniques to format fields and sections in a report.

☑ Highlighting Expert
☑ Apply conditional formats to fields
☑ Create If Then Else statements
☑ Suppressing fields and sections
☑ Section Expert

LESSON 10

Absolute Formatting Overview

The formatting techniques that you learned in Lesson 4 are known as **ABSOLUTE FORMATTING** because they are applied to every occurrence of the object. As you will learn, you may not always need to apply the formatting that you create. The options on the Format Editor and Section Expert if checked, turn on what is known as Absolute Formatting, which means that the format will be applied to all values in the field. Absolute Formatting is not on if the option is not checked. This also applies to drop-down lists and text fields on these dialog boxes.

Conditional Formatting Overview

In Lesson 4 you learned basic formatting techniques. In Lesson 9 you learned that data could be formatted or manipulated using formulas and functions. The techniques covered in those two lessons will handle a large percent of your report formatting needs. What you may have noticed is that the formatting that you have learned to create so far is applied to every detail record. There will be times when the report does not need or require the same formatting to be applied to every detail record. Conditional formatting starts off as absolute formatting, but goes a step further by setting up criteria to determine when the formatting should be applied.

There are formatting techniques that you can use that will give you the option of applying the formatting only if a condition is met. This is known as **CONDITIONAL FORMATTING**. Examples of conditional formatting include the following:

① Highlighting records when the data in one field is greater than a constant value.
② Highlighting records with a specific color that have data missing in a field.
③ Check the value or length of a field and apply different formatting, depending on the value or length of the field.
④ Print a background color on every other detail record on the report.
⑤ Formatting one field with a border based on the value in another field.

> Conditional formatting is created using the Highlighting Expert or Formula Editor. Conditional formatting overrides absolute formatting that is created with the Format Editor because you can set the "on" and "off" properties conditionally.

Highlighting Expert Overview

The Highlighting Expert allows you to easily create and apply font, background and border conditional formatting to fields on a report without having to write any code. It is a scaled down version of the Format Editor. One downside is that it does not provide a lot of options. The Highlighting Expert allows you to bring attention to certain values on the report. The way that the Highlighting Expert allows you to conditionally bring attention to values on the report is by changing one or some of the following:

☑ Font style
☑ Font color
☑ Background color
☑ Border style

> Conditional formatting that is created by the Highlighting Expert cannot be modified in the Formula Workshop that you learned about in Lesson 9.

An example of when to use the Highlighting Expert would be if you wanted to highlight the order amount if it is more than $1,000. The first two exercises in this lesson will show you how to highlight data using the Highlighting Expert.

Right-clicking on the field that needs to meet a condition and selecting the Highlighting Expert option will open the dialog box shown in Figure 10-1.

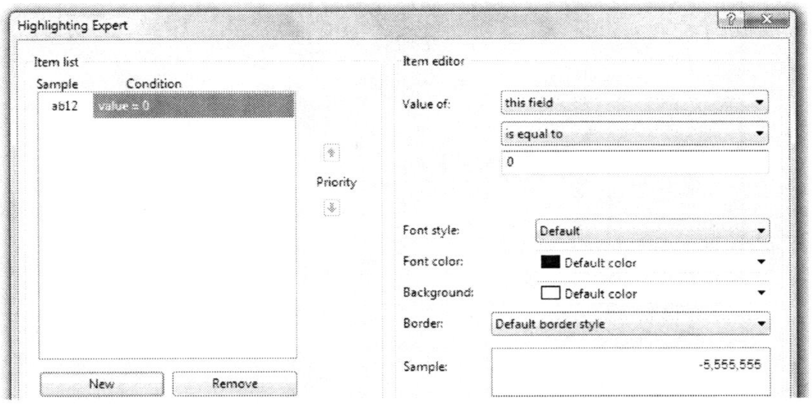

Figure 10-1 Highlighting Expert

The Highlighting Expert does not work with **PARAMETER FIELDS**, which you will learn about in Lesson 12. To set the conditional formatting the Highlighting Expert can only compare data in a table.

The Highlighting Expert is similar to the Select Expert. One difference that I noticed is that the Highlighting Expert does not have as many operators as the Select Expert has.

As shown in Figure 10-1, the Highlighting Expert has the following two sections:

① **Item List** Displays the conditional formatting formulas created by the Highlighting Expert for the field that is selected.
② **Item Editor** Allows you to create and view the conditional formatting formulas.
This section has the **SAMPLE** column that will let you see the highlighting that will be applied. The **CONDITION** column displays the formula that will create the formatting.

Item Editor Options

① The **VALUE OF** drop-down list contains the fields, formulas and functions that are on the report or that are connected to the report, as shown in Figure 10-2. These are the fields that you can use to create the conditions for.

The **THIS FIELD** option in the Value of field lets you use the field that was selected before the Highlighting Expert was opened. Selecting a different field then the one that was selected prior to opening the Highlighting Expert means that you want to apply the formatting to the field selected prior to opening the Highlighting Expert, but you want the condition to be set based on the value in a different field.

The last option in the drop-down list illustrated in Figure 10-2, **OTHER FIELDS** opens the Choose Field dialog box, which you can use to select another field from any data source connected to the report to use to create highlighting criteria for.

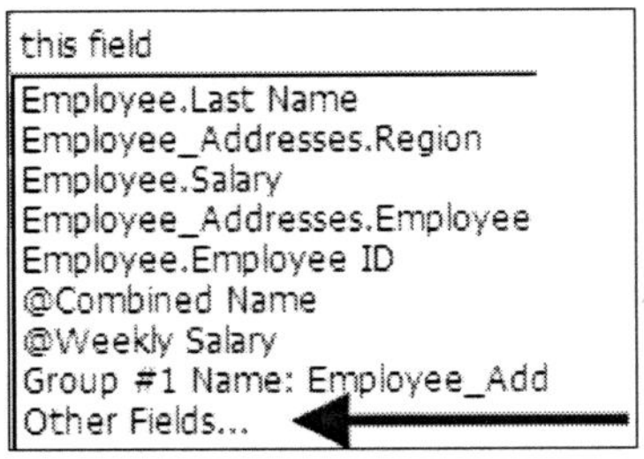

Figure 10-2 Field selection drop-down list

② The **COMPARISON** drop-down list is the second field in the Item Editor section. It contains the selection criteria options shown in Figure 10-3. You can use these operators to select which records will be highlighted.

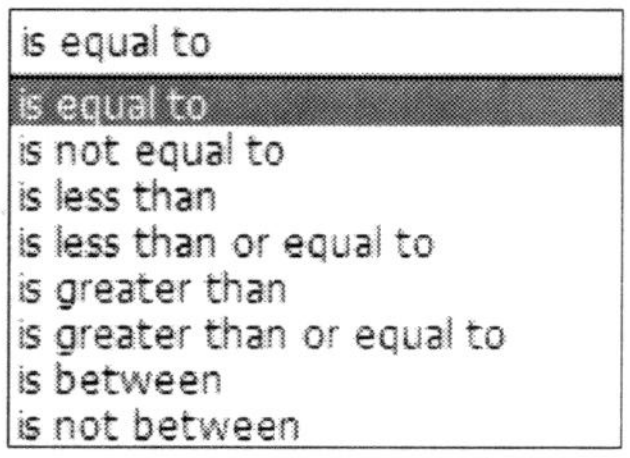

Figure 10-3 Comparison drop-down list operators

③ The **COMPARE TO** drop-down list is the third field from the top. It will display the values in the field that you select in the Value Of drop-down list. This is like the Browse Data window. You can also type in the value that you want.

Item List Options

① The **PRIORITY** buttons let you change the order that the highlighting will be applied. Priority is important when there are multiple conditions set for the same field. For example, if you want to set the background of a date field to green if it is greater than 1/1/01 and another condition to place a border around the same date field if the date is greater than 6/24/02. If the date is 1/24/03, which of the two formatting conditions should be applied to the date field? If the greater than 1/1/01 is the first condition, all of the records that are greater than 1/1/01 would have a green background applied, even if the date is greater than 6/24/02. In some instances, multiple conditions can conflict. This is why setting a priority is important. It is how Crystal Reports resolves the conflicts.

② The **REMOVE** button will delete the highlighting criteria that is displayed in the Item List.

Exercise 10.1: Use The Background Highlighting Option

In this exercise you will modify a report to highlight the background of the Delay In Days To Ship field for orders that were not shipped in two days or less.

1. Save the L9.10 report as
   `L10.1 Highlight order delay shipping time conditionally.`

2. Right-click on the Delay In Days To Ship formula field and select **HIGHLIGHTING EXPERT**, then click the **NEW** button on the Highlighting Expert dialog box.

3. Open the Comparison drop-down list and select **IS GREATER THAN OR EQUAL TO**, then type a 3 in the field below.

4. Select **GRAY** as the background color. You should have the options selected that are shown in Figure 10-4.

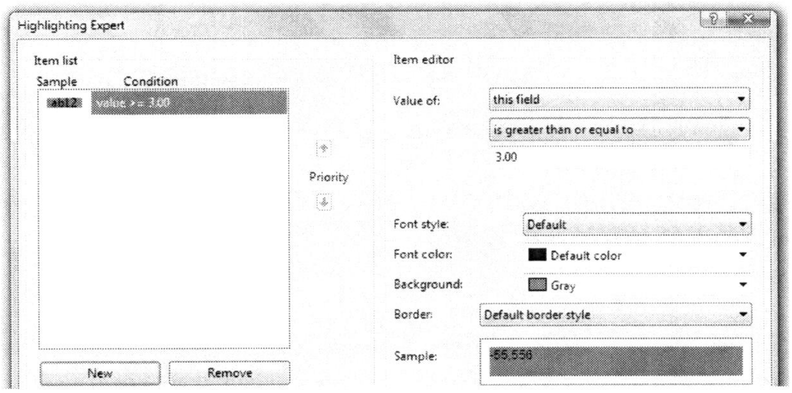

Figure 10-4 Highlighting options

5. Click OK and save the changes. The report should look like the one shown in Figure 10-5. Close the report.

Figure 10-5 L10.1 report with conditional field background highlighting

Exercise 10.2: Use One Field To Highlight Another Field And Set A Priority

The Highlighting Expert allows you to create more than one highlighting condition per field. If a field has multiple conditions, there may be a need to set a priority for the conditions. In this exercise you will create two conditions for the same field and set a priority for the conditions. You will create the following conditions:

① Make the quantity bold if it is greater than or equal to three.
② Italicize the quantity if the unit price is greater than $500.

Create The Quantity Is Greater Than Condition

1. Save the L9.10 report as
   `L10.2 Use multiple conditions to highlight a field.`

2. Right-click on the Quantity field and select Highlighting Expert, then click New.

3. Open the Comparison drop-down list and select **IS GREATER THAN OR EQUAL TO**, then type 3 in the field below.

4. Select the bold Font style. Leave the Highlighting Expert dialog box open to complete the next part of the exercise.

Create The Unit Price Is Greater Than Condition

1. Click New, then open the Value Of drop-down list and select the Unit Price field.

2. Open the Comparison drop-down list and select **IS GREATER THAN**, then type 500 in the last field.

3. Select the bold italic font style, then select red as the font color. Leave the Highlighting Expert dialog box open to complete the next part of the exercise.

Set The Priority

There could be a lot of records that meet both of the conditions that you just created. Unless it doesn't matter which order the conditions are applied to the field, you should set a priority. In this exercise, the most important criteria is for the Unit Price field.

1. Click on the Unit Price condition in the **ITEM LIST**, then click the ⬆ (Priority Up) button. You should have the options selected that are shown in Figure 10-6.

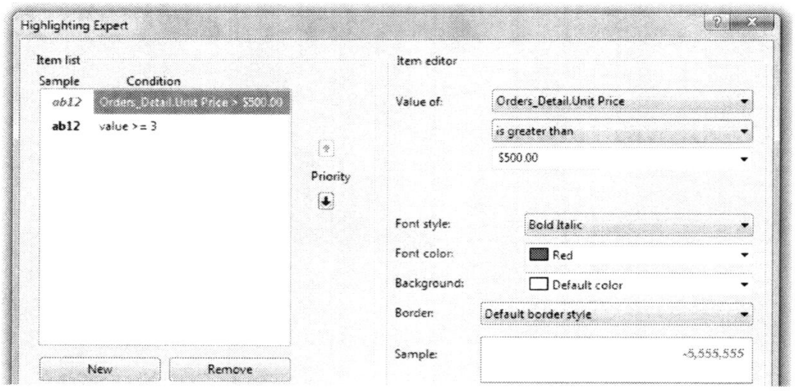

Figure 10-6 Highlighting conditions

2. Click OK and save the changes. The report should look like the one shown in Figure 10-7. I added the words red and bold to the report to indicate what you should see on your report. Close the report.

Customer Name	Order Date	Ship Date	Order ID	Unit Price	Quantity	Delay In Days To Ship
Alley Cat Cycles	06/24/2001	07/02/2001	1,761	$21.90	1	8
Alley Cat Cycles	06/24/2001	07/02/2001	1,761	$539.85	Red 1	8
Alley Cat Cycles	06/24/2001	07/02/2001	1,761	$329.85	Bold 3	8
Piccolo	06/24/2001	06/29/2001	1,762	$2,939.85	Red 2	5
City Cyclists	06/24/2001	06/30/2001	1,763	$41.90	2	6
City Cyclists	06/24/2001	06/30/2001	1,763	$764.85	Red 3	6
Hercules Mountain Bikes	06/24/2001	06/27/2001	1,764	$37.90	2	3
Hercules Mountain Bikes	06/24/2001	06/27/2001	1,764	$23.50	2	3
Hercules Mountain Bikes	06/24/2001	06/27/2001	1,764	$832.35	Red 2	3

Figure 10-7 L10.2 Use multiple conditions to highlight a field report

Highlighting Expert Limitations

Despite being relatively easy to use, there are some features in Crystal Reports in my opinion, that could be improved. [See www.tolana.com/crxi/xi_wishlist.html. This list is based on a newer version of Crystal Reports, but the same issues exist in Crystal Reports Basic for Visual Studio 2008.] The Highlighting Expert is one feature that could be improved, similar to the inherent issues with some of the wizards. You should be aware of the following two facts about the Highlighting Expert.

① Formulas created by the Highlighting Expert override formulas in the Formula Workshop.
② Formulas created by the Highlighting Expert are not accessible or visible in the Formula Workshop. This means that you cannot see the formulas created by the Highlighting Expert and can easily forget that they exist.

Any formula that you can create with the Highlighting Expert can be created in the Formula Editor. It is easier to maintain formulas if they are all in the same place. Take from this what you will.

If...Then...Else Statements

This is one of the most used lines of programming code. This statement lets you set different options based on what you need to happen when the data is evaluated. The syntax below is for an If Then Else statement:

If EXPRESSION/CONDITION Then TRUE STATEMENTS
Else
FALSE STATEMENTS

Parts Of The If Then Else Statement Explained

① The **Expression/Condition** must evaluate to true or false.
② The **True Statements** will execute if the Expression/Condition is true.
③ The **Else** part of the statement is optional. If the Else clause is not included and the Expression/Condition is false, nothing will happen, which may be what you want. By "nothing happens", I mean that the If statement will default to the value for the data type. For example, if Field A is greater than 95, then textfield5 = "Great Job". If the variable "textfield5" was not declared to have a specific default value, the default value for a text field data type is " " (null), which is what would be displayed if Field A is not greater than 95.
④ The **False Statements** will execute if the Expression/Condition is false.

The plain English translation is: IF Choice A meets this condition, THEN do X, ELSE do Y.
Walk through the examples in Table 10-1 to gain a better understanding of If Then Else statements.
Fill in the column on the right based on the numbers in the Choice A column.

If Choice A is greater than 25, then Field B = 100, else Field B = 0.

Choice A	What Does Field B=
26	
1	
25	

Table 10-1 If Then Else examples

It may help to understand If...Then...Else statements if you think of them as a true or false test question. In the example above, the test question can be worded as "Is Choice A greater than 25?" There are two possible answers:

① Yes, it is (True). If it is, Field B would be set to 100.
② No, it isn't (False). If it isn't, Field B would be set to 0.

How Did You Do?

Table 10-2 contains the answers for the second column in Table 10-1. The third column explains the answer.

Choice A	Field B=	Reason
26	100	The answer is 100 because 26 is greater than 25.
1	0	The answer is 0 because 1 is less than 25.
25	0	The answer is 0 because 25 is not greater than 25.

Table 10-2 If Then Else answers for Table 10-1

To complicate If statements even more, there can be multiple true and false statements in the same If Then Else statement. When this is the case, they have to be enclosed in parenthesis, otherwise Crystal Reports will stop processing the statement after the first semi-colon, which often will produce a syntax error. Statements with multiple true and false statements are known as **NESTED IF STATEMENTS**.

Conditional Formatting Tips

When you create a formula for an option, this is known as conditional formatting because the formula will turn the option on and off. Boolean formulas are used for on-off options in conditional formatting. There are two types of properties that conditional formatting can be applied to. The property type determines the type of conditional formula that has to be created. When creating conditional If...Then...Else statements, keep the following in mind:

① **CHECK BOX** formatting options are either on or off. This means that you do not have to type the entire If...Then...Else statement. Crystal Reports will turn the format option on if the test returns a true value. If the formula returns a false value, the formatting is not turned on. **On-Off** properties like the Can Grow option or any option that has a check box on the Format Editor is an example. On-off properties require **BOOLEAN** formulas.

② **DROP-DOWN LISTS** and **TEXT BOXES** and formatting options can have more than one choice. For this type of conditional formatting you have to type the entire If...Then...Else statement to specify what you want to happen if the test is true and if the test is false. **Multiple choice** properties like the border line style option which is a drop-down list on the Line tab of the Format Editor is an example. Multiple choice properties require If Then Else or Select Case statements.

Conditional Formatting Warnings

You should be aware of the following when creating conditional formatting:

① If a field has formatting that is created with the Highlighting Expert and with conditional formatting, the Highlighting Expert formatting takes precedence. If the conditional formatting does not change the formatting created by the Highlighting Expert, the conditional formatting will be applied.

② Conditional formatting overrides absolute formatting even if the result of the conditional formatting is false.

③ Keep in mind that Crystal Reports does not require the "Else" part of an If Then Else statement.

④ If absolute and conditional formatting are applied to a field and the If Then Else statement for the conditional formatting does not have an Else clause and the conditional formatting does not return a "True" value, neither the conditional formatting or the absolute formatting is applied.

⑤ In addition to If Then Else statements you can also use **SELECT CASE** statements as long as the formatting property is in the Function Tree.

As you can see, it can be difficult to apply both absolute and conditional formatting to the same field. Even with the best intentions and code, you can get unexpected results. There are two things that you can do to help ensure that you get the output that you need when you have to combine absolute and conditional formatting. I have found the second option below to be more effective, but if the first option fits your needs, you should use it.

① Use the "Else" clause on If statements or the **DEFAULT** clause on Select Case statements.

② Use the "Else" clause with the **DEFAULTATTRIBUTE** function. To do this, select the default (absolute) option on the Format Editor dialog box and use the DefaultAttribute as the Else part of the If statement. For example, if you need to set the default value for a field to green on the Format Editor, use the following If Then Else statement.

```
If {Employee.Salary}/52 <= 750
    Then crRed
        Else
            DefaultAttribute
```

This formula will display salaries that are less than or equal to $750 in red and the other salaries in green if the salary field is set to green on the Format Editor.

> Formulas are created because the report needs an action to be taken based on the result. Sometimes you always need an action to be taken, regardless of the outcome of the formula. In those cases, you would put what you want to happen in place of the DefaultAttribute in the formula. Use the Default Attribute when you do not want to change the property. It is not a requirement to use this function.

> Unless stated otherwise, when instructed to open a category, the category is in the Functions tree.

Exercise 10.3: Use The If Then Else Statement And IsNull Function

In Exercise 9.15 you created a formula to combine two address fields. The formula that you created in that exercise is fine as long as there is data in both address fields. Unless the fields are required to be filled in on a data entry form, you cannot be 100% sure that they will contain data. In Lesson 2, you learned about Null values in fields. The second address field is an example of a field that can have null values because all addresses do not require two fields.

While the Employee Addresses table only has a few records, you could manually check to see if both address fields contained data before creating the formula. If the table had two million records, checking them manually probably is not a good idea and could be quite time consuming. There are two options discussed below that you can use to prevent a formula from failing, if a field is null (empty).

①　The **ISNULL** function will let you test a field to see if it is null. If it is, you can make a decision on what to do. To make this decision you need to use the If Then Else statement with the IsNull function.

②　Check the **CONVERT DATABASE NULL VALUES TO DEFAULT** option on the Options dialog box. Turning this option on will convert null values to zero for numeric fields or blank for string fields. "Blank" is different than Null.

> While Crystal Reports supports the **CONVERT DATABASE NULL VALUES TO DEFAULT** option, not all databases support it. If you want to use this option, you need to make sure that the database that you are working with supports it. If you can't or don't want to confirm whether or not a database supports this feature, you can use the **ISNULL** function. I personally find it easier to use the IsNull function all the time, so that I can "see" what is going on.

In this exercise you will create a formula that will combine the two employee address fields and check the Address2 field to see if it is null. The majority of the time, the second address field will be the one that will not have data. On the rare occurrence that the first address field is null, you would want the formula to fail so that the field would be blank on the report. Hopefully, the person reading the report will notice this and fix the data. You can also write code that will print a message in the combined address field if either of the address fields is empty.

> The **ISNULL** function has to be placed inside the If Then Else statement because the check that it will perform on the Address2 field is the first part (the test question) that the If Then Else statement is evaluates. In "plain" English the formula that you will create is:
>
> **If** the Address2 field does not have any data
> **then** set the Full Address field (the formula field name) to only display/print the Address1 field
> **else** set the Full Address field to display/print the Address1 field and the Address2 field.

1. Save the L9.15 report as `L10.3 If Then Else Statement`.

2. Open the Full Address formula and delete the formula that is there. (**Hint**: You can right-click on the field in the report and select **EDIT FORMULA**.)

3. Open the **CONTROL STRUCTURES** category in the Operators tree, then double-click on the **IF X THEN Y ELSE Z** statement, as illustrated in Figure 10-8.

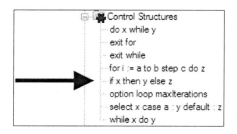

Figure 10-8 If Then Else statement illustrated

4. Open the **PRINT STATE** category, then double-click on the **ISNULL** function, as illustrated in Figure 10-9. With the flashing insertion point between the parenthesis in the formula, double-click on the Address2 field in the Report Fields tree. This is the question part of the **IF** statement.

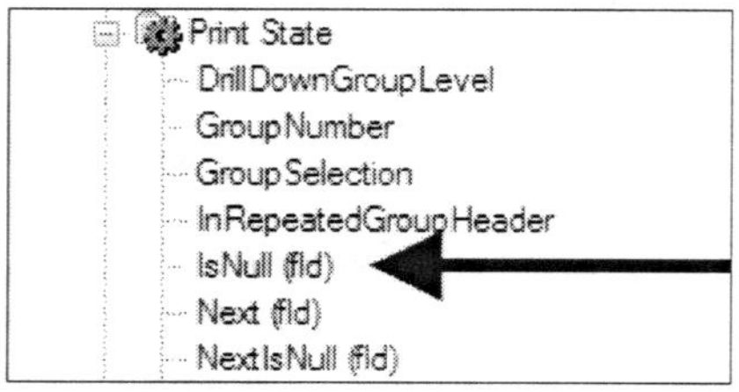

Figure 10-9 IsNull function illustrated

5. Click after the word **THEN** in the formula and double-click on the Address1 field, then press Enter. The word **ELSE** should be on the next line. This is the "true" part of the question, meaning that this is what you want to have print if the Address2 field is null.

6. Click after the word **ELSE** and add the Address1 field, then type + " " +.

7. Add the Address2 field. If you want to add a comment to the formula, you can. Check the formula for errors. It should look like the one shown in Figure 10-10.

```
// formula to check to see if the address2 field is null
if IsNull ({Employee_Addresses.Address2}) then {Employee_Addresses.Address1}
else {Employee_Addresses.Address1}+ " " +{Employee_Addresses.Address2}
```

Figure 10-10 If Then Else and IsNull formula

8. Save the formula and close the Formula Workshop. The report should look like the one shown in Figure 10-11. You will now see data in the Address field. Compare this report to the L9.15 report. Save the changes and close the report.

First Name	Last Name	Address	Weekly Salary	Salary
Steven	Buchanan	14 Garrett Hill	$961.54	$50,000.00
Robert	King	Edgeham Hollow	$711.54	$37,000.00
Anne	Dodsworth	7 Houndstooth Rd.	$673.08	$35,000.00
Michael	Suyama	Coventry House	$576.92	$30,000.00
Totals for region -		# of employees 4	$576.92	$30,000.00
Bas-Rhin				
Justin	Brid	2 impasse du Soleil	$1,442.31	$75,000.00
Xavier	Martin	9 place de la Liberté	$961.54	$50,000.00
Laurent	Pereira	7 rue Nationale	$865.38	$45,000.00
Totals for region -		# of employees 3	$865.38	$45,000.00

Figure 10-11 L10.3 If Then Else Statement report

Exercise 10.4: Use The Length Function

The Length function will check the number of characters in a field. Based on the length, you can assign different actions. For example, if a field has 10 characters you can display one message and if the same field in another record has 12 characters, you can display a different message.

In Exercise 9.9 you created a formula to format a phone number field. What you saw was that all of the phone numbers were not the same length. This caused some of the phone numbers to not be formatted properly. Using the Length function on the phone number field will allow you to use different formatting options based on the number of characters in the field. If you look at the data in the Phone field you will see that phone numbers are 12, 14 or 15 characters long.

In this exercise you will modify the Supplier Information report to check the number of characters in the Phone number field for each record and format the field based on the number of characters in the field.

Create A Formula For 12 Character Phone Numbers

In this part of the exercise you will create the formula that checks for 12 characters and creates the formatting for 12 character phone numbers.

1. Save the L9.9 report and as `L10.4 Length function`.

2. Open the Supplier Phone formula field and delete the formula, then open the **CONTROL STRUCTURES** category in the Operators tree and double-click on the If x then y else z statement.

3. Open the **STRINGS** category then double-click on the **LENGTH(STR)** function, as shown in Figure 10-12. With the flashing insertion point between the parenthesis in the formula, add the Phone field, then click outside of the parenthesis on the right and type `=12` before the word "then".

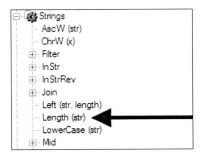

Figure 10-12 Length function illustrated

4. Click in front of the word **ELSE** and press Enter. Open the **ADDITIONAL FUNCTIONS** category, then open the **SAMP1** category and double-click on the **PICTURE** function.

5. Double-click on the Phone field in the Report Fields tree, then click after the comma in the formula and type " (XXX)XXXXXXX". (There are seven X's after the parenthesis.)

6. Click in front of the word ELSE and press Enter. Leave the Formula Workshop open to complete the next part of the exercise.

Create A Formula For 15 Character Phone Numbers

In this part of the exercise you will create the formula that checks for 15 characters and creates the formatting for phone numbers that have 15 characters. Most of the formula is the same as the one that you created for 12 characters. It is easier to copy the formula and change what's needed, then it is to create it again from scratch.

1. Copy the 12 character formula and paste it below the word ELSE.

2. Change the second =12 to =15, then change the Picture to XX-XXX-XXXXXXX.

In this exercise if the phone number is not 12 or 15 characters, you just want the phone number printed without any formatting. You have complete control over which lengths you want to provide formatting for and which ones you don't.

3. Add the Phone field after the last ELSE in the formula. Your formula should look like the one shown in Figure 10-13. Check for syntax errors.

```
//This formula formats the phone number field
if Length ({Supplier.Phone})=12 then
Picture ({Supplier.Phone},"(XXX)XXXXXXX" )
else
if Length ({Supplier.Phone})=15 then
Picture ({Supplier.Phone}," XX-XXX-XXXXXXX" )
else
{Supplier.Phone}
```

Figure 10-13 Phone number formula

4. Save the changes and close the Formula Workshop. The report should look like the one shown in Figure 10-14. Compare this report to the L9.9 report. Usually, phone numbers are entered with formatting so that they are lined up better then the data in the Supplier table. An example of this is the Customer Phone Number field in the Customers table. Save the changes and close the report.

Supplier ID & Name	Supplier Phone
1 - Active Outdoors	(503) 555-9931
2 - Triumph	(313) 555-5735
3 - Guardian	81 3 3555-5011
4 - InFlux	81 6 431-7877
5 - Craze	(604) 681 3435
6 - Roadster	44- 17-1 555-2222
7 - Vesper	(514) 555-9022

Figure 10-14 L10.4 Length function report

Exercise 10.5: Using Nested If Statements In Formulas

In the previous exercise the formula that you created contained more than one If statement. This type of If statement is known as a NESTED IF statement. You can have as many If statements in a formula as you need. In this exercise you will create a Nested If statement to give customers a different discount on their next order based on the total amount of their last order.

1. Save the L4.2 report as L10.5 Nested If Statement.

2. Delete the first and last name fields from the report.

3. Create a formula field and name it `Order Discount`, then add the If Then Else statement to the formula.

4. Add the Order Amount field, then click outside of the brackets and type `>=10000`.

5. Click after the word **THEN** and type `"10% discount"`.

6. Copy the formula and paste it twice.

7. Change the middle Order Amount line of code to `>=5000`, then change the discount to `15%`. Change the last Order Amount line of code to `>=2500`, then change the discount to `20%`.

8. Click after the last **ELSE**, press Enter and type `"25% discount"`. Your formula should look like the one shown in Figure 10-15.

```
if {Orders.Order Amount} >=10000 then "10% discount" else
if {Orders.Order Amount} >=5000 then "15% discount" else
if {Orders.Order Amount} >=2500 then "20% discount" else
"25% discount"
```

Figure 10-15 Order Discount formula

9. Save the formula and close the Formula Workshop, then add the Order Discount formula field to the report after the Ship Via field. The report should look like the one shown in Figure 10-16. Save the changes and close the report.

Customer Orders Report					
Customer Name	Order #	Order Date	Order Amount	Ship Via	Order Discount
City Cyclists	1	12/2/00	$41.90	UPS	25% discount
Deals on Wheels	1002	12/2/00	$5,060.28	Pickup	15% discount
Warsaw Sports, Inc.	1003	12/2/00	$186.87	UPS	25% discount
Bikes and Trikes	1004	12/2/00	$823.05	Pickup	25% discount
SAB Mountain	1005	12/3/00	$29.00	Loomis	25% discount
Poser Cycles	1006	12/3/00	$64.90	Purolator	25% discount
Spokes	1007	12/3/00	$49.50	Parcel Post	25% discount
Clean Air Transporta	1008	12/3/00	$2,214.94	Purolator	25% discount
Extreme Cycling	1009	12/3/00	$29.00	Loomis	25% discount
Cyclopath	1010	12/3/00	$14,872.30	UPS	10% discount

Figure 10-16 L10.5 Nested If Statement report

Because the Order Amount field is evaluated for each record, it will only match one of the If statements when the statement is set up correctly. If the Order Amount is $3,000, the formula will stop processing after the third statement. If the Order Amount is $6,500, the formula will stop processing after the second statement.

The order that you place the criteria values in is very important. If the statements were in a different order, the formula would not return the correct result because it is possible that the order amount would meet the criteria of another statement. For example, if the >=2,500 portion of the statement was above the >=10,000 portion of the statement and the order amount is $6,500, the formula would stop processing after the first If statement because $6,500 is >=2,500. That is not the outcome that you want though. You really want the $6,500 order to receive a 15% discount.

The rule of thumb is to put the criteria in high to low order. The option after the last else statement is the "catch all" statement. Sometimes, this will be an error message. In the example above, the customer would receive a 25% discount off of their next order if their last order was less than $2,500. In this example, the company is going to offer larger discounts to customers that placed smaller orders in hopes of having them place a larger order the next time that they order.

Suppressing Fields And Sections

There are times when there is no need to print the same data over and over again on a report. Sometimes not repeating the same data makes the report easier to read. There are also times when you will need to suppress a section of the report. Like the Highlighting Expert, the suppression of fields and sections in a report can be suppressed based on a condition. These conditions are created using Boolean formulas.

Exercise 10.6: Suppressing Fields

In this exercise you will learn how to suppress fields by creating a conditional formula for a field that has a salary greater than $50,000.

1. Save the L6.12 report as `L10.6 Suppress salary GT 50000`.

2. Right-click on the Salary field and select Format Object. On the Common tab check the **SUPPRESS** option as illustrated in Figure 10-17.

As you see in Figure 10-17, most of the options have this ![x-2 button] button.
This button will open the **FORMAT FORMULA EDITOR**.

The default color for the Formula button is blue, which means that the option does not have a formula. If the button is red, it means that the option does have a formula.

You will also notice that the pencil is in a different position when the option has a formula. ![pencil icon]

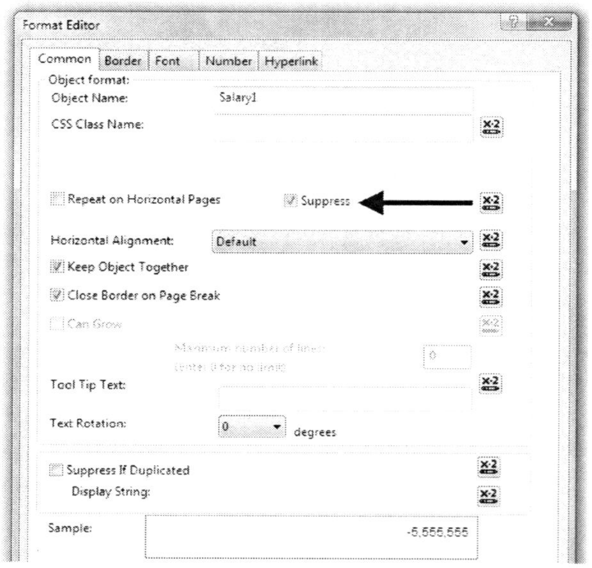

Figure 10-17 Common tab on the Format Editor

> Formatting formulas that you create with the Section Expert or Format Editor will be applied whether or not the property option that it is attached to is checked. As long as the Formula button is red, which means that the property has a formula, the formula will be applied.

3. Click the **FORMULA** button across from the Suppress option on the Format Editor. You will see the Formula Workshop. Create a formula to suppress the salary if it is greater than $50,000. Add a comment that explains what the formula does. Save the changes and close the Formula Workshop.

4. Notice that the button across from the **SUPPRESS** option has red text. Click OK to close the Format Editor. Notice that the Salary field is dimmed out in the design window. This lets you know that this field will not always print on the report because of the suppression criteria. The report should look like the one shown in Figure 10-18. If your report does not look like the one shown, make sure that your formula looks like the one shown in Figure 10-19. You can refer back to Lesson 6, Figure 6-72 to see what the report looks like without the conditional formatting. Save the changes and close the report.

First Name	Last Name	Address1	Region	Salary
Steven	Buchanan	14 Garrett Hill		$50,000.00
Robert	King	Edgeham Hollow		$37,000.00
Anne	Dodsworth	7 Houndstooth Rd.		$35,000.00
Michael	Suyama	Coventry House		$30,000.00
Bas-Rhin				
Justin	Brid	2 impasse du Soleil	Bas-Rhin	← Suppressed
Xavier	Martin	9 place de la Liberté	Bas-Rhin	$50,000.00
Laurent	Pereira	7 rue Nationale	Bas-Rhin	$45,000.00
BC				
Andrew	Fuller	908 W. Capital Way	BC	← Suppressed
Albert	Hellstern	13920 S.E. 40th Street	BC	← Suppressed
Laura	Callahan	4726 - 11th Ave. N.E.	BC	$45,000.00

Figure 10-18 L10.6 Suppress salary GT $50000 report

```
// This formula will suppress the salary if it is > 50000
{Employee.Salary} >50000
```

Figure 10-19 Suppression formula

Comparison Conditional Formatting

You can use one field for the comparison criteria and a different field to apply the conditional formatting to. You will learn how to do this in the next three exercises.

Exercise 10.7: Compare Customer Averages

In Exercise 6.3 you created a report that printed the average order amount for each customer and the average order amount for all of the customers on the report. In this exercise you will modify that report to display a message if a customers average order amount is greater than the average order amount for all customers on the report. If the average order amount is less, no message will print. In order to print a message based on a condition, the formula has to use the **DISPLAY STRING** option on the Format Editor.

 If you open the Formula Workshop from the Format Editor dialog box, you cannot create a different type of formula. You also cannot modify or delete existing formulas.

1. Save the L6.3 report as `L10.7 Display string conditional formatting`.

2. Right-click on the Average Order Amount field in the group footer section and select Format Object.

3. On the Common tab click the Formula button across from the **DISPLAY STRING** option, then double-click on the If Then Else statement.

4. After the word **IF**, add the Group 1 Average Order Amount field, then type `>=` after the field.

5. Add the Report Area:Average Of Orders.Order Amount field, then press Enter.

6. Click after the word **THEN** and add the ToText(x) function.

7. Add the Group 1 Avg of Orders.Order Amount field inside of the ToText(x) function. Click outside of the parenthesis and type `+ " ** Above report average"`, then press Enter.

8. Copy the ToText portion of the formula and paste it after the **ELSE** clause, then type `+ " "` at the end of the formula. Your formula should look like the one shown in Figure 10-20.

```
if Average ({Orders.Order Amount}, {Customer.Customer Name})>= Average ({Orders.Order Amount})
then ToText (Average ({Orders.Order Amount}, {Customer.Customer Name}))+" ** Above report average"
else ToText (Average ({Orders.Order Amount}, {Customer.Customer Name}))+ " "
```

Figure 10-20 Customer average comparison formula

9. Save the changes and close the Formula Workshop, then click OK to close the Format Editor.

10. Make the Average Order Amount field in the group footer section longer. Left align the field, then preview the report. Page 1 should look like the one shown in Figure 10-21.
The last page of the report should look like the one shown in Figure 10-22. Notice that there is no message next to these averages. This is because the customer average amount is less than $5,625.32, which is the average order amount for the report.

Save the changes and leave the report open to complete the next exercise.

	Order Date	Ship Date	Order Amount	Order #	Unit Price
Alley Cat Cycles					
	09/28/2001	09/30/2001	$2,559.63	2157	$539.85
	09/28/2001	09/30/2001	$2,559.63	2157	$313.36
	10/27/2001	11/06/2001	$2,699.55	2272	$899.85
	01/31/2002	02/03/2002	$9,290.30	2664	$455.86
	01/31/2002	02/03/2002	$9,290.30	2664	$2,792.86
	02/19/2002	02/22/2002	$8,819.55	2735	$2,939.85
	02/19/2002	02/22/2002	$8,819.55	2735	$2,939.85
Total # orders - 7		Total $ amount of orders - $ 44,038.51			
	Average order amount for the customer - $6,291.22 ** Above report average				
Backpedal Cycle Shop					
	07/02/2001	07/04/2001	$3,479.70	1802	$1,739.85
	08/15/2001	08/19/2001	$3,415.95	1972	$479.85
	08/15/2001	08/19/2001	$3,415.95	1972	$764.85
	08/15/2001	08/19/2001	$3,415.95	1972	$53.90
	11/16/2001	11/18/2001	$10,798.95	2358	$2,939.85
	11/16/2001	11/18/2001	$10,798.95	2358	$479.85
	11/16/2001	11/18/2001	$10,798.95	2358	$1,739.85
	12/18/2001	12/19/2001	$6,226.05	2507	$16.50
	12/18/2001	12/19/2001	$6,226.05	2507	$329.85
	12/18/2001	12/19/2001	$6,226.05	2507	$2,939.85
	01/04/2002	01/05/2002	$9,612.47	2560	$2,792.86
	01/04/2002	01/05/2002	$9,612.47	2560	$764.85
	01/04/2002	01/05/2002	$9,612.47	2560	$832.35
	02/02/2002	02/02/2002	$8,819.55	2685	$2,939.85
Total # orders - 14		Total $ amount of orders - $ 102,459.51			
	Average order amount for the customer - $7,318.54 ** Above report average				

Figure 10-21 Page 1 of the L10.7 Display string conditional formatting report

	Order Date	Ship Date	Order Amount	Order #	Unit Price
	01/30/2002	01/31/2002	$8,819.55	2662	$2,939.85
	02/28/2002	03/06/2002	$5,321.25	2770	$33.90
	02/28/2002	03/06/2002	$5,321.25	2770	$1,739.85
	02/28/2002	03/06/2002	$5,321.25	2770	$33.90
Total # orders - 9		Total $ amount of orders - $ 59,951.48			
	Average order amount for the customer - $6,661.28 ** Above report average				

Total # of customers on this report - 78
Grand Total # of orders - 724
Grand Total $ amount of all orders - $ 4,015,868.71
Average order amount for all customers - $ 5,546.78

Figure 10-22 Last page of the L10.7 Display string conditional formatting report

Exercise 10.8: Font Color Conditional Formatting

In the previous exercise you compared the customer average amount to the average amount for the report. Detail records that are below the report average were not formatted. It may be helpful to change the color of customers that have an average less than the report average.

1. Save the L0.7 report as L10.8 Font color conditional formatting.

2. Right-click on the Average Customer Order Amount field in the group footer section and select Format Object. On the Font tab click the Formula button across from the **COLOR** option.

The formula that you need to create to change the font color is the opposite of the formula that you created in the previous exercise. Rather than type it in again, you can copy the formula that you created in the previous exercise and change it as needed.

3. Open the **FORMATTING FORMULAS** folder in the Workshop Tree. Under the Avg Of Order Amount1 section you should see the **DISPLAY STRING** formula, as illustrated in Figure 10-23. Click on the Display String formula and select (highlight) the formula up to the first ToText function, then press the **CTRL + C** keys.

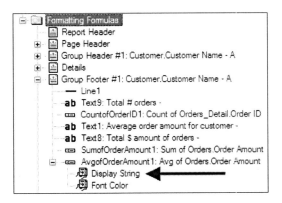

Figure 10-23 Formatting Formulas folder

4. Click on the Font color formula in the Workshop Tree, then scroll to the end of the comments and paste the formula in by pressing the **CTRL + V** keys.

5. Change the >= to <=, then type `crRed` after the word **THEN**. Save the changes and close the Formula Workshop. Click OK to close the Format Editor.

6. Go to the last or next to last page of the report. You should see the customer average dollar amounts in red. If you do not see the color red on the last few pages of the report, compare your font color formula to the one shown in Figure 10-24. Save the changes and close the report.

```
//
if Average ({Orders.Order Amount}, {Customer.Customer Name})<= Average ({Orders.Order Amount})
then crRed
```

Figure 10-24 Font color formula

Exercise 10.9: Suppress Currency Formatting

Every detail record on the L10.7 report prints the dollar sign for the Order Amount field. The report may look better if the dollar sign only printed for the first detail record for the customer. In this exercise you will create conditional formatting to suppress the dollar sign on any record other than the first one for each customer.

1. Save the L10.7 report as `L10.9 Suppress currency formatting`.

2. Right-click on the Order Amount field in the details section and select Format Object. Click on the Customize button on the Number tab. Click on the **CURRENCY SYMBOL** tab.

3. Click the Formula button across from the **ENABLE CURRENCY SYMBOL** option and add the If Then Else statement to the Formula text section.

4. Click after the word **IF** and add the **ONFIRSTRECORD** function, which is under the Print State category. Type the word `or`, then press the space bar.

5. Add the Customer Name field, then type `<> Previous`. Add the Customer Name field again and press Enter.

6. Delete the word **ELSE** and add the **CRFLOATINGCURRENCYSYMBOL** function.

7. Type two left parenthesis in front of the first Customer Name field and one parenthesis after the field. Type two left parenthesis in front of the second Customer Name field and three after the field. You may want to add a comment so that when you look at the formula later, you will know what it does.

8. Save and close the formula. Click OK twice to close both dialog boxes. The report should look like the one shown in Figure 10-25. As you can see, the dollar sign for the Order Amount field only prints on the first detail record for each customer. If your report does not look like the one shown, compare your formula to the one shown in Figure 10-26. Save the changes and close the report.

	Order Date	Ship Date	Order Amount	Order #	Unit Price
Alley Cat Cycles					
	09/28/2001	09/30/2001	$2,559.63	2157	$539.85
	09/28/2001	09/30/2001	2,559.63	2157	$313.36
	10/27/2001	11/06/2001	2,699.55	2272	$899.85
	01/31/2002	02/03/2002	9,290.30	2664	$455.86
	01/31/2002	02/03/2002	9,290.30	2664	$2,792.86
	02/19/2002	02/22/2002	8,819.55	2735	$2,939.85
	02/19/2002	02/22/2002	8,819.55	2735	$2,939.85
Total # orders - 7		Total $ amount of orders - $ 44,038.51			

Average order amount for the customer - $6,291.22 ** Above report average

Figure 10-25 L10.9 Suppress currency formatting report

```
// This formula will suppress the dollar sign on all detail records
// in each group, except for the first record
if OnFirstRecord or (({Customer.Customer Name}) <> Previous (({Customer.Customer Name})))
then crFloatingCurrencySymbol
```

Figure 10-26 Dollar sign suppression formula

Formula Wrap Up

So how did you do creating and understanding the logic behind If Then Else statements? Hopefully you did okay. The reason that I am asking is because if you can understand and create If Then Else statements, you are on your way to becoming a Crystal Reports power report writer or a computer programmer. If you are curious about other statements that you can use, check out the following in the Help file: For Loop and my favorite, the Select Case statement.

Select Case Statement

Select Case is similar to If Then Else. I personally find Select Case statement easier to read and understand, especially easier then Nested If statements. For example, in Exercise 10.5 you created the nested If statement shown in Figure 10-27.

```
if {Orders.Order Amount} >=10000 then "10% discount" else
if {Orders.Order Amount} >=5000 then "15% discount" else
if {Orders.Order Amount} >=2500 then "20% discount" else
"25% discount"
```

Figure 10-27 Nested If statement

The following Select Case statement provides the same logic as the Nested If statement shown above in Figure 10-27. For whatever reason, I find this easier to read and understand.

```
Select {Orders.Order Amount}
    Case Is  >= 10000:
        "10% discount"
    Case Is >= 5000:
        "15% discount"
    Case Is >= 2500:
        "20% discount"
    Default:
        "25% discount"
```

Boolean Formulas

In Lesson 2 you learned that Boolean fields have values of true/false or yes/no. **BOOLEAN EXPRESSIONS** return a value of true or false. In Lesson 4 you learned how to format a Boolean field. Earlier in this lesson I said that one way to understand If Then Else statements is to think of them as a true or false question. A Boolean formula is the test question portion of an If Then Else statement. Boolean formulas do not have to be created on Boolean fields. The value that a Boolean formula returns is either true or false. You can then format the result of the Boolean formula like you did in Exercise 4.5.

In Exercise 10.6 you created a formula that would suppress the salary if it was greater than $50,000. If the salary is greater than $50,000, the salary did not print. A Boolean formula could have been used to accomplish the same result. Figure 10-28 shows the formula. The difference would be the values printed in the salary field in the L10.6 report. Instead of printing the salary for some records and nothing for other records as shown earlier in Figure 10-18, the values **TRUE** or **FALSE** would have printed as shown in Figure 10-29. [See the L10 With Boolean Suppression formula report in the zip file]

```
{Employee.Salary} > 50000
```

Figure 10-28 Boolean formula

First Name	Last Name	Address1	Region	Salary > 50K
Steven	Buchanan	14 Garrett Hill		False
Robert	King	Edgeham Hollow		False
Anne	Dodsworth	7 Houndstooth Rd.		False
Michael	Suyama	Coventry House		False
Bas-Rhin				
Justin	Brid	2 impasse du Soleil	Bas-Rhin	True
Xavier	Martin	9 place de la Liberté	Bas-Rhin	False
Laurent	Pereira	7 rue Nationale	Bas-Rhin	False

Figure 10-29 L10 With Boolean suppression formula report

The Section Expert

So far, all of the formatting techniques that you have learned were to change individual objects on the report. You can use the Section Expert to format an entire section of the report similar to how the Format Editor lets you format fields. You can also create formulas for many of the options on the Section Expert which is shown in Figure 10-30. With section formatting you can make the following types of changes to a report.

    ① Force each group to start at the top of a new page.
    ② Change the line spacing in the details section to something other than single spacing.
    ③ Create page breaks.
    ④ Conditionally suppress a section of the report.

Formatting options that are not available for the section of the report that is selected are dimmed out.

For example, in Figure 10-30, the **NEW PAGE BEFORE** option is not available for the report header section. There are three ways to open the Section Expert as discussed below.

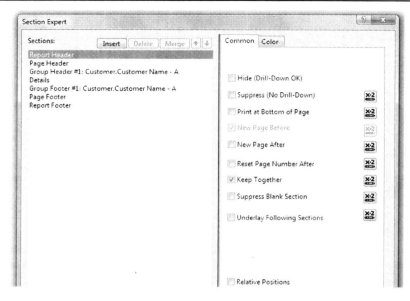

Figure 10-30 Section Expert

① Right-click on the section bar and select Section Expert as shown in Figure 10-31. If there is more than one of the same section, for example page header a and page header b, you will see the shortcut menu shown in Figure 10-32, which has additional options. Table 10-3 explains the options on this shortcut menu.

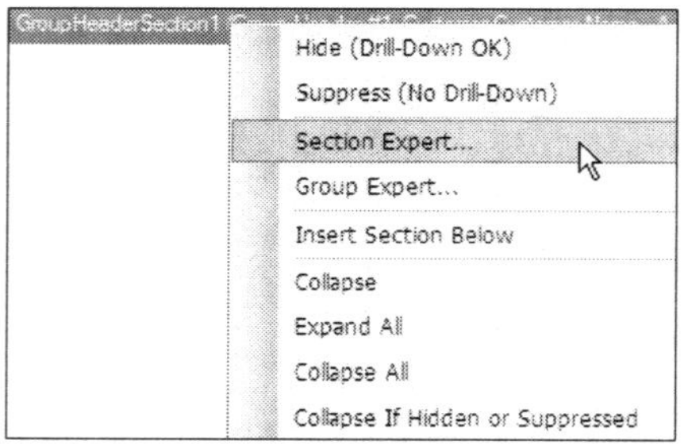

Figure 10-31 Section shortcut menu

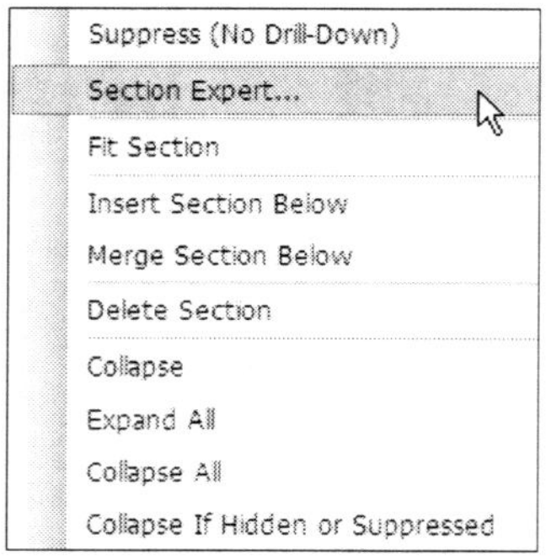

Figure 10-32 Multiple section shortcut menu

② Right-click on a blank section of the report, then Report ⇒ Section Expert.
③ Crystal Reports ⇒ Report ⇒ Section Expert.

Option	Description
Fit Section	Removes vertical unused space from a section. This option is not available on the header or footer subsection (a).
Merge Section Below	Moves the fields in the section below to the selected section, then deletes the section below. This option is not available on the last header or footer subsection in the group.
Delete Section	Deletes the selected section of the report.

Table 10-3 Multiple section shortcut menu options explained

The advantage to using the first option above to open the Section Expert is that the section will be highlighted on the left side of the Section Expert dialog box when it is opened. Table 10-4 explains the section formatting options on the Common tab. Table 10-5 explains the section options that are only available for a specific section of the report.

Option	Description
Hide (Drill-Down OK)	Hides the objects in the section when the report is printed. The section can be viewed on the preview window. If the section of the report that this option is applied to is part of a higher level group and the group is drilled into, the objects in the section will be visible on the drill-down tab. This option is not available for subsections.
Suppress (No Drill-Down)	The section that this option is applied to will not be printed and does not allow drill-down and cannot be viewed on the preview window, even if a higher level section is drilled-down. This option is available for subsections.
Print at Bottom of Page	This option forces the section to be printed as close to the bottom of the page as possible, even if the detail records stop printing half way down the page.
New Page Before	This option forces a page break before the section prints. (1)
New Page After	This option forces a page break after the section prints. (1)
Reset Page Number After	Resets the page number back to one after the section has printed. This option also resets the Total Page Count special field.
Keep Together	Keeps the section together on the same page when printed. This option is sometimes confused with the Keep Group Together option on the Group Expert dialog box. These options produce different results. [See Lesson 6, Using The Group Expert]
Suppress Blank Section	Prevents the section from printing when all of the objects in the section are blank.
Underlay Following Sections	This option causes the section to print next to the section below it. For example, this option will allow charts or images to print next to detail records.
Relative Positions	This option will lock an object next to another object like a cross-tab. If the cross-tab grows, the object will be repositioned so that it remains aligned with the other object.
Background Color	This option is on the Color tab. It lets you select a color for the background of the section. This is different then the formatting that objects in the section have. You learned how to use this option in Exercise 4.9.

Table 10-4 Common and Color tab section formatting options explained

(1) This option is often used to force each group to start on a new page.

Section	Option	Description
Page Footer	Reserve Minimum Page Footer	Select this option when you need to remove space in the page footer section to gain more space on the printed page.
Details	Format With Multiple Columns	This option allows you to display data in columns similar to a newspaper layout, instead of down the page. When checked, a new tab called **LAYOUT** will open as shown in Figure 10-33. The options on the Layout tab let you set the size of the columns.

Table 10-5 Section specific formatting options explained

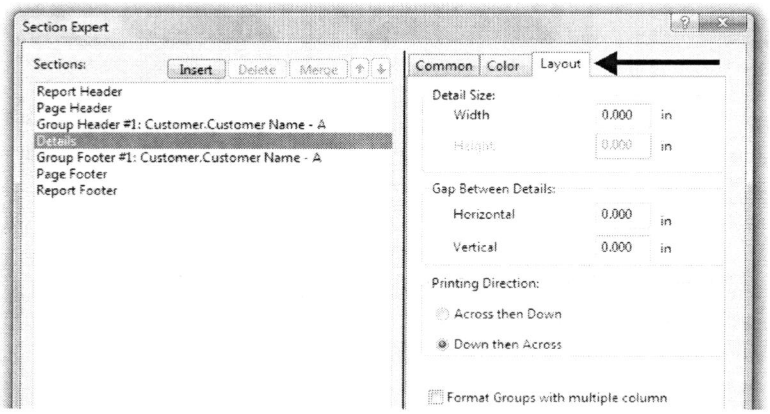

Figure 10-33 Layout tab illustrated

> If all of the detail sections have the Hide or Suppress option checked, the result is a Summary report.

Exercise 10.10: Conditionally Format A Page Break

Page breaks are one of the most used section formatting techniques. While the concept appears straight forward, it can be tricky and can produce unexpected results. Many page breaks are created when another group starts on a report. In this exercise you will add a page break to a report that prints orders by month. The objective is to force a page break when the month of the order date changes in the group header section of the report.

Hopefully you are asking yourself what is different about the first group of data. You may have looked through the functions to see if there is a function that you can use. If you have looked for a function, you won't find any that are specifically for sections on a report or for page breaks. You could create your own formula, but what would you write? You may have to think outside of the box on this one.

In case you are thinking that you could use the **NEW PAGE AFTER** option for the group header section, this option would cause the detail records to start on a different page, but the group header information would remain on the previous page, as shown in Figure 10-34.

2001 Orders By Month			
Salesperson	Order Date	Order #	Order Amount
January			

Figure 10-34 New Page After option turned on for the group header section

I know what you are thinking: Use the **NEW PAGE AFTER** option on the group footer section. That will give you the desired output of having each group start on a new page. The downside is that if the report has data in the report footer section, it will not print on the same page as the last group footer section of information. The information in the report footer section will be forced to a new page. If the report that you are creating does not have data in the report footer section or you want the information in the report footer section to print on a page by itself, using the New Page After option on the group footer section will work.

In Exercise 10.9 you used a function called **ONFIRSTRECORD**. You could write code to see if the group contains the first record in the report. If it does, do not force a page break. This will work because only one group per report will contain the first record on the report. It just so happens that the first record is in the first group, which is the group that currently has a page break before it. Creating a formula to not force a break on the first record will cause the formatting, in this case a page break, to be turned off on the first group. This is what you want to have happen.

1. Save the L6.7 report as `L10.10 Conditional page break`.

2. Open the Section Expert and click on the Formula button across from the New Page Before option for the group header section.

3. Type `Not` and press the space bar, then add the OnFirstRecord function, or you can type the function in. Save and close the formula, then click OK to close the Section Expert.

4. Save the changes, then preview the report. The first group (January), should be on page 1 of the report. If you click on any of the months in the group tree you will see that the data for the month starts on a new page. If you look at the last page of the report, you will see that the report footer information is not on a page by itself.

> **Using The New Page After Option To Format A Page Break**
>
> Earlier, the idea of using the New Page After option was discussed as a way to force a page break. Adding the **NOTONLASTRECORD** function to the New Page After option on the group footer section will force each group to start on a new page, just like the exercise that you just completed.

Exercise 10.11: Resetting Page Numbers

Depending on the type of report that you create, you may have the need to have the page number reset after a certain condition has been met. A report that you may need this for is one that will be distributed to more than one person. An example of this would be a report like the monthly order report by sales rep that you created in Exercise 6.13. Resetting the page number to one when orders for a different sales rep prints, would allow the report to be distributed to each rep and have the page numbers make sense to each rep. Can you imagine receiving a report that started on page 75? You may think that you were missing pages. Using the **RESET PAGE NUMBER** section formatting option would prevent that from happening. In this exercise you will learn how to use this option.

1. Save the L6.13 report as `L10.11 Reset page number`.

2. Create a page break formula that does not cause a page break on the first record of the report, for the group header section.

3. Check the **RESET PAGE NUMBER AFTER** option for the group footer section, then click OK. The first page of the report should start on page 1.

4. In the group tree, click on Group 3. You will see that the page number is 1. If you go to the next page, it will be page 2. This is what should happen. Save the changes and leave the report open to complete the next exercise.

Exercise 10.12: Using The Change Group Dialog Box Options

If you look at the second page for any group in the report that you just modified, you will notice that the group header information (the Salespersons name) only prints on the first page of each group. Figure 10-35 shows the second page of the first group. The report would look better if the group name printed on every page. Options on the **CHANGE GROUP** dialog box will let you force the group header information to print on every page.

Salesperson	Order Date	Order ID	Product ID	Unit Price	Quantity
	11/17/2001	2362	303221	$329.85	2
	11/17/2001	2362	201201	$832.35	3
	11/15/2001	2356	6401	$12.00	2
	11/14/2001	2352	303181	$329.85	3

Figure 10-35 Second page of the first group on the L10.11 Reset page number report

1. Save the L10.11 report as `L10.12 Use Repeat Group Header option`.

2. Right-click on the group header section bar and select **GROUP EXPERT**, then click the Options button. Notice the Field Name at the top of the shortcut menu.

3. On the Options tab check the **REPEAT GROUP HEADER ON EACH PAGE** option as shown in Figure 10-36. This option will cause the group header information to print on every page of the report.

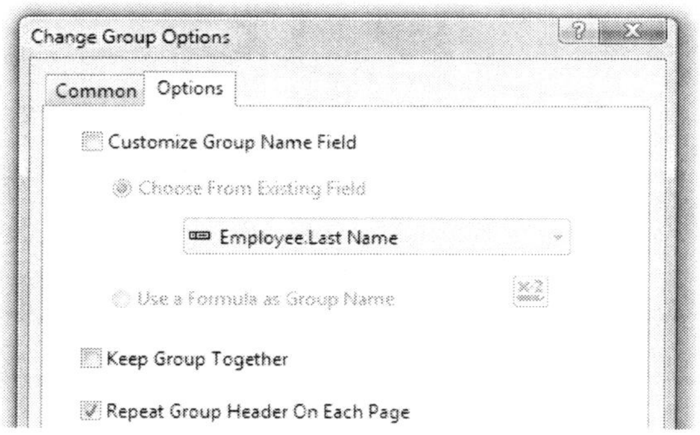

Figure 10-36 Change Group Options dialog box

4. Click OK twice to close both dialog boxes. If you go to any page after the first page of a group, you will see the group header information, just like it is on the first page of each group. Save the changes and leave the report open to complete the next exercise.

How The Change Group Options Work

If checked, the **CUSTOMIZE GROUP NAME FIELD** option will let you create the name for the group as you want it to appear in the group header section, or a different section if you copy or move the group header field to it.

 Do not check this option if you only want to display the data that is in the field that is being grouped on.

The **USE A FORMULA AS GROUP NAME** option will let you write a formula that will control what appears in the Group Name field. This option is very helpful if you need to change what prints in the group name field based on data that appears in the report or data in a table that is connected to the report.

The **REPEAT GROUP HEADER ON EACH PAGE** option will cause the group header section to be printed at the top of each page. This will let you know which group the details records and totals are for.

The purpose of the **KEEP GROUP TOGETHER** option shown above in Figure 10-36 is to force all records that are in the same group to print on the same page. If this option is checked and the first group on the report does not fit on the first page, the group will start printing on the second page and the first page of the report will be blank. If this happens, clear the **RESPECT KEEP GROUP TOGETHER ON FIRST PAGE** option on the Report Options dialog box.

The Keep Group Together option if checked, will cause all of the group sections (the group header, group footer and detail section for the group) to be printed on the same page. If all three sections will not fit on the current page, they will start printing on the next page. This is different then the **KEEP TOGETHER** option on the Section Expert, which only causes the section that the option is applied to, to print on the same page. [See Table 10-4] These options are best suited for reports that do not have a lot of detail records in each group. Groups that have a lot of records may require more than one page, which may result in the report having breaks in unexpected places.

Exercise 10.13: Using The InRepeatedGroupHeader Function

Prior to changing the group options in the previous exercise, it was easy to tell which was the first page for each group in the report. For this report, that is not exactly true because each group starts on page 1, but pretend that the page numbers are not reset. To help make reading the report easier, adding text on the pages in the group, other than the first page would resolve this issue. The **INREPEATEDGROUPHEADER** function will let you add conditional formatting to a group header or footer when the group prints on more than one page.

1. Save the L10.12 report as `L10.13 Use the InRepeatedGroupHeader function.`

2. Add a text object to the right of the Last Name field in the group header section and type `(Continued)` in the object. Change the font size of the text object to 8.

3. Right-click on the text object and select Format Object, then click the Formula button across from the Suppress option. Type `Not InRepeatedGroupHeader` in the Formula text window.

4. Save the formula and close the Formula Workshop. Click OK to close the Format Editor and save the changes. Go to page 2 of the report. You should see (Continued) next to the salespersons name, as shown in Figure 10-37. Close the report.

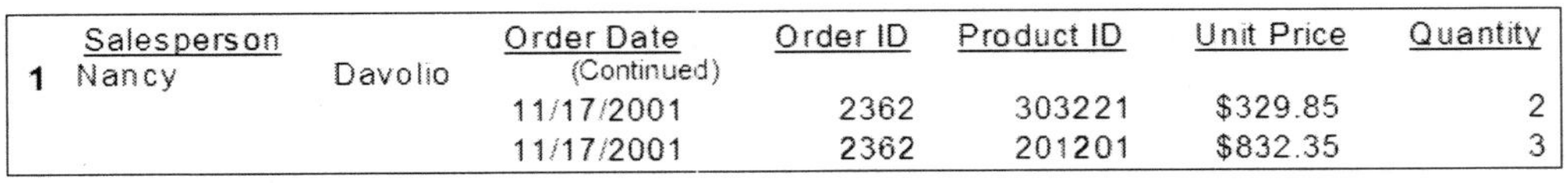

	Salesperson		Order Date	Order ID	Product ID	Unit Price	Quantity
1	Nancy	Davolio	(Continued)				
			11/17/2001	2362	303221	$329.85	2
			11/17/2001	2362	201201	$832.35	3

Figure 10-37 Page 2 of the L10.13 Use the InRepeatedGroupHeader function report

Exercise 10.14: Suppress A Section Of The Report

There will be times when you need to permanently hide a section of a report. Often, this is done (on a second copy of an existing report) when you do not want some users to see certain information on a report. An example that comes to mind is the L6.13 Skills monthly orders by sales rep report that you modified in Exercise 10.11. Because the goal of the report in Exercise 10.11 was to distribute the sections of the report to the appropriate sales rep, there is no reason to display the Report Total information in the report footer section. You will learn how to suppress a section of the report in this exercise.

1. Save the L10.11 report as `L10.14 Report footer suppressed.`

2. Right-click on the report footer section bar and select the **HIDE (DRILL-DOWN OK)** option. The report footer section should look like the one shown in Figure 10-38. The slanted lines indicate that the section is suppressed.

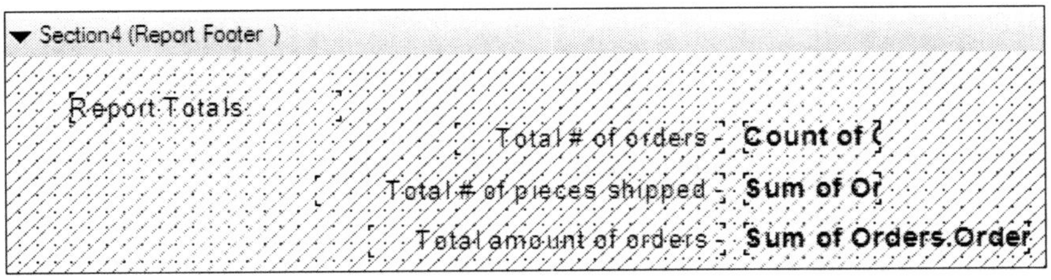

Section4 (Report Footer)

Report Totals

Total # of orders - Count of (
Total # of pieces shipped - Sum of Or
Total amount of orders - Sum of Orders.Order

Figure 10-38 Report footer section suppressed

> You can also turn the suppression options on or off by selecting the option on the Section Expert dialog box.

3. On the last page of the report you should not see the report totals at the end of the report. Save the changes and close the report.

How To Use Section Suppression With Address Fields

In Lesson 4 you learned how to add sections to a report. In the exercise that you just completed, you learned how to suppress a section of the report. If you have the need to create a report that uses more than one address field, often they are placed on separate rows in the details section. The second address field is often blank, which means that a blank row will print for the records when the second address field is blank, as illustrated in Figure 10-39.

When combined, the Suppress (No Drill-Down) section option and adding a section with conditional formatting will allow you to suppress a section of the report based on a condition. You can combine these options and place the second address field in a section by itself, then conditionally hide the section if the second address field is blank.

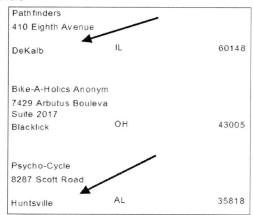

Figure 10-39 Blank row illustrated

Remember that if you suppress a field in a section that has other objects, the entire section will be suppressed if the condition is true. Often, this is not what you want. If you move the second address field to its own section of the report as shown in Figure 10-40, you can suppress the section if the address field is blank. This will cause the report to print like the one shown in Figure 10-41 instead of the one shown above in Figure 10-39.

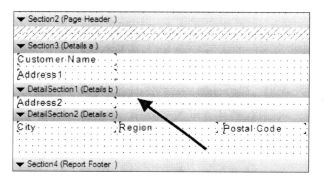

Figure 10-40 Address 2 field in a section by itself

Figure 10-41 Report with the Address 2 field suppressed

Exercise 10.15: Suppress A Group

Depending on the amount of data that is displayed on a report, not all users may need to view all of the records. In this exercise you will modify a report to only print groups of data that meet specific criteria. You will modify a customer average report to only print groups that have a group total average amount that is less than $2,500. This report also has record selection criteria that needs to be removed.

Modify The Existing Record Selection Criteria And Total Fields

1. Save the L6.3 report as
   `L10.15 Suppress group if avg customer amount LT 2500K.`
   (LT is my abbreviation for less than.)

2. Delete the Order Amount record selection criteria.

3. Change the Order Date selection criteria to only include orders in 2001.

4. Change the Total # of orders field in the group footer section to use the Order ID field in the Orders table. Change the summary type to Distinct count.

5. In the Report Footer section change the Grand Total # of orders summary field to Distinct count.

Add The Suppression Criteria

1. Open the Section Expert and add the formula shown in Figure 10-42 to the Suppress (No Drill-Down) option for the group header, details and group footer sections.

```
// This formula will suppress groups on the report where the
// average order amount of the customer is less than $2,500
//
// This formula is used on the Group Header, Details
// and Group Footer report sections
Average ({Orders.Order Amount}, {Customer.Customer Name})< 2500
```

Figure 10-42 Suppress group formula

Notice that the Formula Workshop displays the format option Suppress (No Drill-Down) in the title bar as shown in Figure 10-43.

Formula Workshop - Format Formula Editor - Suppress (No Drill-Down)

Figure 10-43 Format Workshop title bar

2. Save the formulas and close the Formula Workshop. Click OK to close the Section Expert. The first page of the report should look like the one shown in Figure 10-44. Some of the groups (customers) that you should not see are AIC Childrens, Alley Cat Cycles and Belgium Bike Co. Save the changes.

	Order Date	Ship Date	Order Amount	Order #	Unit Price
Aruba Sport					
	06/05/2001	06/08/2001	$5,879.70	3079	$2,939.85
Total # orders - 1		Total $ amount of orders -	$5,879.70		
		Average order amount for the customer -	$5,879.70		
Athens Bicycle Co.					
	06/08/2001	06/18/2001	$8,819.55	3097	$2,939.85
Total # orders - 1		Total $ amount of orders -	$8,819.55		
		Average order amount for the customer -	$8,819.55		
Backpedal Cycle Shop					
	02/08/2001	02/09/2001	$3,544.20	1279	$12.00
	02/08/2001	02/09/2001	$3,544.20	1279	$1,739.85
	02/08/2001	02/09/2001	$3,544.20	1279	$13.50
	02/19/2001	02/19/2001	$6,233.05	1311	$329.85

Figure 10-44 L10.15 Suppress group if avg customer amount LT 2500K report

Figure 10-45 shows the grand totals for the report. The report has suppression criteria to not display a group if the average customer order amount is less than $2,500.

Order Date	Ship Date	Order Amount
Total # of customers on this report - 256		
Grand Total # of orders - 1,564		
Grand Total $ amount of all orders - $ 5,859,400.27		
Average order amount for all customers - $ 2,236.41 ◄		

Figure 10-45 Report totals

Remember that records that are suppressed are still included in the total fields on the report. Some people consider this a flaw so to speak, of how data is processed. To correct this problem, running total fields should be used instead of summary fields in the group and report footer sections. In Lesson 13 you will learn how to fix this report so that the customers who averages are less than $2,500 are not counted in any total amount field on the report.

Exercise 10.16: Using The Color Tab Section Expert Options

One of the more popular uses of the Color tab on the Section Expert is to add a color background to every other detail record on the report. If you have ever seen what is known as "green bar" computer paper, you understand the color effect that you will create in this exercise.

1. Save the L4.14 report as `L10.16 Add color to rows`.

2. Open the Section Expert. Click on the details section, then click on the Color tab.

3. Click the Formula button and type the formula shown at the bottom of Figure 10-46.

```
// This formula will print a silver background for all
// even number rows in the Details section of the report.
//
// RecordNumber mod 2 will return 0 for even row numbers
// and 1 for odd number row numbers
//
// DefaultAttribute is the default row color
//
If RecordNumber mod 2 = 0
then crSilver
Else DefaultAttribute
```

Figure 10-46 Row color formula

4. Save the formula and close the Formula Workshop. Click OK to close the Section Expert. The report should look like the one shown in Figure 10-47. Save the changes and close the report.

Customer Orders Report						
Customer Name	Order #	Order Date	Order Amount	Ship Via	First Name	Last Name
City Cyclists	1	12/2/00	$41.90	UPS	Nancy	Davolio
Deals on Wheels	1002	12/2/00	$5,060.28	Pickup	Janet	Leverling
Warsaw Sports, Inc.	1003	12/2/00	$186.87	UPS	Margaret	Peacock
Bikes and Trikes	1004	12/2/00	$823.05	Pickup	Margaret	Peacock
SAB Mountain	1005	12/3/00	$29.00	Loomis	Janet	Leverling
Poser Cycles	1006	12/3/00	$64.90	Purolator	Margaret	Peacock
Spokes	1007	12/3/00	$49.50	Parcel Post	Anne	Dodsworth
Clean Air Transportation Co.	1008	12/3/00	$2,214.94	Purolator	Margaret	Peacock
Extreme Cycling	1009	12/3/00	$29.00	Loomis	Margaret	Peacock

Figure 10-47 L10.16 Add color to rows report

How The Row Color Formula Works

Now that you have created the row color formula, knowing how it works will be helpful because you can modify the formula to create other patterns.

RECORDNUMBER is a special field that counts records in the details section.

MOD divides one number by another number and returns the remainder, instead of the result of the division.

IF RECORDNUMBER MOD 2=0 means to divide the record number by 2. If the remainder is zero, meaning that if the record number is evenly divisible by two, apply the color to the background of the detail row.

If the report that you are applying the background row color formatting to has background formatting for objects in the section of the report that will have a background color, you should use **NOCOLOR** for the Else clause instead of using the color white because NoColor produces a result that is similar to being transparent, which is what you want. Using the color white will cause the background color applied to individual fields to produce results that are not always visually appealing. If the report does not have any fields with background color formatting, using the **DEFAULT ATTRIBUTE** is acceptable.

You can change this formula to create a background pattern different then every other row.

Example #1
If RecordNumber mod 5 = 0 will shade every fifth row as shown in Figure 10-48.

Customer Name	Order #	Order Date	Order Amount	Ship Via	First Name	Last Name
City Cyclists	1	12/2/00	$41.90	UPS	Nancy	Davolio
Deals on Wheels	1002	12/2/00	$5,060.28	Pickup	Janet	Leverling
Warsaw Sports, Inc.	1003	12/2/00	$186.87	UPS	Margaret	Peacock
Bikes and Trikes	1004	12/2/00	$823.05	Pickup	Margaret	Peacock
SAB Mountain	1005	12/3/00	$29.00	Loomis	Janet	Leverling
Poser Cycles	1006	12/3/00	$64.90	Purolator	Margaret	Peacock
Spokes	1007	12/3/00	$49.50	Parcel Post	Anne	Dodsworth
Clean Air Transportation Co.	1008	12/3/00	$2,214.94	Purolator	Margaret	Peacock
Extreme Cycling	1009	12/3/00	$29.00	Loomis	Margaret	Peacock
Cyclopath	1010	12/3/00	$14,872.30	UPS	Nancy	Davolio
BBS Pty	1011	12/3/00	$29.00	Purolator	Margaret	Peacock
Piccolo	1012	12/3/00	$10,259.10	Loomis	Nancy	Davolio
Pedals Inc.	1013	12/3/00	$1,142.13	Parcel Post	Margaret	Peacock
Spokes 'N Wheels Ltd.	1014	12/4/00	$29.00	Purolator	Nancy	Davolio
Cycle City Rome	1015	12/4/00	$43.50	UPS	Anne	Dodsworth
SAB Mountain	1016	12/4/00	$563.70	FedEx	Janet	Leverling

Figure 10-48 Mod 5 = 0 output

Example #2
If RecordNumber mod 3 in [1,2] will shade the first two rows out of every three rows, as shown in Figure 10-49. Figure 10-50 shows the formula.

Customer Name	Order #	Order Date	Order Amount	Ship Via	First Name	Last Name
City Cyclists	1	12/2/00	$41.90	UPS	Nancy	Davolio
Deals on Wheels	1002	12/2/00	$5,060.28	Pickup	Janet	Leverling
Warsaw Sports, Inc.	1003	12/2/00	$186.87	UPS	Margaret	Peacock
Bikes and Trikes	1004	12/2/00	$823.05	Pickup	Margaret	Peacock
SAB Mountain	1005	12/3/00	$29.00	Loomis	Janet	Leverling
Poser Cycles	1006	12/3/00	$64.90	Purolator	Margaret	Peacock
Spokes	1007	12/3/00	$49.50	Parcel Post	Anne	Dodsworth
Clean Air Transportation Co.	1008	12/3/00	$2,214.94	Purolator	Margaret	Peacock
Extreme Cycling	1009	12/3/00	$29.00	Loomis	Margaret	Peacock

Figure 10-49 Mod 3 in [1,2] output

```
If RecordNumber mod 3 in [1,2]
then crSilver
Else DefaultAttribute
```

Figure 10-50 Mod 3 in [1,2] formula

Example #3
If RecordNumber mod 10 in [3,5] will shade the third and fifth rows out of every ten rows, as shown in Figure 10-51.

Customer Name	Order #	Order Date	Order Amount	Ship Via	First Name	Last Name
City Cyclists	1	12/2/00	$41.90	UPS	Nancy	Davolio
Deals on Wheels	1002	12/2/00	$5,060.28	Pickup	Janet	Leverling
Warsaw Sports, Inc.	1003	12/2/00	$186.87	UPS	Margaret	Peacock
Bikes and Trikes	1004	12/2/00	$823.05	Pickup	Margaret	Peacock
SAB Mountain	1005	12/3/00	$29.00	Loomis	Janet	Leverling
Poser Cycles	1006	12/3/00	$64.90	Purolator	Margaret	Peacock
Spokes	1007	12/3/00	$49.50	Parcel Post	Anne	Dodsworth
Clean Air Transportation Co	1008	12/3/00	$2,214.94	Purolator	Margaret	Peacock
Extreme Cycling	1009	12/3/00	$29.00	Loomis	Margaret	Peacock
Cyclopath	1010	12/3/00	$14,872.30	UPS	Nancy	Davolio
BBS Pty	1011	12/3/00	$29.00	Purolator	Margaret	Peacock
Piccolo	1012	12/3/00	$10,259.10	Loomis	Nancy	Davolio
Pedals Inc.	1013	12/3/00	$1,142.13	Parcel Post	Margaret	Peacock

Figure 10-51 Mod 10 in [3,5] output

Exercise 10.17: Create Odd And Even Page Headers

As more and more word processing mail merge documents are being converted to reports, the need for odd and even page headers and footers is becoming more popular in reports. Some of these documents have header and footer information similar to the pages in this workbook. Documents that fall into this category are also often printed on printers that can print two pages on one sheet of paper automatically on duplex printers.

In the previous exercise you learned that the MOD function can be used with a special field to determine an action based on the current record number. Creating odd and even page headers is similar. The difference is that for the page header, you need two page header sections and each one requires its own conditional MOD formula. These formulas are for the page number and determine if the current page number is odd or even. Each page of the report only needs either the odd page header information or the even page header information. Therefore, each page header section has to be suppressed when the other page header section prints.

 Even page numbers have a remainder of zero. Odd page numbers have a remainder of one.

1. Open a new report and save it as L10.17 Odd even page headers. Add the Customer Name and Address fields from the Customer table as shown below in Figure 10-52.

2. Create another page header section, then delete the print date field.

3. In the first page header section add a text object, then type This is the right page header and should have an odd page number in the object.

4. Add the Page Number field to the right corner of the Page Header a section, then place the text object to the left of the page number field.

5. Copy everything in the Page Header a section to the Page Header b section. Make sure that the field headings in both page header sections are lined up with the fields in the details section.

6. In the second page header section change the text object to This is the left page header and should have an even page number in the object. Move the Page Number field to the left corner, then place the text object to the right of the page number field. The report layout should look like the one shown in Figure 10-52.

Section2 (Page Header a)				
		This is the right page header and should have an odd page number	Page	
Customer Name	Address	Address	City	Postal Code
PageHeaderSection1 (Page Header b)				
ber This is the left page header and should have an even page number				
Customer Name	Address1	Address2	City	Postal Code
Section3 (Details)				
Customer Name	Address1	Address2	City	Postal Code

Figure 10-52 L10.17 report layout

7. Add the following formula PageNumber mod 2 = 0 to the Page Header a Suppress (No Drill-Down) option on the Section Expert. You are adding this to the right page header section so that the left page header section will be suppressed when the right page header information is printed. Because the report does not have any groups, you do not have to check the Suppress (No Drill-Down) option.

8. Add the following formula PageNumber mod 2 = 1 to the Page Header b Suppress (No Drill-Down) option on the Section Expert. Save the changes. The report should look like the one shown in Figures 10-53 and 10-54. Close the report.

			This is the right page header and should have an odd page number 1	
Customer Name	Address	Address	City	Postal Code
City Cyclists	7464 South Kingsway	Suite 2006	Sterling Heights	48358
Pathfinders	410 Eighth Avenue		DeKalb	60148

Figure 10-53 L10.17 report - odd page number

2 This is the left page header and should have an even page number				
Customer Name	Address1	Address2	City	Postal Code
Feel Great Bikes Inc.	3015 Delta Place	Suite 2601	Eden Prairie	55367
SAB Mountain	Hauptstr. 29		Bern	CH-3006

Figure 10-54 L10.17 report - even page number

Exercise 10.18: Print Symbols Conditionally

In this exercise you will create a report that will print a check mark next to the quantity if it is less than 250. This can be used as a visual reminder of which products need to be reordered. In Exercise 4.4 you learned how to use the Character Map. You will use an image from the Character Map to indicate that a product needs to be reordered.

1. Create a new report and save it as `L10.18 Print symbols conditionally`.

2. Add the Product and Purchases tables to the report. Add the fields shown in the report.

3. Add the logo and this title `Reorder Report` to the page header section.

4. Create a formula field named Reorder Product, then type the code shown below.

   ```
   // Chr( 252) is the character code for a check mark
   If {Purchases.Units in Stock} <= 250 Then Chr(252)
   ```

5. Add the Reorder Product formula field to the report to the right of the Units in Stock field. Select the Wingdings font, then change the font size to 12. Save the changes. The report should look like the one shown in Figure 10-55.

Product ID	Product Name	Price (SRP)	Units in Stock	Reorder Product
1,101	Active Outdoors Crochet Glove	$14.50	220	✓
1,102	Active Outdoors Crochet Glove	$14.50	450	
1,103	Active Outdoors Crochet Glove	$14.50	325	
1,104	Active Outdoors Crochet Glove	$14.50	265	
1,105	Active Outdoors Crochet Glove	$14.50	367	
1,106	Active Outdoors Lycra Glove	$16.50	440	
1,107	Active Outdoors Lycra Glove	$16.50	358	
1,108	Active Outdoors Lycra Glove	$16.50	266	
1,109	Active Outdoors Lycra Glove	$16.50	750	
1,110	Active Outdoors Lycra Glove	$16.50	112	✓
1,111	Active Outdoors Lycra Glove	$16.50	686	
2,201	Triumph Pro Helmet	$41.90	78	✓
2,202	Triumph Pro Helmet	$41.90	80	✓

Figure 10-55 Symbols conditionally added to the report

Test Your Skills

Use the Highlighting Expert to complete the first three skills exercises.

1. Save the L5.6 report as `L10.19 Skills US orders not shipped`.

   - Highlight the order amount field in bold and red if the order amount is >=1500. Your report should look like the one shown in Figure 10-56. The second and third order amounts (plus others) should have the conditional formatting.

Customer Name	Country	Order Date	Order Amount	Shipped
City Cyclists	USA	04/29/2002	$63.90	False
Pathfinders	USA	04/26/2002	$3,185.42	False
Rockshocks for Jocks	USA	04/25/2002	$8,933.25	False
Rockshocks for Jocks	USA	04/30/2002	$31.00	False
Poser Cycles	USA	04/14/2002	$83.80	False
Trail Blazer's Place	USA	04/18/2002	$107.80	False
Trail Blazer's Place	USA	04/25/2002	$39.80	False
Hooked on Helmets	USA	04/20/2002	$2,797.25	False
Hooked on Helmets	USA	04/25/2002	$1,971.53	False

Figure 10-56 L10.19 Skills US orders not shipped report

2. Save the L9.10 report as `L10.20 Skills Order delay highlight`.

   - Add a single box around the Order ID field if the Delay In Days To Ship field is >=5. Your report should look like the one shown in Figure 10-57.

Customer Name	Order Date	Ship Date	Order ID	Unit Price	Quantity	Delay In Days To Ship
Alley Cat Cycles	06/24/2001	07/02/2001	1,761	$21.90	1	8
Alley Cat Cycles	06/24/2001	07/02/2001	1,761	$539.85	1	8
Alley Cat Cycles	06/24/2001	07/02/2001	1,761	$329.85	3	8
Piccolo	06/24/2001	06/29/2001	1,762	$2,939.85	2	5
City Cyclists	06/24/2001	06/30/2001	1,763	$41.90	2	6
City Cyclists	06/24/2001	06/30/2001	1,763	$764.85	3	6
Hercules Mountain Bikes	06/24/2001	06/27/2001	1,764	$37.90	2	3
Hercules Mountain Bikes	06/24/2001	06/27/2001	1,764	$23.50	2	3

Figure 10-57 L10.20 Skills Order delay highlight report

3. Save the L10.5 report as `L10.21 Skills Customer discount`.

   - Place a double underline border on the Order Amount field if the order discount is 15%.
   - Place a yellow background on the Order Amount field if the order discount is 10%. This should be the first priority. Your report should look like the one shown in Figure 10-58.

Customer Name	Order #	Order Date	Order Amount	Ship Via	Order Discount
City Cyclists	1	12/2/00	$41.90	UPS	25% discount
Deals on Wheels	1002	12/2/00	$5,060.28	Pickup	15% discount
Warsaw Sports, Inc.	1003	12/2/00	$186.87	UPS	25% discount
Bikes and Trikes	1004	12/2/00	$823.05	Pickup	25% discount
SAB Mountain	1005	12/3/00	$29.00	Loomis	25% discount
Poser Cycles	1006	12/3/00	$64.90	Purolator	25% discount
Spokes	1007	12/3/00	$49.50	Parcel Post	25% discount
Clean Air Transporta	1008	12/3/00	$2,214.94	Purolator	25% discount
Extreme Cycling	1009	12/3/00	$29.00	Loomis	25% discount
Cyclopath	1010	12/3/00	$14,872.30	UPS	10% discount
BBS Pty	1011	12/3/00	$29.00	Purolator	25% discount
Piccolo	1012	12/3/00	$10,259.10	Loomis	10% discount

Figure 10-58 L10.21 Skills Customer discount report

4. Save the L5.14 report as `L10.22 Skills Modify row color`.

    -   Print the odd number detail rows with a Yellow background. Your report should look like the one shown in Figure 10-59. Compare this report to one shown earlier in Figure 10-47.

Customer Name	Order ID	Order Date	Order Amount	Ship Via	First Name	Last Name
City Cyclists	1	12/02/2000	$41.90	UPS	Nancy	Davolio
Deals on Wheels	1,002	12/02/2000	$5,060.28	Pickup	Janet	Leverling
Warsaw Sports, Inc.	1,003	12/02/2000	$186.87	UPS	Margaret	Peacock
Bikes and Trikes	1,004	12/02/2000	$823.05	Pickup	Margaret	Peacock
SAB Mountain	1,005	12/03/2000	$29.00	Loomis	Janet	Leverling

Figure 10-59 L10.22 Skills Modify row color report

5. Save the L9.14 report as `L10.23 Skills Next discount`.

    -   Delete the selection criteria.
    -   Create a formula called `Next Discount`. The purpose of this formula is to show the discount the customer will receive on their next order. The discount is based on their previous order.
    -   The Next Discount formula needs the following criteria:
        -   Print "10% off your next order", if the quantity = 3.
        -   Print "15% off your next order", if the quantity = 2.
        -   Print "20% off your next order", if the quantity = 1.
    -   Delete the Unit Price field from the report.
    -   Add the Next Discount formula field after the Customer Name field. Your report should look like the one shown in Figure 10-60.

Customer Name	Next Discount	Order Date	Ship Date	Order ID	Quantity	Delay In Days To Ship
City Cyclists		12/02/2000	12/10/2000	1	1	8
Deals on Wheels	15% off your next order	12/02/2000	12/02/2000	1,002	3	0
Deals on Wheels	15% off your next order	12/02/2000	12/02/2000	1,002	3	0
Warsaw Sports, Inc.	15% off your next order	12/02/2000	12/05/2000	1,003	3	3
Warsaw Sports, Inc.	15% off your next order	12/02/2000	12/05/2000	1,003	3	3
Bikes and Trikes	15% off your next order	12/02/2000	12/02/2000	1,004	3	0
SAB Mountain	20% off your next order	12/03/2000	12/03/2000	1,005	2	0
Poser Cycles		12/03/2000	12/05/2000	1,006	1	2
Poser Cycles		12/03/2000	12/05/2000	1,006	1	2
Poser Cycles		12/03/2000	12/05/2000	1,006	1	2
Spokes	15% off your next order	12/03/2000	12/03/2000	1,007	3	0

Figure 10-60 L10.23 Skills Next discount report

6. Modify the L10.7 report to print the group header information at the top of the page if the group prints on more than one page. Save the report as `L10.24 Skills Modify group header options`.

    -   Suppress the dollar sign on the Order Amount field on all but the first record in each group. Make the dollar sign fixed.

    The bottom of page 1 should look like the one shown in Figure 10-61. Notice where the dollar sign is. The top of page 2 should look like the one shown in Figure 10-62.

Belgium Bike Co						
	07/01/2001	07/04/2001	$ 3,327.67	1801	$32.21	
	07/01/2001	07/04/2001	3,327.67	1801	$899.85	
	07/01/2001	07/04/2001	3,327.67	1801	$281.85	
	07/02/2001	07/02/2001	3,420.64	1805	$832.35	
	07/02/2001	07/02/2001	3,420.64	1805	$296.87	
	07/02/2001	07/02/2001	3,420.64	1805	$329.85	
	07/18/2001	07/18/2001	5,485.40	1867	$726.61	
	07/18/2001	07/18/2001	5,485.40	1867	$2,645.87	
	07/18/2001	07/18/2001	5,485.40	1867	$329.85	
	08/11/2001	08/16/2001	2,753.45	1960	$53.90	
	08/11/2001	08/16/2001	2,753.45	1960	$899.85	
						Page 1 of 19

Figure 10-61 L10.24 Skills Modify group header options report - bottom of page 1

	Order Date	Ship Date	Order Amount	Order #	Unit Price
Belgium Bike Co.					
	08/11/2001	08/16/2001	2,753.45	1960	$899.85
	11/08/2001	11/13/2001	4,111.86	2341	$329.85
	11/08/2001	11/13/2001	4,111.86	2341	$485.87
	11/08/2001	11/13/2001	4,111.86	2341	$832.35
	11/17/2001	11/23/2001	2,979.66	2359	$2,939.85
	11/17/2001	11/23/2001	2,979.66	2359	$39.81
	11/23/2001	11/23/2001	3,505.80	2413	$13.05
	11/23/2001	11/23/2001	3,505.80	2413	$1,739.85
	04/20/2002	04/28/2002	6,839.40	2952	$2,939.85
	04/20/2002	04/28/2002	6,839.40	2952	$479.85
Total # orders - 21		Total $ amount of orders -	$83,946.78		
		Average order amount for the customer -	$3,997.47		

Figure 10-62 L10.24 Skills Modify group header options report - top of page 2

7. Modify the L6.11 report so that each quarter starts on a new page. Save the report as L10.25 Skills 2001 orders by quarter with page break.

   - Reset the page number when a new quarter begins. Each quarter should start on a new page.
   - When you view the first page of each quarter of the report, it should have a page number 1.

8. Modify the L10.14 report to display the Employee First and Last name in the group tree instead of the Employee ID. Save the report as L10.26 Skills Modify group tree view.

   - Do not display the Employee ID field in the group header section.
   - **Hint**: Create a formula to combine the employee first and last name fields on the Change Group options dialog box.

   Page 2 of your report should look like the one shown in Figure 10-63. Notice the options in the group tree. Compare this to the L10.13 report.

Nancy Davolio	Salesperson		Order Date	Order ID	Product ID	Unit Price	Quantity
Janet Leverling	Nancy	Davolio	(Continued)				
Margaret Peacock			11/17/2001	2362	303221	$329.85	2
Michael Suyama			11/17/2001	2362	201201	$832.35	3
Robert King			11/15/2001	2356	6401	$12.00	2
Anne Dodsworth			11/14/2001	2352	303181	$329.85	3

Figure 10-63 L10.26 Skills Modify group tree view report

9. Modify the L6.2 report to be used as a summary report. Save the report as L10.27 Skills Summary report with conditional formatting.

   - Suppress the field headings.
   - Remove the border from the Order Amount field in the group footer section.
   - Hide the details section.
   - Change the report title to Summary Of Customer Orders.
   - Remove the bold from all of the objects in the group footer section.
   - Display the text Level 1 Customer if the Total $ Amount Of Orders field is > $75,000. (**Hint**: Use comparison conditional formatting.)
   - Page one of your report should look like the one shown in Figure 10-64.

Summary Of Customer Orders	
	2/12/2008
Alley Cat Cycles	
Total # orders - 7	Total $ amount of orders - $44,038.51
Backpedal Cycle Shop	
Total # orders - 14	Total $ amount of orders - $102,459.51 Level 1 Customer
BBS Pty	
Total # orders - 11	Total $ amount of orders - $58,289.14
Belgium Bike Co.	
Total # orders - 21	Total $ amount of orders - $83,946.78 Level 1 Customer

Figure 10-64 L10.27 Skills Summary report with conditional formatting

CHARTS

Crystal Reports has an expert that you can use to create charts. There are 15 types of charts that you can create, including pie, bar and line. In this lesson you will learn the following:

☑ How to create all 15 chart types using the Chart Expert
☑ Basic chart formatting and editing techniques

LESSON 11

Charts Overview

In addition to being able to format data in reports, charts allow you to present data in a graphical format which often makes the data easier to understand by visually displaying the relationship between the data. Charts also allow data to be presented in formats that text-only reports cannot do as well. For example charts can show trends over time, relationships or how one set of data compares to another set of data.

In previous lessons you created basic charts using a report wizard. As you saw, the chart options were very limited. When you need to create or modify charts that require more detail then the wizards provide, you should use the Chart Expert. It is very easy to get carried away when creating charts. Try to create charts that present the data in a meaningful way. Remember that sometimes, less is more.

There are four ways to open the Chart Expert as discussed below.

    ① Click the **CHART** button on the Crystal Reports - Insert toolbar.
    ② Right-click on the report, then Insert ⇒ Chart.
    ③ Crystal Reports ⇒ Insert ⇒ Chart.
    ④ Right-click on an existing chart and select Chart Expert.

Chart Considerations

There are two areas that need to be addressed before you start to create the chart. The two areas are the chart type and the source of the data for the chart. You will select the chart type on the Type tab on the Chart Expert, which is discussed below. Changing the chart type is easy. If you are not sure which chart type is the most appropriate, with a few mouse clicks, you can try out a few chart types and variations to see which is the best one for the data. Charts should enhance the ability to understand the data and make it easy to see the differences. The data source for the chart comes from one of the following: records in the details section of the report, a cross-tab or summary data.

I teach a technical writing class and one of the assignments has students create three charts to visually present data. Overall, the students do a good job on the charts. However, it is easy to tell which students have never created a chart before for at least one of the reasons listed below.

    ① The wrong chart type was selected. Newsflash: Bar charts are not the best option for all types of data, especially data that shows trends or needs to show how data has changed over time.
    ② The values on the X and Y axes are backwards. Dollar amounts, quantity, percents, usually go on the Y axis and time, dates and categories usually go on the X axis.
    ③ Not understanding the data that the chart will use.

The Chart Expert

This is the tool that allows you to create new charts and modify charts. It has wizard like characteristics because you click on the tabs to accomplish different tasks associated with creating and editing a chart. The biggest benefit of using the Chart Expert instead of the chart options on a wizard is that you have a lot of the chart options available from the beginning and the chart does not have to be based on data that will be printed on the report, like the wizards require. The options on each tab are covered in detail in this lesson because not understanding what all of the options are or not knowing where they are, will take you longer to create a chart. As you read about the Chart Expert, you may gain a better understanding of the options if you have the Chart Expert open.

The five tabs on the Chart Expert (Type, Data, Axes, Options and Text) contain options for a variety of features that you can use to make the chart as effective as possible. Keep in mind that not all of these tabs are available for all chart types. The tabs and options are discussed below.

> You do not have to create a chart from an existing report. You can select the fields that you need on the Chart Expert.

Type Tab

The options on this tab let you select what the chart will look like. The 15 chart types that you can select from are shown on the left side of Figure 11-1. Many of these chart types have variations that you can select, which gives you more chart options.

Each chart type is explained in Table 11-1.

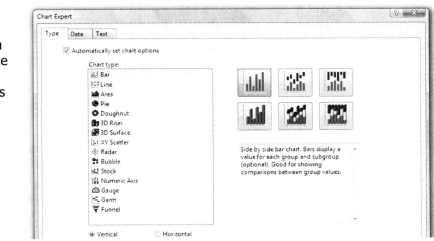

Figure 11-1 Chart Expert Type tab options

> If checked, the **AUTOMATICALLY SET CHART OPTIONS**, removes the Axes and Options tabs from the Chart Expert.

In previous lessons you created a pie and bar chart using a wizard. If you have created charts in spreadsheet software, you are probably familiar with many of the chart types in Crystal Reports. When selecting the chart type, the most important consideration should be to select the chart type that will best display the data that will be presented in the chart. This is the first thing that you have to do. When you click on the chart type on the left you will see variations of the chart on the right. Click on the chart style (variation) on the right that you want to use. Under the chart variations you will see a description of the chart type.

Chart Type Options

At the bottom of the Type tab shown above in Figure 11-1, you will see the two options discussed below for the bar, line and area chart types.

① **Vertical** This is the default option. The elements will start at the bottom of the chart, as shown on the right side of Figure 11-1, shown above.
② **Horizontal** If selected, this option will change the direction of the elements on the chart. The bars will start on the left, instead of the bottom, as shown in Figure 11-2.

Figure 11-2 Horizontal chart options

Chart Type	Description
Bar	Bar charts, as shown in Figure 11-3, show differences between items and relationships between grouped data. This is probably the most used chart type. Stacked bar charts show each item as a percent of the total.
Line	Line charts show trends and changes over a period of time. The markers on the bottom three line chart types indicate the exact values. In Figure 11-4, the data is represented with lines. A good use of **3D LINE CHARTS** is when the data lines cross each other often. This makes a line chart easier to read. (1)
Area	Area charts show how the data has changed over a period of time. Figure 11-5 shows how the four types of income (mail order, store, kiosk and Internet) make up the total income and how the income changes over the months. Area charts are almost identical to stacked line charts. The difference is that area charts are filled in below the trendline. Area charts are probably best suited for a few groups of data. (1)
Pie	Pie charts only show information for one point in time. Figure 11-6 shows the various types of income for July. Each slice of the pie represents the percent for the item. The Multiple pie chart type will create a chart for each group. (2)
Doughnut	This chart type is similar to pie charts. The difference is that there is a hole in the center, which contains the grand total of the data presented in the chart. (2)
3D Riser	This is the 3D version of bar charts that shows data values side by side, separately or stacked. It can display several groups of data in shapes like a pyramid or octagon.
3D Surface	This is the 3D version of area charts. This chart type uses three sets of data. The surface of the chart has a curve and shows trends in relation to time.
XY Scatter	XY Scatter charts show how two values are related (like month of year and order amount) and how a change in one value affects the other value, as shown in Figure 11-7. This chart type lets you see the correlation between the items. The X and Y axis must display numeric data. If data like dates or months can be converted to numeric data, it can be used in this chart type.
Radar	Radar charts compare sets of data relative to a center point and shows how far the data value is from the standard (the center point value). The values that are often used are group subtotals. The data from the X axis is usually plotted in a circle and the Y values are plotted from the center of the circle out.
Bubble	This chart type is similar to XY Scatter charts because it plots individual points. The difference is that bubble charts use different size plot points based on the data value. The larger the data value, the larger the size the plot point is.
Stock	This chart type is similar to bar charts. The difference is that the bars in stock charts do not have to touch the bottom of the chart. This type of chart is often used to display the minimum and maximum of stock prices, where each bar represents a different stock. Stock charts plot the first and last trade of the day or the high and low values for each element.
Numeric Axis	This chart type does not use a fixed X axis value or interval like many other chart types do. You can use a date/time field or numeric value for the X axis. This chart type is another way to create bar, line and area charts.
Gauge	This chart type looks like a gauge in a car as shown in Figure 11-8. The needle in the chart points to the value that is being represented. If there is more than one value or group being represented, a gauge chart is created for each value or group. Multiple needles in one gauge means that there is more than one "On change of" value.
Gantt	This chart type is primarily used to display project management data like the start and end dates of tasks on a project plan. Gantt charts only work with date and date/time fields.

Table 11-1 Chart types explained

Chart Type	Description
Funnel	This chart type is similar to stacked bar charts because they show each item as a percent of the total. The difference is that the bars are in the shape of a funnel. The height of the bar represents the percent of the data. The width of the bar does not represent anything.

Table 11-1 Chart types explained (Continued)

(1) This chart type requires at least two sets of data.
(2) This chart type only uses one value because it shows how the whole (100%) is divided.

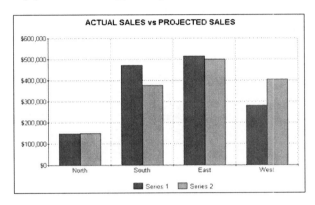

Figure 11-3 Bar chart

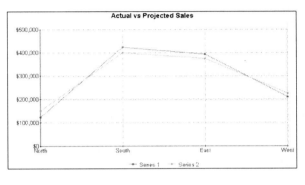

Figure 11-4 Line chart

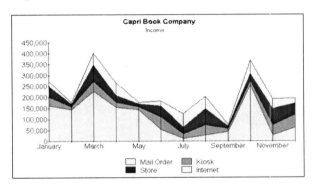

Figure 11-5 Area chart

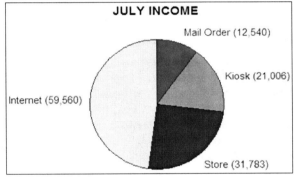

Figure 11-6 Pie chart

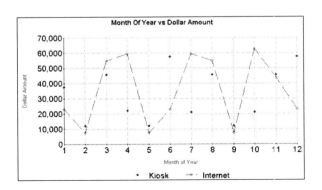

Figure 11-7 XY Scatter chart

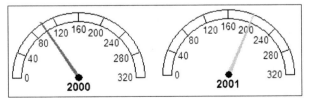

Figure 11-8 Gauge chart

It would be very helpful and a big time saver to me if at least one of the tabs on the Chart Expert would display the chart with the options that are selected, similar to what you see when you use the Chart Options dialog box to modify the chart. You will learn how to use the Chart Options dialog box later in this lesson.

Data Tab

The options on this tab let you select the source of the data for the chart. This is the second area that needs to be addressed before you create the chart. There are four ways (called layout options) to chart data, as discussed below. Depending on the chart type that was selected, not all of the data layout options will be available.

Each layout type works independently of the others. You can only select one layout type. If you select one and make changes on that screen, then select a different layout type and make changes, the only information that will be saved, will be the layout that you changed last.

All four layout options have the **ON CHANGE OF** drop-down list. The options in this list are how you decide when a new element (bar, slice of pie, point on a line, etc) will be added to the chart. This option lets Crystal Reports know that when the value in the field(s) listed below this option changes, you want a new element on the chart to be created.

The options in the Placement section including the **PLACE CHART** drop-down list lets you select where the chart will be placed in the report. The **ONCE PER REPORT** option places the chart in the report header or footer section. If the report has groups, you will see the options shown in Figure 11-9 in the drop-down list.

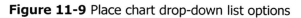

Figure 11-9 Place chart drop-down list options

The reason that you see three **FOR EACH** options is because the report has three groups. Charts are placed at least one section in the report above the data that is on the chart. Advanced, group, cross-tab and OLAP charts cannot be placed in the details section of a report.

Advanced Layout Options

This layout option is always available. Out of the four layout options, this is probably the most complex because it allows you to create a chart that is not based on data that will print on the report. If you created a report using the Blank Report option and have not added any fields to the report, the options on this tab will let you select the fields for the chart. This is how you would create a report that only has a chart. If you need to a create a chart based on records in the details section of the report, click on the Advanced layout option on the Data tab. You will see the options shown in Figure 11-10.

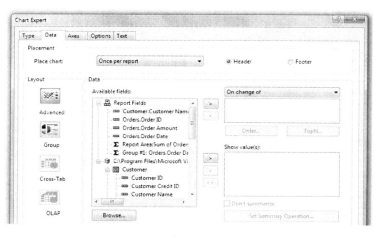

Figure 11-10 Chart Expert Data tab - Advanced options

> When you are working on exercises that use the options on the Advanced tab, you will see this instruction: **ADD THE FIELD TO THE FIRST LIST**. This means to add the field to the list that is under the On Change Of option shown above in Figure 11-10.

> If the report already has groups defined, you can still create an advanced chart because the options on this tab are not affected by the groups that are on the report.

The **AVAILABLE FIELDS** section of the Data tab contains the fields that are already on the report, including the summary, formula, running total fields, as well as, all of the fields in the tables associated with the report. This section is only available if the On Change of option is selected in the drop-down list on the right.

| The summary and running total fields can only be added to the SHOW VALUE(S) list.

The ON CHANGE OF option allows you to select up to two fields to group the data in the chart on. This group is not a real group like the ones that you learned how to create earlier in this workbook. When the value in the field changes a new element is created. Each element on the chart represents one group.

If you wanted to create a chart that displayed the orders by sales rep, you would add the sales rep (Employee Last Name) field to the list box below this drop-down list. The Order Amount field would be added to the Show Value(s) list to get a total for each sales rep. Figure 11-11 shows this report.

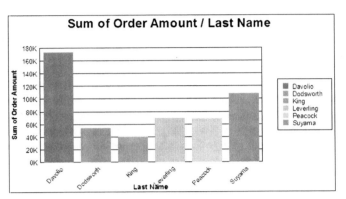

Figure 11-11 Sales reps orders chart

The On Change Of option works like the group option because it summarizes the values in the group. The difference is that the groups in the chart do not have an effect on the report. If you select multiple fields to group on, the data from each group will be displayed (side by side or stacked, based on the chart type that is selected). If the order date was added to the Evaluate option as shown in Figure 11-12, the report would look like the one shown in Figure 11-13.

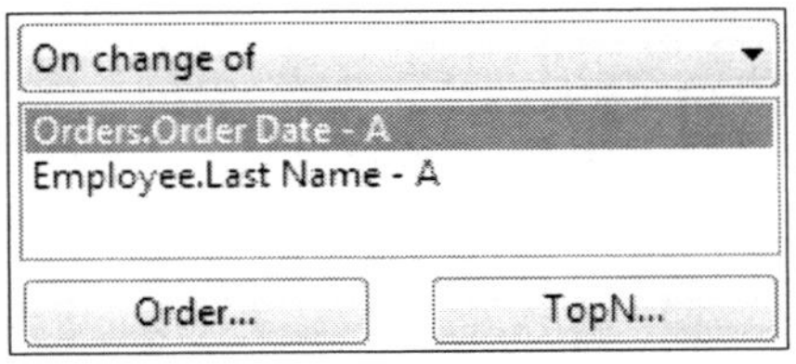

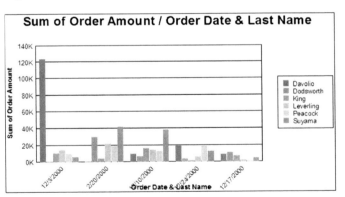

Figure 11-12 On change of options

Figure 11-13 Sales reps orders chart with additional options

The first field below the drop-down list is the primary group and determines how the data is grouped. The second field creates the elements in the primary group. In the example shown above in Figure 11-12, the order date field is the primary group. The Employee last name field is the secondary group. Putting the fields in this order groups the records by date. Each element in the date group is a different sales rep.

The FOR EACH RECORD option in the drop-down list will cause a new element to be added to the chart for every record that would print on the report. If this option is selected, only one field can be added to the box below this drop-down list. If there is not a lot of data in the table that the field that you select is in, it is okay to select this option because the chart will be legible. If there are a lot of records, more than likely it would be hard to read the chart if this option is selected. If this option is selected, fields that are added to the **SHOW VALUE(S)** list will not be summarized, the actual value in the field is what will appear in the chart.

You can reduce the records that are used to create the chart by using the Select Expert that you learned about in Lesson 5. If you realize that you need to do this, you can create the selection criteria after the chart has been created. You will learn how to do this later in this lesson.

 Gantt charts have to use the **FOR EACH RECORD** option. A start and end date must be added to the Show value(s) list.

The **FOR ALL RECORDS** option creates a chart with only one element, which is a grand total for all of the records that are on the report. You cannot add any fields to the box below the drop-down list if this option is selected.

The **SHOW VALUE(S)** list contains the field(s) that the chart will create a summary for. The actual value or the value from the summary calculation will be used as an element on the chart. Which value is used is determined by the option selected in the evaluation option drop-down list. Table 11-2 explains the type of summary value each of the evaluation options causes to be created. If you add more than one field to this list, the chart will plot a separate line or bar for example, for each field in this list. Each chart type allows at least one field in the Show Value(s) list. In the Orders by sales rep example, if you add the Order Amount field to the Show value(s) list, a total (summary) for each sales rep would be created.

Option	Show Value Summary Type
On change of	Summary for each group.
For each record	Actual value for each record.
For all records	One summary value for the entire report.

Table 11-2 Evaluation options explained

Summary Calculations

Table 11-3 explains the default type of summary calculations that the Show Value option applies to different field types. You can change the summary calculation type by following the steps below.

Field Type	Default Calculation Type
Number	Summary
Currency	Summary
All others	Count

Table 11-3 Default summary calculations

① Click on the field that you want to change the calculation for in the Show value(s) list.
② Click the **SET SUMMARY OPERATION** button shown earlier in Figure 11-10. You will see the Edit Summary dialog box shown in Figure 11-14. You learned about this dialog box in Lesson 6.
③ The options in the **CALCULATE THIS SUMMARY** drop-down list are the ones that are available for the data type of the field that you are changing. Select the type of calculation that you want.

The **ORDER** button on the Data tab will open the Chart Sort Order dialog box shown in Figure 11-15. The options on this dialog box work the same way that the options on the Insert Group dialog box work that you learned about in Lesson 6. These options let you select the sort order for the element in the chart.

In the orders by sales rep example, if you selected the Order Amount field and then clicked the Order button you would be able to select how you wanted the total order amount for each rep to be displayed. If you were creating a bar chart and wanted to see the sales reps in order from high to low based on sales, you would select **DESCENDING**.

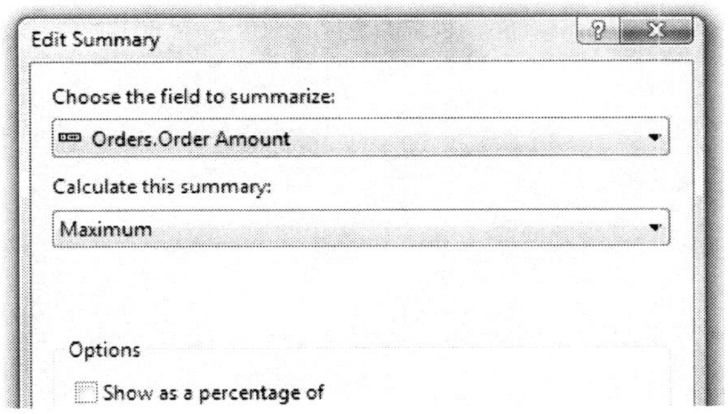

Figure 11-14 Edit Summary dialog box

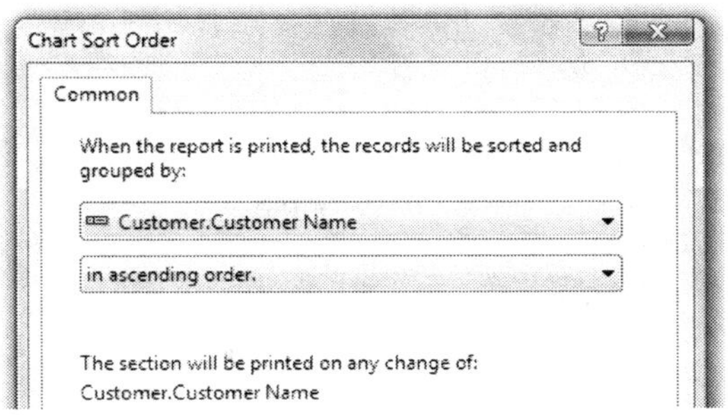

Figure 11-15 Chart Sort Order dialog box

Group Sort Expert

The **TOP N** button will open the Group Sort Expert, shown in Figure 11-16. The options on this dialog box are similar the ones on the **OTHERS** tab on the Change Group Options dialog box. [See Lesson 6, Figure 6-66] If you only wanted to include the top or bottom N records, groups or percents, you would select the options here. The options selected in Figure 11-16 will display the five sales reps that had the lowest number of sales.

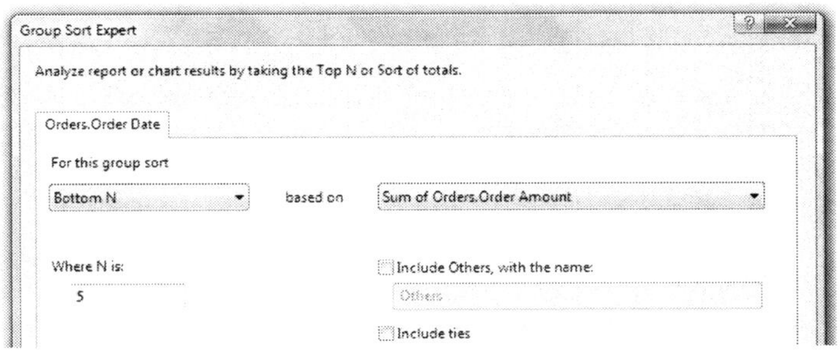

Figure 11-16 Group Sort Expert

If you want to include groups that are not part of the group sort, you can by checking the appropriate **INCLUDE** options on the right side of the dialog box. If checked, the **INCLUDE TIES** option will include groups that have the same summarized value if they meet the other selection criteria.

Group Layout Options

The group layout options create a chart that is based off of fields in a group header or footer section of the report. This chart layout type is only available if both of the conditions discussed below have been met.

① The chart must be placed in the report header or footer or in a group header or footer section that is on a higher level then the data in the group that the chart will be based on.
② The report has to have one group that has a summary or total field.

The options shown in Figure 11-17 let you select how the data in the group will be displayed in the chart. The options are explained below.

The options in the **ON CHANGE OF** drop-down list are the fields (that have a summary or total field) that are in a lower level then the section of the report that the chart has been placed in. This option lets you select the group that the chart will be based on.

The 2001 Orders by shipping method report that you created in Exercise 6.4 has two groups: the Ship Via group and the Customer Name group. Both of these groups have summary fields.

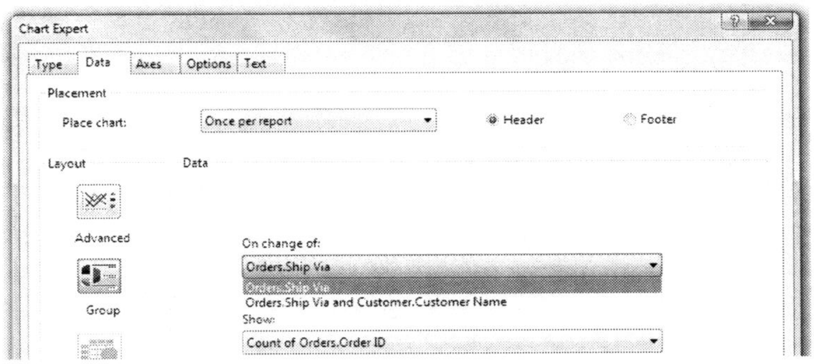

Figure 11-17 Chart Expert Data tab - Group options
(On Change Of options for the two groups below the chart)

If you put the chart in the report header or footer section, the On Change Of drop-down list will have the options shown above in Figure 11-17.

If the report has three groups with a summary or total field and you place the chart in the first group section, you would see the summary or total fields for the two groups below it. Just by looking at the options in Figure 11-18, you do not know if the chart is in a report or group section.

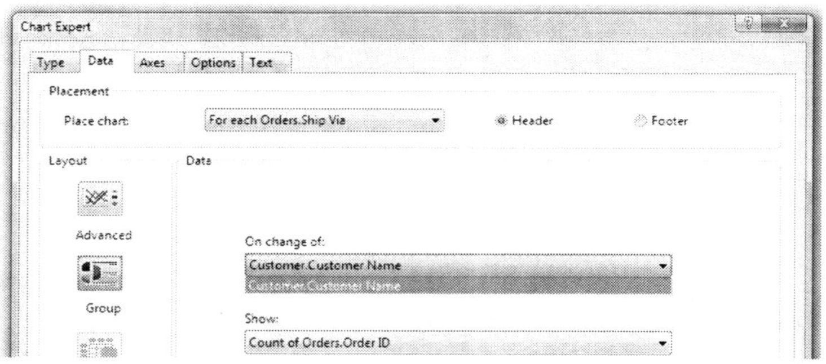

Figure 11-18 On Change Of options for one group below the chart

If you put the chart in the first group header or footer section or the report header or footer section and there is only one group below it that has a summary or total field, you would only see one option in the On Change Of drop-down list as shown above in Figure 11-18. These are the summary fields in the group header or footer section in the report.

The fields in the **SHOW** drop-down list are the summary and subtotal fields in the group that is selected in the On Change Of field. This is how you select the summary field in the group that will be used in the chart.

Cross-Tab Layout Options

This layout option is only available if the report has a cross-tab object in the same or corresponding section of the report that the chart is placed in. By corresponding section, I mean if the cross-tab that the chart will be based off of is in the Group 2 footer section, the chart can be placed in the Group 2 header or footer section. The options shown in Figure 11-19 let you create a chart based on the data in the cross-tab.

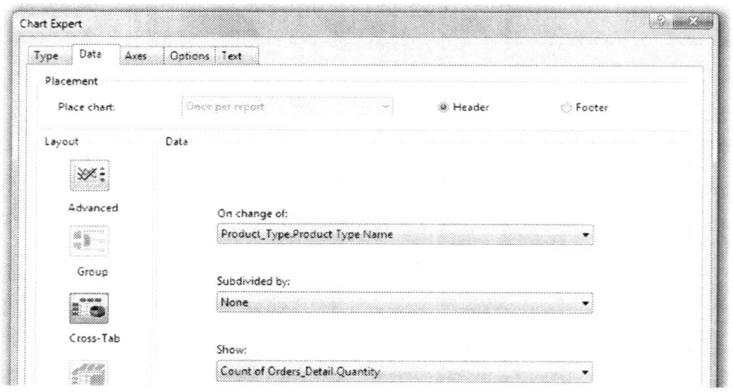

Figure 11-19 Chart Expert Data tab - Cross-Tab options

Earlier you learned that cross-tab charts cannot be placed in the details section. If you move the cross-tab object to a different section after a cross-tab chart has been created, the report will automatically be moved to the new section also.

If the report has more than one cross-tab object, you have to select the cross-tab object that you want to create the chart off of before you open the Chart Expert.

The options in the **ON CHANGE OF** drop-down list are the first fields in the Rows and Columns sections of the Cross-Tab Expert or Wizard, regardless of how many fields each of these sections have. [See Exercise 7.10] The field selected in this drop-down list is the first (or only) element that will be used as the primary X axis value.

Selecting a field in the **SUBDIVIDED BY** drop-down list is optional, which is why the default option is **NONE**. The only field that is available in the Subdivided By drop-down list is the one that was not selected in the On Change Of drop-down list. Selecting a field will create a second X value, which will add a second series of data to the chart. This will let you create a chart that does a side by side comparison. Figure 11-20 shows a line chart with the first field in the Row section and the first field in the Column section from the cross-tab selected.

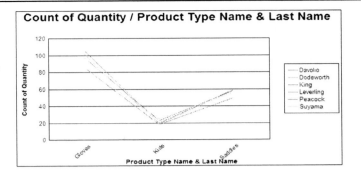

Figure 11-20 Line chart with the row and column fields selected

The options in the **SHOW** drop-down list are the fields that are in the Summary Fields section of the Cross-Tab window. They are the fields that you select from to summarize the report on, like the Show Value option on the Advanced Layout screen.

Axes Tab

Depending on the chart type that is selected, you may not see the Axes tab shown in Figure 11-21. You will see this tab if the chart type selected uses the X and Y axis. For example, bar, line, area and radar charts use the X and Y axis. Pie, doughnut and Gantt chart types do not.

The options on this tab let you select how the chart will display the data values that you see across the bottom of the chart (the X axis) and on the left side of the chart (the Y axis). If you are creating a 3D chart you can also select the data values for the Z axis.

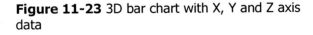

Figure 11-21 Chart Expert - Axes tab

If the chart that you are creating needed to display order totals by month, like the report that you created in Exercise 6.7, the months would be placed on the X axis because the report is grouped by month and the totals would be placed on the Y axis because they represent the quantity, as shown in Figure 11-22. If you were creating the same chart, but selected a 3D layout, the chart would look like the one shown in Figure 11-23, which also includes the data axis (the Z axis).

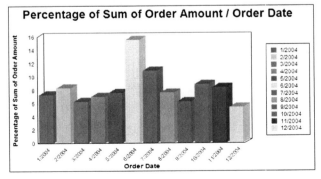

Figure 11-22 Bar chart with X and Y axis data

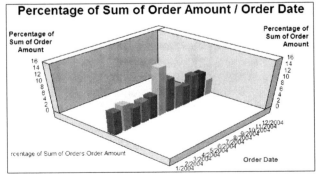

Figure 11-23 3D bar chart with X, Y and Z axis data

Show Gridlines Options

You will see two or three axis options in this section depending on whether the chart is two or three dimensional.

The **Group Axis** option corresponds to the ON CHANGE OF field on the Advanced Layout section of the Data tab.
The **Series Axis** will only appear for three dimensional chart types.
The **Data Axis** option corresponds to the SHOW field on the Advanced Layout section of the Data tab.

If checked, the major and minor options will add gridlines to the chart. The MAJOR option will place the gridlines (with labels) on the axis, as shown in Figure 11-24. The MINOR option can only be used with numeric labels and will place the gridlines between the labels on the axis.

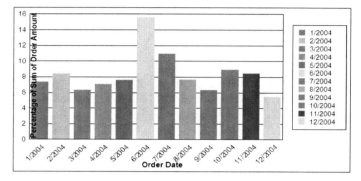

Figure 11-24 Bar chart with major gridlines added

 Some chart types will have a gridline on the Group axis whether you select the option or not.

Data Values Options

The options in this section of the Axes tab let you customize the **VALUES** on the Data axis.

The **AUTO RANGE** option is the default and lets Crystal Reports use the chart values to set the starting and ending values for the Data axis. If you want to customize the values, clear this option and enter the Min, Max and Number formats that you want.

MIN is the lowest value that you want to see on the axis. Usually this is zero, but you may have the need to use a different starting value.

MAX is the highest value that you want to see on the Axis. This value is usually larger than the largest value of the data on the axis.

The danger in changing the max value in my opinion is that you would be basing the change on the current values that are displayed on the chart. If the report is run later and for whatever reason has a larger value than the value that you entered in this field, the chart would not capture the largest value, thus making the data on the chart inaccurate.

The **NUMBER FORMAT** option is only available if the Auto Range option is not checked. The options in the drop-down list shown in Figure 11-25 let you select the format for the numbers that will be displayed on the chart.

Figure 11-25 Number Format options

If you change the data value options and then recheck the **AUTO RANGE** option, the changes that you made will still be in effect, even though the options are not enabled.

If checked, the **AUTO SCALE** option lets you select the starting numeric value that the chart will use.

Number Of Division Options

The options in this section let you customize the number of gridlines (intervals) and labels that the data axis will have. Select the **MANUAL** option if you want to set the intervals.

Options Tab

Figures 11-26 to 11-28 show various versions of the Options tab. The options are different depending on the chart type that is selected.

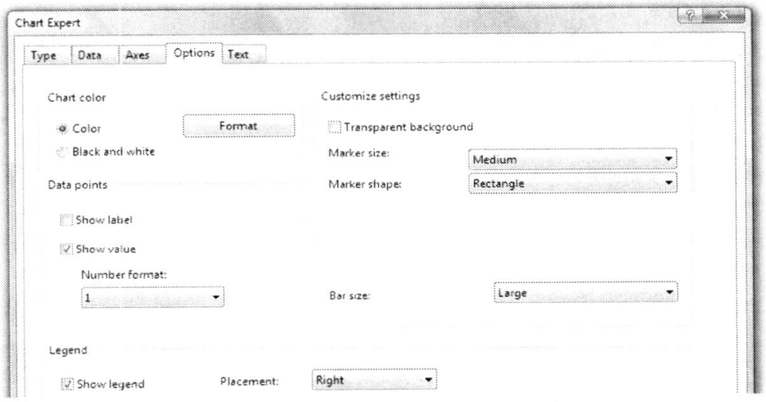

Figure 11-26 Options tab for a bar chart

The options in the **CUSTOMIZE SETTINGS** section let you select the size and shape for the legend in some chart types or the shape of the markers for bar and line charts. The **MARKERS** are the points on a chart that are connected by lines. This feature is often used in line charts, as you saw earlier in Figure 11-4. The last size option in this section lets you select the size of the element. For example, the size of a slice of the pie or the size of the bar as shown in Figures 11-27 and 11-28.

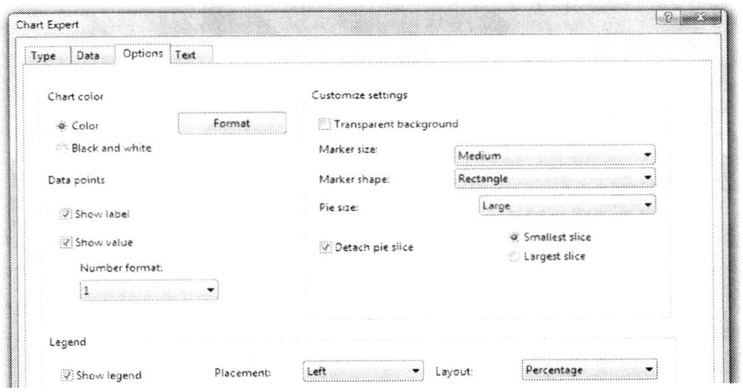

Figure 11-27 Options tab for a pie chart

The options in the **DATA POINTS** section let you select whether or not labels and values (the actual data) are displayed with the elements. Each element (slice) in the pie chart shown earlier in Figure 11-6 has a label and value. The value is in parenthesis for illustration purposes.

The options in the **LEGEND** section let you turn the legend on and off, as well as, select where you want the legend placed in reference to the chart. The legend is the color coded key that lets you know what the elements on the chart are referencing.

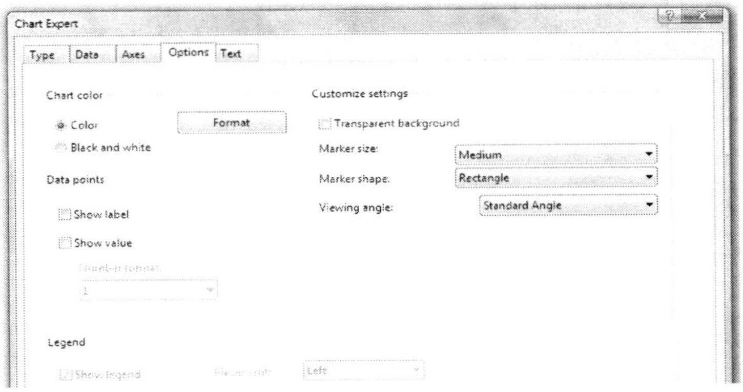

Figure 11-28 Options tab for a 3D Riser chart

The area chart shown earlier in Figure 11-5 has the legend at the bottom of the chart. In Figure 11-27 above, the legend will be placed on the left side of the chart. Notice in Figure 11-28 above that the legend options are dimmed out. That means that the chart type cannot have a legend. There are also times when a chart looks better without a legend.

Chart Color Format Expert

Click the Format button on the Options tab. The options on this dialog box allow you to conditionally format the colors for the elements on a chart. The options shown in Figure 11-29 should look familiar because they are similar to the options on the Highlighting Expert that you learned about in Lesson 10. The difference between them is that the Highlighting Expert works with objects on the report and the options on the Chart Color Format Expert work with elements on a chart.

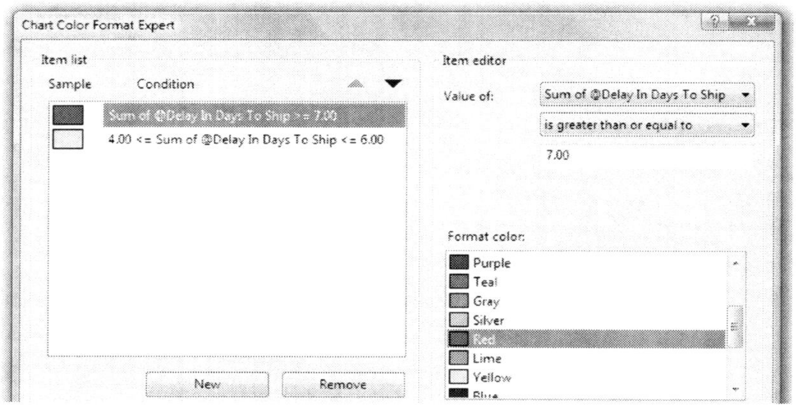

Figure 11-29 Color Format Expert options

The conditional formatting that you apply to an element does not change if the data for that element changes. For example, if you apply conditional formatting to the bottom section (for example, the mail order section) of the area chart shown earlier in Figure 11-5 and the data changes and the mail order element is no longer on the bottom, the formatting for the mail order element does not change. The new data that is in the bottom section of the area chart will change.

In my opinion, conditional formatting usually looks better on charts that are using data that is grouped.

Text Tab

The options on this tab will let you add text to a chart. As shown in Figure 11-30, the **AUTO TEXT** option is checked for all of the title fields and the text fields are dimmed out. This is because Crystal Reports automatically creates many of the titles based on the field names that the chart is being created from. You saw this when you created charts with the wizards in Lesson 7. To change a title, clear the check mark next to the title that you want to change and type in the title that you want. It is not a requirement to have titles. You can change the font of a title by clicking on the title that you want to change in the **FORMAT** section and then click the Font button. Figure 11-31 shows the font options.

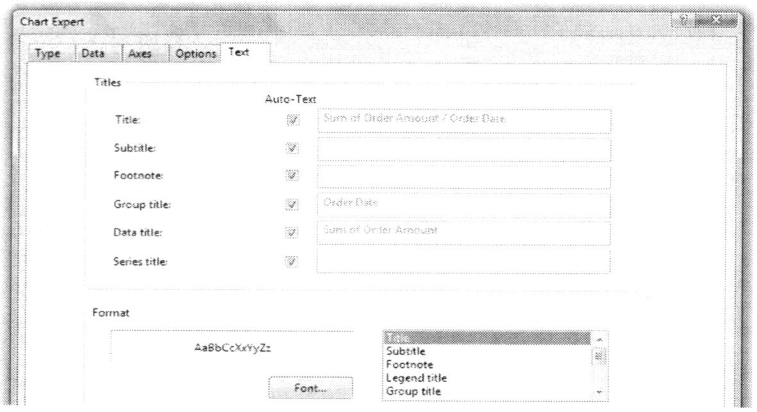

Figure 11-30 Text tab chart options

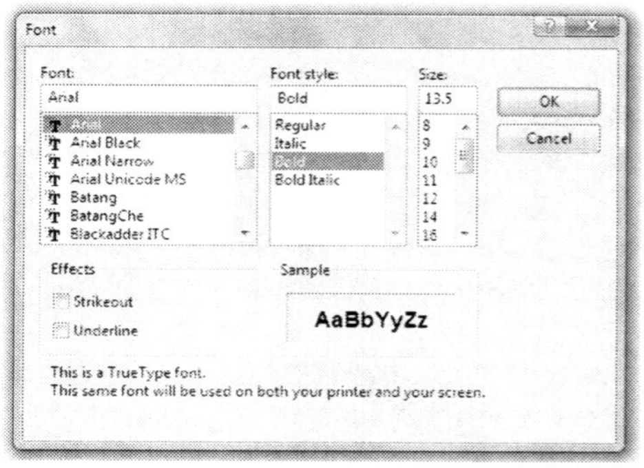

Figure 11-31 Font options

Parts Of A Chart

Charts can contain all or any of the options discussed below. It is important that you understand these options. These options can be added or deleted as needed. Figure 11-32 illustrates many of the parts of a chart that have already been discussed in this lesson. The parts of the chart are explained below.

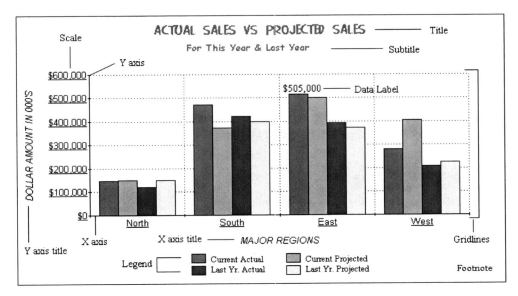

Figure 11-32 Parts of a chart illustrated

Title and **Subtitle** are a description of what type of data the chart is displaying.

X and **Y Axis** represent the vertical (Y) axis and horizontal (X) axis of the chart. The X axis often represents quantities or percents.

Gridlines make the chart easier to read if the values are close in range. You can have horizontal and vertical gridlines.

Scale shows the unit of measurement. The scale range is taken from the data that is displayed on the report. The scale is automatically created for you, but you can change it. Crystal Reports uses the Auto Scale and Auto Range options on the Chart Expert Axes tab to create the scale.

The **Legend** is used to help make the chart easier to read. Legends are color coded representations of different data elements on the chart.

 Chart Exercise Tips

① Unless stated otherwise, if the exercises in this lesson do not create a new report, open the Chart Expert after step 1 in each exercise and place the chart in the report header section of the report.
② If the instruction to select a chart type says to select the line chart with markers data points for example, you would select the line chart type from the list on the left of the Type tab on the Chart Expert dialog box. You would then click on the icon on the right that has the words markers data points.

 When you view a chart on the design tab, you may see fields that you did not select. You will see real data on the preview tab. The chart in the design window does not represent data in the tables that the chart is using. I am telling you this because I do not want you to think that you are losing your mind when you see a chart in the design window that doesn't display what you are expecting.

Exercise 11.1: Create A Bar Chart

1. Save the L7.8 report as `L11.1 Bar chart`.

2. Delete the existing chart. Open the Chart Expert, then select the Side by side bar chart type.

3. On the Data tab select the Group data layout option, if it is not already selected. Select the Order Date field from the On Change Of drop-down list if it is not already selected, then select the Order Amount field in the Show drop-down list.

4. On the Axes tab add a major gridline to the Group axis option.

5. On the Options tab select the Show value Data Points option, then change the Number format to $1. Place the Legend at the bottom of the chart. You should have the options selected that are shown in Figure 11-33.

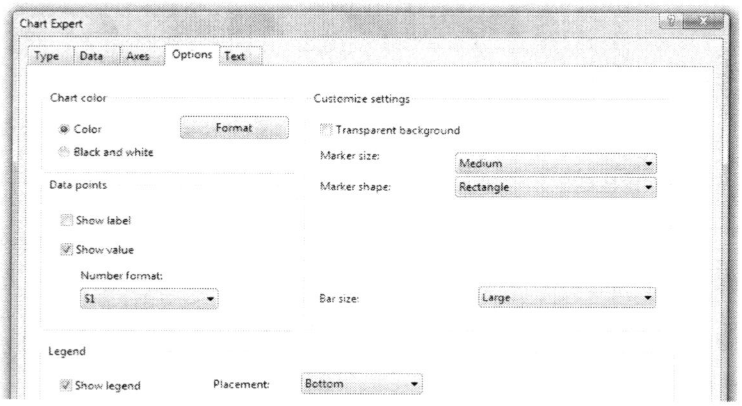

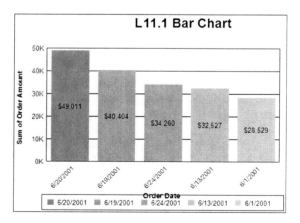

Figure 11-33 Options for the bar chart

6. On the Text tab change the Title to `L11.1 Bar Chart`. Click OK and save the changes. The chart should look like the one shown in Figure 11-34. The chart looks good, but with a few changes, it would look better. Later in this lesson you will learn how to modify a chart.

Figure 11-34 L11.1 Bar chart

Exercise 11.2: Copy A Chart To A Group Section

Earlier you learned that if the same chart is placed in a group section of the report that it will only display data for the group. In this exercise, you will copy the chart that you created in Exercise 11.1 and place the copy in the group footer section of the report.

1. Save the L11.1 report as `L11.2 Chart in group footer section`.

2. Open the Section expert, click on the group footer section and click the **INSERT** button, then click OK. You should now see a group footer 1b section on the report.

3. Right-click on the chart and select Copy. Right-click and select Paste, then click in the group footer 1b section.

4. Open the Chart Expert for the chart in the group footer 1b section. On the Data tab add the Customer Name field to the first list, then add the Order Amount field to the Show value(s) list.

5. Clear the Show value option on the Options tab.

6. Change the Title to `L11.2 Chart in Group Footer Section`.
   Change the Subtitle to `Customer Orders By Day`.
   Delete the text in the Group title field. Click OK and save the changes. The chart should look like the one shown in Figure 11-35. At the end of every group on the report you will see a chart that only contains data for the records in that group. If you didn't want the chart in the report header section, you could delete it.

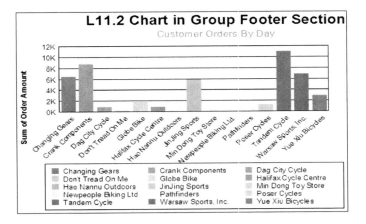

Figure 11-35 L11.2 Chart in group footer section

Exercise 11.3: Create A Line Chart

In this exercise you will create a chart that displays order totals by month.

1. Save the L6.7 report as `L11.3 Line chart`.

2. Select the Line chart type with markers at data points, then select the Group layout option on the Data tab.

3. Select the Sum Order Amount field in the Show drop-down list.

4. Place the legend on the right side of the chart. Select the large **MARKER SIZE** and the **DIAMOND** Marker shape.

5. Change the Subtitle to `L11.3 Line Chart`. Click OK and save the changes. The chart should look like the one shown in Figure 11-36.

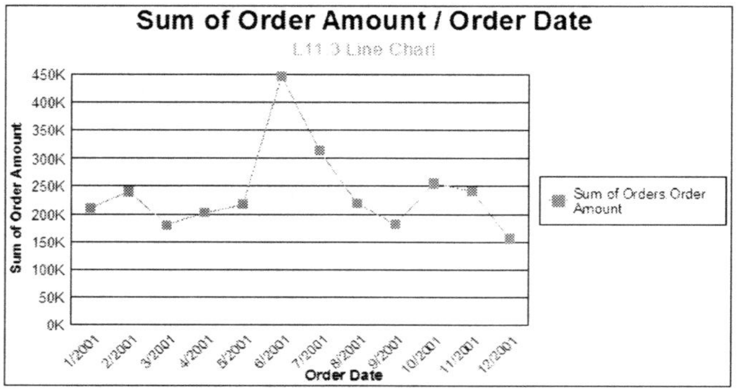

Figure 11-36 L11.3 Line chart

Exercise 11.4: Create An Area Chart

As mentioned earlier, you can add a chart to a report that does not have any data. You will learn how to do that in this exercise by creating a report that charts the sum of last years sales by region.

1. Create a new report and save it as L11.4 Area chart. Add the Customer table.

2. Select the Stacked Area chart type with 3D visual effect.

3. On the Data tab add the Region and Customer Name fields to the first list, then add the Last Year's Sales field to the Show value(s) list. You should have the options shown in Figure 11-37.

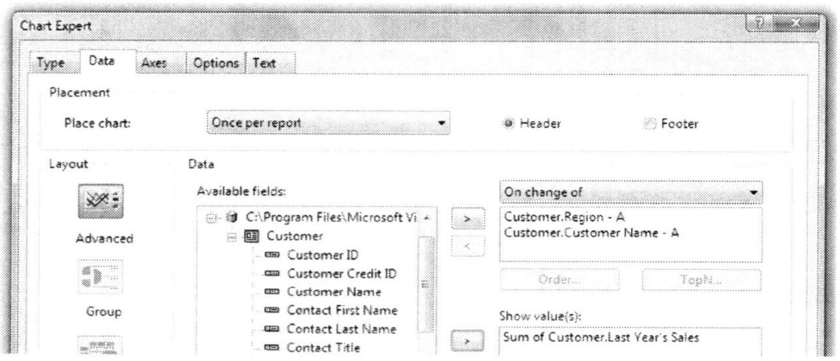

Figure 11-37 Area chart data tab options

4. Add a major gridline to the Group axis option. Change the option to show the legend at the bottom of the chart.

5. Change the Subtitle to L11.4 Area Chart. Delete the Group title, then click OK. Make the chart at least 6.5 inches wide.

Add The Selection Criteria

In addition to being able to create a report that does not have any other information besides a chart, you can also select the records that you want the chart to be based on.

1. Open the Select Expert. Select the Region field, then click OK.

2. Select the **IS ONE OF** value, then add the following regions: CA, NY, PA and BC. Click OK and save the changes. The chart should look like the one shown in Figure 11-38.

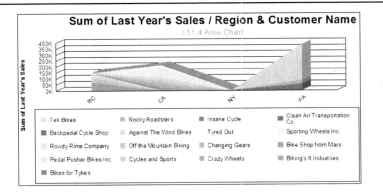

Figure 11-38 L11.4 Area chart

Exercise 11.5: Create A Pie Chart

In this exercise you will create a chart that displays the order totals for 2001, by quarter.

1. Save the L6.11 report as `L11.5 Pie chart`.

2. Select the Pie chart type with visual 3D effect.

3. Check the Show label and Show value options. Change the Number format to 1. Select **BOTH** for the Legend layout option.

4. Change the Title to `L11.5 Pie Chart`. Add the Footnote `2001 Orders By Quarter`, then make the footnote italic. Click OK twice to close both dialog boxes and save the changes. The chart should look like the one shown in Figure 11-39. The number under the date on each slice of the pie is the number of orders for that quarter.

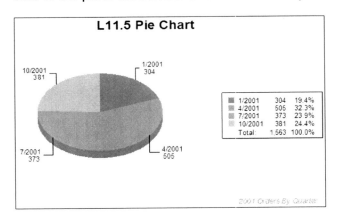

Figure 11-39 L11.4 Pie chart

Exercise 11.6: Detach A Slice Of A Pie Chart

One way to emphasize a slice of a pie chart is to pull it away from the rest of the chart. This is sometimes referred to as "Exploding" a slice of a pie chart.

1. Save the L11.5 report as `L11.6 Explode a slice of the pie chart`.

2. Right-click on the chart and select Chart Expert.

3. On the Options tab check the option **DETACH PIE SLICE**, then select the **LARGEST SLICE** option.

4. Change the Title to `L11.6 Explode a slice of a pie chart`. Click OK and save the changes. The chart should look like the one shown in Figure 11-40.

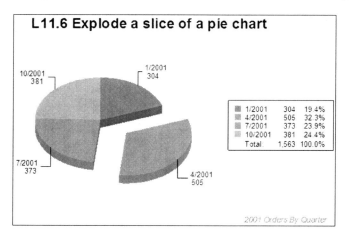

Figure 11-40 L11.6 Explode a slice of the pie chart

Exercise 11.7: Create A Doughnut Chart

In this exercise you will modify the pie chart that you created in Exercise 11.5 so that it will be a doughnut chart.

1. Save the L11.5 report as `L11.7 Doughnut chart`.

2. Select the Doughnut chart type.

3. Change the Title to `L11.7 Doughnut Chart`. Click OK and save the changes. The chart should look like the one shown in Figure 11-41.

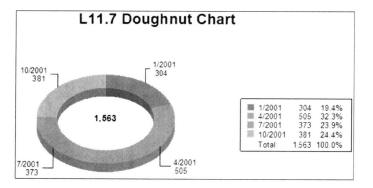

Figure 11-41 L11.7 Doughnut chart

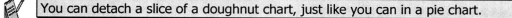

You can detach a slice of a doughnut chart, just like you can in a pie chart.

Exercise 11.8: Create A 3D Riser Chart

In this exercise you will create a chart that shows last years sales for three states (regions) that are over a certain dollar amount. In order to do that the report will need selection criteria.

1. Save the L11.4 report as `L11.8 3D Riser chart`.

2. Use the Select Expert to create the criteria shown in Figure 11-42.

{Customer.Region} in ["MA", "PA", "WI"] and
{Customer.Last Year's Sales} >= $35000.00

Figure 11-42 Selection criteria

3. Select the 3D Riser bar chart type.

4. Display major gridlines for all axes. Show minor gridlines for the Data axis. Clear the Auto Scale option.

5. Change the Title to L11.8 3D Riser Chart.
   Change the Subtitle to Last Year's Sales >= 35,000. Click OK and save the changes. The chart should look like the one shown in Figure 11-43.

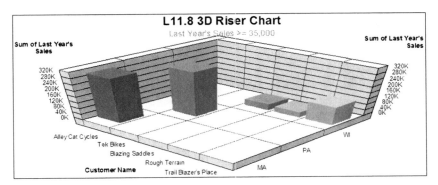

Figure 11-43 L11.8 3D Riser chart

Exercise 11.9: Create A 3D Surface Chart

In this exercise you will create a chart that shows a count of orders and order total amount by sales rep.

1. Save the L6.13 report as L11.9 3D Surface chart.

2. Select the 3D Surface honeycomb surface chart type, then select the Advanced layout option on the Data tab.

3. Add the Employee ID field to the first list, then add the Order Amount and Group 1 Count Of Orders.Order ID fields to the Show value(s) list.

4. Add a major gridline to all axes.

5. Change the Viewing angle on the Options tab to **MAX VIEW**.

6. Add the Title L11.9 3D Surface Chart.
   Add the Subtitle Sum of orders by Sales Rep.
   Add the Footnote For 2001. Click OK and save the changes. The chart should look like the one shown in Figure 11-44.

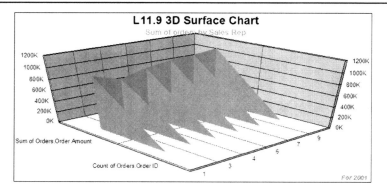

Figure 11-44 L11.9 3D Surface chart

Exercise 11.10: Create An XY Scatter Chart

In this exercise you will create a chart that plots the number of orders in 2001 by month and total dollar amount.

1. Save the L6.7 report as L11.10 XY Scatter chart.

2. Select the XY Scatter chart type, then select the Advanced layout option.

3. Add the Order Date field to the first list, then add the Group 1 Distinct Count Of Orders.Order ID and Order Amount fields to the Show value(s) list.

4. On the Options tab change the Marker shape to **DIAMOND**.

5. Change the Title to L11.10 XY Scatter Chart.
   Add the Subtitle 2001 Orders By Month. Click OK and save the changes. The chart should look like the one shown in Figure 11-45. As you can see, the markers are not diamond shaped. This option does not seem to work on the Chart Expert. You will learn how to fix this later in this lesson. If your report has diamond markers, there was a software update after this book was published.

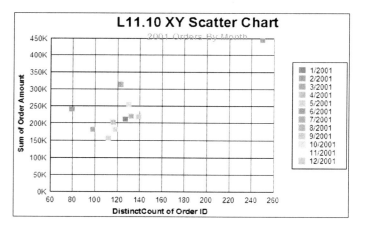

Figure 11-45 L11.10 XY Scatter chart

Exercise 11.11: Show The Bottom 20% Of Orders

In the exercise that you just completed, the chart plotted the data for all 12 months. If the marketing department wanted to create a campaign to increase sales in the months that had the lowest number of sales, it could be difficult to tell which months fall into that category. If the chart was modified to only display the months that are in the bottom 20% of sales based on the total order amount by month, the chart would be easier for the marketing department to use.

You have already created a report that displayed the top five orders for a month. To create a report for the bottom 20% is very similar.

1. Save the L11.10 report as `L11.11 Bottom 20 percent chart`.

2. Right-click on the chart and select Chart Expert, then click on the Data tab.

3. Click on the Order Date field on the top list on the right, then click the **TOP N** button.

4. Open the Group Sort drop-down list and select **BOTTOM PERCENTAGE**. Change the Percentage field to `20`, then check the **INCLUDE TIES** option. The options that are shown in Figure 11-46 will display the months that are in the bottom 20%, based on the number of orders placed that month. Click OK.

5. Change the Title to `L11.11 Bottom 20% Of Orders`.
   Delete the Subtitle.
   Change the Group title to `Number of orders`.
   Change the Data title to `Total monthly order amount`. Click OK and save the changes.
   The chart should look like the one shown in Figure 11-47.

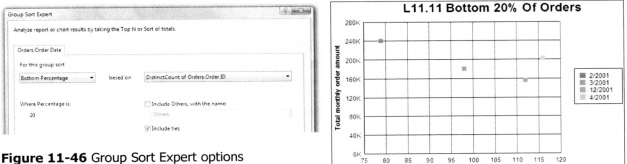

Figure 11-46 Group Sort Expert options

Figure 11-47 L11.11 Bottom 20 percent chart

If you create a Top N report and do not add the records on the report that do not meet the Top N criteria to the "Others" group option, any grand total fields that are placed in the report footer will include totals for all records that meet the report criteria, whether or not they appear on the report. This means that if the records that do not meet the Top N criteria are not added to the "Others" option, the report grand totals will not be accurate because they will include amounts for detail records that are not on the report. This may not be what you want. If you only want the grand totals to include records that print on the report, in this case the Top N records, you have to create running total fields and place them in the report footer instead of summary fields.
[See Lesson 13, Running Totals]

Exercise 11.12: Create A Radar Chart

In this exercise you will create a chart that plots the order totals in 2001 by quarter.

1. Save the L6.11 report as `L11.12 Radar chart`.

2. Select the Radar chart type, then select the Group layout option, if it is not already selected.

3. Select the Sum of Orders.Order Amount field in the Show drop-down list.

4. Check the Show value option, then select the circle Marker shape.

5. Change the Title to `L11.12 Radar Chart`.
Add the Subtitle `Sum of 2001 Orders By Quarter`. Click OK and save the changes.
The chart should look like the one shown in Figure 11-48. This is a good example of not selecting the appropriate chart type for the data. This chart is somewhat hard to read.

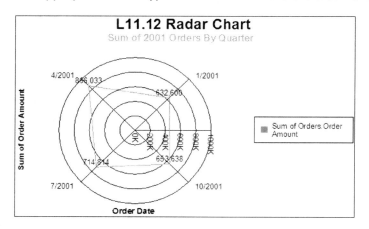

Figure 11-48 L11.12 Radar chart

Exercise 11.13: Create A Bubble Chart

In this exercise you will create a chart that plots the orders between 6/1/2001 and 6/15/2001. Even though the Bubble chart is similar to the XY Scatter chart, the Bubble chart requires three fields in the Show value(s) list.

1. Save the L7.2 report as `L11.13 Bubble chart`.

2. Change the Order Date selection criteria to between 6/1/2001 and 6/15/2001, then delete the Order Amount criteria.

3. Select the Bubble chart type.

4. Add the Order Date to the first list, then add the Order Amount field to the Show value(s) list.

5. Add the Order ID field to the Show value(s) list. Click on the field, then click the Set Summary Operation button. Change the summary type to Count and click OK.

6. Add the Order Amount field to the Show value(s) list again. Click on the field, then click the Set Summary Operation button. Change the summary type to Average and click OK.

7. Add a major gridline to the Group axis option.

8. Change the Title to `L11.13 Bubble Chart`.
Add the Subtitle `For orders between 6/1/2001 and 6/15/2001`, then click OK. Save the changes. The chart should look like the one shown in Figure 11-49.

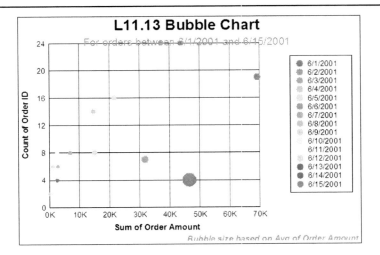

Figure 11-49 L11.13 Bubble chart

Exercise 11.14: Create A Stock Chart

The stock report that you will create will show the average order amount for five regions and the largest order in each region. Stock charts plot minimum and maximum values. The average value will be used as the minimum value and the largest order amount will be used as the maximum value.

The reason that I am using the average value for the minimum is because the lowest value would touch the bottom of the chart which defeats the purpose of the exercise of showing you how a stock chart really does look different then a bar chart.

Create The Selection Criteria

1. Create a new report and save it as L11.14 Stock chart. Add the Customer and Orders tables to the report.

2. On the Links tab the tables should be joined on the Customer ID field. If they aren't, create the link by clicking on the Customer ID field in the Orders table and dragging it to the Customer ID field in the Customer table. To make sure that link is correct, right-click on the link between the tables and select **LINK OPTIONS**. You will see the dialog box shown in Figure 11-50. Make sure that the link is exactly like the one illustrated. Close both dialog boxes.

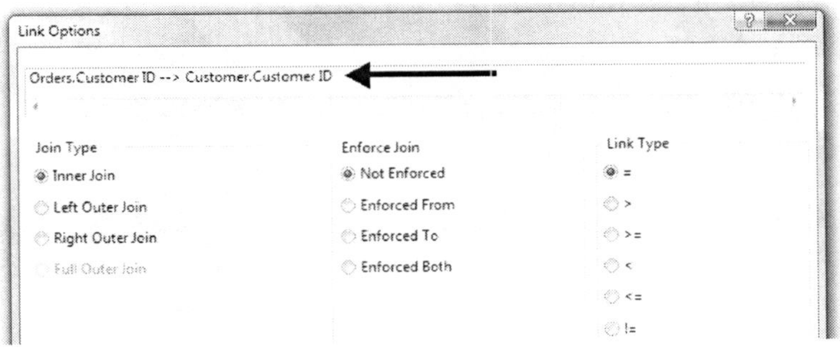

Figure 11-50 Link Options dialog box

3. Create selection criteria to only include customers in the following regions: MA, PA, AL, ID, WI.

Create The Chart

1. Open the Chart Expert and select the Stock High-Low stock chart.

2. Add the Region field to the first list.

3. Add the Order Amount field to the Show value(s) list. Click on the field, then click the Set Summary Operation button. Change the summary type to Maximum, then click OK.

4. Add the Order Amount field to the Show value(s) list again. Click on the field, then click the Set Summary Operation button. Change the summary type to Average, then click OK.

5. Check the Show value option. Do not display a legend.

6. Change the Title to `L11.14 Stock Chart`.
    Add the Subtitle `Avg & Max order amounts for 5 states`. Click OK and save the changes. The chart should look like the one shown in Figure 11-51.

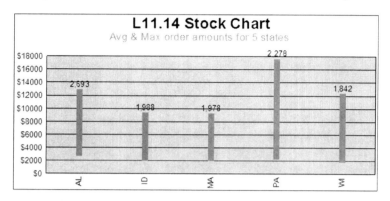

Figure 11-51 L11.14 Stock chart

Exercise 11.15: Create A Numeric Axis Chart

In this exercise you will create a chart that displays the sum of orders for one company during a specific date range. You will use the options on the Chart Sort Order dialog box to set the frequency of the On Change Of option.

Create The Report

1. Create a new report and save it as `L11.15 Numeric Axis chart`. Add the Customer and Orders tables to the report. Make sure the tables are linked liked they were in Exercise 11.14.

2. Create selection criteria for the Order Date field. The dates should be between 6/1/2001 and 6/7/2001. Create selection criteria that limits the report to only display information for the customer, To The Limit Biking Co.

3. Add the Order Date and Order Amount fields to the details section. Delete the date field from the page header section if it's there.

4. Change the format of the Order Date field to XX/XX/XXXX, then sort the Order Date field in ascending order.

Create The Chart

1. Open the Chart Expert. Select the Numeric Axis - Date axis bar chart type.

2. Add the Order Date field to the first list. Click on the field, then click the **ORDER** button.
    Make sure the last option on the Chart Sort Order dialog box is set to **FOR EACH DAY**, then click OK.

3. Add the Order Amount field to the Show value(s) list.

4. Add a minor gridline to the Data axis option.

5. Check the Show value option, then select the $1 Number format.

6. Change the Title to L11.15 Numeric Axis Chart.
   Add the subtitle To The Limit Biking Co - June 2001. Click OK and save the changes. The chart should look like the one shown in Figure 11-52.

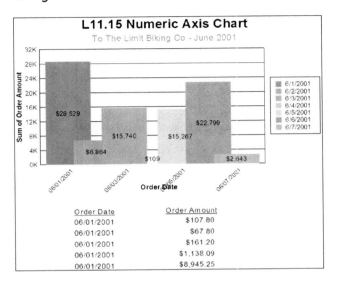

Figure 11-52 L11.15 Numeric Axis chart

Exercise 11.16: Create A Gauge Chart

In Lesson 10 you read how to create a report that displayed the words True or False in a Boolean field based on the employees salary. [See Lesson 10, Boolean Formulas] This was done to keep the employees actual salary private. In this exercise you will create a chart that will plot how many employees salaries are greater than 50K.

1. Save the L10 With a Boolean suppression formula report as L11.16 Gauge chart.
   This report is one that I created and is in the zip file that you downloaded.

2. Select the Gauge chart type.

3. Add the **BOOLEAN_STYLE** formula field to the first list, then add the Employee ID field to the Show value(s) list.

4. Click on the Employee ID field, then click the Set Summary Operation button. Change the summary type to Count and click OK.

5. Change the Title to L11.16 Gauge Chart.
   Add the Subtitle Employee salary over 50K. Click OK and save the changes. The chart should look like the one shown in Figure 11-53. The company has 15 employees. If you look at the needles on the chart, you will see that when added together, they equal 15.

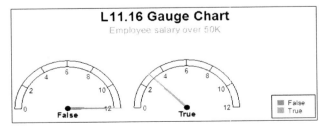

Figure 11-53 L11.16 Gauge chart

Exercise 11.17: Create A Gantt Chart

In Lesson 9 you created a report that calculated how many days it took to ship the customer orders. Gantt charts require a start and end date. In this exercise you will use the order date as the start date and the ship date as the end date.

The L9.10 Calculate order processing time report currently only has criteria that the order date is greater than or equal to a specific date. The Gantt chart would not be readable if all of the records that are currently on the report were displayed on the chart. To make the chart readable, you will select a few Order ID numbers to display on the chart.

1. Save the L9.10 report as `L11.17 Gantt chart`.

2. Create selection criteria that limits the report to the following Order ID numbers from the Orders Detail table: 1, 1015, 1020, 1069 and 1090.

3. Change the order date criteria to 6/24/2000.

4. Open the Chart Expert and select the Gantt chart layout.

5. Select the **FOR EACH RECORD** option from the drop-down list on the Data tab, then add the Customer Name field to the first list.

6. Add the Order Date and Ship Date fields to the Show value(s) list.

7. Add the Title `L11.17 Gantt Chart`. Add the Subtitle `Delay in shipping`. Click OK. Save the changes and refresh the data. The chart should look like the one shown in Figure 11-54.

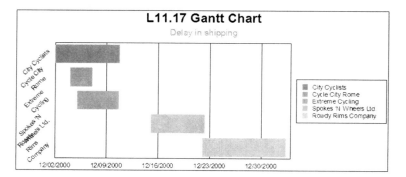

Figure 11-54 L11.17 Gantt chart

Exercise 11.18: Create A Funnel Chart

In this exercise you will create a chart that will display the daily order totals for the top five order days in June 2001.

1. Save the L7.8 report as `L11.18 Funnel chart`.

2. Delete the existing chart, then open the Chart Expert.

3. Select the Funnel chart type, then select the Advanced layout option.

4. Add the Order Date field to the first list, then add the Order Amount field to the Show value(s) list.

5. Change the Legend layout option to **BOTH**.

6. Change the Title to L11.18 Funnel Chart.
    Add the Subtitle With total order amounts by day.
    Add the Footnote For the top 5 order days in June 2001. Click OK and save the
    changes. The chart should look like the one shown in Figure 11-55. Leave the report open to
    complete the next exercise.

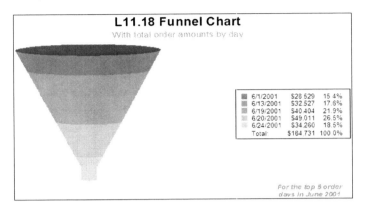

Figure 11-55 L11.18 Funnel chart

Exercise 11.19: Modify The Funnel Chart

In the previous exercise, the legend displayed the daily order total and the percent. The chart may be
easier to read if it also had information. In this exercise you will display the order date and the number
of orders per day next to each bar on the chart.

1. Save the L11.18 report as L11.19 Modified Funnel chart.

2. Open the Chart Expert for the existing chart.

3. Delete the Order Amount field from the Show value(s) list and add the Order ID field to the
    Show value(s) list.

4. Click on the Sum Of Orders.Order ID field, then click the Set Summary Operation button.
    Change the summary type to Count and click OK.

5. Check the Show label and Show value options, then change the Legend layout option to
    Percentage.

6. Change the Title to L11.19 Funnel Chart.
    Change the Subtitle to With total number of orders per day.
    Click OK and save the changes. The chart should look like the one shown in Figure 11-56.

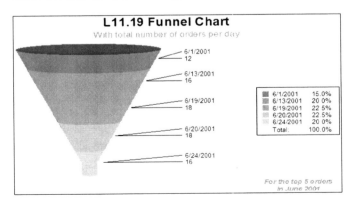

Figure 11-56 L11.19 Modified Funnel chart

Exercise 11.20: Create Charts From Cross-Tab Data

Charts that are created from cross-tab data are often easier to create because the data has already been summarized. In this exercise you will create three charts and save them in the same report. Often, cross-tab data is stored in the report header. I find it easier to create additional report header sections and place each report in it's own section. That keeps the charts from overlapping when the report is viewed or printed.

Add More Report Header Sections

1. Save the L7.10 report as `L11.20 Cross-Tab data charts`.

2. Open the Section Expert and add three more report header sections.

Create The Quantity Sold By Product Type Chart

1. Right-click in the report header b section and insert a chart. Select the Side by side bar chart type and Horizontal position option.

2. Make sure that the On Change Of option on the Cross-Tab layout window has the Product Type Name field selected. The Subdivided By field should be set to None and the Show drop-down list should have the Quantity count field selected.

3. Check the Show value option on the Options tab.

4. Change the Title to `Qty Sold By Product Type`.
   Add the Footnote `Report Header B`.
   Change the Group title to `Product Type`.
   Change the Data title to `Qty Sold`. Click OK and save the changes. The chart should look like the one shown in Figure 11-57.

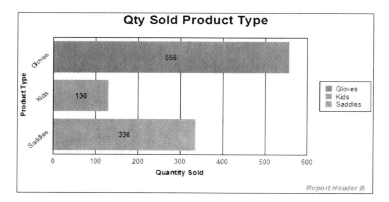

Figure 11-57 L11.20 Quantity sold by product type chart (Report Header B)

Create The Quantity Sold By Product Type By Sales Rep Chart

The chart that you just created provides a high level overview of how many of each product type was sold. The numbers shown represent the totals across the bottom of the cross-tab. [See Lesson 7, Figure 7-34] The chart that you will create in this part of the exercise will display how many of each product type was sold by each sales rep.

1. Right-click in the report header c section and insert a chart. Select the Stacked bar chart type and Horizontal position option.

2. Select the Employee Last Name field in the Subdivided By drop-down list on the Cross-Tab data layout window.

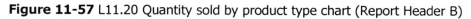

3. Add a major gridline to the Group axis option, then check the Show value option on the Options tab.

4. Change the Title to `Product Type & Qty Sold By Sales Rep`.
   Add the Footnote `Report Header C`.
   Change the Group title to `Product Type`.
   Change the Data title to `Qty Sold`. Click OK and save the changes. The chart should look like the one shown in Figure 11-58. What you will notice is that each block on the chart is a running total, meaning that the sales rep Dodsworth did not have 186 glove sales. Instead, the sales rep sold the difference between 186 and 85 gloves.

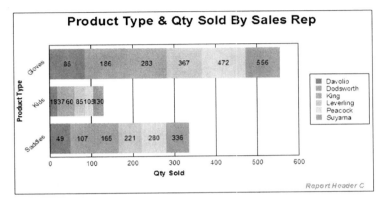

Figure 11-58 L11.20 Product type & Quantity Sold By Sales Rep chart (Report Header C)

Create The Percent Of Quantity Sold Chart

The chart that you will create in this part of the exercise will display the total quantity of products each sales rep sold and what percent of the total product quantity their sales represent.

1. Right-click in the report header d section and insert a chart. Select the Pie chart type with visual 3D effect option.

2. Add the Employee Last Name field to the first list on the Advanced tab. Add the Quantity field to the Show value(s) list, then change the summary type to Count.

3. Check the Show label and Show value options, then change the Legend layout option to Percentage. Explode the largest slice of the pie.

4. Change the Title to `Percent Of Qty Sold`.
   Add the Subtitle `The #'s on the chart represent the qty`.
   Add the Footnote `Report Header D`. Click OK and save the changes. The chart is on page 2 and should look like the one shown in Figure 11-59.

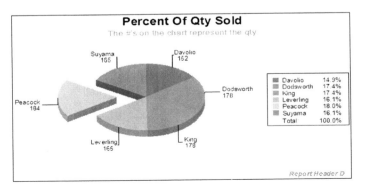

Figure 11-59 L11.20 Percent of Quantity Sold chart (Report Header D)

Exercise 11.21: Create A Color Highlighting Chart

In this exercise you will create a chart that will change the color of the bars on the chart to red, if the delay in ship time is greater than or equal to seven days or yellow if the delay in ship time is between four and six days. To reduce the number of order days to something that will make the chart readable, you will add selection criteria to the report.

1. Save the L9.10 report as L11.21 Highlighted chart.

2. Add selection criteria to the report so that only orders with an order date between 12/02/2001 and 12/05/2001 will appear on the report.

3. Add selection criteria to the report to only display orders that have a delay in days to ship greater than or equal to two.

4. Select the Side by side bar chart type with visual 3D effect option.

5. Add the Order ID field to the first list, then add the Days To Ship formula field to the Show value(s) list.

6. Change the Title to L11.21 Color highlighting chart.
    Add the Subtitle Yellow = 4-6 day delay, Red = 7+ day delay.
    Add the Footnote Orders between 12/2/2001 & 12/5/2001.
    Change the Group title to Order Number.
    Change the Data title to Delay In Days To Ship.
    Leave the Chart Expert open to complete the next part of the exercise.

Add The Color Highlighting To The Chart

In this part of the exercise you will create the criteria that will change the colors of the bars on the chart to red or yellow depending on the value in the Delay in Days To Ship field.

1. On the Options tab click the Format button, then click the New button.

2. Open the first drop-down list and select the Delay in Days To Ship field, then open the second drop-down list and select Is greater than or equal to. Type a 7 in the last field.

3. Select Red as the Format color, then click the New button.

4. Open the first drop-down list and select the Delay in Days To Ship field, then open the second drop-down list and select Is between. Type a 4 in the first field and a 6 in the last field.

5. Select Yellow as the Format color. Click OK twice to close both dialog boxes and save the changes. The chart should look like the one shown in Figure 11-60.

The second, third, sixth and seventh bars should be red.

The fourth and fifth bars should be yellow.

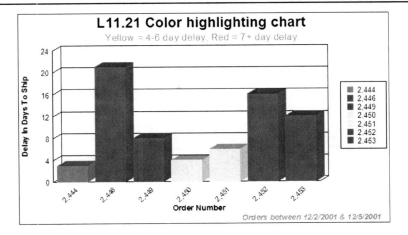

Figure 11-60 L11.21 Highlighted chart

Formatting And Editing Charts

There are a variety of techniques available to format and edit charts as a whole or individual parts of a chart, like the legend and axis titles. The majority of these options are on the Chart Options dialog box.

Exercise 11.22: Resizing Charts

Charts have the same sizing handles that images have. Like images, you can drag the chart to another section of the report or to a different location in the section that it is currently in.

Resize The Entire Chart

If the default size of the chart is too small or too large, you can resize the chart by following the steps below.

1. Save the L11.18 report as L11.22 Resized chart.

2. Click on the chart, then place the mouse pointer in the lower right corner of the chart and drag it to the 6 inch mark on the ruler. Save the changes.

 You can place the mouse pointer any place on the highlighted border of the chart to resize the chart in any direction that you need.

As you saw earlier in Figure 11-55, the text in the footnote was cut off. There is no way to select an individual object on the chart and resize it. The only solution is to make the chart wider or longer as shown in Figure 11-61.

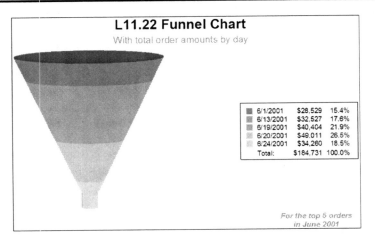

Figure 11-61 L11.22 Resized chart

More Chart Types

As mentioned earlier in this lesson there are more chart types then the ones on the Type tab on the Chart Expert. If you want to apply a different chart type, follow the steps below.

1. Right-click on the chart in a report that you want to change and select Chart Options ⇒ Template. Click on the Custom tab. You should see the dialog box shown in Figure 11-62.

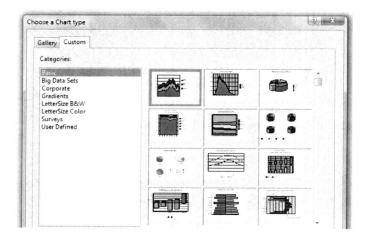

Figure 11-62 Choose a Chart type dialog box

2. Click on a category on the left to view the chart types, then select the chart type that you want to use on the right and click OK.

3. Customize the chart as needed.

Exercise 11.23: Using The Underlay Following Sections Option

As you learned in Lesson 10, this option will let you place the content in one section of the report next to the content in the section below it. In this exercise you will apply this option so that the chart will print next to the data that it represents. This is often used with charts that are in the group header section of a report so that the records in the details section will print next to the chart.

The **UNDERLAY FOLLOWING SECTIONS** option on the Section Expert is better suited for reports that do not have a lot of fields in the details section. If you cannot get the chart and the fields in the details section to fit, you can select the landscape print option to have more space across the page.

In Exercise 11.2 you copied a chart to the group footer section. You will modify this report and apply the Underlay option to the group header section.

1. Save the L11.2 report as L11.23 Chart with underlay option.

2. Delete the group name field in the group header section.

3. Copy the chart in the group footer 1b section to the group header section and place it as far left as possible. Delete the chart in the group footer 1b section.

4. Resize the chart so that it ends at the 3.5 inch mark on the ruler.

5. Change the Title to L11.23 Chart With Underlay Option.

6. Change the format of the Order Date field to only display the date.

7. Move the fields in the details and group footer 1a sections over to the right so that they are on the right of the chart as shown in Figure 11-63.

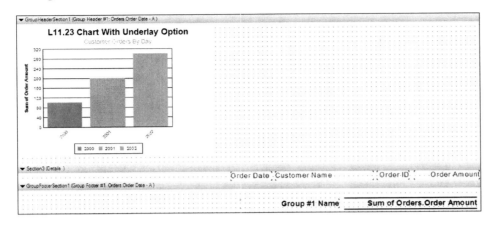

Figure 11-63 Modified details and group footer layout

8. Open the Section Expert and apply the **UNDERLAY FOLLOWING SECTIONS** option to the group header section. Delete the group footer 1b section. Click OK and save the changes. The chart should look like the one shown in Figure 11-64.

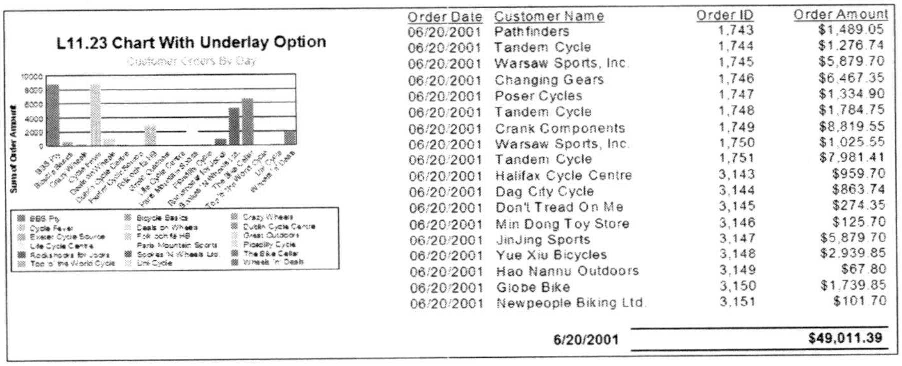

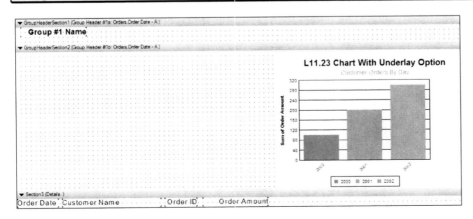

Figure 11-64 L11.23 Chart with the Underlay option applied

If there is information in the group header section that you do not want to include in the underlay, create another group header section and place the chart in the new group header section as shown in Figure 11-65. You would still apply the underlay option to the group header section with the chart. The report would look like the one shown in Figure 11-66. Notice that the information in the first group header section (the Group #1 Name field) did not move.

Figure 11-65 L11.23 Sample report layout for the chart in it's own group header section

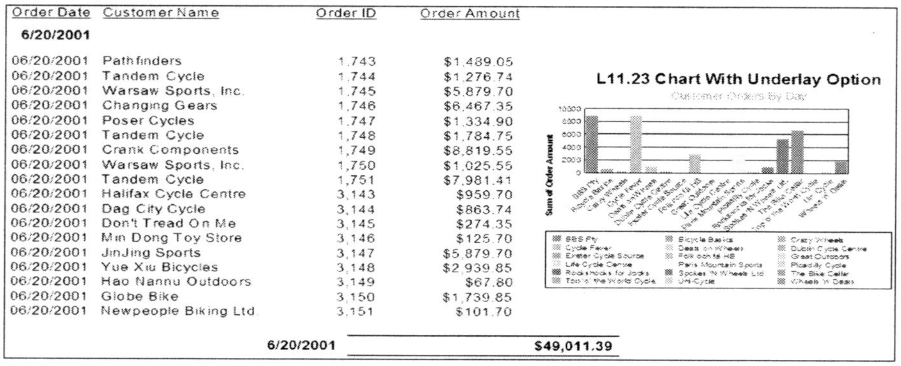

Order Date	Customer Name	Order ID	Order Amount
6/20/2001			
06/20/2001	Pathfinders	1,743	$1,489.05
06/20/2001	Tandem Cycle	1,744	$1,276.74
06/20/2001	Warsaw Sports, Inc.	1,745	$5,879.70
06/20/2001	Changing Gears	1,746	$6,467.35
06/20/2001	Poser Cycles	1,747	$1,334.90
06/20/2001	Tandem Cycle	1,748	$1,784.75
06/20/2001	Crank Components	1,749	$8,819.55
06/20/2001	Warsaw Sports, Inc.	1,750	$1,025.55
06/20/2001	Tandem Cycle	1,751	$7,981.41
06/20/2001	Halifax Cycle Centre	3,143	$959.70
06/20/2001	Dag City Cycle	3,144	$863.74
06/20/2001	Don't Tread On Me	3,145	$274.35
06/20/2001	Min Dong Toy Store	3,146	$125.70
06/20/2001	JinJing Sports	3,147	$5,879.70
06/20/2001	Yue Xiu Bicycles	3,148	$2,939.85
06/20/2001	Hao Nannu Outdoors	3,149	$67.80
06/20/2001	Globe Bike	3,150	$1,739.85
06/20/2001	Newpeople Biking Ltd	3,151	$101.70
	6/20/2001		**$49,011.39**

Figure 11-66 L11.23 Sample report with chart in it's own group header section

Chart Options Dialog Box

The options on this dialog box pick up where the options on the Chart Expert leave off. I would like to see the following dialog boxes added to the Chart Expert: Chart Options, Choose A Chart and Numeric Axis Grids and Scales. I think that would make creating and modifying charts easier.

Depending on the chart type, you will see slightly different options on the Chart Options dialog box. The options let you change the overall look of the chart. What I like most about the Chart Options dialog box is that you can see what your changes will look like without having to preview the report. This is very helpful when you need to experiment with several options. To open the dialog box right-click on the chart and select Chart Options ⇒ General. Many of the options on this dialog box are also on the Chart Expert.

Many of the options on the Chart Options dialog box are the same as the ones on the Chart Expert. The figures that follow show the tabs that you are most likely to use.

General Tab

The options on this tab effect the general look of the chart. Figures 11-67 to 11-69 show the appearance options for three types of charts.

In Exercise 11.10 you created an XY Scatter chart and were expecting the markers to have a diamond shape. If you want to change the markers shape, open the report, then open the Chart Options dialog box and select Diamond from the Shape drop-down list.

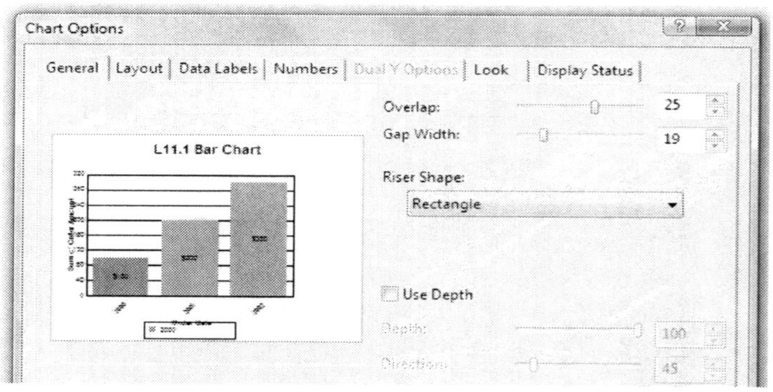

Figure 11-67 Bar chart general tab options

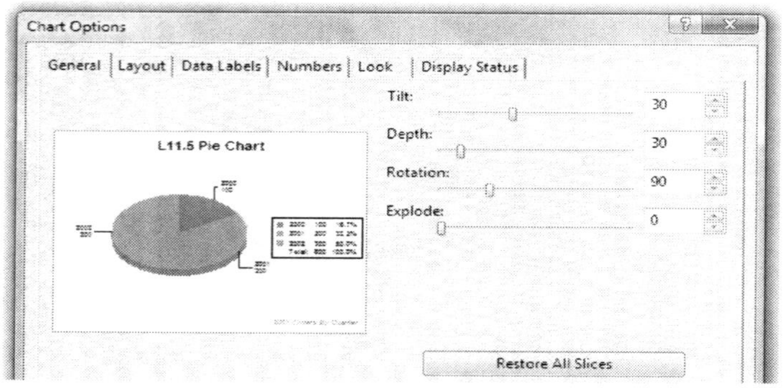

Figure 11-68 Pie chart general tab options

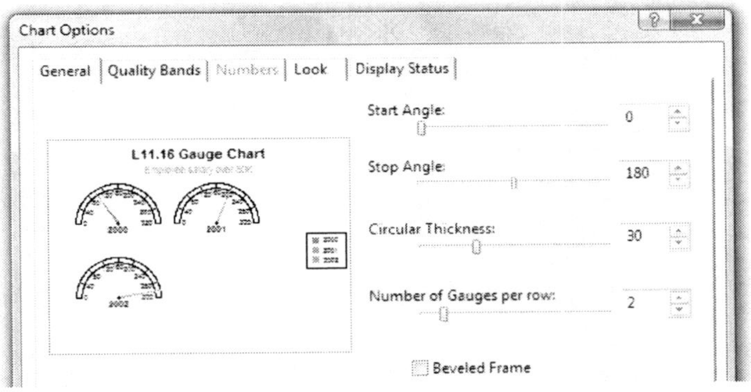

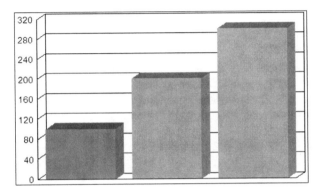

Figure 11-69 Gauge chart general tab options

Use Depth This option is on the Bar chart general tab. If checked, this option will display the chart in 3D format, as shown in Figure 11-70.

Figure 11-70 Use Depth option applied to a chart

Layout Tab

The options shown in Figure 11-71 let you add or modify the appearance of the chart type. For example, in the figure a 3D bar chart is shown. Selecting the Stacked option will change the chart so that it looks like the one shown in Figure 11-72.

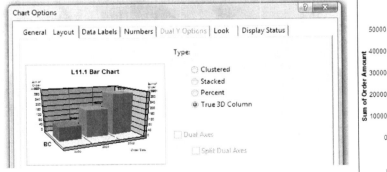

Figure 11-71 Layout tab options

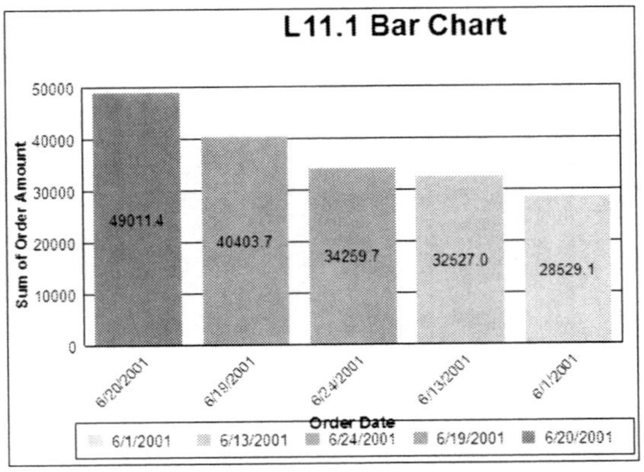

Figure 11-72 Stacked layout option

Data Labels Tab

The options shown in Figure 11-73 let you add data labels to the chart, change the location of the labels and what the label will display.

The options displayed on this tab depend on the options selected on the Layout tab.

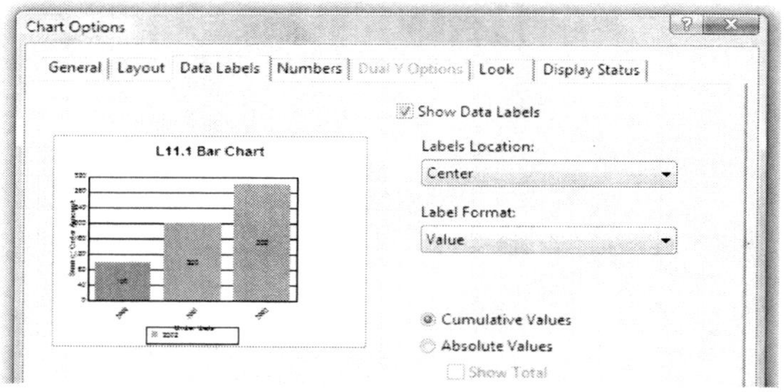

Figure 11-73 Data Labels tab options

Numbers Tab

The options shown in Figure 11-74 let you format the numbers on the chart. The category drop-down list lets you select the type of number that you want to format.

Figure 11-75 shows the Date formats.

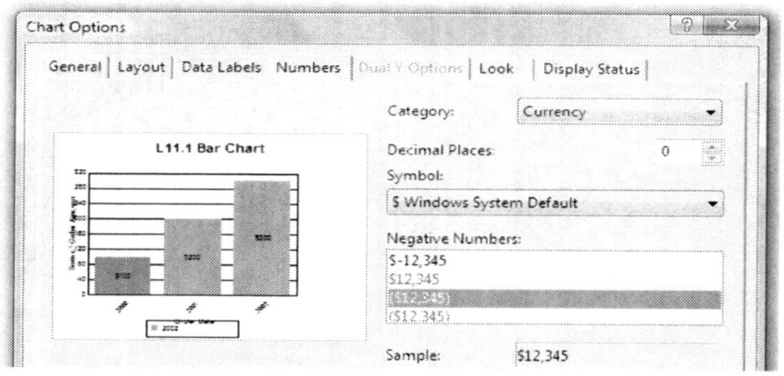

Figure 11-74 Currency format options

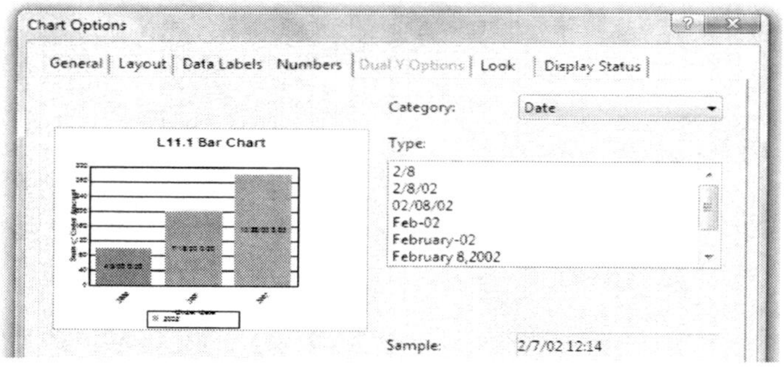

Figure 11-75 Date format options

Dual Y Options Tab

The options shown in Figure 11-76 let you add a second set of data to the report. The L11.10 XY Scatter chart that you created will let you use these options. To enable this tab, check the **DUAL AXES** option on the Layout tab. This chart is currently plotting data for only one year. If you want to plot data for another year, select it from the Secondary (Y2) Axis list.

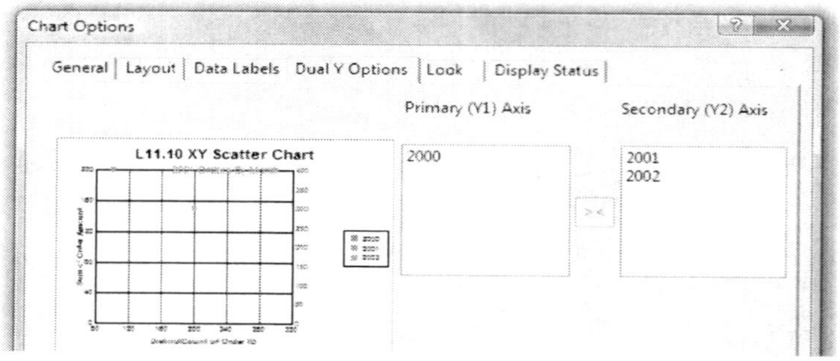

Figure 11-76 Dual Y Options tab options

Look Tab

The options shown in Figure 11-77 let you modify the legend and change the color of the items in the legend.

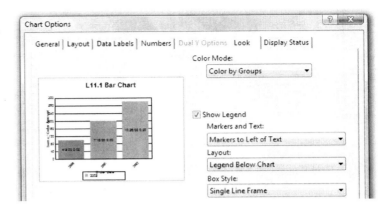

Figure 11-77 Look tab options

Display Status Tab

The options shown in Figure 11-78 let you add and remove major and minor gridlines for the group and data axis. You can also select whether or not to display the legend or data labels.

Figure 11-78 Display Status tab options

Other Chart Options Menu Items

In addition to the Chart Options dialog box, the following options are also available to modify a chart.

① **TEMPLATE** opens the Gallery tab of the Choose A Chart Type dialog box, as shown in Figure 11-79.
② **TITLES** opens the dialog box shown in Figure 11-80.
③ **GRID** opens the dialog box shown in Figure 11-81.

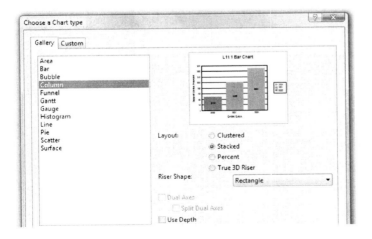

Figure 11-79 Chart type gallery options

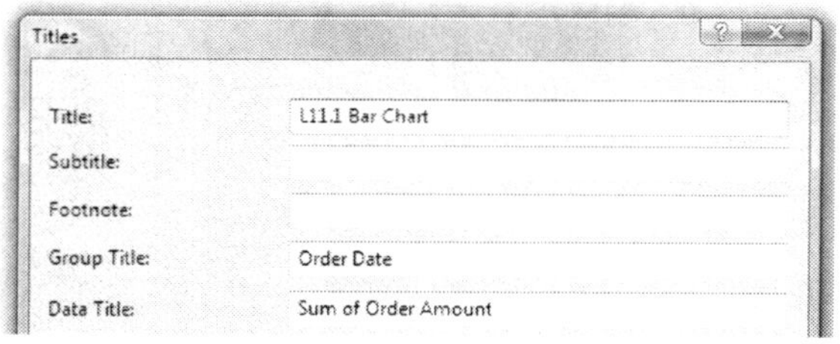

Figure 11-80 Titles dialog box

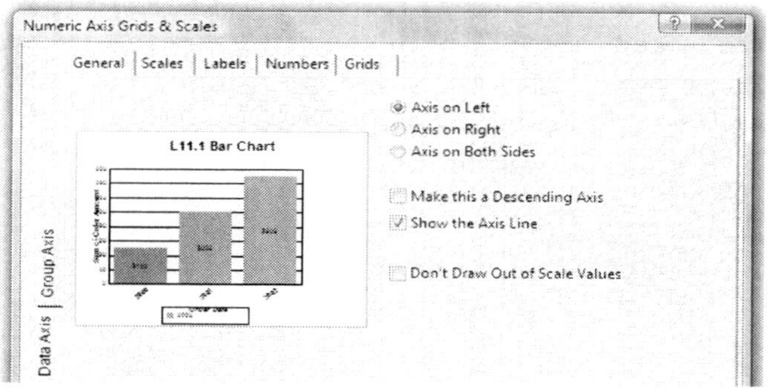

Figure 11-81 Numeric Axis Grids & Scales dialog box

Customizing 3D Charts

As you saw earlier in Figure 11-68, the General tab options let you tilt and rotate charts. If you want or need more 3D chart formatting options, right-click on a chart like the 3D Surface or 3D Riser chart and select Chart Options ⇒ Viewing Angle. You will see the dialog box shown in Figure 11-82.

You can scroll through the list of viewing angles to find one that you like. If clicked, the **ADVANCED OPTIONS** button displays additional options that let you customize the viewing angle even more, as shown in Figure 11-83. You can also view the Preset Viewing Angles on the left by clicking on the forward and backward (VCR style) buttons below the chart thumbnail and to the left of the Duplicate button. Another way to view them is by opening the drop-down list under the chart thumbnail. The options on the **ROTATE, PAN, WALLS** and **MORE** tabs allow you to customize additional 3D options.

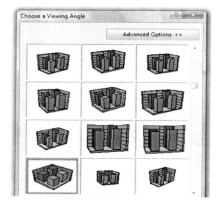

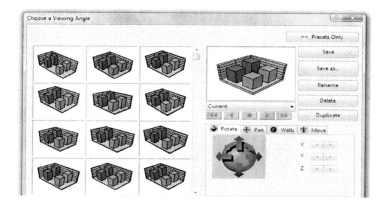

Figure 11-82 Choose A Viewing Angle dialog box

Figure 11-83 Advanced viewing angle customization options

> If you make any manual changes to a viewing angle, you will be prompted to save the changes with a new viewing angle preset name when you click OK. Entering a name on this dialog box will let you save a new viewing angle or replace an existing one. You do not have to do this to apply the changes that you have selected on the Choose a Viewing Angle dialog box. If you want to apply the changes to the chart without saving them as a viewing angle, click the Cancel button on the **ENTER 3D VIEWING ANGLE PRESET NAME** dialog box shown in Figure 11-84 and the changes will still be applied to the chart.

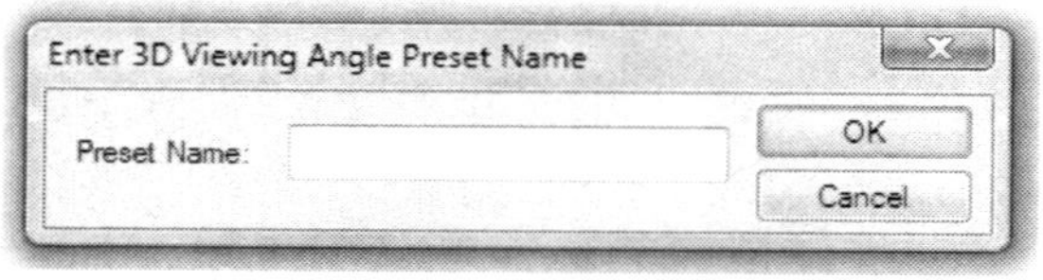

Figure 11-84 Enter 3D Viewing Angle Preset Name dialog box

Test Your Skills

1. Create a new report that includes the following information for a chart. It should look like the one shown in Figure 11-85.

   - Save the report as L11.24 Skills bar chart.
   - Add the Customer and Orders tables to the report.
   - Create a side by side horizontal bar chart. Apply the Use depth effect on the Chart Options dialog box.
   - Use the Region field as the On Change Of option.
   - Use the Last Year's Sales and Order Amount fields as the Show value(s) options.
   - Add the Title L11.24 Skills Bar Chart. Use the font size 14, no bold and the Comic Sans MS font. Add the Subtitle December 2000 Orders.
   - Add major gridlines to the Group and Data axis.
   - Use the Manual data axis option with an interval of 6.
   - Use the large Bar Size on the Options tab.
   - Only display orders in December 2000 that are in the CA, PA, NJ and WI regions.
   - Use the Numeric Axis Grids & Scales dialog box to change the Abbreviation option on the Numbers tab to thousands, no separator.

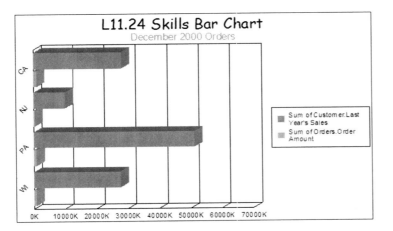

Figure 11-85 L11.24 Skills bar chart

2. Create a new report for a 3D Riser bar chart like the one shown in Figure 11-86.

   - Save the report as
     L11.25 Skills Orders for three shipping methods chart.
   - The chart should show the total order amount for orders between December 1-10, 2000 for these three shipping methods: Loomis, Purolator and Parcel Post.
   - Change the Title to L11.25 Skills Orders For 3 Shipping Methods. Change the Subtitle to December 1-10, 2000.
   - Display major gridlines for all axes.

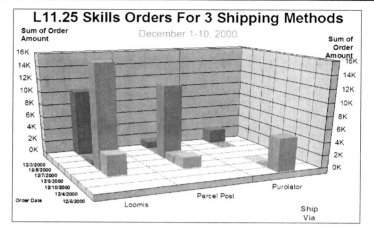

Figure 11-86 L11.25 Skills Orders for three shipping methods chart

3. Modify the L11.11 report. When finished, the report should look like the one shown in Figure 11-87.

- Save the report as L11.26 Skills Top 10 orders chart.
- Insert a group header section under the existing one and create a pie chart that shows the top 10 orders for the month.
- Show the values for each slice of the pie. Detach the smallest slice of the pie.
- Include any top 10 ties.
- Place the legend at the bottom of the chart.
- Use the $1 Number format.
- Change the Title to L11.26 Top 10 Orders For the Month. Change the font size to 9.
- Sort the detail records in descending order on the Order Amount field.

The first 10 orders that are shown in Figure 11-87 are the same records that are on the chart.

	Salesperson	Order Date	Order #	Order Amount
January				
Janet	Leverling	01/15/2001	1177	$10,886.79
Michael	Suyama	01/13/2001	1167	$9,353.30
Janet	Leverling	01/10/2001	1159	$8,910.95
Margaret	Peacock	01/23/2001	1225	$8,819.55
Anne	Dodsworth	01/27/2001	1232	$8,174.25
Anne	Dodsworth	01/23/2001	1222	$6,116.82
Margaret	Peacock	01/05/2001	1137	$6,040.95
Robert	King	01/15/2001	1181	$5,912.96
Janet	Leverling	01/08/2001	1151	$5,879.70
Michael	Suyama	01/18/2001	1197	$5,879.70
Nancy	Davolio	01/22/2001	1220	$5,879.70
Nancy	Davolio	01/23/2001	1223	$5,362.48
Anne	Dodsworth	01/22/2001	1221	$5,341.24
Janet	Leverling	01/02/2001	1123	$5,219.55
Nancy	Davolio	01/10/2001	1155	$5,219.55
Anne	Dodsworth	01/11/2001	1160	$5,219.55
Robert	King	01/28/2001	1241	$4,849.86
Robert	King	01/22/2001	1217	$4,602.90
Margaret	Peacock	01/30/2001	1246	$3,884.25
Anne	Dodsworth	01/02/2001	1126	$3,842.55
Nancy	Davolio	01/12/2001	1165	$3,712.60
Robert	King	01/28/2001	1240	$3,635.34
Michael	Suyama	01/30/2001	1245	$3,419.25

L11.26 Top 10 Orders For The Month

$5,879.70	18.1%
$5,219.55	16.1%
$10,886.79	11.2%
$9,353.30	9.6%
$8,910.95	9.1%
$8,819.55	9.0%
$8,174.25	8.4%
$6,116.82	6.3%
$6,040.95	6.2%
$5,912.96	6.1%
Total	100.0%

Figure 11-87 L11.26 Skills Top 10 orders chart

PARAMETER FIELDS

Parameter fields add interaction between the person running the report and the report. Parameter fields allow you to customize reports to better meet the users needs.

In this lesson you will learn how to do the following:

- ☑ Use the Create Parameter Field dialog box
- ☑ Create a list of static values for a parameter field
- ☑ Use parameter fields with the Select and Section Experts
- ☑ Create formulas for parameter fields

LESSON 12

Parameter Fields Overview

The reports that you have learned to create so far in this workbook did not require any input from the people that would run them. In Lesson 2 you learned that different users may need slightly different versions of the same report. Based on the report creation techniques that you have learned so far, especially the Select Expert, if one group of people needed to see a customer report for a specific date range and another group of people need to see the same report for specific customers, you would have to create two reports. This is the largest downside to only using the Select Expert to create selection criteria. Using parameter fields to pass data to the Select Expert, is a much better solution.

Think about this. If a user requested a report to only show data for one year, the date range would be entered as the criteria on the Select Expert. Now, the same user or a different user needs to see the same report, but for a different date range and specific customers. The easiest thing to do based on the report techniques that you have learned so far is to open the existing report and save it with a new file name and change the selection criteria to the new date range and add customer criteria. As you can see, this could get out of hand rather quickly. If the original report used parameter fields to get the criteria from the person running the report, the report could be used for any date range and any customer. Another thing to think about is maintaining all of these reports. If a field needs to be added, you would have to add the field to more than one report.

If you created two parameter fields for the report, one for a date range and another one to select customers, both groups of people could use the same report. A popular type of parameter field is one that passes data to the Select Expert. In addition to being able to pass data to the Select Expert, a parameter field can also pass data to conditional and other types of formulas. This allows the person running the report to have control over the records that will appear on the report without having to know how to use the Select Expert or how to create formulas. The reports that you create that have criteria on the Select Expert can be enhanced by using parameter fields in place of specific (hard coded) values from a table or the value that you type in the second drop-down list on the Select Expert. This would give the reports a lot more flexibility.

To help the person that will run a report that has parameter fields, you can include features like default values and drop-down lists. For example, if you were creating a parameter field that needed to allow the user to select a country, you could set a default country if the report is often run using a specific country. You could also create a drop-down list field that contains all of the countries and let the user select the country that they wanted to run the report for. In the workplace you may hear this drop-down list referred to as a **PICK LIST** when referencing a parameter field.

An example of a pick list and how to combine existing reports (which means less reports for you to create or maintain) would be the reports that you created in Exercises 5.1 and 5.2. The report in Exercise 5.1 used the Select Expert to only display customers in one region. The report that you created in Exercise 5.2 displayed customers in two regions. These reports could easily be combined with the use of a parameter field. What would you do if the user needed to run the reports that you created in Exercise 5.1 or 5.2 for different regions next week? Someone, probably you, would have to save the current report with a new name and change the selection criteria for the new regions.

How Do Parameter Fields Work?

When a report is run that has a parameter field you will be prompted to select options, which creates all or part of the criteria that is needed to run the report. The information that is gathered from the parameter fields is passed on to various portions of the report like the Select Expert or a formula. The data in the parameter field is used to run the report.

Like the Select Expert, parameter fields ask questions that will determine what data will be displayed on the report. Using parameter fields, the following questions can be answered: Which three months do you want to see the sales reps totals for? Which country do you want to see sales for? Which customers ordered hats in December?

In addition to using parameter fields to gather the report selection criteria, parameter fields can be used to customize and format the report. For example, parameter fields can be used to select the sorting or grouping options, which you will learn how to do in this lesson or highlight records that meet a certain condition. If a report has confidential information, one of the parameter fields can require the person running the report to enter their User ID by using a special field as the basis for a parameter field. Based on the User ID, parts of the report would be hidden.

While parameter fields are a good way to get input from the person running the report, they are not the best solution because they lack functionality that you may need. If you are a programmer, you can create a form in Visual Basic or Visual C++ for example, to get user input. This also allows you to create more validation rules.

The Create Parameter Field Dialog Box

Now that you know what parameter fields are and how they work, it is time to learn about the dialog box shown in Figure 12-1, which is used to create parameter fields.

Table 12-1 explains the options on the Create Parameter dialog box. Reports can and often do have more than one parameter field. Right-click on the Parameter Fields category in the Field Explorer, then select NEW to open the dialog box shown in Figure 12-1.

Figure 12-1 Create Parameter Field dialog box

Option	Description
Name	This option lets you name the parameter field. The name is how you would reference the parameter field. Try to use as descriptive a name as possible, while keeping the name as short as possible. You can use the name of the field in the table that the parameter field will query. You can also use the name of an existing formula. As you learned in Lesson 3, Crystal Reports adds a question mark to the beginning of parameter field names. [See Lesson 3, Field Type Symbols And Naming Conventions] (1)
Prompting Text	Enter text that tells the user what to enter or select in the parameter field.
Value Type	This option lets you select the data type for the parameter field. You should select the same data type as the field or data that the parameter field will be compared to. (1)
Allow multiple values	Lets the parameter field accept more than one value if the Discrete values option is selected. If this option and the Range Value(s) option is selected, more than one range can be entered in the parameter field.
Discrete value(s)	Only allows one value to be entered in the parameter field.
Range value(s)	Beginning and ending values must be entered for a range. This option is often used for a date range like the Is Between record selection operator.
Discrete and Range Values	Allows discrete or range values or both to be entered in the parameter field.
Allow editing of default values . . .	If this option is checked, it will allow the person running the report to select from default values and enter their own values.
Default Values button	This button opens the Set Default Values dialog box, which is explained later in this lesson.

Table 12-1 Create Parameter Field dialog box options explained

(1) This is a required option to create a parameter field.

Data Types

The data type that you select determines how the parameter field will be used in the report. For example, you cannot select a string data type to use for a parameter field that will be used in a comparison with a date/time field. Number, currency and string data types do not have the limitations that date, date/time and Boolean data types have.

Number and Currency data types can only use the numbers zero to nine and the minus sign. Any other values will generate an error message.

String data types can use all of the number data type options, plus letters and special characters.

Date And Time Data Types

Date fields, especially when used for a range as shown in Figure 12-2 may be the most used data type to limit the records that are on a report.

When you use the Select Expert to create criteria for a date field, you have several options including "Is greater than", "Is greater than or equal to" and "Is between". The Create Parameter Field dialog box does not have the same exact options in terms of their names.

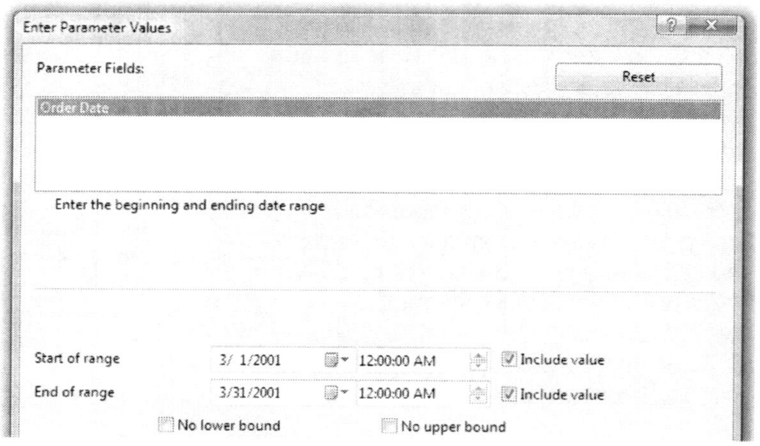

Figure 12-2 Date/Time parameter field options

The following three options will let you specify how to use dates on a parameter field. Figure 12-2 above, shows the options available for date/time parameter fields when the report is run.

   ① **INCLUDE VALUE** If checked, this option will include the date that is entered in the parameter field as part of the selection process. Checking this option on the Start of range field is the equivalent of the "Is greater than or equal to" Select Expert operator. Checking this option on the Start and End of range fields is the equivalent of the "Is between" Select Expert operator.

   ② **NO LOWER BOUND** If checked, the value in the Start of range field will not be used. (2)

   ③ **NO UPPER BOUND** If checked, the value in the End of range field will not be used. (2)

(2) You cannot select both of these options at the same time. If you type 1/1/05 in the Start of range field and 6/1/05 in the End of range field and clear the No lower bound option, all records that have a value that is less than the value in the End of range field will be included on the report, even though a date was entered in the Start of range field. If the No upper bound option is checked, all records that have a date greater than 1/1/05 will be included in the report.

If you need to create a date range, you have to select the **RANGE VALUE(S)** option on the Create Parameter Field dialog box. By default, this option is not selected because the **DISCRETE VALUE(S)** option is the default. These two options are mutually exclusive, meaning that only one of them can be selected for the parameter field.

Boolean Parameter Fields

Boolean parameter fields are very similar to the Boolean formulas that you learned how to create in Lesson 10. Like Boolean formulas, Boolean parameter fields are used with a Boolean field in a table, which has one of two values: True or False.

Figure 12-3 shows the options that are available for Boolean parameter fields. In addition to being able to select a default value of true or false for the Boolean parameter field, you can enter a description for the true and false options. The description should help the person running the report decide which option is appropriate for the report.

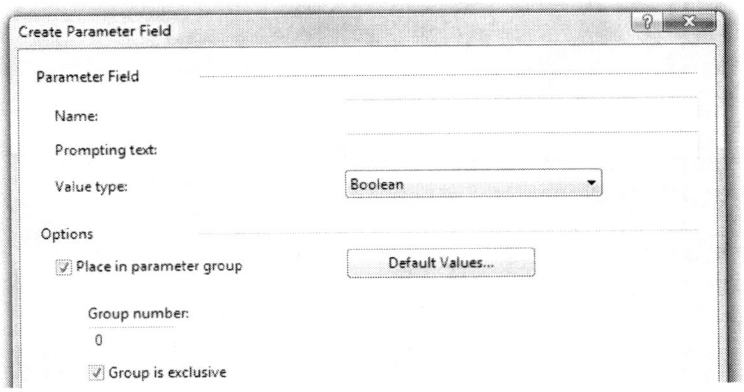

Figure 12-3 Boolean parameter field options

The **PLACE IN PARAMETER GROUP** option if checked, lets you include the parameter field as part of a group.

The **GROUP NUMBER** option allows you to add the Boolean parameter field to a group of other Boolean parameter fields. Creating a Boolean group will remind you of a group of radio buttons that you have probably seen on dialog boxes in other applications, like the print range options on the dialog box shown in Figure 12-4.

The number that you enter in the field is the Boolean group that the parameter field that you are creating or editing should be associated with. If the report has five Boolean fields and two are needed to create one Boolean group, you would enter the same number in this field for these two parameter fields. The three options in Figure 12-4 would have the same Boolean group number.

This is similar to how summary fields appear on the Data tab of the Chart Expert, as shown in Figure 12-5. Notice how there are three fields that are in the Group #1 section and three fields in the Group #2 section. That would be the equivalent of two Boolean groups.

The **GROUP IS EXCLUSIVE** option shown above in Figure 12-3 works with the Boolean groups on the report. This option lets you select whether or not only one option in the Boolean group can be selected. If checked, this option will only allow one option in the group to be selected. That option will be set to true and the other options will return a value of false.

Figure 12-4 is an example of this because you can only select one of the print range options. Not selecting this option will allow more than one option in the group to be selected. Each option selected will be set to true and the others will be set to false. This option lets you create check boxes like the ones shown in Figure 12-6.

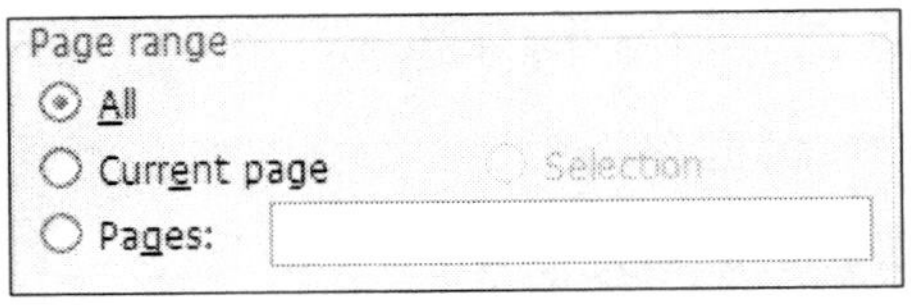

Figure 12-4 Radio button group example

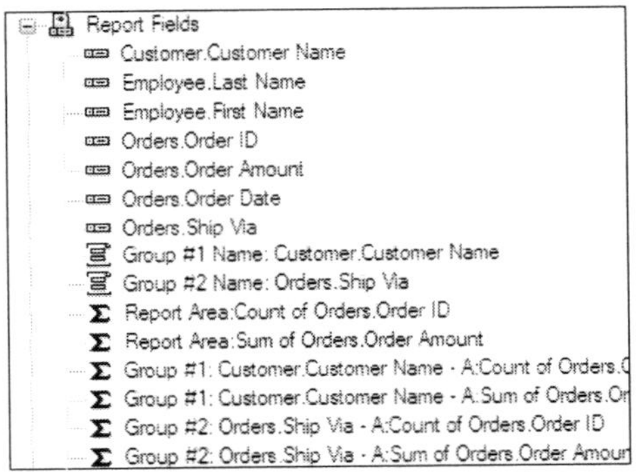

Figure 12-5 Available group fields in a chart

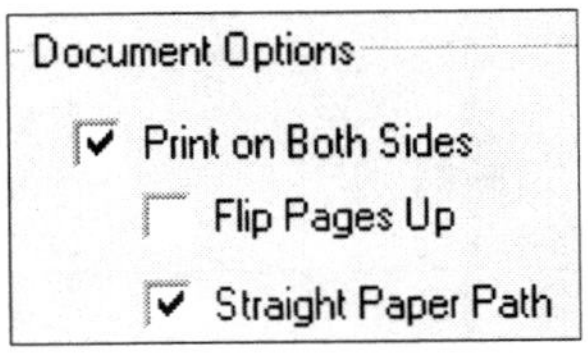

Figure 12-6 Check box options

Set Default Values Dialog Box

The options on the dialog box shown in Figure 12-7 let you set up the default values for the parameter field.

Table 12-2 explains the options on the dialog box

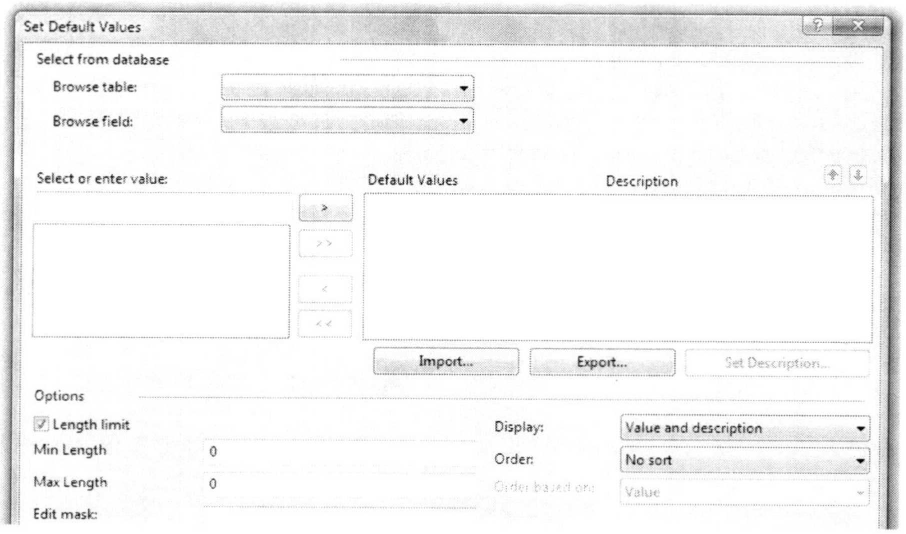

Figure 12-7 Set Default Values dialog box

Option	Description
Browse table	Lets you select the table that has the field that you want to use for the default values for the parameter field.
Browse field	Lets you select the field that has the default values for the parameter field.
Select or enter value	Lets you select values from a field to use as default values or type in the values. The values will be moved to the default VALUES COLUMN.
Description column	Lets you enter text that will be displayed next to the value in the list. This is helpful when the value field option is an ID field. Often, the person running the report will not understand the values in an ID field. For example, you may need to use the Customer ID field, but display either the Customer ID field and the Customer Name field or display the Customer Name field by itself. The Customer Name field contains data that the person running the report understands.
Import	This button lets you select the file that has the data for the default values for the parameter field.
Export	This button lets you copy the existing list of default values to a file.
Set Description	This button lets you set up a description for a default value.
Length limit	Lets you set the minimum and maximum length of data that can be entered in a parameter field for a string data type field. For numeric fields you enter a range that the value entered in the parameter field must be between.
Edit mask	Lets you set the format that the data has to be entered in the parameter field. [See Edit Masks later in this lesson]
Display	The options in this drop-down list let you select what will be displayed, the value or the value and the description.
Order	Lets you select how the default values will appear on the Enter Parameter Values dialog box when the report is run.
Order based on	Lets you select the sort order for how the values will appear on the Enter Parameter Values dialog box. They can be sorted by the value or by the description.

Table 12-2 Set Default Values dialog box options explained

I can hear you saying to yourself that the options on this dialog box will be very helpful to create default values. While that is true, keep in mind that the values are stored in a separate file, even the values that come from a table that is connected to the report. It takes additional processing power to retrieve the data from the file.

Once you select options on the Set Default dialog box and go back to the Create Parameter Field dialog box, the **ALLOW EDITING OF DEFAULT VALUES . . .** option is automatically checked. If the parameter field that you are creating requires that the value has to be selected from the list of values, clear this option.

Using Parameter Fields With The Select Expert

This combination may be the most used parameter field option. Many of the reports that you have created in this workbook used the Select Expert to specify which records appear on the report. In programming terminology, these reports are known as "hard coded" because all of the options needed to run the report are coded into the report. At one time this was the primary programming option that was used. Today, there are other options and parameter fields is one of these options.

After you create the parameter fields, open the Select Expert and select the parameter field instead of the actual values in the table. For example, in Exercise 5.2 you created the criteria shown in Figure 12-8. Instead of selecting the specific states (regions) FL and OH, which is the hard coding that I was referring to earlier, you would select the parameter field from the drop-down list. That is how the value in the parameter field is passed to the Select Expert.

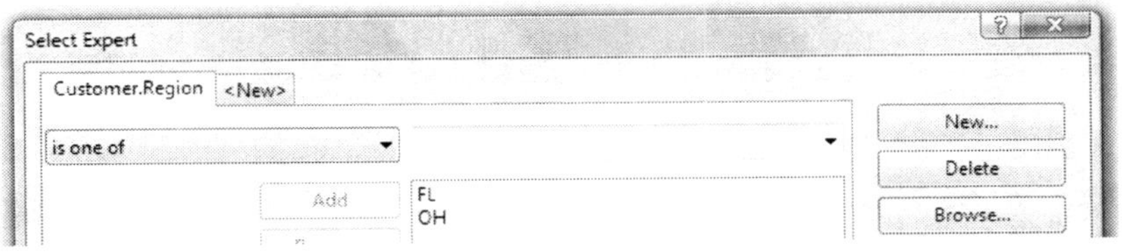

Figure 12-8 Select Expert criteria

What you will find is that you cannot always use the same operator (Is greater than, Is between, etc) with parameter fields that you would when selecting actual values from a field. The majority of the time you will use the "Is equal to" operator with parameter fields on the Select Expert even when the parameter field will be used for a range of values like "Is between 1/1/04 and 1/31/04" or when the parameter field is used to select multiple values like "Is one of FL or OH".

When you open the drop-down list on the Select Expert as shown in Figure 12-9, you will see all of the parameter fields that have the same data type as the field from the table. Parameter fields are always at the top of the list.

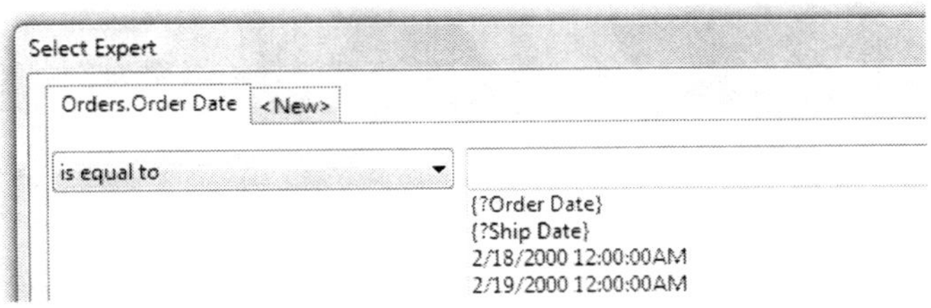

Figure 12-9 Select Expert with parameter field options

If you do not see the parameter field that you are looking for when you open the drop-down list on the right of the Select Expert, it usually means one of two things: 1) that you selected the wrong data type when you created the parameter field or 2) you associated the parameter field with the wrong field. Open the Edit Parameter Field dialog box, change the data type or field that the parameter field is associated to, then re-open the Select Expert.

You will see the terms "pick list", "list of values" and "prompt". Depending on who wrote the article or documentation, these words when used in conjunction with parameter fields can be used interchangeably. To me, the first two mean the same thing, but prompt, refers to the questions asked on the Enter Parameter Values dialog box.

Enter Parameter Values Dialog Box

This dialog box contains all of the parameter fields for a report as you saw earlier in Figure 12-2. Parameter fields appear on the Enter Parameter Values dialog box in the order that they are created.

Tip For Parameter Field Exercises

After saving the existing report with a new report name in step 1 of the parameter field exercises, open the Create Parameter Field dialog box by right-clicking on the Parameter Fields option in the Field Explorer and selecting New unless instructed otherwise.

Exercise 12.1: Create An "Is Equal To" Parameter Field

In this exercise you will enhance the L5.1 Region = CA report by creating a parameter field that will prompt for the state that will be used to run the report.

1. Save the L5.1 report as `L12.1 Is Equal To parameter field`.

2. Type `Region` in the Name field, then type `Enter the region` in the Prompting text field.

3. Change the Value type to String, if it is not already selected. Select the Discrete value(s) option, then click OK.

4. Open the Select Expert, then open the second drop-down list. At the top of the list you will see the parameter field that you just created, as illustrated in Figure 12-10. Select the Region parameter field and click OK.

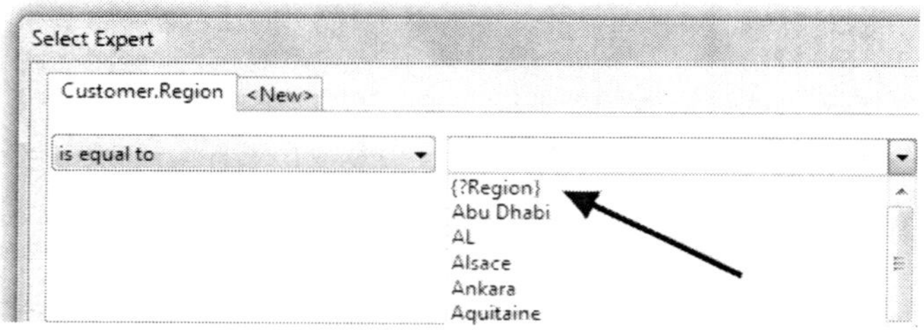

Figure 12-10 Parameter field illustrated on the Select Expert

5. Save the changes, then preview the report. You will see the dialog box shown in Figure 12-11. This dialog box is created based on the parameter field(s) that the report has.

Figure 12-11 Enter Parameter Values dialog box

6. Type `CA` in the Region field and press Enter or click OK.

Unless the parameter field has an edit mask, string fields are not case sensitive, which means that you can type "CA" or "ca" and get the same results. If you were running this report against live data, I would refresh the report every time it is run to make sure that I had the most current data. You will now see the six records in the CA region.

Run The Report Again

1. Click the REFRESH button on the toolbar above the report.

2. Type your first name in the Region field and press Enter. You should not get any output. Close the report and save the changes.

Unless your first name is a region in the table, you will not see any data on the report. This isn't what you want to happen. The majority of reports are created to retrieve data, not produce empty reports. If this report used a list of values for the region field, you would have been able to select a region from a list instead of typing it in. That is a better solution.

Exercise 12.2: Create An "Is Greater Than" Parameter Field

In this exercise you will enhance the L5.3 Order Date GTE 6-24-01 report by creating a parameter field that will prompt for the Order Date that will be used to run the report. This will allow the report to use any date.

1. Save the L5.3 report as `L12.2 Is Greater Than parameter field`.

2. Type `Order Date` in the Name field, then type `Enter the beginning order date` in the Prompting text field.

3. Change the Value type to Date and click OK.

4. Open the Select Expert, then open the second drop-down list.

As you will notice, you do not see the parameter field that you just created. That is because the Order Date field is a date/time field. I did this to demonstrate that Crystal Reports does try to help you as much as possible.

5. Close the Select Expert and reopen the parameter field dialog box by right-clicking on the Order Date parameter field in the Field Explorer and selecting Edit. Change the Type to Date Time and click OK.

6. Open the Select Expert. Select the Order Date parameter field in the second drop-down list and click OK. Preview the report. You will see the Enter Parameter Values dialog box shown in Figure 12-12.

The default date/time displayed in the Discrete Value field is the current one.

If you entered data in a parameter field that isn't valid, the report would run, but not return any records, which would cause the report to be empty. This is why it is a good idea that parameter fields have a list of values as often as possible. All fields on the Enter Parameter Values dialog box are not required.

Figure 12-12 Enter Parameter Values dialog box

I have noticed that if you leave some types of fields empty and click OK, you will not get an error message that says that you have not selected at least one value. Date fields force you to enter a valid date.

> If you click on the arrow at the end of the date field you will see the calendar shown in Figure 12-13. Instead of typing in the date, you can use the calendar to select the date.

7. Select June 24, 2001 in the calendar. Change the time to 12:00:00 AM. You should now see the date and time on the dialog box as shown in Figure 12-14.

Figure 12-13 Calendar control

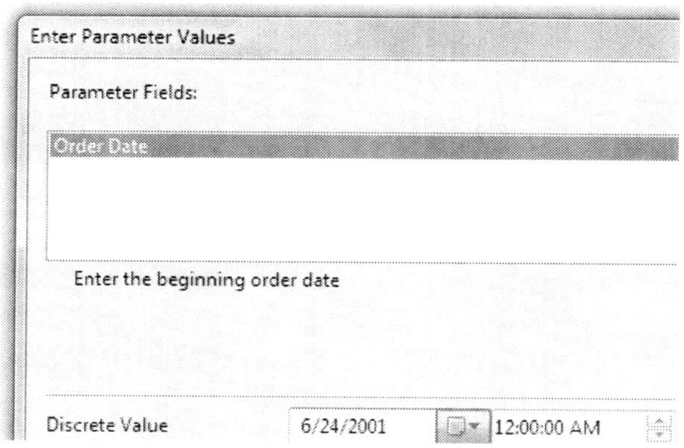

Figure 12-14 Order Date entered

8. Click OK. The report should have 2,199 records like the report shown in Exercise 5.3. Save the changes and leave the report open to complete the next exercise.

How To Use The Calendar Control

Navigating in this calendar is similar to other electronic calendars that you may have used. If you need a date in the month and year that is displayed on the calendar, click on the date in the calendar. The options are explained below.

   ① The left arrow button moves to the previous month.
   ② The right arrow button moves to the next month.
   ③ The current date, which is shaded.

Exercise 12.3: Set A Default Date For A Parameter Field

If you know that the majority of times that a report is run that a certain value will be selected, you can set that value as the default. Setting a default value will still let another value be selected when the report is run. Default values are usually created to save time. In this exercise you will set a default date for the parameter field in the L12.2 report.

1. Save the L12.2 report as L12.3 Parameter field with a default value.

2. Open the parameter dialog box for the Order Date field. Click the Default Values button.

3. Type 6/24/2001 in the Date field and 12:00:00 AM in the Time field. Click the right arrow button. The date and time should be on the right.

4. Click the Set Description button. Type This is the default value in the Description field as shown in Figure 12-15 and click OK. You should have the options shown in Figure 12-16.

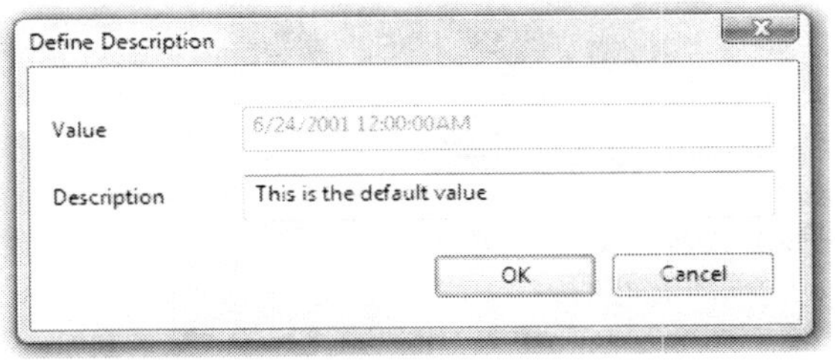

Figure 12-15 Define Description dialog box

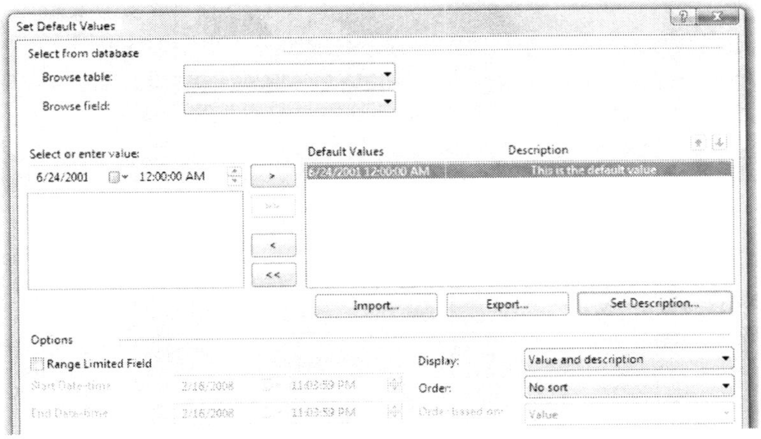

Figure 12-16 Default Value option illustrated

5. Click OK twice to close both dialog boxes. Save the changes and preview the report. You will see the default date that you just added to the parameter field as shown in Figure 12-17.

If you want to run the report with the default value, leave the **PICK FROM DEFAULTS** option checked and click OK.

If you want to select a different date, clear the Pick from defaults option and select the date.

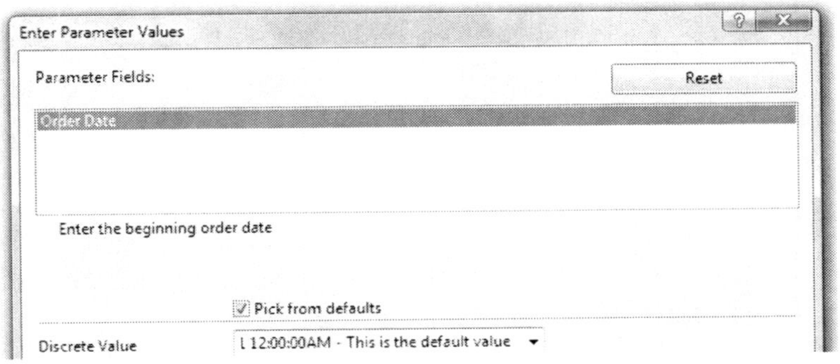

Figure 12-17 Date parameter field options

6. Select the date 7/15/2001 from the calendar and click OK. The report should have 1,977 records. Save the changes and close the report.

List Of Values

As you learned in Exercise 12.1, if a parameter field does not have a default value or a drop-down list with values, it is possible that the person running the report will type in the values incorrectly. As much as possible, you should avoid creating parameter fields that allow this to happen. Instead, you should provide a list of values for the parameter field.

A list of values is the data that the person running the report will select from. You can use the same list of values for different prompts in the same report. For example, if the report prompted for a customer "Bill to" state and a "Ship to" state, you could use the same list of states for both parameter fields.

Static List Of Values

Static lists are best suited for values that do not change or for data that is not stored in a field. An example of a static list of values would be a list of states. Keep in mind that static lists do not change unless you change them. This is the biggest drawback of a static list of values. If the static list of values comes from a field in a table and new values are added or existing values are deleted, the list for the parameter field should be updated.

As you can imagine, this could take several hours a week to keep these lists updated. This is better controlled by a form in the application. The reason that I refer to this list as a static list is for the reasons discussed below.

① The values do not change unless you change them or re-import them from a table or file.
② The full version of Crystal Reports (Crystal Reports XI or Crystal Reports 2008) supports dynamic lists which retrieve data directly from the table in addition to static lists.

There are three ways to create a static list of values as discussed below. You can use any combination of these options to create the list that you need.

① Import the values from a field in a table.
② Type the list of values in manually.
③ Import the list of values from a text file.

Exercise 12.4: Create A Static List Of Values Manually

In this exercise you will create a static list of values manually. In Exercise 5.2, the report was limited to two regions; OH and FL. In this exercise you will limit the regions to five, but you will be able to select which of the five regions that you want to appear on the report from a drop-down list.

1. Save the L5.2 report as `L12.4 Manual static list of values`.

2. Type `Region` in the Name field, then type `Select the region(s)` in the Prompting text field.

3. Check the **ALLOW MULTIPLE VALUES** option, then click the Default Values button. In this report, you are only going to allow the report to be run for one of the regions that you add to the static list of values.

4. Type `OH` in the Select or enter value field, then click the right arrow button. Click the Set Description button and type `Ohio` and click OK.

If the data in the Default Values column contains an ID number, abbreviation or other data that the person running the report may not be familiar with, you should enter a brief explanation in the Description column. The information that you enter in the Description column will appear in the drop-down list next to the content in the Value column. The description is only used for display purposes.

> 💡 You do not have to enter a value in the Description column for every option in the list, only those that you think the person running the report may not understand.

If you have entered a description for every value in the list, you can change the **DISPLAY** option at the bottom of the dialog box to Description as shown in Figure 12-18.

Display: [Description ▼]

Figure 12-18 Default value display option

If you do this, the only values that will appear in the list will be the values in the Description column. If there is data in a report that you do not want everyone to see, you can create a list of values that will prevent everyone from seeing all of the data. For example, you may not want all sales reps to see sales outside of their region. In this example, you would create a parameter field with a list of values that has the regions that you want the sales reps to be able to view.

5. Add the following regions to the Default Values column: CA, PA, WI and FL. You should have the options shown in Figure 12-19.

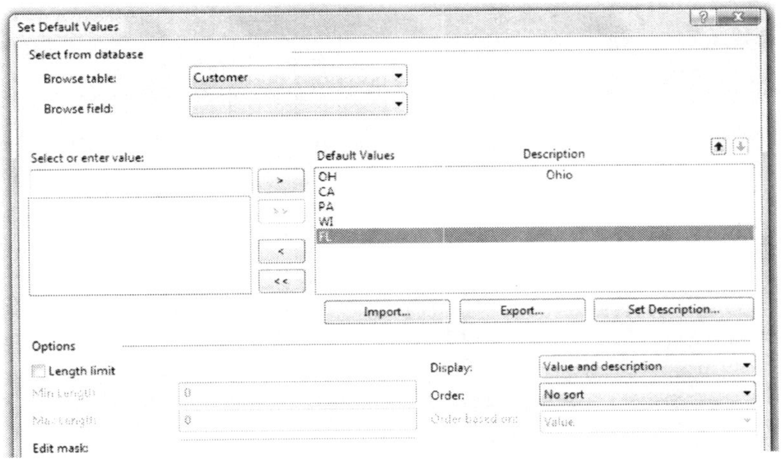

Figure 12-19 Default values for the parameter field

6. Click OK. Clear the Allow Editing of default values option and click OK.

7. Open the Select Expert and change the selection criteria to Is equal to. Select the Region parameter field, then click OK. Save the changes and preview the report.

You will see the Enter Parameter Values dialog box. If you open the Discrete Values drop-down list, you will see the values that you added to the list of values as shown in Figure 12-20. As you can see, the first option also displays the description that you entered. If you try to type in a value you will see that you can't.

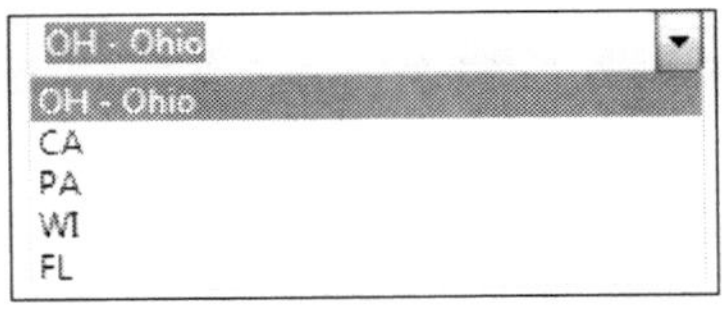

Figure 12-20 List of values

That is because the **ALLOW EDITING OF DEFAULT VALUES** option is not selected on the Create Parameter field dialog box. Also notice that the values are not in alphabetical order. They are in the order that they were added to the Value/Description table. In the next exercise you will learn how to change the order of values in a static list of values.

If the **ALLOW EDITING OF DEFAULT VALUES** option was checked on the Create Parameter Field dialog box shown earlier in Figure 12-1, you would be able to type values in the Discrete Values field. The person running the report could select an option from the drop-down list and/or type in the value that they want. This would be useful for example, if the static list contained the 10 most used options, which would keep the list small, while providing additional flexibility.

8. Select PA from the list, then click the Add button. Click OK. You should have five records on the report. Save the changes and leave the report open to complete the next exercise.

Exercise 12.5: Change The Sort Order Of The Static List Of Values

> There are two ways to change the sort order of a list of values. The instructions in this exercise are best suited for a list that does not need a lot of changes or for a list that you do not necessarily want in alphabetical order, but just in a different order then the list is currently in.
>
> An example of this would be if you wanted to put a specific value at the top of the list because it is the most used option and then put the rest of the list in alphabetical order. You may have seen this on a web-based form for a country field. You would see "USA" at the top of the drop-down list because the company knows that most of their subscribers are in the USA. Below that option, the rest of the countries are in alphabetical order.

As you saw in the previous exercise, the states are not in alphabetical order on the parameter dialog box. Most lists are in alphabetical order because it is easier to find the value that you need. In this exercise you will learn how to change the order of the items in the list.

1.   Save the L12.4 report as `L12.5 Sorted static list of values`.

2.   Open the Edit Parameter dialog box for the Region field, then click the Default Values button.

3.   Open the Order drop-down list and select **ALPHABETICAL ASCENDING** as shown in Figure 12-21. Click OK twice to close both dialog boxes. If you run the report you will see that the options in the drop-down list are in alphabetical order. Save the changes and close the report.

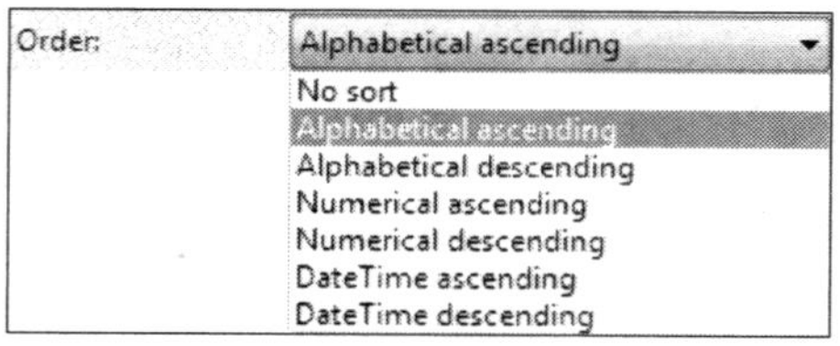

Figure 12-21 Reorder buttons illustrated

How To Manually Sort The List Of Values

If you want the values in a specific order, opposed to alphabetical, numerical or date time, you can put the values in the order that you want, on the Set Default Values dialog box. Figure 12-22 shows the values in alphabetical order. If PA was the state that would be selected most, you could put it at the top of the list by clicking on the value, then click the Up button illustrated in Figure 12-23 until PA is at the top of the list.

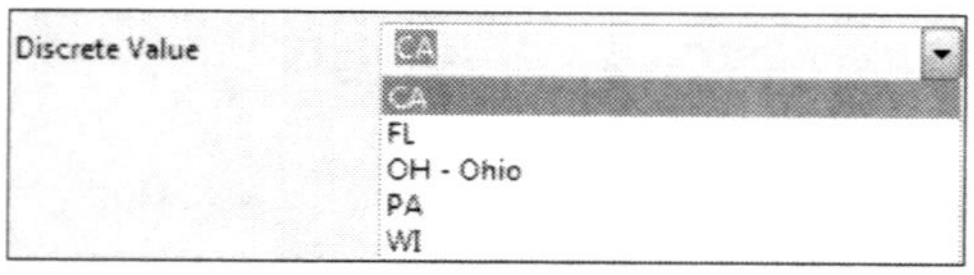

Figure 12-22 Values in alphabetical order

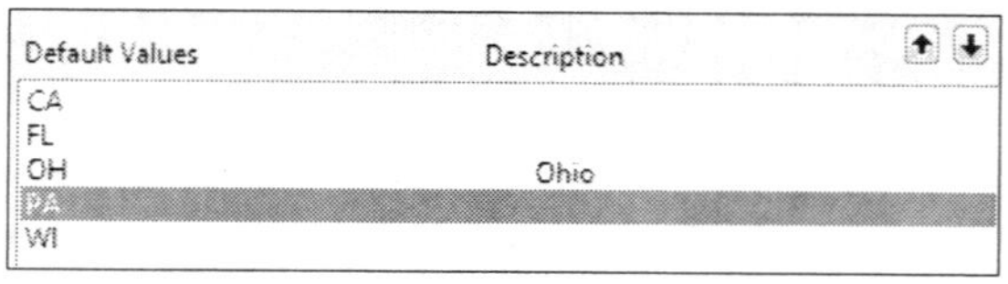

Figure 12-23 How to rearrange the order of the values

Importing A Static List Of Values

The list of values that you created manually in Exercise 12.4 was small, so it did not take a lot of time to set up. Often, that is not the case and you could have 100 or more values for a static list. If the data for the static list exists in a table or text document, it is easier to import the list. If you know that you do not need all of the values in the list that you will import, you have the two options discussed below for removing the values that you do not need. You will have to evaluate which option is best, on a list by list basis.

① Import the list as is, then manually delete or change the options as needed on the Set Default Values dialog box.

② Delete the values or make the changes to the list before importing it as a list of values. If the data that will be imported is in a table, it may not be possible or feasible to change the live data.

> If the list of values has a description it will also be imported, if all of the values are imported. If the values are added individually from a database, the Description column will not be imported.

Exercise 12.6: Create An Imported Static List Of Values From A Table

In this exercise you will import values from a field in a table to create a static list of values.

1. Save the L5.2 report as `L12.6 Imported static list of values from a table`.

2. Type `Region` in the Name field, then click the Default Values button.

3. The Customer table should be in the Browse table field. Open the **BROWSE FIELD** drop-down list and select Region.

You will now see all of the values from the Region field from the Customer table. If there were values in the list that you did not want or need, you can delete them by clicking on the value that you do not want and then click the Delete button.

4. Click the Add All button. All of the entries should be in the Default Values list as shown in Figure 12-24.

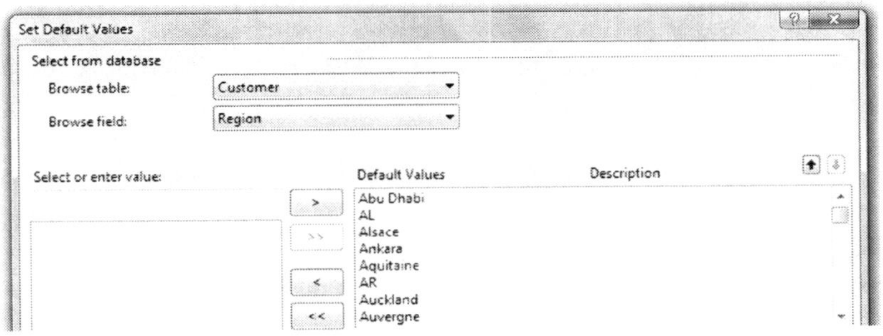

Figure 12-24 Values from a field added to the default values list

5. Click OK. Clear the Allow editing of default values . . . option, then check the Allow multiple values option. Click OK.

6. Open the Select Expert. Select the Is Equal To operator, then select the parameter field. Remove the other values from the list and click OK. Save the changes and close the report.

When you open this parameter drop-down list you will see all of the values from the field in the table. If you changed any values, you will see the changes in the drop-down list. The data in the table was not changed.

Exercise 12.7: Import A List Of Values From A File

In the previous exercise you imported values from a table in the database. You can create an external file and import the values. This may be helpful if you have a need to modify the values frequently and do not have access to the database.

1. Save the L5.2 report as `L12.7 Imported static list of values from a file`.

2. Type `Region` in the Name field. Click the Default Values button.

3. Click the **IMPORT** button. Navigate to your project folder and double-click on the Imported List.txt file.

You should see six entries in the default values list. You can import data from more than one file. If there are duplicates, they will not be added to the list twice. The second list that you will import has the following values: CA, MN, VA, MI, WI and TX. The current list of values has VA, MI and TX. When the second list is imported, these values will not be imported again.

4. Click the Import button and double-click on the Imported List2.txt file. Notice that there are no duplicate entries in the default values list.

5. Sort the list in alphabetical ascending order, then click OK twice to close both dialog boxes. Save the changes and test the parameter field.

Exercise 12.8: Create Parameter Fields For Countries And Regions

In this exercise you will create two prompts. The first one is for the country, the second one is for the region. The L6.6 report currently displays all countries and regions. The parameter fields that you will create for this report will allow a specific country and specific region to be selected when the report is run. The only downside to this report is if a region is selected that is not in the country that is selected, the report will produce strange output.

1. Save the L6.6 report as `L12.8 Parameters for countries and regions`.

2. Type `Country` in the Name field.

3. Type `Select a country` in the Prompting text field, then click the Default Values button.

4. Add all of the countries from the Customer table as default values, then click OK twice to close both dialog boxes.

5. Create a parameter field named `Region`, then type `Select the region(s) for the country` in the Prompting text field.

6. Check the Allow multiple values option, then add all of the regions from the Customer table as default values for the parameter field. Put USA at the top of the list.

7. Open the Select Expert. Select the Country field and click OK. Select the Is equal to operator, then select the Country parameter field.

8. Add criteria for the Region field. Select the Is equal to operator, then select the Region parameter field.

9. Save the changes and run the report. You should see the dialog box shown in Figure 12-25. USA should be at the top of the country drop-down list.

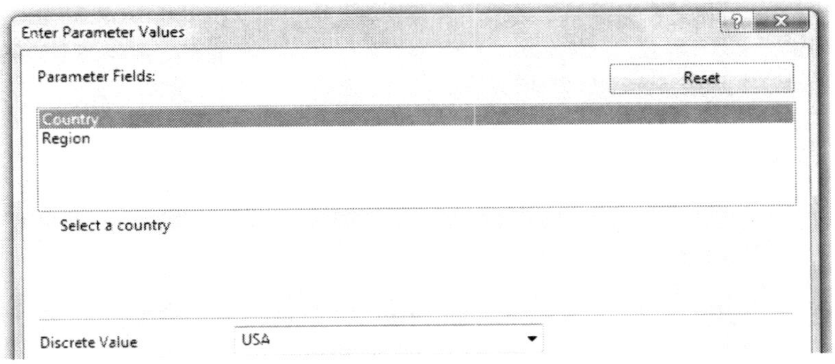

Figure 12-25 Options for a report with two parameter fields

10. Click on the Region parameter field and select CA.

11. Run the report with the options in Table 12-3.

Country	Region	Output
USA	CA and PA	You should see records in both states.
USA	Abu Dhabi	You should not get any output because the region is not in the country.
USA	Abu Dhabi and AL	You should only see records for AL.

Table 12-3 Report options for the L12.8 report

Range Values And Allow Multiple Values Options

The reports that you have created parameter fields for in this lesson have added a lot of interactivity between the user and the report. This allows the person running the report to have more control over the records that will appear on the report. What you have probably noticed is that each parameter field that you have created only allows one option to be selected. In some instances this can limit the data that displays on reports in a way that is not best suited for the user.

The Create Parameter Field dialog box has two options that will allow more flexibility. The **RANGE VALUES** option allows the parameter field to accept high and low values, like the "Is between" Select Expert operator. A good use of this option would be for a date range. The **ALLOW MULTIPLE VALUES** option allows more than one value to be selected from the parameter field. A good use of this option would be if you need to select more than one value from the same field. An example is if you needed to select several products to see which ones are not selling.

Range Values Option

When you select this option you will be able to use one parameter field to accept two values, a start of range value and an end of range value. More than likely, you will use this to allow date ranges to be entered. When a parameter field has this option selected on the Select Expert you have to select the "Is equal to" operator, because the parameter field contains the start and end values in one field. A parameter field with the range value is the equivalent of the "Is between" Select Expert operator.

By default, the start and end of range fields have the **INCLUDE VALUE** option checked. This means that the values entered in both fields will be included in the record selection process. If you clear this option for either field, the value will not be included in the record selection process. This is the equivalent of the "Is greater than" and "Is less than" Select Expert operators.

Earlier in this lesson you learned about the **NO LOWER BOUND** and **NO UPPER BOUND** options. When the Range values option is selected, these options are not checked. This means that only records that have a value between the start and end range values will be included in the record selection process.

These options were also discussed earlier in conjunction with date fields. These options also work with non date field ranges. If either of these options are checked, the input field is disabled and you can't enter anything in the field. These options can also be used like the "Is greater than" and "Is less than" Select Expert operators.

Only entering a value in the Start of range input field and checking the No lower bound option will retrieve all records that have a value greater than (or equal to, if the Include value option is also checked for the field) the value in the Start of range field.

Only entering a value in the End of range input field and checking the No lower bound option will retrieve all records that have a value less than (or equal to, if the Include value option is also checked for the field) the value in the End of range field.

Exercise 12.9: Use The Range Values Option With Dates

In Exercise 12.2 you created a parameter field that only allowed one date to be entered. In this exercise you will modify that parameter field to allow a date range to be entered.

1. Save the L12.2 report as L12.9 Date range parameter field.

2. Open the Order Date parameter dialog box. Change the Prompting text to Enter the beginning and ending date range.

3. At the bottom of the dialog box select the Range value(s) option and click OK.

4. Open the Select Expert. Change the Order Date operator to "Is equal to", then select the parameter field and click OK. Save the changes.

You can also use the "Is not equal to" operator with range value parameter fields.

5. Preview the report. Use the calendar control to select the start date 3/1/2001 and the end date 3/31/2001. Change the time on both fields to 12:00:00 AM. You should have the options selected that are shown in Figure 12-26. Click OK. The report should have 159 records. Close the report.

If you ran the report again and cleared the INCLUDE VALUE option on the Start of range field, there would be 139 records on the report. That means that 20 orders were placed on 3/1/2001.

To verify that, check the Include value option on the Start of range field, then change the End of range value to 3/2/2001 and clear the Include value option on the End of range field. In the real world, the time portion of a date/time field would probably have a value.

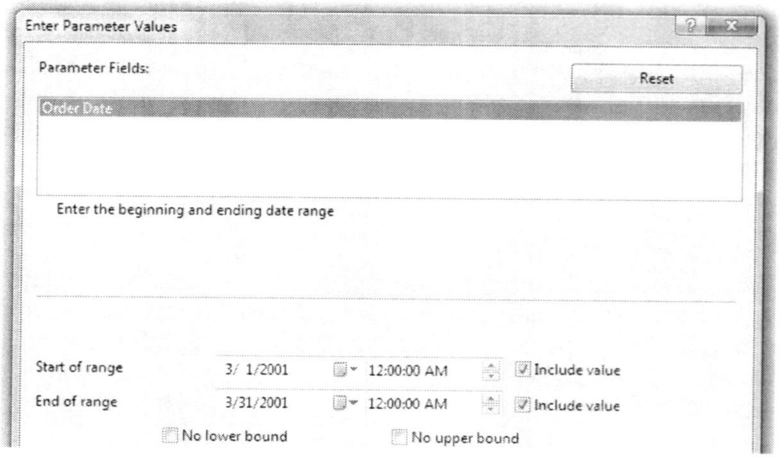

Figure 12-26 Date range parameter options

If you wanted to run the report for one day, you would enter the same date in the start and end of range fields. You would have to include the equivalent of 11:59:59 PM on the End of range field or you could enter the next day and use a time of 12:00:00 AM.

> If you are running a monthly report and do not know if there are 30 or 31 days in the month, enter the first day of the month after the month you are running the report for in the End of range field and use a time of 12:00:00 AM and clear the Include value option. Doing this will include all records for the prior month.

Using Range Values For Non Date Data

A lot of the time, the range value parameter field is used for dates. You can use range parameter fields for other types of data. Two other uses that come to mind are to only print records in a zip code range. Another use is if you wanted to print a list of customers whose last name started with a specific letter or was in a range of letters, like customers whose last name started with A through D.

Exercise 12.10: Use The Range Values Option With Currency

In the previous exercise you used the Range values option with a date field. You can also use this option with numeric and currency fields. In this exercise you will use the option to find all orders that are within a certain dollar amount range.

1. Save the L6.7 report as `L12.10 Currency range parameter field`.

2. Change the following options, then click OK.
   Type `Order Amount Range` in the Name field.
   Type `Enter the order amount range for the report:` in the Prompting text field.
   Change the Type to Currency.
   Select the Range values option.

3. Add the Order Amount values to the Default value column. Clear the Allow editing of default values option.

4. Open the Select Expert and click on the **NEW** tab. Select the Order Amount field and click OK. Select the "Is equal to" operator, then select the Order Amount Range parameter field and click OK. Save the changes.

5. Select the first order amount over $500 for the Start of range value. Select the first order amount over $1,000 for the End of range value.

6. Clear the Include value option for the End of range field. Doing this will only display orders that have an order amount between $500 and $1,000. You should have the options shown in Figure 12-27. Click OK. There should be 28 records on the report. Save the changes and close the report.

The options selected for the Order Amount Range parameter field will not let the person running the report enter the values that they want. They would have to select values from the drop-down list. This could pose a problem if there are more than 500 unique values in the drop-down list. If there are, all of the values would not be able to be accessed. In this exercise the last value in the drop-down list is $1,186.07. There are orders in the table that have an order amount greater than that.

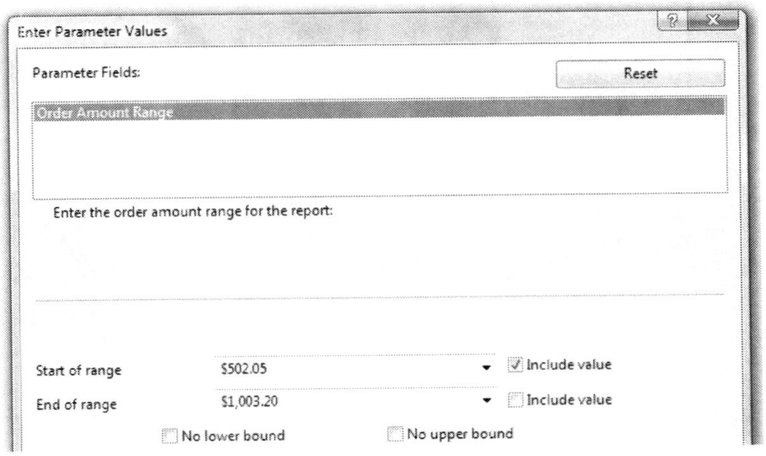

Figure 12-27 Currency range parameter options

The way that this parameter field is currently set up, you could not run a report to select orders greater than that amount. In order to be able to select any value the Allow editing of default values option must be selected.

Allow Multiple Values Option

When you select this option you will be able to select more than one value to the parameter field. This is the equivalent of the "Is one of" Select Expert operator. You may often have a report request that requires that more than one value be included in the selection process. When the Allow multiple values option checked, you are creating what is called an ARRAY. This means that the field can contain more than one value.

Exercise 12.11: Use The Allow Multiple Values Option With A Static List Of Values

In Exercise 12.4 you created a static list of values by manually entering them. As you just learned, selecting the Allow multiple values and the Allow editing of default values options will allow the person running the report to select values from the static list and type in other values.

In this exercise you will modify the parameter field to allow multiple values to be selected from the static list and allow other values to be entered.

1. Save the L12.5 report as `L12.11 Customer multi value parameter field`.

2. Open the Parameter dialog box for the Region field.

3. Change the following options and click OK.
   Prompting text - `Select the region(s) or type them in below:`
   Select the Allow editing of default values . . . option.

4. Open the Select Expert. Select the "Is equal to" operator on the Region parameter field and click OK. Save the changes.

5. Select the FL and PA regions from the Discrete Value list and add them to the Value list.

6. Manually add the TX and NY regions to the Value list by typing a value in the Discrete Value field and then click the Add button at the end of the field. Your dialog box should have the options shown in Figure 12-28. Click OK. There should be nine records on the report. Save the changes and close the report.

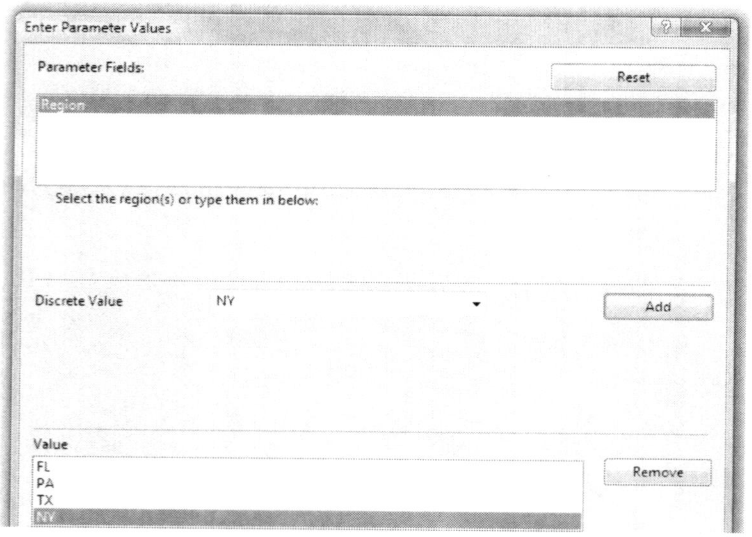

Figure 12-28 Multiple and custom value parameter field options

Combining Range And Multiple Values

What may not initially be apparent is that these two options can be combined on the same parameter field. Doing this allows for maximum flexibility and options when the report is run. On a report that uses a date parameter field, you can allow multiple date ranges to be entered. For example, if you wanted to be able to compare the orders for the first five days of three months, you could enter 1/1/01 to 1/5/01, 3/1/01 to 3/5/01 and 5/1/01 to 5/5/01 on the same parameter field. Another example would be if you wanted to see orders 1001 to 1050 and 1100 to 1124 on the same report. Setting the Range values and Allow multiple values options would allow you to create parameter fields for both of the examples just discussed.

Exercise 12.12: Combine Range And Multiple Values For A Date Field

In Exercise 12.9 the parameter field that you created only allowed one date range to be entered. In this exercise you will modify that parameter field to allow multiple date ranges to be entered.

1. Save the L12.9 report as `L12.12 Multiple date range parameter field`.

2. Open the Order Date parameter field dialog box.
   Change the following options and click OK.
   Prompting text - `Enter the Order Date range(s):`
   Select the Allow multiple values option.

3. Save the changes and preview the report. Add the following date ranges to the Value list. 1/1/01 to 1/5/01, 3/1/01 to 3/5/01 and 5/1/01 to 5/5/01. After you add the End of range date, click the **ADD** button, then add the next date range. Change the time on all dates to 12:00:00 AM.

4. Your dialog box should have the options shown in Figure 12-29. Click OK. There should be 95 records on the report. Save the changes and close the report.

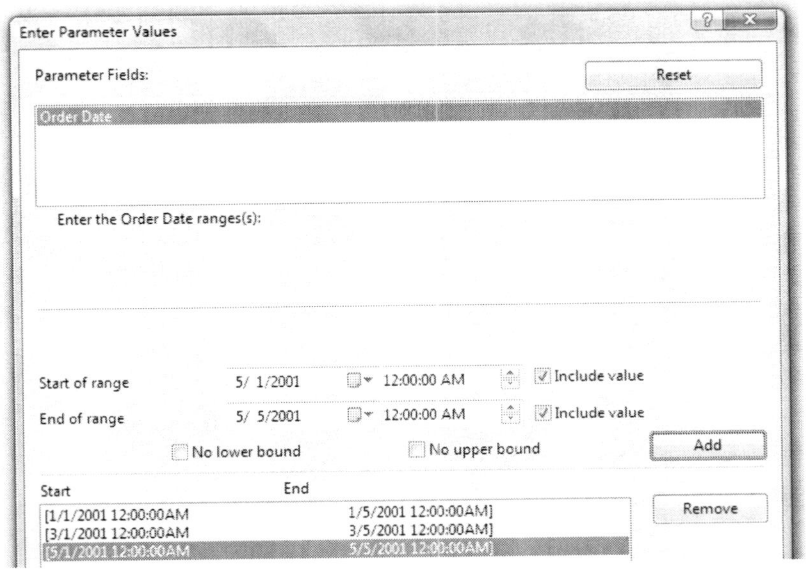

Figure 12-29 Range and multiple values parameter field options

Using Formula Fields In Parameter Fields

All of the formulas that you have created in this workbook have been static or hard coded, meaning that they do not change each time the report is run. There will be times when hard coded formulas will not produce the results that are needed. One way to tell if is you get requests for several reports that are very similar. This is often the case for reports that are used in what is known as "What-If" analysis.

For example, someone wants to see the potential revenue gain if they raise the price of the products by 5, 7 or 8%. Hard coded formulas could possibly require you to create three reports, one for each of the potential percent increases. Creating a parameter field that prompted for the percent of increase, allows the report to be flexible and not have to be changed.

A parameter field that is based off of a formula field will allow the user to be able to sort or group the report the way that best meets their needs. Instead of selecting a field name on the Record Sort Expert or Insert Group dialog box, you would select the formula field.

In addition to using formula fields for What-If analysis, you can also base parameter fields off of formula fields that are used to conditionally format data. An example of this is the suppression of data as shown in the L10.6 Suppress Salary GT 50000 report. Another example would be the conditional formatting that you created using the Highlighting Expert in Exercises 10.1 and 10.2.

Using Parameter Fields To Highlight Data

In Exercise 10.1 you used the Highlighting Expert to conditionally format data when a certain condition was met. The report created in that exercise may be more helpful if an option existed to select the value, in this case, the threshold to use for applying the conditional formatting. The report currently highlights records if the value in the Delay in Days To Ship field is greater than or equal to three.

Exercise 12.13: Create A Parameter Field To Highlight Rows Of Data

In this exercise you will modify the L9.10 report to prompt to select the delay in days to ship. You will also add a date range parameter. The background color of the row will change to yellow if the record meets the condition.

Create The Order Date Range Parameter Field

1. Save the L9.10 report as `L12.13 Highlight rows of data parameter field`.

2. Change the following options and click OK.
   Type `Date Range` in the Name field.
   Prompting text - `Select the date range that you want to see orders for:`
   Change the Value type to Date Time.
   Select the Range values option.

Create The Highlight Rows Of Data Parameter Field

1. Open a new parameter field dialog box. Type `Delay in Days` in the Name field.

2. Change the following options:
   Prompting text - `Enter the minimum number of Delay in Days To Ship that you want to see:`
   Change the Value type to Number.
   Change the Default Value option to 3.
   Change the Min Value option to 1.
   Change the Max Value option to 100. (This can be any number that you want that is greater than the Min value.)
   You should have the options shown in Figure 12-30. Click OK.

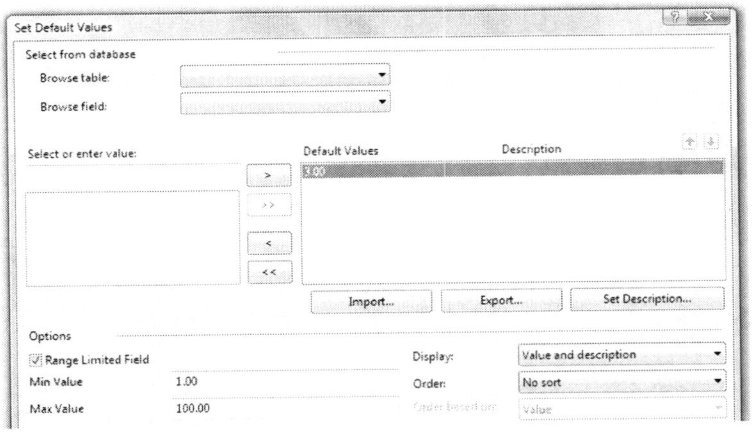

Set Default Values

Select from database

Browse table:

Browse field:

Select or enter value: | Default Values | Description

3.00

>

> >

<

<<

Import...   Export...   Set Description...

Options

☑ Range Limited Field   Display: Value and description

Min Value   1.00   Order: No sort

Max Value   100.00   Order based on Value

Figure 12-30 Delay in days parameter field options

Create The Row Color Formula

In this part of the exercise you will create the formula that will change the background to yellow for the rows that have a days to ship number greater than or equal to the number that is entered on the parameter field that you just created.

1. Open the Section Expert and click on the details section, then click on the Color tab.

2. Click the Formula button and open the Report Fields tree.

Notice on the left side of the Formula Workshop that the conditional formatting formula that you are creating is being applied to the background color option of the details section.

3. Type `If` in the Formula Text window, then press the space bar. Double-click on the Delay in Days To Ship formula field in the Report Fields section.

4. Press the space bar and type >=, then press the space bar.

5. Double-click on the Delay in Days parameter field in the Report Fields section, then press the space bar and type `Then crYellow Else crNoColor`. Your formula should look like the one shown in Figure 12-31. Click the Save and close button. Click OK to close the Section Expert.

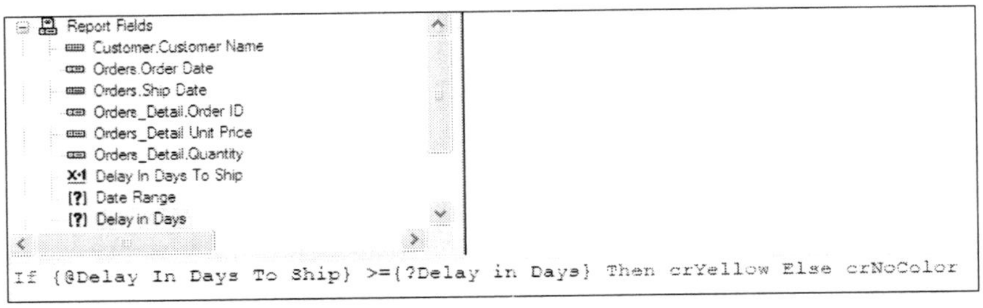

Report Fields
  Customer.Customer Name
  Orders.Order Date
  Orders.Ship Date
  Orders_Detail.Order ID
  Orders_Detail.Unit Price
  Orders_Detail.Quantity
  Delay In Days To Ship
  [?] Date Range
  [?] Delay in Days

`If {@Delay In Days To Ship} >={?Delay in Days} Then crYellow Else crNoColor`

Figure 12-31 Parameter field formula

 If you did not add the crNoColor option, rows that did not meet the criteria would have a black background and you would not be able to see the text.

Add The Date Range Parameter Field To The Select Expert

If you look at the Parameter Fields section of the Field Explorer you will see that the Date Range field does not have a green check mark next to it. That is because the field is currently not being used on the report.

1. Open the Select Expert and select the "Is equal to" operator for the Order Date field.

2. Open the next drop-down list and select the Date Range parameter field, then click OK. Save the changes.

Test The Parameter Fields

1. Select the first date in 2001 for the Start of range value, then select the last date in 2001 for the End of range value.

2. Change the time to 12:00:00 AM for both dates.

3. Click on the Delay in Days parameter field. Notice that the default value that you set is in the Delay in Days field. Click OK. The top of the first page of the report should look like the one shown in Figure 12-32. Every row that has a value of three or greater in the Delay in Days To Ship field has a yellow background.

Customer Name	Order Date	Ship Date	Order ID	Unit Price	Quantity	Delay In Days To Ship
Rough Terrain	01/01/2001	01/01/2001	1,121	$41.90	1	0
Rough Terrain	01/01/2001	01/01/2001	1,121	$809.87	1	0
Hooked on Helmets	01/01/2001	01/08/2001	1,122	$21.90	3	7
Hooked on Helmets	01/01/2001	01/08/2001	1,122	$479.85	2	7
Clean Air Transportation	01/02/2001	01/02/2001	1,123	$1,739.85	3	0
Off the Mountain Biking	01/02/2001	01/09/2001	1,124	$19.90	3	7
Road Runners Paradise	01/02/2001	01/03/2001	1,125	$19.71	2	1
Road Runners Paradise	01/02/2001	01/03/2001	1,125	$36.00	1	1
Platou Sport	01/02/2001	01/02/2001	1,126	$16.50	2	0
Platou Sport	01/02/2001	01/02/2001	1,126	$1,739.85	2	0
Platou Sport	01/02/2001	01/02/2001	1,126	$329.85	1	0
BBS Pty	01/02/2001	01/10/2001	1,127	$13.50	3	8
BBS Pty	01/02/2001	01/10/2001	1,127	$479.85	1	8

Figure 12-32 L12.13 Highlight rows of data parameter field report

4. Run the report again with the dates 6/1/01 to 6/30/01. Select 5 as the delay in days. The report should look like the one shown in Figure 12-33.

Customer Name	Order Date	Ship Date	Order ID	Unit Price	Quantity	Delay In Days To Ship
To The Limit Biking Co.	06/01/2001	06/04/2001	1,665	$14.50	1	3
To The Limit Biking Co.	06/01/2001	06/04/2001	1,665	$16.50	2	3
To The Limit Biking Co.	06/01/2001	06/04/2001	1,665	$37.90	3	3
The Great Bike Shop	06/01/2001	06/01/2001	1,666	$14.50	3	0
The Great Bike Shop	06/01/2001	06/01/2001	1,666	$2,939.85	3	0
The Great Bike Shop	06/01/2001	06/01/2001	1,666	$899.85	2	0
To The Limit Biking Co.	06/01/2001	06/01/2001	1,667	$479.85	2	0
Psycho-Cycle	06/01/2001	06/09/2001	1,668	$431.87	2	8
Psycho-Cycle	06/01/2001	06/09/2001	1,668	$274.35	1	8
Tandem Cycle	06/01/2001	06/05/2001	1,669	$41.90	3	4
Tandem Cycle	06/01/2001	06/05/2001	1,669	$2,939.85	2	4
Tandem Cycle	06/01/2001	06/05/2001	1,669	$2,939.85	1	4
Tek Bikes	06/01/2001	06/01/2001	1,670	$33.90	2	0
Belgium Bike Co.	06/02/2001	06/02/2001	1,671	$1,739.85	1	0
Extreme Cycling	06/02/2001	06/12/2001	1,672	$33.90	3	10

Figure 12-33 Highlighting report with different parameter options selected

Using Parameter Fields To Select The Sorting And Grouping Options

In Lesson 6 you learned how to sort and group data by selecting options on the Record Sort Expert and Insert Group dialog boxes. There will be times when a report needs to be sorted or grouped in several different ways. Rather then hard code this information and have to create several reports, one for each field the report needs to be sorted or grouped on, you can create a parameter field that will be used to find out what field the person wants the report to be sorted or grouped on. The value collected from the parameter field will be passed to the Record Sort Expert or Insert Group dialog box.

Parameter fields cannot retrieve a formula or table name. Therefore, you have to create a formula that uses the value in the parameter field as the field to sort or group on. The formula field is what you will select on the sorting or grouping dialog box.

Exercise 12.14: Create A Parameter Field To Sort The Records

In Exercise 3.1 you created a customer information report. As it is, the report is not sorted or grouped. In this exercise you will create a formula and parameter field that will allow the report to be sorted on one of the following three fields: Customer Name, Region or Country.

Create The Sort By Parameter Field

1. Save the L3.1 report as `L12.14 Sort records parameter field`.

2. Type `Sort By Field` in the Name field.

3. Change the following options and click OK.
    Prompting text - `Select the field that you want to sort by:`
    Select String in the Value type drop-down list.
    Add the following default values `Customer Name`, `Region` and `Country` to the Value column.
    Type `State` in the Description column of the Region value.

Create The Sort Formula And Add It To The Parameter Field

1. Open the Formula Editor and create a new formula. Type `SortBy` as the formula name.

2. Type the formula shown below, then click the Save and close button.

```
If {?Sort By Field} = "Customer Name" Then
{Customer.Customer Name}
Else
If {?Sort By Field} = "Region" Then {Customer.Region}
Else
{Customer.Country}
```

3. Open the Record Sort Expert. Add the SortBy formula field to the Sort Fields list and click OK. Save the changes.

Test The Sort Parameter

1. Preview the report. The Enter Parameter Values dialog box shown in Figure 12-34 will open. Select the Customer Name option from the drop-down list, then click OK. The report should be sorted in Customer Name order.

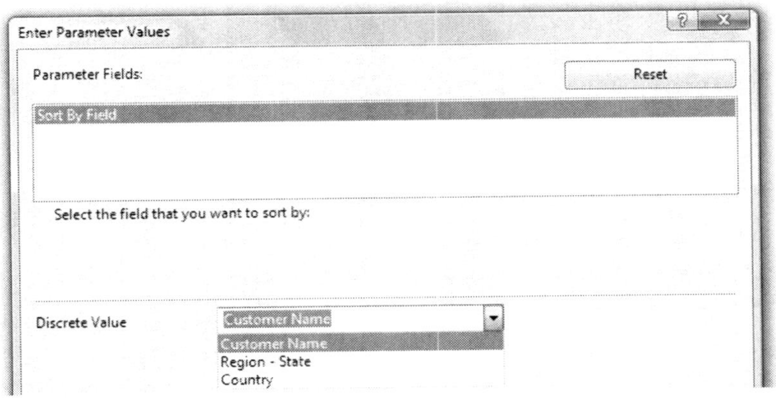

Figure 12-34 SortBy options

2. Save the changes, then run the report again and sort the report by Region. Leave the report open to complete the next exercise.

Exercise 12.15: Create A Parameter Field To Group Data

In the previous exercise you learned how to sort the detail records using a parameter field. Selecting the field to group on via a parameter field basically works the same way. The difference is that you attach the formula field to the Insert Group dialog box instead of the Record Sort Expert.

In this exercise you will create a group for the customer information report from the previous exercise. One parameter field that you will create in this exercise will let you select which of the three fields; Customer Name, Region or Country to group on.

Create The Group Sort Parameter Field

1. Save the L12.14 report as `L12.15 Group data parameter field`.

2. Type `Group By Field` in the Name field.

3. Change the following options and click OK.
   Prompting text - `Select the field that you want to group by:`
   Add the following default values `Customer Name`, `Region` and `Country` to the Value column.
   Type `State` in the Description column of the Region value.
   Clear the Allow editing of default values option.

Create The Group Formula And Add It To The Parameter Field

1. Open the Formula Editor and create a new formula. Type `GroupBy` as the formula name.

2. Click on the SortBy formula field under the Formula Fields node on the left of the Formula Workshop. Copy and paste the SortBy formula into the GroupBy formula.

3. Change the word "Sort" to `Group` in two places in the formula, then click the Save and close button.

Test The Parameter Field

1. Save the changes and preview the report. You should see the dialog box shown in Figure 12-35.

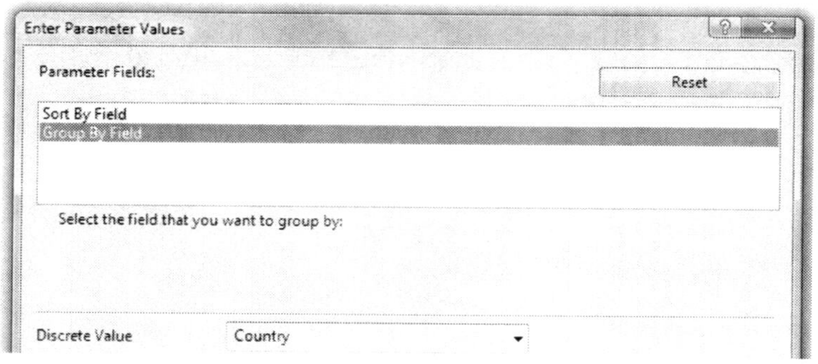

Figure 12-35 Group and field sort parameter options

2. Run the report a few times, selecting different options.

Boolean Parameter Fields

In Lesson 10 you learned how to create Boolean formulas. Boolean parameter fields, like Boolean formulas, can only have two values: True and False. Like Boolean formulas, you do not have to display the options as true and false in a parameter field. If the Boolean parameter field is not a group, you can use the Description column to enter the text that you want to display in the drop-down list instead of the values, true and false.

Interestingly enough, you cannot use the Description column to change what is displayed in the drop-down list on Boolean group parameter fields. Instead, the name of the Parameter field is used. Therefore, make good use of the name field.

Using A Parameter Field To Suppress Data

You have learned how to conditionally suppress data on a report. Suppression is often done with a Boolean field. Suppressing data is popular on reports that have a lot of detail records. Being able to select whether or not to suppress detail records allows one to run the report and only see the summary information. Doing this means that a report can be a detail report or a summary report. The Suppress (No Drill-Down) option on the Section Expert requires a Boolean formula when it will be used conditionally.

Exercise 12.16: Conditional Section Suppression Using A Parameter Field

In the last skills exercise in Lesson 10, the details section was manually suppressed to create a summary report. In this exercise you will modify a report so that it can be run as a detailed report or a summary only report.

Create The Suppress Parameter Field

1. Save the L6.2 report as `L12.16 Suppress section parameter field`.

2. Type `Summary Report` in the Name field.

3. Change the following options and click OK.
   Prompting text - `Do you want to run a Summary Only report?`
   Add the default values Yes and No.

Modify The Section Expert Options

1. Open the Section Expert and add another page header section.

You need the additional page header section because the field headings will also have to be suppressed if the report will be run as a summary report.

2. Click on the Formula button for the Suppress (No Drill-Down) option for the page header b section, then type the formula shown below.

   ```
   If {?Summary Report} = "Yes" Then True
   ```

This formula checks to see if the Summary Report parameter field has the value Yes. If it does, the page header b and details sections will be suppressed.

3. Highlight the formula and press CTRL + C, then click the Save and close button. This will let you copy the formula.

4. Click on the details section in the Section Expert, then click the Formula button across from the Suppress (No Drill-Down) option. Paste (Press CTRL + V) the formula into the Formula Text window, then click the Save and close button. Click OK to close the Section Expert.

Modify The Report

As mentioned earlier, when the report is run in the summary only mode, the field headings should not print. This is why you created the second page header section and added the suppression formula to the second page header section.

1. Move the field headings to the page header b section and save the changes. Preview the report. You should see the dialog box shown in Figure 12-36.

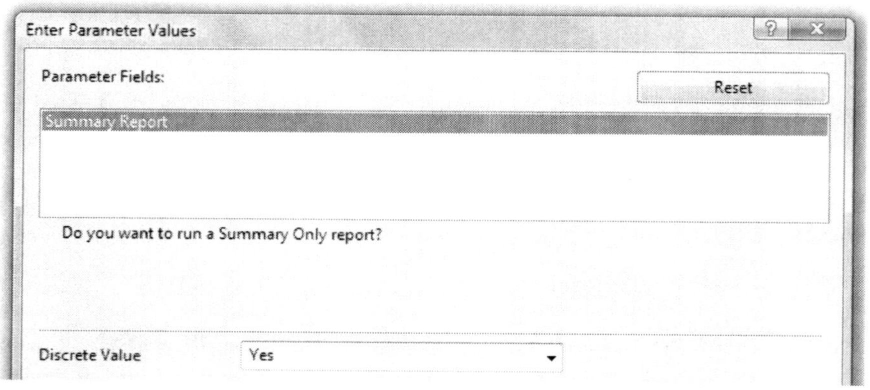

Figure 12-36 Summary only parameter dialog box

2. Select Yes to run a summary report. You should only see summary information on the report. Run the report again and select No.

Managing Data Entry In Parameter Fields

You have created several parameter fields in this lesson. While you took care and entered the data in the parameter fields correctly, it is unrealistic to think that people that run the reports will always enter the correct information in the parameter fields. If the reports are going to be part of an application, there are more options available for helping and guiding users to enter the data in parameter fields correctly then Crystal Reports provides. Crystal Reports does provide three types of options that you can use to help users enter data in the parameter fields correctly. These options are Min and Max field lengths, which use a range of values to limit the data. You have already used these options on date fields. The other options are Min and Max value and Edit Masks.

On string parameter fields the **MIN LENGTH** and **MAX LENGTH** options are used. The length refers to how many characters can be entered in the field. The number that you enter in the Max Length field should not be larger then the actual length of the corresponding field in the table. Any items in the Value column have to meet the min and max requirements.

The range limits **MIN VALUE** and **MAX VALUE** are primarily used for number and date fields. These options require that the data entered in the field be in a specific range. For example, if the min value is one and the max value is five, any number less than one or greater than five would not be accepted.

> If a number parameter field is populated with a static list of values and you do not want all of the values to be available, open the Set Default Values dialog box and enter the min and max values for the range of data that you want to keep and click OK. You will see a message that says that you are about to lose data. Click OK. Any records that are not in the range that you selected will be deleted from the default values list for the parameter field.

Edit Masks

In Lessons 9 and 10 you learned about masks. You learned that they are placeholders that determine how data will be displayed on a report. The edit mask feature for parameter fields is similar. Edit masks are used to set the rules for how data has to be entered into a field. If an edit mask has 10 placeholders, that that no more than 10 characters can be entered into the field. Each of the edit mask characters has its own rule. The characters can be combined in the same field as needed. For example, if you were going to use an edit mask for a country field, you may want to force the first character to be an upper case letter and the other characters could be a combination of upper and lower case letters.

Table 12-4 lists the mask characters that you can use. Edit masks provide a lot of flexibility for managing the data that is entered in parameter fields. An edit mask is a series of characters (placeholders) that control the type of data that can be entered in **STRING** parameter fields. The Edit mask field was shown earlier at the bottom of Figure 12-19.

The edit mask **>AA** could be used for a state field. AA forces two alphanumeric characters to be entered in the field. **>** forces the characters to be upper case.

If the values entered are not correct, you will see an error message. Often, the error messages are cryptic and can confuse the person that is trying to run the report. If I use an edit mask on a parameter field, I put as much information in the Prompting text field as possible to help the person enter the correct data.

Character	Description
A	Requires that an alphanumeric character be entered.
a	Allows an alphanumeric character, but is not required.
0 (zero)	Requires a numeric character to be entered.
9	Allows a numeric character, but is not required.
#	Allows a digit, space, plus sign or minis sign, but is not required.
L	Requires a letter to be entered.
?	Allows a letter, but is not required.
&	Allows any character or space, but is required.
C	Allows any character or space, but is not required.
. , : ; - /	Allows separator characters, but is not required.
<	Converts the characters in the field to lower case.
>	Converts the characters in the field to upper case.
\	Causes the character that follows the \ to be taken as a literal.
Password	Does not display actual characters that are entered. Instead, circles appear when text is entered into this field.

Table 12-4 Edit mask characters

Adding Parameter Field Criteria To A Report

You have learned how to create parameter fields that add a lot of interaction. The one thing that is missing is adding the parameter field criteria to a report. With all of the parameter field selection combinations that a report can have, including the parameter field selection criteria on the report would be helpful. Single value parameter fields can be dragged from the Field Explorer on to the report like other fields.

 Range value and multiple value parameter fields cannot be dragged onto the report and printed like single value parameter fields. If these fields are added to the report, they will not print. Printing solutions for these types of parameter fields are discussed below.

Printing Parameter Range Fields

There are two functions, **MINIMUM()** and **MAXIMUM()** in Crystal Reports that let you print the range in a parameter field. These functions return the beginning and ending values. The formula below will print the date range on the report as long as the **NO LOWER BOUND** and **NO UPPER BOUND** options are not checked on the Enter Parameter Values dialog box. Replace the {?Date_Parameter} field with the name of the field that you need.

"Starting Date " & Minimum ({?Date_Parameter}) & " and Ending Date " & Maximum ({?Date_Parameter})

You can use the Minimum and Maximum functions for any type of range parameter field data. It is not just for date ranges.

Exercise 12.17: Print Parameter Range Fields

1. Save the L12.14 report as L12.17 Print Parameter Range fields.

2. Create a formula field called Print Date Range. Type the code shown below and save the formula. Type the formula all on one line.

   "Starting Date " & Minimum ({?Date Range}) & " and Ending Date " & Maximum ({?Date Range})

3. Add the Print Date Range formula field to the top of the page header section. Make the field at least four inches long, then save the changes. Preview the report. You should see the date range at the top of the report, similar to the one shown in Figure 12-37. You will have different data on the report.

Starting Date 2/3/2001	4:24:47PM and Ending Date 12/3/2007		4:24:47PM	
Customer Name	Order Date	Ship Date	Order ID	Unit Price
Pathfinders	02/04/2001	02/04/2001	1,256	$23.50
Uni-Cycle	02/04/2001	02/04/2001	1,257	$9.00

Figure 12-37 Parameter field range printed on the report

Printing Multi Value Parameter Fields Using The Join Function

If you drag a multi value parameter field to a report, the only value that will print will be the first one. All of the values that are selected in a multi value parameter field are stored in one field and are separated by a comma in the array. The **JOIN** function will print all of the values in the array. The formula below will let you print all of the values in a multiple value parameter field. Replace the {?ShipVia} field with the name of the field that you need.

"Shipping Methods Selected: " + Join ({?ShipVia}, ", ")

Exercise 12.18: Print Multi Value Parameter Fields

1. Save the L12.11 report as L12.18 Print Multi Value Parameter fields.

2. Create a formula field called Print Regions. Type the code shown below and save the formula.

   "Regions Selected: " + Join ({?Region}, " , ")

3. Add the Print Regions formula field to the top of the page header section. Make the field longer, then save the changes.

4. Preview the report. Select two regions from the list and type in two other regions. Your report should look similar to the one shown in Figure 12-38. You will have different data on the report.

Regions Selected: CA , FL , PA , TX			
Customer Name	Address1	Region	Country
Sporting Wheels Inc.	480 Grant Way	CA	USA
Rockshocks for Jocks	1984 Sydney Street	TX	USA
Rowdy Rims Company	4861 Second Road	CA	USA
Clean Air Transportation C	1867 Thurlow Lane	PA	USA

Figure 12-38 Multi value parameter field printed on the report

Deleting Parameter Fields From A Report

You may need to delete a parameter field from a report. If you do, follow the steps below.

1. Right-click on the parameter field in the Field Explorer that you want to delete and select **DELETE**. You will see the message shown in Figure 12-39. This message is letting you know that once you delete the field it cannot be undone.

Figure 12-39 Delete parameter field message

2. Click Yes. You may see the message shown in Figure 12-40.

Figure 12-40 Unable to delete field message

This message is letting you know that the parameter field can't be deleted now because it is being used in the report. Before you can delete a parameter field, you have to delete it from the place(s) that it is being used in the report. In this example, it is being used on the Select Expert. If it was being used on the report to display the criteria that was used to run the report, you would have to delete it from there. The parameter field could also be used in a formula.

3. Click OK and delete the parameter field from all of the places that it is being used in the report. Once you do that, repeat step 1 above and the parameter field will be deleted, then save the changes.

Test Your Skills

1. Modify the L4.6 report to prompt to select a country.

   - The country prompt should allow multiple values.
   - Save the report as `L12.19 Skills select a country parameter field`.
   - The Enter Parameter Values dialog box should look like the one shown in Figure 12-41.

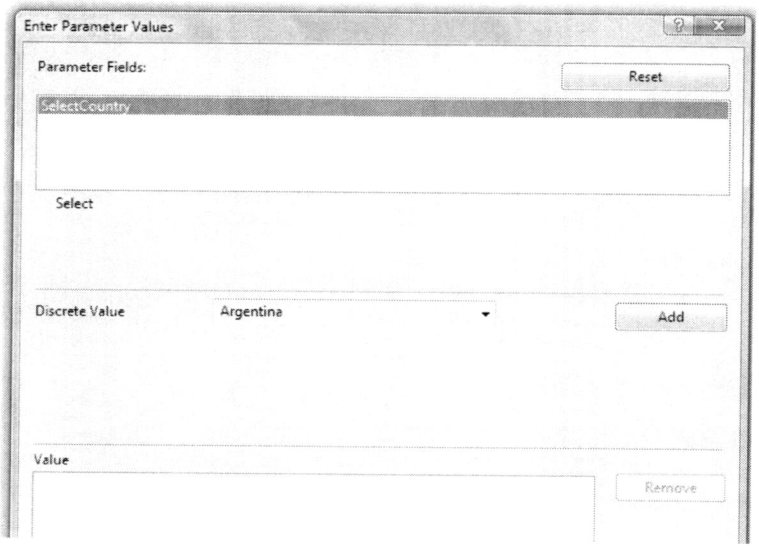

Figure 12-41 Enter Parameter Values dialog box options

2. Create parameter prompts for the L9.6 report.

   - Save the report as `L12.20 Skills sales rep parameter field`.
   - Create parameter fields for the sales rep and order date fields.
   - The parameter fields should let you select a sales rep by last name and an order date greater than or equal to the date selected on the Enter Parameter Values dialog box. For example, run the report and select the sales rep Janet Leverling and the date, 1/2/2001. The first page of the report should look like the one shown in Figure 12-42.

Employee	Order Date	Order #	Customer #	Product #	Unit Price	Quantity	Line Item Total
3 Janet Leverling							
12/31/2000							
11							
	01/02/2001	1123	11	102171	$1,739.85	3	$5,219.55
	Total order amount for customer - **$ 5,219.55**						
55							
	01/02/2001	1128	55	3304	$21.90	3	$65.70
	Total order amount for customer - **$ 65.70**						
Daily Totals	# of orders for the day - **2**						
	Total order amount for customer - **$ 5,285.25**						

Figure 12-42 L12.20 Skills sales rep parameter field report

3. Modify the L5.3 report to allow a range of order numbers like 1002 to 1050 and 1100 to 1124 to be entered.

- Save the report as L12.21 Skills order number range.
- Delete the Order Date selection criteria.
- If you run the report with the order number ranges listed above, there should be 100 records on the report. Figure 12-43 shows the Enter Parameter Values dialog box.

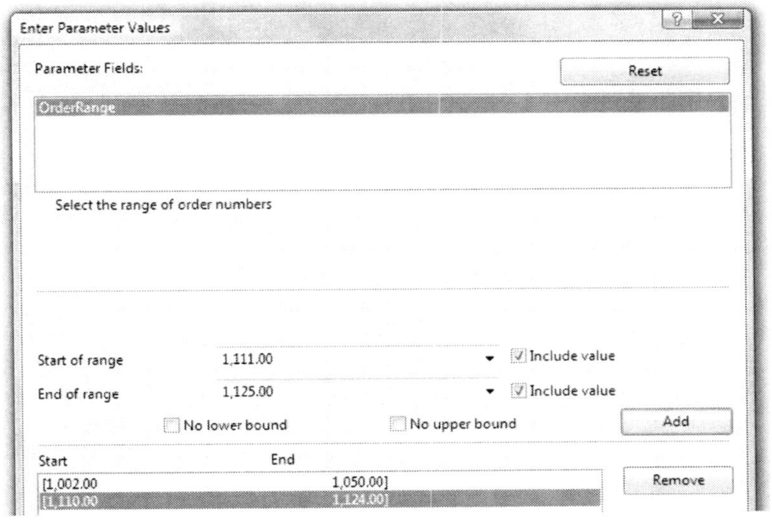

Figure 12-43 Order number range options

ADDITIONAL CRYSTAL REPORTS FUNCTIONALITY

Believe it or not, this workbook only covers a little more than half of the functionality that Crystal Reports has to offer report designers. You may be thinking that you have learned enough in the first 12 lessons to create all of the reports that you need. Some of the topics covered in this lesson, like the cross-tab and drill-down reports build on what you have already learned in previous lessons. Other topics are being introduced for the first time. Many of the reports that you learn how to create in this lesson are known as or referred to as "Non standard report types".

In this lesson you will learn how to:

- ☑ Use the Cross-Tab Expert
- ☑ Apply conditional formatting to a cross-tab object
- ☑ Add hyperlinks to a report
- ☑ Create Running Total reports
- ☑ Create a Hierarchical Group report
- ☑ Use the Group Sort Expert
- ☑ Create a form letter
- ☑ Add a watermark to a report

LESSON 13

Cross-Tab Expert Overview

In Lesson 7 you learned how to create a cross-tab report using a wizard. In this lesson you will learn more about cross-tab reports by learning how to use the Cross-Tab Expert. Cross-Tab reports let you summarize large amounts of data in columnar format, in a relatively small amount of space. Cross-Tab reports do not have to be the only object on the report. You can add a cross-tab object to a report that has standard data. In addition to using the Cross-Tab wizard, there are two ways to add a Cross-Tab object to a report as discussed below.

① Right-click on a blank space on the report and select Insert ⇒ Cross-Tab, then click in the report section where you want to place the cross-tab.
② Crystal Reports ⇒ Insert ⇒ Cross-Tab.

The Cross-Tab Expert has three tabs: Cross-Tab, Style and Customize Style. Many of the options on the first two tabs are on the Cross-Tab wizard.

Figure 13-1 shows the Cross-Tab tab.
Table 13-1 explains the buttons that are not on the Cross-Tab wizard.
Figure 13-4 shows the Style tab. The options on this tab are the same as the ones on the wizard.
Figure 13-5 shows the Customize Style tab. Tables 13-2 to 13-4 explain the options on this tab.

Cross-Tab Tab

The options shown in Figure 13-1 let you select the fields that will be used to create the cross-tab.

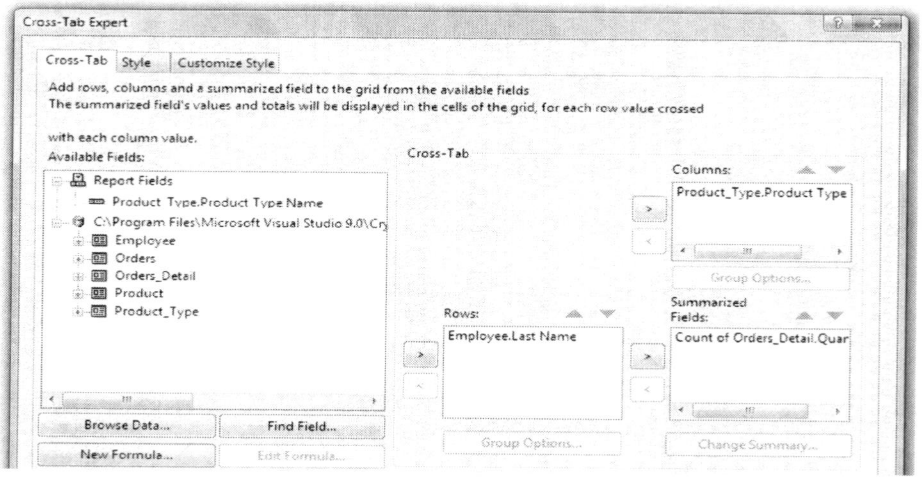

Figure 13-1 Cross-Tab options

Button	Description
New Formula	Opens the Formula Editor so that you can create a formula that is needed for the cross-tab report.
Edit Formula	Opens the Formula Editor so that you can edit an existing formula. You can edit a formula that has been added to the cross-tab or a formula that is listed in the Available Fields list.
Group Options	Opens the Cross-Tab Group Options dialog box shown in Figure 13-2. It is similar to the Insert Group dialog box that you have already learned about. After you click on a field in the Rows or Columns section, this button will be enabled and you can change the group options for the field.
Change Summary	Opens the Edit Summary dialog box shown in Figure 13-3. It works the same way that the Insert Summary dialog box works and will let you change the default summary type that was selected when the field was added to the Summarized Fields section.

Table 13-1 Buttons on the Cross-Tab tab explained

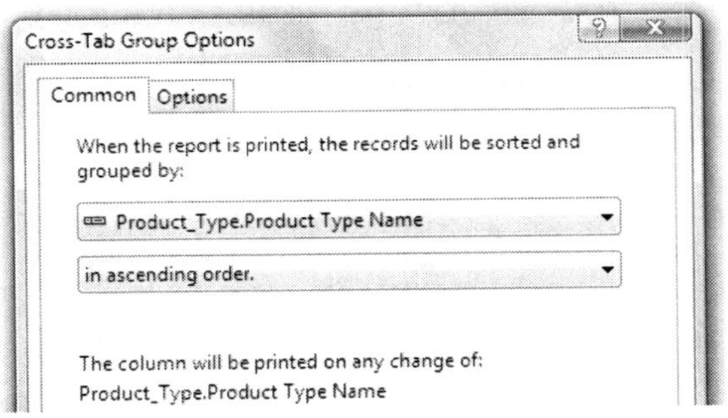

Figure 13-2 Cross-Tab Group Options dialog box

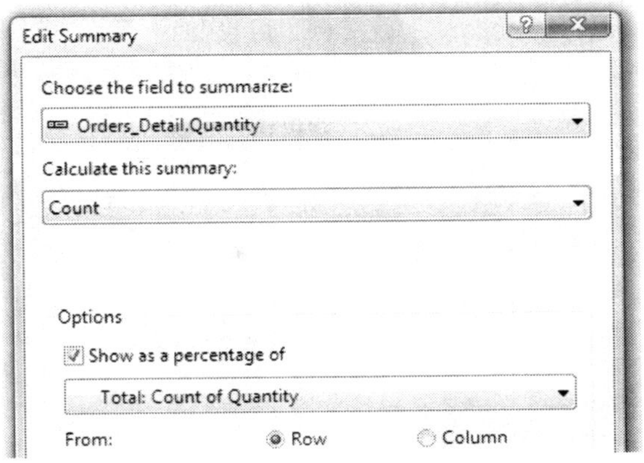

Figure 13-3 Edit Summary dialog box

Cross-Tab Tips

① It is best not to place any other objects in the same report section as the cross-tab, as they will probably be overwritten.
② When more than one field is added to the rows, columns or summarized fields sections, the values will be stacked in the cell.
③ If you want the cross-tab to capture all of the data in the report, place it in the report header section.
④ It is better to position fields so that there are more rows than columns. Doing this will help keep the cross-tab from being forced to print on more than one page.

Style Tab

The options shown in Figure 13-4 are the style templates that you can use to format the entire cross-tab object at one time. These are the same styles that are on the Cross-Tab wizard.

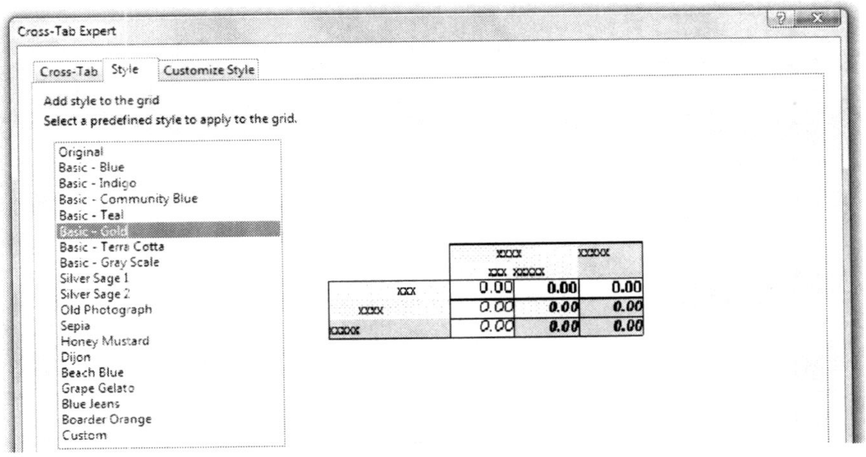

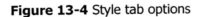

Figure 13-4 Style tab options

If there is a style that is close to what you need, select it then click on the Customize Style tab. Make the changes that you want to the style. If you want to save the style changes that you make, click Yes when prompted and create a name for your style. The style that you created will appear on the Style tab with the name "Custom". I could not find a way to rename the style.

Customize Style Tab

The options shown in Figure 13-5 let you apply formatting to a specific section of the cross-tab like a row or to the entire cross-tab object. Each field in the Rows and Columns sections represent a group.

The options in the Grid Options section are applied to the entire cross-tab.

The options in the Group Options section can be applied to each field.

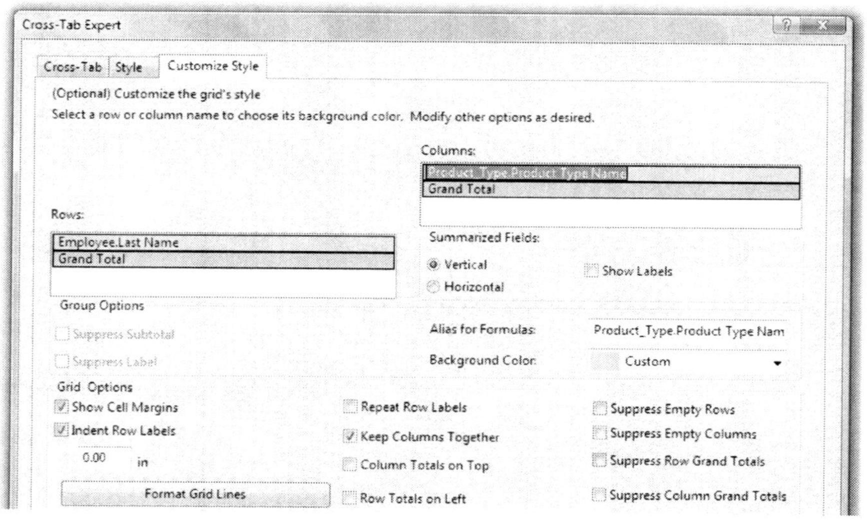

Figure 13-5 Customize Style tab options

Option	Description
Vertical/Horizontal	These options determine how the summarized fields will be displayed. There has to be at least two summarized fields to select one of these options. The **VERTICAL** option will stack the summarized fields in the same cell. This is the default option. The **HORIZONTAL** option will place the summarized fields side by side.
Show Labels	If checked, this option will display the summarized field name in the row or column header.

Table 13-2 Summarized Field options explained

Option	Description
Suppress Subtotal	This option is only available if there are two or more fields in the Rows section or two or more fields in the Columns section. This option cannot be used on grand total fields. If checked, this option will suppress the subtotal for the row or column that is selected.
Suppress Label	This option is only available if the Suppress Subtotal option is checked. If checked, this option will suppress the Group By fields label.
Alias for Formulas	This option lets you enter a different name for the field that is used on the cross-tab. The name entered in this field can be used in conditional formatting formulas instead of the name in the table.
Background Color	This drop-down list box will let you select a background color for the row or column of data.

Table 13-3 Group Options explained

Option	Description
Indent Row Labels	Allows you to set how much space you want to indent the row labels.
Repeat Row Labels	This option is only available if the Keep Columns together option is checked. This option will force the row labels to be repeated on other pages when the width of the cross-tab requires more than one page.
Keep Columns Together	This option will prevent a column from being split across two pages.
Column Totals on Top	This option will cause column totals to print at the top of the column.
Row Totals on Left	If checked, this option will cause the row totals to print on the left of the cross-tab object.
Suppress Empty Rows	If checked, rows that do not have data will not appear in the cross-tab.
Suppress Empty Columns	If checked, columns that do not have data will not appear in the cross-tab.
Suppress Row Grand Totals	If checked, the grand total row will not appear in the cross-tab.
Suppress Column Grand Totals	If checked, the grand total column will not appear in the cross-tab.
Format Grid Lines button	Clicking this button will open the Format Grid Lines dialog box shown in Figure 13-6. Table 13-5 explains the options on this dialog box.

Table 13-4 Grid Options explained

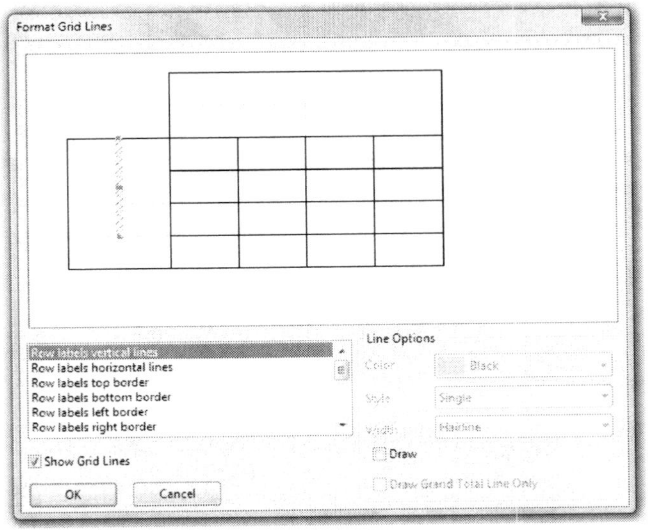

Figure 13-6 Format Grid Lines dialog box

Option	Description
Grid Line	Lets you select the grid line in the list box that you want to modify. The grid line(s) that you select will be highlighted in the grid at the top of the dialog box.
Show Grid Lines	Lets you turn the grid lines on or off.
Color	Lets you select a color for the grid lines.
Style	Lets you select a style for the grid lines.
Width	Lets you select a width for the grid lines.
Draw	Lets you select a specific grid line to hide.
Draw Grand Total Line Only	If checked, this option will only display grid lines on grand total rows or columns.

Table 13-5 Format Grid Lines dialog box options explained

Sample Cross-Tab Report

In Lesson 7 the cross-tab reports that you created only had one field in the rows, columns and summarized fields sections. When additional fields are added to the rows or columns sections of the Cross-Tab Expert it is the same as creating additional groups on a report. If the customers country field is added to the rows section, the L7.10 report will look like the one shown in Figure 13-7. [See the L13 Cross-Tab multi row report in the zip file]

		Gloves	Kids	Saddles	Total
Davolio	Canada	2	1	2	5
	USA	69	15	35	119
	Total	71	16	37	124
Dodsworth	Canada	7	3	3	13
	USA	69	14	40	123
	Total	76	17	43	136
King	Canada	8	2	2	12
	USA	68	13	39	120
	Total	76	15	41	132

Figure 13-7 L7.10 report with another row added

Formatting Formulas

You can create conditional formatting formulas in a cross-tab using the Format Editor, similar to how conditional formatting formulas are created for other fields on a report. The **CURRENTFIELDVALUE** function is similar to the **DEFAULTATTRIBUTE** that you learned about in Lesson 10. You can use the CurrentFieldValue function in a formula for the field that is currently being evaluated instead of typing in the table and field name, as you will see in Example 1 below.

In addition to being able to use the CurrentFieldValue and DefaultAttribute functions, cross-tabs can also use the **GRIDROWCOLUMNVALUE** function. This function lets you create a formula that depends on the value in a row that is related to the current cell. An advantage to using the GridRowColumnValue function is that you can use the Alias field name instead of the real field name. The examples below demonstrate how these functions can be used in a cross-tab or OLAP grid.

Example #1 The formula below will set the current field (cell) to yellow if it is greater than or equal to 25.

If CurrentFieldValue >= 25 Then crYellow Else DefaultAttribute

Example #2 The formula below will set the current field (cell) to yellow if it is greater than or equal to 100 and the Product Name is "Gloves".

If GridRowColumnValue {Product.Product Name} = "Gloves" and CurrentFieldValue >= 100 Then crYellow Else DefaultAttribute

 You can use the **HIGHLIGHTING EXPERT** to format data fields in a cross-tab.

Exercise 13.1: Use The Cross-Tab Expert

In this exercise you will recreate the cross-tab report that you created in Exercise 7.10. You will enhance the report by adding the following:

① Indenting the row labels.
② Modifying the grid lines.
③ Applying conditional formatting to change the background of cells that meet a specific condition.
④ Create a formula to calculate the total dollar amount of sales per product, per sales rep.

Create The Product Type Selection Criteria

The Cross-Tab wizard has a Record Selection screen that lets you create selection criteria. If you use the Cross-Tab Expert, you have different options. You can create a formula or create the selection criteria using the Select Expert.

1. Create a new report and save it as `L13.1 Cross-Tab`. Add the following tables to the report: Employee, Orders, Orders Detail, Product and Product Type, then click Finish.

2. Select the Cross-Tab Expert, then click OK.

3. Open the Select Expert. Select the Product Type Name field in the Product Type table and click OK. Select the "Is one of" operator, then add the gloves, kids and saddles options, then click OK.

Create The Cross-Tab

1. Add a cross-tab object to the report header. Right-click on the report header section bar and select **DON'T SUPPRESS**.

2. Move the Last Name field in the Employee table to the **ROWS** section.

3. Move the Product Type Name field in the Product Type table to the **COLUMNS** section.

4. Move the Quantity field in the Orders Detail table to the **SUMMARIZED FIELDS** section.

5. Click the **CHANGE SUMMARY** button and change the summary type to Count, then click OK.

Customize The Cross-Tab

The Customize Style tab has several options that you can use to change the appearance of the cross-tab.

1. On the Customize Style tab, clear the **COLUMN TOTALS ON TOP** and **ROW TOTALS ON LEFT** options, if they are selected.

2. Check the Indent Row Labels option and type `.25` in the box below it.

3. Click the Format Grid Lines button.

4. Scroll down the list and select the **COLUMN LABEL BOTTOM BORDER** option, then select **DASHED** from the Style drop-down list.

5. Click OK to close the Format Gridlines dialog box, then click OK to close the Cross-Tab Expert.

6. Save the changes. The report should look like the one shown in Figure 13-8. Leave the report open to complete the next part of the exercise.

	Gloves	Kids	Saddles	Total
Davolio	85	18	49	152
Dodsworth	101	19	58	178
King	97	23	58	178
Leverling	84	25	56	165
Peacock	105	20	59	184
Suyama	84	25	56	165
Total	556	130	336	1,022

Figure 13-8 L13.1 Cross-Tab report

Add Another Row Of Data To The Cross-Tab

In this part of the exercise you will create a formula that will calculate the total of each product that each sales report sold.

1. Open the Cross-Tab Expert and click the New Formula button.

2. Type `Line Item` as the formula name, then click the Use Editor button. Type the formula shown below.

   `{Orders_Detail.Unit Price} * {Orders_Detail.Quantity}`

3. Save the formula, then click on the field in the Available Fields list on the Cross-Tab Expert and add it to the Summarized Fields section. Click OK.

4. Make the row and column headings bold, then remove the bold from the other fields.
   (**Hint**: You can select all of the headings first, then add the bold formatting.) Save the changes. The cross-tab should look like the one shown in Figure 13-9.

If you are wondering why sales reps have the same quantity sold of a product but have different totals for the product, like the sales reps Leverling and Suyama do in the gloves column, it is because the products listed are categories of products, meaning that there are different types of gloves and each type of glove has a different price. I thought the same thing at first, that there could be something wrong with the Line Item formula, so I created a detail report and looked at the raw data for the gloves and saw that there are different priced gloves.

	Gloves	Kids	Saddles	Total
Davolio	85 $2,735.59	18 $11,498.14	49 $1,929.29	152 $16,163.02
Dodsworth	101 $3,404.30	19 $11,625.66	58 $2,492.96	178 $17,522.92
King	97 $2,933.57	23 $15,069.70	58 $2,348.04	178 $20,351.31
Leverling	84 $2,668.06	25 $13,833.10	56 $2,235.63	165 $18,736.79
Peacock	105 $3,174.88	20 $10,830.79	59 $2,647.96	184 $16,653.63
Suyama	84 $2,486.31	25 $13,532.76	56 $2,026.98	165 $18,046.05
Total	556 $17,402.71	130 $76,390.15	336 $13,680.86	1,022 $107,473.72

Figure 13-9 Second row of data added to the cross-tab

When you see data that does not look right or somehow catches your attention, you should take the time to look at the raw data to see if you can find out why the data looks the way that it does. [See the L13 Cross-Tab check data report in the zip file] This is the report that I created to figure out if there was really a problem with the formula.

Exercise 13.2: Creating Conditional Formatting In Cross-Tabs

Creating conditional formatting in cross-tabs is not that much different then creating conditional formatting in other types of reports. In this exercise you will create conditional formatting on the quantity cells in the gloves column to change the background color to yellow if the quantity is greater than or equal to 100. This would be helpful to quickly be able to see which sales reps sold the most of this particular product.

1. Save the L13.1 report as `L13.2 Conditional formatting Cross-Tab.`

2. In the first column of the cross-tab, right-click on the detail Quantity field and select Format Field.

3. On the Border tab click the Formula button across from the Background option.

4. Type the formula shown below, then click the Save and close button.

```
If GridRowColumnValue("Product_Type.Product Type Name") = "Gloves"
and CurrentFieldValue >= 100 Then crYellow Else DefaultAttribute
```

5. Click OK and save the changes. The gloves quantity for two sales reps should have a yellow background.

Cross-Tab Printing Issues

Cross-tab objects can have printing issues, in particular cross-tab objects that require more than one page to print horizontally. The Cross-Tab Expert has the Repeat Row Labels and Keep Columns Together options that you learned about earlier in Table 13-4, that you can use to resolve some printing issues. If there are horizontal printing issues, there are some options that you can use to resolve them.

① **Repeat Horizontal Pages** This option is on the Common tab on the Format Editor dialog box. If checked, this option will force objects in the page header or page footer section to print on every horizontal page.

② **Relative Positions** This option is on the Common tab on the Section Expert. Use it to control an object that is to the right of a cross-tab object. If checked, this option will cause the object next to the cross-tab to stay in the same relative position, regardless of how much the cross-tab grows.

Hyperlinks

If you have used the Internet, you have used hyperlinks, which are often called "Links". Crystal Reports has hyperlink functionality that you can add to reports. You may have already seen the Hyperlink tab shown in Figure 13-10, on the Format Editor.

In addition to being able to create a hyperlink to a website or email address, you can create a hyperlink to a file. You can also create hyperlinks to websites and email addresses that are stored in a table. Hyperlinks can be attached to objects like a chart or logo on the report.

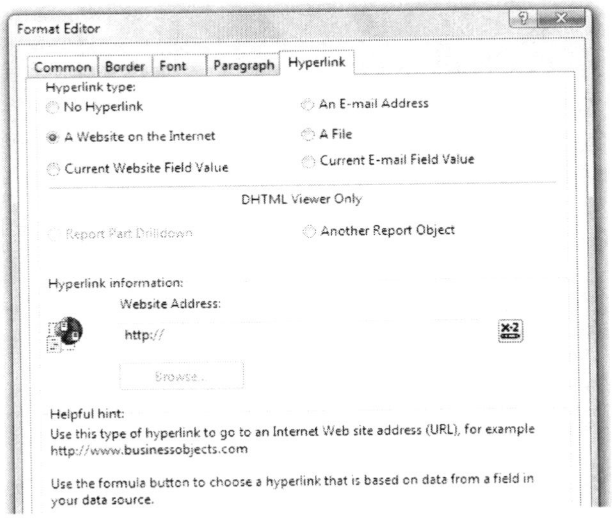

Figure 13-10 Hyperlink tab on the Format Editor

Hyperlink Options

Before opening this tab, you have to select the object that you want to use for the hyperlink.

No Hyperlink Select this option to remove the hyperlink.

A Web Site On The Internet This option will allow you to create a hyperlink to a specific page on a web site.

Current Website Field Value This option lets you create a hyperlink for website addresses that are stored in a field. Each record that appears on the report that has a web site will have a hyperlink to the web site.

An Email Address This option will allow you to create a hyperlink to a specific email address.

A File This option allows you to create a hyperlink to a file. This file can be another report or a document. The only stipulation is that the file has to reside in a location that the person running the report can access. Unless the person running the report has access to your hard drive, you should not create a hyperlink to a file on your hard drive.

Current E-mail Field Value This option lets you create a hyperlink for email addresses that are stored in a field. Each record that appears on the report that has an email address will have a hyperlink to the email address.

Exercise 13.3: Create Hyperlinks

In this exercise you will create the following types of hyperlinks.

       ① A website on the Internet.
       ② An email address.
       ③ To a file.
       ④ To an email address stored in a field in a table.
       ⑤ To a website address stored in a field in a table.

1. Create a new report and save it as `L13.3 Hyperlinks`.

2. Select the Standard Expert, then add the Customer Name, Web Site and E-mail address fields from the Customer table to the report.

3. Add the Xtreme logo image to the report header section.

Create A Hyperlink To A Website

1. Right-click on the logo and select Format Object.

2. On the Hyperlink tab, select the option, A website on the Internet.

3. Click after the http:// in the Website address field and type `www.tolanapublishing.com`. You should have the options shown in Figure 13-11. Click OK and save the changes.

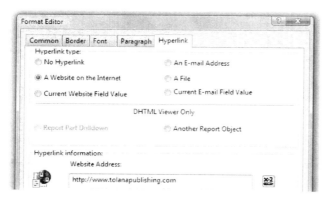

Figure 13-11 Website hyperlink options

Create A Tool Tip For A Hyperlink

1. Right-click on the logo and select Format Object.

2. Type `Go to www.tolanapublishing.com` in the **TOOL TIP TEXT** field on the Common tab and click OK.

Create A Hyperlink To An Email Address

1. Add a text object to the report header section and type
   `Click here to send an email to` and your first name.

2. Right-click on the text object and select Format Object.

3. On the Hyperlink tab select the An Email Address option, then type your email address in the E-mail Address field after the words MAIL TO:. You should have the options shown in Figure 13-12. The only difference should be the email address. Click OK and save the changes.

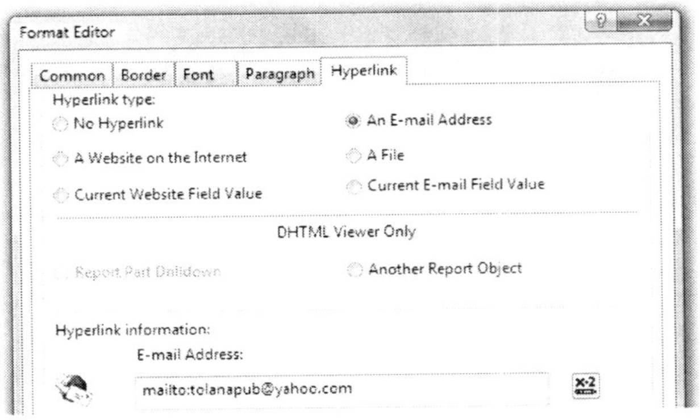

Figure 13-12 E-mail Address hyperlink options

Create A Hyperlink To A File

In this part of the exercise you are going to pretend that your hard drive is a network server and create a hyperlink to a file on your hard drive. Yes, I know this contradicts what I said earlier about not creating links to a file on your hard drive, but everyone reading this workbook does not have access to the same server.

1. Add a text object to the report header section and type
   `Click here to open the L8.6 Orders PDF file.`

2. Right-click on the text object and select Format Object.

3. On the Hyperlink tab select the option, A File, then click the BROWSE button.

4. Navigate to your project folder and double-click on the L8.6 Skills Top 5 orders PDF export file. You may have to change the Files of Type option to All files, to see the PDF file. You should have the options shown in Figure 13-13. Click OK and save the changes.

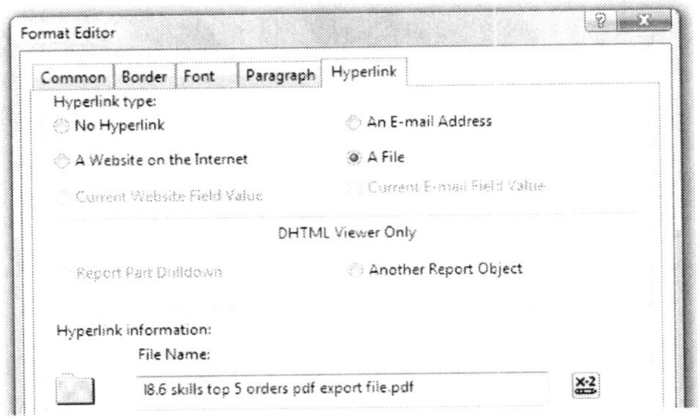

Figure 13-13 File hyperlink options

Create A Hyperlink To An Email Address In A Field

1. Right-click on the E-mail field in the details section and select Format Object.

2. On the Hyperlink tab select the Current E-Mail Field Value option. Notice that the section where you normally type in the information is dimmed out. That is because this type of hyperlink is tied to a field in the table. You should have the options shown in Figure 13-14. Click OK and save the changes.

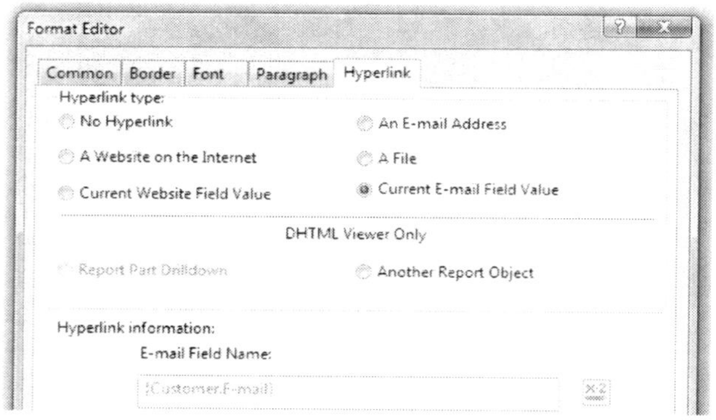

Figure 13-14 Email address field hyperlink options

Create A Hyperlink To A Website Address In A Field

1. Right-click on the Website address field and select Format Object.

2. On the Hyperlink tab select the Current Website Field Value option. You should have the options shown in Figure 13-15. Click OK and save the changes.

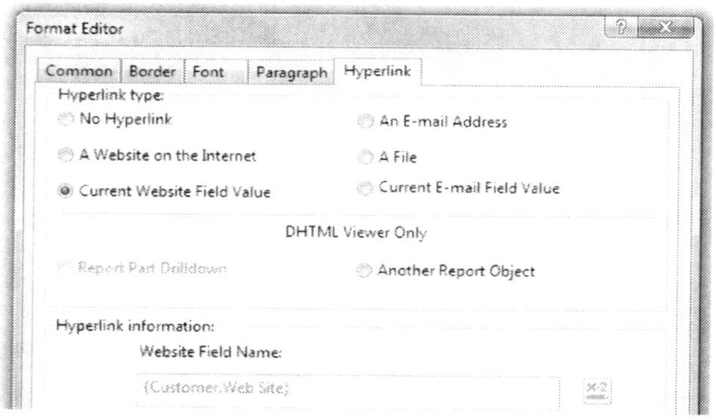

Figure 13-15 Website address field hyperlink options

Test The Hyperlinks

1. The report should look like the one shown in Figure 13-16. If you hold the mouse pointer over the logo you should see the tool tip. The tool tip did not display for me. If you are connected to the Internet, click on the logo. You should see the home page of Tolana Publishing.

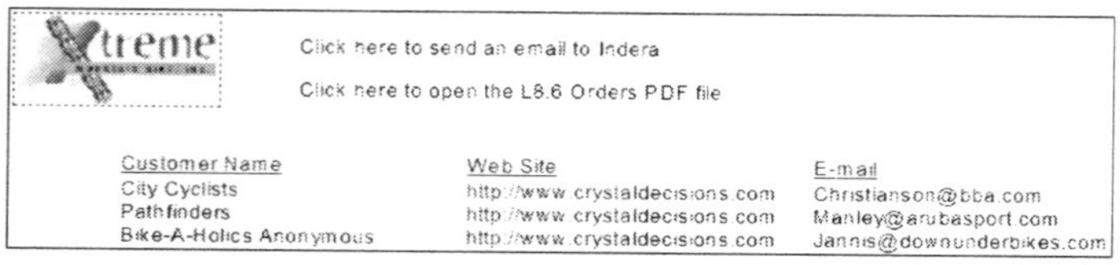

Figure 13-16 L13.3 Hyperlinks report

2. Click on the Email address text object in the report header. Your email software and a new email window should open. If it doesn't and you are sure that you created the hyperlink correctly, this could mean that your email software is not configured to open from a hyperlink.

3. Click on the hyperlink for the L8.6 file. The PDF file will open if you have Adobe Acrobat or the free Adobe reader installed.

4. Click on the Email address for Pathfinders. If your email software did not open in step 2 above, it probably will not open when you click on this link.

5. Click on the Web Site address for City Cyclists. The Business Objects web site should open. Some readers have let me know that a different web site opens. I haven't been able to duplicate the problem.

Running Total Fields

Running total fields are similar to the summary fields that you have already learned to create. While running total fields are similar to summary fields, they provide more options which allows you more flexibility over the total fields that you create. There are five differences between running total and summary fields, as discussed below.

① Running total fields only calculate data that is displayed.
② Running total fields can be placed in the details section of the report, which would display a total up to the current record.
③ Running total fields are only evaluated/calculated during the **WHILE PRINTING RECORDS** pass of the report is taking place. Crystal Reports uses a three pass system. This means that records in the "Others" group will not be counted in grand totals.
④ Running total fields are calculated at the detail level (record by record) and summary fields are calculated by group.
⑤ If a running total field is placed in the group header section, it will only include a total for the first record in the group because the other records in the group have not been processed at this point.

As you learned in Lesson 11, Top N reports do not have to include records that do not meet the Top N criteria. Records that do not meet the Top N criteria can be placed in the "Others" group. It is important to note that records in the "Others" group will be included in any grand totals on the report, whether or not the records in the "Others" group are printed on the report.

This is something that needs to be addressed during the report design phase. You have to find out if the people requesting the report want grand totals only for the records that meet the Top N requirements or all records including those in the "Others" category. Figure 13-17 shows the Create Running Total Field dialog box. If you only want report or grand totals for the records that meet the Top N condition, you have to use a running total field instead of a summary field.

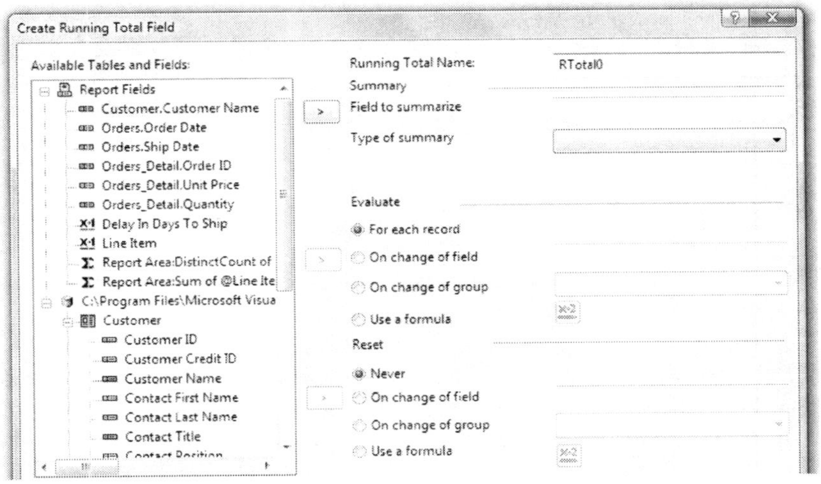

Figure 13-17 Create Running Total Field dialog box

You have probably figured out that there are a lot of good reasons to use running total fields instead of summary fields. You have also probably realized that selecting the appropriate type of total field (summary or running total) requires some thought. The other item that you have to consider is where the running total field will be placed on the report. Table 13-6 explains what the running total field will calculate depending on which section of the report it is placed in. The output will change depending on the **EVALUATE** option that is selected.

Section	Which Records Will Be Calculated
Report Header	The first record on the report.
Page Header	All records up to the first record that will be printed on the current page.
Group Header	All records up to the first record of the current group.
Details	All records up to the current detail record.
Group Footer	All records up to the last record in the current group.
Page Footer	All records up to the first record on the next page.
Report Footer	All records on the report.

Table 13-6 Running total field output options explained

Like other dialog boxes that you have used, the Available Tables and Fields section contains the fields and formulas that you can use to create running total fields. The options in the **SUMMARY** section at the top on the right let you enter a name for the running total field, select a field to base the running total field on and select the type of summary. The options in the **TYPE OF SUMMARY** field drop-down list are the same as the ones for summary fields. The name of this field can be misleading because as you can see, a running total field does more then create totals. Like summary fields, it can provide counts, averages, percents and more.

The options in the **EVALUATE** section let you select when you want the running total field to be incremented. The **FOR EACH RECORD** option is most like a summary field calculation because the running total field is incremented after each detail record is processed.

The **ON CHANGE OF FIELD** option performs the running total field calculation when the value in the field is different then the value from the previous record. This is useful when the field that the running total is using can have several records that have the same value and you only want to count the value once. This is like the Distinct Count summary type that you have already used. If you are using a field like the Order ID field and the report uses the Orders and Orders Details tables, most of the time you should select the Order ID field from the parent table, which in this example is the Orders table.

When selecting this evaluation option, give some thought to the data that is in the field that you are using because records other then the first one that has the same data will not increment the running total field because this option excludes records. The key to using this option successfully is to select a field that has a lot of unique values in it.

 If you are going to use the **ON CHANGE OF FIELD** option, make sure that the records are sorted correctly, otherwise you will end up with unexpected results.

The **ON CHANGE OF GROUP** option can only be used on a report that has a group. This option will evaluate (increment) the running total field when the group changes.

If you need the running total field to be incremented based on a condition, select the **USE A FORMULA** option and click the Formula button next to the field. Then create a formula that the records must meet in order for the running total field to be incremented. An example of this would be if the report needed a total of orders that were not shipped in three days. The formula would check the Delay In Days To Ship formula field. If it was greater than three, add the order total to the running total field. If you needed a count of how many orders were not shipped that had an Delay In Days To Ship amount greater than three, you would create another running total field, use the count summary type and use the same formula for this running total field.

The options in the **RESET** section let you select when you want the running total field to be reset to zero. If you were using the running total field to get group totals, you would select the **ON CHANGE OF GROUP** option, then select the group from the drop-down list. You could also create a formula that determined when to reset the running total field.

 You should also use a running total field on reports that suppress records if there is a group selection formula. Report grand totals are calculated **BEFORE** the group selection formulas that have suppression are calculated.

There are two ways to open the Create Running Total Field dialog box as discussed below.

    ① Right-click on the field in the details section that you want to create a running total for and select Insert ⇒ Running Total.
    ② Right-click on the Running Total Fields category in the Field Explorer and select New.

Exercise 13.4: Create Two Delay In Shipping Running Total Fields

In this exercise you will create two running total fields. You will create one to get an order total amount of orders that were not shipped in three days. The second running total field will count the number of orders that were not shipped in three days.

1. Save the L9.10 report as `L13.4 Delay in shipping running totals`.

2. Create the Line Item formula field that you created earlier in Exercise 13.1 and add it to the report after the Quantity field. Wrap the Delay In Days To Ship field heading to two lines.

Create The Order Total Amount Running Total Field

In this part of the exercise you will create a running total field that will only count the Unit of Price amount if the Delay in Shipping is greater than three days.

1. Right-click on the Line Item formula field and select Insert ⇒ Running Total.

2. Type `Order Total Delay Amount` in the Running Total Name field.

3. Select the Sum Type of Summary, if it is not already selected.

4. Select the **USE A FORMULA** Evaluate option, then click the Formula button.

5. Double-click on the Delay In Days To Ship field, then type `> 3` as the criteria.

6. Highlight the formula and press the Ctrl + C keys. This will let you paste the code into the next formula that you will create.

7. Click the Save and close button, then click OK and save the changes.

Create The Order Count Running Total Field

In this part of the exercise you will create a running total field to get a count of the number of orders that were not shipped in three days.

If you preview the report you will see duplicate values in the Customer Name and Order ID fields. This means that some orders have more than one item. If this were live data, often the items that are in stock will ship immediately and the items that are not, will be delayed. Whatever the case is, you only want to count each order once. Therefore, using the Count summary option would not work. You would have to use the Distinct Count option on the Order ID field.

1. Open the Create Running Total Field dialog box and type `Order Count` in the Running Total Name field.

2. Select the Order ID field as the Field to summarize.

3. Select the Distinct Count Type of Summary.

4. Select the Use a formula Evaluate option, then click the Formula button.

5. Paste the formula in by pressing the Ctrl + V keys.

6. Click the Save and close button, then click OK and save the changes.

> You could get the same results without a formula if the report was sorted on the Order ID field and you selected the **ON CHANGE OF FIELD** Evaluate option.

Add The Running Total Fields To The Report

1. Drag the Order Count running total field to the report footer section. Move the Order Total Delay Amount field to the report footer section. Create headings for the fields.

2. Format the Order Total Delay Amount field to have a floating dollar sign. Delete the Record Number field from the report footer. Save the changes. The totals on the last page of the report should look like the ones shown in Figure 13-18.

Bicicletas de Montaña C	06/26/2001	06/26/2001	3,179	$764.85	3	$2,294.55	0
Guadalajara en ruedas	06/26/2001	06/27/2001	3,180	$790.73	3	$2,372.19	1
Total # of orders > 3 days shipping	422			Total order amount of orders > 3 days shipping		$ 792,498.58	

Figure 13-18 L13.4 Delay in shipping running totals report

Modify The Report

If you look in the Delay in Days to Ship column, you will see records that have a value that is less than three. These records are not counted in the running total fields. The person reading the report may or may not know or remember this. For example, they may think that the total order amount for all of the records that are on the report is almost $800,000.00. That is not true. That amount only includes the records that were not shipped in three days.

To help clarify these running total fields on the report, you could print a message that says that the totals only include orders not shipped in three days. If you do that, more than likely, the person would ask you to include totals for all of the records on the report as well, so it's better to be proactive and add the fields up front.

1. Create a Distinct Count summary field based on the Order ID field and place it below the Total number of orders running total field in the report footer section. Format it so that it only displays whole numbers with a comma.

2. Create a summary field based on the Line Item formula field and place it below the Total order amount running total field in the report footer section.

3. Create a title for the Order ID summary field called `Total # of orders on the report.`

4. Create a title for the Line Item formula field called `Total order amount of all orders on the report.`

5. Remove the bold from all fields in the report footer section. Save the changes. The last page of the report should look like the one shown in Figure 13-19.

Customer Name	Order Date	Ship Date	Order ID	Unit Price	Quantity	Line Item	Delay In Days To Ship
Total # of orders > 3 days shipping		422	Total order amount of orders > 3 days shipping				$792,498.58
Total # of orders on the report		1,260	Total order amount of all orders on the report				$2,441,325.43

Figure 13-19 L13.4 Revised report footer section

As you can see, there is a rather large difference in count and amount of the orders that were not shipped in three days versus the orders that are printed on the report.

Exercise 13.5: Use Running Total Fields With Parameter Fields

As you learned in Lesson 12, parameter fields allow you to not hard code selection criteria, which makes the report much more flexible. The report that you created in Exercise 12.13 allows the user to select the date range and number of delay in days to ship. In this exercise you will modify that report to include the running total fields that you created in Exercise 13.4. You will also create summary fields that provide totals for the entire report. These fields will demonstrate the difference between summary and running total fields.

1. Save the L12.13 report as `L13.5 Running total and parameter fields`.

2. Create the Line Item formula field, the Order Total Delay Amount and Order Count running total fields that you created in Exercise 13.4. Add the fields to the report footer section.

3. Create two summary fields, one for a distinct count of orders and one for the total order amount of all records. Place these fields in the report footer section under the running total fields.

4. Create titles for these fields as shown below.

5. Run the report for all of 2001, with a delay in shipping days that is greater than or equal to four. Save the changes. The last page of the report should look like the one shown in Figure 13-20.

Customer Name	Order Date	Ship Date	Order ID	Unit Price	Quantity	Line Item	Delay In Days To Ship
Number of orders with a delay in shipping		529	Total order amount of delayed orders			$ 950,860.65	
Total number of orders		2,616	Total order amount of all orders			$ 2,861,205.48	

Figure 13-20 L13.5 Running total and parameter fields report

Running Total And Summary Field Limitation

The one limitation that both field types have is that they will not produce the correct result if the report suppresses data because by default both fields will calculate the suppressed records that will not be printed on the report. This happens because both fields perform calculations without taking into account conditional formatting formulas that the suppress option may have.

In Exercise 10.15 you modified a report and added a formula to the Suppress (No Drill-Down) option on three sections of the report. This was done because the report requirement was to only display groups that met a condition. You have to follow the same process for a running total field. The reason that you have to do this is because you only want running total fields to include records that will actually appear on the report. To fix the L10.15 report add the same formula to the running total fields.

Figure 13-21 shows the last page of the L10.15 report. This version of the report has summary fields and running totals in the report footer section.
[See the L13 Suppression report in the zip file]

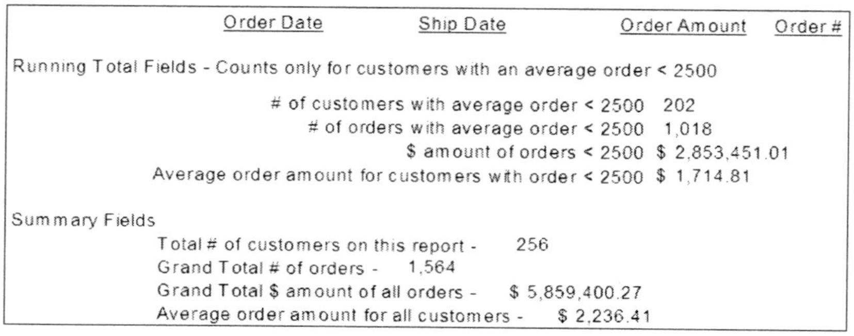

Order Date	Ship Date	Order Amount	Order #

Running Total Fields - Counts only for customers with an average order < 2500

# of customers with average order < 2500   202
# of orders with average order < 2500   1,018
$ amount of orders < 2500 $ 2,853,451.01
Average order amount for customers with order < 2500 $ 1,714.81

Summary Fields

Total # of customers on this report -   256
Grand Total # of orders -   1,564
Grand Total $ amount of all orders - $ 5,859,400.27
Average order amount for all customers - $ 2,236.41

Figure 13-21 Running total fields added to the L10.15 report

Notice that the amounts are different. The summary fields did not produce the amounts that you expected because it includes values not printed on the report. Running total fields only include values that are printed on the report. The reason that the summary field totals are larger is because it includes records that are not printed on the report. As you read, summary fields are calculated in the first pass of the report. Filtering and suppression are done on the second pass.

Hierarchical Group Reports

A hierarchical group is a special type of parent-child, one-to-many relationship. It shows the relationship between records that are in the same table. If it helps, think of the parent field as the field that is displayed in the group header section and the child fields will be displayed in the details section of the report. In Lesson 3 you learned about **RECURSIVE JOINS**. This type of join is required to create hierarchical reports. [See Lesson 3, Recursive Joins]

Hierarchical groups are useful when you need to create a report where two fields in the same table relate to each other. This is what Crystal Reports refers to as a hierarchical group. This is how you can create organizational charts. The Employee table lists the employees that work for the company. It also contains who each employee reports to. Remember that the person that has someone reporting to them is also an employee.

In this example, the people that have someone reporting to them is the "parent" portion of the relationship. Employees that do not have anyone reporting to them is the "child" portion of the relationship. The Hierarchical Group Options dialog box shown in Figure 13-22 is used to create hierarchical group reports.

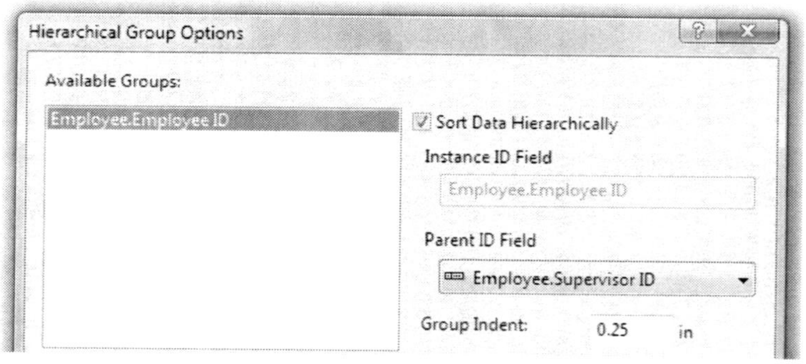

Figure 13-22 Hierarchical Group Options dialog box

The **AVAILABLE GROUPS** list contains all of the groups that the report has. The hierarchical report must be created using one of the groups that are listed in this section.

Once you select a group, check the **SORT DATA HIERARCHICALLY** option to indicate that you want to apply hierarchical sorting to the group that is selected.

The **INSTANCE ID FIELD** contains the field that will be used as the child field.

The **PARENT ID FIELD** contains the fields that can be used as the parent field. The parent record (in this example, the supervisor) will print first and then the employees that report to the supervisor will print below. All of the fields in this drop-down list are the same data type as the group field.

The **GROUP INDENT** option lets you select how much the child records should be indented. Using this feature is optional. If the columns do not contain a lot of data and the Group Indent option is greater than zero, it is possible that some data will not line up properly with the field headings. One way to fix this is to make the Group Indent number smaller. Another option is to resize some of the fields on the report. Leaving this option set to zero means that the child records will not be indented, which will make it difficult to see who reports to who.

Hierarchical Report Requirements

In order to create a hierarchical report, the following three requirements must be met.

① The table must have two fields that represent the same data. This allows the data in one field to point to another record in the same table.

② The parent and child fields must have the same data type.

③ The report must be grouped on the child field.

Exercise 13.6: Create A Hierarchical Group Report

In this exercise you will create an organizational report that shows who each employee reports to.

1. Create a new report and save it as `L13.6 Hierarchical report`. Add the Employee table, but do not add any fields to the report.

2. Create a group on the Employee ID field. Use the Options tab to create a group name formula that combines the Employee first and last name fields. [See Exercise 9.6]

3. Crystal Reports ⇒ Report ⇒ Hierarchical Grouping Options. You will see the Hierarchical Group Options dialog box.

4. Check the Sort Data Hierarchically option, then select the Supervisor ID field from the Parent ID Field drop-down list.

5. Change the Group Indent option to `.25`. You should have the options shown above in Figure 13-22. Click OK.

6. Add the Position and Hire Date fields to the group header section, then format the Hire Date field so that the time will not be displayed. Save the changes. The report should look like the one shown in Figure 13-23.

Andrew Fuller	Vice President, Sales	07/12/1991
Steven Buchanan	Sales Manager	09/13/1992
Nancy Davolio	Sales Representative	03/29/1991
Janet Leverling	Sales Representative	02/27/1991
Margaret Peacock	Sales Representative	03/30/1992
Michael Suyama	Sales Representative	09/13/1992
Robert King	Sales Representative	11/29/1992
Laura Callahan	Inside Sales Coordinator	01/30/1993
Anne Dodsworth	Sales Representative	10/12/1993
Albert Hellstern	Business Manager	03/01/1993
Tim Smith	Mail Clerk	01/15/1993
Caroline Patterson	Receptionist	05/15/1993
Justin Brid	Marketing Director	01/01/1994
Xavier Martin	Marketing Associate	01/15/1994
Laurent Pereira	Advertising Specialist	02/01/1994

Figure 13-23 L13.6 Hierarchical report

The Group Sort Expert

You have already used the Group Sort Expert to create and modify Top N reports. In addition to being able to create and modify Top N reports, the Group Sort Expert allows you to sort groups in ways other than ascending or descending order. You can sort groups based on values in a summary field in the group.

For example, in Exercise 6.2, you created a report that grouped the orders by customer. You also created two summary fields for the customer group; one for the customers total dollar amount of orders and one for the total number of orders. If someone needed to see the orders in high to low or low to high order based on the total dollar amount of the customer, you could sort the customer group on the Order Amount summary field. If you sorted the Order Amount summary field in ascending order, the customers with the lowest total dollar amount would appear at the beginning of the group.

In Exercise 6.7 you created a report that grouped the orders in 2001 by month. If you wanted to show the months with the highest monthly totals at the beginning of the report, you would sort the month group in descending order on the Order Amount summary field. You will modify these two reports in this lesson.

Figure 13-24 shows the Group Sort Expert dialog box. When you open the dialog box you will see a tab for each group that the report has. You can sort on as many of the summary values in the groups as needed. Keep in mind that the sorting starts with the first tab and works it's way across the tabs.

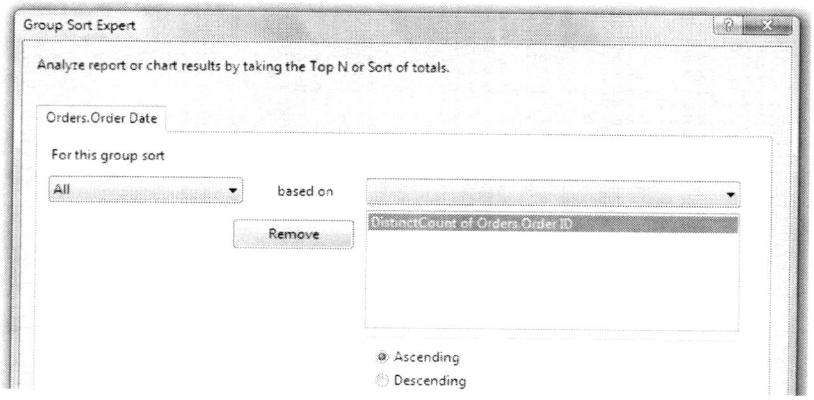

Figure 13-24 Group Sort Expert dialog box

In addition to the Top N, Bottom N, Top and Bottom Percentage options which you have already learned about, the **FOR THIS GROUP SORT** drop-down list has the following options:

NO SORT, which is the default and will use the sort options that were set up when the group was created.

The **ALL** option will include all of the groups and not suppress any groups like the Top N, Bottom N, Top Percentage and Bottom Percentage options will.

The options in the **BASED ON** drop-down list are the summary fields that are in a group section of the report.

To create a Top or Bottom N report, the report must have the two items discussed below, before opening the Group Sort Expert.

    ① The report must have at least one group.
    ② The group that you want to use for the Top or Bottom N report must have a summary field in it.

The way that you know that the report has both of the options discussed above is that you can open the Group Sort Expert. Reports that do not meet the criteria will have the option to open the Group Sort Expert dimmed out.

There are two ways to open the Group Sort Expert as discussed below.

① Click the Group Sort Expert button on the Crystal Reports - Main toolbar.
② Crystal Reports ⇒ Report ⇒ Group Sort Expert.

Multiple Top/Bottom N Criteria

You can create different Top or Bottom N criteria for each tab on the Group Sort Expert. In Figure 13-24 shown above you could create three top or bottom N sets of criteria. In Exercise 6.4 the report is grouped on the Ship Via and Customer Name fields. If you selected the Top 5 option for the Ship Via field and the Top 10 percent option for the Customer Name field, the report would look like the one shown in Figure 13-25.

This report shows the top five shipping methods based on the total shipping amount and the top 20% of customers based on their order amount per shipping method. [See the L13 Top N criteria report in the zip file]

Loomis
- Cyclopath
- Hooked on
- Platou Spo
- Rough Terr
- Blazing Sad
- Canal City (
- Extreme C
- Warsaw Sp
- Bike-A-Holi

Parcel Post
FedEx
UPS
Purolator

	Order #	Order Date	Order Amount	Salesperson	
Loomis					
Cyclopath					
	1283	02/10/2001	$53.90	Janet	Leverling
	1727	06/17/2001	$18.00	Janet	Leverling
	1931	08/04/2001	$4,602.47	Michael	Suyama
	2101	09/14/2001	$65.70	Nancy	Davolio
	2141	09/25/2001	$845.55	Margaret	Peacock
	2145	09/25/2001	$5,651.42	Anne	Dodsworth
	2394	11/21/2001	$1,619.55	Margaret	Peacock
	Total # of orders for customer - 7			Total order amount for customer - $ 12,856.59	
Hooked on Helmets					
	1122	01/01/2001	$1,025.40	Michael	Suyama
	1183	01/15/2001	$36.00	Janet	Leverling
	1628	05/18/2001	$6,005.00	Nancy	Davolio
	1826	07/04/2001	$6,095.30	Janet	Leverling
	1836	07/07/2001	$1,799.70	Robert	King
	1889	07/22/2001	$1,529.70	Janet	Leverling
	2380	11/19/2001	$1,870.20	Margaret	Peacock
	Total # of orders for customer - 7			Total order amount for customer - $ 18,361.30	

Figure 13-25 Report with multiple Top N criteria

Exercise 13.7: Sort The Report On The Customer Group By Order Amount Field

In this exercise you will change the sort order of the groups to show the groups that have customers with the lowest total order amounts at the top of this report. You will also sort the groups by the number of orders in descending order. This sort will happen within the order amount sort. This is helpful if two or more customers have the same order total amount.

1. Save the L6.2 report as `L13.7 Group sorted on two fields.`

2. Open the Group Sort Expert and select the All option from the drop-down list.

3. Select the Order Amount summary field, then select the Ascending option.

4. Select the Order ID count field, then select Descending and click OK. Save the changes. The report should look like the one shown in Figure 13-26. As you look through the report, you should see all customers with the lowest order amount totals at the beginning of the report.

As the report designer, it may be obvious to you how a report is sorted and grouped. Unlike the reports that you have created earlier in this workbook that have groups, reports that have groups that are sorted by a value in a summary field, may not be as easy for the reader to figure out how the report is grouped and sorted just by looking at it.

	Order Date	Ship Date	Order Amount	Order #	Unit Price
Super Bike	06/24/2001	06/26/2001	$2,699.55	3166	$899.85
Total # orders - 1		**Total $ amount of orders -**	**$ 2,699.55**		
Deals on Wheels	02/01/2002	02/05/2002	$5,879.70	2667	$2,939.85
Total # orders - 1		**Total $ amount of orders -**	**$ 5,879.70**		
Piccolo	06/24/2001	06/29/2001	$5,879.70	1762	$2,939.85
Total # orders - 1		**Total $ amount of orders -**	**$ 5,879.70**		
Tyred Out	06/26/2001	06/26/2001	$8,819.55	1777	$2,939.85
Total # orders - 1		**Total $ amount of orders -**	**$ 8,819.55**		

Figure 13-26 L13.7 Group sorted on two fields report

If you look at the report shown above in Figure 13-26, you will see the group name (the company name field) in the group header section. Many people will think that this is how the report is sorted even though the report is sorted by the values in the order amount summary field. You should do something to make sure that the person reading the report is aware of how the report is sorted or grouped. There are three options that I select from to help clarify how a report presents data. You can use any of the options below or come up with a different solution.

① Add how the report is grouped and sorted as a subtitle on the report. For example, Grouped by (field name) and sorted by (field name). You fill in the field name.
② Add how the report is grouped and sorted to the page or report footer section.
③ Add the summary value field to the group header section.

Exercise 13.8: Sort The Month Groups In Descending Order

In this exercise you will sort the groups in descending order by the total monthly order amount.

1. Save the L6.7 report as `L13.8 Sorted month groups`.

2. Open the Group Sort Expert and select the All option.

3. Delete the Distinct Count of Orders ID criteria.

4. Select the Order Amount summary field, then select the Descending option. Save the changes. The report should look like the one shown in Figure 13-27. If you look in the group tree, you will be able to tell which month had the highest order amount, because it is at the top of the list.

6/2001					
7/2001	Nancy	Davolio	06/29/2001	1796	$83.80
10/2001	Michael	Suyama	06/29/2001	1797	$1,773.75
11/2001	Robert	King	06/30/2001	1798	$798.75
2/2001					
8/2001	Totals For: June				
5/2001					
1/2001	Total # of orders for the month - **250**				
4/2001	Total order amount for the month - **$446,198.19**				
9/2001	Percent of yearly sales - **15.56%**				
3/2001					
12/2001					

Figure 13-27 L13.8 Sorted month groups report

Creating Group Selection Formulas

Group selection formulas are used to filter groups that do not meet a condition. The formulas can be created by using the values in a group summary field or by using the values in the Group Name field. To use a Group Name field (which are stored in the Group Names Field folder in the Field Explorer), you have to use the Group Name function. The only time that you need to use this function is if the report has custom group names.

To create a group selection formula, select a summary field on the Select Expert instead of a detail field. In Exercise 13.7, you modified the report to sort the groups in ascending order. If you only wanted to see groups (in this example, customers) that have an order summary total amount less than $10,000 and are in the USA, you would create two selection criteria options; one on the Order summary total amount, which is a group summary field and one on the Country field.

Exercise 13.9: Create A Group Selection Formula

1. Save the L6.2 report as `L13.9 Group selection formula`.

2. Right-click on the Order Amount summary field in the group footer section and select the Select Expert option. Select the "Is less than" operator, then type `10000` in the next drop-down list. This is the group selection formula.

3. Click on the New tab and select the Country field. Select the "Is equal to" operator, then select the USA region.

4. Delete the Order Amount greater than 2499.99 criteria and Order Date criteria.

5. Click on the Order Amount tab, then click the Show Formula button. The group selection formula should look like the one shown in Figure 13-28. Click OK and save the changes. The report should look like the one shown in Figure 13-29.

○ Record Selection ◉ Group Selection

```
Sum ({Orders.Order Amount}, {Customer.Customer Name}) < $10000.00
```

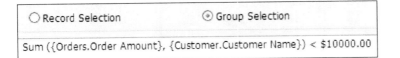

Figure 13-28 Group selection formula

	Order Date	Ship Date	Order Amount	Order #	Unit Price
AIC Childrens	06/21/2001	06/21/2001	$101.70	3153	$33.90
Total # orders - 1		Total $ amount of orders -	$ 101.70		
Ankara Bicycle Company	06/13/2001	06/15/2001	$959.70	3112	$479.85
Total # orders - 1		Total $ amount of orders -	$ 959.70		
Arsenault et Maurier	05/15/2001	05/25/2001	$1,739.85	3022	$1,739.85
Total # orders - 1		Total $ amount of orders -	$ 1,739.85		
Aruba Sport	06/05/2001	06/08/2001	$5,879.70	3079	$2,939.85
Total # orders - 1		Total $ amount of orders -	$ 5,879.70		

Figure 13-29 L13.9 Group selection formula report

As you may expect, group selection formulas will suppress groups that do not meet the selection criteria. What I find interesting is that the summary field group totals are the same as if there were no suppressed groups. This is because there is a difference between suppressing groups and filtering records. Keep this in mind when creating group selection formulas.

Form Letters

Crystal Reports is being used more and more to create form letters instead of using word processing software. Form letters are usually customized for each person or company that they will be sent to. If a report already has the selection criteria that is needed for the form letters, make a copy of the report and delete the objects that are not needed.

Exercise 13.10: Create A Form Letter

In this exercise you will create a basic form letter similar to one that you have probably received in the mail. If you want, you can add other items like a company logo and date to a form letter.

1. Save the L12.14 report as `L13.10 Form letter.`

2. Delete all of the fields in the details section.

3. Open the Section Expert and click on the details section. Click on the Color tab, then click on the Formula button. Delete the formula at the bottom of the window, then click the Save and close button.

4. On the Common tab check the **NEW PAGE AFTER** option in the details section. Click OK to close the Section Expert.

5. Add the Customer Name and Address1 fields from the Customer table to the top of the details section.

6. Create a formula to combine the City, State and Zip Code fields. Save the formula as `ComboCityStZip`. Add a comma and space after the City field and a space after the State field.

7. Create a formula named `Salutation`. Type the word `Dear`, then add the Customer Name field.

8. Create a formula named `Body Of Letter`. Enter the formula shown in Figure 13-30.

```
"We want to thank you for your order on "
& DateValue ({Orders.Order Date})
& " in the amount of "
& {Orders.Order Amount}
& ". We realize that this order took "
& ToText ({?Delay in Days},0)
& " days to ship. The 15% off coupon at the bottom of this letter is
our way of saying thank you for not canceling the order. We really
appreciate your business."
```

Figure 13-30 Body of letter formula

9. Add these formulas to the report as shown in Figure 13-31, then save the changes.

```
▼ Section3 (Details )
Customer Name
Address1
@ ComboCitySTZip

@ Salutation

@ BodyOfLetter
```

Figure 13-31 Formula fields added to the report

10. Preview the report. Use the date range 1/1/2001 to 1/31/2001. Change the time to 12:00:00 AM for the start date and 11:59:59 PM for the ending date. Select 4 as the Delay In Days To Ship. The first form letter should look like the one shown in Figure 13-32. There should be 127 records (form letters).

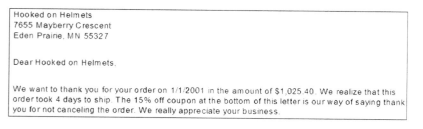

```
Hooked on Helmets
7655 Mayberry Crescent
Eden Prairie, MN 55327


Dear Hooked on Helmets.


We want to thank you for your order on 1/1/2001 in the amount of $1,025.40. We realize that this
order took 4 days to ship. The 15% off coupon at the bottom of this letter is our way of saying thank
you for not canceling the order. We really appreciate your business.
```

Figure 13-32 L13.10 Form letter

Multi-Column Reports

In Lesson 7 you used the Mail Label Report wizard which let you create multi-column labels. You can use the options on the Layout tab shown in Figure 13-33, on the Section Expert to create multi-column reports.

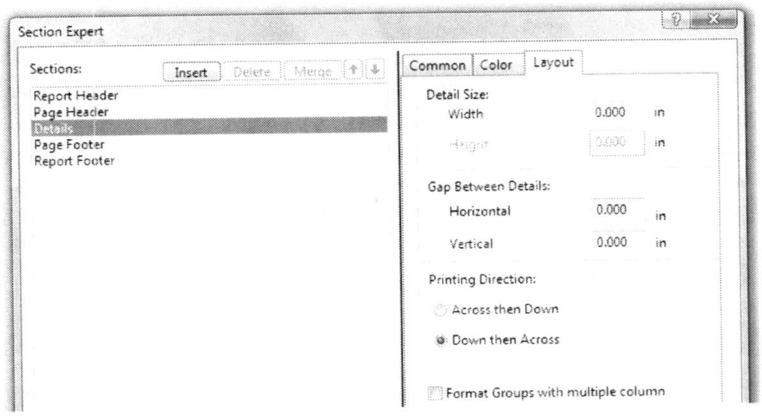

Figure 13-33 Layout tab options

The options on the Layout tab will let you create columns like the Mail Label wizard does. Unlike word processing software that often has a "Number of columns" option, the Layout tab does not. You create the columns by using the **DETAIL SIZE** and **GAP BETWEEN DETAILS** options.

The **FORMAT GROUPS WITH MULTIPLE COLUMN** option if checked, will cause the group headers and footers to have the same width as the details section.

Summary Reports

The majority of reports that you have created in this workbook contained detail level records. This is the type of report that many people are use to seeing. Detail level reports provide a lot of information. There are times when this is too much information and someone will want to only see summary information. The L10.27 report that you created is a summary report. There are two main ways to create summary reports as discussed below.

① Use the Hide or Suppress report section options.
② Use a Parameter field.

Drill-Down Reports

Drill-down reports initially look like summary reports. The difference is that drill-down reports do not use the Suppress (No Drill-Down) option. Keep in mind that the only data that will print or be exported when using the drill-down feature is what is displayed on the selected preview tab.

Drill-Down Report Problems

There are two problems that you may encounter when designing reports that will use the drill-down feature as discussed below.

① Problems with the group headers.
② Problems with the column headings.

What I have noticed on reports that have at least three groups is that when you drill-down, you will see more headers then you probably want or need. When you drill-down on the top level group (group 1), you will see the headers for the second group. This may not be what you want when you drill-down to the third level.

Using the Hide (Drill-Down OK) option on the Section Expert doesn't work well.
The **DRILLDOWNGROUPLEVEL** function will allow you to control when group headers are suppressed.

This function is used for printing. The original preview window will return a zero when this function is used. If you are drilling down on group 2, the function will return a 2.

When you drill-down on the first group, you usually don't have a need to see the headers for the second group. To prevent this from happening, you would use the formula shown below to conditionally suppress the second level group headers. You would place this formula on the Suppress (No Drill-Down) option. In this example you would place it on the group 2 header. When this formula is applied, the group 2 header will not appear when you drill-down on the first level. The group 2 header will appear when you drill-down on the third level, which is what you want to have happen.

```
DrillDownGroupLevel = 1
```

Column Heading Problems

On the first preview tab you will see column headings but no detail records if you use the Hide or Suppress option on the Section Expert. This happens when the column headings are in the page header section. When you drill-down to the detail level, the data in the page header section does not appear. Yes, I was confused when I realized this also.

The number of groups on the report determines the solution. If the report only has one group, move the column headings to the group header section. Decide if they look better above or below the group name field if the group name field is on the report.

If the report has more than one group, create a second details section and move the detail fields to the second section, then move the column headings to the first detail section and select the **SUPPRESS BLANK SECTION** option on the Section Expert.

Exercise 13.11: Drill-Down Report

In Exercise 10.27 you created a summary report that displayed the number of orders and total amount of orders for each customer. In this exercise you will modify this report so that the field headings are displayed when the report is drilled down.

Use The Drill-Down Feature

1. Save the L10.27 report as `L13.11 Drill-Down report`.

2. Double-click on the first company name in preview mode, which is a group header field. You should see the tab shown in Figure 13-34. Notice that there are no field headings on this tab. Look at the bottom of the window. You will see a tab with the name of company.

Alley Cat Cycles					
Alley Cat Cycles					
	09/28/2001	09/30/2001	$2,559.63	2157	$539.85
	09/28/2001	09/30/2001	$2,559.63	2157	$313.36
	10/27/2001	11/06/2001	$2,699.55	2272	$899.85
	01/31/2002	02/03/2002	$9,290.30	2664	$455.86
	01/31/2002	02/03/2002	$9,290.30	2664	$2,792.86
	02/19/2002	02/22/2002	$8,819.55	2735	$2,939.85
	02/19/2002	02/22/2002	$8,819.55	2735	$2,939.85
Total # orders - 7		Total $ amount of orders - $44,038.51			

Figure 13-34 Detail records tab

Modify The Summary Report

In this part of the exercise you will move the field headers to the group header section so that they will appear on the drill-down tabs.

1. Make the group header section longer, then drag the field headings to the group header section below the group field as shown in Figure 13-35.

▼ GroupHeaderSection1 (Group Header #1: Customer.Customer Name - A)

Group #1 Name

Order Date   Ship Date   Order Amount   Order #   Unit Price

▼ Section3 (Details)

Order Date   Ship Date   rder Amount   Order·ID   Unit·Price

▼ GroupFooterSection1 (Group Footer #1: Customer.Customer Name - A)

Figure 13-35 Field headings moved to the group header section

2. Select all of the field headings, then open the Format Editor. Clear the suppress option on the Common tab, then click OK.

3. Save the changes. If you double-click on the first company name, the new tab should display the field headings as shown in Figure 13-36. Like the full report, you can print the data on the detail records drill-down tab.

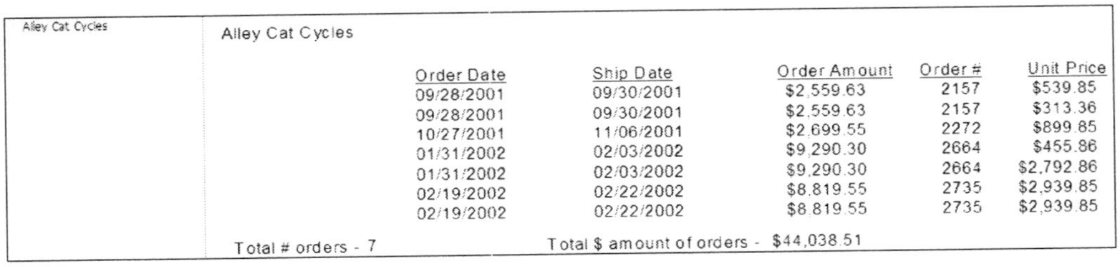

Alley Cat Cycles					
	Alley Cat Cycles				
	Order Date	Ship Date	Order Amount	Order #	Unit Price
	09/28/2001	09/30/2001	$2,559.63	2157	$539.85
	09/28/2001	09/30/2001	$2,559.63	2157	$313.36
	10/27/2001	11/06/2001	$2,699.55	2272	$899.85
	01/31/2002	02/03/2002	$9,290.30	2664	$455.86
	01/31/2002	02/03/2002	$9,290.30	2664	$2,792.86
	02/19/2002	02/22/2002	$8,819.55	2735	$2,939.85
	02/19/2002	02/22/2002	$8,819.55	2735	$2,939.85
	Total # orders - 7	Total $ amount of orders - $44,038.51			

Figure 13-36 Field headings displayed on the drill-down tab

Exercise 13.12: Add A Watermark To A Report

In Exercise 11.23 you learned how to use the Underlay option. In this exercise you will use the Underlay option to add a watermark to a report.

1. Save the L3.3 report as L13.12 Watermark report.

2. Create another page header section. Move the field headings to the new page header section.

3. Add the draft logo from the zip file for this book to the page header a section. Place the logo in the center of the section, then make it larger as shown in Figure 13-37.

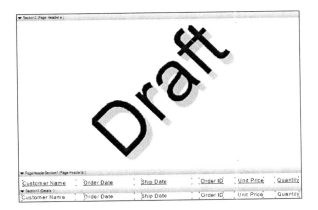

Figure 13-37 Logo added to the first page header section

4. Open the Section Expert for the page header a section. Select the Underlay following sections option and click OK. Save the changes and preview the report. It should look like the one shown in Figure 13-38.

Customer Name	Order Date	Ship Date	Order ID	Unit Price	Quantity
C-Gate Cycle Shopp	12/31/2000 12:00:C	12/31/2000	1,119	$17.50	2
SAB Mountain	12/31/2000 12:00:C	1/2/2001 10:	1,120	$16.50	2
SAB Mountain	12/31/2000 12:00:C	1/2/2001 10:4	1,120	$41.90	1
Rough Terrain	1/1/2001 12:00:00/	1/1/2001 7:31	1,1	$41.90	1
Rough Terrain	1/1/2001 12:00:00/	1/1/2001 7:31:21A	1,121	$809.87	1
Hooked on Helmets	1/1/2001 12:00:00/	1/8/2001 7P	1,122	$21.90	3
Hooked on Helmets	1/1/2001 12:00:00/	1/8/200 7:30	1,122	$479.85	2
Clean Air Transporte	1/2/2001 12:00:00/	1/2/200 2	1,123	$1,739.85	3
Off the Mountain Bik	1/2/2001 12:00:00/	1/2/001 3:59	1,124	$19.90	3
Road Runners Parac	1/2/2001 12:00:00/	1/2001 3:2	1,125	$19.71	2
Road Runners Parac	1/2/2001 12:00:00/	1/2001 A	1,125	$36.00	1
Platou Sport	1/2/2001	2001 1:29:59A	1,126	$16.50	2
Platou Sport	1/2/20 12:00:0	1/2/1 1:29:59A	1,126	$1,739.85	2
Platou Sport	1/2/2 12:00:00/	2/200 1:29:59A	1,126	$329.85	1
BBS Pty	1/2/2 1 12:00:00/	0/2001 2:31:27	1,127	$13.50	3
BBS Pty	1/2/2 12:00:00/	0/2001 2:31:27	1,127	$479.85	1
Tandem Cycle	1/2/200 :00:00/	3/2001 11:59:21/	1,128	$21.90	3
The Bike Cellar	1/2/2001 0:00	1/2/2001 9:22:35A	1,129	$33.90	1
The Bike Cellar	1/2/2001 12	1/2/2001 9:22:35A	1,129	$23.50	1
The Bike Cellar	1/2/2001 12:00:00/	1/2/2001 9:22:35A	1,129	$2,939.85	1
Rowdy Rims Compa	1/3/2001 12:00:00/	1/4/2001 3:47:10A	1,130	$23.50	1

Figure 13-38 Watermark added to the report

Test Your Skills

1. Apply conditional formatting to the L7.11 Cross-Tab report.

   - Save the report as `L13.13 Skills Cross-Tab`.
   - Modify the report to include a group for Country = USA for each sales rep.
     Use the Customer table. Combine all other sales in a different group, called Other.
   - Remove the bold from the group names.
   - The report should look like the one shown in Figure 13-39.

		2000	2001	2002	Total
Davolio	USA	$39,485.69	$278,893.25	$109,053.25	$427,432.19
	Other	$32,377.01	$171,972.58	$28,975.17	$233,324.76
	Total	**$71,862.70**	**$450,865.83**	**$138,028.42**	**$660,756.95**
Dodsworth	USA	$23,107.06	$359,523.99	$119,880.97	$502,512.02
	Other	$5,942.88	$154,021.53	$20,372.78	$180,337.19
	Total	**$29,049.94**	**$513,545.52**	**$140,253.75**	**$682,849.21**
King	USA	$10,460.46	$335,306.18	$152,761.39	$498,528.03
	Other	$10,633.29	$177,100.42	$62,494.20	$250,227.91
	Total	**$21,093.75**	**$512,406.60**	**$215,255.59**	**$748,755.94**
Leverling	USA	$26,055.91	$324,864.09	$133,904.53	$484,824.53
	Other	$18,065.73	$116,491.40	$23,840.63	$158,397.76
	Total	**$44,121.64**	**$441,355.49**	**$157,745.16**	**$643,222.29**
Peacock	USA	$24,508.97	$295,308.43	$120,391.01	$440,208.41
	Other	$13,949.42	$150,842.13	$26,799.81	$191,591.36
	Total	**$38,458.39**	**$446,150.56**	**$147,190.82**	**$631,799.77**
Suyama	USA	$47,602.06	$347,551.55	$135,243.28	$530,396.89
	Other	$7,202.16	$149,329.93	$23,472.50	$180,004.59
	Total	**$54,804.22**	**$496,881.48**	**$158,715.78**	**$710,401.48**
Total		**$259,390.64**	**$2,861,205.48**	**$957,189.52**	**$4,077,785.64**

Figure 13-39 L13.13 Skills Cross-Tab report

2. Add running total fields to the L6.1 report.

   - Save the report as `L13.14 Skills Running totals`.
   - Create two running total fields and place them in the report footer section. Create one for all USA orders and one for all Canadian orders.
   - The last page of the report should look like the one shown in Figure 13-40.

Customer Name	Address
	Grand Total # of customers on this report - 269
	Total # of orders in the USA - 90
	Total # of orders in the Canada - 10

Figure 13-40 L13.14 Skills Running totals report

3. Sort the L6.3 report by groups.

   - Save the report as `L13.15 Skills Group sort`.
   - Sort the groups by the Total amount of orders summary field in descending order.
   - Filter the groups so that only customers with a total amount of orders over $50,000 appear on the report.
   - The first customer on the report should be the one shown in Figure 13-41.

	Order Date	Ship Date	Order Amount	Order #	Unit Price
Backpedal Cycle Shop					
	07/02/2001	07/04/2001	$3,479.70	1802	$1,739.85
	08/15/2001	08/19/2001	$3,415.95	1972	$479.85
	08/15/2001	08/19/2001	$3,415.95	1972	$764.85
	08/15/2001	08/19/2001	$3,415.95	1972	$53.90
	11/16/2001	11/18/2001	$10,798.95	2358	$2,939.85
	11/16/2001	11/18/2001	$10,798.95	2358	$479.85
	11/16/2001	11/18/2001	$10,798.95	2358	$1,739.85
	12/18/2001	12/19/2001	$6,226.05	2507	$16.50
	12/18/2001	12/19/2001	$6,226.05	2507	$329.85
	12/18/2001	12/19/2001	$6,226.05	2507	$2,939.85
	01/04/2002	01/05/2002	$9,612.47	2560	$2,792.86
	01/04/2002	01/05/2002	$9,612.47	2560	$764.85
	01/04/2002	01/05/2002	$9,612.47	2560	$832.35
	02/02/2002	02/02/2002	$8,819.55	2685	$2,939.85

Total # orders - 14   Total $ amount of orders - $ 102,459.51

Average order amount for the customer - $ 7,318.54

Figure 13-41 L13.15 Skills Group sort report

4. Add hyperlinks to the L13.3 report.

   - Save the report as `L13.16 Skills hyperlink`.
   - Create another report header section for the hyperlinks that you will create in this exercise.
   - Use the Wingdings envelope and open folder images in the first row of the Character Map as the objects for the hyperlinks.
   - Use the envelope image to create an email hyperlink that opens an email window with your email address in the To field.
   - Use the folder image to create a file hyperlink that opens the L13.1 report.
   - Change the font size of both text objects to 28. The images should be larger.
   - Add the appropriate text to the hyperlinks, so that the person running the report will know what the images link to.
   - The report header section should look like the one shown in Figure 13-42.

Figure 13-42 L13.16 Skills hyperlink report

The End!

If you are reading this paragraph, I hope it means that you have completed all of the exercises in this workbook. If so, congratulations because you have covered a lot of material. If some topics seem a little fuzzy right now, that is to be expected. Hopefully you have gained some valuable Crystal Reports skills and techniques. As you have probably figured out, unless you are creating a basic list report, there are a lot of options and features at your disposal to create reports that people will "like" to use.

INDEX

No Stress Tech Guides

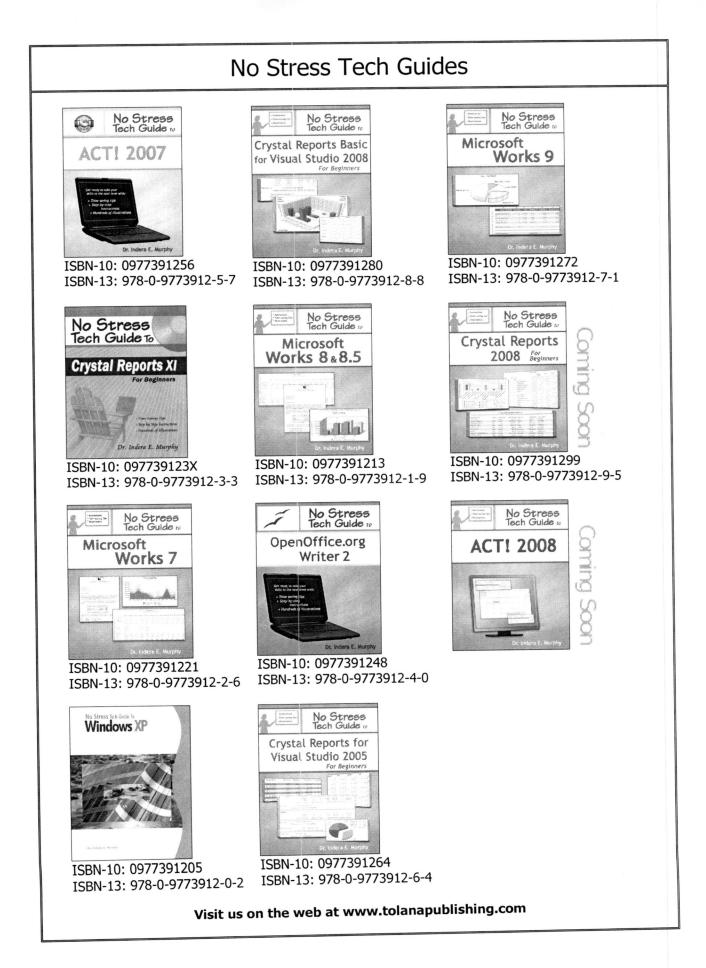

No Stress Tech Guide to ACT! 2007
ISBN-10: 0977391256
ISBN-13: 978-0-9773912-5-7

No Stress Tech Guide to Crystal Reports Basic for Visual Studio 2008 For Beginners
ISBN-10: 0977391280
ISBN-13: 978-0-9773912-8-8

No Stress Tech Guide to Microsoft Works 9
ISBN-10: 0977391272
ISBN-13: 978-0-9773912-7-1

No Stress Tech Guide To Crystal Reports XI For Beginners
ISBN-10: 097739123X
ISBN-13: 978-0-9773912-3-3

No Stress Tech Guide to Microsoft Works 8 & 8.5
ISBN-10: 0977391213
ISBN-13: 978-0-9773912-1-9

No Stress Tech Guide to Crystal Reports 2008 For Beginners — Coming Soon
ISBN-10: 0977391299
ISBN-13: 978-0-9773912-9-5

No Stress Tech Guide to Microsoft Works 7
ISBN-10: 0977391221
ISBN-13: 978-0-9773912-2-6

No Stress Tech Guide to OpenOffice.org Writer 2
ISBN-10: 0977391248
ISBN-13: 978-0-9773912-4-0

No Stress Tech Guide to ACT! 2008 — Coming Soon

No Stress Tech Guide To Windows XP
ISBN-10: 0977391205
ISBN-13: 978-0-9773912-0-2

No Stress Tech Guide to Crystal Reports for Visual Studio 2005 For Beginners
ISBN-10: 0977391264
ISBN-13: 978-0-9773912-6-4

Visit us on the web at www.tolanapublishing.com

Printed in the United States
201904BV00005B/73-264/P

9 780977 391288